Lecture Notes in Computer Science 9023

Commenced Publication in 1973
Founding and Former Series Editors:
Gerhard Goos, Juris Hartmanis, and Jan van Leeuwen

More information about this series at http://www.springer.com/series/7410

Yun-Qing Shi · Hyoung Joong Kim
Fernando Pérez-González · Ching-Nung Yang (Eds.)

Digital-Forensics and Watermarking

13th International Workshop, IWDW 2014
Taipei, Taiwan, October 1–4, 2014
Revised Selected Papers

 Springer

Editors

Yun-Qing Shi
NJIT
Newark, NJ
USA

Hyoung Joong Kim
Korea University
Seoul
Korea, Republic of (South Korea)

Fernando Pérez-González
Universidad de La Laguna
La Laguna
Spain

Ching-Nung Yang
Department of Computer Science
and Information Engineering
National Dong Hwa University
Hualien
Taiwan

ISSN 0302-9743   ISSN 1611-3349   (electronic)
Lecture Notes in Computer Science
ISBN 978-3-319-19320-5   ISBN 978-3-319-19321-2   (eBook)
DOI 10.1007/978-3-319-19321-2

Library of Congress Control Number: 2015939424

LNCS Sublibrary: SL4 – Security and Cryptology

Springer International Publishing AG Switzerland is part of Springer Science+Business Media
(www.springer.com)

Preface

The International Workshop on Digital-forensics and Watermarking 2014 (IWDW 2014), the 13th IWDW, hosted by the National Dong Hwa University, was held in the National Taipei University of Business, Taipei, Taiwan during October 1–4, 2014. The IWDW 2014, following the tradition of IWDW, aimed to provide a technical program covering the state-of-the-art theoretical and practical developments in the field of digital watermarking, steganography and steganalysis, forensics and antiforensics, and other multimedia-related security. With 79 submissions, from 17 different countries and areas, the Technical Committee has selected 47 papers (32 oral and 14 poster presentations, and one keynote speech) for publication, including one paper for the best student paper award, and one for the best paper award. Besides these papers, the workshop has been featured by the opening talk delivered by the three invited lectures titled "A Watermarking Scheme for Categorical Relational Databases," "Multimedia Forensics: A Game Theoretic Approach," and "Past, Present and Future of Reversible Watermark" presented, respectively, by Professor C.C. Chang, Professor Mauro Barni, and Professor Oscar C. Au; and a one-hour open discussion among all the participants.

First of all, we would like to thank all the authors, reviewers, lecturers, and participants for their valuable contributions to the success of IWDW 2014. Our sincere gratitude also goes to all the members of Technical Program Committee, International Publicity Liaisons, and our local volunteers for their careful and hard work, and effort made in the wonderful organization of this workshop. We do appreciate the generous support from the National Dong Hwa University and the National Taipei University of Business in Taiwan, Korea Institute of Information Security and Cryptography (KIISC). Finally, we hope that the readers will enjoy reading this volume and that it will provide inspiration and opportunities for the future research.

January 2015

Yun-Qing Shi
Hyoung Joong Kim
Fernando Pérez-González
Ching-Nung Yang

Organization

Honorary Chairs

Heekuck Oh   KIISC, Korea
Ruay-Shiung Chang   National Taipei University of Business, Taiwan

General Chairs

Ching-Nung Yang   National Dong Hwa University, Taiwan
Chin-Chen Chang   Feng Chia University, Taiwan

Technical Program Chairs

Yun-Qing Shi   New Jersey Institute of Technology, USA
Hyoung Joong Kim   Korea University, Korea
Fernando Pérez-González University of Vigo, Spain

Technical Program Committee

Rainer Boehme   University of Muenster, Germany
Lee-Ming Cheng   City University of Hong Kong, China
Claude Delpha   Paris-SuD XI University, France
Jana Dittmann   Magdeburg University, Germany
Isao Echizen   National Institute of Informatics, Japan
Dongdong Fu   Intel, USA
Miroslav Goljan   Binghamton University, USA
Ton Kalker   DTS Inc., USA
Xiangui Kang   Sun Yat-sen University, China
Mohan S. Kankanhalli   National University of Singapore, Singapore
Anja Keskinarkaus   University of Oulu, Finland
Alex Kot   Nanyang Technological University, Singapore
Chang-Tsun Li   Warwick University, UK
Li Li   Hangzhou Dianzi University, China
Shenghong Li   Shanghai Jiaotong University, China
Chia-Chen Lin   Providence University, Taiwan
Zheming Lu   Zhejiang University, China
Jiang Qun Ni   Sun Yat-sen University, China
Sheng-Lung Peng   National Dong Hwa University, Taiwan
Alessandro Piva   Florence University, Italy
Yong-Man Ro   Korea Advanced Institute of Science and Technology,
             Korea

Vasiliy Sachnev	Catholic University, Korea
Kouichi Sakurai	Kyushu University, Japan
Shiuh-Jeng Wang	Central Police University, Taiwan
Andreas Westfeld	HTW Dresden, Germany
Xinpeng Zhang	Shanghai University, China
Yao Zhao	Beijing Jiao Tung University, China

International Publicity Liaisons

Asia

Heung-Kyu Lee	Korea Advanced Institute of Science and Technology, Korea
Jiwu Huang	Shenzhen University, China

Europe

Anthony TS Ho	Surrey University, UK
Mauro Barni	Siena University, Italy

America

C.-C. Jay Kuo	University of Southern California, USA
Nasir Memon	New York University Polytechnic School of Engineering, USA

Organizing Chairs

Jou-Ming Chang	National Taipei University of Business, Taiwan
An-Hang Chen	National Taipei University of Business, Taiwan
Sheng-Lung Peng	National Dong Hwa University, Taiwan

Organizing Committee

Guanling Lee	National Dong Hwa University, Taiwan
Shou-Chih Lo	National Dong Hwa University, Taiwan
Hung-Lung Wang	National Taipei University of Business, Taiwan
Jinn-Shyong Yang	National Taipei University of Business, Taiwan

Contents

Reversible Data Hiding

Visual Cryptography

Poster Session

Steganography and Steganalysis

Forensics

New Developments in Image Tampering Detection

Guanshuo Xu$^{(\boxtimes)}$, Jingyu Ye, and Yun-Qing Shi

New Jersey Institute of Technology, Newark, NJ 07102, USA
{gx3,jy58,shi}@njit.edu

Abstract. Statistical feature-based pattern recognition approach has been proved to be useful in digital image forgery detection. In this paper, we first present this approach adopted in Phase 1 of the first IEEE IFS-TC Image Forensics Challenge, in which the task is to classify the tampered images from the original ones, together with the experimental results. Several different kinds of statistical features and their combinations have been tested. Finally, we have chosen to use co-occurrence matrices calculated from the rich model of noise residual images. Furthermore we have selected a subset of the rich model to further enhance the testing accuracy by about 2 % so as to reach a high detection accuracy of 93.7 %. In Phase 2 of the competition, the task is to localize the tampered regions by identifying the tampered pixels. For this purpose, we have introduced the Hamming distance of Local Binary Patterns as similarity measure to tackle the tampering without post-processing on copy-moved regions. The PatchMatch algorithm has been adopted as an efficient search algorithm for block-matching. We have also applied a simple usage of the scale-invariant feature transform (SIFT) when other kinds of processing such as rotation and scaling have been performed on the copy-moved region. The achieved f-score in identifying tampered pixels is 0.267. In summary, some success has been achieved apparently. However, much more efforts are called for to move image tampering detection ahead.

Keywords: Image tampering detection · Forgery detection · Digital forensics · Natural image modeling

1 Introduction

Living in our digital age, manipulating digital images becomes much easier than before. Fake images are often found in the news media nowadays such that one cannot simply believe that the image they see represents what really have taken place like before. Therefore, image tampering detection becomes an urgent and important issue in the research of image forensics. People need to tell if a given image has been tampered or not, and if the image has been tampered then where it has been tampered without a priori knowledge. In the past more than one decade, researchers have made efforts on image tampering detection and quite a number of methods have been proposed. In [1, 2], two early algorithms to detect tampering and duplicated regions in images have been proposed. Later, image lighting inconsistency [3], camera parameters [4], bicoherence statistics [5], Hilbert-Huang transform [6], and statistics of 2-D phase

© Springer International Publishing Switzerland 2015
Y.-Q. Shi et al. (Eds.): IWDW 2014, LNCS 9023, pp. 3–17, 2015.
DOI: 10.1007/978-3-319-19321-2_1

congruency [7] have been used to detect tampered images. According to what kind of features is utilized, there are two main approaches to image tampering detection research: one is the specific approach (designed to detect the tampering caused by some specific method) and another is the general approach (designed for the tampering caused by various methods).

Columbia Image Splicing Detection Evaluation Dataset [8] was established in 2004. As the first public domain available dataset, it has been playing an important role in moving ahead the research on image tampering detection. The blind splicing detection methods [6, 7, 9] have achieved success detection rates of 72 %, 80 %, and 82 %, respectively. The more advanced statistical models further moved the detection rate to slightly above 91 %, [10, 11]. It was reported that the detection rate has reached 93 % [12] with additional features derived from wavelet transform domain.

However, the total number of spliced images and that of original images in the Columbia dataset are not large enough (each is slightly less than 1000) to allow researchers to apply high-dimensional feature set. That is, the more advanced statistical modeling cannot be applied to image splicing detection. Furthermore, the original images from which the dataset was established are JPEG images. Hence, there are some JPEG artifacts remaining, which have in fact somehow un-reliably boosted the detection rate. This partially explained the fact that while the tampering detectors well trained can perform well in the dataset, they cannot achieve high detection rates on real testing images. Specifically, the system trained in the Columbia dataset which achieved a detection rate at 91 % could only achieve a detection rate of 66 % on a group of 60 tampered images collected from the open domain [13].

To actively move the research on image tampering detection ahead, the Technical Committee (TC) of Information Forensics and Security (IFS) at IEEE Signal Processing Society successfully organized a competition on Image Tampering Detection in the summer and fall of 2013 [14]. The competition is worldwide and consists of two stages. In the first stage, there are 1500 images for training and 5713 images for testing. That is, the participants could use the training images to train and test their trained classifiers. Afterwards, the research teams who participated in the competition were expected to decide if each image in the test dataset has been tampered or not. To allow the dataset to be used continuously in the website even after the competition in 2013, the organizers have not announced the true-false ground truth for these test images even after the competition. Instead, the organizers have only provided the test scores on the performance according to the test results submitted by the joining teams. In the second stage, each team worked on a set of tampered images, and was requested to tell for each tampered image where the tampering took place in the accuracy of pixels. At the end of the competition, the organizers of the TC of IFS, IEEE Signal Processing Society awarded the first two teams as the Winner and the Runner-up, respectively.

The authors of this paper have won the second position (Runner-up) in the competition in both the 1st stage and the 2nd stage [14]. In this paper, we first report what we have used in the 1st stage of competition, i.e., a blind and effective image tampering detection method based on advanced image statistical modeling. The statistical modeling we used is based on what derived from the advanced steganalytic research with some modification to reduce feature dimensionality drastically. Then, in the 2nd stage of competition, we used two different technologies popularly used in copy-move detection, which have complimented each other. It is expected that by providing the newest technologies utilized in image tampering detection as well as a summary for the past research along this direction, this paper is useful for further moving the re-search on image tampering detection ahead.

The rest of the paper is organized as follows. In Sect. 2, we discuss how we have detected if a give image has been tampered or not. In Sect. 3, given an image which has been identified as a tampered image, we present our approaches to identifying which portions in the accuracy of pixel-level have been tampered. Discussion and summary are given in Sect. 4.

2 Statistical Feature Based Machine Learning Approach

In the first stage of the IEEE competition mentioned above, three schemes have been developed in a row by our group. It turns out that the one which has achieved the best performance among the three utilizes a subset of high-dimensional feature set originally designed and used for the modern steganalysis.

2.1 Local Binary Patterns (LBP)

Local Binary Patterns (LBP) [15] was proposed as an effective texture classification technology, and has been utilized for face recognition and image forensics, including steganalysis [16] and camera model classification [17]. In the 1st stage of the competition, we applied LBP technology, and thus derived LBP histograms from the images are used as the statistical features.

Note that most of the images provided by the organizers of the competition are color images. Thus, before we start the feature extraction process, color images were transferred to gray images using Matlab's 'rgb2gray' function.

As said, there are 1050 images in 'pristine' class (negative) and 450 images in 'fake' class (positive), provided by the organizers. The latest version of Libsvm [18] of polynomial kernel was served as the classifier for this experiment. Performance on the training set thus derived is provided in Tables 1 and 2, respectively. The accuracy (ACC) is the balanced training accuracy. In Table 2, all the LBP features were used, while in Table 1, only the so-called 'uniformity' features of LBP were considered and the dimensionality was reduced from 256-D to 59-D. However, a significant performance drop was observed comparing with the original 256-D, which was mainly brought by the low TP rate. Therefore, we chose to use the classifier trained by 256-D LBP to test the testing dataset, which contains 5,713 images. The accuracy provided by the online system was around 85 %. This first trying was encouraging. Later we got better results in our attempts.

2.2 Combination of LBP and LDP with Other Two Types of Features

Given the initial success by using the LBP, it is naturally to enhance its performance by building more advanced and hence complicated statistical models. In [10, 11], the

Table 1. TP and TN using uniform lbp (59D)

ACC = 0.715	Predicted negative	Predicted positive
Actual negative	0.9437	0.0563
Actual positive	0.5133	0.4867

Table 2. TP and TN using lbp (256D)

ACC = 0.912	Predicted negative	Predicted positive
Actual negative	0.9491	0.0509
Actual positive	0.1247	0.8753

moments of 1-D and 2-D characteristic functions and Markov transition probability matrices extracted from multi-size block DCT coefficients of images have been combined together. This statistical model has achieved success based on experimental results on Columbia dataset [8]. Inspired by the success of [10, 11], we designed an even more complex statistical model which contained mainly the following four parts:

- LBP [15] calculated from original image (256D).
- LDP [19] calculated from original image (512D).
- Moments of characteristic functions features calculated from original image and multi-block DCT 2D arrays [10] (168D).
- Markov transition probability matrices calculated from multi-block DCT 2D arrays [10, 20] (972D).

The Local Derivative Patterns (LDP) is another set of statistical features, proposed in [19], which captures directional changes of derivatives of neighboring pixels against central pixel. In [19], the performance of LDP was claimed to outperform LBP in face recognition. Thus, we involved the LDP as our second set of features in this statistical model. As the feature size was large, only horizontal and vertical directions were considered here, resulting in $2 \times 256 = 512D$ features.

Moments of characteristic functions and Markov transition probability matrices have been successfully used in [10, 11, 20]. Here, Markov features were calculated from all the 2×2, 4×4 and 8×8 DCT coefficients arrays.

The block diagram of this statistical model is shown in Fig. 1. Total feature dimension is 1,908D.

We used the same training process as in our first attempt mentioned above (applying LBP alone). The result is shown in Table 3. The training accuracy boosted from 91.2 % to 94.9 %, making us confident that the accuracy should also improve for testing set. However, surprisingly, the feedback result was only around 81 %. Most likely, however, this abnormality was caused by a bug in testing score calculation which was reported by some of the participants and fixed later on by the organizers.

2.3   Advanced Statistical Models

Through the experiments reported above, we realized that features derived from spatial domain could have more detection capability to images tampered in spatial domain.

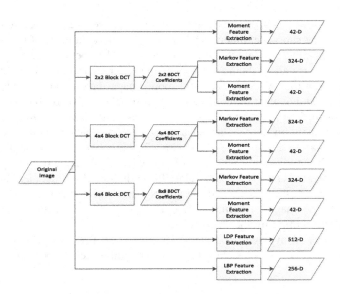

Fig. 1. The combined statistical model

Table 3. TP and TN using combined model (1908D)

ACC = 0.949	Predicted negative	Predicted positive
Actual negative	0.9726	0.0274
Actual positive	0.0747	0.9253

In [21], Fridrich and Kodovský proposed to combine co-occurrence arrays extracted from various quantized and truncated noise residuals to break one of the most powerful spatial-domain-steganographic algorithms. The total feature dimensionality utilized was 12,753-D. Although steganalysis and tampering detection are different research areas, they have similar characteristics of pixel manipulation. The previous works [10, 11] have shown that the methods designed for steganalysis could work well for tampering detection if trained by the samples of image tampering. Furthermore, the statistical model used in [21] contains the desired high-order statistical features that we need, i.e., more powerful statistical features in the spatial domain. Therefore, we applied the statistical model in [21] to this research.

We made some changes in the experimental settings this time. From the results in Tables 1, 2 and 3, we notice that the accuracies for positive (TP) and negative (TN) classes are imbalanced. Very likely the imbalance was caused by not having enough training data for positive class (fake images). As there was no mandatory requirement on using only the provided training set for training purpose, we added all the 700 images in phase 2 of this competition to positive class for training because they are claimed to be fake. Hence, we had more data for positive class and the training set becomes much more balanced (1050 negative and 1150 positive). The ensemble classifier [22], which was used in [21] for classification, was also inherited to replace the SVMs to classify high-dimensional features.

In all the following experiments, in the training phase, we set the training/testing ratio to 0.8/0.2, the subspace dimensionality to 300, and the number of splits to 13. All the other settings remained default. Note that there could be better choice of parameters and we could not try all of them. Apart from the feature subspace ensemble, we also applied data ensemble. As there was 100 more image data in positive class and the classifier required equivalent training size, a random selection of 1050 out of 1150 data was carried on before the start of training process. The data ensemble made sense because the competition used balanced accuracy for evaluation. Thus, there was no reason to have bias on training size of any class. The number of data ensemble was also 13 and during the training process, 13 × 13 = 169 classifiers have been built. Training errors were generated and averaged by classifying the rest 20 % data available for the training stage. Then, the 169 trained classifiers were used for classifying test dataset consisting of 5,713 images. The final decisions made on the 5,731 testing images were made by majority voting by the 169 decisions.

Table 4 shows the average error rate (0.5 × FP + 0.5 × FN) using the full feature set in [1]. The training accuracy reaches 96.35 %. The online feedback testing result was around 91.7 %.

Table 4. Average error rate using rich model (12,753D)

Average error	False negative	False positive
0.0366	0.0383	0.0349

So far we have shown that the full set of features (12,753-D) generated from the rich model worked quite well. In spite of this success, we doubt that not all the features in this rich model have had positive contribution. Furthermore, the image tampering and the image steganography have some different behavior and hence make different changes to the original image. Last but not the least, lowering feature dimensionality is attractive because of the lacking of enough training images for allowing high feature dimensionality. Hence, we took one step further to select a subset of the whole feature set in [21] aiming at improving accuracy.

Our selection steps are shown as follows:

- Divide the whole rich model (12,753-D) into groups.
- Find classification errors and standard deviations (STD) on training data of each group.
- Select and combine groups by simultaneously considering classification errors and the STD.

When forming groups, we basically followed the residual types, i.e., first order (S1), second order (S2), third order (S3), edge 3 × 3 (S3 × 3), edge 5 × 5 (S5 × 5), and 3 × 3, 5 × 5 spam (S35_spam). Features calculated from 'spam' and 'minmax' residuals were grouped separately. For details of the residual types, please refer to [21]. The reason we included STD into our feature selection was that all of the features generated are from co-occurrence arrays, and some of them had quite uneven distributions, and some even had a lot of zeroes which implied lower population of histogram bins.

As the mean of each co-occurrence array was the same (or close considering that the minmax occurrence matrices have 325 bins and spam occurrence matrices have 338 bins), it was natural to use standard deviation to measure the distribution of co-occurrence values. Here we assumed that lower STD implied better distribution and higher STD implied worse distribution.

Table 5 shows the error rates and STD corresponding to each group of the residual images. By considering both of these two factors, we chose three groups: S3_spam, S3 × 3_spam and S3 × 3_minmax, and the total feature dimensionality thus reduce to 1,976D. As the feature size was still high in S3 × 3_minmax (1,300D), we performed backward selection on all the four sub-groups (four co-occurrence matrices), i.e., each time we remove one 325D matrix. Only one 325D (S3 × 3_minmax24) was removed. We could probably remove more, which could be done in our future research. The details of this backward selection are shown in Table 6. The total dimensionality now has been reduced to 1,651D. This 1,651D feature set served as our final feature set for this competition. To make it clear, the final set we use is S3_spam (338D) + S3 × 3_spam (338D) + S3 × 3_minmax22h (325D) + S3 × 3_minmax22v (325D) + S3 × 3_minmax41 (325D) = 1,651D. The online feedback testing accuracy was around 93.8 % - 94.0 %. There was about a 2 % increase compared with the whole feature set of rich model. Although this might not be the optimal subset, it is the best we could do within the limited period of time.

Table 5. Errors and std on training data for each group

Residual type	Dimension	STD	AVG ERR	FN	FP
S1_minmax	3250	0.0630	0.0503	0.0397	0.0608
S2_minmax	1625	0.0360	0.0447	0.0434	0.0460
S3_minmax	3250	0.0497	0.0442	0.0444	0.0439
S3 × 3_minmax	1300	0.0345	0.0438	0.0417	0.0459
S5 × 5_minmax	1300	0.0371	0.0437	0.0349	0.0524
S1_spam	338	0.0299	0.0659	0.0661	0.0656
S2_spam	338	0.0263	0.0640	0.0698	0.0582
S3_spam	338	0.0275	0.0559	0.0514	0.0604
S35_spam	338	0.0288	0.0677	0.0630	0.0725
S3 × 3_spam	338	0.0254	0.0526	0.0439	0.0614
S5 × 5_spam	338	0.0273	0.0579	0.0497	0.0661

Table 6. Errors and std on training data for each group

	AVG ERR	FN	FP
without S3 × 3_minmax22h	0.0392	0.0386	0.0397
without S3 × 3_minmax22v	0.0397	0.0402	0.0392
without S3 × 3_minmax24	0.0376	0.0397	0.0355
without S3 × 3_minmax41	0.0450	0.0397	0.0355

3   Tampering Localization

In Phase 2 of the competition, the participants were required to locate the tampered region pixel-wisely on images provided by the organizers which had all been tampered. Before starting the research, an analysis was made based on the training data about the major tampering methods. By observing the training data and the ground truth masks in training set, the tampering methods can be classified into two major categories. In plain language, tampered regions could either be originated from the same images (copy-move), or from different images (splicing). Figure 2 shows one example for splicing and one for copy-move. It was noticed that these two categories might not cover all the tampering cases, but they were definitely the main stream.

Fig. 2. From left to right: splicing example, mask of the splicing example, copy-move example, mask of the copy-move example.

Once we have defined the tampering methods to work with, the next step was to design corresponding forensic methods. The major idea of our algorithm design was to break big problem into smaller problems and to design specific algorithms to solve each small problem. Each algorithm was expected to work independently and the last step was to fuse the outputs.

The copy-move problem can be separately into three categories based on the copied content, i.e., smooth area, texture area, and object. And the copied content can be further processed, e.g., scaling and rotation. To solve the problem that tampered areas are directly copy-moved (without further processing), similarity is compared between image blocks (or patches). We propose a new distance measure that counts the total hamming distance of LBP [15] calculated from pixels inside patches. Similarity is measured based on the count of hamming distance. This distance measure has the advantage that copied regions can be detected even in smooth regions due to camera sensor noise, not to say textured region and objects, as long as there is no other processing. As most of the images have more than 1024×768 pixels, the searching process could be rather slow. To speed up the searching process, we adopted the PatchMatch algorithm [23, 24]. For copy-move cases that has involved further processing on tampered region, we used the popular scale-invariant feature transform (SIFT) [25] features and designed a somewhat naive method to use it. As we know, the SIFT does not work for smooth areas. Fortunately, based on our observation and study of popular image editing software, smooth areas, most likely, have not gone through any further processing. Table 7 shows the different copy-move cases versus our forensic methods. Because we entered the competition rather late, we have only designed algorithms for copy-move tampering localization. Splicing localization has to be future work.

Table 7. Copy-move cases versus forensic methods

Forensic method	Copy-move cases					
	Smooth (wo)	Texture (wo)	Object (wo)	Smooth (w)	Texture (w)	Object (w)
Hamming distance of LBP	YES	YES	YES	N/A	NO	NO
Euclidian distance of SIFT	NO	YES	YES	N/A	YES	YES

w = with further processing, wo = without further processing

3.1 PatchMatch and Hamming Distance Measure

3.1.1 PatchMatch Fast Searching Algorithm

In this Section, we introduce our forensic algorithm for copy-move without further processing.

Copy-move forgery detection is one of the most popular topics in image tampering detection. The survey in [26] provides valuable evaluation on most of the methods developed to address this topic. There are three key elements in almost all of these algorithms, i.e., feature extraction from each block (patch), similarity (distance) measure between features extracted from two blocks, fast searching algorithm for block matching. The method to calculate features has main impact on the accuracy of block-matching. It also has influence on searching speed. The fast searching algorithms speed up the searching process. Before we introduce our feature extraction method and distance measure. We first introduce the PatchMatch [23, 24], which had been served as our fast searching algorithm.

PatchMatch was initially proposed as an efficient method to search for most similar patches between different images or different parts of images [23]. The algorithm of PatchMatch contains mainly three steps.

1. To match the patches in image A with the patches in image B according to similarity measure, there is an initialization process that assigns each patch in A with one patch in B. The most convenient assignment is randomization, which was the initialization method adopted in our algorithm. The size of the patches can be user defined. In our work, we considered sizes 5×5, 7×7, 9×9 and 11×11.
2. Assume one patch in A has been assigned a patch in B with small similarity between them. However, one of its neighbor (in A) is assigned a patch with larger similarity, the patch then looks for the better patch in the corresponding position in B according to the correspondence of its neighbor. This process is referred to as propagation. By doing this for all the pixels in image A, the similarity of each patch can be greatly improved.
3. Better correspondence of each patch in image A can be found by search nearby areas of its current match in image B.

Steps two and three are performed iteratively to guarantee the best matches of each patch in A.

In [24], PatchMatch was extended to copy-move detection by finding k-NN (k > 1) for each patch, and constructing a graph and identifying connected components from the graph to find the copy-move region.

In our work, we took the approach by randomizing the tampered image, assigning each patch one of the randomized patch in the same image, and performing the three steps in [23], described above. Only 1-NN was considered for each patch. In order to avoid assigning the most similar patch to itself, we set a minimal distance as a limitation.

3.1.2   Hamming Distance Between LBP Patterns

Now we discuss the features and the similarity measure (distance). In the original PatchMatch paper [23, 24], the average Euclidean distance of all the pixel values in corresponding patches was used as similarity measure. This similarity measure would create a lot of false positives in smooth areas. As the authors of [23, 24] mentioned that any distance could be used to replace the Euclidean distance, we adopted a new similarity measure. This similarity measure should work no matter the copy-moved region is smooth area, texture area or object, as long as there is no further processing as mentioned in the Introduction Section. Note that in [26], a lot of features and distance measures in literature have been evaluated. We have not applied them on the data in the competition yet. This should be our future work.

The features that we used were the Local Binary Patterns (LBP) [15]. The similarity measure we used was Hamming distance between two LBPs of corresponding positions within two image patches. More specifically, for each pixel in a patch, LBP was calculated as an 8-bit binary string and the hamming distance between corresponding pixels were summed. The summation of hamming distances served as similarity measures of two patches. The reason we used LBP was that in smooth regions, sensor noise would likely dominate the pixel-value variation within a patch which could be well captured by LBP, for LBP considers the relative relationships of 8-neighbors with respect to the central pixel. If the copy-moved area is texture or object, LBP should also work intuitively. Figure 3 shows an example of Hamming distance calculation for one pixel (central pixel). In Figs. 6, 7, 8 and 9, the four images in the center of the upper row of each figure are the output with patch size 5×5, 7×7, 9×9, 11×11. Note that sometimes the detected tampered areas were different with different patch sizes. The four outputs were processed and combined which is shown in the lower rows.

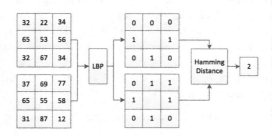

Fig. 3. Calculation of LBP and hamming distance

Fig. 4. Left to right: original image, output with patch size 5 × 5, ground truth, processed output

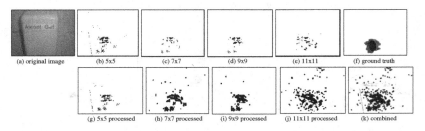

Fig. 5. Smooth area: example 1

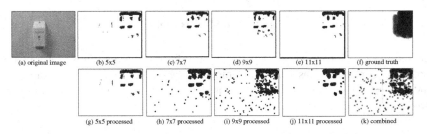

Fig. 6. Smooth area: example 2

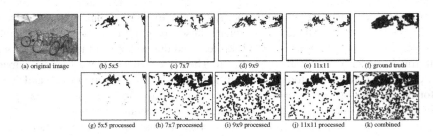

Fig. 7. Texture area: example 1

3.1.3 Post Processing

The output could be noisy (see Figs. 5, 6, 7 and 8). To alleviate this problem, we removed connected components with small areas. Then, a dilation operation was performed on all the rest of the connected components to make sure that the output mask covered all of tampered region. The lower rows in Figs. 6, 7, 8 and 9 are the

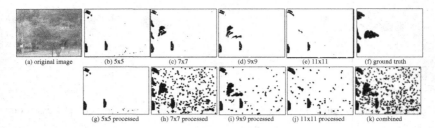

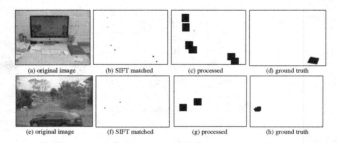

Fig. 8. Texture area: example 2

Fig. 9. Two SIFT examples

processed masks. Note that there are still a lot of false positives. Those false positives are mainly from (1) areas that the tampered regions copied from (2) areas near boundaries of image content. More research should be done to control those false positives.

3.1.4   Limitation and Bonus

We have noticed that when images contain apparent JPEG 8×8 grids (decompressed from a JPEG format and resaved to '.png'), our distance measure failed as it is sensitive to those periodic patterns. Figure 4 (Upper Right image) is the output with patch size of 5×5. We can see that there are so many false positives that we cannot tolerate. However, the tampered region has not been reported due to the fact that JPEG grid was weak (or no JPEG grid) in tampered region. Therefore, whenever we found an image with clear JPEG grids. We took a different approach, i.e., we inverted the 0 and 1 and performed a morphological open followed by a dilation to filter out the tampered region. This was kind of a by-product (bonus) of our distance measure.

The method we used to detect JPEG grid was proposed in [27]. For details please refer to [27]. We note that in the testing phase, this adjustment of the algorithm caused a lot of false positives. Sometimes all the pixels were reported as tampered.

3.2   A Simple Usage of SIFT and Euclidian Distance

In this Section, we discuss how we used SIFT [25] to solve the problem when the copy-moved region had been further processed. We realize that there are a few publications that have addressed this problem using SIFT. Again, this should be our future work to evaluate them on this dataset. At the time of the competition, a simple (somewhat naïve) usage of SIFT was adopted.

A simple implementation of SIFT [28] was adopted as feature extraction tool. For each detected feature points, a 128-D feature vector was generated. We performed a brute force search to find the matched points by calculating the Euclidean distance between feature vectors. A threshold was set to filter out the points that located the copy-moved region. Two examples are shown in Fig. 9. After that, morphological dilations were performed on each point with a square of size min(height, width)/8 to include all the areas of tampered region. This usage was quite coarse and naïve with still acceptable performance.

3.3   Combining Strategies

The two algorithms for copy-move localization have been performed on all the test data. The strategy to combine the output was that any pixel that has been voted as fake by any algorithm was decided as fake in the final output.

4   Discussion and Conclusion

In Phase 1 of the competition organized by IEEE IFS-TC, the winner team took the strategy of merging two tampering detection methods [29], i.e., the statistical-model based classification and the copy-move detection. Similar to our approach, they also used a subset of the rich model as features. While we used ensemble classifiers and simultaneously considered classification performance and standard deviations of features and came up with an efficient subset of the original rich model, they used the SVM as classifier and the area under the receiver operating curve as the measure for feature selection. It was discovered that the tampering detection by using the statistical model generated a lot of miss detections. This problem was alleviated by introducing a copy-move detector which by their experiments could efficiently 'catch' the miss detections by the statistical classifier. Eventually, the two tampering detection methods were merged and their testing score in Phase 1 has boosted to 94.2 %.

In Phase 2 of the competition, the winner team adopted and fused three methods [30], i.e., PRNU based tampering detection, copy-move detection, and statistical model based classification. Comparing with the other two, the PRNU based detector was the most reliable one, as information of the camera noise was used. Although the camera information and noise patterns were unavailable, they were successfully extracted by the winner team using a noise-based fingerprint clustering methods on the training data. However, there were some camera mismatch between training and testing da-taset. Also, the PRNU based methods became unreliable at dark, saturated or highly textured regions. Hence, they adopted a copy-move detector as the second approach. The original version of Patch-Match was used which includes capability of detecting rotated and scaled copy-move regions. In their statistical-based method, the same feature set was used as was developed during Phase 1 of the competition. Combined with a sliding window approach, the statistical-based approach specifically targeted at splicing detection, although the reliability was deemed by the team as the lowest among the three methods.

In summary, the competition organized by the Technical Committee of Information Forensics and Security, IEEE Signal Processing Society has largely boosted the capability of image tampering detection by providing a large dataset and organizing the competition. The research on image tampering detection has thus been moved ahead by a big step. Many challenges, in particular, how to more reliably detect the tampered regions, however, remain. And more advanced research is called for.

References

1. Farid, H., Lyu, S.: Higher-order wavelet statistics and their application to digital forensics. In: IEEE Workshop on Statistical Analysis in Computer Vision, vol. 8, p. 94, June 2003
2. Fridrich, J., Soukal, D., Lukáš, J.: Detection of copy-move forgery in digital images. In: Proceedings of Digital Forensic Research Workshop (2003)
3. Johnson, K., Farid, H.: Exposing digital forgeries by detecting inconsistencies in lighting. In: Proceedings of the 7th Workshop on Multimedia and Security, pp. 1–10. ACM, August 2005
4. Huang, Y.: Can digital image forgery detection be unevadable? a case study: color filter array interpolation statistical feature recovery. In: Visual Communications and Image Processing 2005, pp. 59602 W–59602 W. International Society for Optics and Photonics, July 2005
5. Ng, T., Chang, F., Sun, Q.: Blind detection of photomontage using higher order statistics. In: Proceedings of the 2004 International Symposium on Circuits and Systems, ISCAS 2004, vol. 5, pp. V–688. IEEE, May 2004
6. Fu, D., Shi, Y.Q., Su, W.: Detection of image splicing based on Hilbert-Huang transform and moments of characteristic functions with wavelet decomposition. In: Shi, Y.Q., Jeon, B. (eds.) IWDW 2006. LNCS, vol. 4283, pp. 177–187. Springer, Heidelberg (2006)
7. Chen, W., Shi, Y.Q., Su, W.: Image splicing detection using 2-D phase congruency and statistical moments of characteristic function. In: Society of Photo-Optical Instrumentation Engineers (SPIE) Conference Series, vol. 6505, p. 26, February 2007
8. DVMM Research Lab. Columbia Image Splicing Detection Evaluation Dataset (2004). http://www.ee.columbia.edu/ln/dvmm/downloads/AuthSplicedDataSet/AuthSplicedDataSet.htm
9. Ng, T.-T., Chang, F., Sun, Q.: Blind detection of photomontage using higher order statistics. In: Proceedings of the 2004 International Symposium on Circuits and Systems, ISCAS 2004, vol. 5, pp. V–688. IEEE, May 2004
10. Shi, Y.Q., Chen, C., Chen, W.: A natural image model approach to splicing detection. In: Proceedings of the 9th Workshop on Multimedia & Security, pp. 51–62. ACM, September 2007
11. Shi, Y.Q., Chen, C.-H., Xuan, G., Su, W.: Steganalysis versus splicing detection. In: Shi, Y.Q., Kim, H.-J., Katzenbeisser, S. (eds.) IWDW 2007. LNCS, vol. 5041, pp. 158–172. Springer, Heidelberg (2008)
12. He, Z., Lu, W., Sun, W., Huang, J.: Digital image splicing detection based on Markov features in DCT and DWT domain. Pattern Recogn. **45**(12), 4292–4299 (2012)
13. http://web.njit.edu/~shi/tech-report (2009)

14. http://ifc.recod.ic.unicamp.br/
15. Ojala, T., Pietikainen, M., Maenpaa, T.: Multiresolution gray-scale and rotation invariant texture classification with local binary patterns. IEEE Trans. Pattern Anal. Mach. Intell. **24** (7), 971–987 (2002)
16. Shi, Y.Q., Sutthiwan, P., Chen, L.: Textural features for steganalysis. In: Kirchner, M., Ghosal, D. (eds.) IH 2012. LNCS, vol. 7692, pp. 63–77. Springer, Heidelberg (2013)
17. Xu, G., Shi, Y.Q.: Camera model identification using local binary patterns. In: IEEE International Conference on Multimedia and Expo (ICME), pp. 392–397. IEEE, July 2012
18. Chang, C.-C., Lin, C.-J.: LIBSVM: a library for support vector machines. ACM Trans. Intell. Syst. Technol. 2, 27:1–27:27 (2011). http://www.csie.ntu.edu.tw/ ∼ cjlin/libsvm
19. Zhang, B., Gao, Y., Zhao, S., Liu, J.: Local derivative pattern versus local binary pattern: face recognition with high-order local pattern descriptor. IEEE Trans. Image Proc. **19**(2), 533–544 (2010)
20. Sutthiwan, P., Shi, Y.Q., Zhao, H., Ng, T.-T., Su, W.: Markovian rake transform for digital image tampering detection. In: Shi, Y.Q., Emmanuel, S., Kankanhalli, M.S., Chang, S.-F., Radhakrishnan, R., Ma, F., Zhao, L. (eds.) Transactions on Data Hiding and Multimedia Security VI. LNCS, vol. 6730, pp. 1–17. Springer, Heidelberg (2011)
21. Fridrich, J., Kodovsky, J.: Rich models for steganalysis of digital images. IEEE Trans. Inf. Forensics Secur. **7**(3), 868–882 (2012)
22. Kodovsky, J., Fridrich, J., Holub, V.: Ensemble classifiers for steganalysis of digital media. IEEE Trans. Inf. Forensics Secur. **7**(2), 432–444 (2012)
23. Barnes, C., Shechtman, E., Finkelstein, A., Goldman, D.: PatchMatch: a randomized correspondence algorithm for structural image editing. ACM Trans. Graph. -TOG **28**(3), 24 (2009)
24. Barnes, C., Shechtman, E., Goldman, D.B., Finkelstein, A.: The generalized patchmatch correspondence algorithm. In: Daniilidis, K., Maragos, P., Paragios, N. (eds.) ECCV 2010, Part III. LNCS, vol. 6313, pp. 29–43. Springer, Heidelberg (2010)
25. Lowe, D.G.: Distinctive image features from scale-invariant keypoints. Int. J. Comput. Vis. **60**(2), 91–110 (2004)
26. Christlein, V., Riess, C., Jordan, J., Angelopoulou, E.: An evaluation of popular copy-move forgery detection approaches. IEEE Trans. Inf. Forensics Secur. 7(6), 1841–1854 (2012)
27. Fan, Z., de Queiroz, R.L.: Identification of bitmap compression history: JPEG detection and quantizer estimation. IEEE Trans. Image Proc. **12**(2), 230–235 (2003)
28. http://www.robots.ox.ac.uk/ ∼ vedaldi/code/sift.html
29. Cozzolino, D., Gragnaniello, D., Verdoliva, L.: Image forgery detection through residual-based local descriptors and block-matching. In: IEEE International Conference on Image Processing (ICIP) (2014)
30. Cozzolino, D., Gragnaniello, D., Verdoliva, L.: Image forgery localization through the fusion of camera-based, feature-based and pixel-based techniques. In: IEEE International Conference on Image Processing (ICIP) (2014)

Inter-frame Video Forgery Detection Based on Block-Wise Brightness Variance Descriptor

Lu Zheng[2], Tanfeng Sun[1,2(✉)], and Yun-Qing Shi[2]

[1] School of Electronic Information and Electrical Engineering,
Shanghai Jiao Tong University, Shanghai, People's Republic of China
tfsun@sjtu.edu.cn
[2] Department of Electrical and Computer Engineering,
New Jersey Institute of Technology, Newark, NJ, USA

Abstract. Video forensics becomes more and more important than ever before. In this paper a new methodology based on Block-wise Brightness Variance Descriptor (BBVD) is proposed. It is capable of fast detecting video inter-frame forgery. Our proposed algorithm has been tested on a database consisting of 240 original and forged videos. The experiments have demonstrated that the precision rate is about 94.09 % in detecting the insertion forgery and the precision rate is 79.45 % in the forgery localization. Moreover, the time utilized for forgery detecting is shorter than the time used for video replay. On average the time of forgery detection is only about 73.4 % in video replay.

Keywords: Video forensics · Inter-frame forgery · Block-wise brightness variance descriptor

1 Introduction

Recently, due to availability of inexpensive and easily-operable multimedia tools, digital multimedia technology has experienced drastic advancements. At the same time, video forgery becomes much easier and it is more difficult to validate video content. Consequently, the origin and integrity of video can no longer be taken for granted. With these reasons, video forensics is becoming increasingly important, especially when the digital video content is used for legal support.

Currently, there are two types of forgery detection [1]: active detection (e.g., using watermark) and passive detection (e.g., blind detection). As for the active detection, the tampered region can be identified using a pre-embedded "semi"-fragile watermark in the video stream [2]. With the passive detection, also called blind detection, there is no need to embed any watermark into the protected files. On the contrary, the intrinsic features of the video itself can be used for forgery detection. As known, a digital video contains a large amount of information both in spatial domain and in temporal domain, Examples include, for examples, the correlation or similarity between neighboring frames.

Moreover, since the videos with watermarks embedded are sometimes can be considered as some kinds of forgery, the passive video forgery detection becomes more attractive and prevalent. In recent years, more and more approaches have been

Y.-Q. Shi et al. (Eds.): IWDW 2014, LNCS 9023, pp. 18–30, 2015.
DOI: 10.1007/978-3-319-19321-2_2

developed for passive forgery video detection. There are three main categories for video forensic methods [3]. The first category is based on the video acquisition analysis, namely noise model or intrinsic parameters of CCD methods. One example in this regard is the methodology to use the non-uniformity of the dark current of CCD chips for camcorder identification proposed by Kurosawa et al. [4]. The second category is the detecting methods with video compression. For example, Tagliasacchi et al. [5] developed a method to detect block boundary for tampering trace by using estimation of the QP parameters. The last category is the video doctoring detection, including **copy-move detection in videos, which is based on inconsistencies in content, video editing and so on.** It was proposed to detect the copy-move operation in the video firstly by Wang and Farid [6]. They developed a method to detect frame duplication based on the correlation coefficient. The method based on inconsistencies in content is reported by Chao et al. [7]. They introduced an approach based on optical flow which is computed for each pixel to find out the discontinuity caused by inter-frame insertion or deletion during the forgery. It can detect frame insertion and deletion with high precision in large-scale testing. But it is so complicated that the computational expense is too much to meet the requirements of practical applications.

To sum up, there are only a small number of algorithms to detect video inter-frame forgery. In this paper, a novel algorithm which is block-wise based using the brightness variance descriptor is proposed. It is highly efficient because of the algorithm's low computational complexity. The remaining paper is divided into four sections. Section 2 is about feature extraction. The propose scheme is presented in Sect. 3. Section 4 contains experiment results and discussion. The conclusion is drawn in Sect. 5.

2   Feature Extraction

In this paper, a new feature, called the block-wise brightness variance descriptor (BBVD) in consistent video sequence, is proposed for video inter-frame forgery detection. The main idea is that the consistency of the ratio of the BBVD in equal time intervals will be disturbed in frame forgery videos. This method can not only detect whether the video is tampered or not, but also detect the location of the frame forgery.

2.1   Base of the Proposed New Features

As is known, digital video not only contains a large amount of information in the spatial domain, but also in the temporal domain. In the temporal domain, the correlation of adjacent frames is very high, which means the corresponding variation is relatively rather low. So if some frames are inserted or deleted to tamper the original content of the original videos, the variance of brightness should often be changed largely.

A new idea can be obtained according to Weber's Law [8], which describes the perceptual difference between the increment stimulus and the original stimulus. The ratio of the variation can be defined as the follows:

$$R = \frac{\Delta B}{B} \tag{1}$$

where B is the brightness or the gray value of a pixel in one frame and ΔB is the variant value from different pixels, R is the ratio of the variation of the brightness versus original brightness. The R is a constant in the equation.

So a constant or slow variable of brightness ratio should be obtained from consecutive frames in the video frames sequence.

Moreover, due to the persistence phenomenon of human vision [9], the image can be retained in the human visual system for about 0.1 to 0.4 s after its disappearance. So, in order to guarantee the consistency of the video content, any two frames with some short time intervals such as 0.4 s must have only small variation. As for the common video frame rate, i.e. 24 frames per second, the minimum value of time interval is as follows:

$$24 \text{ fps } \times 0.4 \text{ s } = 9.6 \text{ frame} \approx 10 \text{ frame} \tag{2}$$

that means every two frames with an interval within approximately 10 frames still have a correlation to some degree.

Here a constant or slow variable of brightness ratio should be kept from non-consecutive but rather adjacent frames, such as 10-frames interval in the video frames sequence, i.e.,

$$R_{BVD} = \frac{\Delta B_f}{B_f} \tag{3}$$

where B_f is the brightness or gray value of the first frame and ΔB_f is the difference of first frame versus its adjacent 10th frame. R_{BVD} is the ratio the difference of two frames versus first frame. For an original video, the ratio between the two frames with a certain time interval is usually a constant or tardily variable. However, this consistency will be disturbed in the inter-frame forgery video. The feature used in the paper is based on the R_{BVD}.

2.2   Sub-sequences Group Generation

Before feature extraction, the whole video sequence needs to be partitioned into several short temporal sub-sequences with a same duration. In this experiment, the full-length video sequence is partitioned into a series of short overlapping sub-sequences groups, i.e. $G = \{g_1, g_2, g_3 \dots g_j \dots g_n\}$, where n is the total number of the sub-sequence group. The length of the each sub-sequence is 15 frames with 5 frames overlapping to satisfy the persistence phenomenon of vision for human eye [9], that is,

(1) 1st sub-sequence group: 1st frame to 15th frame;
(2) 2nd sub-sequence group: 11th frame to 25th frame
(3) 3rd sub-sequence group: 21st frame to 35th frame

    ......

(j) j^{th} sub-sequence group: wth frame to $(w + 15)^{th}$ frame, where $w = [(j-1) \times 10 + 1]$.

Short-temporal video sequences analysis, rather than frame by frame analysis, is performed to accelerate forgery detection.

2.3   Feature Model Based on Sub-block

In the paper, the new feature, R_{BVD}, calculated from each so called sub-sequence group $\{g_n\}$ is used to determine whether a test video has been tampered or not. In order to reduce the negative influence of the mutation or fluctuation in some part of the frame, each frame is partitioned into a series of 16 (4×4) sub-blocks, denoted as $B_{sblock} = \{b_1, b_2, b_3, \ldots, b_{16}\}$. For each sub-sequence group, taking the jth sub-sequence group as an example, obtained the first frame $(w^{th}$ frame) and the last frame $((w + 15)^{th}$ frame) in the current sub-sequence group. According to Eq. (3), compute R_{BBVD} between each sub-block in the first frame and the corresponding sub-block in the last frame in each sub-sequence group. Then calculated the average value of the all the ratio of BBVD in the current sub-sequence.

$$R_{BBVD} = \frac{\Delta B_{sblock}}{B_{ave}} = \frac{1}{M \times N} \sum_{i=1}^{M} \sum_{j=1}^{N} \frac{Bf_{ij} - Bl_{ij}}{B_{ave}} \qquad (4)$$

where, R_{BBVD} represents the ratio of BBVD between the each block in the first frame and the corresponding block in the last frame in each sub-sequence group. ΔB_{sblock} is defined as the variation of the gray value of pixels in the corresponding sub-blocks. Bf_{ij} and Bl_{ij} represent the gray value in each pixel of the current block in the first frame and the last frame of the current sub-sequence group respectively. M and N represent the number of the pixel in row and column in each block. B_{ave} is the average gray value of pixels in the current block of the first frame in each sub-sequence group and B_{ave} can be defined as follows:

$$B_{ave} = \frac{1}{M \times N} \sum_{i=1}^{M} \sum_{j=1}^{N} Bf_{ij} \qquad (5)$$

As the R_{BBVD} of each block in the corresponding two frames has been calculated in each group, calculate the average of these series R_{BVD}, value defined as R_{BVD}, in each sub-sequence.

$$R_{BVD} = \frac{1}{16} \sum_{i=1}^{16} R_{bi} \qquad (6)$$

R_{BVD} is our new feature for detecting video inter-frame forgery. R_{bi} is an element value of a 8×8 block. The process of algorithm is introduced in the following section.

3 Proposed Scheme

The new feature is proposed in the previous section. In this section, we describe the proposed scheme.

3.1 Assumptions Made for the Proposed Scheme

As mentioned above, human eyes can not perceive video content modification if only very few frames have been modified. In this paper, only the meaningful video frame insertion is concerned, by meaningful, it means the forgery content can be perceived by human eye. Thus, it is based on several assumptions as listed below:

1. Each test video sequence is one shot video sequence taken by the stationary video camera.
2. Each forged video has only one of the following two type of forgery: frame insertion or frame deletion.
3. In frame insertion or frame deletion, the number of the inserted or deleted frame is more than 10.
4. Each frame insertion or deletion video only has been performed once.

3.2 Framework

In Fig. 1, the proposed framework is presented. The main process of forgery detection includes short-temporal frame sequence partitioning, sub-block division in each frame, R_{BVD} obtained extraction, adaptive self-threshold selection, fast detection, forgery type detection and forgery localization. The detailed process will be described in the following subsections.

3.3 Feature Extraction

The detailed steps of feature extraction are given as follows:

1. Given a test video, parse it into a series of frames.
2. Partition the full-length video sequence into short overlapping sub-sequence groups as we discussed before, i.e. $G = \{g_1, g_2, g_3 \dots g_j \dots g_n\}$. Note that there is some frames overlap between consecutive groups.
3. For each frame, partition it into 4×4 blocks, denoted as $B = \{b_1, b_2, b_3 \dots b_i \dots b_{16}\}$.
4. By using Eq. (4), calculate the ratio of BBVD for each group.
5. By utilizing Eqs. (5) and (6), the average value of ratio of BBVD, denoted as R_{BVD}, is calculated.

In this way, a series of R_{BVD} is calculated in the whole-length video sequence as the shown in Fig. 1. Among a series value of R_{BVD}, there are two obvious peak points. As mentioned before, the ratio of BBVD is close to a constant in a normal video and this consistency will be disturbed in the frame insertion video. As shown in Fig. 1,

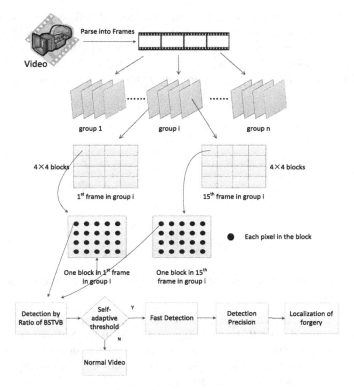

Fig. 1. Framework of proposed scheme

the corresponding sub-sequences to these two peak points must contain the original frame and the insertion frame. Although it is easy to determine the peak point from the figure, how to get a self-adaptive threshold is important.

3.4 Self-adaptive Threshold Selection Method

The so-called 3σ Rule is the common criteria of gross error detection in the probability theory. Its basic assumption is that the random error obey the normal distribution, and then the absolute value of error mainly concentrated in the vicinity of the its mean. It can be expressed as follows:

$$P(-3\sigma < z - \mu < 3\sigma) = 0.9974 \tag{7}$$

where $z \sim N(\mu, \sigma^2)$, σ is the standard deviation of z. Equation (7) implies that data can be treated as the gross error is more than 3σ.

When applying the 3σ Rule to our method, if the ratio of BBVD is more than 3σ, where σ refers to the standard deviation of a sequence of ratio of BBVD derived from every two frames with the equal time interval in a video, this value can be treated as the gross error. That means these two frames are no longer subordinated to consistency of those frames with equal time intervals, which indicating the existence of the insertion frames. In this way, the approximate location of the insertion frame will be found.

As mentioned above, whether R_{BBVD} is subordinated to the Gaussian distribution needs to be justified before applying the 3σ Rule to our method. The verified results are given in Fig. 2.

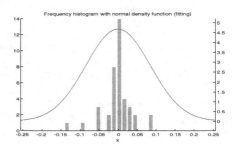

Fig. 2. The curve-fitting of frequency histogram conform to Gaussian distribution of R_{BBVD}.

From Fig. 2, it is obvious that the series of R_{BBVD}, is subordinated to Gaussian distribution and thus the 3σ Rule can be applied to the BBVD sequence. Since most R_{BBVD}, are close to 0, only few values have large numerical deviation which can be treated as the gross error. Usually, the gross error implies that the corresponding sub-sequence frames contain either inserted frames or deleted frames.

After validation, we can calculate the standard deviation of the series of R_{BVD}, i.e., $\{R_{BVD1}, R_{BVD2}, R_{BVD3}\ldots\ldots.R_{BVDn}\}$ in the in the whole-length video sequence as follows.

$$\mu_{BVD} = \frac{1}{N}\sum\nolimits_{i=1}^{N} R_{BVDi} \tag{8}$$

$$\sigma_{BVD} = \sqrt{\frac{1}{N}\sum\nolimits_{i=1}^{n} (R_{BVDi} - u)^2} \tag{9}$$

where μ_{BVD} is the mean value of the R_{BVD}, σ_{BVD} is the standard deviation of series R_{BVD}. So we can obtain the self-adaptive threshold from the testing video frame sequence.

3.5 Inter-frame Forgery Type Detection

The details of the inter-frame forgery detection is as follows:

1. According to the 3σ Rule, if the value of R_{BVD} is more than 3σ, this value can be treated as a gross error.
2. If none of R_{BVD} is more than 3σ, the test video is determined as a normal video.

3. If the number of the gross error is one peak, the test video is frame deletion video.
4. If the number of the gross error is more than two, the test video is a frame insertion video.

As for the frame insertion video, the ratio of BBVD at the beginning and the end of the insertion frame has a greater volatility than other normal frames. As shown in Fig. 3, two distinct peak points occur in the whole series of R_{BVD}. Thus, it is easy to conclude that the corresponding sub-sequence group of these two peak points must contain the insertion frame and original frame. Some videos have abrupt change to result in false detection will be analyzed in the experiment. As for the deletion video, only just one peak point can be found if only one deleting operation was done. Furthermore, the peak value of the deletion usually is less than that of the insertion.

Fig. 3. The sampling of the ratio of BBVD with frame insertion forgery in each sub-sequence

3.6 Forgery Localization

The process of the insertion forgery localization is the same as the deletion forgery localization. So the forgery localization of the insertion detection was given as an explanation. Since two maximum peak points have been found, it is easy to figure out the corresponding sub-sequences. Each sub-sequence has 15 frames, which contains the normal frames and insertion frames. To specify the accurate location of the frame insertion, the ratio of BBVD for frame to frame needs to be calculated further.

The details of the insertion forgery localization is as follows:

Step 1. Select the first frame, i.e., f_i, as a reference position in the sub-sequence which includes the peak point.

Step 2. Select 40 adjacent frames of which 20 frames are ahead of f_i and the other 20 frames are behind.

Step 3. Calculate the ration of BBVD of each two adjacent frames by utilizing Eqs. (4) and (5). In this way, two new series of ratio of BBVD frame by frame can be calculated, each of which is corresponding to a peak point. The results are shown in Fig. 4.

The variation between two adjacent frames in non-tampered frame sequence is extremely low which implies that the ratio of BBVD is close to 0. Only two corresponding

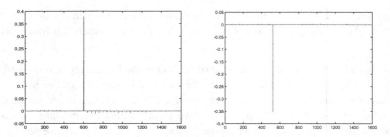

Fig. 4. Results of the ratio of BBVD calculated by frame to frame

frames are from different video frame subsequences can lead to a sudden volatility. As shown in Fig. 4, all the values except one point are nearly equal to 0 in each figure. Those points of which values equal to 0 mean that the corresponding two frames are the continuous and original frame sequence. And the point with a sudden volatility means the corresponding frames contain the original frame and insertion frame. Thus, select the maximum value of each result and find the corresponding frames to this result. The localization of frame is the accurate location of the frame insertion. The deletion detection is the same process as the insertion detection.

4   Experimental Results and Discussion

The scheme of the inter-frame video forgery detection has been presented above. Here experimental works are presented to verify that our algorithm is feasible and has good performance.

4.1   Video Database

The original videos are from the Recognition of Human Actions Database [9]. The video database contains six types of human actions (walking, jogging, running, boxing, hand waving and hand clapping) in four different scenarios: outdoors s1, outdoors with scale variation s2, outdoors with different clothes s3, and indoors s4, as illustrated below.

All sequences were taken over homogeneous backgrounds with a static camera with 25 fps frame rate. The format of all the video sequence is AVI file format [9].

The insertion forgery database used in our work follows Chao et al. [7] scheme for fair comparison. The test video database is generated with TRECVID Content Based Copy Detection (CBCD) scripts. The CBCD scripts can generate frame insertion videos automatically with random length. In our approach, 220 frame insertion video sequences and 20 normal video sequences are selected for testing. Each frame is of 240 × 320 pixels in size and the length of each video sequence is ranged from 375 frames to 625 frames (approximately 15 to 25 s).

4.2   Evaluation Parameter

To evaluate the detection efficiency, two criterions called the recall rate, R_r, and the precision rate, R_p, are used. The recall rate is the proportion of correctly detected videos among all tampered videos. The precision rate refers to the percentage of correctly detected video among all the detected videos. The recall rate, R_r, and the precision rate, R_p, are defined as follows:

$$R_r = \frac{N_c}{N_c + N_m} \times 100\,\% \tag{10}$$

$$R_p = \frac{N_c}{N_c + N_f} \times 100\,\% \tag{11}$$

where N_c is the number of correctly detected video forgeries; N_m is the number of missed video forgeries; N_f is the number of falsely detected video forgeries.

4.3   Experiments on Frame Insertion Detection

Video Frame Insertion Detection. As for validation of the video frame insertion, the recall rate reaches 98.67 % and the precision rate reaches 94.09 % as shown in Table 1.

Table 1. Test results for validation of video frame insertion

	N_c	N_m	N_f	R_r (%)	R_p (%)
Our scheme	223	3	14	98.67	94.09
Chao scheme [7]	2863	137	140	95.43	95.34

From Table 1, we can conclude: Our scheme has a higher recall rate than that achieved by Chao scheme [7], but a lower precision rate to some extent. That is our scheme pay more attention to efficiency than to precision.

Above comparison is not peer to peer, because the Chao [7] is using more than 3000 forgery video sequence, but only 220 forgery video sequences are used in our scheme. So we just perform qualitative analysis.

Video Frame Insertion Localization. For the localization of frame insertion, the recall rate reaches 89.23 % and the precision rate reaches 79.45 %.

Since the localization of frame insertion detection is not discussed in Chao [7], the localization performance is not compared between the two schemes. From Table 1, we can conclude that the proposed scheme can detect most localizations of insertion forgery. From the above data, there are some deviation in frame insertion localization. Because there are some constraints on the test videos which are based on the several assumptions mentioned before, this algorithm has susceptibility to some extent. That is, if the object moves too fast, some values of R_{BBVD} will has a bigger and abrupt variation, which is not caused by the frame insertion.

4.4 Real-Time Applications

There are 10 video sequences with different lengths and sizes used in experiment and shown in Table 2. Table 2 describes the relationship between the tested video length and the test duration (namely computational cost). For a video of 2.85 MB lasting 45 s long, it takes about 8.4 s to detect the frame insertion. The time-cost of our scheme is shown in Table 2. There is no time cost discussed in Chao [7], however the processing time of their scheme is usually longer than the video length because of its complexity of pixel-based optical flow calculation.

Table 2. Time-cost of computing in our scheme among different length videos[a]

Number	Video length (s)	Video size (MB)	Average time-cost (s)	Ratio of real-time (%)
1	45	2.85	8.4	0.19
2	35	2.15	7.4	0.21
3	31	1.93	7.1	0.23
4	27	1.68	6.7	0.25
5	26	1.67	7.3	0.28
6	21	1.39	6.2	0.30
7	20	1.24	5.7	0.29
8	19	1.18	4.6	0.24
9	17	0.75	5.6	0.33
10	16	1.00	5.5	0.34

[a]with CPU i7-2820, 4 GB RAM, Win7 64bit, and Matlab2012b.

Form Table 2, we can conclude that the gross trend of time-cost of our scheme is directly in proportion to the video length. It is 73.4 % short than video length on average. There are some exceptional cases, such as number 4 and 5 in Table 2. As a result, our scheme can satisfy real-time request in most applications.

4.5 Frame Insertion with Different Insertion Number

Two hundred forgery video sequences are generated with TRECVID Content Based Copy Detection (CBCD) scripts and are selected to test the detection efficiency with different frame insertion numbers. Those video sequences can be classified into two groups. The 100 video sequences are those with less than 25-frame insertion and the other 100 video sequences are those with more than 25-frame insertion.

According to the results listed in Table 3, we can conclude as follows. In term of detection precision, R_p, our scheme is 11.6 % lower than that achieved by Chao [7]. In term of detection recall, our scheme is compatible to than achieved by Chao [7]. The proposed approach is more efficient than Chao [7] in real-time applications. Moreover, it is obvious that both recall rate and precision rate will drop down with fewer frames insertion. Frame insertion forgery with more than 25-frame insertion will lead to a higher detection accuracy. It is in accord with Chao's conclusion.

Table 3. Test results with different frame insertion numbers

	Insertion frames	$N_c + N_m + N_f$	N_c	N_m	N_f	R_r (%)	R_p (%)
Our scheme	$N \leq 25$	100	66	13	21	83.5	75.8
	$N > 25$	100	82	5	13	94.25	86.32
Chao scheme[7]	$N = 25$	608	566	44	8	92.67	95.58
	$N = 100$	612	566	34	12	94.33	97.92

5 Conclusion

In this paper, a novel feature, called block-wise brightness variance descriptor (BBVD), is proposed. And a fast scheme for video frame forgery detection based on the new feature is developed. Experiments have shown that the recall rate in detecting video frame insertion reaches 98.67 % and the precision rate reaches 94.09 % as shown in Table 1. As for the detecting the location of the frame insertion, the recall rate reaches 89.23 % and the precision rate reaches 79.45 %. It is more suitable for real-time processing than Chao et al.'s scheme [7].

Future work will focus on improving the robustness when detecting the location of video frame insertion and enhancing its recall rate and precision rate.

Acknowledgements. This work was supported by the Project of International Cooperation and Exchanges by Shanghai Committee of Science and Technology (No. 12510708500). And it is also partially supported by the National Natural Science Foundation of China (No. 61272249, 61272439), the Specialized Research Fund for the Doctoral Program of Higher Education (No. 20120073110053).

References

1. Rocha, A., Scheirer, W., Boult, T., Goldenstein, S.: Vision of the unseen: Current trends and challenges in digital image and video forensics. ACM Comput. Surv. **43**, 26 (2011)
2. Roy, S.D., Li, X., Shoshan, Y., Fish, A., Yadid-Pecht, O.: Hardware Implementation of a digital watermarking system for video authentication. IEEE Trans. Circuits Syst. Video Technol. **23**(2), 289–301 (2013)
3. Bestagini, P., Fontani, M., Milani, S., Barni, M., Piva, A., Tagliasacchi, M., Tubaro, K.S.: An overview on video forensics. In: Proceedings of European Signal Processing Conference (EUSIPCO 2012), pp. 1229–1233, Bucharest, Romania (2012)
4. Kurosawa, K., Kuroki, K., Saitoh, N.: CCD fingerprint method-identification of a video camera from videotaped image. In: International Conference on Image Processing, pp. 537–540 (1999)
5. Tagliasacchi, M., Tubaro, S.: Blind estimation of the QP parameter in H.264/AVC decoded video. In: 2010 11th International Workshop on Image Analysis for Multimedia Interactive Services (WIAMIS) (2010)
6. Wang, W., Farid, H.: Exposing digital forgeries in video by detecting duplication. In: Proceedings of the 9th Workshop on Multimedia and Security, pp. 35–42. ACM (2007)

7. Chao, J., Jiang, X., Sun, T.: A novel video inter-frame forgery model detection scheme based on optical flow consistency. In: Shi, Y.Q., Kim, H.-J., Pérez-González, F. (eds.) IWDW 2012. LNCS, vol. 7809, pp. 267–281. Springer, Heidelberg (2013)
8. Comesana, P., Pérez-González, F.: Weber's law-based side-informed data hiding. In: 2011 IEEE International Conference on Acoustics, Speech and Signal Processing (ICASSP), pp. 1840–1843. IEEE. (2007)
9. KTH database: http://www.nada.kth.se/cvap/actions

Universal Counterforensics of Multiple Compressed JPEG Images

Mauro Barni, Marco Fontani, and Benedetta Tondi[✉]

Department of Information Engineering and Mathematics,
University of Siena, Siena, Italy
barni@dii.unisi.it, marco.fontani@unisi.it, benedettatondi@gmail.com

Abstract. Detection of multiple JPEG compression of digital images has been attracting more and more interest in the field of multimedia forensics. On the other side, techniques to conceal the traces of multiple compression are being proposed as well. Motivated by a recent trend towards the adoption of universal approaches, we propose a counterforensic technique that makes multiple compression undetectable for any forensic detector based on the analysis of the histograms of quantized DCT coefficients. Experimental results show the effectiveness of our approach in removing the artifacts of double and also triple compression, while maintaining a good quality of the image.

1 Introduction

In the last years the supremacy of images as the most direct and trustful mean of communication has been threatened by the widespread availability of photo manipulation software. The research community has tackled with this problem in several ways: at the beginning, only active approaches like image watermarking and digital signatures were investigated; lately, Multimedia Forensics emerged as the discipline that tries to infer as much information as possible about the processing history of an image without having access to any further information.

Shortly afterwards the birth of Multimedia Forensics, counter-forensic methods started to be investigated as well, whose goal is to conceal the evidence of manipulation when a user alters an image by means of processing tools for malicious purposes. As we will discuss in the paper, most of the state-of-the-art approaches are targeted at deceiving a specific forensic detector, by erasing the traces it searches for. On the contrary, universal approaches exist that, instead of deceiving a fixed detector, attempt at making the doctored image undetectable for *any* detector, at least within a certain class [8]. While the literature is rich of targeted counter forensic schemes, the first universal approaches have been proposed only recently [2,5]; this fact witnesses the higher complexity of developing universal CF methods. In this paper, we propose a universal counter forensic approach for concealing traces of multiple JPEG compression. From a forensic point of view, JPEG compression is one of the most important stages in the processing chain of a digital image, because it leaves peculiar statistical footprints that can be used as a telltale of tampering. In particular, traces left by

© Springer International Publishing Switzerland 2015
Y.-Q. Shi et al. (Eds.): IWDW 2014, LNCS 9023, pp. 31–46, 2015.
DOI: 10.1007/978-3-319-19321-2_3

multiple JPEG compressions are usually a powerful tool in analyzing the authenticity of an image. Therefore, the method proposed in this paper establishes a new challenge for future forensic detectors.

The paper is organized as follows: Sect. 1.1 briefly reviews related works and clarify our contribution; a summary of the effects of multiple JPEG compressions in the frequency domain is given in Sect. 2. In Sect. 3 we introduce the theoretical framework behind our method, while Sect. 4 is devoted to a detailed description of all the phases of the algorithm. Experimental validation is finally reported in Sect. 5.

1.1 Related Works and Contribution

The interest of forensic researchers in the detection of multiple compressions is motivated by the fact that when JPEG images are manipulated by a photo-editing software and later re-saved in JPEG format, artifacts are introduced in the image. Popescu et al. [14] showed that multiple quantization steps introduce periodic artifacts into the histograms of DCT coefficients, which can then be searched for in order to detect a manipulation. Inspired by this work, many techniques for detecting double JPEG compression have been proposed, which analyze the first order statistics of the DCT coefficients, e.g., [13]. Many recently proposed forensic approaches rely on the analysis of the first significant digits (FSD) of the DCT coefficients. Specifically, the distribution of the FSDs in the frequency domain is investigated in order to tell apart single compressed images from double compressed [10] and, more in general, multiple compressed ones [11]. On the other hand, counterforensic schemes have been developed in order to remove or disguise the artifacts of multiple compression in the FSD distributions, like in [12]. A unifying characteristic of these anti-forensic methods is that they are targeted to deceive a specific forensic detector (*targeted approaches*). As such, they do not guarantee that a possible different detector, even based on the analysis of the same statistic, would be defeated in turn; in fact, the analyst may develop a modified version of the detector that is robust to the counter-forensic approach, thus pushing forward the cat-and-mouse game.

To overcome this limitation, that is inherent in the use of targeted couter-forensic techniques, a recent trend has turned to *universal approaches*, see [5] and [2], for which the optimality under certain criteria is discussed. In particular, in [2], a universal technique for concealing manipulations of gray-scale images in the spatial domain is proposed. The general idea behind this method is the following: in order to avoid the introduction of new traces, the attacker should try to make *the statistics* of the image as close as possible to the statistics of an untouched image. In this way, in principle, the tampering would be statistically undetectable for any forensic detector, whatever are the traces it looks for in the image, thus definitively ending the cat and mouse loop. The rigorous theoretical framework behind such an approach is provided in [1], where the general problem of hypothesis testing in presence of an adversary is addressed, thus opening the door to the applicability of the method to many different scenarios, like watermarking, fingerprinting, spam filtering, secure classification, reputation systems, and so on. Of course, it is very hard to devise a universal technique that is capable of "fixing" every statistic of the processed signal; in [1] the first steps have been taken by assuming some limitations on the resources available to the forensic investigator. Specifically, the optimum strategies for the forensic analyst and the attacker are found under the assumption that the analyst relies on first order statistics to perform the decision. Although this limitation might sound restrictive, it holds in many realistic scenarios, like in the image forensic scenario, and permits to cope with an entire class of forensic detectors. Leveraging on the theoretical results in [1], the universal attacking strategy proposed in [2] is optimum against any forensic detector based on the analysis of the histogram of the image.

In this paper, we want to extend the *universal* counterforensic algorithm developed in [2] to the frequency (DCT) domain, at the purpose of countering the detection of multiple JPEG compressions. In order to do so, we will exploit the results which come from the extension of the adversarial hypothesis testing to the case of multiple observations, addressed in [3]. To the best of our knowledge, the proposed techniques is also the first that has been applied for concealing traces left by any number of compression stages. On top of that, the very good results obtained in terms of visual quality of the attacked image are a strength of our method.

2   JPEG-Based Image Forensics and Watson's Model

The JPEG standard is today the most widely used method for storing digital images. Despite its lossy nature, JPEG compression is designed not to introduce annoying artifacts in pixels, at least for reasonable compression ratios. On the other hand, appreciable artifacts are introduced in the Discrete Cosine Transform (DCT) domain, where most of the computation is carried, and this fact fostered the development of a whole branch of image forensic techniques. For this reason, we find it worthy to introduce the basic concepts of JPEG coding and briefly describe how JPEG-based forensic algorithms work.

To begin with, we revisit the procedure of compression of a gray-scale image according to the JPEG standard. As a first operation, the input is divided into blocks of 8×8 pixels each. For each block, the two dimensional DCT is computed. Let $X(i, j)$, $1 \leq i, j \leq 8$, denote the DCT coefficient in position (i, j) of the block. The DCT coefficients are then quantized into integer-valued quantization levels $X_q(i, j)$ as follows:

$$X_q(i, j) = \text{sign}(X(i, j))\text{round} \left(\frac{|X(i, j)|}{q(i, j)} \right), \tag{1}$$

where the quantization steps $q(i, j)$ are given by a predetermined (chosen) quantization matrix $Q = \{q(i, j)\}_{i,j=1}^{8}$. After quantization, the values $X_q(i, j)$ of the block are ordered by zig-zag scanning and finally compressed by a lossless encoder. Viceversa, in the decompression procedure, first the bit stream is decoded, and the integer coefficients $X_q(i, j)$ are rearranged back into blocks.

Then, the de-quantized DCT coefficients are recovered by multiplying the coefficients with the corresponding entry of the quantization matrix, i.e., $X_q(i,j) \cdot q(i,j)$. Due to the quantization step, the compression procedure is not invertible and the dequantized coefficients assume only values which are integer multiples of the corresponding quantization step. Finally, the inverse DCT of each block is computed and the result is rounded and truncated so that the integer values range in $[0, 255]$. The quantization factor is the parameter which determines the amount of approximation introduced by the compression, thus affecting both the compression ratio and the quality of the reconstructed image. Typically, the quantization matrix is fixed by selecting a quality factor (QF), in $[0, 100]$; a high quality factor corresponds to a high quality of the reconstructed image, which also means lower values for the quantization coefficients.

Now let us suppose that an image is compressed twice. Let $X_{q_1}(i,j)$ denote the quantized value in position (i,j) after the first encoding with quantization step $q_1(i,j)$. When the image goes through a second compression stage, the resulting quantization level is:

$$X_{q_2}(i,j) = \text{sign}(X_{q_1}(i,j))\text{round}\left(\frac{|X_{q_1}(i,j) \cdot q_1(i,j)|}{q_2(i,j)}\right), \qquad (2)$$

where $q_2(i,j)$ is the quantization step of the second encoding. Popescu et al. [14] observed that double quantization, and more in general consecutive quantizations, introduce periodic artifacts in the histogram of DCT coefficients. Such a periodic pattern depends on the ratio between the quantization steps, that is, on the ratio between the quality factor of first and second compression. More specifically, when the step size decreases (i.e., QF increases) some bins in the histograms are empty, whereas when it increases (i.e., QF decreases) some bins contain a large number of samples and some other bins only few. It is proper to observe that forensic analysers have usually to deal with the first kind of artifacts, since in many application the goal of the attacker is to pass off a lower quality image as an image of higher quality. For this reason, in this paper we consider the case of multiple compression with increasing quality factors; however it is proper to stress that, being universal, our technique can equivalently be applied in the other case.

Below, we give a brief description of the Watson's model that we will use to characterize the distortion constraint of the DCT coefficients, that is for the estimation of the Just Noticeable Difference (JND) of the block-based DCT coefficients [17].

The Watson's DCT-based Visual Model. This model establishes a link between modifications in the (unquantized) DCT domain and their impact in the pixel domain. To account for the sensitivity of the Human Visual System (HVS) to different frequencies, the model defines a *sensitivity table*, which is an 8×8 matrix W whose element $W(i,j)$ gives the amount of modification for coefficient (i,j) that produces a JND in the pixel domain. Lower values in the matrix correspond to higher sensibility for the HVS to that frequency. For our experimental evaluations, we use the matrix of standard values provided in

[6]. The sensitivity table is the simplest estimation of the JND, as it does not take into account the local properties of the image. To obtain a more accurate evaluation of the JND for a DCT coefficient we need to consider two more effects: the *luminance masking* and the *contrast masking*.

The luminance masking effect is due to the fact that, according to the HVS, a bright background hides more noise that a dark background. To account for such an effect, Watson's model modifies the matrix for each block of the image on the basis of the value of the DC coefficient (mean luminance intensity of the block). The refined threshold for the (i, j) DCT coefficient of the k-th block is given by

$$T_L(i, j; k) = W(i, j) \cdot \left[\frac{C(1, 1; k)}{\overline{C}} \right]^{\alpha},$$
(3)

where $C(1, 1; k)$ is the DC value of the k-th block, $\overline{C}$ is the mean intensity of the image, and α is a constant. The value suggested by Watson is $\alpha = 0.649$.

Watson's model further refines the estimation of the JND by considering also the contrast masking effect. This is done by evaluating the influence that the AC energy has in the DCT coefficients. The threshold for the DCT coefficient (i, j) of the k-th block is then given by:

$$T(i, j; k) = \max\{T_L(i, j; k), |C(i, j; k)|^{\eta} \cdot T_L(i, j; k)^{1-\eta}\},$$
(4)

where η is a constant between 0 and 1 (Watson suggests $\eta = 0.7$).

3   Theoretical Background for the Proposed Work

Before diving into the proposed scheme we need to give a brief overview of the theoretical framework behind it. A universal counter-forensic method is derived by modelling and studying the struggle between the forensic analyst (or defender D) and the attacker (A). In the general case, D wants to tell apart modified and untouched images, while A aims at making the decision fail. More specifically, after generating the manipulated image with the desired properties, A wants to slightly modify it in such a way to prevent D from detecting manipulations, while respecting a distortion constraint. A first theoretical analysis of such an interplay between A and D has been proposed in [1], under the assumption that D only considers first order statistics for the analysis. By formulating the problem as a game and solving it by means of game theoretical tools, the authors derived the optimum strategies for both players (D and A). Interestingly, since there is a dominant strategy for the defender, the optimum attacking strategy results from the resolution of an optimization problem, obtained by assuming that D plays its dominant strategy. These theoretical findings have been put in practice in the image forensic scenario for designing a universal counter-forensic (U-CF) method, able to fool *any* forensic detector based on the image histogram, whatever the trace it looks for (e.g., footprints left by contrast enhancement operations, cut and paste, splicing, and so on) [2]. According to this technique, starting from the processed image y with histogram h_Y, A produces the attacked image

z in three steps: *retrieval* of a target histogram from a database of untouched histograms, *computation of the optimum mapping* and *implementation of the mapping* into the image. The overall scheme is preserved in the algorithm proposed in this paper; however, working in the DCT domain poses several new challenges that need to be solved, especially in the second and the third phase.

With a specific reference to the JPEG forensic scenario, the D/A interplay can be described as follows: on one side, D wants to tell apart single compressed from multiple compressed images while, on the other side, A aims at hiding the effect of multiple compressions so that the image looks like a single compressed one. We assume that, as an extension of the previous case, the defender relies the decision on the analysis of the histograms of the DCT coefficients; this hypothesis actually holds for most of the existing forensic tools. The main difference with respect to the previous case is that now the forensic analyst has to combine the information brought by 64 histograms, one for each DCT frequency (i, j). At the same time, A has 64 histograms to act upon in order to fool D, while preserving the constraint on the visual distortion of the image *in the spatial domain*. It should now be evident that, although having similarities with the analogous problem in the pixel domain, the case under analysis cannot be treated with the theoretical tools proposed in [1]. Instead, the detection of JPEG multiple compression in frequency domain finds an appropriate background in [3], where the case of *multiple observations* is considered, and then D bases the decision on a number S of features (or summaries) each one extracted from an observed sequence which describes the status of a system. This is exactly the case with the JPEG forensic methods, since they separately analyse coefficients belonging to different DCT frequencies. Let x be a reference single compressed image on which D bases the decision; we denote by $h_{X_{ij}}$ the histogram of the quantized DCT coefficients in position (i, j) and with $v_{X_{ij}}$ the normalized one. Moreover, we indicate with v_{ij}, for $1 \leq i, j \leq 8$, the normalized histograms of the image under analysis. Because of the decorrelation property of the DCT transform, the dependence among DCT coefficients in different subbands is low (intrablock dependence), and then we can approximately assume them independent. Exploiting this fact in the analysis in [3], it is easy to show that the optimum log-likelihood function of the Neyman-Pearson test performed by D (under the assumption of resources limited to the first order analysis) can be noticeably simplified, becoming

$$\sum_{i,j=1}^{8} \mathcal{D}(v_{ij} || v_{X_{ij}}), \tag{5}$$

where $\mathcal{D}(\cdot || \cdot)$ is the Kullback-Leibler (KL) divergence. Given two probability distributions R and Q defined over the same alphabet, the KL divergence is defined as

$$\mathcal{D}(R||Q) = \sum_{a} R(a) \log \frac{R(a)}{Q(a)}.$$

According to the game theoretical analysis, expression (5) is the optimum objective function that A has to minimize in producing the forgery [3].

4   Universal JPEG Counter-Forensic Algorithm

In this section we describe in detail each phase of the proposed counter-forensic algorithm. The attacker owns an image which has been compressed two or more times with increasing quality factor, i.e., with $QF_k > QF_{k-1}$, where k denotes the number of times that the image has undergone a compression stage. In order to pass off the image as a single compressed image, the attacker runs the universal counter-forensic algorithm schematized in Fig. 1. Before entering the details of each step, let us introduce some necessary notation. For simplicity, the capital letter X is used to denote image x in the transformed domain and X_q for the quantized version. In addition, $X_q(i,j)$ indicates the transformed coefficient in position (i,j) of a generic block; when a particular block k is addressed we denote it by $X_q(i,j;k)$.

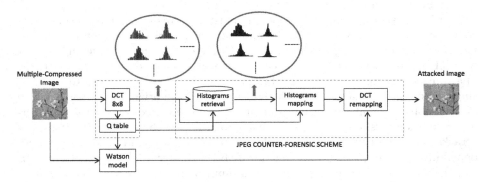

Fig. 1. The block scheme of the proposed universal JPEG counter-forensic algorithm.

4.1   Retrieval Phase

The proposed counter-forensic scheme assumes that the attacker owns a database (DB) of images that have been JPEG compressed only once. Given the multiple compressed image Y_q with quantization matrix $Q_Y = \{q_Y(i,j)\}_{i,j=1}^8$, A searches in the adapted DB of images the one whose vector of DCT histograms is the most similar to the histogram vector $h_Y = (h_{Y_{11}}, h_{Y_{12}}, ..., h_{Y_{88}})$.

For any frequency subband (or block position) (i,j), the similarity between an histogram $h_{X_{ij}}$ and $h_{Y_{ij}}$ is measured by the chi-square distance χ^2, defined as follows:

$$\chi^2(h_{X_{ij}}, h_{Y_{ij}}) = \frac{1}{2} \sum_{m \in \mathcal{C}} \frac{(h_{X_{ij}}(m) - h_{Y_{ij}}(m))^2}{(h_{X_{ij}}(m) + h_{Y_{ij}}(m))},$$

where $\mathcal{C}$ denotes the set of all the values taken by the DCT coefficients[1]. While in the spatial domain these values range from 0 to 255 (pixel values), in the frequency domain the DCT coefficients vary in $[-1024, 1023]$.

---

[1] Experiments show that using χ^2 in place of $\mathcal{D}$ in this phase lightens the computation without significantly affecting the results.

We can distinguish between two methods for performing the choice of the 64 DCT target histograms, depending on how the overall χ^2 distance is computed:

- *average distance:* for each image X in the DB the attacker sums each contribution $\chi^2(h_{X_{ij}}, h_{Y_{ij}})$ provided by each couple of histograms[2] and chooses the vector of 64 DCT histograms minimizing the overall distance. That is, the attacker looks for the vector h_X which minimizes $\sum_{(i,j)} \chi^2(h_{X_{ij}}, h_{Y_{ij}})$;
- *separate distance for each subband:* for each DCT subband, A searches the DB for the histogram associated with the minimum of the χ^2 distance; i.e., for each (i,j), the A chooses the $h_{X_{ij}}$ which minimizes $\chi^2(h_{X_{ij}}, h_{Y_{ij}})$.

It is evident that, in the second case, the target DCT histograms retrieved from the DB probably belong to different images, i.e., different histogram vectors of the DB. However, in our model, which is confined to the analysis of first-order statistics, this fact does not arise any contradiction, being consistent with the optimum strategy for A. Besides, it must be stressed that performing the choice in the second way allows to find, for each subband, target histograms which are closer to the processed ones with respect to those found in the first way. There are some important considerations we need to do about the retrieval phase. First, we notice that the attacker can hardly resort directly to a DB of single compressed images, since the corresponding quantization matrices would be probably different from the input quantization matrix Q_Y. Instead of storing thousands versions of the same image quantized with all possible tables, the attacker can more practically consider a DB of never-compressed images and, depending on the quantization matrix of the Y_q under analysis, adapt the DB "on-the-fly". This means that, for a given input image Y_q, the attacker *simulates* the (single) JPEG compression by quantizing the DCT coefficients according to the input quantization matrix Q_Y. The second observation still concerns practicality: since the search is conducted on the vector of DCT histograms and not on images, only the histograms of unquantized DCT coefficients need to be stored in the DB. This allows to reduce both the size of the dataset and the execution time.

4.2 Mapping Phase

According to our previous discussion, in this phase the attacker has to determine the histograms $v_{Z_{i,j}}$ which minimizes the quantity $\sum_{(i,j)} \mathcal{D}(v_{Z_{ij}} || v_{X_{ij}})$, subject to a distortion constraint imposed in order to maintain the final image visually similar to the initial one. In order to characterize this constraint in the frequency domain we rely on the concept of Just Noticeable Distortion (JND), defined as the maximum modification of the DCT coefficients which is visually undetectable. Then, it is reasonable to take the JND as maximum value for the distortion that A can introduce in the coefficients of the transformed image Y. A commonly used model for the JND is Watson's model [17], described in Sect. 2,

---

[2] Each contribution may be possibly weighted by some coefficients in order to give more importance to the low frequency coefficients.

which provides a 8×8 sensitivity matrix $W = \{W(i,j)\}_{i,j=1}^8$. Each entry of the matrix $W_q(i,j)$ provides the maximum amount of distortion which can be introduced in the quantized DCT coefficients of the subband (i,j) without generating annoying artifacts. Let $W_q = \{\text{round}(W(i,j)/q_Y(i,j))\}_{i,j=1}^8$ denote the quantized Watson's matrix, approximated to integer values[3]. The maximum distortion for the (i,j) coefficient is given by $K(i,j) = W_q(i,j) \cdot D_{\max}$ for some $D_{\max} \geq 1$ (larger $D_{\max}$ allow to obtain more accurate mapping at the price of a higher visual distortion). Interestingly, since distortion constraints are defined subband-wise, the problem can be solved as 64 separate minimizations:

$$\min_{|Z(i,j)-Y(i,j)| \leq K(i,j)} \mathcal{D}(v_{Z_{ij}} || v_{X_{ij}}), \quad \forall (i,j), 1 \leq i,j \leq 8. \tag{6}$$

Let us focus on a single DCT subband and analyze the corresponding problem. It is useful to introduce the *transportation matrix* $N_{ij} = \{n_{ij}(m \to r)\}_{m,r=1}^{|\mathcal{C}|}$, where each term $n_{ij}(m \to r)$ indicates the number of elements in $h_{Y_{ij}}$ which must be moved from the m-th to the r-th bin. Let n_{ij} be the total number of blocks in the image (i.e., the number of DCT coefficients for each position (i,j)). Each constrained optimization problem in (6) is quite similar to the one in [2] and, similarly, can be rephrased in function of the $n_{ij}(m \to n)$ variables as follows:

$$\min_{n_{ij}(m \to r)} \sum_{r=1}^{|\mathcal{C}|} \frac{(\sum_m n_{ij}(m \to r))}{n} \cdot \log \frac{(\sum_m n_{ij}(m \to r))}{n v_{X_{ij}}(r)}, \tag{7}$$

subject to

$$\begin{cases} \sum_r n_{ij}(m \to r) = h_{Y_{ij}}(m) \; \forall i \\ n_{ij}(m \to r) = 0, \; \forall (m,r) \in \mathcal{I} : |m-r| > K(i,j) \\ n_{ij}(m \to r) \geq 0 \quad \forall m, r \\ n_{ij}(m \to r) \in \mathbb{N} \end{cases} \tag{8}$$

where the histogram $h_{Y_{ij}}$ and the distortion constraint were rewritten in terms of $n_{ij}(m \to r)$ variables. Solving problem (7)–(8) provides the optimum map N_{ij}^*, from which we obtain the final attacked histogram $h_{Z_{ij}}$ by computing $\sum_m n_{ij}^*(m \to r)$ for each r. Problem (7)–(8) is a convex mixed integer non-linear problem (MINLP) [4] for which a global optimum solution exists and efficient solvers are available for the resolution. It is worth observing that the number of optimization variables is given by $|\mathcal{C}|$, that is the cardinality of the alphabet of the DCT coefficients ($|\mathcal{C}| = 2048$), and it does not depend on the size of the image. This value seems to be significantly larger compared to the one in the pixel domain (i.e., 256); however, since the statistics of the DCT coefficients are usually peaked around the mean value [9], the number of variables can be noticeably reduced by cutting off the bins below $m_{\min}$ (where $m_{\min}$ is s.t. $h_{Y_{ij}}(m) = 0$ $\forall m < m_{\min}$) and above $m_{\max}$ (where $m_{\max}$ is s.t. $h_{Y_{ij}}(m) = 0$ $\forall m > m_{\min}$).

---

[3] Performing the rounding for computing W_q may cause a slight violation of the JND constraint, but it is preferable for the remapping operation.

Let $\mathcal{E}$ be the set of the empty bins within the interval $[m_{\min}, m_{\max}]$. It is easy to argue that the actual complexity/number of variables of the (i,j)-th minimization is $2K(i,j) \cdot ((m_{\max} - m_{\min}) - |\mathcal{E}|)$, which is usually much lower than $|\mathcal{C}|$. Moreover, since the JPEG compression quantizes more strongly the high-frequency DCT coefficients, the complexity of the minimizations will decrease at higher frequencies, because histograms will tend to cluster around zero. Experiments showed that, except for the very low-frequency subbands, the complexity of the minimizations is often smaller than the one for the spatial domain.

It is interesting to note that problem (7)–(8) has very close ties with the *transportation problem* (TP) [15]. The difference with the classical TP is that, according to the definition of the attacker's strategy, the attacker is satisfied with any distortion less than $K(i,j)$, that is, he/she is not concerned about minimizing the distortion provided that it is less that $K(i,j)$.[4] In this way, the optimum attacking strategy in (7)–(8) provides the optimum map even when the classical transportation problem, which moves $v_{Y_{ij}}$ exactly into $v_{Z_{ij}}$, would introduce too much distortion into the image (i.e., more than $K(i,j)$).

To sum up, the mapping phase provides the attacker with the 64 matrixes N_{ij}^*, $1 \leq i,j \leq 8$; each matrix N_{ij}^* defines the modifications that must be made on the DCT coefficients in position (i,j) in order to obtain the optimum attacked histogram $h_{Z_{ij}}$.

4.3   Implementation of the Mapping

After obtaining the transportation matrixes, it is necessary for the attacker to implement the mapping in such a way that reduces as much as possible the visual distortion introduced in the image. Notice that, since the forensic detector relies on the histograms of the DCT coefficients, the result of the attack in terms of detectability of the produced forgery only depends on the results of the mapping phase, and it is not affected by the modifications performed in this phase. In the following, we describe an approach that allows the attacker to implement the modifications set by the matrixes N_{ij}^*'s in a perceptually convenient way. The basic idea is to exploit the different sensitivity of the Human Visual System to the DCT coefficients of the different blocks in order to first modify the coefficients in those blocks where the HVS is less sensitive. To do so, we exploit the threshold (refined) values of the JND provided by Watson's model which, as described in Sect. 2, are indeed block-dependent. Again, modifications are implemented separately on the DCT coefficients of each frequency subband. Below, we describe the main steps of the proposed scheme for the implementation of the transportation matrix N_{ij}^* in the generic subband (i,j):

1. Set all the coefficients as "admissible";
2. Rank the blocks based on the value of the threshold $T(i,j)$ in decreasing order: block k such that $T(i,j;k)$ is maximum is ranked first, and so on;

---

[4] In the transportation problem the objective function of the minimization problem would be the distortion (cost of the transportation), which in our formulation is instead a constraint.

3. For each couple of values (m, r) such that $n_{ij}(m \to r) \neq 0$ proceed as follows:
   (a) find the blocks with admissible DCT coefficients having value m;
   (b) select the first $n_{ij}(m \to r)$ according to the order established by the ranking;
   (c) substitute them with r;
   (d) remove selected coefficients from the admissible ones[5];

The procedure is applied to all the 64 DCT subbands. Notice that, according to the above scheme, the attacker computes the thresholds of the JND only once, without updating them to account for the variations caused by incremental modifications. In principle, lower distortion can be introduced by iteratively updating the thresholds. However, since Watson's model is mainly concerned about average luminance and energy of each block, the benefit obtained by iterative updating is not relevant enough to justify the increased computational complexity, and for this reason this feature was not implemented. At the end of the procedure, the adversary gets the transformed image Z_q with the quantized lq remapped' DCT coefficients, whose DCT histograms are, by construction, the 64 target histograms $h_{Z_{ij}}$, $1 \leq i, j \leq 8$, obtained in the mapping phase. Computing the de-quantized coefficients and applying the inverse DCT transform yields the final attacked image z in the pixel domain. The image will appear visually close to the input one, but its histograms will show traces of just one compression step.

5   Experimental Validation

In this section we put the proposed technique to work, in order to show that it actually conceals the traces of multiple compression in all the histograms of the DCT coefficients. Besides, we evaluate the perceptual similarity between the input image and the one obtained after the implementation of the mapping.

To generate the database for the attacker, we computed the histograms of each DCT coefficient from 2000 grayscale uncompressed images, obtaining 64 histograms per image. Then, 25 grayscale uncompressed images were chosen from different sources for performing tests. Both the database and the test images are available on our research group website[6]. For a multiple compressed image, consistently with the notation introduced in Sect. 4, we denote by $\{QF_1, QF_2, : ., QF_k\}$ the quality factor used for the first, second, ..., k-th compression step. Each test image was used to generate, using the `imwrite` function of Matlab, the following images:0 three double-compressed versions of the image, with quality couples $\{65, 85\}$, $\{75, 90\}$ and $\{85, 95\}$; five triple-compressed versions, with quality triplets $\{65, 85, 90\}$, $\{70, 75, 95\}$, $\{70, 80, 95\}$, $\{75, 85, 95\}$, $\{80, 85, 95\}$; for each of the above multiple-compressed images, one single-compressed image with quality given by QF_1 (these images serve to test the discrimination capability of a forensic detector).

---

[5] This avoids multiple substitutions of the same coefficients.

[6] http://clem.dii.unisi.it/~vipp/index.php/download/imagerepository.

We applied the JPEG counter-forensic scheme to each of the above images, using $D_{max} = 4$; the experiment was performed using both the *separate* and *average* search (as defined in Sect. 4.1) in order to compare performance. To test the effectiveness of the proposed scheme, we implemented a simple double compression detector based on the so-called calibration technique [7]. Calibration is a procedure allowing to estimate the original distribution of a quantized signal by removing a small number of rows/column to disrupt the structure of JPEG blocks. The calibration-based detector simply works by calculating the "expected" histograms for quantized DCT coefficients and comparing them to the histograms of observed DCT coefficients in the given image.[7] If the image was compressed only once, the expected histogram is quite similar to the observed one (the χ^2 distance is used to compare histograms); on the other hand, if multiple compressions were performed, the expected histogram differs significantly from the observed one. We limit the detector to consider the first 12 DCT coefficients (in the JPEG zig-zag ordering), because higher frequency coefficients are not reliable for this kind of analysis, due to the sparsity of histograms induced by quantization. It is proper to stress again that, since the proposed scheme is *universal*, it is not tailored for deceiving this specific detector.

Let us describe the experiments we conducted. In the first experiment, the detector was used to discriminate between double-compressed and single-compressed images, generated according to points 1. and 3. of the above list. To test the performance of the proposed scheme, we computed the Receiver Operating Characteristic (ROC) curve of the detector before and after the application of our JPEG counter-forensic attack, along with the Area Under the Curve (AUC). As we can see in Fig. 2(a), the detector behaves reasonably well in absence of counter-forensic schemes, while its performance dramatically drop after application of the proposed scheme. Moreover, we see that both the *separate* and *average* search methods lead to reasonably good performance in terms of deceiving the calibration-based detector, with the former slightly favored at small probabilities of false alarm, that counts the most in forensic scenarios.

In the second experiment we tried to discriminate between single- vs. triple-compressed images, both before and after application of the CF method. Results are plotted in Fig. 2(b): we see that good CF performance are obtained in the leftmost part of the ROC, corresponding to low false alarm probability. For false alarm probabilities over 0.4, the detector manage to distinguish between single- and triple- compressed images even in presence of counter forensic. This fact is mainly due to the different distribution of quality factors between triple compressed and single compressed images in the considered experiments; from a forensic point of view, however, false alarm probabilities as high as 0.4 are not of interest.

---

[7] The expected histogram is obtained by estimating the histograms of unquantized coefficients (using calibration), then quantizing them according to the quantization factors available in the JPEG header of the file.

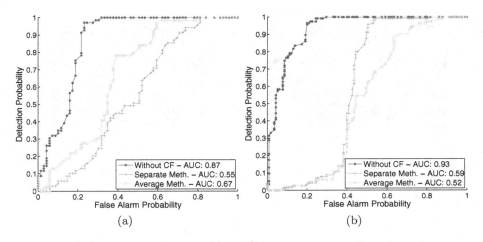

Fig. 2. ROC curve for the calibration-based detector for single-vs-double (a) and single-vs-triple (b), before and after application of the proposed method.

Table 1. Performance of the proposed method in term of perceptual quality. Each row shows the mean and the standard deviation of the SSIM obtained for a given experiment. For double compression a total of 75 images were processed, while the number raises to 125 for triple compression.

Experiment	Mean SSIM	Std. dev. SSIM
Double compr - Separate	0.920	0.033
Double compr - Average	0.903	0.046
Triple compr - Separate	0.945	0.025
Triple compr - Average	0.935	0.027

Let us now turn to consider the perceptual quality of produced images. We evaluated the quality by means of the Structural Similarity (SSIM) index [16], computed between the input and the output to the proposed scheme. Results are given in Table 1. We can confirm that using the separate search on the database (as defined in Sect. 4.1) allows the attacker to obtain better results in terms of perceptual quality of the produced image. It may seem counter-intuitive to the reader that a better similarity was obtained in the case of triple compression: this is actually not surprising if we keep in mind that the similarity is computed between the input and the output of the CF scheme, and it is easier to keep fidelity to an image whose quality was not so high from the beginning (as it is a triple compressed images). A practical comparison between a multiple-compressed image and the counter-forensic version is shown in Fig. 3.

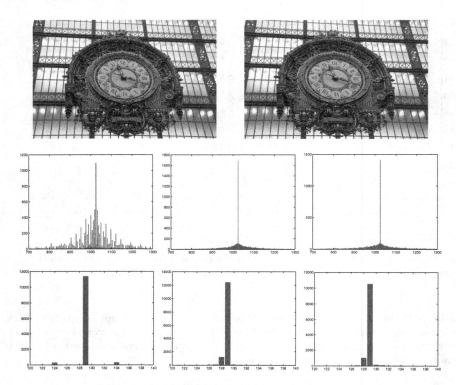

Fig. 3. Upper row: comparison between a triple-compressed image with qualities {70, 80, 95 } (left) and its counter-forensic version (right). Middle row: the histogram of DCT coefficients in position (1,2) coming from the above multiple-compressed image (left), the target from the DB (middle), and the remapped version obtained with the proposed scheme (right). Bottom row: histograms of DCT coefficients in position (3,4), ordered as in the previous line.

6   Conclusions

In this paper we have presented a universal counter forensic technique for hiding traces of multiple compression in JPEG images. The described method is proposed as an extension of the counter forensic algorithm developed in [2] for concealing the manipulation of tampered image in the spatial domain. With respect to most of the state-of-the-art techniques, which aim at deceiving a targeted detector by removing the specific artifacts of multiple compression it searches for, the proposed method attempts to make the image look like a single compressed one working on the first order statistics of the image. The main strength of this method is that it can be applied for concealing any number of compression stages that the image may have undergone and with any quality factor. We showed that our method provides good results in terms of quality of the attacked image and degradation of detection performances. As a challenge for the future, it would be interesting to devise universal counter-forensic methods against detectors whose analysis is based on higher order statistics (e.g., the joint RGB histograms for color images).

Acknowledgments. This work was partially supported by the European Office of Aerospace Research and Development under Grant FA8655-12-1- 2138: AMULET - A multi-clue approach to image forensics.

References

1. Barni, M., Tondi, B.: The source identification game: an information-theoretic perspective. IEEE Trans. Inf. Forensics Secur. **8**(3), 450–463 (2013)
2. Barni, M., Fontani, M., Tondi, B.: A universal technique to hide traces of histogram-based image manipulations. In: Proceedings of MM&Sec 2012, 14th ACM workshop on Multimedia & Security, pp. 97–104. ACM, New York (2012)
3. Barni, M., Tondi, B.: Multiple-observation hypothesis testing under adversarial conditions. In: Proceedings of WIFS 2013, IEEE International Workshop on Information Forensics and Security, pp. 91–96, November 2013
4. Bonami, P., Kilinc, M., Linderoth, J., et al.: Algorithms and software for convex mixed integer nonlinear programs. Computer Sciences Department, University of Wisconsin-Madison. Techical report (2009)
5. Comesana-Alfaro, P., Perez-Gonzalez, F.: Optimal counterforensics for histogram-based forensics. In: Proceedings of ICASSP 2013, IEEE International Conference on Acoustics, Speech and Signal Processing, pp. 3048–3052, May 2013
6. Cox, I., Miller, M., Bloom, J., Fridrich, J., Kalker, T.: Digital Watermarking and Steganography, 2nd edn. Morgan Kaufmann Publishers Inc., San Francisco (2008)
7. Fridrich, J., Goljan, M., Hogea, D.: Steganalysis of JPEG images: breaking the F5 algorithm. In: Petitcolas, F.A.P. (ed.) IH 2002. LNCS, vol. 2578, pp. 310–323. Springer, Heidelberg (2003)
8. Kirchner, M., Böhme, R.: Tamper hiding: defeating image forensics. In: Furon, T., Cayre, F., Doërr, G., Bas, P. (eds.) IH 2007. LNCS, vol. 4567, pp. 326–341. Springer, Heidelberg (2008)
9. Lam, E.Y., Goodman, J.W.: A mathematical analysis of the DCT coefficient distributions for images. IEEE Trans. Image Process. **9**(10), 1661–1666 (2000)
10. Li, B., Shi, Y., Huang, J.: Detecting doubly compressed JPEG images by using mode based first digit features. In: Proceedings of MMSP 2008, IEEE Workshop on Multimedia Signal Processing, pp. 730–735, October 2008
11. Milani, S., Tagliasacchi, M., Tubaro, S.: Discriminating multiple JPEG compression using first digit features. In: Proceedings of ICASSP 2012, IEEE International Conference on Acoustics, Speech and Signal Processing, pp. 2253–2256, March 2012
12. Milani, S., Tagliasacchi, M., Tubaro, S.: Antiforensics attacks to benford's law for the detection of double compressed images. In: Proceedings of ICASSP 2013, IEEE International Conference on Acoustics, Speech and Signal Processing, pp. 3053–3057, May 2013
13. Pevný, T., Fridrich, J.: Estimation of primary quantization matrix for steganalysis of double-compressed JPEG images. In: Proceedings of SPIE, vol. 6819, pp. 681911–681911-13 (2008). http://dx.doi.org/10.1117/12.759155
14. Popescu, A.C., Farid, H.: Statistical tools for digital forensics. In: Fridrich, J. (ed.) IH 2004. LNCS, vol. 3200, pp. 128–147. Springer, Heidelberg (2004)

15. Rachev, S.T.: Mass Transportation Problems: Volume I: Theory. Springer, New York (1998)
16. Wang, Z., Bovik, A.C., Sheikh, H.R., Simoncelli, E.P.: Image quality assessment: from error visibility to structural similarity. IEEE Trans. Image Process. **13**(4), 600–612 (2004)
17. Watson, A.B.: DCT quantization matrices visually optimized for individual images. In: Proceedings of IS&T/SPIE's Symposium on Electronic Imaging: Science and Technology, pp. 202–216. International Society for Optics and Photonics (1993)

Determination of Stop-Criterion for Incremental Methods Constructing Camera Sensor Fingerprint

Babak Mahdian[✉], Adam Novozámský,
and Stanislav Saic

Institute of Information Theory and Automation of ASCR,
Prague, Czech Republic
{mahdian,novozamsky,ssaic}@utia.cas.cz

Abstract. This paper aims to find the minimum sample size of the camera reference image set that is needed to build a sensor fingerprint of a high performance. Today's methods for building sensor fingerprints do rely on having a sufficient number of camera reference images. But, there is no clear answer to the question of how many camera reference images are really needed? In this paper, we will analyze and find out how to determine the minimum needed number of reference images to remove the mentioned uncertainty. We will introduce a quantitative measure (a stop-criterion) stating how many photos should be used to create a high-performance sensor fingerprint. This stop-criterion will directly reflect the confidence level that we would like to achieve. By considering that the number of digital images used to construct the camera sensor fingerprint can have a direct impact on performance of the sensor fingerprint, it is apparent that this, so far underestimated, topic is of major importance.

Keywords: Image ballistics · Source camera verification · Pattern noise · PRNU · Fingerprint performance · Laplace distribution

1 Introduction

Generally, there are two essential tasks in forensics analysis of digital images and videos: their integrity verification (genuineness analysis) and ballistics analyzes. In this paper we will deal with image (video) ballistics which does address the problem of linking digital images (videos) under investigation to the exact source imaging device that has been used to capture photos (videos) under investigation. Since image ballistics makes possible to differentiate between source cameras of the same make and model, it became especially useful in the forensic, law enforcement, insurance, and media industries.

Although past research was mainly focused on data hiding and digital watermarking approaches [1–3] to perform digital image integrity verification and image ballistics, today there is a relatively new approach called passive one which

© Springer International Publishing Switzerland 2015
Y.-Q. Shi et al. (Eds.): IWDW 2014, LNCS 9023, pp. 47–59, 2015.
DOI: 10.1007/978-3-319-19321-2_4

does not need embedding any secondary data into the image [4]. In contrast to active methods, the passive approach does not need any prior information about the image being analyzed. There have been methods developed to detect image splicing [5,6], traces of non-consistencies in color filter array interpolation [7], traces of geometric transformations, [8], cloning [9], computer graphics generated photos [10], JPEG compression inconsistencies [11], etc. Typically, pointed out methods are based on the fact that digital image editing brings specific detectable statistical changes into the image.

In the image ballistics area, methods mainly focused on camera sensor noise and systematic artifacts that are brought into the image [12–18]. These artifacts have been used to link a digital image to its exact acquisition device.

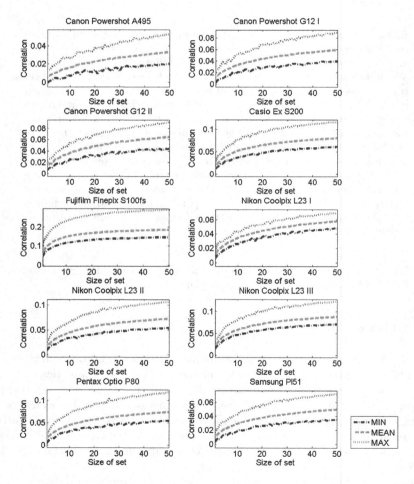

Fig. 1. Performance of camera sensor fingerprint constructed using camera reference sets of different sizes and 100 test images for each camera.

1.1   Motivation

When linking a digital image to an exact camera (or a video signal to camcorder), typically the following procedure is used. First, the camera sensor fingerprint is constructed [12, 13]. Second, the constructed fingerprint and image under investigation are matched (usually through a correlation measurement). This indicates if the digital image has been captured by this camera. The sensor fingerprint is constructed incrementally by using many camera reference images. Camera reference images are recommended to be of a uniformly illuminated surface. Usually, an edge-preserving denoising filter is applied on camera reference images. Residuals of digital images and their denoised versions are put together (e.g., by averaging) to construct the basic version of sensor fingerprint.

The problem is how many photos should be used to form the camera reference images so there will be a high confidence that the constructed fingerprint is of a high performance? Is the optimal size of this set 10, 50, or even 250? The topic is of major importance. The reason is that number of digital images used to construct the camera sensor fingerprint, typically, has a direct impact on performance of the sensor fingerprint. Insufficient number of reference images cause a poor performance of the fingerprint. To this end, most authors rather recommended to employ a fixed and higher number of reference images to be safe in terms of having a good performing fingerprint (in published literature we have, typically, observed recommended sizes of reference images ranging from 30 to 150).

To remove the uncertainty about the size of sets of camera reference images, we will introduce a quantitative measure determining how many photos should be used to create the sensor fingerprint to have a high performing fingerprint. In other words, we are going to search for the optimal number of reference images that will reflect our the confidence level and accuracy we want to achieve. To address the problem we will search for a stop-criterion stating that no more images are needed to be added to the set of camera reference images.

Before going on, we also explicitly define what is a fingerprint of good (high) or poor performance. A fingerprint with a good performance is such a fingerprint that enables a successful recognition of the exact source cameras when inspecting photos of various scenes, lighting conditions, etc. When a non-sufficient number of images are used to create the sensor fingerprint, the measured fingerprint is of poor performance (often random noise components dominate in there) and hence the image source verification task generate weak results. By weak results we mean lower rate of true positives. Figure 1 demonstrates performance of 10 different camera sensor fingerprints constructed by $1 \cdots 50$ reference images of uniformly illuminated surface (a white paper). The figure demonstrates obtained correlation (obtained by using Eq. 3) between 100 test images (natural images captured by same cameras) and associated camera fingerprints (minimal, maximal and mean values of obtained correlation values are shown). Apparently size of camera reference sets have a direct impact on results obtained. For the sake of completeness, we point out that false positive states for mistakenly pinpointing

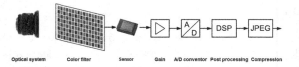

Fig. 2. A typical digital camera system.

the source camera. By true positive we mean correctly pinpointing a digital image to the source camera.

2   Basic Notations and Preliminaries

A typical camera consists of several different components (see Fig. 2). As pointed out in [19], the core of every digital camera is the imaging sensor. The sensor (e.g., CCD or CMOS) is consisted on small elements called pixels that collect photons and convert them into voltages that are subsequently sampled to a digital signal in an A/D converter. Generally, before the light from the scene which is being photographed reaches the sensor it also passes through the camera lenses, an antialiasing (blurring) filter, and then through a color filter array (CFA). The CFA is a mosaic of tiny color filters placed over the pixel of an image sensor to capture color information. Color filters are needed because typical consumer cameras only have one sensor which cannot separate color information. Most commonly, Bayer color filter is used.

The resulting signal is then further processed using color correction and white balance adjustment. Additional processing includes gamma correction to adjust for the linear response of the imaging sensor, noise reduction, and filtering operations to visually enhance the final image. Finally, the digital image might be compressed stored and stored in a specific image format like JPEG.

What is important in terms of forensic analyzes of digital images is that different components of camera leave different kind of artifacts or fingerprints useful for integrity verification of photos or ballistics analysis. Typically, artifacts (fingerprints) left by CFA, post processing, and compression parts are in common for cameras of same make and model. In other words, assuming that we know their value and behavior for a particular camera make and model and based on the fact that digital image editing (e.g., photoshopping) change these values (fingerprints), they can be employed for verification of the originality of digital images.

On the other hand, each camera has its own unique sensor which consists of millions of pixels each of unique properties. Hence, if we are able to find kind of information brought into image by the sensor and which will remain stable and present in all images captured by that sensor and cannot be found in no image captured by any other sensor, then we can call it fingerprint of that sensor or camera. Such a camera sensor fingerprint can be employed to link digital images to particular digital cameras which captured them.

2.1 Sensor as a Camera Fingerprint

Image sensors suffer from several fundamental and technology related imperfections resulting in their performance limitations and noise. As pointed out in [19], if we take a picture of an absolutely evenly lit scene, the resulting digital image will still exhibit small changes in intensity among individual pixels which is partly because of pattern noise, readout noise or shot noise. While readout noise or shot noise are random components, the pattern noise is deterministic and remain approximately the same if multiple pictures of the same scene are taken. As a result, pattern noise can be the fingerprint of sensors which we are searching for.

Pattern Noise (PN) is consisted of two components called Fixed Pattern Noise (FPN) and photo response non-uniformity (PRNU). FPN is independent of pixel signal, it is an additive noise, and some high-end consumer cameras can suppress it. The FPN also depends on exposure and temperature. PRNU is formed by varying pixel dimensions and inhomogeneities in silicon resulting in pixel output variations. It is a multiplicative noise. Moreover, it is not dependent on temperature and seems to be stable over time. The values of PRNU noise increases with the signal level (it is more visible in pixels showing light scenes). In other words, in very dark areas PRNU noise is suppressed. Moreover, PRNU is not present in completely saturated areas of an image. Thus, such images should be ignored when searching for PRNU noise.

There has not been performed a lot of studies analyzing the PRNU noise in deeper details. Despite this, it has been shown that it has a dominant presence in the pattern noise component found in digital images. This made possible Fridrich et al. [12,13] to employ PRNU noise to identify exact source cameras. In other words, PRNU noise is employed as the fingerprint of camera sensors. Generally, it can be claimed that state-of-the-art source identification methods are mostly based on methods proposed by Fridrich et al. (e.g., [12,13,20,21]). There have been published some additional papers by others authors(e.g., [14–18]) aiming to improve accuracy of results. Typically, they brought modifications to the original paper of Fridrich et al. [12,13] based on some new theoretical or empirical findings. Nonetheless, the key concept of how to measure sensor's fingerprint has remained unchanged.

2.2 Modeling and Extracting PRNU

Let us model the image acquisition process in the following way:

$$I_{i,j} = I_{i,j}^o + I_{i,j}^o \cdot \varGamma_{i,j} + \varUpsilon_{i,j} \tag{1}$$

Here, $I_{i,j}$ denotes the image pixel at position (i,j) produced by the camera, $I_{i,j}^o$ denotes the noise-free image (perfect image of the scene), $\varGamma_{i,j}$ denotes PRNU noise and $\varUpsilon_{i,j}$ stands for all additive or negligible noise components.

Following the approach proposed by [12,13], the PRNU component is estimated in the following way. For a given camera, PRNU noise is estimated by averaging multiple images I_k, $k = 1, \cdots, N$ captured by this camera. The process is sped up by suppressing the scene content from the image prior to averaging. This is achieved by using a denoising filter $\mathcal{F}$ and averaging the noise residuals instead. We will denote residuals by $\hat{I}_k$ (i.e., $\hat{I}_k = I_k - \mathcal{F}(I_k)$). In other words, deterministic components of sensor noise of the camera C are computed in the following way:

$$\Gamma_{sensor} = \frac{1}{N} \sum_{k=1}^{N} \hat{I}_k = \frac{1}{N} \sum_{k=1}^{N} I_k - \mathcal{F}(I_k) \tag{2}$$

Alternatively, for example, maximum likelihood estimation (MLE) instead of simple averaging can be employed.

To reduce the false positive rate, sensor fingerprint are enhanced by Wiener filtering in the frequency domain (e.g., to reduce JPEG compression artifacts) and linear pattern removal through zero-mean operation (e.g., to remove traces of CFA interpolation) [12]. Pointed out Γ_{sensor} is the basic version of sensor fingerprint of camera. To achieve accurate results and minimize the false positive rate, it is necessary to perform additional frequency filtering, fingerprint enhancement and correction, suppressing dominant traces of camera embedded software, filtering JPEG artifacts, etc. Without such a correction, typically, a high rate of false positives is obtained (because of camera operations such as gamma correction, CFA interpolation, color enhancement, geometric deformation corrections, compression, additional embedded camera software functionalities, etc.) This part often depends on specific camera brands under investigation.

Linking of a digital image to an exact camera is carried out by performing a similarity measure of two sensor fingerprints. One is obtained from the image under investigation and second from the set of camera reference images. This can be carried out, for example, by employing a simple correlation measure. Having available two different sensor fingerprints Γ_{s_1} and Γ_{s_2}, we measure their similarity by employing a normalized correlation:

$$corr(\Gamma_{s_1}, \Gamma_{s_2}) = \frac{(\Gamma_{s_1} - \overline{\Gamma_{s_1}}) \odot (\Gamma_{s_2} - \overline{\Gamma_{s_2}})}{(\|\Gamma_{s_1} - \overline{\Gamma_{s_1}}\|) \cdot (\|\Gamma_{s_2} - \overline{\Gamma_{s_2}}\|)} \tag{3}$$

where $\overline{X}$ denotes mean of the vector X, $\odot$ stands for dot product of vectors defined as $X \odot Y = \sum_{k=1}^{N} X(k)X(k)$ and $\|X\|$ denotes L_2 norm of X defined as $\|X\| = \sqrt{X \odot X}$.

There has been carried out studies about the specific choice and effectiveness of denoising filters (e.g., [14]). It is important to note that there is no general perfect denoising filter. All of them have t heir advantages and disadvantages. Moreover, it is interesting to note that when applying the proposed PRNU estimation method on a larger set of digital images or when analyzing digital video signals consisted of thousands of individual frames, the computational time becomes a drawback of the method. It has been shown that the computational time of the method can effectively be enhanced by using GPU-accelerated version of the algorithm. For example, in [22,23] a parallel CUDA implementation of Γ_{sensor} has been built achieving remarkable speedup in fingerprint computation (up to 5–6 times).

3   Laplacian Distributed Residuals

As pointed out in last section, for a given camera C, deterministic components of sensor noise can be estimated by averaging multiple images captured by this camera, I_k, $k = 1, \cdots, N$. The process is sped up by suppressing the scene content from the image prior to averaging by using a denoising filter $\mathcal{F}$ and averaging the noise residuals $\hat{I}_k$ instead.

Apparently samples of residuals, $\hat{I}_k$, and their corresponding averaged versions $\frac{1}{N} \sum_{k=1}^{N} \hat{I}_k$ are the key information forming the sensor fingerprint of camera, Γ_C. Let us first to find an appropriate form for the probability density function (p.d.f.) of the distribution of residual values so that they can be efficiently modeled. Figure 3 demonstrates the histogram of residuals $\frac{1}{N} \sum_{k=1}^{N} \hat{I}_k$, obtained using a typical set of reference images of sizes $N = 1, 5, 10, 15, 20, 25$.

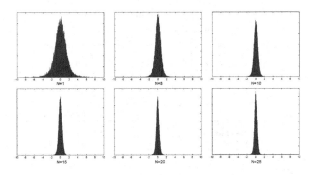

Fig. 3. Distribution of averaged residuals Γ_C constructed using a typical camera reference image set of different sizes $N = 1, 5, 10, 15, 20, 25$.

These figures demonstrate that the Laplacian p.d.f. fits the observed distribution well. Γ_C has a Laplace (μ, b) distribution if its probability density function is

$$f(\Gamma_{C_{i,j}} | \mu, b) = \frac{1}{2b} \exp\left(-\frac{|\Gamma_{C_{i,j}} - \mu|}{b}\right) \tag{4}$$

where μ is a location parameter and $b \geq 0$ is sometimes referred to as the diversity.

To estimate parameters of the Laplace distribution, maximum likelihood estimator is used. Maximum likelihood estimator of b can be obtained by:

$$\hat{b} = \frac{1}{M} \sum_{i=1}^{M} |\Gamma_{C_{i,j}} - \hat{\mu}| \tag{5}$$

Having Laplacian-distributed residuals, $\hat{I}_k$, we easily can estimate parameters the of associated p.d.f. Specifically, we focus on parameter b and will analyze its behavior during computation process of the sensor fingerprint. Figure 4 demonstrates values of b for different number camera reference images of 10 different cameras. Apparently, b follows a descending trend. Specifically, we can see that b descends as the number of camera reference images grows. It is important to note that the descending trend is steep in the beginning. On the other hand, b becomes almost stable for higher number of images.

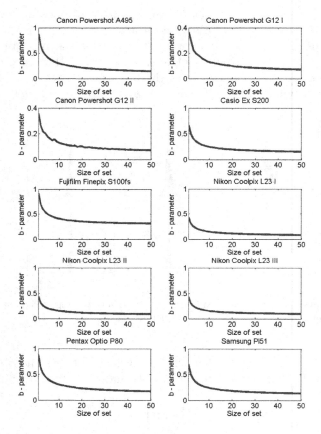

Fig. 4. Estimated parameter b for 10 different sensor fingerprints constructed using camera reference image sets of sizes $N = 1 \cdots 50$.

4   Determination of Stop-Criterion for Size of Reference Images

The uncertainty which is addressed in this paper is about the needed number of reference images, N, that is needed to construct a sensor fingerprint, Γ_{sensor}, of high performance. As pointed out previously, in literature, it is often pointed out that $N \to \infty$ brings a more accurate sensor fingerprint and suppressed Υ.

In last section we introduced the parameter b that is based on Laplace distribution modeling of residuals. Moreover, we have shown that b has a specific behavior and descends as the number of camera reference images grows. It has been shown that the descending trend of b is steep in the beginning. On the other hand, b becomes almost stable for higher number of images.

The question is what is the relation between b and the performance of the sensor fingerprint and how can we employ b to predict the future performance level of the fingerprint in terms of true positives? Here, we will use a differential operator to quantify the behavior of b. In other words, having $\Gamma_C = \frac{1}{N} \sum_{k=1}^{N} \hat{I}_k$, we will measure the rate at which the value of the b changes with respect to change of k:

$$\Delta b_k = b_{k+1} - b_k \tag{6}$$

To create a stop-criterion, we collected 25 different cameras and for each of them created a camera reference image sets of 50 images and a test image sets of 100. We constructed 50 sensor fingerprints Γ_C by using $1 \cdots 50$ reference images per camera. Reference photos have been selected randomly. Having 50 different sensor fingerprints constructed using a different size of reference image sets, we carried out an image ballistics test using Eq. 3 that calculated the true positive rate for all test images. A global threshold has been employed for the classification part of this part. At the same time we also measured Eq. 6 for all camera fingerprints (to remove local outliers, a low-pass filter always have always been applied on Δb). Having available 50 different true positive rates as well as 50 values of b for each camera sensor fingerprint, we analyzed their relation and empirically gained an optimal b for different rates of true positives. Efficiency that can be obtained by using b as the stop-criterion is shown the next section. In this study, we selected the false positive rate to be 0.1 percent. For the sake of simplicity, for the parameter searching and experimental part, there only have been chosen cameras that are distinguishable using the basic version of sensor fingerprint enhanced by Wiener filtering in the frequency domain (e.g., to reduce JPEG compression artifacts) and linear pattern removal through zero-mean operation as recommended in [12].

Figure 5 demonstrates a portion of results of our analysis. Specifically, shown is performance of fingerprint constructed by sets of reference images of sizes $N = 1 \cdots 50$. Also shown is the associated and estimated b.

5   Experimental Results

Table 1 demonstrates efficiency of using Δb for 10 test camera sensor fingerprints. These cameras have not been used in the process of determination of optimal Δb. We have selected our true positive rate to be 99.99 percent with having false positive rate of 0.01 percent. Considering these desired true and false positive rates we have computed the optimal Δb. As mentioned in last section, this stop-criterion has been calculated using a 25 different cameras and associated sets of reference images of sizes $N = 1 \cdots 50$. In our case, optimal Δb was 0.0050. For each test camera, Table 1 shows gained true positive rate and associated size

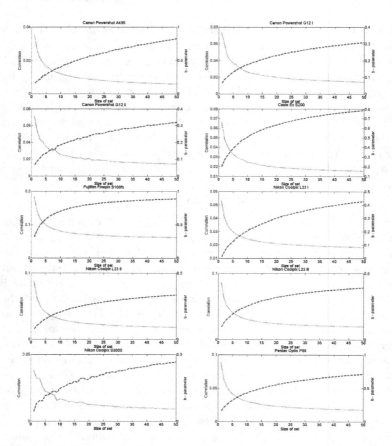

Fig. 5. Shown is performance of fingerprint constructed by sets of reference images of sizes $N = 1 \cdots 50$. Also shown is the associated and estimated b.

Table 1. Sown is performance (%) of sensor fingerprints based on different values of Δb. Shown is also associated number of reference images used to construct the sensor fingerprint (shown in square brackets).

Δb	0.0400	0.0300	0.0200	0.0100	0.0050	0.0040	0.0030
canon-powershot-g12-III	73 [3]	84 [4]	99 [6]	100 [9]	100 [14]	100 [16]	100 [19]
canon-powershot-g12-IV	75 [2]	97 [4]	100 [7]	100 [10]	100 [11]	100 [13]	100 [22]
fujifilm-finepix-s100fs-II	100 [4]	100 [5]	100 [6]	100 [10]	100 [14]	100 [21]	100 [25]
nikon-coolpix-l23-IV	81 [3]	93 [5]	97 [6]	100 [8]	100 [11]	100 [15]	100 [19]
nikon-coolpix-l23-V	100 [4]	100 [5]	100 [5]	100 [7]	100 [11]	100 [17]	100 [24]
nikon-coolpix-l23-VI	100 [3]	100 [4]	100 [6]	100 [7]	100 [12]	100 [14]	100 [21]
pentax-optio-p80-II	97 [4]	100 [5]	100 [7]	100 [11]	100 [18]	100 [22]	100 [27]
iphone-3GS	18 [5]	28 [6]	28 [7]	62 [12]	94 [20]	100 [27]	100 [35]
iphone-4s-I	86 [4]	98 [5]	100 [6]	100 [10]	100 [15]	100 [20]	100 [23]
iphone-4s-II	95 [4]	100 [6]	100 [8]	100 [9]	100 [12]	100 [21]	100 [28]

of camera reference image set (shown in square brackets). In this experiment, we gained 0 percent false positive rate.

Table 1 demonstrates gained true positive rates for 100 test images per camera. Moreover, size of camera reference images used to construct the camera sensor fingerprint is shown either. For the sake of completeness, we also show different values of Δb and associated results obtained.

6 Discussion and Conclusion

In this paper we addressed the problem of uncertainty of how many reference images should be used to construct a high performance camera sensor fingerprint. Typically, papers dealing with construction of sensor fingerprints proposed to incrementally use about 40–50 images of a uniformly illuminated surfaces. Some others simply recommended to use as much as possible.

In last sections, we have introduced a quantitative measure stating how many photos should be used. We searched for an the minimal number of camera reference images that will directly reflect the confidence and accuracy level we want to achieve. To address the problem, we introduced a stop-criterion that can determine if more images are needed to be added to the set of reference images to get the desired true positive rate.

It also has been shown that a small number of reference images available for construction a sensor fingerprint is not always a limiting factor for constructing a well performing fingerprint. It should be noted that employing camera reference image sets of N when $N \to \infty$ does not necessarily convert to a perfect sensor fingerprint. By a perfect sensor fingerprint we mean a signal that only and only consists of deterministic noise components unique for each sensor. Digital images captured by today's consumer cameras and smartphones suffer from a set of systematic and non-systematic imperfections and enhancements (sensor noise, gamma correction, CFA interpolation, color enhancement, geometric deformation corrections, and a number of additional embedded camera software functionalities) that bring a number of correlated and uncorrelated artifacts into digital images which cannot be overcome using N, $N \to \infty$, number of camera reference image.

Acknowledgments. This work has been supported by the Czech Science Foundation under Project no. GACR 13-28462S.

References

1. Sencar, H.T., Ramkumar, M., Akansu, A.N.: Data Hiding Fundamentals and Applications: Content Security in Digital Multimedia. Academic Press Inc., Orlando (2004)
2. Arnold, M., Schmucker, M., Wolthusen, S.D.: Techniques and Applications of Digital Watermarking and Content Protection. Artech House Inc., Norwood (2003)
3. Nikolaidis, N., Pitas, I.: Robust image watermarking in the spatial domain. Signal Process. **66**(3), 385–403 (1998)

4. Mahdian, B., Saic, S.: A bibliography on blind methods for identifying image forgery. Image Commun. **25**(6), 389–399 (2010)
5. Ng, T.-T., Tsui, M.-P.: Camera response function signature for digital forensics - part i: theory and data selection. In: IEEE Workshop on Information Forensics and Security, December 2009, pp. 156–160 (2009)
6. Lint, Z., Wang, R., Tang, X., Shum, H.-Y.: Detecting doctored images using camera response normality and consistency. In: CVPR 2005: Proceedings of the 2005 IEEE Computer Society Conference on Computer Vision and Pattern Recognition (CVPR 2005) - Volume 1, Washington, pp. 1087–1092. IEEE Computer Society (2005)
7. Popescu, A., Farid, H.: Exposing digital forgeries in color filter array interpolated images. IEEE Trans. Signal Process. **53**(10), 3948–3959 (2005). www.cs.dartmouth.edu/farid/publications/sp05a.html. [Online]
8. Mahdian, B., Saic, S.: Blind authentication using periodic properties of interpolation. IEEE Trans. Inf. Forensics Secur. **3**(3), 529–538 (2008)
9. Mahdian, B., Saic, S.: Detection of copy-move forgery using a method based on blur moment invariants. Forensic Sci. Int. **17**(2–3), 180–189 (2007)
10. Dirik, A.E., Bayram, S., Sencar, H.T., Memon, N.: New features to identify computer generated images. In: IEEE International Conference on Image Processing, ICIP 2007, vol. 4, pp. 433–436 (2007)
11. Fridrich, J., Pevny, T.: Detection of double-compression for applications in steganography. IEEE Trans. Inf. Sec. Forensics **3**(2), 247–258 (2008)
12. Chen, M., Goljan, M., Lukas, J.: Determining image origin and integrity using sensor noise. IEEE Trans. Inf. Forensics Secur. **3**(1), 74–90 (2008)
13. Lukas, J., Fridrich, J., Goljan, M.: Digital camera identification from sensor pattern noise. IEEE Trans. Inf. Forensics Secur. **1**(2), 205–214 (2006)
14. Amerini, I., Caldelli, R., Cappellini, V., Picchioni, F., Piva, A.: Analysis of denoising filters for photo response non uniformity noise extraction in source camera identification. In: Proceedings of the 16th International Conference on Digital Signal Processing, Series DSP 2009, Piscataway, pp. 511–517. IEEE Press (2009). Available: http://dl.acm.org/citation.cfm?id=1700307.1700392. [Online]
15. Alles, E.J., Geradts, Z.J.M.H., Veenman, C.J.: Source camera identification for heavily JPEG compressed low resolution still images. J. Forensic Sci. **54**(3), pp. 628–638 (2009). Available: http://www.science.uva.nl/research/publications/2009/AllesJFS2009. [Online]
16. Yongjian Hu, C.J., Yu, B.: Source camera identification using large components of sensor pattern noise. In: 2nd International Conference on Computer Science and Its Applications, CSA 2009, Jeju Island, Korea (2009)
17. Li, Y., Li, C.-T.: Decomposed photo response non-uniformity for digital forensic analysis. In: Sorell, M. (ed.) e-Forensics 2009. LNICST, vol. 8, pp. 166–172. Springer, Heidelberg (2009)
18. Hu, Y., Jian, C., Li, C.-T.: Using improved imaging sensor pattern noise for source camera identification. In: ICME, pp. 1481–1486 (2010)
19. Lukas, J., Fridrich, J., Goljan, M.: Detecting digital image forgeries using sensor pattern noise. In: Proceedings of the SPIE, West, p. 2006 (2006)
20. Chen, M., Fridrich, J., Goljan, M., Luk, J.: Source digital camcorder identification using sensor photo-response nonuniformity. In: Proceedings of SPIE Electronic Imaging, Photonics West (2007)
21. Chen, M., Fridrich, J., Goljan, M.: Digital imaging sensor identification (further study). In: Delp, E.J., III; Wong, P. W. (ed.) Security, Steganography, and Watermarking of Multimedia Contents IX. Proceedings of the SPIE, vol. 6505 (2007)

22. Williams, D., Codreanu, V., Yang, P., Liu, B., Dong, F., Yasar, B., Mahdian, B., Chiarini, A., Zhao, X., Roerdink, J.: Evaluation of autoparallelization toolkits for commodity graphics hardware. In: 10th International Conference on Parallel Processing and Applied Mathematics. Springer, Warsaw, Poland (2013)(to appear)
23. Williams, D., Codreanu, V., Roerdink, J.B., Yang, P., Liu, B., Dong, F., Chiarini, A.: Accelerating colonic polyp detection using commodity graphics hardware. In: Proceedings of the International Conference on Computer Medical Applications, Sousse, Tunisia, pp. 1–6 (2013)

Combination of SIFT Feature and Convex Region-Based Global Context Feature for Image Copy Detection

Zhili Zhou[✉], Xingming Sun, Yunlong Wang, Zhangjie Fu,
and Yun-Qing Shi

School of Computer and Software & Jiangsu Engineering Center of Network
Monitoring, Nanjing University of Information Science and Technology,
Nanjing 210044, China
{zhou_zhili,sunnudt}@163.com, 1018485761@qq.com,
wwwfzj@126.com, shi@njit.edu

Abstract. The conventional content-based image copy detection methods concentrate on finding either global or local features to handle the copy detection task. Unfortunately, the global features are not robust to the cropping attack, while the local features cannot substantially capture context information and thus are not discriminative enough. To address these issues, this paper proposes a novel image copy detection method, which combines both the global and the local features. Firstly, SIFT (scale invariant feature transform) features are extracted and then initially matched between images. Secondly, the SIFT matches are verified by the proposed convex region-based global context (CRGC) features, which describe the global context information around the SIFT features, to effectively remove the false matches. Finally, the number of the surviving SIFT matches is used to determinate whether a test image from image databases is a copy of a given query image. Experimental results have demonstrated the effectiveness of our proposed method in terms of both robustness and discriminability.

Keywords: Image copy detection · Copy attacks · Convex region · Global context information

1 Introduction

Due to the rapid development of network communications and the widespread application of digital images, more and more image content is distributed and shared on networks. However, with the wide use of various powerful image processing tools, digital images are getting easier to be replicated and modified. Therefore, copyright protection for digital images has become an important issue.

Generally, there are two typical technologies for protecting owners against unauthorized (re)use of their image content: digital watermarking and content-based image copy detection [1, 2]. Digital watermarking technology embeds the copyright information into the protected images before distribution. Thus, all copies of the protected images contain the watermark, which can later be extracted to prove the

© Springer International Publishing Switzerland 2015
Y.-Q. Shi et al. (Eds.): IWDW 2014, LNCS 9023, pp. 60–71, 2015.
DOI: 10.1007/978-3-319-19321-2_5

ownership. Different from watermarking, the image copy detection technology only employs the image itself, which already contains unique information for identifying illegal image copies. Generally, given an original image registered by its owner, the image copy detection system extracts its feature and that of each suspect image from web image databases, respectively. Then, the extracted features are compared to determine if a suspect image is a copy version of the original. If the suspect image is an illegal copy of the original, this will be sent to the content owner for a consideration about taking lawsuits against the illegal user. The advantage of the image copy detection lies in that it does not need to embed any additional information prior to distribution [2]. Therefore, this paper will focus on image copy detection.

Generally, the image copy detection technique is close to common content-based image retrieval (CBIR). There are also differences between the two. They both comprise two similar parts: feature extraction and feature matching. The main difference is that their objectives are not the same. The goal of image copy detection is to detect the copies of a given query image, which can be regarded as the transformed versions generated by some copy attacks [3], while that of CBVR is to find the ones similar to the query image. It is worth noting that the similar images may not be copies. For example, if the query image and a test image are captured from the same scene but from different camera locations, or share the same or similar semantics, the test image will be similar to but not a copy of the query image. That is because the test image is not a transformed version of the query image. In Fig. 1 (b), we can see that the test image on the right is similar to the query image on the left, but it is not a copy of the query image.

Generally, an ideal image copy detection method should be robust to most of the common copy attacks and discriminative enough to distinguish copies from non-copies. To meet the requirements, many image copy detection methods have been proposed. The traditional image copy detection methods concentrate on finding either global or local features to handle the copy detection task.

The early image copy detection works are usually based on the global features, such as the ordinal measure [1], ellipse track-based feature [4], edge-based signature [5], which are usually extracted from the whole or nearly the whole image region. However, all of these global features are not robust to the copping attack. That is because, due to the loss of spatial information caused by the cropping, the global features extracted from the cropped image may be quite different from those extracted from its original. Therefore, the global features suffer from the robustness issue. This greatly decreases the recall of copy detection, since many image copies after the copping attack cannot be effectively detected by using these global features any more.

To address the robustness issue of the global features, many recent image copy detection studies [6] have investigated the keypoint-based local features, such as scale invariant feature transform (SIFT) [7], principle components analysis on SIFT (PCA-SIFT) [8], and speeded up robust feature (SURF) [9]. They usually extract the local image features, each of which usually consists of two components: a keypoint and a corresponding descriptor. Then the local features between different images are matched by comparing their local descriptors for copy detection. Although these local features have achieved good robustness to most of the common attacks, they are not discriminative enough since they depend on the gradient statistics of small local patches and thus do not substantially capture the context information [10–13]. The discriminability

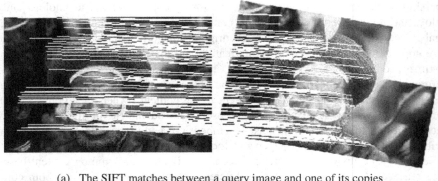

(a)   The SIFT matches between a query image and one of its copies

(b)   The SIFT matches between a query image and one of its similar images

Fig. 1. Two examples of the SIFT matches between different images

issue may cause many false matches between images, and therefore greatly reduces the performance of copy detection. Consequently, it is not suitable to directly apply these local features for copy detection. To enhance the detection performance, some improved keypoint-based local features, such as multi-resolution histogram descriptor (MHD) [11], Polar-Mapping of Discrete Fourier Transform (PM-DFT) [12], and Multiscale-SIFT [13], have been proposed to improve the discriminability. Although these local features can achieve better detection performance than the traditional ones, they do not adequately address the issue of discriminability since they are also based on small local patches.

From the above discussion, we found that the global features are not robust enough but they encode the spatial context information, which will be beneficial to obtain good discriminability, while the local features are robust to most of the common attacks but suffer from discriminability. Since either the global or the local features are hard to satisfy the demands of image copy detection individually, we attempt to combine both global and local features so as to take full of their merits. In this paper, we propose a novel copy detection method based on combination of the SIFT feature and the convex region-based global context (CRGC) feature.

Our method consists of three main steps, which are initial matching of SIFT features, verification for SIFT matches by using CRGC features, and copy detection by using the number of the surviving matches. Firstly, we extract the local image features (namely the SIFT features) for image representation, and find SIFT matches between images. Generally, a SIFT feature consists of two important components: a keypoint and a corresponding 128-D descriptor. The keypoint is characterized with three property elements: a dominant orientation, a characteristic scale, and its coordinates. Secondly, by utilizing the property values of keypoints of SIFT features, we propose the global features (namely the CRGC features), which describe the global context information of the SIFT features, to verify the SIFT matches and remove false positives. Finally, the number of the surviving matches can be used for copy detection. Since the GRGC features encode the global context information, the use of them will help the SIFT features to enhance the discriminability for image copy detection. By utilizing the property values of keypoints of SIFT features, the CRGC feature can achieve invariance to the geometric transformations such as rotation, scaling and translation. Therefore, in our method, the two types of features can complement each other well for image copy detection.

The rest of the paper is organized as follows. Section 2 introduces the proposed copy detection method in detail. In Sect. 3, the experiments are presented and discussed. Conclusions are drawn in Sect. 4.

2 Proposed Method

2.1 Initial Matching of SIFT Features

SIFT [7] is one of most famous local feature extraction algorithms. Since SIFT feature has good robustness to a variety of image transformations, such as rotation, scaling, and brightness change, the algorithm has been successfully applied in many computer applications, such as image retrieval, object categorization, and facial recognition.

The good robustness of SIFT feature will also be beneficial for resisting most of the common attacks including various geometric transformations and signal manipulations. Therefore, in our method, we adopt SIFT algorithm [7] to extract local features. As introduced in the previous section, a SIFT feature consists of two important components: a keypoint and a corresponding 128-D descriptor, where the keypoint is characterized with three property values: a dominant orientation, a characteristic scale, and its coordinates. The procedure of SIFT feature extraction can be described as follows. Firstly, for a given image, keypoints are detected by difference-of-Gaussian (DOG) detector. Then, the surrounding local patches of each keypoint is characterized by a 128-D SIFT descriptor.

For each image, we extract the SIFT features. Hundreds of keypoints and the associated local descriptors are obtained. Next, we match the SIFT features between different images by computing the distances of their descriptors. In our method, the matching strategy from [7], which employs the ratio between distance of the closest neighbor to that of the second closest, is adopted for the initial matching of SIFT features.

For example, we suppose that SF_A and SF_B are the SIFT feature sets of image A and B, respectively. For a feature sf_{Ai} in SF_A, let sf_{Bj} be its closest neighbor and sf_{Bk} its second closest neighbor in SF_B. And, the distances from sf_{Ai} to sf_{Bj} and sf_{Bk} are denoted as d_{ij} and d_{ik}, respectively, where the distance between features can be obtained by computing the Euclidean distance of their 128-D SIFT descriptors. If $d_{ij}/d_{ik} < Dratio$, the feature sf_{Ai} and sf_{Bj} can be regarded as a pair of matched SIFT features, else they are not. Here the threshold $Dratio$ is appropriately set as 0.6, according to [7]. Figure 1 shows two examples of the SIFT matches between different images, where each pair of matched SIFT features are displayed by connecting the corresponding keypoints of the SIFT features with lines.

2.2 Verification for SIFT Matches

After the initial matching of SIFT features, we can obtain a set of SIFT matches between two different images. However, due to the discriminability issue of SIFT features [12–14], many false positive matches will occur when there exist many similar local patches, typically found between similar images, as shown in Fig. 1 (b). As the number of the initial matches is commonly used to determine copies, many similar images will be incorrectly detected as copies. Consequently, the performance of copy detection will be greatly reduced. Since the false SIFT matches will have negative influence for image copy detection, the verification for SIFT matches is demanded.

The verification for local feature matches is the post-processing strategy used to remove false matches between images. In the traditional verification methods, such as [15–17], the geometric consistency is usually explored to filter false matches. Among these methods, the random sample consensus (RANSAC) algorithm [17] is one of most famous algorithms of geometric verification for local feature matches. However, since many false SIFT matches between similar images are geometrically consistent, these false matches can not be effectively removed by the verification of geometric consistency. As shown in Fig. 2, after verification for the SIFT matches between the two images of Fig. 1 (b) by using the RANSAC algorithm, there also exist many false matches, which are geometrically consistent but can not be effectively removed. Consequently, the similar images will also be incorrectly detected as copies, and thus these methods are not suitable for image copy detection.

Nonetheless, it is worth noting that although many falsely matched SIFT features between similar images might be similar, their global context information is usually

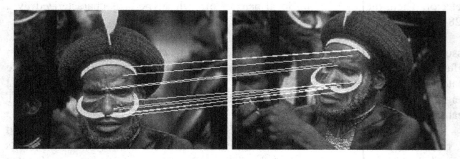

Fig. 2. The SIFT matches after using RANSAC algorithm

quite different. If the global context of SIFT features is explored to verify the initial matching results, false positives will be effectively removed and thus the performance of copy detection will be greatly improved. Therefore, the global context of SIFT features is encoded by the proposed global context features, namely CRGC features, for verification of initial SIFT matches. The procedure of the verification can be divided into three parts: convex region construction, CRGC feature extraction, feature comparison. Next, each of them is presented in detail.

2.2.1 Convex Region Construction

For a pair of matched SIFT features between two different images, the global context feature of each of the two is extracted by characterizing a reliable region around the SIFT feature. Their extracted reliable regions should cover the same or approximately the same image content under the copy attacks of various geometric transformations, such as rotation, scaling, translation and cropping. These reliable regions are the guarantee and basis for the extraction of robust global context features. In our method, we construct the reliable convex regions by two main steps: image normalization and computation of the reliable convex region.

From [7], we know that as the keypoints of SIFT features are detected based on image properties, their property values change covariantly with the geometric transformations including rotation, scaling and translation. To illustrate this point, for a pair of matched SIFT features sf_A and sf_B between images A and B. Their corresponding keypoints, denoted as p_A and p_B, can be regarded as a pair of matched keypoints. In Fig. 3 (a), the arrows from the images are used to represent the keypoints and their property values. The origin positions of the arrows represent the positions of the keypoints, and the lengths and orientations of the arrows indicate the characteristic scales and dominant orientations of the keypoints, respectively. From Fig. 3 (a), we can see that image B is generated from image A with the rotation and scaling transformations. For the keypoint p_B from image B, its dominant orientation and characteristic scale also change covariantly to the rotation and scaling transformations, respectively. Therefore, if f_A and f_B are a true match, the scales and orientations of image A and B can be normalized according to the property values of their keypoints. The step of image normalization is described as follows.

Taking image A for example, its keypoint p_A is treated as the origin. The image A is normalized according to the dominant orientation ϕ_A and characteristic scale s_A of the keypoint. The normalized image A' is formulated as

$$A' = s_0/s_A \begin{pmatrix} \cos(\phi_A) & -\sin(\phi_A) \\ \sin(\phi_A) & \cos(\phi_A) \end{pmatrix} A \qquad (1)$$

Where, the rotation angle is equal to the dominant orientation ϕ_A of the keypoint, and s_0 is a constant which is equal to 4. In the same way, we can normalize the image B to image B' according to the dominant orientation and characteristic scale of the keypoint p_B. Consequently, image A and B are normalized and their orientations and scales are consistent, as shown in Fig. 3 (b).

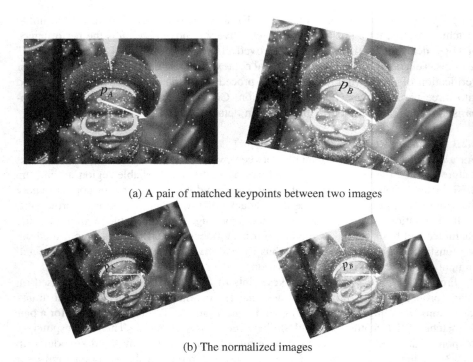

(a) A pair of matched keypoints between two images

(b) The normalized images

Fig. 3. Two images are normalized according to the property values of a pair of matched keypoints

After image normalization, for the pair of matched SIFT features denoted as sf_A and sf_B, we now compute their reliable convex regions. From the above step, the images are normalized by the rotation and scaling transformations, and thus the coordinates of all of their keypoints are changed with the same degree of rotation and scaling transformations. By using the new coordinates of these keypoints, we can generate two initial convex regions around feature sf_A and sf_B by the algorithm of convex hull computation [18], as shown in Fig. 4 (a). There are two reasons to generate the regions in this way. The first one is that these convex regions can avoid covering the border region of the images, which usually only contain some slight textures and will negatively influence discriminability. The second one being both of the two convex regions rarely contain the cropped regions, which will affect the extraction of our robust global context features. Note that since a proportion of keypoints may be unstable under image transformations, the two convex regions will cover different image content. To address this problem, by aligning the coordinates of p_A and p_B, we compute the common region of the two convex regions to generate the reliable convex regions of sf_A and sf_B, as shown in Fig. 4 (b).

As a result, the constructed convex regions of the two images cover the same image content under the geometric transformations including scaling, rotation and translation, while covering approximately the same image content with cropping, as shown in Fig. 4 (b). Therefore, the reliable regions will be beneficial to the extraction of our robust global context features.

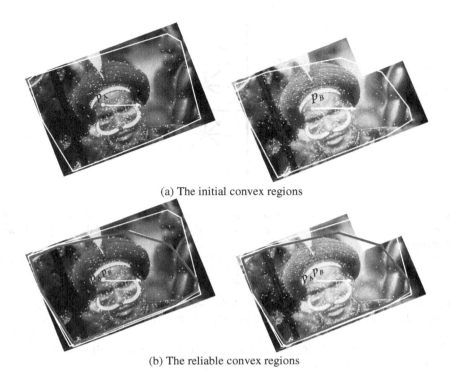

(a) The initial convex regions

(b) The reliable convex regions

Fig. 4. The construction of the reliable convex regions

2.2.2 CRGC Feature Extraction

Since the Histogram of Orientation Gradients (HOGs) [7, 19] can effectively charac-terize the image content, we extract the global context features, namely CRGC features, from the constructed convex regions using HOGs. The extraction of the CRGC features is described as follows.

For a SIFT feature, we unequally divide its convex region into 2 × 2 non-over-lapping subregions by using the rectangular coordinate system, as shown in Fig. 5. Then, for each subregion, we compute the gradient magnitude and orientation at each pixel point, and the gradient magnitudes of these pixel points are accumulated into an orientation histogram with 8 orientation bins. Next, an 8 dimensional feature vector is formed from the values of all the orientation histogram entries, corresponding to the lengths of the arrows in Fig. 5. Finally, the 8 × 2 × 2 (32) dimensional feature vector is generated by concatenating the four feature vectors from the 2 × 2 subregions, and the 32-D feature vector is normalized to unit length to form the CRGC feature of the convex region around the SIFT feature.

Since the convex regions are rotation, scale and translation invariant and the HOGs have been proven to be robust to the copy attacks of brightness change, noise adding, and so on, our CRGC features are robust to most of the common copy attacks.

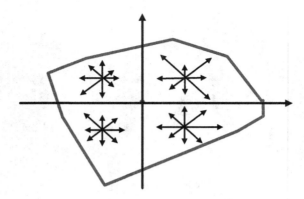

Fig. 5. For each subregion, an orientation histogram is constructed by accumulating the gradient magnitudes near that direction, and the lengths of the arrows represent the entries of the orientation histogram

2.2.3   Feature Comparison

In this section, for the pair of matched SIFT features sf_A and sf_B, we will compare their corresponding GRGC features to determine whether the SIFT features are a true match or not.

We denote the two CRGC features as cf_A and cf_B. The similarity of the context features is computed by cosine similarity:

$$sim = \frac{\sum_{i=1}^{32} \left(cf_A^i \times cf_B^i \right)}{\sqrt{\sum_{i=1}^{32} \left(cf_A^i \right)^2} \times \sqrt{\sum_{i=1}^{32} \left(cf_B^i \right)^2}} \tag{2}$$

Where, cf_A^i and cf_B^i denote the i-th element values of cf_A and cf_B, respectively, and i ranges from 1 to 32. If the similarity satisfies the following rule, the SIFT match can be regarded as a false match and then it will be removed.

$$sim < sim_{TH} \tag{3}$$

Where sim_{TH} is a preset threshold. After removing these false matches, the number of the surviving SIFT matches will be used for copy detection.

2.3   Copy Detection

In this section, we will discuss how to perform image copy detection by using the number of the surviving SIFT matches.

Let the number of the surviving matches between an original (query) image Q and a test image T be N_{QT}. Then, copy detection between the two images can be implemented using Formula (4).

$$N_{QT} \geq N_{TH} \tag{4}$$

Where, N_{TH} is a preset threshold. If N_{QT} is no less than the preset threshold N_{TH}, we accept that the test image is a copy version of the original, else we reject it.

3 Experiments

In the experiments, we adopt the image database downloaded from [20]. The image database includes 1,000 images with the size of 384 × 256 or 256 × 384, which are saved in JPEG format. Firstly, 30 images are randomly chosen from the image database. Then, each chosen image is modified by 30 image attacks using Adobe Photoshop 7.0. Thus, 900 image copies are generated for our experiments. These 30 copy attacks are the most commonly used ones, including rotations with 5, 10, 20, 90 and 180 degrees, scaling with the scaling factor are 0.5, 2 and 4, translation with -10 and +10 pixels, cropping 2 %, 5 %, 10 %, 20 % percentages, Guassian noise adding and so on. To evaluate the performances of our method and other methods, the precision and recall curve (P-R curve) is adopted in our experiments. The similarity threshold value sim_{TH} is empirically set as 0.88 for the SIFT match verification in our method.

In the experiment, the 30 randomly chosen original images serve as query images. The 900 image copies are inserted into the test image database and making there a total of 1900 test images in the database. We compare the performance of our method (SIFT + CRGC) with that of SIFT, Multiscale-SIFT and SIFT + RANSAC methods. SIFT method represent the method which matches SIFT features between images and then uses the number of matches for copy detection, and Multiscale-SIFT represents the method which detects image copies in a similar way but uses the Multiscale-SIFT features instead of the SIFT features. The SIFT + RANSAC method is also similar to SIFT method, but it adds the step of SIFT match verification by using RANSAC algorithm.

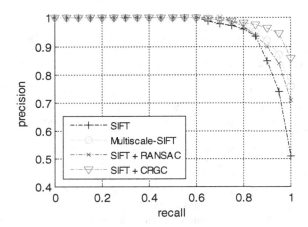

Fig. 6. The PR curves of different methods

For each method, the PR curve is obtained by varying the value of its detection threshold. Figure 6 presents the P-R curves of these methods. From Fig. 6, we can see that the precision and recall rates of our method are up to about 95 %, while the three other methods can achieve about 88 %, 91 % and 90 %, respectively. Our method (SIFT + CRGC) can achieve better recall and precision than other methods. As we know, the precision and the recall represent the performances in terms of robustness and discriminability, respectively. Therefore, our method combining the SIFT and CRGC features can achieve desirable performance and outperform other methods in terms of both robustness and discriminability.

4   Conclusion

In this paper, a novel image copy detection method based on combination of the global and local features has been presented. It takes good robustness possessed by SIFT features and high discriminability of GRGC features. Experimental results have shown that our method can achieve desirable performances for image copy detection in terms of both robustness and discriminability. However, the initially matching SIFT features between images is a time-consuming step because hundreds of SIFT features with high dimensions will be extracted from every image. Future work will be aimed to improve the efficiency of copy detection by using indexing methods.

Acknowledgements. This work is supported by the NSFC (61232016, 61173141, 61173142, 61173136, 61103215, 61373132, 61373133), GYHY201206033, 201301030, 2013DFG12860, BC2013012, PAPD fund, Hunan province science and technology plan project fund (2012GK3120), the Scientific Research Fund of Hunan Provincial Education Department (10C0944), and the Prospective Research Project on Future Networks of Jiangsu Future Networks Innovation Institute (BY2013095-4-10)

References

1. Kim, C.: Content-based image copy detection. Sig. Process. Image Commun. **18**(3), 169–184 (2003)
2. Hsiao, J.-H., et al.: A new approach to image copy detection based on extended feature sets. IEEE Trans. Image Process. **16**(8), 2069–2079 (2007)
3. Joly, A., et al.: Content-based copy retrieval using distortion-based probabilistic similarity search. IEEE Trans. Multimedia **9**(2), 293–305 (2007)
4. Wu, M.-N., et al.: Novel image copy detection with rotating tolerance. J. Syst. Softw. **80**(7), 1057–1069 (2007)
5. Lin, C.-C., Wang, S.-S.: An edge-based image copy detection scheme. Fundamenta Informaticae **83**(3), 299–318 (2008)
6. Sukthankar. R., Ke, Y., Huston, L.: Efficient near-duplicate detection and subimage retrieval, In: Proceedings of the 12th ACM International Conference on Multimedia (Multimedia), pp. 869–876, New York (2004)
7. Lowe, D.G.: Distinctive image features from scale-invariant keypoints. Int. J. Comput. Vision **60**(2), 91–110 (2004)

8. Ke, Y., Sukthankar, R.: PCA-SIFT: a more distinctive representation for local image descriptors. In: Proceedings of the 2004 IEEE Computer Society Conference on Computer Vision and Pattern Recognition, 27 June–2 July 2004, Los Alamitos, pp. 506-513 (2004)

9. Bay, H., et al.: Speeded-up robust features (SURF). Comput. Vis. Image Underst. **110**, 346–359 (2008)

10. Mortensen, E.N., et al.: A SIFT descriptor with global context. In: 2005 IEEE Computer Society Conference on Computer Vision and Pattern Recognition, CVPR 2005, 20–25, June, 2005, San Diego, CA, United states, pp. 184–190 (2005)

11. Xu, Z., et al.: A novel image copy detection scheme based on the local multi-resolution histogram descriptor. Multimedia Tools Appl. **52**(2–3), 445–463 (2011)

12. Ling, H.F., et al.: PM-DFT: a new local invariant descriptor towards image copy detection. J. Comput. Sci. Technol. **26**(3), 558–567 (2011)

13. Ling, H., et al.: Efficient image copy detection using multiscale fingerprints. IEEE Multimedia **19**, 60–69 (2012)

14. Mikolajczyk, K., et al.: A comparison of affine region detectors. Int. J. Comput. Vision **65** (1–2), 43–72 (2005)

15. Zhou, W., et al.: Spatial coding for large scale partial-duplicate web image search. In: 18th ACM International Conference on Multimedia ACM Multimedia 2010, MM 2010, 25–29 October 2010, Firenze, Italy, pp. 511–520 (2010)

16. Jegou, H., Douze, M., Schmid, C.: Hamming embedding and weak geometric consistency for large scale image search. In: Forsyth, D., Torr, P., Zisserman, A. (eds.) ECCV 2008, Part I. LNCS, vol. 5302, pp. 304–317. Springer, Heidelberg (2008)

17. Fischler, M.A., Bolles, R.C.: Random sample consensus: a paradigm for model fitting with applications to image analysis and automated cartography. Commun. ACM **24**(6), 381–395 (1981)

18. Graham, R.L.: An efficient algorithm for determining the convex hull of a finite planar set. Inf. Process. Lett. **1**, 132–133 (1972)

19. Dalal, N., Triggs, B.: Histograms of oriented gradients for human detection. In: Schmid, C. (ed.) IEEE Computer Society Conference on Computer Vision and Pattern Recognition, vol. 1, pp. 886–893. IEEE Computer Soc, Los Alamitos (2005)

20. Li, J.: http://sites.stat.psu.edu/jiali/, 2003

Watermarking

A Blind Robust Reversible Watermark Scheme for Textual Relational Databases with Virtual Primary Key

Chin-Chen Chang[1,2(✉)], Thai-Son Nguyen[1,3], and Chia-Chen Lin[4]

[1] Department of Information Engineering and Computer Science,
Feng Chia University, Taichung 40724, Taiwan, R.O.C
alan3c@gmail.com, thaison@tvu.edu.vn
[2] Department of Computer Science and Information Engineering,
Asia University, Taichung, Taiwan, R.O.C
[3] Department of Information Technology, Travinh University,
Travinh City, Travinh Province, Vietnam
[4] Department of Computer Science and Information Management,
Providence University, Taichung 43301, Taiwan, R.O.C
mhlin3@pu.edu.tw

Abstract. In recent years, many researchers have studied reversible watermarking techniques for relational databases. Most of the developed schemes have been based on a primary key attribute in order to determine the selected tuples and attributes to carry the watermark bits. What happens, however, when the primary key attribute does not exist for a relational database? In this paper, we propose a blind robust reversible watermarking scheme for a textual relational database. This scheme does not rely on the primary key attribute. To avoid the absolute dependence on the primary key attribute, as in existing schemes, in the proposed scheme the content of textual attributes are used to generate the virtual primary attribute that is applied in tuple and attribute selections. Moreover, the selection of attributes does not depend on the order of attributes in the relational database. Model and robustness analysis demonstrate that our proposed scheme achieves a high resilience against different types of tuple attacks, i.e., tuple attacks and attribute attacks. The experimental results also confirm that the proposed scheme is more secure and robust than other existing schemes.

Keywords: Blind · Reversible watermark · Relational database · Robustness · Textual attribute · Virtual primary key

1 Introduction

With the rapid development of computer network and digitalization techniques, both fingerprinting and watermarking are two critical solutions against piracy and malicious operations in the modern digital world. Fingerprinting [1, 2] is a branch of data hiding that is used to protect data from threats, i.e., unauthorized disclosure. Meanwhile watermarking [3–17] is another branch of data hiding that can help authorized users to identify source or ownership of purchased or received digital data.

© Springer International Publishing Switzerland 2015
Y.-Q. Shi et al. (Eds.): IWDW 2014, LNCS 9023, pp. 75–89, 2015.
DOI: 10.1007/978-3-319-19321-2_6

Watermarking provides copyright protection and content authentication for various digital multimedia objects, i.e., text, image, video, and audio [3–7] by embedding some owner information (i.e., owner's signature, company logo) into the original form of the data without causing degradation of visual quality and maintaining the hidden information in such a way as to prevent it from being maliciously erased. Similarly, over the last decade, due to the increasing number of applications with relational databases, researchers have looked at how to apply watermarking to ensure the security of relational databases [8–16]. One critical issue of relational database watermarking is how to derive enough space from relational databases to embed watermarks since this is often precluded compared with other digital multimedia objects, such as image, text, video, etc. Moreover, the acceptable data distortion of watermarked relational databases is significantly less since a relational database needs to provide data for daily work and since human visual systems do not treat the modified data as identical to the original data, as may be the case with images or video. Once the amount of distortion is increased, the referential ability of a relational database is decreased. For example, when the price of one piece of cloth is changed from $10 to $100 after embedding a watermarking bit, the modified price may create some misunderstanding among customers.

Recently, many watermarking schemes have been proposed. In 2002, Agrawal and Kiernan [8] proposed a well-known relational database watermarking scheme by embedding the watermark into the least significant bits (LSBs) of the selected numerical attribute. Their scheme withstands various attacks, i.e., tuple deletion, tuple alteration, tuple insertion, and tuple sorting attacks. In addition, their scheme ensures that the minimum different value between the original means and the modified means and variances of all numerical attributes are obtained. However, this scheme cannot be applied directly to a textual relational database. One reason is that any modification in the bits of textual attributes could make these values meaningless. In [9], Sion et al. expanded a watermarking technique for the categorical attributes of relational databases. It is unlike Agrawal and Kiernan's scheme in that the numerical attribute is used for carrying a watermarking bit. Similarly, Sion et al. used categorical attributes to embed the watermark. To embed a watermark bit, the current value of the categorical attribute was modified to different values of the categorical attributes. This scheme tolerates the small distortion imposed by the relational database. The small distortion did not have a significant effect on the content of the categorical relational database. In [10], Al-Haj and Odeh introduced a new relational database watermarking scheme using non-numerical, multi-word attributes, attributes of a selected number of tuples, instead of using numerical or categorical attributes as in [8] and [9], respectively. In their scheme, a binary image was used as watermark that was embedded into the relational database. Their scheme obtained robustness. It was able to resist the attempts of an attacker in respect to removing or weakening the embedded watermark data. In addition, this scheme maintained a blind capability, meaning that it does not require the original database when the embedded watermark was extracted or verified. However, Al-Haj and Odeh's scheme does not ensure against all malicious attacks. Take a modification attack as an example; their scheme only detects completely the embedded watermark with 100 % accuracy when an attacker modified less than 10 % of the watermarked relational database.

In [11], Shehab et al. proposed another watermarking scheme based on an optimization technique for a numerical relational database. Shehab et al.'s scheme was highly robust against various data attacks. To obtain this, their scheme first divides the relational database into several non-overlapping partitions. Then each partition is used to embed one watermark bit. Their scheme was robust against tuple deletion, tuple alteration, and tuple insertion attacks, as well as a tuple sorting attack. However, Shehab et al.'s scheme is only efficient when small modifications are accepted in the relational database used by an application. In addition, their scheme cannot ensure that the original relational database is reconstructed after the embedded watermark has been extracted and verified.

In 2013, to obtain reversibility in relational database watermarking and further improve resilience against various tuple attacks, Farfoura et al. [12] introduced into their scheme a new, blind, reversible watermarking technique that applied a reversible data hiding scheme as proposed in 2004 by Thodi et al. [18], called "prediction-error expansion." Farfoura et al.'s scheme obtains the high resilience against tuple database attacks. For instance, Farfoura et al.'s scheme can detect fully the embedded watermark in a tuple alteration attack, even when the content of the watermarked relational database has been modified by up to 60 %. However, this scheme cannot achieve a high robustness against tuple addition attacks. For such an attack, Farfoura et al.'s scheme only detects the entire embedded watermark correctly when less than 50 % of the tuples from other database sources are used in a mixture with the current watermarked relational database. To ensure minimum distortion of the watermark relational database, their scheme only used a fractional portion of the numerical attributes to carry watermark bits. As a result, their scheme cannot be used for embedding watermark bits if the numerical attributes do not contain the fractional portion.

These above schemes [8–12] are based on important assumptions that the relational database must have a primary key attribute and that the order of attributes in the relational database cannot be changed. As a result, if the content of the primary key attribute is modified or deleted, the watermark cannot be verified. Furthermore, these schemes cannot withstand attribute attacks that alter the order of attributes in the relational database.

To apply a watermarking scheme to a textual relational database and further improve robustness against different types of attacks, i.e., tuple attacker and attribute attacks, this paper proposes a new blind watermarking scheme for a textual attribute. Our scheme limits the watermark to being embedded only into textual attributes. To achieve strong robustness, meaning that the watermark to survive under varieties of data attacks, such as tuple attacks and attribute attacks, in the proposed scheme, actual content of the attributes is used to generate the virtual primary key, which is different for each tuple. As a consequence, even when the relational database does not contain the primary key attribute, the proposed scheme also ensures that the watermark is embedded, extracted and verified in the relational database. In addition, the proposed scheme obtains reversibility. The experimental results show that malicious attackers must alter or remove a huge number of tuples or attributes in order to modify or delete the embedded watermark in the proposed scheme.

The paper is organized as follows. Section 2 presents the proposed watermarking scheme, including watermark embedding and watermark detection procedures. The details of our tests are given in Sect. 3. Finally, conclusions and suggestions for future work are given in Sect. 4.

2 The Proposed Watermarking Scheme

To embed a watermark into a relational database in existing schemes [10–13], the relational database must contain a primary key attribute. The main reason is that these existing schemes depended critically on the primary key attribute for embedding and detecting a watermark. Therefore, these schemes assumed that the order of the entire candidate attributes and the primary key attribute cannot be changed by attackers. If the primary key attribute is changed, the integrity and availability of the relational database will be violated, making the relational database unusable. However, any changes or deletion of the primary key reduces the effectiveness of these schemes. These schemes cannot embed/extract the watermark successfully without the primary key attribute. Moreover, these schemes are vulnerable to attacks that delete or add attributes. In addition, if the order of the candidate attributes in the watermarked relational database is modified, these schemes cannot extract and verify the embedded watermark.

In order to address these vulnerabilities in existing schemes and to obtain more satisfactory properties, we propose a new robust reversible watermarking scheme for a textual relational database. We restrict the watermarking to embedding into the textual value of candidate attributes to achieve strong robustness, which ensures that the watermark can withstand a variety of data attacks, i.e., tuple attacks and attribute attacks. Figure 1 shows the flowchart of the main steps in our proposed scheme.

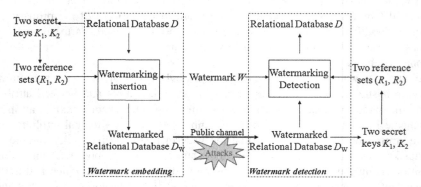

Fig. 1. Flowchart of the main processes in the proposed scheme

In comparison to some existing watermarking schemes [10–13] that use a primary key attribute for embedding and verifying watermark data, we propose a new watermarking scheme that does not depend on the primary key attribute. Assume that a relational database D without the primary key attribute that is defined as D ($V_0, V_1 \ldots, V_{\alpha-1}$) is used for embedding watermark W, where α attributes, $V_0, V_1 \ldots, V_{\alpha-1}$, are textual attributes. These textual attributes are candidates for embedding watermark information. For each attribute V_j, we partition the value of attribute V_j into two parts: (i) V_j^1: the last word of the attribute V_j within which a watermark bit may be embedded; and (ii) V_j^{-1}: the value of V_j without the last word, which is used to determine whether the tuple and the attribute are used for carrying watermark bit or not. Table 1 provides the critical parameters used in this section.

Table 1. Notations used in our proposed scheme

Symbols	Description
D	Original relational database
D_W	Watermarked relational database
V_j	Attribute j in relational database D
K_1 and K_2	Two secret keys
α	Number of attributes in the relational database available for embedding the watermark
L	The length of watermark W
g	In g tuples, one tuple is used to carry watermark bit

In our proposed scheme, the string of the textual attributes V_j in tuple t_i is separated into two parts: $t_i V_j^1$ and $t_i V_j^{-1}$. We use the results of a one-way hash cryptography function that is computed by the value of $t_i V_j^{-1}$ and two secret keys K_1 and K_2 to determine whether a tuple is selected or not for embedding a watermark bit. Two secret keys are critical in both the watermark embedding and detection of the proposed scheme. Therefore, for security reasons, two secret keys K_1 and K_2 are calculated by Eqs. (1) and (2), respectively.

$$K_1 = H(DB\_Version°DB\_Name°DB\_Inf.°\ldots). \tag{1}$$

$$K_2 = H\big(K_1°H(DB\_Version°DB\_Name°DB\_Inf.°\ldots)\big). \tag{2}$$

where $°$ indicates the concatenation function; DB_Name is the name of the database; $DB\_Version$ is the version of the database; $DB\_Inf.$ is the database information, i.e., the number of attributes, the number of tuples of the relational database D; and $H()$ is a one-way cryptography hash function. Several hash functions, i.e., MD5 [19] and SHA [19], are the best choices for use in our proposed scheme.

For watermark W to be embedded into the relational database D, W should be secretly chosen to be a meaningful image or is generated in a secure and random manner in Eq. (3) to thwart various data attacks.

$$W = H(K_1°K_2°H(DB\_Version°DB\_Name°DB\_Inf.°DOI°\ldots)). \tag{3}$$

In our scheme, we assume that α is equal to or larger than 2. For each tuple t in the relational database D, we calculate the virtual primary key, vt_iP, by combining the two smallest results of a hash function in $\{H\big(K_1°H\big(K_2°V_j^{-1}\big)\big)|j=0,1,\ldots,\alpha-1\}$. In general, we may use more than two results of the hash function to ensure optimization of the construction of the virtual primary key value.

2.1   Reference Set Generation

In this section, we present how to construct two reference sets, i.e., R_1 and R_2, by using two secret keys K_1 and K_2. Two reference sets are used to refer to when a secret bit is embedded into the selected attribute. These reference sets are important to embed, extract and verify the watermark in both watermark embedding and watermark detection phases. The procedure for reference set generation is as follows:

```
Reference set generation procedure
Input: Two embedding keys K₁ and K₂
Output: Two reference sets, R₁ and R₂
Step 1: Generate two random sequences S₁ and S₂; // using
a pseudo-random generator with the seed value K₁ and K₂,
respectively. S₁ and S₂ have twenty-six distinct elements,
and their values are from 0 to 25.
Step 2: Let OriginalSet1 and OriginalSet2 be {a, b,...,
z} and {A, B, ..., Z}, respectively.
Step 3: For each i from 0 to 25, let R₁[i] =
OriginalSet1[S₁[i]] and R₂[i] = OriginalSet2[S₂[i]].
```

2.2   Watermark Embedding

In this section, we demonstrate the main processes of the watermark embedding procedure. The bit-encoding procedure describes the process of encoding one watermark bit into a textual attribute. The two reference sets, R_1 and R_2, are determined by using the reference set generator procedure. The last word V_j^1 is extracted from the selected attribute for embedding watermark bit b by referring to two reference sets, R_1 and R_2. The Bit encoding procedure is as follows:

```
Bit_encoding procedure:
Input: Watermark bit b, the last word of the selected at-
tribute j: Vⱼ¹, and two reference sets, R₁ and R₂
Output: The watermarked word of the selected attribute j:
Vⱼ¹*
Step 1:  Extract the last letter A of Vⱼ¹.
Step 2: Get the index idx of the last letter A in the
OriginalSet1 set.
Step 3: If b = 0, set A to be R₁[idx]; otherwise, set A to
be R₂[idx].
Step 4: Generate Vⱼ¹* by updating Vⱼ¹ with new value of the
letter A.
```

A watermark is set of L bits $W = \{b_0, b_1,... b_{L-1}\}$ that is secretly chosen from meaningful images (i.e., company logo) or is generated by using Eq. (3). To embed watermark W into the relational database, a watermark embedding procedure is conducted to determine whether tuples and attributes will be used to contain the watermark bit. Note that in some existing schemes [10–13], the order of attributes in relational data does not change, otherwise it cannot be recovered. Therefore, if there are any changes of the order of attributes, the embedded watermark cannot be extracted and verified. To avoid this, in our proposed scheme, we use a part of the attribute value into determining whether or not tuple and attribute are selected. As a result, our scheme achieves strong robustness against various attribute attacks related to the order of attributes in a relational database, i.e., attribute deletion, attribute addition, and attribute sorting attacks. The watermark embedding procedure is as follows:

```
Watermark embedding procedure:
Input: Relational database D
Output: Watermarked relational database D_w, two secret
keys K_1 and K_2
Step 1: Generate two secret keys K_1 and K_2 using Equations
(1) and (2), respectively.
Step 2: Generate watermark W using Equation (3).
Step 3: For each t_i in the relational database D, calcu-
late the virtual primary key vt_iP.
Step 4: If vt_iP mod g = 0, this tuple is selected for em-
bedding a watermark bit. Then the following steps are
processed:
Step 4.1: Attribute V_j in tuple t_i is selected for embed-
ding a watermark bit if the result of hash function |H
(K_2H (K_2 V_j^{-1}))|is the smallest one among α attributes.
Multiple attributes are selected if there are multiple
attributes that are the same smallest hash value. For
each, the selected attribute V_j, the last word V_j^1 is ex-
tracted.
Step 4.2: Compute the mark_bit_idx = vt_iP mod L, and read
the corresponding watermark bit b from the watermark W as
b = W[mark_bit_idx]. Then, the bit_encoding procedure is
used to embed b into the last word V_j^1 of the selected at-
tribute V_j.
Step 5: Repeat Steps 3 and 4 until all the tuples in the
relational database D are processed.
```

In the watermark embedding procedure, Step 4 decides whether the tuple will be selected for embedding a watermark, and Step 4.1 determines whether the attribute will be used to carry the watermark bit. This is unlike existing schemes that depend on the primary key and on the order of attributes. Our scheme generates a virtual primary key by using the content of attributes. This generation is dynamic and content based. It is dynamic because of the different tuples in which we select the different attribute to generate the virtual primary key. In addition, without knowing how the two secret keys, K_1 and K_2, are generated, a malicious attacker cannot detect whether the tuple is selected in the relational database D. The generation is also content-based because it depends on the results of a hash function of the attributes' content rather than the order of attributes. As a result of two these properties, a malicious attacker cannot remove all virtual primary keys by modifying the value of an attribute if the attacker does not alter or delete a large amount of attributes in the relational database.

2.3   Watermark Detection

In this section, we demonstrate the details of a watermark detection procedure that can be used in two scenarios: (i) If Jane suspects that the published relational database Q is illegally copied or tampered from her watermark relational database, she can use the watermark detection procedure to extract and verify the embedded watermark to prove ownership of the published relational database. (ii) Jane utilizes the trial version of a database application and she wants to buy a license to use the full version of the relational database.

To extract and verify the embedded watermark, W, the same selected tuples and selected attributes should be determined as used in the watermark embedding proce-dure. Therefore, secret parameters, i.e., g, α, and L, are required in addition to two secret keys, K_1 and K_2, because of the identical distribution of a one-way hash function. To ensure accuracy of the extracted watermark bit, the two reference sets R_1 and R_2 are generated by using the same secret keys, K_1 and K_2, respectively. Then, the Bit_coding procedure is subsequently used to extract the embedded watermark bit. This is shown in the following:

```
Watermark_bit_extracting algorithm:
Input: The last word of the selected watermarked attrib-
ute j: V_j^{1*}, and two reference sets, R_1 and RS_2
Output: The watermark bit b and the recovered value of
the last word of the selected watermarked attribute j: V_j^1
Step 1:   Extract the last letter A of V_j^{1*}.
Step 2: If A∈R_1, the embedded watermark bit b = 0, get
index idx of the letter A from the set R_1.
Step 3: Otherwise, (A∈R_2), the embedded watermark bit b =
1, get index idx of the letter A from the set R_2.
Step 4: Reconstruct V_j^1 by updating V_j^{1*} by replacing the
letter A by OriginalSet1[idx].
```

Our watermark detection procedure is used to extract and detect the entire embedded watermark W from the watermarked relational database D_W. In the water-mark detection procedure, for each tuple t_i, the same virtual primary key attribute as used in the watermark embedding procedure should be computed by using the content of attributes and two secret keys K_1 and K_2. Then, all the tuples of a watermarked relational database D_W are processed to extract the embedded watermark bits. When all embedded watermark bits have been completely checked, to determine the final extracted watermark, the procedure uses the majority voting mechanism (MVM), as shown in Step 8. This is because watermark W is embedded several times into the relational database D in the watermark embedding procedure.

```
Watermark detection algorithm:
Input: Relational database D_w, parameters g, α, and L
Output: Watermarked status ∈ {true, false}
Step 1: Generate two secret keys K_1 and K_2 using Equations
(1) and (2), respectively.
Step 2: Generate watermark W using Equation (3).
Step 3: Set count[i][0] to 0, and count[i][1] to 0 for
all i from 0 to L-1.
Step 4: For each t_i in the relational database D, calcu-
late the virtual primary key vt_iP.
Step 5: If vt_iP mod g = 0, this tuple has been embedded
the watermark bit. Then, the following steps are pro-
cessed:
Step 5.1: Attribute V_j in the tuple t_i is selected for ex-
tracting watermark bit if its result of hash function |H
(K_1 ℋ (K_2 ℋ V_j^{-1})) |is the smallest one among α attributes.
Multiple attributes are selected if there are multiple
attributes of the same smallest hash value. For each the
selected attribute V_j, the last word V_j^1 is extracted.
Step 5.2: Compute the mark_bit_inx = vt_iP mod L. Then,
extract b' from the last word in the selected attribute
by using the bit_decoding procedure.
Step 6: Set count[mark_bit_idx][b'] to
count[mark_bit_idx][b'] + 1.
Step 7: Repeat Steps 3 to 5 until all tuples in R_w are
processed.
// Majority voting mechanism
Step 8: For each i from 0 to L - 1, do the following
steps:
Step 8.1: If count[i][0] + count[i][1] = 0,set W'[i] = -1.
Step 8.2: If count[i][1] > count[i][0], set W'[i] = 1.
Step 8.3: Otherwise, (count[i][1] ≤ count[i][0]), set
W'[i] = 0.
Step 8.4: If W'[i] = W[i], then add matchcount to 1.
Step 9: If matchcount = L. This means that the original
relational database D has been recovered successfully,
then return true.
Step 9: Otherwise (matchcount ≠ L), meaning that the
original relational database D cannot be recovered, and
then return false.
```

In this procedure, we use two counting variables count[L][0] and count[L][1] to indicate the number of times that the extracted watermark bit is 0 or 1, respectively. After all watermark bits are extracted, the procedure assigns 0 (or 1, respectively) to the corresponding final watermark bit, if count[i][1] $\leq$ count[i][0]) (or count[i][1] > count [i][0]). In our proposed scheme, if the virtual primary key attribute, vt_iP, is unique to every tuple t, on average N/g bits are embedded into the relational database D. In other words, each watermark bit is embedded on average $N/(gL)$ times. In fact, some watermark bits may be embedded fewer times than others.

3   Experimental Results

The performance of the proposed scheme is compared in this section to four existing schemes, i.e., Al-Haj and Odeh's scheme [10], Shehab et al.'s scheme [11], Farfoura et al.'s scheme [12], and Chang et al.'s scheme [13]. All experiments were performed on a PC with an Intel(R) Core™ i7-3770 CPU @ 3.4 GHz and an 8 GB RAM. The operating system used for this testing was Windows 7 Professional 64-bit, and all of the algorithms were implemented by Microsoft Visual Studio 2005 C# using the ADO component to connect with a Microsoft SQL Server 2005 database. In these experiments, the eight candidate attributes for the four existing schemes and for the proposed scheme were numerical attributes and textual attributes that were generated artificially, respectively. Size N of the generated relational database D was 80,000 tuples, and the values of the parameters used in our experiments were $g = 6$, $\alpha = 8$, and $L = 60$. For each result in the experiments, we tested 50 times, and calculated the average value of all of the successful watermark matches.

In this section, we did not compare the proposed scheme with the other three existing schemes in a tuple sorting attack. The major reason for this is that a tuple sorting attack is completely ineffective against the proposed scheme and three of the other existing schemes [11–13]. In other words, the same results would be obtained by all four of these schemes to such an attack. This is because all four schemes use the results of a one-way hash function to independently select the tuples and attributes for embedding watermark bits. Only for Al-Haj and Odeh.'s scheme [10], such an attack is always effective because in their scheme the m short strings are embedded into the sub-set in order. As a result, when the order of tuples is rearranged, the watermark is almost removed.

As mentioned above, four existing schemes [10–13] depended critically on a primary key attribute. Thus, the relational database must contain a primary key attribute that is important to determine whether the tuple and attribute are selected for embedding a watermark. Therefore, alterations to the primary key attribute cause significant degradation in the effectiveness of the relational database. In addition to the primary key attribute based approach; these four existing schemes depended on order of attributes in the relational database to determine attributes for carrying a watermark bit. Therefore, when attackers try to add some new attributes into, or delete some attributes from watermarked relational database, as well as sorting the order of attributes, these existing schemes cannot extract and verify the embedded watermark. This means that these four existing schemes [10–13] are not robust against attribute attacks. In contrast, the resilience of the proposed scheme against these attribute attacks, this is because some attributes are selected randomly to generate the virtual primary key, which is different for each tuple. As a consequence, even when the primary key attribute is not existed in the relational database or some attributes are added or deleted from the relational database, the proposed scheme still ensures that the watermark is embedded, extracted and verified in the relational database. Therefore, in this section, we only compare the proposed scheme with four existing schemes [10–13] in term of tuple attacks, i.e., tuple deletion, tuple alteration, and tuple insertion attacks, and time execution cost.

3.1   Turtle Deletion Attack

Figure 2 presents the performance of the proposed scheme and four other existing schemes in terms of a tuple deleted attack. The proposed scheme obtains a higher robustness to this attack than the other four existing schemes. The proposed scheme can successfully detect the embedded watermark, even when more than 95 % of tuples in the watermarked relational database were randomly deleted. Figure 2 shows that Al-Haj and Odeh's scheme was the worst among the five schemes because their scheme embeds m sub-strings of the watermark into each m-tuple subset of the relational database. As a result, when attackers delete the subset, m corresponding substrings of the watermark are also erased from the relational database.

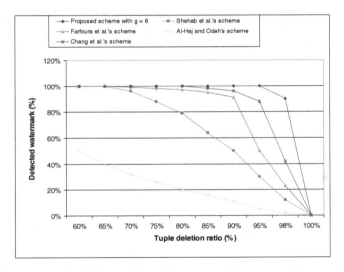

Fig. 2. Resilience to tuple deletion attacks of the proposed scheme and four existing schemes

3.2   Tuple Alteration Attack

To simulate this attack on the five schemes, we randomly modified the ratio of tuples in the watermarked relational database. Figure 3 shows the resilience to this attack for the five schemes. As we can see in Fig. 3, the embedded watermark can be detected with 100 % accuracy in the proposed scheme and in Chang et al.'s scheme, even when up to 80 % of tuples are altered. This shows the strong resilience of the proposed scheme and

Chang et al.'s scheme to this type of attack. Although, the proposed scheme and Chang et al.'s scheme both applied the MVM technique, the proposed scheme slightly outperforms Chang et al.'s scheme against this attack. Once 90 % of tuples of the watermarked relational database in the proposed scheme and in Chang et al.' scheme are altered, the embedded watermark will be modified around 5 % and 9 %, respectively. The main reason for this is that the proposed scheme is based on the content of the attributes to determine the selected attributes. For each selected tuple, the attribute is selected for embedding a watermark bit, when its result of hash function $|H(K_1^\circ H(K_2^\circ V_j^{-1}))|$ is the smallest one among α attributes. If there are multiple attributes that have the same smallest hash value, more than one attribute is selected for carrying a watermark bit. This means that more watermark bits will be embedded in the proposed scheme. In contrast, Chang et al.'s scheme is based on histogram-shifting technique to embed a watermark into the numerical attributes. In Chang et al.'s scheme, the primary key attribute is used to determine the selected attributes. Then the selected attribute is used for embedding watermark bits, and only if the last two digits of the selected attributes are of the high-frequency value. In other words, one watermark bit will be embedded fewer times in Chang et al.'s scheme than in the proposed scheme. Therefore, the proposed scheme always obtains a higher accuracy for each reconstructed watermark bit than Chang et al.'s scheme.

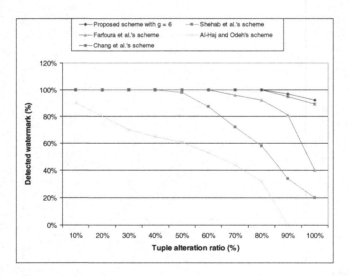

Fig. 3. Resilience to tuple alteration attacks of the proposed scheme and four existing schemes

3.3 Tuple Insertion Attack

In a tuple insertion attack, to weaken the accuracy of the extracted watermark, attackers attempt to mix a ratio q of tuples from other sources and some ratio tuple from the watermarked relational database to generate their own relational database with the same size as the watermarked relational database. Figure 4 shows a comparison between our proposed scheme and four existing schemes in this attack. Figure 4 shows that Shehab et al.'s scheme outperforms the other two schemes, i.e., Farfoura et al.'s scheme, and Al-Haj and Odeh.'s scheme. Shehab et al.'s scheme can detect the embedded watermark successfully; even when only 50 % of the tuples in the watermarked relational database are used. However, Fig. 4 also shows that even when ratio q is up to 60 % of the relational database size, it does not prevent both our proposed scheme and Chang et al.'s scheme from extracting the embedded watermark with 100 % accuracy. This means that our scheme and Chang et al.'s scheme are superior to Shehab et al.'s scheme [11] and the two other schemes [10, 12] in this attack. The reason for this is that in Shehab et al.'s scheme, the statistics of one partition is computed and then is modified to embed the watermark bit. Therefore, when a higher ratio of tuples from another source is used than the ratio of tuples from the watermarked relational database, the statistical results will be changed and cannot maintain the accuracy of the extracted watermark bit. In comparison, a MVM technique is applied in the proposed scheme and in Chang et al.'s scheme to ensure the high accuracy of the extracted watermark bit. Although, the proposed scheme and Chang et al.'s scheme obtain the same results in this type of attack, nevertheless, Chang et al.'s scheme is based on using the primary key attribute. Therefore, when a relational database does not have a primary key attribute, or the primary key attribute is deleted, the watermark cannot be embedded into the original relational watermark, or extracted from watermarked relational databases. In contrast, the proposed scheme constructs a virtual primary key that is used to independently determine the selected tuples and the selected attributes. Therefore, the proposed scheme has improved robustness against data attacks over the Chang et al. scheme.

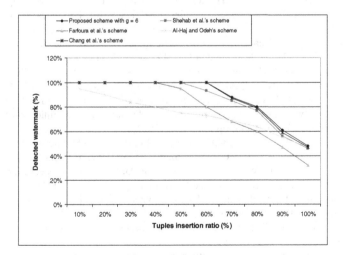

Fig. 4. Resilience to tuple insertion attacks of the proposed scheme and four existing schemes

4   Conclusions

In this paper, we proposed a new blind, reversible, robust watermarking technique for a textual relational database. The proposed scheme makes use of the content of textual attributes to generate a virtual primary key attribute. As a result, the proposed scheme does not rely on the primary key attribute. Therefore, our proposed scheme can embed a watermark into a relational database that does not contain the primary key attribute. In terms of attacks, the order of attributes on a watermarked relational database can be modified; however, the watermark is still extracted correctly in the proposed scheme. Moreover, in comparisons of the proposed scheme to four existing schemes, all of the results confirmed that the proposed scheme achieves a higher resilience than the four existing schemes under various data attacks, such as tuple attacks and attribute attacks. Therefore, the proposed scheme is the most secure and robust among the five tested schemes. An interesting expansion of our work is to propose an optimal algorithm to generate a virtual primary key that is used to enhance the level of robustness of a watermarking scheme for relational databases.

References

1. Li, Y., Swarup, V., Jajodia, S.: Fingerprinting relational databases: schemes and specialties. IEEE Trans. Dependable Secur. Comput. 2(1), 34–45 (2005)
2. Li, Y., Swarup, V., Jajodia, S.: Constructing a virtual primary key for fingerprinting relational data. In: Proceedings of the ACM Workshop Digital Rights Management (DRM), pp. 133–141 (2003)
3. Mansouri, A., Aznaveh, A.M., Torkamani, F., Kurugollu, F.: A low complexity video watermarking in H.264 compressed domain. IEEE Trans. Inf. Forensics Secur. 5(4), 649–657 (2010)
4. Kang, X.G., Yang, R., Huang, J.W.: Geometric invariant audio watermarking based on an LCM feature. IEEE Trans. Multimed. 13(2), 181–190 (2011)
5. Nguyen, T.S., Chang, C.C., Chung, T.F.: A tamper-detection scheme for BTC-compressed images with high-quality images. KSII Trans. Internet Inf. Syst. 8(6), 2005–2012 (2014)
6. Mali, M.L., Patil, N.N., Patil, J.B.: Implementation of text watermarking technique using natural language watermarks. In: International Conference on Communication Systems and Network Technologies (CSNT), pp. 482–486 (2013)
7. Nguyen, T.S., Chang, C.C., Lin, M.C.: Adaptive Lossless Data Hiding Scheme for SMVQ-Compressed Images using SOC Coding. Smart Comput. Rev. 4(3), 230–245 (2014)
8. Agrawal, R., Kiernan, J.: Watermarking relational databases. In: Proceedings of the 28th International Conference on Very Large Databases, pp. 155–166 (2002)
9. Sion, R., Atallah, M., Prabhakar, S.: Rights protection for categorical data. IEEE Trans. Knowl. Data Eng. 17(7), 912–926 (2005)
10. Al-Haj, A., Odeh, A.: Robust and blind watermarking of relational database systems. J. Comput. Sci. 4(12), 1024–1029 (2008)
11. Shehab, M., Bertino, E., Ghafoor, A.: Watermarking relational databases using optimization-based techniques. IEEE Trans. Knowl. Data Eng. 20(1), 116–129 (2008)

12. Farfoura, M.E., Horng, S.J., Lai, J.L., Run, R.S., Chen, R.J., Khan, M.K.: A blind reversible method for watermarking relational databases based on a time-stamping. Expert Syst. Appl. **39**, 3185–3196 (2012)
13. Chang, C.C., Nguyen, T.S., Lin, C.C.: A blind reversible robust watermarking scheme for relational database. Sci. World J. **2013**, 1–12 (2013)
14. Rao, U.P., Patel, D.R., Vikani, P.M.: Relational database watermarking for ownership protection. In: 2nd International Conference on Communication, Computing & Security, India, pp. 988–995 (2012)
15. Prasannakumari, V.: A robust tamperproof watermarking for data integrity in relational databases. Res. J. Inf. Technol. **1**(3), 115–121 (2009)
16. Khan, A., Husain, S.A.: A fragile zero watermarking scheme to detect and characterize malicious modification in database relation. Sci. World J. **2013**, 1–16 (2013)
17. Bhattacharya, S., Cortesi, A.: A generic distortion free watermarking technique for relational databases. In: Prakash, A., Sen Gupta, I. (eds.) ICISS 2009. LNCS, vol. 5905, pp. 252–264. Springer, Heidelberg (2009)
18. Thodi, D.M., Rodriguez, J.J.: Expansion embedding techniques for reversible watermarking. IEEE Trans. Image Process. **16**, 721–730 (2007)
19. Schneier, B.: Applied Cryptography, 2nd edn. Wiley, New York (1996)

Image Descriptor Based Digital Semi-blind Watermarking for DIBR 3D Images

Hsin Miao[1], Yu-Hsun Lin[2,3]([✉]), and Ja-Ling Wu[2]

[1] Department of CSIE, National Taiwan University, Taipei, Taiwan
[2] GINM, National Taiwan University, Taipei, Taiwan
{klchchottf,lymanblue,wjl}@cmlab.csie.ntu.edu.tw
[3] Intel-NTU Connected Context Computing Center, Taipei, Taiwan

Abstract. Content protection for 3D multimedia data is essential to assure property rights. The depth-image-based rendering (DIBR) operation is one of the ways to synthesize arbitrary virtual views from color-plus-depth 3D data. In this work, a novel semi-blind watermarking scheme is proposed to protect DIBR 3D images. The watermarking system utilizes image descriptors as side information to compensate the distortion produced by DIBR operations. The compensation process (aka resynchronization) estimates the disparity map between the views and recovers the synthesized virtual view back to the watermark embedded view. As compared with the existing related work, the proposed method is able to detect embedded watermark on arbitrary DIBR synthesized virtual views. We also investigate the effects of choosing different image descriptors as the side information for resynchronization. Furthermore, experimental results show that the proposed scheme is robust to against JPEG compression plus DIBR attack (i.e., DIBR operation performed on the JPEG compressed 3D images). Finally, the robustness of our work against HEVC (i.e., H.265) 3D compression plus DIBR is also investigated.

Keywords: Blind watermarking · Color-plus-depth 3D image · Depth-image-based rendering (DIBR) · Image descriptor · Resynchronization

1 Introduction

The 3D multi-view color-plus-depth (3D MVD) image format, generated by limited number of cameras, has been selected as 3D data format for the emerging HEVC 3D compression standard by MPEG [1] due to the considerations of storage size and rendering capability (i.e. the number of synthesized virtual views). Users are able to utilize DIBR technique to synthesize multiple virtual views. These virtual views are then showed on a 3D display to provide 3D views. In general, it requires 2 views and 8 views for stereo 3D display and autostereoscopic 3D (i.e. 3D viewing without special 3D glasses) display devices, respectively.

For the purpose of protecting intellectual property rights, multimedia content owners rely on digital watermarking systems to prevent right-claimed contents from illegal distribution. Although there are some effective approaches to embed

© Springer International Publishing Switzerland 2015
Y.-Q. Shi et al. (Eds.): IWDW 2014, LNCS 9023, pp. 90–104, 2015.
DOI: 10.1007/978-3-319-19321-2_7

Fig. 1. A DIBR 3D image watermarking scheme.

watermarks on 2D images, it is still difficult to detect the embedded watermark on the virtual-view images synthesized by DIBR. Malicious users might distribute these virtual-view images illicitly, so 3D content owners should find a way to protect not only the MVD images but also the synthesized virtual-view images, which are rendered on the basis of DIBR algorithms. Therefore, an effective watermarking scheme for DIBR 3D images is worthy of investigation.

There are research works focused on DIBR 3D image watermarking schemes [2,3]. These works require the original image or the watermarked image without noise during the watermark detection process. However, a semi-blind watermarking system in which the embedded watermark can be detected without the aid of original image (e.g. color or depth image) is more preferable, because a semi-blind watermarking scheme can avoid exposing the original 3D content to the public.

In addition, the number of synthesized virtual views plays an important role in designing a semi-blind watermarking system for DIBR 3D images. The study [4] proposed a blind watermarking system for DIBR 3D images; however, the scheme can only be used to detect embedded watermarks on 2-virtual-view 3D images synthesized by DIBR. This is because in [4], the number of required watermarks is linearly proportional to the number of synthesized virtual-view images; therefore, direct applying it to protect the 3D MVD image will easily introduce visible artifacts. In contrast to previous works, we propose a semi-blind watermarking scheme that can efficiently detect the embedded watermarks from any one of the multiple virtual-view images synthesized by DIBR algorithms.

A resynchronization process, as illustrated in Fig. 1, to overcome the challenges of watermarking arbitrarily synthesized multiple virtual-view images is realized and investigated in this work. The resynchronization process utilizes a widely adopted image descriptor (e.g. SIFT descriptor) to estimate the effects introduced by DIBR process (e.g. the disparity map) on a suspected view (which is one of the synthesized virtual-view images), and warp the suspected view back to the resynchronized view, which is expected to be similar to the original watermark embedded view. After the resynchronization process, an estimate of the embedded watermark can be extracted from or detected on the resynchronized view. The proposed resynchronization process consists of 4 modules: (1) feature point matching, (2) disparity map estimation, (3) view warping, and (4) view selection. The details of each one of the 4 modules will be addressed in Sect. 4-C.

The contributions of this work can be summarized as follows:

- An image descriptor based resynchronization scheme is proposed to compensate the negative effects caused by DIBR process.

– On the basis of the above resynchronization scheme, a semi-blind watermarking framework for DIBR 3D images is presented, in which the embedded
watermark can be extracted from or detected on anyone of the virtual views
synthesized by DIBR.

2   Related Work

In general, watermarking schemes for DIBR 3D images can be categorized into
informed watermarking and *blind watermarking*. Informed DIBR 3D image
watermarking schemes were proposed in [2,3]. These works require the original
image or the depth map during the watermark detection process. Unfortunately,
this requirement poses a risk in exposing the valuable 3D contents to the public. An effective blind watermarking scheme for color-plus-depth 3D image was
proposed in [4] which embeds multiple watermarks to the pixels that are pre-
estimated as the involved embedding blocks of virtual-view images during the
watermarking embedding process. The approach in [4] can detect the watermark embedded on the virtual-view image without the aid of the original color
image or depth map. However, it can only address very limited virtual-view
image synthesis scenarios because the distortion caused by embedding multiple
watermarks will be quite serious when the number of synthesized views becomes
large. Moreover, there are research works [5] utilizing specific statistical properties and/or the characteristics of wavelet transformation such that the resultant
watermarking schemes are robust to limited DIBR shifting operation. Nevertheless, the scenario applicable to detect embedded watermarks from anyone of the
synthesized virtual-view images has never been considered in these works.

The DIBR operation of virtual-view image synthesis shifts the pixels based
on the corresponding depth values [6] which makes one kind of local geometric attacks on the embedded watermarks. Although the spread spectrum (SS)
watermarking [7], which embeds messages into different frequency bands of a
given image, is robust to different kinds of attacks (e.g. compression, additive Gaussian noise), the transformation operations (e.g. DCT and/or DFT) in
the frequency domain based watermarking scheme is vulnerable to the above-
mentioned local geometric attack. The reason is that local geometric deformation destroys the synchronization necessary for making SS-based watermark
detection successful [8,9]. In order to resist local geometric attacks, the resynchronization method presented in [10], is taken into account in designing our
resynchronization scheme.

The emerging HEVC 3D standard takes the virtual-view image quality into
consideration in which the virtual-view image is synthesized by using the suggested view synthesis software [6]. In order to support the advanced autostereoscopic 3D display, the number of virtual-view images can go up to 6 views based
on the provided color-plus-depth 3D data with a limited given camera number
(i.e. 2-view). To the best of our knowledge, this work is the first one addressing
the problem of watermark detection on arbitrary virtual-view (i.e. multi-view)
image synthesized by DIBR operations.

3   Background

The key components of the proposed watermarking scheme, DIBR operations and the involved image descriptors, are briefly reviewed in this Section.

3.1   Depth-Image-Based Rendering (DIBR) Operation

A virtual-view image represents the projected image of an object from a different viewing angle that is not captured in the current reference-view images. We are able to warp the current reference-view image to the synthesized virtual-view image based on the physical relations provided by the reference-view color image and the corresponding depth map. Actually, DIBR operation is a simplified synthesis process where the virtual-view image is constructed by shifting the pixels horizontally based on the computed disparity map.

The View Synthesis Reference Software, shorten as VSRS [6], is developed by MPEG to be the reference software for synthesizing multiple virtual-view images on the basis of 2-view color-plus-depth 3D image inputs. In VSRS, the pixels in the reference-view image will be shifted as

$$u_t = u_s + \frac{f_u \left(t_{u,t} - t_{u,s}\right)}{z_s} + d_t - d_s, \tag{1}$$

where u_t and u_s are respectively the horizontal coordinates of synthesized virtual-view and reference-view images, $t_{u,t}$ and $t_{u,s}$ denote the horizontal translations in camara extrinsic parameters, f_u denotes the horizontal focal length, d_t and d_s denote the coordinates of intersection with the optical axis of the image, and z_s denotes the depth value, respectively.

3.2   Image Descriptors

Image descriptors usually played important roles in the computer vision research area. Among the numerous image descriptors, we focused only on the most widely used one and the one needs the lowest bit rate, in this sub-section.

The Scale-Invariant Feature Transform (SIFT) descriptor [11] is the most widely used image descriptor that is robust or even invariant to the translation, rotation, and scaling of the target image. SIFT descriptor is a 128 dimensional vector (i.e. 128 bytes) that consists of 16 gradient-histograms, where each gradient-histogram is a vector of 8 dimensions to express the gradient distributions within an image block. SIFT descriptor is adopted, of course, for its high robustness against DIBR induced affine-transformation attack.

On the other hand, the Compressed Histogram of Gradient (CHoG) descriptor [12] has been proposed to describe a target image with lower bit rate, where the size of a CHoG image descriptor can be reduced to less than 15 bytes. In this work, CHOG descriptor is chosen as a reference for benchmarking the effect of descriptor size in watermarking detectability.

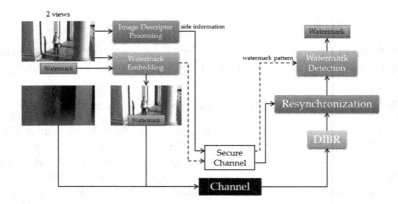

Fig. 2. The block diagram of the proposed 3D watermarking framework.

4   The Proposed Watermarking System

In this Section, with the aid of side information (i.e. image descriptors), a semi-blind watermarking scheme for compensating the effects of view synthesis process is proposed. The resynchronization process warps the given virtual-view (i.e. the suspected view) image to one of the 2-view input color images based on the estimated view synthesis effects. Then, we detect the embedded watermark from the synthesis-compensated-view (i.e. resynchronized view) image.

The proposed watermarking scheme consists of the following modules: Watermark Embedding module, Image Descriptor module, Resynchronization module, and Watermark Detection module.

Figure 2 illustrates the proposed scheme, and each one of the above-mentioned modules will be detailed in the following sub-sections, successively.

4.1   Watermark Embedding Module

A linear approximation of the Improved Spread Spectrum (ISS) watermarking technique [13] is used in this module to embed watermarks on the 2-view input color images. Mathematically, an ISS watermark embedding scheme can be represented as:

$$\mathbf{X'} = \mathbf{X} + \mathbf{w}_k(\alpha b - \lambda c), \tag{2}$$

where $\mathbf{X}$ is the original signal, $\mathbf{X'}$ is the watermark embedded signal, $\mathbf{w}_k$ is a reference pattern (i.e. the valid key for a registered user), b represents the inserted bit ($b = +1$ or -1 to respectively represent bit '1' or bit '0'), and α controls the strength of the embedded 1-bit side information b. The introduction of parameter λ removes the interference from the original signal $\mathbf{X}$ during the watermark decoding process. Finally, c denotes the normalized correlation between $\mathbf{X}$ and $\mathbf{w}_k$. The detailed properties of ISS technique can be found in [13].

4.2   Image Descriptor Module

A set of image descriptors $\mathbf{P}$ are extracted from the 2-view input color images as the side information for the resynchronization process. An image descriptor (or a feature point) p is represented by a descriptor vector $\mathbf{V}_p$.

For a given image with 500×500 pixels, we can extract 2000 SIFT descriptors where the total data size may be more than that of the given image itself (one SIFT descriptor costs 128 bytes). Therefore, further processing is required for reducing the total data size of the extracted SIFT descriptors.

The following approaches are introduced in this module to achieve the goal.

1. Image Descriptor Selection. The image descriptor is utilized to estimate the effects of rendering operation (e.g. to find an estimated disparity map). So, we construct a sparse image descriptor set in which the required data size is small and still capable of estimating the disparity map. We choose the image descriptors $\mathbf{P_D}$ from the image descriptor set $\mathbf{P}$ such that the Euclidean distance between each image descriptor pair in $\mathbf{P_D}$ is larger than a predefined threshold D, that is:

$$\overline{p_i p_j} > D, \forall p_i, p_j \in \mathbf{P_D}, \tag{3}$$

where $\overline{p_i p_j}$ represents the Euclidean distance between the image descriptors p_i and p_j.

2. Image Descriptor Quantization. The data size of image descriptors are further reduced by applying a quantization operation. For a given descriptor vector V_p, the quantization is performed as

$$\mathbf{V'_P} = \text{round}\left(\frac{\mathbf{V}_p}{2^k}\right) \times 2^k, k = 1...6, \tag{4}$$

where round$(\cdot)$ quantizes the target quantity to the nearest integer. For example, if $k = 4$ in Eq. (4), we can reduce $50\,\%$ size of $\mathbf{V_P}$ since each tuple element in the vector is reduced from 8 bits to 4 bits.

4.3   Resynchronization Module

As pre-described, the resynchronization process is used to compensate the local geometric distortions introduced by DIBR rendering operations. Figure 3 illustrates the proposed resynchronization module which is consists of the following 4 steps: Feature Points Matching, Disparity Map Estimation, View Warping using Disparity Map, and View Selection.

Feature Points Matching. The disparity between two feature points of each matching pair are calculated, where the disparity is defined as the horizontal translation of a feature point between two images.

We perform the image descriptor matching between the side information (i.e. the image descriptor set $\mathbf{P_D}$) and the suspected-view image. That is, we match the descriptors in $\mathbf{P_D}$ and the descriptors $\mathbf{U}$ extracted from the suspected-view image, where L_2 norm is used as the matching criterion.

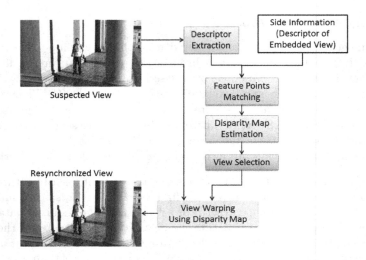

Fig. 3. The proposed resynchronization processes.

For a synthesized virtual-view image, the rendering process only introduces horizontal (disparity) shifting to the input image. Therefore, a *Vertical Constraint* is taken to improve the matching performance, that is, we only match the descriptor pair where the difference in vertical coordinates is less than a give threshold T. By applying the constraint, we can remove the outliers that decrease the quality of estimated disparity map.

Disparity Map Estimation. Disparity map represents the disparity values of all pixels between the suspected view and the reference view. Since we have reduced the data size of side information, only a sparse disparity map needs to be computed (i.e. only few disparity values are produced) from the limited descriptor pairs. In order to estimate the whole disparity map from these sparse disparity values, a segmentation-based disparity map reconstruction process is proposed. We segment the suspected image by a superpixel segmentation method presented in [14]. The disparity value of each segment is estimated as follows:

- Segment with several disparity values. For a segment q with several disparity values, the disparity of the whole segment, d_q, is the average of these available disparity values.
- Segment without disparity value. For a segment q has no disparity value available, we assign the nearest available disparity value to this segment.

View Warping Using Disparity Map. In this step, we compensate the rendering process of the suspected image according to the estimated disparity map, that is

$$I_{sync}(u, v) = I_{sus}(u - d_{(u,v)}, v),\tag{5}$$

where I_{sus} is the suspected view, I_{sync} denotes the resynchronized view, and $d_{x,y}$ is the estimated disparity of point (u, v) on the disparity map.

View Selection. Under the multi-view scenario, the resynchronization process for each virtual-view image depends on the relative distance between the synthesized view and the two original input color images. For a suspected image, we can compute 2 disparity maps based on the provided side information with respect to the 2 input color images. Obviously, the estimated disparity map with smaller averaged disparity value will be chosen, which means the suspected image should be physically closer to the selected input image; and therefore, the estimated disparity values would be more reliable than that of the other one.

4.4   Watermark Detection

For a watermark embedded signal $\mathbf{X}'$, in Eq. (2), attacked by an additive noise $\mathbf{n}$, we have a corrupted watermarked signal $\mathbf{Y} = \mathbf{X}' + \mathbf{n}$. The embedded bit b can be extracted from the corrupted watermarked signal $\mathbf{Y}$ as

$$\begin{aligned}
b' &= \text{sign}(\langle \mathbf{Y}, \mathbf{w}_k \rangle) \\
&= \text{sign}(\alpha b + (1 - \lambda)c + \langle \mathbf{n}, \mathbf{w}_k \rangle),
\end{aligned}\tag{6}$$

where $\text{sign}(\cdot)$ represents the sign of the computed result (i.e. $b' = +1$ for bit '1' and $b' = -1$ for bit '0') and $\langle , \rangle$ denotes a normalized inner product of two vectors.

There are 2 major sources of the noise $\mathbf{n}$, that is

$$\mathbf{n} = n_c + n_R \tag{7}$$

where n_c is the noise from the channel and n_R represents the noise from the rendering process.

The proposed framework can eliminate the effect of rendering operations with the aid of side information. In other words, we try to make $n_R \approx 0$ and improve the quality of the decoded watermark.

5   Experimental Results

5.1   Experiment Settings

In order to evaluate the effectiveness of the proposed 3D watermarking framework, six color-plus-depth 3D images taken from the 3D video coding standard [15] proposed by MPEG are adopted, including *Dancer*, *Poznanhall2*, *Poznanstreet*, *Balloons*, *Kendo*, and *Newspaper*.

To evaluate the performance of the proposed watermarking system, we take bit-error-rate (BER) as the evaluation metric. For an N-bit watermark detection unit, BER is defined by

$$\text{BER}\ (I, \mathbf{w}_k) = \frac{\text{number of } (b_i' \in M' \neq b_i \in M)}{N}, \tag{8}$$

where M and M' are respectively the embedded and the extracted watermark messages of the given image I using watermark pattern $\mathbf{w}_k$, while b_i and b_i' denote the i_{th} bits in M and M', respectively.

5.2   The Effects of DIBR Operation

In our work, BER of the embedded watermark detected from the suspected-view image is used to examine the effect of DIBR operations. The suspected-view is an intermediate view of a pair of input views synthesized by VSRS, and without loss of generality, the watermark message is assumed to be embedded in the left input-view image. The experimental parameters are empirically set as follows: the blocksize controlling both watermark strength and watermark capacity is set to 32, the length of watermark pattern $\mathbf{w}_k$ is set to 400 bits, and the watermark strength controller α is set to 7.

Table 1. Bit Error Rates of the benchmarking approaches and the proposed approach

BER (%)	Dancer	Poznanhall2	Poznanstreet	Balloons	Kendo	Newspaper
Direct approach	43.38	29.51	40.20	62.43	54.36	37.30
Global translation	24.61	33.63	26.62	16.34	22.46	18.16
Proposed	**3.62**	**10.14**	**6.96**	**3.71**	**7.62**	**10.48**

For benchmarking, the direct approach and the global translation approach are implemented and compared with the proposed approach, in terms of BER defined in Eq. (8). In the direct approach, we extracted the watermark directly on the suspected-view image. In the global translation approach, the following relation between the resynchronized-view image and the suspected-view image is assumed:

$$I_{sync}(u, v) = I_{sus}(u - t_x, v), \tag{9}$$

where I_{sync} denotes the translated-view image, I_{sus} is the suspected-view image, and t_x is the amount of global translation. In other words, the resynchronized view can be generated by horizontally shifting the suspected view by t_x pixels, where t_x is set to be -20 to 20 pixels in our experiments. Because different translation t_x leads to different resynchronized-view images $I_{sync}(u, v)$, the corresponding BER's are therefore varied. Since the quality of resynchronized-view images should be inversely proportional to the associated BER values, the one with respect to the minimum BER is our best choice.

Table 2. PSNRs of the embedded images

Dancer	Poznanhall2	Poznanstreet	Balloons	Kendo	Newspaper
35.13	35.22	35.22	35.18	35.18	35.04

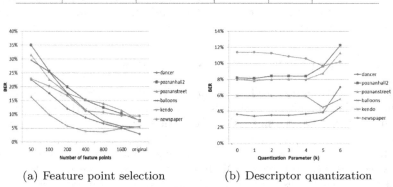

(a) Feature point selection   (b) Descriptor quantization

Fig. 4. The effects of (a) the feature point selection and (b) the descriptor quantization.

Table 1 shows BER's of the compared approaches on different test images, and Table 2 presents the corresponding PSNR's of the embedded images. From Table 1, it is clear that BER's of the proposed approach are much lower than that of the other two approaches. Notice that BER's of the direct approach are closer to 0.5 in most cases, which shows the proposed resynchronization process is indeed compensating the distortion produced by DIBR operations. Besides, although the global translation approach performs better than the directly approach, the resultant performance is still not satisfiable. Comparing with the other two benchmark approaches, the proposed watermarking scheme achieved much lower BER's, which implies that the watermark extracted by the proposed approach ought to be much more correct than that of the others.

5.3   The Effects of Image Descriptor Module

In this sub-section we evaluate the BER performance on each step of the proposed image descriptor module.

Feature Point Selection. Figure 4(a) shows the BER performance of the proposed feature point selection algorithm. The results show that if we use more feature points, BER's of extracted watermarks are lowered in most cases. It implies that there is a trade-off between the size of side information and the accuracy of extracted watermark; therefore, the owner of 3D images is able to flexibly choose suitable size of side information to obtain the required BER performance with the aid of the proposed image descriptor selection step.

Descriptor Quantization. Figure 4(b) shows the BER performance with respect to different quantization parameters k, defined in Eq. (4). The results show that BER's of extracted watermarks do not change significantly, for $k = 1$ to 4, in almost all the test images. For example, if we set k to 4, the BER performance is nearly the same as the original one while the size of side information has been reduced by half. This result shows that the proposed descriptor quantization process is effective in reducing the size of side information but keeps the quality of extracted watermark intact.

5.4   The Effect of Multiple-View Synthesizing

This sub-section evaluates the effects of multiple-virtual-view rendering by VSRS. The configuration of multiple virtual-view synthesizing is illustrated in Fig. 5. Different virtual views are synthesized by different vitual cameras in different locations. Figure 6 shows the BER performance (only for test sequences Balloon and Dancer here due to the page limit) of the view selection step where the multiple virtual views are synthesized by DIBR through VSRS. The three lines in the figure stand for the cases using side information from the left view, the right view, and the proposed view selection step, respectively. The results show that, after view selection, BER's of the extracted watermarks approach to the minimum of BER's obtainable from the left view and the right view for most of the input images. Because using side information from the nearer view leads to lower BER, if a watermark is embedded on both input views, view selection module is capable of choosing the side information from the nearer view on the basis of the suspected view in most cases.

This result shows that the proposed process is specifically effective in protecting 3D images. The reason is that malicious users could illegally distribute a DIBR synthesized virtual view, and if the side information is provided from one input view only, the farther the distance between the suspected view and the input view, the worse the accuracy of the detected watermark.

5.5   Effectiveness of Descriptors

By comparing BER's with the same size of side information, the effectiveness of descriptors including SIFT and CHoG are evaluated in this subsection. Although CHoG is designated as a compressed descriptor, the results given in Fig. 7 show that the proposed feature point selection and descriptor quantization steps produce lower BER's in most cases (only the results of test sequences Balloon and Dancer are presented here due to the page limit). This experiment shows that the proposed side information reduction process is effective.

In addition, the same figure also illustrates that the performance is correlated with the size of side information in the proposed approach. If there are more feature points, the size of side information is getting larger, and BER's of extracted watermarks become lower. This result implies that there is certain flexibility in the proposed system: users are able to sacrifice the performance in BER by reducing the size of side information.

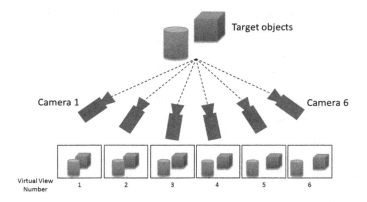

Fig. 5. The multiple virtual-view synthesizing configuration.

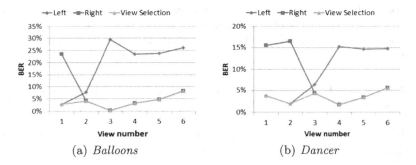

(a) Balloons   (b) Dancer

Fig. 6. The effects of view selection, in terms of BER's.

5.6   Proposed Method vs. Previous Work

This sub-section illustrates the comparison between the proposed watermarking scheme and the most related previous work [4]. DIBR scheme used in the previous work is to synthesize two stereo views from one center view, which can be represented as:

$$
\begin{cases}
u_L = u_C + \left(\frac{t_x}{2} \times \frac{f}{Z}\right) \\
u_R = u_C - \left(\frac{t_x}{2} \times \frac{f}{Z}\right).
\end{cases}
\tag{10}
$$

where u_C denotes the horizontal position of a pixel in the center view, u_L and u_R are the corresponding pixels in the left and right views, f is the focal length of the camera, t_x is the baseline distance and is set to 5 % of the image width, and Z represents the depth value of the pixel in the center view.

Table 3 shows the comparisons in terms of BER's and PSNR's, respectively. Clearly, from Table 3, the proposed watermarking scheme achieves a comparable or better BER performance to [4]. In addition, the averaged PSNR of the proposed framework is 4 dB higher than that of [4]. This result shows that the

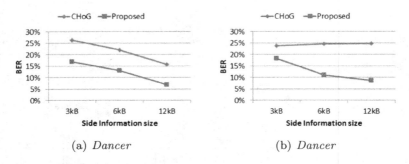

(a) *Dancer*   (b) *Dancer*

Fig. 7. The effects of side information and involved descriptors, in terms of BER's.

proposed system is capable of obtaining higher image quality after watermark embedding, under the same robustness conditions to DIBR operations.

Although [4] did not require side information to extract the embedded watermark, it cannot detect the embedded watermark from the arbitrarily synthesized virtual-view image, generated by the latest DIBR algorithm suggested in MPEG standard.

Table 3. BER and PSNR comparisons between Lin's method [4] and the proposed approach, under DIBR scheme given in Eq. (10).

BER (%)	Dancer	Poznanhall2	Poznanstreet	Balloons	Kendo	Newspaper
Lin's method [4]	4.95	1.32	4.75	5.73	4.95	8.20
Proposed	4.36	0.20	1.81	2.28	1.63	3.97
PSNR (dB)	Dancer	Poznanhall2	Poznanstreet	Balloons	Kendo	Newspaper
Lin's method [4]	30.44	30.35	30.48	30.28	30.36	30.30
Proposed	35.21	35.28	35.09	35.19	35.23	35.02

5.7 The Effects of DIBR and Compression

Due to the consideration of storage size, 3D images are usually compressed in multimedia applications. This means that the embedded watermark on a 3D image is always attacked by both DIBR and compression operations. This subsection evaluate the performance of the case that both DIBR and compression attacks are taken into account. Two compression algorithms, including JPEG and HEVC, are considered in the experiments.

Figure 8(a) illustrates BER's of the extracted watermarks distorted by both VSRS and different degrees of JPEG compression. The result shows the proposed watermark scheme is robust to both VSRS operation and JPEG compression with quality factor larger than 30. In other words, the proposed watermarking scheme is capable of resisting not only DIBR rendering but also JPEG compression attacks.

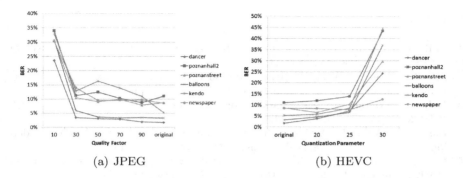

(a) JPEG   (b) HEVC

Fig. 8. BER performances of the proposed watermarking scheme under both VSRS and (a) for JPEG and (b) for HEVC compression attacks.

Figure 8(b) illustrates BER's of the extracted watermark distorted by both VSRS and different degrees of HEVC compression. The result shows the proposed watermarking scheme is robust to HEVC compression with quantization parameter less than 25. However, as shown in Fig. 8(b), BER's of the extracted watermarks are not acceptable for HEVC compression with quantization parameter larger than 30. In other words, further investigations about how to increase the ability of the proposed watermarking scheme resisting to both VSRS and high degree HEVC compression is a must.

6   Conclusion

In this paper, a semi-blind watermarking scheme capable of resisting the latest rendering operations, suggested by MPEG standard, is proposed to protect DIBR 3D images. The proposed resynchronization process utilizes image descriptors as side information to estimate the disparity map between the embedded view image and the suspected view image. The resynchronization process effectively compensates the distortion produced by DIBR operations, and makes it possible to detect the embedded watermark in anyone of the synthesized virtual-view images.

Experimental results show that the proposed system is able to resist both DIBR and compression attacks. In addition, effects on the size of side information have been investigated. Compared with related works, the proposed watermarking scheme is feasible for detecting watermarks on more types of DIBR 3D images. Besides, simulation results also show the proposed watermarking scheme performs better in terms of BER and PSNR for DIBR synthesized 3D images.

In the future, the improvement in disparity map estimation will be studied further. In addition, the properties of multi-view synthesizing images will be utilized to enhance the performance of the proposed watermarking scheme. Furthermore, exploration on more robust watermarking schemes against HEVC compression plus DIBR attack will also be studied.

References

1. Call for Proposals on 3D Video Coding Technology. ISO/IEC JTC1/SC29/WG11 MPEG2011/N12036, March 2011
2. Zhu, N., Ding, G., Wang, J.: A novel digital watermarking method for new viewpoint video based on depth map. In: ISDA 2008, vol. 2, pp. 3–7 (2008)
3. Halici, E., Alatan, A.: Watermarking for depth-image-based rendering. In: IEEE ICIP 2009, pp. 4217–4220 (2009)
4. Lin, Y.-H., Wu, J.-L.: A digital blind watermarking for depth-image-based rendering 3d images. IEEE Trans. Broadcast. **57**(2), 602–611 (2011)
5. Kim, H.-D., Lee, J.-W., Oh, T.-W., Lee, H.-K.: Robust dt-cwt watermarking for DIBR 3D images. IEEE Trans. Broadcast. **58**(4), 533–543 (2012)
6. Test Model under Consideration for HEVC based 3D video coding. ISO/IEC JTC1/SC29/WG11 MPEG2011/M12350, November 2011
7. Cox, I.J., Kilian, J., Leighton, F., Shamoon, T.: Secure spread spectrum watermarking for multimedia. IEEE Trans. Image Process. **6**(12), 1673–1687 (1997)
8. Dong, P., Brankov, J.G., Galatsanos, N.P., Yang, Y., Davoine, F.: Digital watermarking robust to geometric distortions. IEEE Trans. Image Process. **14**, 2140–2150 (2005)
9. Bas, P., Chassery, J.-M., Macq, B.: Geometrically invariant watermarking using feature points. IEEE Trans. Image Process. **11**(9), 1014–1028 (2002)
10. Dugelay, J., Roche, S., Rey, C., Doerr, G.: Still-image watermarking robust to local geometric distortions. IEEE Trans. Image Process. **15**(9), 2831–2842 (2006)
11. Lowe, D.G.: Distinctive image features from scale-invariant keypoints. IJCV **60**(2), 91–110 (2004)
12. Chandrasekhar, V., Takacs, G., Chen, D., Tsai, S., Reznik, Y., Grzeszczuk, R., Girod, B.: Compressed histogram of gradients: a low-bitrate descriptor. IJCV **96**(3), 384–399 (2012)
13. Malvar, H., Florencio, D.: Improved spread spectrum: a new modulation technique for robust watermarking. IEEE Trans. Signal Process. **51**(4), 898–905 (2003)
14. Liu, M.-Y., Tuzel, O., Ramalingam, S., Chellappa, R.: Entropy rate superpixel segmentation. In: IEEE CVPR 2011, pp. 2097–2104 (2011)
15. Descriptions of exploration experiments in 3-d video coding, JTC 1/SC 29/WG11, no. N10173, October 2008

Watermarking for Digital Audio Based on Adaptive Phase Modulation

Nhut Minh Ngo$^{(\boxtimes)}$ and Masashi Unoki

Japan Advanced Institute of Science and Technology, 1-1 Asahidai,
Nomi, Ishikawa 923-1292, Japan
{nmnhut,unoki}@jaist.ac.jp

Abstract. This paper proposes a novel blind watermarking method for digital audio based on adaptive phase modulation. Audio signals are usually non-stationary, i.e., their own characteristics are time-variant. The features for watermarking have not been selected by combining the principle of variability, which affects the performance of the whole watermarking system. The proposed method embeds a watermark into an audio signal by adaptively modulating its phase with the embedded bit '0' or '1' using two all-pass filters. The frequency location of the filter pole-zero which characterizes the transfer function of the filter is adapted to distribution of signal power spectrum. The filter pole-zero locations are adapted in such a way that phase modulation causes the least distortion in watermarked signals to achieve the best sound quality. The experimental results show that the proposed method could embed inaudible watermark into various kinds of audio signals and correctly detect watermark without the aid of original signals. The proposed method has the ability to embed watermark into audio signals up to 150 bits per second with the bit error rate of less than 10 %.

Keywords: Audio watermarking · Blind detection · Adaptive phase modulation · All-pass filter

1 Introduction

With the advances of multimedia and the Internet technologies, security of digital audio has faced with many risks. The ease of reproducing, modifying, and sharing multimedia data has led to demand on preventing copyright infringement. Copyright protection based on encryption is inadequate because our data need to be decrypted before being played back. The technique of inserting copyright codes into the file header is insecure because the codes can easily be removed once the file header is analyzed. Contrary to these techniques, audio watermarking hides special codes into the actual content without any effect on its normal use [1]. Watermarking has become a promising technique for copyright protection. Other applications of digital watermarking have also been considered such as copy control, tamper detection, and covert communication [2].

© Springer International Publishing Switzerland 2015
Y.-Q. Shi et al. (Eds.): IWDW 2014, LNCS 9023, pp. 105–119, 2015.
DOI: 10.1007/978-3-319-19321-2_8

To be effectively used in practical applications, an audio watermarking method must satisfy the following basic requirements [1]: inaudibility, blindness, robustness, and high embedding capacity. Inaudibility keeps watermark in the watermarked audio imperceptible to listeners during normal use. Blindness is required to increase applicability in practice. Watermark must be robust against signal processing operations or intentional attacks from illegal users. High capacity is required for data hiding applications such as covert communication. Among these requirements, inaudibility and robustness for audio watermarking are the most challenging because they conflict each other. It is straightforward that to provide an inaudible watermark, perceptually insensitive features of the audio should be exploited for embedding. However, robustness against attacks such as lossy compression is then difficult to achieve because the watermark could be easily removed without distorting the audio. We usually meet a trade-off among these requirements when implementing a watermarking system for digital audio.

Audio watermarking methods could be categorized as methods in time domain and methods in transformed domain. Typical methods in time domain embed watermarks by modifying least significant bits (LSB) or insert watermarks which are perceptually shaped according to the human auditory system (HAS) [3,4]. Although these methods could be used to embed inaudible watermarks into audio signals, they are not robust against attacks (e.g., LSB) or have low embedding capacity [4]. Methods in transformed domain exploit advantages of frequency masking characteristics of HAS [5,6] to embed inaudible watermarks. It has been reported that controlled phase alteration results in inaudible change in sound to HAS [7,8]. This characteristic of HAS is potential and has been exploited for inaudible audio watermarking [9–13].

Unoki and Hamada [14] proposed an audio watermarking method based on the cochlear delay (CD) characteristic. Experimental results show that CD-based audio watermarking method has high sound quality and robustness against attacks in non-blind detection scheme. However, sound quality is degraded in blind detection scheme [15] due to the effect of click sounds at framing points, especially in low-pitch sounds. Takahashi et al. [16] proposed a method based on periodical phase modulation (PPM). This method provides high sound quality as well as robustness because it was based on HAS property that PPM is relatively inaudible to human ears. However, as PPM modifies the phase spectra of components at high frequencies, watermarks in pulse-like sounds or around rapid onsets in musical sounds could be detected. Real world audio signals are usually non-stationary, hence their perceptually insignificant features which are potentially suitable for embedding inaudible watermarks also vary in time. As a result, the watermark is transparent for some signals but audible for others. This property has not been taken into consideration for designing a watermark embedding algorithm. In a nutshell, these proposed methods have a shortcoming that the embedding scheme is not adjusted according to the audio's own characteristics, which drastically influences the performance of the whole watermarking system.

Tackling the above issues, this paper proposes a novel blind watermarking method for digital audio based on adaptive phase modulation. Depending on a local characteristic of each signal frame, a suitable phase modulator is chosen in order to ensure the least distortion in watermarked audio. More precisely, portion of modification for watermark embedding in phase spectral domain is adapted to local signal energy distribution so that human perceives the watermark as the slightest distortion. The experimental results showed that the proposed method can produce watermarked sound with better sound quality in comparison with other static watermarking methods. The proposed method can embed up to around 150 bits per second. The proposed approach also has the ability to balance inaudibility and robustness by adjusting the phase modulation scheme.

The rest of this paper is organized as follows. Section 2 describes the concept of the proposed method, the details of watermark embedding and detection processes, and an illustrative example for these two processes. We present the results of evaluations with regard to effectiveness of the proposed adaptive scheme, inaudibility, robustness, and comparison with conventional watermarking methods in Sect. 3. Limitations on the proposed method are discussed in Sect. 4. Section 5 gives some concluding remarks and suggests a number of directions for future research.

2   Proposed Method

2.1   Concept of Adaptive Phase Modulation

Real world audio signals are non-stationary, i.e., their characteristics are variant with time. For this reason, acoustic signal processing applications usually divide signals into frames for non-stationary signal analysis. An obvious example of the variability characteristic of audio signals is that their power distribution over frequency components is time-variant. Figure 1 shows two pieces of music with their power distribution in frequency domain. The top plots show the waveforms and the bottoms show their power spectrogram. For the left signal, there are some periods having power distributed over the whole range of frequencies and the others having power distributed in only low frequencies. For the right signal, most of the periods have power distributed on low and high region of frequencies. The variability characteristic of audio signals should be taken into account for designing a watermarking algorithm to achieve the best performance.

Audio watermarking methods based on phase modulation usually take the advantage of controlled phase alteration resulting in perceptually transparent change to human ears [7,8]. The phase of an audio signal can be manipulated by an all-pass filter (APF). An APF passes all the frequency components equally but changes the phase according to the filter phase response. The principle of watermark embedding is as follows. The audio signal is split into frames in which a watermark bit is embedded into a frame. According to the embedded bit, an APF corresponding to the bit is designed. The bit is then encoded into a frame by using the designed filter to enhance the phase spectrum of the audio frame. Since enhancing the audio phase by an APF results in no perceptual change, the

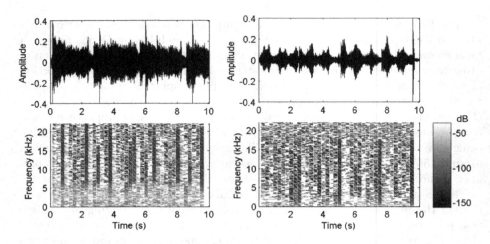

Fig. 1. Waveform and power spectrogram of two pieces of music

watermarked frame is perceived without any difference. However, an issue occurring is that sound quality is affected because of the abrupt change at framing points of the whole watermarked signal due to phase shift. This issue should be thoroughly taken into consideration when implementing a watermarking method based on phase modulation.

In practice, a second-order APF can be used to flexibly control phase change in audio signals by adjusting the modulus and angle of the filter's poles and zeros. A second-order infinite impulse response (IIR) APF is represented as follows:

$$H(z) = \left(\frac{-\beta^* + z^{-1}}{1 - z^{-1}\beta}\right) \left(\frac{-\beta + z^{-1}}{1 - z^{-1}\beta^*}\right) \tag{1}$$

where $\beta = re^{j\theta}$ and β^* is complex conjugate of β. It has a pair of zeros ($\frac{1}{\beta}$ and $\frac{1}{\beta^*}$) and a pair of poles (β and β^*) that are symmetric on the real axis in z-plane. A second-order APF can be characterized by the modulus and angle of its poles and zeros, i.e., r and θ, respectively. Figure 2 shows the phase characteristics and pole-zero locations of second-order APFs with respect to the pole-zero frequency θ. Because of the nature of APFs, the magnitude spectrum of a filtered signal is not manipulated but its phase spectrum is changed as follows.

$$\angle Y(e^{j\omega}) = \angle X(e^{j\omega}) + \angle H(e^{j\omega}) \tag{2}$$

where $\angle X(e^{j\omega})$, $\angle Y(e^{j\omega})$, and $\angle H(e^{j\omega})$ are phase spectra of an input signal and an output signal and phase response of the APF, respectively.

The absolute phase response and the group delay have a peak at the frequency that corresponds to the angle of the filter pole-zero θ (referred to hereafter as pole-zero frequency). According to (2), this frequency can be interpreted as the location where the signal is modified the most in phase spectrum. We have observed that the region around the pole-zero frequency is more affected than the outside region. In other words, if a signal has its energy concentrating at

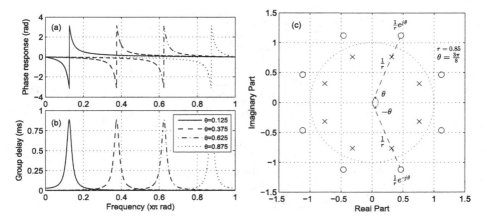

Fig. 2. Characteristics of second-order APFs with respect to θ: (a) phase response, (b) group delay, and (c) pole-zero locations in z-plane

the pole-zero frequency then the filtered signal has faster disruption at framing points than the signal having its energy outside of the pole-zero frequency. From these observations, we found that we can design an APF with its pole-zero frequency lying on low energy region in spectrum domain to achieve the best sound quality for a specific signal. This is the key principle for our proposed watermarking method based on frame-adaptive phase modulation.

2.2 Watermark Embedding

Adaptive Phase Modulator. Second-order APFs are used to realize the adaptive phase modulation scheme. The pole-zero modulus r of the APF is modulated with the embedded bit '0' or '1', i.e., to embed bit '0', r_0 is used and to embed bit '1', r_1 is used. The pole-zero angle θ is adapted to the power distribution of the audio frames in subbands. In each frame, the pole-zero angle θ is determined by the center frequency of the lowest power subband.

Figure 3 depicts a block diagram of the proposed watermark embedding process. Watermark $s[i]$ is embedded into an original signal $x[n]$ as follows.

Step 1. Original signal $x[n]$ is first split into frames, $x_i[n]$ in which the frame length $N = f_s/N_{bit}$; f_s is the sampling frequency and N_{bit} is the number of watermark bit per second. Each frame is filtered by the APF which is designed by the next two steps.

Step 2. Frame $x_i[n]$ is then decomposed into K sub-bands. Power of each subband is calculated and the lowest power sub-band k is identified by (3). The output of this step is the parameter θ, i.e., the center frequency of the sub-band k which is calculated by (4).

$$k = \arg\min_l \left\{ 10\log_{10}\left(\sum_\omega |X_{il}(e^{j\omega})|^2 \right) \right\} \qquad (3)$$

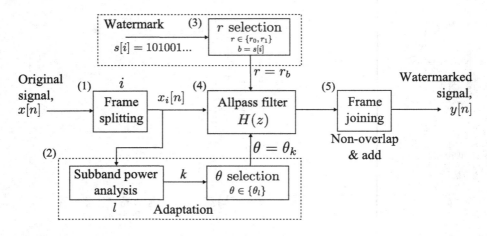

Fig. 3. Watermarking based on phase modulation: embedding process

where $X_{il}(e^{j\omega})$ is the Fourier transform of the l-th sub-band of the frame $x_i[n]$.

$$\theta_k = \frac{(2k-1)\pi}{2K} \quad \text{(rad)} \tag{4}$$

Step 3. The watermark bit which is represented by the filter parameter r is encoded into a frame in this step. Two values of the parameter r, r_0 and r_1 are earlier determined by experimental analysis. According to watermark bit $s[i]$, either r_0 or r_1 is set to r: $r = r_b$, where $b = s[i]$.

Step 4. Filter $H(z)$ is designed with the two parameters, r and θ, by (1). Then, frame $x_i[n]$ is filtered by $H(z)$.

Step 5. Finally, the filtered frames are joined together by non-overlap and add (non-OLA) technique to yield watermarked signal, $y[n]$.

These steps are repeated until we reach the final frame.

2.3 Watermark Detection

To detect an embedded watermark, each watermarked frame will be analyzed to determine the filter that was used to process that frame in embedding process. It should be noted that the filtering process can be performed in frequency domain as follows.

$$Y_i(z) = X_i(z)H(z) \tag{5}$$

where $X_i(z)$ and $Y_i(z)$ are z-transform of the original frame and the watermarked frame, respectively. Let z_0 be a zero of the filter $H(z)$. As the definition of a zero of an IIR filter, $H(z_0) = 0$. Hence, $Y_i(z_0) = 0$. This is a hint for blind watermark detection. We can use chirp-z transformation (CZT) [17] to calculate $Y_i(z_0)$ by (6).

$$Y_i(z) = \sum_{n=0}^{N-1} y_i[n]z^{-n} \tag{6}$$

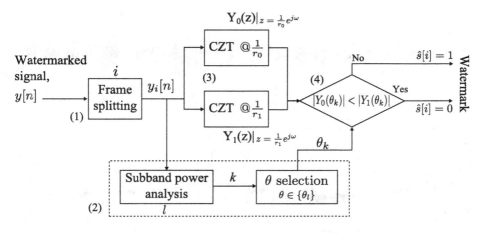

Fig. 4. Watermarking based on phase modulation: detection process

CZT over the zero location of the APF exposes a minimum at the pole-zero frequency which corresponds to the pole-zero angle θ in the power spectrum. Based on the zero location over which the minimum occurs, we can determine which APF was used and then decode the embedded bit.

Figure 4 depicts a block diagram of the proposed detection process. Watermark is detected in four steps as follows.

Step 1. Watermarked signal $y[n]$ is first split into the frames $y_i[n]$ in which the frame length is as same as that in embedding process.

Step 2. Parameter θ_k is determined in the same manner as in the second step of the embedding process. Since the APF does not change power spectrum of the output signal, the power distribution of the watermarked frames in subbands could be obtained as same as that of the original frames.

Step 3. Frame $y_i(n)$ is then analyzed by two types of CZT over two contours with radii of $1/r_0$ and $1/r_1$, respectively. The outputs are $Y_0(z)$ and $Y_1(z)$, respectively.

Step 4. The magnitudes at θ_k, $|Y_0(\theta_k)|$ and $|Y_1(\theta_k)|$, are compared to decode watermark $\hat{s}[i]$ by (7).

These steps are repeated for the total number of frames.

$$\hat{s}[i] = \begin{cases} 0 & \text{if } |Y_0(\theta_k)| < |Y_1(\theta_k)| \\ 1 & \text{otherwise} \end{cases} \tag{7}$$

where $Y_0(\theta_k) = Y_0(z)|_{z=\frac{1}{r_0}e^{j\theta_k}}$ and $Y_1(\theta_k) = Y_1(z)|_{z=\frac{1}{r_1}e^{j\theta_k}}$.

2.4 Example

Figure 5 shows an example of watermark embedding at the bit rate of 4 bits per second bps. Watermark bits $s[i]=$'1001' were embedded into the first four frames.

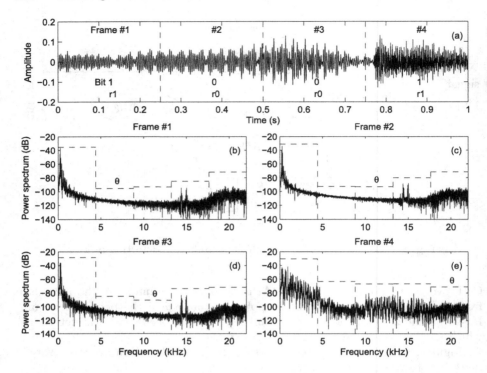

Fig. 5. Example on modulation of r with embedded bits and adaptively adjusting θ: (a) shows four audio frames and the value of r in each frame; (b), (c), (d), and (e) respectively show power spectrum of frame #1, frame #2, frame #3, and frame #4 and determination of θ in each frame.

Parameter r was set to either r_0 or r_1 based on $s[i]$. Number of subbands K is five. Parameter θ was set differently for each frame based on its power distribution in subbands. For example, frame #1 has $\theta_{\#1} = \frac{3\pi}{10}$ and frame #2 has $\theta_{\#2} = \frac{\pi}{2}$ as shown in Figs. 5(b) and (c).

Figure 6 shows an example of watermark detection. The pole-zero frequency θ was determined by the same way as in the embedding process. The CZT of $y_1[n]$ over $\frac{1}{r_1}$ exposes a minimum at $\theta_{\#1}$ which decodes a bit '1' while the CZT of $y_2[n]$ over $\frac{1}{r_0}$ exposes a minimum at $\theta_{\#2}$ which decodes a bit '0'. The two embedded bits were correctly detected.

3   Evaluation

We carried out several experiments to evaluate the proposed method with the RWC music database [18] which consists of 102 music tracks of various music genres. Each music track has a sampling frequency of 44.1 kHz and 16-bit quantization. The bit rates were chosen from 6 to 400 bps. The watermark was set as random binary data. The detection process is blind, i.e., only the watermarked audio

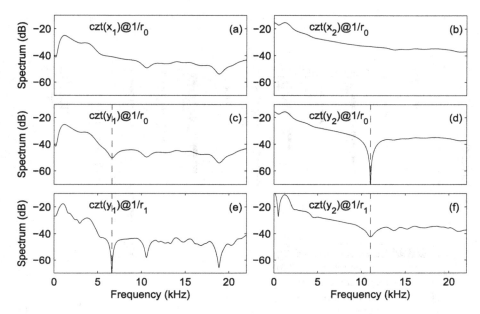

Fig. 6. Minima in CZT spectra of watermarked signals: (a) and (b) show CZT of original frames #1 and #2 over $\frac{1}{r_0}$, (c) and (e) show CZT of watermarked frame #1 over $\frac{1}{r_0}$ and $\frac{1}{r_1}$, respectively, and (d) and (f) show CZT of watermarked frame #2 over $\frac{1}{r_0}$ and $\frac{1}{r_1}$, respectively. Bits of '1' and '0' were embedded into $y_1[n]$ and $y_2[n]$, respectively. Minima at $\theta_{\#1}$ in (d) and at $\theta_{\#2}$ in (e) indicate that the watermark bits were correctly detected.

Table 1. Quality degradation of sound and PEAQ (ODG)

Quality degradation	ODG
Imperceptible	0
Perceptible, but not annoying	−1
Slightly annoying	−2
Annoying	−3
Very annoying	−4

signal is used for detecting. Inaudibility of the proposed method is objectively tested by perceptual evaluation of audio quality (PEAQ) [19]. PEAQ is used to measure degradation in audio according to the objective difference grade (ODG). The ODG indicates sound quality of target signals as shown in Table 1. The evaluation criterion for PEAQ is set to an average ODG of −2 (slightly annoying) which is recommended by [20]. The watermark detection accuracy is measured by bit detection rate (BDR) which is defined as the ratio between the number of correctly detected bits and the total number of embedded bits. The evaluation threshold for average BDR is chosen as a common rate of 90 % in this paper.

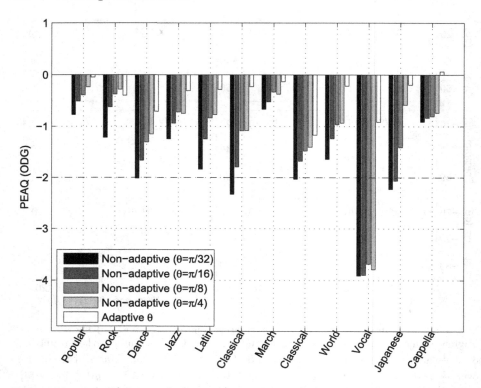

Fig. 7. Objective evaluation on inaudibility of the proposed method in different musical categories

3.1   Effectiveness of the Proposed Method

In order to confirm the adaptation effectiveness of the proposed method, we comparatively evaluated the proposed adaptive phase modulation scheme with non-adaptive phase modulation schemes. Non-adaptive phase modulation schemes were implemented by setting a fixed value of APF parameter θ instead of frame-variant parameter θ in the adaptive scheme. θs of $\pi/32$, $\pi/16$, $\pi/8$, and $\pi/4$ were chosen in the non-adaptive schemes. Figure 7 shows the average ODG in different musical categories for the proposed method in comparison with non-adaptive phase modulation-based watermarking schemes. The bit rate was set to 6 bps in this experiment. The proposed method has good sound quality (ODG ≥ -2) for all the categories while some of the non-adaptive schemes have a few categories with bad quality. For all the categories, the proposed method has better sound quality than the non-adaptive schemes. The proposed method has a total average ODG of -0.24 and 95 % of all the songs have ODG greater than or equal to -2. The non-adaptive schemes seem to have a trend that when θ increases, the ODGs also increase. However, for the jazz, march, and vocal categories, the best case of sound quality is when θ is equal to $\pi/8$.

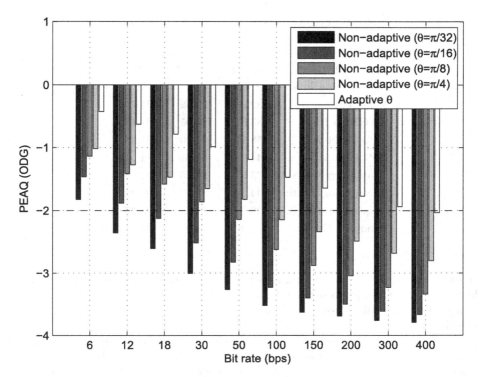

Fig. 8. Objective evaluation on inaudibility of the proposed method with respect to bit rate

Figure 8 depicts the average ODGs with respect to bit rate. For all the conditions of bit rates, the adaptive scheme satisfies the evaluation criterion and has better sound quality performance in comparison with the non-adaptive schemes. When the bit rate increases, the sound quality of both the adaptive scheme and non-adaptive schemes decrease. This is because the more bits are embedded into audio signals, the more quality degradation the watermarked signals suffer.

3.2 Robustness Evaluation

We carried out experiments to evaluate robustness of the proposed method against the following processing: addition of white Gaussian noise (AWGN) with an SNR of 36 dB, MP3 compression at 128 kbps, MPEG4 HE-ACC (MP4) compression at 96 kbps, re-quantization to 8 bits, re-sampling to 22 kHz and 16 kHz, and bandpass filtering with the passband between 100 Hz and 6 kHz and the stopband of −12 dB per octave. We set up the robustness test with three different configurations of adaptive phase modulation schemes to investigate the trade-off between the inaudibility and robustness of the proposed method. The default configuration (Config. 1) which was described earlier in Sect. 2 is the scheme we adjust parameter θ to the lowest power subband. Since the least sensitive portion of audio

Table 2. Inaudibility and robustness evaluation with several configurations

Measure	Config. 1	Config. 2	Config. 3
PEAQ (ODG)	−0.42	−1.12	−1.23
Bit detection rate (%)			
No processing	99.09	99.52	99.75
AWGN 36 dB	83.07	88.95	97.43
MP3 128 kbps	58.17	91.86	94.98
MP4 96 kbps	44.09	68.51	94.51
Re-quantization 8 bits	73.97	84.25	92.06
Re-sampling 22 kHz	44.34	89.87	99.22
Re-sampling 16 kHz	43.97	88.87	98.27
Bandpass filtering	46.29	59.26	61.26

signal is modified, the sound quality is the best but the robustness may be quite low. We investigated two other schemes of adaptation in which parameter θ is adjusted to the medium power subband (Config. 2) and the highest power subband (Config. 3).

Table 2 shows the average BDR of the watermark detector in three configurations. For the first configuration, the BDRs are all lower than 90 % except for bandpass filtering but the PEAQ is close to imperceptible grade. By contrast, the third configuration has all the BDRs greater than 90 % but the PEAQ is quite lower than that of the first. On the other hand, the second configuration has PEAQ a little higher than the third and all the BDRs almost acceptable except for MP4 and bandpass filtering. These results suggested that we can trade inaudibility for robustness toward a robust watermarking system with the proposed approach. However, a further investigation should be done to figure out the most balanced scheme for both inaudibility and robustness.

3.3   Comparative Evaluation

We compared our proposed method with three other conventional methods: the CD-based method (CD) [15], the direct spread spectrum method (DSS) [5], and the echo hiding method (ECHO) [13]. All these methods detect watermark using a blind detection scheme. In this experiment, the default adaptive scheme (Config. 1) was used and there is no processing applied to watermarked signals. Figure 9 plots the average ODG and BDR of the proposed method and the compared methods with respect to bit rate. For all the conditions of bit rates, ODGs of the proposed method are higher than those of the compared methods in which ODGs of the compared methods are mostly lower than −2. On the other hand, the CD-based method has all the BDRs greater than 99 % while the BDRs of the proposed method satisfy the evaluation threshold (90 %) for the bit rates not greater than 150 bps. The DSS method satisfies the evaluation

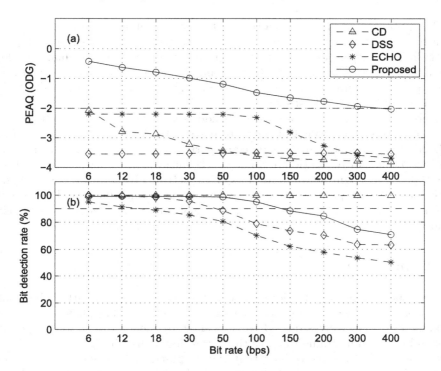

Fig. 9. Comparative evaluation on ODG and BDR with respect to bit rate

threshold for the bit rates less than 50 bps and the ECHO method satisfies for the bit rates less than 18 bps.

The results of PEAQ and BDR suggested that the proposed method can embed watermarks into various kinds of audio signals with good inaudibility and blindly detect embedded watermarks. Compared with conventional water-marking methods, the proposed adaptive watermarking method provides better sound quality of watermarked audio signals.

4   Discussion

Phase modulation itself does not actually make sound quality of each frame degraded but introduces discontinuity at framing points in the whole signal. Discontinuity causes click sounds in watermarked signals which could be per-ceived as annoying distortion. OLA technique is usually employed to eliminate discontinuity in conventional signal processing applications. However, OLA does not work with the proposed method because it destroys the audio samples around the framing points which are a key factor for blind detection by CZT. For that reason, the proposed method modifies the least significant portion to embed watermark instead of using OLA technique.

The proposed method meets a trade-off between inaudibility and robustness. To achieve the best sound quality, the proposed method chooses the least perceptually insensitive portion of audio signals for embedding watermark at the expense of weakness against signal processing operations. Further investigations are required to figure out a more effective adaptive scheme in order to satisfy both inaudibility and robustness.

Another issue with the proposed method is that we assumed all the frame positions could be identified in the watermark detection process. However, the embedded watermark cannot be detected correctly without frame synchronization. An avenue for realization of frame synchronization is to perform exhaustive search of local magnitude minima in CZT spectrum. In addition, the current work has not incorporated security parameter into embedding and detection processes. A key should be used to encrypt embedding watermarks to increase security. These issues will be thoroughly considered in future work.

5   Conclusion

In this paper, we proposed a novel blind watermarking method with high sound quality based on the concept of adaptive phase modulation. The phase modulator parameter is adaptively adjusted to the center frequency of the lowest power subband of an audio frame to make the disruption at framing points negligible. The experimental results verified that the proposed method can achieve high inaudibility for many kinds of audio signals and precisely detect watermark from watermarked audio signals by a blind scheme. Robustness could be achieved with the proposed approach at the expense of slightly reducing sound quality. Besides, the proposed method has high embedding capacity, i.e., bit rate of 150 bps. We plan to figure out an effective adaptive scheme for satisfying both inaudibility and robustness and implement a frame synchronization scheme for watermark detection in next stages.

Acknowledgement. This work was supported by a Grant-in-Aid for Scientific Research (B) (No. 23300070) and an A3 foresight program made available by the Japan Society for the Promotion of Science.

References

1. Cvejic, N., Seppänen, T.: Digital Audio Watermarking Techniques and Technologies. IGI Global, USA (2007)
2. Podilchuk, C.I., Delp, E.J.: Digital watermarking: Algorithms and applications. IEEE Signal Proc. Mag. **18**, 33–46 (2001)
3. Chen, B., Wornell, G.W.: Quantization index modulation: A class of provably good methods for digital watermarking and information embedding. IEEE Trans. Inf. Theory **47**, 1423–1443 (2001)
4. Bassia, P., Pitas, I., Nikolaidis, N.: Robust audio watermarking in the time domain. IEEE Trans. Multimedia **3**, 232–241 (2001)

5. Cox, I.J., Kilian, J., Leighton, T., Shamoon, T.: Secure spread spectrum watermarking for multimedia. IEEE Trans. Image Process. **6**, 1673–1687 (1997)
6. Swanson, M.D., Zhu, B., Tewfik, A.H., Boney, L.: Robust audio watermarking using perceptual masking. Elservier Signal Proc. **66**, 337–355 (1988). Spec. Issue on Copyright Prot. and Access Cont
7. Moore, B.C.J.: An Introduction to the Psychology of Hearing, 6th edn. Brill Academic Pub, London (2013)
8. Nelson, D.A., Bilger, R.: Pure-tone octave masking in normal-hearing listeners. J. Speech Hear. Res. **17**, 223–251 (1974)
9. Bender, W., Gruhl, D., Morimoto, N., Lu, A.: Techniques for data hiding. IBM Syst. J. **35**, 313–336 (1996)
10. Dong, X., Bocko, M.F., Ignjatovic, Z.: Data hiding via phase manipulation of audio signals. In: Proceedings of IEEE International Conference Acoustics, Speech, Signal Process, vol. 5, pp. 377–380 (2004)
11. Arnold, M., Baum, P.G., Voeßing, W.: A phase modulation audio watermarking technique. In: Katzenbeisser, S., Sadeghi, A.-R. (eds.) IH 2009. LNCS, vol. 5806, pp. 102–116. Springer, Heidelberg (2009)
12. Chen, X.M., Doerr, G., Arnold, M., Baum, P.G.: Efficient coherent phase quantization for audio watermarking. In: Proceedings of IEEE Internatioal Conference Acoustics, Speech, Signal Process, pp. 1844–1847 (2011)
13. Gruhl, D., Lu, A., Bender, W.: Echo hiding. In: Anderson, R. (ed.) IH 1996. LNCS, vol. 1174, pp. 295–315. Springer, Heidelberg (1996)
14. Unoki, M., Hamada, D.: Method of digital-audio watermarking based on cochlear delay characteristics. Int. J. Innovative Comput., Inf. Control **6**, 1325–1346 (2010)
15. Unoki, M., Miyauchi, R.: Reversible watermarking for digital audio based on cochlear delay characteristics. In: Proceedings of IIHMSP 2011 (2011)
16. Takahashi, A., Nishimura, R., Suzuki, Y.: Multiple watermarks for stereo audio signals using phase-modulation techniques. IEEE Trans. Sig. Process. **53**, 806–815 (2005)
17. Rabiner, L.R., Schafer, R.W., Rader, C.M.: The chirp z-transform algorithm. IEEE Trans. Audio Electroacoust. **17**, 86–92 (1969)
18. Goto, M., Hashiguchi, H., Nishimura, T., Oka, R.: Music genre database and musical instrument sound database. In: Proceedings of ISMIR 2003, pp. 229–230 (2003)
19. Kabal, P.: An examination and interpretation of itu-rbs.1387: Perceptual evaluation of audio quality. Technical report, Dept, Elect. Comp. Eng. (2002)
20. Nishimura, A., Unoki, M., Kondo, K., Ogihara, A.: Objective evaluation of sound quality for attacks on robust audio watermarking. In: Proceedings of Meeting on Acoustics, pp. 1–9 (2013)

Adapted Quantization Index Modulation
for Database Watermarking

Javier Franco-Contreras[1,4], Gouenou Coatrieux[1,4(✉)],
Nora Cuppens-Boulahia[2,4], Frédéric Cuppens[2,4], and Christian Roux[3]

[1] Institut Mines-TELECOM, TELECOM Bretagne,
Inserm U1101 LaTIM, 29238 Brest, France
{javier.francocontreras,gouenou.coatrieux}@telecom-bretagne.eu
[2] Institut Mines-TELECOM, TELECOM Bretagne, UMR CNRS 3192 Lab-STICC,
35576 Cesson Sévigné, France
[3] Institut Mines-TELECOM, Mines Saint-Étienne, 62362 Saint-Étienne, France
[4] Université Européenne de Bretagne, Rennes, France

Abstract. In this paper, we adapt the robust Quantization Index Modulation (QIM) originally proposed by Chen and Wornell for images to the protection of relational databases. In order to embed a bit of the watermark, we modulate the relative angular position of the circular histogram center of mass of one numerical attribute. We experimentally verify the suitability of our scheme in terms of distortion, robustness and complexity within the framework of one medical database of more than one half million of inpatient hospital stay records. Our solution is very robust against most common database attacks (tuple deletion and insertion and attribute value modifications), and the embedded message can be error free retrieved even after a suppression or addition of 80 % of the database tuples, making it suitable for database copyright protection, owner identification and traitor tracing.

Keywords: Watermarking · Database security · Quantization Index Modulation (QIM)

1 Introduction

The last two decades have seen an increasing attention paid to the transfer and sharing of relational databases along with their growing economical and decisional value, related in part to the progress of data-mining [1] and assisted decision tools [2]. At the same time, the easier the access to data, the more important are the risks in terms of security. Data records may be redistributed or modified without authorization. Even in highly sensitive domains like healthcare [3] and defense [4], an important number of data leaks is reported each year. Existing security mechanisms such as access control or encryption protect data from external threats, avoiding non-authorized users to access information, but once these mechanisms are bypassed or more simply when the access is granted, data are no longer protected.

© Springer International Publishing Switzerland 2015
Y.-Q. Shi et al. (Eds.): IWDW 2014, LNCS 9023, pp. 120–134, 2015.
DOI: 10.1007/978-3-319-19321-2_9

In this context, watermarking has been proposed as a complementary security mechanism offering an *"a posteriori"* protection. It allows the user accessing the data and normally working with them while keeping them protected. To do so, watermarking basically consists in the embedding of a message (some security attributes) or a watermark into a host multimedia document (e.g. an image, a database) based on the principle of controlled distortion. More clearly, host data are modified so as to encode a message in an imperceptible way within them. The embedded message can be used for various security objectives (e.g. copyright protection, data authenticity). Multiple examples of image, audio or video watermarking exist (see [5]). Database watermarking was introduced by Agrawal *et al.* [6] in 2002. Since then, several methods have been proposed [7–9] that can be distinguished in two main classes: (i) "robust" methods, commonly employed in copyright or fingerprinting/traitor tracing frameworks [10,11] where the embedded message should survive database modifications being innocent or malevolent; (ii) "fragile" methods the watermarks of which should not survive data modifications. Fragility is an interesting property for database authentication [12–15]. Herein, we are interested in robust watermarking.

Regarding the embedding process or the watermarking modulation the above methods exploit, they can be differentiated into "attribute-distortion-free" methods and "attribute-distortion-based". Basically, the formers modulate the order of tuples within a relation preserving the database attribute's values [12,13]. However, such a technique makes the watermark dependent on the way the database is stored, inducing constraints on the database management system. Notice that a tuple reordering may be enough to eliminate the watermark. Thus the range of applications this family of methods can be used for is limited.

Regarding "attribute-distortion-based" methods, their authors assume some data distortion (e.g. modification of attributes' values) can be carried out for message insertion without perturbing any *a posteriori* usages of data. As example in [6], Agrawal *et al.* proposed to modify the numerical attribute's least significant bits (LSBs) in secretly selected tuples so as to embed a binary sequence pattern. As the position of the modified tuples is only known of the database owner, the pattern detection consists in verifying that the LSBs of secret tuples respect the expected LSBs distribution. In order to achieve higher robustness against tuple deletion and modification attacks, Sion *et al.* [7] propose an embedding method based on the modification of the statistics of one numerical attribute in non-overlapping groups of tuples. In their scheme, tuples in a group are modified in a way such as a certain number of them have their attribute values greater or smaller than a threshold so as to encode 0 or a 1, respectively. Other embedding modulations considered in the literature are histogram shifting of attribute's values [16], difference expansion [17] or the modification of the relative position of circular histograms in groups of tuples [11]. However, to our knowledge, a classic robust modulation such as Quantization Index Modulation (QIM), originally introduced by Chen and Wornell [18] has not been considered in database watermarking yet. In this work, we propose to extend and adapt this modulation by modulating the angle of the center of mass of the circular histogram of an attribute in groups of tuples. As we will show the resulting modulation outperforms the solutions by Sion *et al.* [7] and Franco-Contreras *et al.* [11] in terms of robustness against tuple insertion and tuple deletion attacks.

The rest of this paper is organized as follows. In Sect. 2 we present the main steps of a common chain of database watermarking before introducing our complete watermarking scheme in Sect. 3. We then evaluate the robustness and distortion performance of our scheme and compare it to the ones by Sion et al. [7] and Franco-Contreras *et al.* [11] in Sect. 4 by means of experiments conducted on one real medical database of more than half million of inpatient stay records.

2   Database Watermarking

Formally, a database is a collection of data organized into a finite set of relations $\{R_i\}_{i=1,...,N_R}$. From here on and for sake of simplicity, we will consider one database composed of one single relation constituted of N unordered tuples $\{t_u\}_{u=1,...,N}$, each of M attributes $\{A_1, A_2, \ldots, A_M\}$. The attribute A_n takes its values within a set called attribute domain, with $t_u.A_n$ referring to the value of the nth attribute of the uth tuple. Each tuple is uniquely identified by either one attribute or a set of attributes, we call its primary key $t_u.PK$.

The main stages of the majority of database watermarking schemes are presented in Fig. 1. On the embedding side, a pretreatment process is first applied so as to make the watermark insertion/extraction independent of the database storage structure. Ordinarily, it consists in a group construction operation that creates a set of N_g non-intersecting groups of tuples $\{G^i\}_{i=1,...,N_g}$.

Typically, the group number for one tuple is obtained from the result of a cryptographic hash function applied to its primary key $t_u.PK$, concatenated with a secret watermarking key K_S as exposed in (1) where '|' represents the concatenation operator [7,9]. The use of a cryptographic hash function, e.g. Secure Hash Algorithm (SHA), ensures the secure and equal distribution of tuples into groups.

$$n_u = H(K_S|H(K_S|t_u.PK))mod N_g \qquad (1)$$

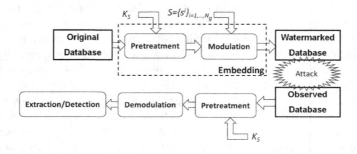

Fig. 1. A common database watermarking chain.

Then, if N is the total number of tuples in the database, each group will approximately contain $\frac{N}{N_g}$ tuples. By next, one bit or symbol of a message S is embedded per group. To do so, the values of one or several attributes are modified accordingly to the used watermarking modulation. Thus, one may expect to embed a message corresponding to a sequence of N_g symbols $S = \{s_i\}_{i=1,...,N_g}$.

Watermark extraction works in a similar way. First, tuples are distributed into the N_g groups. Depending on the watermarking modulation, one symbol is extracted/detected from each of these groups. If tuple primary keys are not modified, the knowledge of the watermarking key ensures synchronization between embedding and reading stages.

3   Proposed Scheme

The scheme we propose is based on Quantization Index Modulation (QIM) introduced by Chen and Wornell in [18]. This modulation allows us embedding and extracting a sequence of bits, a sequence which is robust against classic database attacks. In the sequel, we first recall QIM principles and its use in the case of signal watermarking. We then explain how we adapt it to the phase angle of the vector associated to the center of mass of the circular histogram of one numerical attribute in one group of tuples so as to embed one bit of message.

3.1   QIM Modulation and Signals

Quantization index modulation (QIM) is based on the quantization of the components of a host signal (samples, group of samples or transformed coefficients) according to a set of quantizers based on codebooks in order to embed the symbols of a message. More clearly, to each symbol s^i issued from a finite set $S = \{s^i_u\}_{u=0,...,U}$ QIM associates a codebook $\{C_{s^i_u}\}_{u=0,...,U}$ such that:

$$C_{s^i_u} \bigcap C_{s^i_v} = \emptyset \text{ if } u \neq v \tag{2}$$

The symbol s^i_u is embedded into one component X of the signal by replacing X by X_W which corresponds to the nearest element of X in the codebook $C_{s^i_u}$:

$$X_W = Q(X, s^i_u) \tag{3}$$

where Q is a function that returns the nearest element to X in $C_{s^i_u}$. Notice that the watermarking distortion corresponds to the distance between X and X_W. For illustration purpose, let us consider one pixel X of an image, which takes its values from a one-dimensional space $[0, 255]$. This scalar space is then subdivided into non overlapping intervals or cells of equal size. Each cell is then associated to only one codebook $\{C_{s^i_u}\}_{u=0,...,U}$ so as to satisfy (2). Consequently, each symbol s^i_u has several representations in $[0, 255]$ and Q can be defined as a scalar quantizer. In the insertion process, if X belongs to a cell that encodes the desired symbol s^i_u, its watermarked version X_W corresponds to the centroid of

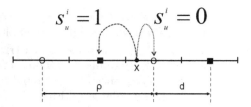

Fig. 2. Example of QIM in the case where X is a scalar value for the embedding of a binary sequence. Codebooks are based on an uniform quantization of step ρ. Cells centered on squares represent $C_0(s_u^i = 0)$ whereas cells centered on circles represent $C_1(s_u^i = 1)$. $d = \rho/2$ establishes the measure of robustness to signal perturbations.

this cell. Otherwise, X is replaced by the centroid of the nearest cell encoding s_u^i. The knowledge of the cell to which X_W belongs is enough for the detector to identify the embedded symbol in X. Figure 2 illustrates such an embedding process in the case of a binary message, i.e. $s_u^i \in 0, 1$ and two codebooks C_0 and C_1 the cells of which are defined based on uniform scalar quantization of quantization step ρ.

An extension of this approach is Compensated QIM (DM-DC) [18], where a fraction of the quantization error is added back to the quantized value so as to better manage the watermark robustness/imperceptibility tradeoff. Although this approach is not considered in this work, it could be applied in order to reduce the number of modified tuples at the price however of a lower robustness.

3.2 QIM Watermarking and Circular Histogram of an Attribute

In this work, we modulate the angle of the vector associated to the center of mass of the circular histogram of an attribute in a group of tuples. Working with circular histogram center of mass provides a more robust embedding space against tuple deletion, insertion and modification attacks than working directly on tuples. More clearly, this feature is less sensitive to such attacks.

In the following, we come back on how to compute this center of mass before explaining QIM codebook construction and present our whole scheme.

Calculation of the Center of Mass. Let us consider one group of tuples G^i secretly built as depicted in Sect. 2. Let us also consider A_t be the numerical attribute selected for embedding and that its attribute domain corresponds to the integer range $[0, L\text{-}1]$, where L is the number of integer values A_t can take. The histogram of the attribute A_t is calculated and mapped onto a circle. Then, and as illustrated in Fig. 3(a), the histogram center of mass Cm^i of the group G^i and its associated vector V^i are calculated. The module and phase of V^i can be calculated from its Cartesian coordinates given by:

$$X_i = \frac{1}{Mass_i} \sum_{l=0}^{L-1} n_l \cos(\frac{2\pi l}{L})$$
$$Y_i = \frac{1}{Mass_i} \sum_{l=0}^{L-1} n_l \sin(\frac{2\pi l}{L}) \tag{4}$$
$$Mass_i = \sum_{l=0}^{L-1} n_l$$

where n_l is the cardinality of the circular histogram class l of G^i (i.e. when A_t takes the integer value l). As a consequence, the module of V^i equals $R = \sqrt{X^2 + Y^2}$ and its phase μ_i, is given by (5), where $\text{sgn}(Y)$ is the sign of Y:

$$\mu_i = \begin{cases} \arctan(Y/X) \text{ if } X > 0 \\ \text{sgn}(Y)\frac{\pi}{2} \text{ if } X = 0 \\ \pi + \arctan(Y/X) \text{ else} \end{cases} \tag{5}$$

In the sequel, in order to embed a symbol s^i into a group G^i, we modulate the value of μ_i which is generally called mean direction.

Construction of the Codebooks. For sake of simplicity, the message we consider in this work is a sequence of bits $S = \{0, 1\}$. Two codebooks are thus necessary: C_0 and C_1. Another simplification we made in this work is that each codebook only contains one cell, as illustrated in Fig. 3(b). The questions to answer are then to determine cells boundaries and their centroids.

Let us define μ as the mean direction of A_t calculated over all the tuples of the database. Based on the fact attribute circular histograms of tuple groups are all positioned around this mean direction, we decided to define the cells' frontiers as the intersection between μ and the unit circle as illustrated in Fig. 3(b). So in order to encode 0 or 1 the histogram will be rotated to the left or to the right of this frontier.

Unlike the previously presented QIM which is based on uniform scalar quantization, the centroids C_{q0} and C_{q1} of our cells C_0 and C_1, respectively, do not correspond to the cells' centers in order to minimize and better control data distortion. They are defined such as (see Fig. 3(b)):

$$C_{q0} = \mu - \Delta; \; C_{q1} = \mu + \Delta \tag{6}$$

where Δ represents the rotation angle shift, a parameter that allows us controlling the compromise robustness/distortion. The main difference of this modulation with compensated QIM exposed above stands in the cell centroid position which is no longer at the center of the cell.

To sum up, each codebook corresponds to one cell (see Fig. 3(b)) defined as:

$$C_0 = (\mu - \pi, \mu); \; C_1 = (\mu, \mu + \pi) \tag{7}$$

Message Embedding and Detection - The Whole Scheme. If we now consider the embedding of the binary sequence symbol $\{s^i\}_{i=0,...,N_g-1} = \{0/1\}$ into the database, N_g groups of tuples $\{G^i\}_{i=0,...,N_g-1}$ are first constituted and one symbol $s_i = \{0, 1\}$ is then inserted per group. As stated above, the mean direction value μ_i of G^i is replaced by the centroid of the cell that encodes the value of s^i. This embedding process can be synthesized as:

$$\mu_i^w = \mu + (2s^i - 1)\Delta \tag{8}$$

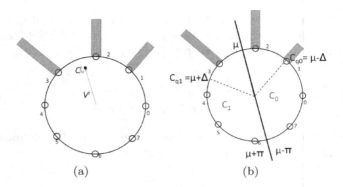

Fig. 3. (a) Mapping of one group G^i histogram onto a circle. The angle of the vector pointing its center of mass is modulated so as to embed one message symbol $s^i = \{0, 1\}$. (b) C_{q0} and C_{q1} are the centroids of the cells of each codebook unique cell C_0 and C_1. The intersection between μ and the unit circle represents the boundary between cells.

where μ_w is the watermarked mean direction, Δ is the rotation angle shift that allows the rotation of V^i so as to align it onto the cell centroid. This rotation is performed in the linear domain, i.e. on the attribute histogram, by modifying the attribute's values of certain tuples of G^i. We come back on this manipulation with more detail in Sect. 3.3.

Regarding message extraction, groups of tuples are reconstructed and angles μ_i^{det} are calculated from each group. It is important to notice that in order to extract the message, the value of μ should be known of the detector so as to make it possible to reconstruct the codebooks C_0 and C_1. μ can be sent to the reader as part of the watermarking key, as example.

In the case the watermarked database has been attacked, the value of μ_i^{det} can differ from μ_i^w. Whatever the situation, the cell to which μ_i^{det} belongs allows us the extraction of one bit s^i:

$$s^{i,det} = \begin{cases} 0 \text{ if } \mu_i^{det} \in C_0 \\ 1 \text{ if } \mu_i^{det} \in C_1 \end{cases} \tag{9}$$

3.3   Linear Histogram Modification

As stated above, a rotation of the center of mass vector V^i corresponds to an alteration of the values of the attribute A_t in a certain number of tuples of G^i. For example, if we call α the elementary angle between two consecutive bins of the circular histogram of A_t, i.e. $\alpha = \frac{2\pi}{L}$, modifying μ_i of α in the clockwise direction results in adding -1 to all the attribute's values in G^i. Notice that $+1$ (resp. -1) is the minimal perturbation that can be applied to an integer value.

In practice, we conduct an iterative process, modifying the attribute's values in G^i so as to rotate V^i onto C_{q0} or C_{q1}. In one iteration, the values in the group are increased of $+1$ (resp. -1) so as to rotate μ_i^w positively (resp. negatively) to make it converge to C_{q1} (resp. C_{q0}). To do so, one can compute the number

n_{mods} of tuples to be modified with the minimal perturbation $+1$ (resp. -1), depending on the elementary angle α and of the number of tuples N_{G^i} in G^i:

$$n_{mods} = round(\frac{|\mu_i^w - C_{q0}|}{\alpha} N_{G^i}) \qquad (10)$$

As exposed, after each iteration the distance between μ^w and C_{q1} (resp. C_{q0}) decreases. However because A_t is an integer attribute, being at least modifiable of ±1, μ_i^w may not reach the codebook cell centroid after an infinite number of iterations. This is why we introduced a user defined parameter ε, such as our algorithm stop when $|\mu_i^w - C_{q0}| < \epsilon$. The minimum value of ϵ depends on the attribute. In our example, A_t is an integer, the circular histogram center of mass of which can be rotated ad minima of $\frac{2\pi}{L}\frac{N_g}{N} = \alpha\frac{N_g}{N}$ (i.e. a modification of ±1 of one individual attribute's value). This results in a minimum value of ϵ for this attribute of a half of this rotation, $\epsilon_{min} = \frac{\alpha}{2}\frac{N_g}{N}$.

4   Experimental Results

In this section we evaluate the performance of our scheme in terms of database distortion, watermark robustness and complexity. We also compare it in terms of robustness with the efficient schemes proposed by Sion *et al.* [7] and Franco-Contreras *et al.* [11] so as to demonstrate the gain of performance it can provide.

4.1   Experimental Dataset

Our test database is constituted of one relation of 508000 tuples issued from one real medical database containing pieces of information related to inpatient stays in French hospitals. In this table, each tuple associates fifteen attributes like the hospital identifier (*id_hospital*), the patient stay identifier (*id_stay*), the patient age (*age*), the stay duration (*dur_stay*) and several other data useful for statistical analysis of hospital activities.

In order to constitute the groups of tuples (see Sect. 2), the attributes *id_stay* and *id_hospital* were concatenated so as to constitute the tuple primary key. Two numerical attributes were then considered for message embedding: patient age (*age*) and stay duration (*dur_stay*). These attributes were chosen because of their intrinsic properties. Indeed, the attribute *age* has slightly uniform distribution, while the attribute *dur_stay* presents an exponential distribution concentrated on the lower values of its domain.

4.2   Performance Criteria

In the sequel, the performance of our scheme is evaluated in terms of statistical distortion, robustness against tuple suppression and insertion attacks and complexity. In order to get a global vision of the variation of the attribute's distribution, we quantify its statistical distortion through the variations of its mean and standard deviation, the Kullback-Leibler divergence (D_{KL} - see (11)) and the mean absolute error (MAE) between histograms (see (12)) of the attribute before and after watermark embedding. If we call h_{A_t} and $h_{A_t^w}$ the histograms of the original attribute A_t and of its watermarked version A_t^w respectively, we have:

$$D_{\text{KL}}(h_{A_t} \| h_{A_t^w}) = \sum_{l=0}^{L-1} \frac{1}{N} \ln\left(\frac{h_{A_t}(l)}{h_{A_t^w}(l)}\right) h_{A_t}(l) \tag{11}$$

$$\text{MAE} = \frac{1}{L \cdot N} \sum_{l=0}^{L-1} \left| h_{A_t}(l) - h_{A_t^w}(l) \right| \tag{12}$$

We recall that the attribute domain for A_t corresponds to the integer range $[0, L-1]$ and N is the total number of tuples in the database. Robustness is evaluated by means of the bit error rate (BER), i.e. the probability the value of an extracted symbol is incorrect after an attack, we compute as:

$$\text{BER} = \frac{\sum_{i=1}^{N_g}(s^i \oplus s^{i,det})}{N_g}; \tag{13}$$

Complexity is established as the computation time or more clearly, the amount of time taken by the execution of the insertion and the extraction processes. It is important to notice that all of the following results are given in average after 30 random simulations with the same parameterization but different group configuration. Given computation times are those of an implementation of our scheme made with Matlab® running on a Intel® Xeon® E5504 running at 2 Ghz with 3 GB of physical memory and four cores.

4.3   Statistical Distortion Results

As stated above, we evaluate the statistical distortion over the attribute's values through the variations of the mean, the standard deviation, the Kullback-Leibler divergence (D_{KL}) and attribute's histograms MAE. These variations depend on the value of the rotation angle shift Δ of the center of mass on which depend the codebook cell centroids and of the number of tuples per group, established by the number of groups N_g (notice that the number of tuples in the database N is fixed). Distortion measurements are given in Table 1 considering the attribute *Age* for different number of groups $N_g = 100, 1000$ and values of Δ. We recall that Δ can only take values multiple of the elementary angle α (see Sect. 3.3). As it can be seen, the mean and standard deviation of the attribute grow with the value of Δ but their variations remain below 1 % of the original values. It is the same for the D_{KL} and the histograms MAE which quantify the distortion of the attribute's distribution. All these measures grow with the number of groups, but the variation is not significant. As exposed, our scheme induces low statistical distortions and may not bias most data-mining operations.

Table 1. Introduced statistical distortion in terms of mean, standard deviation (*Std.dev.*), Kullback-Leibler divergence ($KL - Div$.) and histograms histograms MAE for the attribute *Age*, considering a test database of $N = 508000$ tuples for different number of groups and various rotation angle shifts Δ. α is the elementary angle between classes of the circular histogram (see Sect. 3.3). The original mean and standard deviation of the attribute *Age* are 50.078 and 25.236, respectively. Measures' variations are indicated in parenthesis for the mean and the standard deviation.

Nb.groups		$\Delta = \alpha$	$\Delta = 2\alpha$	$\Delta = 3\alpha$
Mean	100	50.2009 (0.24 %)	50.3265 (0.49 %)	50.4003 (0.64 %)
	1000	50.3071 (0.45 %)	50.3948 (0.63 %)	50.5141 (0.87 %)
Std. dev.	100	25.2 (0.14 %)	25.1865 (0.19 %)	25.1878 (0.19 %)
	1000	25.1562 (0.31 %)	25.1599 (0.3 %)	25.1753 (0.24 %)
KL-Div.	100	0.0188	0.0393	0.0728
	1000	0.0242	0.0349	0.0557
MAE	100	$6.11 \ 10^{-4}$	$9.072 \ 10^{-4}$	$11.4 \ 10^{-4}$
	1000	$7.27 \ 10^{-4}$	$8.745 \ 10^{-4}$	$17 \ 10^{-4}$

4.4 Robustness Results

Robustness of our scheme depends on the rotation angle shift Δ and on the number of tuples per group, established by the number of groups N_g as the number of tuples in the database N is fixed. In a first experiment, the attribute *age* was watermarked with an uniformly distributed binary sequence S varying Δ and N_g. Resulting watermarked databases underwent deletion and insertion attacks with a percentage of suppressed and inserted tuples in the range [20 %, 99 %].

As we can see in Fig. 4(a), in the case of the tuple deletion attack, the bit error rate obviously increases with the percentage of deleted tuples and also along with the number of groups. This is due to the fact that the number of tuples per group decreases when the number of groups is enlarged, perturbing the mean direction estimation and consequently, the robustness of our scheme. On the other hand, a higher value of Δ leads to a lower bit error rate at the price however of an increased distortion, as the distance between the cell centroids and μ (the original mean direction of the attribute and also the codebook cell's frontier) increases (see Sect. 3.2).

A similar experiment was performed in the case of a tuple insertion attack as illustrated in Fig. 4(b). Notice that new added tuple attributes' values follow the original distribution of the attribute. As in the previous case, the bit error rate increases with the number of groups N_g and decreases with the value of Δ. Our scheme better resist this attack due to the fact that new attribute's values modify the mean direction estimator's mean value while increasing at the same time its accuracy (i.e. reducing its variance).

In both cases, the embedded message can be error free extracted when $N_g = 100$ and $\Delta = 3\alpha$ are considered even if 80 % of the database tuples are suppressed or nearly 100 % of new tuples are added.

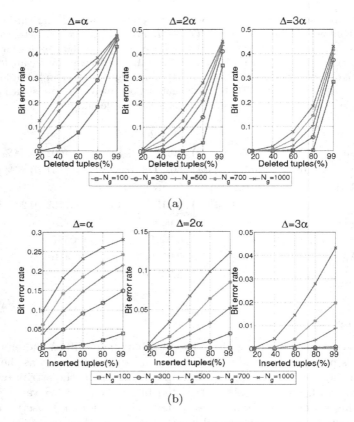

Fig. 4. (a) Bit error rate for the attribute *Age* with different rotation angle shift values Δ taking $N_g = 100, 300, 500, 700$ and 1000 groups for a tuple deletion attack. (b) Bit error rate for the attribute *Age* with different rotation angle shift values Δ taking $N_g = 100, 300, 500, 700$ and 1000 groups for a tuple insertion attack.

A third experiment was conducted so as to evaluate the dependence of the performance of our scheme with the attribute distribution. Attributes *age* and *dur_stay* were then watermarked using the same number of groups $N_g = 1000$ and a rotation angle shift $\Delta = \alpha$. As depicted in Fig. 5, the bit error rate for the attribute *dur_stay* is the lowest one due to the low dispersion of its values around its mean, that makes its mean direction more stable against the addition or suppression of tuples.

We also evaluated the robustness of our scheme against attribute's values modifications in two different manners: (i) Gaussian noise addition of standard deviation $\sigma = 2$; (ii) uniform noise addition of amplitude in $[-4, 4]$. Considering the attribute *age* with a number of groups $N_g = 1000$ and $\Delta = \alpha$, we obtained a BER ≈ 0.04 in the first case and BER ≈ 0.09 in the second, even when 99 % of tuples were modified. The BER decreases for a lower N_g and for a higher Δ. Thus, our scheme can be considered as highly robust against this attack.

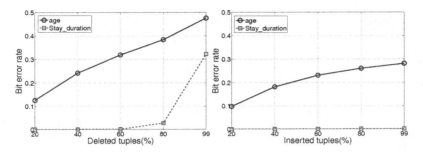

Fig. 5. Bit error rate for the attributes *age* and *dur_stay* with $N_g = 1000$ and $\Delta = \alpha$ considering a tuple deletion attack (left) and a tuple insertion attack (right).

4.5 Robustness/Distortion Comparison Assessments

Finally, we compared the robustness/distortion compromise offered by our scheme and by two efficient methods. First, the method introduced by Sion *et al.* [7] which is based on the modification of the attribute value statistics in a group of tuples G^i so as to embed one bit $s^i = \{0,1\}$ of the message S (see Sect. 2). To do so, a threshold value is first derived from G^i: $Tr = avg + c\sigma$, where avg and σ are the mean and standard deviation values of A_t in G^i and $c \in (0,1)$ is a user defined parameter. The embedded bit value is encoded depending on the number ν_c of watermarked attributes values over or under this threshold. More clearly, for a group of N_t tuples, a bit value 0 is embedded if $\nu_c < N_t\nu_{false}$ and a bit value is embedded if 1 if $\nu_c > N_t\nu_{true}$ where $\nu_{true}, \nu_{false} \in (0,1)$ are user-defined parameters exploited so as to control watermark robustness. At the reading stage, the message is extracted simply by verifying if ν_c is greater or smaller than Tr. Second, we considered the method by Franco-Contreras *et al.* [11]. In this one, each group is divided into two subgroups $G^{A,i}$ and $G^{B,i}$ and the relative angle β_i between vectors associated to their histograms' centers of mass is modulated in order to embed one symbol $s^i = \{0,1\}$ per group of tuples. Depending on the value of s_i, these vectors are rotated in opposite directions with an angle step $\alpha = \frac{2\pi\Delta}{L}$, where Δ corresponds to the shift amplitude of the histogram. More precisely, modifying the angle β_i of $2\alpha(2s_i - 1)$ results in adding $(2s_i - 1)\Delta$ to the attributes of $G^{A,i}$ and $(1 - 2s_i)\Delta$ to those of $G^{B,i}$. At the reading stage, the sign of the watermarked angle β_i^w indicates the embedded symbol in G^i. Notice that because α is a fixed value for reversibility purposes, not all of the groups of tuples can convey one bit of message (non-carriers), see [11] on how handling such a situation.

All the schemes were parameterized in order to obtain the same mean squared error ($MSE = 1.5$) between the original and the watermarked A_t attribute values. The length of the embedded sequence S was set to 100 (i.e. $N_g = 100$). It should be noticed that in [11], the existence of non-carrier groups may result in bit erasures and injections when the database is attacked. In this experiment, these cases are assimilated to bit errors for comparison purposes. As illustrated in Fig. 6 in the case of a tuple deletion attack, our scheme outperforms the others, allowing the extraction of the embedded sequence S with a bit error rate lower

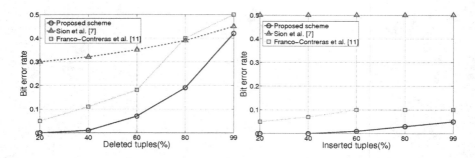

Fig. 6. Bit error rates achieved with our scheme, the one by Sion *et al.* [7] and the one by Franco-Contreras *et al.* [11] in the case of a deletion attack with various intensities (left); an insertion attack with different number of new tuples (right).

than 0.2 even if 80 % of tuples are deleted from the database. The same analysis stands for a tuple insertion attack. As depicted in Fig. 6, in the case of [7], the bit error rate is already close to 0.5 after the insertion of 10 % of new tuples while the other methods resist to insertions of even 100 %, with the proposed scheme offering always a better performance.

4.6   Computation Time

The computation time of our scheme depends on the construction of groups of tuples and of the watermark embedding/extraction processes. The most computationally expensive stage is the construction of groups. It increases with the number of tuples N in the database relation. In this experiment, the attribute *age* was considered for embedding. Table 2 provides the elapsed time for this first task for several values of N considering the SHA-1 hash function. It can be seen that the time logically increases linearly with N.

Table 2. Computation time for the construction of groups using Matlab® running on a Intel® Xeon® E5504 running at 2 Ghz with 3 GB of physical memory and four cores.

Group creation	$N = 200000$	$N = 400000$	$N = 500000$
	67s	134s	170s

The complexity of the insertion process depends on the number of groups N_g, on the value of Δ as well as on the value of the error ϵ manually fixed by the user (see Sect. 3.3). On its side, the extraction stage complexity is essentially related with the number of groups. Indeed, once the groups reconstituted one just has to interpret their center of mass value to decode the message. Results for both processes are given in Table 3. It can be observed that the extraction complexity increases with the number of groups only. The insertion computation time increases also with Δ. Indeed, our scheme iteratively modified the tuples of one group so as to reach at nearly ϵ the codebook cell centroid which encodes

Table 3. Computation time for the insertion ($\epsilon = 10^{-4}$) and the extraction stages using Matlab® running on a Intel® Xeon® E5504 running at 2 Ghz with 3 GB of physical memory and four cores.

Insertion	$N_g = 100$	$N_g = 500$	$N_g = 700$
$\Delta = \alpha$	2s	8.5s	11.3s
$\Delta = 2\alpha$	2.7s	10.4s	14s
Extraction	$N_g = 100$	$N_g = 500$	$N_g = 700$
	0.3s	1s	1.3s

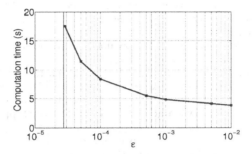

Fig. 7. Computation time for the attribute *Age* with $\Delta = \alpha$ taking $N_g = 500$ and several values of ϵ. The vertical solid line represents the asymptotic value of ϵ for this attribute.

the desired bit (see Sect. 3.3). The smaller ϵ, the more iterations our scheme will have to make. In order to evaluate the influence of ϵ on the computation time, we inserted a watermark into the attribute *Age*, with $N_g = 500$ and $\Delta = \alpha$ and for several values of ϵ. Results are depicted in Fig. 7. As predictable, the computation time inversely grows with ϵ until to reach an asymptote in $\epsilon = 2.79 \cdot 10^{-5}$. This value is directly linked to the attribute specificities (see Sect. 3.3).

5 Conclusion

In this paper, we have proposed a new robust relational database watermarking scheme based on a new modulation derived from Quantization Index Modulation (QIM) originally proposed by Chen and Wornell for images. It embeds one bit of message by modulating the angular position of the center of mass of the circular histogram of one numerical attribute. Obtained experimental results prove its robustness against tuple insertion and deletion and the low statistical distortion it introduces. Our method performs well even under tuple deletion/insertion of extreme conditions. We have shown it is capable to error free extract a message after the suppression of 80 % of the database records while preserving the statistical properties of the watermark attribute. Our scheme is also of low complexity which makes it suitable for copyright protection or traitor tracing applications, where it is necessary to embed robustly a user identifier.

Acknowledgments. This work was supported by the French Armaments Procurement Agency (DGA) - Project DGA RAPID FRAG&TAG - and by the Brittany Region Council. The authors are very grateful to the Department of Medical Information and Archives, CHU Lille; UDSL EA 2694; Univ Lille Nord de France; F-59000 Lille, France, for the experimental data used in this study.

References

1. Allen, H., Gearan, P., Rexer, K.: 5th annual rexer analytics data miner survey. In: Predictive Analytics World (2011)
2. Harvard Business Review Analytic Services: The evolution of decision making: How leading organizations are adopting a data-driven culture (2012)
3. McNickle, M.: Top 10 data security breaches in 2012. In: Healthcare Finance News. Accessed 21 March 2014
4. Rogers, S.: Wikileaks embassy cables: download the key data and see how it breaks down. In: The Gurdian. Accessed 21 March 2014
5. Cox, I., Miller, M., Bloom, J., Fridrich, J., Kalker, T.: Digital Watermarking and Steganography, 2nd edn. Morgan Kaufmann Publishers Inc., San Francisco (2008)
6. Agrawal, R., Kiernan, J.: Chapter 15 - watermarking relational databases. In: International Conference on Very Large Databases VLDB 2002, pp. 155–166. Morgan Kaufmann (2002)
7. Sion, R., Atallah, M., Prabhakar, S.: Rights protection for relational data. IEEE Trans. Knowl. Data Eng. **16**(12), 1509–1525 (2004)
8. Gross-Amblard, D.: Query-preserving watermarking of relational databases and xml documents. ACM Trans. Database Syst. **36**, 3:1–3:24 (2011)
9. Shehab, M., Bertino, E., Ghafoor, A.: Watermarking relational databases using optimization-based techniques. IEEE Trans. Knowl. Data Eng. **20**, 116–129 (2008)
10. Li, Y., Swarup, V., Jajodia, S.: Fingerprinting relational databases: schemes and specialties. IEEE Trans. Dependable Secure Comput. **2**(1), 34–45 (2005)
11. Franco-Contreras, J., Coatrieux, G., Cuppens-Boulahia, N., Cuppens, F., Roux, C.: Robust lossless watermarking of relational databases based on circular histogram modulation. IEEE Trans. Inf. Forensics Secur. **9**(3), 397–410 (2014)
12. Li, Y., Guo, H., Jajodia, S.: Tamper detection and localization for categorical data using fragile watermarks. In: ACM Workshop on DRM, pp. 73–82 (2004)
13. Kamel, I., Kamel, K.: Toward protecting the integrity of relational databases. In: 2011 World Congress on Internet Security (WorldCIS), pp. 258–261. IEEE (2011)
14. Coatrieux, G., Chazard, E., Beuscart, R., Roux, C.: Lossless watermarking of categorical attributes for verifying medical data base integrity. In: 2011 IEEE EMBC, pp. 8195–8198. IEEE (2011)
15. Franco-Contreras, J., Coatrieux, G., Cuppens-Boulahia, N., Cuppens, F., Roux, C.: Authenticity control of relational databases by means of lossless watermarking based on circular histogram modulation. In: Accorsi, R., Ranise, S. (eds.) STM 2013. LNCS, vol. 8203, pp. 207–222. Springer, Heidelberg (2013)
16. Zhang, Y., Niu, X., Yang, B.: Reversible watermarking for relational database authentication. J. Comput. **17**(2), 59–65 (2006)
17. Gupta, G., Pieprzyk, J.: Database relation watermarking resilient against secondary watermarking attacks. In: Prakash, A., Sen Gupta, I. (eds.) ICISS 2009. LNCS, vol. 5905, pp. 222–236. Springer, Heidelberg (2009)
18. Chen, B., Wornell, G.W.: Quantization index modulation: a class of provably good methods for digital watermarking and information embedding. IEEE Trans. Inf. Theory **47**(4), 1423–1443 (1999)

Image Watermarking Based on Various Discrete Fractional Fourier Transforms

Fong-Maw Tsai[1] and Wen-Liang Hsue[1,2(✉)]

[1] Master Program in Communication Engineering,
Chung Yuan Christian University, Chung-Li, Taoyuan City, Taiwan, R.O.C.
nkf40716@gmail.com
[2] Department of Electrical Engineering,
Chung Yuan Christian University, Chung-Li, Taoyuan City, Taiwan, R.O.C.
wlhsue@cycu.edu.tw

Abstract. In this paper, we use discrete fractional Fourier transform (DFRFT) and its other four generalized transforms to embed watermarks and analyze their robustness. The resulting watermarking schemes belong to the transform-domain watermarking schemes. Experiment results show that, among the five transforms, random DFRFT (RDFRFT) is most robust to cropping attack as well as salt-and-pepper noise attack. In general, the two real transforms, real DFRFT and real DFRHT, are good choices for watermark applications because they are not only resistant to cropping and salt-and-pepper noise attacks, but also have the merit of less computations as compared with other three complex DFRFT transforms.

Keywords: Watermarking · Discrete fractional fourier transform · Discrete fractional hartley transform · Robustness

1 Introduction

Because of the wide use of internet, videos, images and other information are digitized and uploaded to the internet. The cases of encroaching upon the intellectual property rights are increased. Therefore, we need to embed the watermark in images and other information for protecting intellectual property rights.

Generally, watermarking schemes are required to have good robustness [1]. Robustness means that after being attacked (for example: the addition of noise, cropping, compression, histogram equalization, and other image processing operations on watermarked images), embedded watermarks can still be successfully extracted from the watermarked images, and extracted watermark can be identified by human vision. The watermarking schemes can be classified as two categories: spatial domain and transform domain watermarkings. But most watermark schemes in the spatial domain are less robust than those in the transform domain. Watermarking in the transform domain also has better imperceptibility feature.

The DFRFT [2] is a generalization of the discrete Fourier transform (DFT), with one free parameter called the fractional parameter. In [3], Pei and Hsue generalized the DFRFT and defined the multiple-parameter discrete fractional Fourier transform (MPDFRFT). If the input data contains N points, the MPDFRFT has N free fractional

© Springer International Publishing Switzerland 2015
Y.-Q. Shi et al. (Eds.): IWDW 2014, LNCS 9023, pp. 135–144, 2015.
DOI: 10.1007/978-3-319-19321-2_10

parameters. In [4], Pei and Hsue further generalized MPDFRFT to define the random discrete fractional Fourier transform (RDFRFT) which has $O(N^2)$ free parameters. Recently, real DFRFT and real DFRHT (discrete fractional Hartley transform) with $O(N^2)$ free parameters are proposed [5]. For transform domain image watermarking, free parameters of DFRFT and its generalizations can be employed as keys to enhance the security. In this paper, we will apply these five transforms to image watermarking schemes and compare their performances.

2   Various Discrete Fractional Fourier Transforms

The $N \times N$ DFT matrix $\mathbf{F}$ is defined as

$$[\mathbf{F}]_{m,n} = \frac{1}{\sqrt{N}} e^{-j(2\pi/N)mn}, \quad 0 \leqq m, n \leqq N - 1. \tag{1}$$

Let an eigendecomposition of the DFT matrix $\mathbf{F}$ be

$$\mathbf{F} = \sum_{k=0}^{N-1} \lambda_k \mathbf{e}_k \mathbf{e}_k^T, \tag{2}$$

where $\mathbf{e}_0, \mathbf{e}_1, \ldots,$ and $\mathbf{e}_{N-1}$ form an orthonormal eigenvector basis of the DFT and $\lambda_0, \lambda_1, \ldots, \lambda_{N-1}$ are the eigenvalues of DFT. $\mathbf{F}$ only has four distinct eigenvalues $\{1, -j, -1, j\}$ [6].

The DFRFT matrix $\mathbf{F}^a$ is defined as [2]:

$$\mathbf{F}^a = \sum_{k=0}^{N-1} \lambda_k^a \mathbf{e}_k \mathbf{e}_k^T, \tag{3}$$

where a is a fractional parameter.

In [3], MPDFRFT is generalized from the DFRFT. MPDFRFT matrix $\mathbf{F}^{\bar{a}}$ is

$$\mathbf{F}^{\bar{a}} = \sum_{k=0}^{N-1} \lambda_k^{a_k} \mathbf{e}_k \mathbf{e}_k^T \tag{4}$$

where $\bar{a}$ is the $1 \times N$ parameter vector: $\bar{a} = [a_0, a_1, \ldots, a_{N-1}]$. In (4), $a_0, a_1, \ldots, a_{N-1}$ can be independent random numbers such that the resulting eigenvalues $\lambda_k^{a_k}, k = 0, 1, \ldots, N - 1$, are random:

$$\lambda_k^{a_k} = \begin{cases} \left(e^{-j2\pi}\right)^{a_k} & \text{if } \lambda_k = 1 \\ \left(e^{-j\pi/2}\right)^{a_k} & \text{if } \lambda_k = -j \\ \left(e^{-j\pi}\right)^{a_k} & \text{if } \lambda_k = -1 \\ \left(e^{-j3\pi/2}\right)^{a_k} & \text{if } \lambda_k = j \end{cases}. \tag{5}$$

In [4], random discrete fractional Fourier transform (RDFRFT) is the further generalization of MPDFRFT. RDFRFT is constructed by random DFT eigenvectors derived from a random DFT-commuting matrix $\mathbf{M}$ [4] and a $1 \times N$ real parameter vector $\bar{a} = [a_0, a_1, \ldots, a_{N-1}]$. Random DFRFT matrix $\mathbf{F}_{\mathbf{M}}^{\bar{a}}$ is

$$\mathbf{F}_{\mathbf{M}}^{\bar{a}} = \sum_{k=0}^{N-1} \lambda_k^{a_k} \mathbf{r}_k \mathbf{r}_k^T \tag{6}$$

where $\lambda_k^{a_k}$ is given by (5), and $\mathbf{r}_k$ are random orthonormal DFT eigenvectors derived by $\mathbf{M}$.

Real DFRFT is a special case of RDFRFT. The $N \times N$ real DFRFT $\mathbf{F}_{\mathbf{M}}^{\bar{a}}$ is defined as [5]:

$$\begin{aligned}
\mathbf{F}_{\mathbf{M}}^{\bar{a}} = &\sum_{k=1}^{m_1} \lambda_1^{a_{1,k}} \mathbf{u}_{1,k} \mathbf{u}_{1,k}^T + \sum_{k=1}^{m_2} \lambda_2^{a_{2,k}} \mathbf{u}_{2,k} \mathbf{u}_{2,k}^T \\
&+ \sum_{k=1}^{m_3} \lambda_3^{a_{3,k}} \mathbf{u}_{3,k} \mathbf{u}_{3,k}^T + \sum_{k=1}^{m_4} \lambda_4^{a_{4,k}} \mathbf{u}_{4,k} \mathbf{u}_{4,k}^T,
\end{aligned} \tag{7}$$

where

$$\begin{aligned}
\lambda_1^{a_{1,k}} &= (e^{-j2\pi})^{a_{1,k}}, & a_{1,k} &= \frac{n_{1,k}}{2} \\
\lambda_2^{a_{2,k}} &= (e^{-j\pi})^{a_{2,k}}, & a_{2,k} &= n_{2,k} \\
\lambda_3^{a_{3,k}} &= (e^{-j\frac{\pi}{2}})^{a_{3,k}}, & a_{3,k} &= 2n_{3,k} \\
\lambda_4^{a_{4,k}} &= (e^{-j\frac{3\pi}{2}})^{a_{4,k}}, & a_{4,k} &= 2n_{4,k}
\end{aligned} \tag{8}$$

with $\lambda_1 = 1$, $\lambda_2 = -1$, $\lambda_3 = -j$, $\lambda_4 = j$, $\bar{a}$ being the $1 \times N$ random parameter vector, $\mathbf{M}$ being the $N \times N$ random DFT-commuting matrix, $n_{1,k}$, $n_{2,k}$, $n_{3,k}$, and $n_{4,k}$ being independent random integers, $\mathbf{u}_{1,k}$, $\mathbf{u}_{2,k}$, $\mathbf{u}_{3,k}$, $\mathbf{u}_{4,k}$ being the random DFT eigenvectors derived from the random DFT-commuting matrix $\mathbf{M}$, which correspond to these DFT eigenvalues respectively: 1, -1, -j, j. m_1, m_2, m_3 and m_4 are the multiplicities of DFT eigenvalues corresponding to 1, -1, -j, j, respectively.

The real DFRFT for one-dimensional and two-dimensional signals can be expressed as $\mathbf{X} = \mathbf{F}_{\mathbf{M}}^{\bar{a}} \cdot \mathbf{x}$ and $\mathbf{P}_{(\bar{a}_1, \mathbf{M}_1, \bar{a}_2, \mathbf{M}_2)} = \mathbf{F}_{\mathbf{M}_1}^{\bar{a}_1} \cdot \mathbf{P} \cdot \mathbf{F}_{\mathbf{M}_2}^{\bar{a}_2}$, where $\mathbf{x}$ is the one-dimensional input and $\mathbf{P}$ is the two-dimensional input.

The real DFRHT is closely related to the real DFRFT. The $N \times N$ real DFRHT $\mathbf{H}_{\mathbf{M}}^{\bar{b}}$ is defined as [5]:

$$\begin{aligned}
\mathbf{H}_{\mathbf{M}}^{\bar{b}} = &\sum_{k=1}^{m_1} \lambda_1^{b_{1,k}} \mathbf{u}_{1,k} \mathbf{u}_{1,k}^T + \sum_{k=1}^{m_2} \lambda_2^{b_{2,k}} \mathbf{u}_{2,k} \mathbf{u}_{2,k}^T \\
&+ \sum_{k=1}^{m_3} \left(\frac{\lambda_3}{-j}\right)^{b_{3,k}} \mathbf{u}_{3,k} \mathbf{u}_{3,k}^T + \sum_{k=1}^{m_4} \left(\frac{\lambda_4}{-j}\right)^{b_{4,k}} \mathbf{u}_{4,k} \mathbf{u}_{4,k}^T,
\end{aligned} \tag{9}$$

where

$$\lambda_1^{b_{1,k}} = (e^{-j2\pi})^{b_{1,k}}, \quad b_{1,k} = \frac{N_{1,k}}{2}$$

$$\lambda_2^{b_{2,k}} = (e^{-j\pi})^{b_{2,k}}, \quad b_{2,k} = N_{2,k}$$

$$\left(\frac{\lambda_3}{-j}\right)^{b_{3,k}} = (e^{-j2\pi})^{b_{3,k}}, \quad b_{3,k} = \frac{N_{3,k}}{2} \tag{10}$$

$$\left(\frac{\lambda_4}{-j}\right)^{b_{4,k}} = (e^{-j\pi})^{b_{4,k}}, \quad b_{4,k} = N_{4,k}$$

with $\lambda_1 = 1, \lambda_2 = -1, \lambda_3 = -j, \lambda_4 = j$, $\overline{b}$ being the random parameter vector, $\mathbf{M}$ being the random DFT-commuting matrix, $N_{1,k}$, $N_{2,k}$, $N_{3,k}$, $N_{4,k}$ being independent random integers, $\mathbf{u}_{1,k}$, $\mathbf{u}_{2,k}$, $\mathbf{u}_{3,k}$, $\mathbf{u}_{4,k}$ being the random DFT eigenvectors derived from the random DFT-commuting matrix $\mathbf{M}$, which correspond to the following DFT eigenvalues respectively: 1, -1, -j, j. m_1, m_2, m_3 and m_4 are the multiplicities of DFT eigenvalues corresponding to 1, -1, -j, j, respectively.

3   Watermarking Scheme

In this paper, the grayscale image "Lena" (256 × 256 pixels) is adopted as the original host image, and the watermark is "CYCU" (50 × 50 pixels) (Fig. 1).

(a)   (b)

Fig. 1.   (a) The original image. (b) The watermark.

In the transform domain, the positions with larger amplitude values are used to embed the watermark [7]. The reason is that if we embed watermark in the positions with larger amplitude values, variations of pixel values in original image will be lower than the case when we embed watermark in positions with smaller amplitude values. So in this way the effect of the watermark embedding on the quality of the original image will be relatively low. Here we employ the method in [7] to embed the watermark:

$$M' = M + kW. \tag{11}$$

In (11), M', M, and W are the transformed outputs of the watermarked image, the original image, and the watermark, respectively. Therefore, the maximum size of the embedded watermark is the same as the size of the original host image. In (11), k is a parameter that can be used to control the strength of the embedded watermark, and it will affect the imperceptibility of watermark. If we use a larger k, the watermark will be stronger and the watermarked image will have greater difference as compared with the original image. If we use a smaller k, the watermark will be weaker and the extracted watermark will be unclear. In this paper, we choose k as 0.2.

The watermark extraction can be done as follows [7]:

$$W' = \frac{M' - M}{k} \tag{12}$$

where W' is the transformed output of the extracted watermark. Finally, by taking the inverse transform of W' into the spatial domain, the watermark can be retrieved. For example, in real DFRFT domain, inverse real DFRFT can be computed by: $\mathbf{Q}_{(-\bar{a}_1, \mathbf{M}_1, -\bar{a}_2, \mathbf{M}_2)} = \mathbf{F}_{\mathbf{M}_1}^{-\bar{a}_1} \cdot \mathbf{P} \cdot \mathbf{F}_{\mathbf{M}_2}^{-\bar{a}_2}$.

We use the peak signal-to-noise ratio (PSNR) between the watermarked and the original images to evaluate quality of the watermarked image. For an $N \times N$ image with 256 grayscales, the PSNR is defined as:

$$\text{PSNR} = 10 \log_{10} \frac{255^2}{\frac{1}{N \times N} \sum_{i=0}^{N-1} \sum_{j=0}^{N-1} (M_{i,j} - M'_{i,j})^2} \tag{13}$$

where $M_{i,j}$ and $M'_{i,j}$ are respectively pixel values of the original image and the watermarked image.

To assess quality of the extracted watermark, we use watermark-to-noise ratio (WNR) [7]. The WNR formula is given by:

$$\text{WNR} = \frac{\sum_{i,j} (W_{i,j})^2}{\sum_{i,j} (W_{i,j} - W'_{i,j})^2} \tag{14}$$

where $W_{i,j}$ and $W'_{i,j}$ are the (i, j)-th pixel values of the original watermark and the extracted watermark, respectively. When the WNR is larger than a threshold, the extracted watermark can be recognized by human eyes. However, the threshold value is subjective, because it is identified by human vision. So setting an appropriate threshold value is very important.

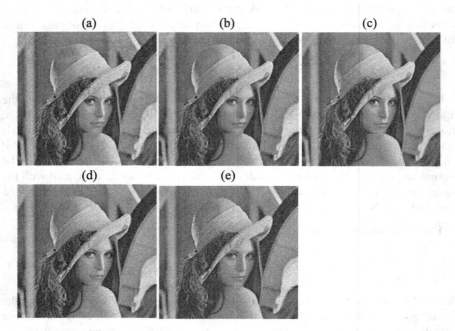

Fig. 2. The watermarked images in different transform domains. (a) DFRFT (PSNR = 31.6055 dB). (b) MPDFRFT (PSNR = 31.6840 dB). (c) RDFRFT (PSNR = 31.6459 dB). (d) Real DFRFT (PSNR = 28.6340 dB). (e) Real DFRHT (PSNR = 28.6342 dB).

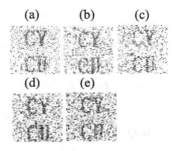

Fig. 3. The extracted watermark from cropped watermarked images. (a) DFRFT (cropping 23 × 23). (b) MPDFRFT (cropping 25 × 25). (c) RDFRFT (cropping 44 × 44). (d) Real DFRFT (cropping 40 × 40). (e) Real DFRHT (cropping 35 × 35).

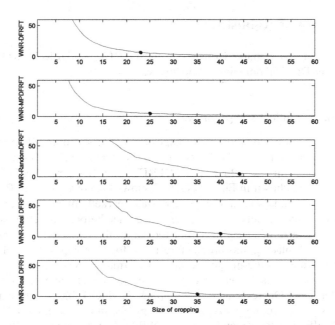

Fig. 4. WNR curves against croppings with DFRFT, MPDFRFT, RDFRFT, real DFRFT, and real DFRHT, respectively.

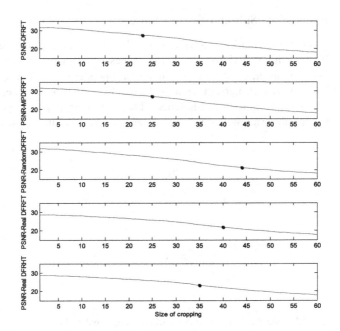

Fig. 5. PSNR curves against croppings with DFRFT, MPDFRFT, RDFRFT, real DFRFT, and real DFRHT, respectively.

4 Comparison of Robustness

Figure 2 shows the watermarked images in the DFRFT, MPDFRFT, RDFRFT, real DFRFT and real DFRHT domains, respectively.

4.1 Robustness Against Cropping

Examples of some extracted watermark images against cropping in different transform domains are shown in Fig. 3. WNR curves of extracted watermarks from cropped watermarked images in the DFRFT, MPDFRFT, RDFRFT, real DFRFT and real DFRHT domains are shown in Fig. 4. Figure 5 shows the corresponding PSNR curves of the watermarked images. In Fig. 4, the watermarked images are cropped with various sizes of square pixels in the upper left corner before extracting watermarks. Figure 4 shows, if size of cropping is not too large, the extracted watermark is recognizable. In Fig. 4, black points are the thresholds for cropping. Prior to the cropping threshold of the watermarked image, extracted watermark is visually recognizable, but if the size of cropping is larger than the threshold, we are unable to identify the extracted watermark. On resistance of cropping, RDFRFT has the best robustness, which can resist up to cropping size of 44 × 44 pixels. In this case, the PSNR value is only about 20 dB. On the other hand, the DFRFT is most fragile, which can only endure 23 × 23 pixels of cropping.

4.2 Robustness Against Salt-and-Pepper Noise

Examples of extracted watermarks from watermarked images with salt-and-pepper noise are shown in Fig. 6. Figure 7 shows the WNR values of extracted watermarks from watermarked images with different densities of salt-and-pepper noise. Because the salt-and-pepper noise randomly changes the pixel values to become 0 or 255 (i.e., minimum and maximum), they has a lot of differences between their adjacent pixel points. Therefore, with increasing salt-and-pepper noise density, WNR value will decrease fast.

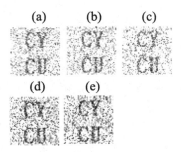

Fig. 6. The extracted watermark from watermarked image with salt-and-pepper noise. (a) DFRFT (density of 0.035). (b) MPDFRFT (density of 0.035). (c) RDFRFT (density of 0.04). (d) Real DFRFT (density of 0.025). (e) Real DFRHT (density of 0.025).

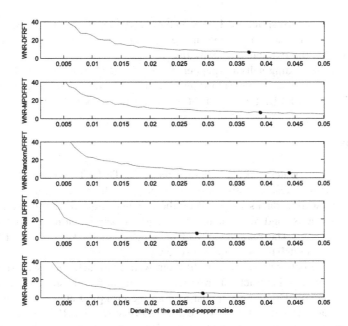

Fig. 7. WNR curves against salt-and-pepper noises with DFRFT, MPDFRFT, RDFRFT, real DFRFT, and real DFRHT, respectively.

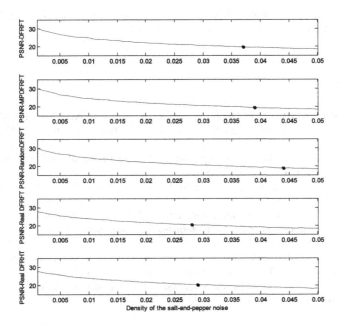

Fig. 8. PSNR curves against salt-and-pepper noises with DFRFT, MPDFRFT, RDFRFT, real DFRFT, and real DFRHT, respectively.

Figure 8 shows corresponding PSNR values against salt-and-pepper noises. From Fig. 8, with increasing salt-and-pepper noise density, PSNR values fast decrease, too. So it tends to blur the extracted watermarks.

On tolerance of adding salt-and-pepper noise to watermarked image, the first three complex transforms have better robustness. Robustness of the other two real transforms, including real DFRFT and real DFRHT, are worse but acceptable.

5 Conclusion

This paper analyzes watermarking schemes based on DFRFT and its other four generalized transforms. These transforms have properties which can be applied to image watermarking as well as data security. With these transforms, we can transform images to transform domains, and we can return images to spatial domain with the same transform parameters. The parameters can be used as secret keys. Therefore, watermarking based on DFRFTs can enhance security.

In order to find better robustness in different watermark schemes, we use these five transforms to embed and extract watermarks. Experiment results show that, among the five transforms, RDFRFT is most robust to both the cropping attack and the salt-and-pepper noise attack. In general, the two real transforms, real DFRFT and real DFRHT, are good choices for watermark applications because they are not only resistant to cropping and salt-and-pepper noise attacks, but also have the merit of less computations as compared with other three complex DFRFT transforms.

Acknowledgements. This work was supported by the Ministry of Science and Technology, R. O. C., under Contract MOST 100-2221-E-033-068-MY3.

References

1. Cox, I., Miller, M., Bloom, J.: Digital Watermarking. Elsevier, New York (2002)
2. Pei, S.C., Yeh, M.H.: Improved discrete fractional fourier transform. Opt. Lett. **22**, 1047–1049 (1997)
3. Pei, S.C., Hsue, W.L.: The multiple-parameter discrete fractional fourier transform. IEEE Signal Process. Lett. **13**, 329–332 (2006)
4. Pei, S.C., Hsue, W.L.: Random discrete fractional fourier transform. IEEE Signal Process. Lett. **16**, 1015–1018 (2009)
5. Hsue, W.L., Chang, W.C.: Multiple-parameter real discrete fractional fourier and hartley transforms. In: Proceedings of the 19th International Conference on Digital Signal Processing, pp. 694–698. Hong Kong (2014)
6. McClellan, J.H., Parks, T.W.: Eigenvalue and eigenvector decomposition of the discrete fourier transform. IEEE Trans. Audio Electroacoust. **20**, 66–74 (1972)
7. Guo, Q., Liu, Z., Liu, S.: Robustness analysis of image watermarking based on discrete fractional random transform. Opt. Eng. **47**, 057003 (2008)

An Audio Watermarking Scheme Based on Singular-Spectrum Analysis

Jessada Karnjana[1,2]($\boxtimes$), Masashi Unoki[1], Pakinee Aimmanee[2],
and Chai Wutiwiwatchai[3]

[1] School of Information Science, Japan Advanced Institute of Science
and Technology, 1-1 Asahidai, Ishikawa, Nomi 923-1292, Japan
{jessada,unoki}@jaist.ac.jp
[2] Sirindhorn International Institute of Technology, Thammasat University,
131 Moo 5, Tiwanont Road, Bangkadi, Pathumthani 12000, Muang, Thailand
pakinee@siit.tu.ac.th
[3] National Electronics and Computer Technology Center, 112 Thailand Science Park,
Phahonyothin Road, Pathumthani 12120, Khlong Luang, Thailand
chai.wutiwiwatchai@nectec.or.th

Abstract. This paper proposes a blind audio watermarking scheme based on singular-spectrum analysis (SSA) which relates to several techniques based on singular value decomposition (SVD). SSA is used to decompose a signal into several additive oscillatory components where each component represents a simple oscillatory mode. The proposed scheme embedded a watermark into a host signal by modifying scaling factors of certain components of the signal. Test results show that the proposed scheme satisfies imperceptibility criterion suggested by IHC with the average ODG of 0.18. It is robust against many attacks, such as MP3 and MP4 compression, band-pass filtering, and re-sampling. This paper does not only propose a new watermarking scheme, it also discusses the singular value and reveals its meaning, which has been deployed and played an important role in all SVD-based schemes.

Keywords: Singular-spectrum analysis · Singular value decomposition · Singular value · Audio watermarking

1 Introduction

Since the late 20th century, the Internet has grown at unprecedented rate, and the spread of digital-multimedia transfer has increased exponentially, especially after we had advanced technologies in data compression, more powerful personal computers, and social communities. This communication channel is somehow a double-edge sword. On one hand, it is very useful and convenient to access gigantic source of data. On the other hand, it could be harmful when it is misused. For example, there are social concerns about authentication, copyright management, copy control, and the like of digital media. These issues have been aware

© Springer International Publishing Switzerland 2015
Y.-Q. Shi et al. (Eds.): IWDW 2014, LNCS 9023, pp. 145–159, 2015.
DOI: 10.1007/978-3-319-19321-2_11

in music industry since 1990s [1]. One of the potential solutions solving this kind of problems in audio domain is to use an audio-watermarking technique.

Watermarking is a scheme of making information unnoticeable; therefore a user is not aware the existence of hidden information. This type of information hiding is called steganography. The other type is cryptography. Both are information hiding techniques; nevertheless, they have a different objective. While steganography deals with making information unnoticeable, the cryptography tries to make it unreadable. The use of watermarking for copyright control is claimed to be the original goal for audio watermark [2]. Besides copyright management and the like, audio watermarking could be used in many other applications where each has its own requirements. There are at least three areas of application, as stated in [2], for audio watermarking: (1) copyright marking and copy control, (2) forensic watermarking, such as digital fingerprinting, and (3) information hiding for annotation and added value. Since the main objective of audio watermarking is to add information into an audio signal transparently, in general, especially for commercial purposes, there are four requirements for an audio-watermarking method: (1) *Inaudibility*: human auditory system should not be able to detect a watermark, thus sound quality comparing between original and watermarked signals should be equal. (2) *Robustness*: it is an ability to survive of a watermark after attacks, such as re-sampling or compression, are applied to the watermarked signal. (3) *Blindness*: it is a property of extracting hidden information from a watermarked signal without the presence of the original in extracting processes. (4) *Confidentiality*: it is a property of concealment of hidden data [3]. In [2,4], the authors have added an additive requirement which is a capacity or quantity of information embedded in the original signal. For example, for the purpose of value adding, increasing capacity is an important issue since the hidden information is not just a short serial number. Naturally, these requirements conflict each other's. The high robustness, for example, normally comes with the cost of low audio quality or semi-transparency. Work of name of author of [4] also concludes similar phenomenal that high capacity implies low robustness. Therefore, in addition to proposing a new effective technique many researches on audio watermarking have focused on how to compromise these conflicts. However, there is no work that can completely solve these problems. Some techniques are good at transparency or inaudibility, but not blind. Some techniques are good at high capacity, but not robust, especially for the certain attacks.

On classification of audio watermarking schemes, name of the author in [5] had categorized watermarking schemes into three categories. The first embeds information in time domain by mostly changing the least significant bit (LSB) of an original signal. The second introduces an echo, and the third embeds information in a certain transform domain such as frequency or wavelet domain. However, classification depends upon a set of criteria. For example, it could be classified into two categories: the one that deploys properties of the human auditory system and the one that does not. Some techniques deploy characteristics of human auditory system as a guideline for hiding information [6]. The others are

based on mathematical manipulation and do not much rely on special characteristics of human auditory system [7]. In this paper, we investigate the later kind
and propose a watermarking scheme based on singular-spectrum analysis (SSA),
which relates to singular value decomposition-based (SVD-based) watermarking
techniques. These techniques rely on a mathematical method of extracting algebraic features called *singular values* (SVs) from a two-dimensional matrix.

The SVD-based watermarking has a lot of advantages [7–23]. The advantages are mainly due to properties of SVs, such as the invariance of SVs under
common signal processing operations. For example, when a small modification is
applied to the original signal represented by a two-dimensional matrix, its SVs
changes unnoticebly. This property of SVs makes the SVD-based techniques
robust against the common signal processing. Besides, it has a low computational complexity comparing with other transform-based methods.

The SVD-based audio watermarking is originally proposed by Özer et al. in
2005 [8] and based on the watermarking technique employed in the image domain
[11]. From our survey, the SVD-based methods could be categorized into two
frameworks based on the stage in extracting processes that it is employed information of a watermark which is from the embedding stage. For example, methods
described in [8–10,21] use information of a watermark in the extracting stage,
therefore they are necessary non-blind methods. Those described in [7,12–15,17–
20,22,23] do not use information of a watermark in extracting processes. They
can be blind or non-blind. For example, [7,15,22,23] are blind while the others
are non-blind. Even though there are two frameworks, both share a common
concept of SVD-based watermarking, i.e. SVs are modified slightly according
to embedding rules. We can also use the positions of modified SVs as a criterion for categorization. For example, methods described in [12–14,18–20] modify
only the largest SV, but the method described in [23] modifies only some small
SVs. Methods in [7,15,17,21,22] modify all SVs. Section 5 shows the effect of
the position of modified SVs on watermarked-sound quality. It is important to
note here that Lamarche et al. have pointed out that the robustness of those in
the first framework are highly likely due to false positive rate [11]. Therefore, to
avoid such kind of problems, our proposed method is designed to be blind.

Interestingly, to the best of our knowledge, there is not much discussion about
the essence or meaning of SVs in previously SVD-based audio-watermarking
techniques. When SV is modified, which audio feature is exactly modified. The
answer does not depends only on the domain representing a signal, we believe,
but also on how a matrix is created. From the view point of SSA, the meaning of
SVs could be clearly explained. We are inspired by the robustness of SVD-based
methods and intrigued by the question of physical meaning of SV in the hope
that knowing the meaning and its relation with other physical features could
help us to overcome the conflicts in requirements of audio watermarking.

The rest of this paper is organized as follows. Section 2 introduces the background of SSA and SVD. Our proposed method is detailed in Sect. 3. Performance evaluation and experimental results are given in Sect. 4. Remarks are
made in Sect. 5. Section 6 summarizes this paper.

2   Singular-Spectrum Analysis

Singular-spectrum analysis (SSA) is a method of identifying and extracting oscillatory components from a signal [24]. There are many types of SSAs. The SSA we are going to describe in this section is called Basic SSA of which our proposed method is based on. SSA is used to decompose a signal (or time series) of interest into several additive oscillatory components. Each oscillatory component represents a simple oscillatory mode. We hypothesize that the relationship between SSA and oscillatory components is somehow similar to that between Empirical Mode Decomposition (EMD) and intrinsic mode functions.

SSA consists of two stages which involve analysis and synthesis. The decomposition stage has two decomposition steps which are *embedding* and *singular value decomposition* (SVD). It should be noted that the name of the first step has nothing to do with embedding a watermark. It is the SSA terminology. In reconstruction stage, there are also two steps which are *grouping* and *diagonal averaging*.

In the *embedding* step, a signal $X = (f_0, f_1, ..., f_{N-1})^T$ of length N is mapped to a trajectory matrix $\boldsymbol{X}$ of size $L \times K$.

$$\boldsymbol{X} = \begin{bmatrix} f_0 & f_1 & f_2 & \cdots & f_{K-1} \\ f_1 & f_2 & f_3 & \cdots & f_K \\ f_2 & f_3 & f_4 & \cdots & f_{K+1} \\ \vdots & \vdots & \vdots & \ddots & \vdots \\ f_{L-1} & f_L & f_{L+1} & \cdots & f_{N-1} \end{bmatrix} \tag{1}$$

Each column vector of $\boldsymbol{X}$ is called a lagged vector. The ith column of X, X_i, is defined as $X_i = (f_{i-1}, f_i, ..., f_{i+L-2})^T$, where L is the *window length* which has a maximum value of N. Therefore, the matrix $\boldsymbol{X}$ consists of $K = N - L + 1$ lagged vectors, i.e. $\boldsymbol{X} = [X_1 X_2 ... X_K]$. Note that L is the only parameter of Basic SSA. Since the trajectory matrix $\boldsymbol{X}$ has equal elements on the diagonals, i.e. $x_{i,j} = x_{i-1,j+1}$ where $x_{i,j}$ is an element at ith row and jth column of $\boldsymbol{X}$, it is considered to be a Hankel matrix.

For the second step, SVD is a step that decomposes a matrix $\boldsymbol{X}$ into a product of three matrices $\boldsymbol{U}$, $\boldsymbol{D}$, and $\boldsymbol{V}$ with the following relationship.

$$\boldsymbol{X} = \boldsymbol{U} \boldsymbol{D} \boldsymbol{V}^T \tag{2}$$

where $\boldsymbol{X}$ is a matrix being decomposed (in this case, it is the trajectory matrix from the first step), $\boldsymbol{U}$ and $\boldsymbol{V}$ are orthogonal matrices, i.e. $\boldsymbol{U} \boldsymbol{U}^T = \boldsymbol{U}^T \boldsymbol{U} = \boldsymbol{V} \boldsymbol{V}^T = \boldsymbol{V}^T \boldsymbol{V} = \boldsymbol{I}$ where $\boldsymbol{I}$ is the identity matrix, and $\boldsymbol{D}$ is a diagonal matrix whose element is called singular value (SV). Columns of $\boldsymbol{U}$ and $\boldsymbol{V}$, U_i and V_i, which are sorted in descending order of corresponding eigenvalues, are eigenvectors of $\boldsymbol{X} \boldsymbol{X}^T$ and $\boldsymbol{X}^T \boldsymbol{X}$ respectively. Then, the elements of $\boldsymbol{D}$ are the square root of the eigenvalues. If the eigenvalues of $\boldsymbol{X} \boldsymbol{X}^T$ (or $\boldsymbol{X}^T \boldsymbol{X}$) is denoted by $\lambda_1, \lambda_2, ...,$ and λ_L, then the trajectory matrix $\boldsymbol{X}$ can be written as

$$\boldsymbol{X} = \boldsymbol{X}_1 + \boldsymbol{X}_2 + ... + \boldsymbol{X}_d \tag{3}$$

where $\boldsymbol{X}_i = \sqrt{\lambda_i}U_iV_i^T$ and $d = \max\{i,$ such that $\lambda_i > 0\}$. Each $\boldsymbol{X}_i$ represents a simple oscillatory component of the signal X.

The third step is *grouping*. In this step, the set of indices $\{1, 2, ..., d\}$ obtained from the previous step is partitioned into m disjoint subsets $I_1, I_2, ..., I_m$. Then, $\boldsymbol{X}_1, \boldsymbol{X}_2, ..., \boldsymbol{X}_d$ are grouped into m groups.

$$X = \boldsymbol{X}_{I_1} + \boldsymbol{X}_{I_2} + ... + \boldsymbol{X}_{I_m} \tag{4}$$

Since the purpose of this step is to separate the time series into meaningful additive sub-series such as trend or noise, according to separability conditions, which is not our watermarking purpose, the step is not included in our proposed method.

The last step is *diagonal averaging*. This last step transforms (*hankelizes*) each matrix $\boldsymbol{X}_{I_j}$ of the grouped decomposition into a new series of length N. The hankelization of matrix $\boldsymbol{Y}$ of dimension $L \times K$ to the series $Y = (g_0, g_1, ..., g_{N-1})^T$ is defined as follows.

$$g_k = \begin{cases} \dfrac{1}{k+1}\displaystyle\sum_{m=1}^{k+1} y^*_{m,k-m+2} & \text{for} \quad 0 \le k < L^* - 1 \\[2mm] \dfrac{1}{L^*}\displaystyle\sum_{m=1}^{L^*} y^*_{m,k-m+2} & \text{for} \quad L^* - 1 \le k < K^* \\[2mm] \dfrac{1}{N-k}\displaystyle\sum_{m=k-K^*+2}^{N-K^*+1} y^*_{m,k-m+2} & \text{for} \quad K^* \le k < N \end{cases} \tag{5}$$

where $L^* = \min(L, K)$, $K^* = \max(L, K)$, $y^*_{ij} = y_{ij}$ if $L < K$, and $y^*_{ij} = y_{ji}$ if $L \ge K$. In our proposed method, $\boldsymbol{Y}$ is a watermarked trajectory matrix, which is a trajectory matrix after its SVs are modified.

3 Proposed Method

3.1 Embedding Process

The embedding process is illustrated in Fig. 1 (left). First, an audio signal is segmented into non-overlapping frames. One bit of the watermark will be embedded into one frame. This also implies that the frame length determines embedding capacity. Then, trajectory matrices representing each frame are created, and SVD is applied on each matrix. A watermark bit is embedded by modifying SVs according to certain rules. In this work, we use simple rules similar to quantization index modulation. The rules can be summarized as follows.

Let $\{\sqrt{\lambda_1}, \sqrt{\lambda_2}, ..., \sqrt{\lambda_d}\}$ be a set of SVs in descending order, where $d = \max\{i,$ such that $\lambda_i > 0\}$, and ϵ be a small real positive number. We use the following criterion to modify values of SVs. If the watermark bit is 0, then $\sqrt{\lambda_u}, \sqrt{\lambda_{u+1}}, ...,$ and $\sqrt{\lambda_l}$ are replaced with $(1 + \epsilon)\sqrt{\lambda_{l+1}}$, and if the watermark bit is 1, then $\sqrt{\lambda_u}, \sqrt{\lambda_{u+1}}, ...,$ and $\sqrt{\lambda_l}$ are replaced with $(1 - \epsilon)\sqrt{\lambda_{u-1}}$ given that $\sqrt{\lambda_u}$ is greater than $\sqrt{\lambda_l}$.

After modifying SVs, each modified trajectory matrix is hankelized. Finally, the watermarked signal is obtained by adding those hankelized frames.

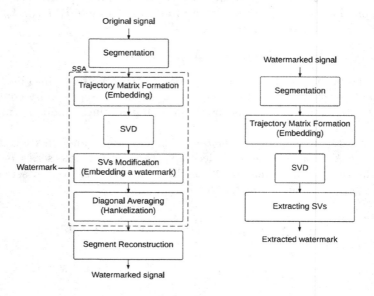

Fig. 1. Embedding and extracting processes

3.2 Extracting Process

The proposed extracting process is shown in Fig. 1 (right). The watermarked signal is segmented into non-overlapping frames. In the same way as embedding process described above, each frame is mapped to a trajectory matrix, and use SVD to extract SVs. The watermark bit is decoded by determining the value of $\sqrt{\lambda_m}$, where $\sqrt{\lambda_m}$ is the median of $\{\sqrt{\lambda_u}, \sqrt{\lambda_{u+1}}, ..., \sqrt{\lambda_l}\}$. If $\sqrt{\lambda_{u-1}} - \sqrt{\lambda_m}$ is greater than $\sqrt{\lambda_m} - \sqrt{\lambda_{l+1}}$, the watermark bit is 1. Otherwise, the watermark bit is 0.

4 Evaluation

Following the evaluation criteria suggested by the committee of Information Hiding and its Criteria (IHC) [25], this work is evaluated in two major dimensions which are objective sound-quality tests of watermarked signals and robustness tests. The perceptual evaluation of audio quality (PEAQ) which is recommended by ITU-R-BS.1387-1 is used to measure the objective different grade (ODG). PEAQ measures the degradation of the watermarked signal being evaluated comparing with the original one and covers a scale from −5 (worst) to 0 (best). IHC suggests that the ODG should be greater than −2.5.

Twelve host signals from RWC music-genre database [26] (Track No. 01, 07, 13, 28, 37, 49, 54, 57, 64, 85, 91, and 100) used in IHC's 2012 audio watermarking competition were used in our experiments. All has a sampling rate of 44.1 kHz, 16-bit quantization, and two channels (stereo). Ninety-bit payloads per 15 seconds of the host signal are embedded into the host. This allows a maximum of 6 bps of embedding capacity.

For robustness evaluation, five attacks were applied to watermarked signals: Gaussian-noise addition with average SNR of 36 dB, re-sampling with 16 and 22.05 kHz, band-pass filtering with 100-6000 Hz and -12 dB/Oct, MP3 compression with 128 kbps joint stereo, and MP4 compression with 96 kbps. We represent extraction precision in term of bit error rate (BER), which is defined by the number of bit errors divided by the total number of embedded bits. Remark that IHC suggests that the BER should be lower than 10 %.

4.1 Singular-Spectrum Analysis and Synthesis

As mentioned in Section 2, SSA can be used to decompose a signal into oscillatory components. In our experiments, the *window length* is set to 500. Figure 2 shows an example of using SSA to decompose a signal. The first panel labeled *Org* is an original signal which is zoomed to observe 300 samples. The second to sixth panels show examples of five oscillatory components corresponding to the 1st, 5th, 50th, 100th, and 200th SVs, respectively. Specifically, the waveform X_1 shown in the second panel is a result of hankelization of the matrix $\boldsymbol{X}_1 = \sqrt{\lambda_1} U_1 V_1^T$, and the waveform X_5 shown in the third panel is a result of hankelization of the matrix $\boldsymbol{X}_5 = \sqrt{\lambda_5} U_5 V_5^T$, and so on. Therefore, SV could be interpreted as a scale factor of each oscillatory component. The lower the component order, the more contribution to the signal. This is because SVs are sorted in descending order. Actually, there are more than 200 components since there are more than 200 SVs that are greater than zero as shown in Fig. 3. The first panel of Fig. 4 shows a waveform of reconstructed signal comparing to the original. The reconstructed signal is constructed from only the first 100 oscillatory components. The second panel shows a residual signal or the difference between the original and reconstructed signals. The more components are added, the smaller the residual signal is. Therefore, it is possible to modify the high-order oscillatory components without affecting sound quality significantly. In this sense, our simple rules are corresponding to changing scale factors of certain components. Figure 5 shows an example of waveform when embedding bit *1* and bit *0* into X_{35}. It can be seen clearly from this example that what is modified is the scale factor of the component waveform.

Although the residual signal is very small when all oscillatory components are added up, it might exists. Thus, we first check ODGs of synthesis signals comparing to the originals. The result is shown in Fig. 6 (light gray). The sound quality of synthesis signals is not different from that of originals.

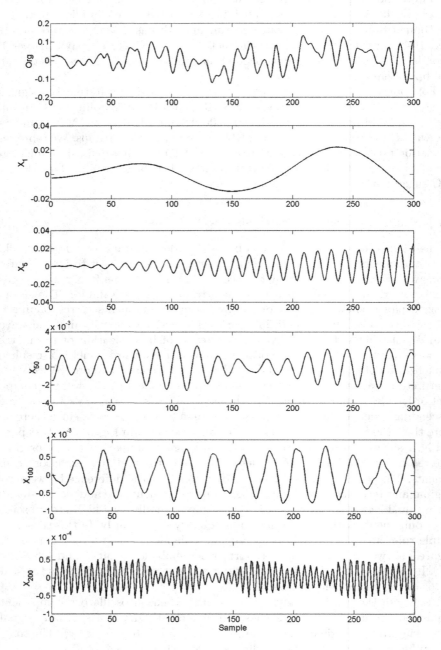

Fig. 2. An example of using SSA to decompose a signal

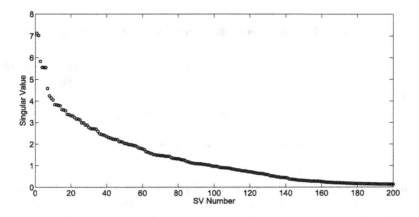

Fig. 3. Singular spectrum (The rst 200 SVs)

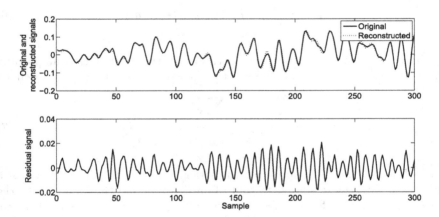

Fig. 4. Original and reconstructed signals (top), Residual signal or the difference between original and reconstructed signals (bottom)

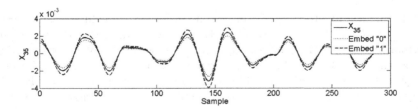

Fig. 5. Embed "0" and "1" into the component X_{35}

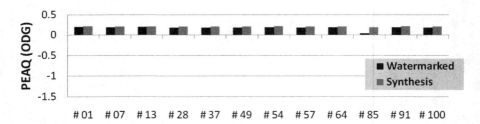

Fig. 6. ODGs of watermarked and synthesis signals

In addition to PEAQ, the log-spectral distance (LSD) and the signal-to-error ratio (SER) were also performed. LSD is a distance or distortion measure between two spectra, which is defined as the following formula given $P(\omega)$ and $\hat{P}(\omega)$ are power spectra of original and synthesis signals respectively.

$$\text{LSD} = \sqrt{\frac{1}{2\pi} \int_{-\pi}^{\pi} \left[10 \log \frac{P(\omega)}{\hat{P}(\omega)} \right]^2 d\omega} \tag{6}$$

SER is the power ratio between a signal and the error. Given amplitudes $A_{\text{sig}}(n)$ and $A_{\text{syn}}(n)$ of original and synthesis signals respectively, SER is defined as follows.

$$\text{SER} = 10 \log \frac{\sum_{n} [A_{\text{sig}}(n)]^2}{\sum_{n} [A_{\text{sig}}(n) - A_{\text{syn}}(n)]^2} \tag{7}$$

The Eqs. (6) and (7) imply that the lower LSD, the power spectrum of a synthesis signal is more similar to that of an original, and the higher SER, the lower error. Therefore, for a perfect reconstruction, the ideal value of LSD is zero, and the ideal value of SER is infinity. The results from our experiment confirm that LSD between any pair of original and a synthesis signals is zero, and SER is inf. Thus, the framework of singular-spectrum analysis-synthesis could be used in audio watermarking.

4.2   Objective Sound-Quality Test

The following parameters are chosen for the proposed embedding rules: $\epsilon = 0.1$, $u = 21$, and $l = 49$, i.e. the 21st to 49th SVs are modified with respect to a watermark bit as described in Sect. 3. Figure 6 shows ODGs of watermarked signals together with ODGs of synthesis signals. From the viewpoint of PEAQ, we can say that our proposed method introduces very small distortion to the sound quality. LSD and SER between original and watermarked signals are shown in Fig. 7. The results indicate that our proposed method satisfies inaudibility criterion.

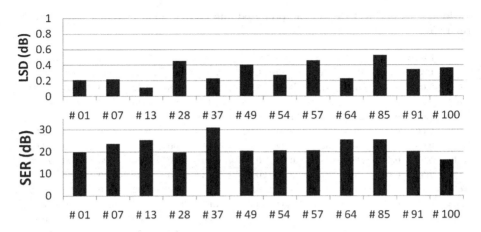

Fig. 7. Log-spectral distance and Signal-to-Error ratio of watermarked signals

4.3   Robustness Test

The results of robustness tests are shown in Table 1. The proposed method is robust against MP3 and MP4 compression, Gaussian-noise addition, band-pass filtering and re-sampling. Furthermore, in order to compare robustness against certain attacks, we implemented the scheme based on [15], which will refer as a conventional method in this paper. The proposed method is more robust against MP3 compression and band-pass filtering than the conventional method.

5   Discussion

The results from our investigation suggest that the robustness could be improved if lower-order oscillatory components are modified instead of the higher-order ones. For example, the robustness against MP3 attack of the proposed scheme increases, as shown in Fig. 9, if values of the 2nd to 9th SVs, instead of the 21st to 49th SVs, are modified to embed a watermark. However, the sound quality of watermarked signals decreases as shown in Fig. 10. It reveals a trade-off between robustness and inaudibility.

Besides the position of modified SVs, the other point we would like to discuss here is the number of SVs which ranges from u to l. If the number of modified SVs increases, then the robustness increases. It is possible that we can keep ODG while BER is decreasing, especially in the case of high orders. For example, when we modify the 51st to 89th SVs, we have an average BER of 13.26 % for MP3 attack. If we set l to 99, we will have the average BER of 10.83 %, and for both cases the average ODG is around 0.18. Therefore, one way to improve the proposed scheme is choosing these parameters appropriately.

We also evaluated the robustness against single-echo addition. It is not a general attack of watermark. We found that both conventional and proposed methods are not robust against this attack as shown in Fig. 8. Because both

Table 1. Comparing BERs of the proposed and conventional methods when attacks are applied

	No Attack		MP3 Attack		AWGN		MP4 Attack		Re-sampling		BP Filtering	
	Prop.	Conv.	Prop.	Conv.	Prop.	Conv.	Prop.	Conv.	Prop.	Conv.	Prop.	Conv.
#01	0.00	0.00	1.67	47.22	0.00	0.00	0.00	0.28	0.42	3.19	1.67	25.83
#07	3.33	0.00	4.17	98.33	3.33	0.00	4.17	0.00	3.75	0.42	4.17	48.61
#13	1.67	0.00	21.67	70.56	1.67	0.00	15.00	13.89	16.67	25.69	36.67	47.78
#28	0.00	0.00	0.00	87.78	0.00	0.00	0.00	0.00	0.00	0.00	0.83	43.61
#37	0.00	0.00	2.50	82.50	0.00	0.00	1.67	0.00	2.50	0.00	5.00	56.67
#49	0.00	0.00	0.83	33.06	0.00	0.00	0.00	0.00	0.00	0.00	0.00	21.39
#54	2.50	0.00	5.83	41.94	2.50	0.00	3.33	0.00	2.08	0.00	4.17	40.56
#57	4.17	0.00	4.17	33.61	4.17	0.00	5.83	0.00	2.92	0.00	10.00	28.89
#64	0.83	0.00	2.50	95.83	0.83	0.00	1.67	0.00	1.25	0.28	2.50	62.22
#85	0.00	0.00	0.00	18.89	0.00	0.00	0.00	0.00	0.00	0.83	0.83	0.83
#91	2.50	0.00	5.00	74.72	2.50	0.00	4.17	0.00	1.67	0.14	5.83	50.56
#100	0.83	0.00	1.67	23.61	0.83	0.00	0.00	0.28	1.25	1.53	0.83	30.00
AV	1.32	0.00	4.17	59.00	1.32	0.00	2.99	1.20	2.70	2.67	6.04	38.08
SD	1.48	0.00	5.83	29.04	1.48	0.00	4.30	3.40	4.56	7.31	10.05	17.30

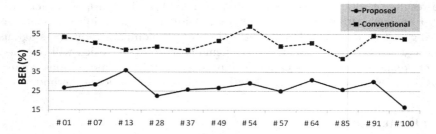

Fig. 8. Comparing BERs of the proposed and conventional methods when single-echo addition with delay time of 100 ms, $-6\,$dB is applied

are time-domain based methods where matrices are created directly from the waveform, thus time-domain processing affects the elements of those matrices in a significant way.

We have verified that our proposed scheme can extend capacity from 6 to 18 bps without affecting both sound quality and a detection rate. The maximum capacity of the proposed scheme given preferred sound quality is determined by N. It could be increased if the parameters such as L, u, l, and ϵ are chosen appropriately similar to a way to improve robustness.

Finally, this is a frame-based method, thus there also exists a problem of frame synchronization. The current proposed scheme assumes to know where to look for hidden information. One possible solution to this problem is using synchronization codes [27,28]. Moreover, in our experiments, we do not claim that the parameters, such as N, L, u, l, and ϵ, are the optimal ones. These are the subjects of our future works.

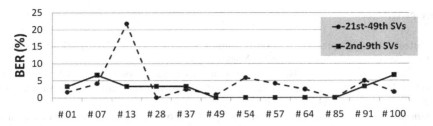

Fig. 9. Comparing BERs, after MP3 attack is applied, when lower-order components are modified to hide information

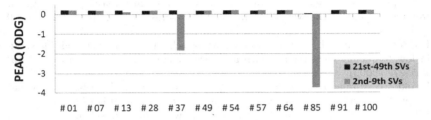

Fig. 10. Comparing ODGs when lower-order components are modified to hide information

6   Conclusion

This paper presented our investigation on deploying SSA for hiding information and proposed audio watermarking scheme based on it. SSA was used to decompose a signal into oscillatory components. Controlling the scale factors which can be done by modifying SVs of some components is the important procedure to embed a watermark. In this SSA view point, we can interpret the physical meaning of SV. We discover that SSA is a perfect analysis-synthesis tool. Although the proposed scheme is robust against many attacks especially MP3 and MP4 compression and satisfies inaudibility criterion, it still has a drawback that involves in audio watermark, for example, it is fragile to single-echo addition. The proposed method is a time-domain SSA-based method so that it seems to be robust against frequency domain processing. Our next interests are as follows: whether a frequency-domain (amplitude and phase spectra) SSA-based method will be robust against time-domain processing such as single-echo addition, and whether a hybrid SSA-based method of time- and frequency-domain will offer a solution to inaudible and robust audio watermarking.

Acknowledgments. This work was supported by a Grant-in-Aid for Scientific Research (B) (No. 23300070) and an A3 foresight program made available by the Japan Society for the Promotion of Science, and under a grant in the SIIT-JAIST-NECTEC Dual Doctoral Degree Program.

References

1. Dutoit, T., Marques, F.: Applied Signal Processing: A MATLAB (TM)-Based Proof of Concept. Springer, New York (2009)
2. Craver, S., Wu, M., Liu, B.: What can we reasonably expect from watermarks? In: IEEE Workshop on Application of Signal Processing to Audio and Acoustics, pp. 223–226. IEEE Press, New York (2001)
3. Unoki, M., Miyauchi, R.: Method of digital-audio watermarking based on cochlear delay characteristics. In: Kondo, K. (ed.) Multimedia Information Hiding Technologies and Methodologies for Controlling Data, pp. 42–70. Information Science Reference, United States (2013)
4. Fallahpour, M., Megias, D.: High capacity audio watermarking using the high frequency band of the wavelet domain. J. Multimed. Tools. Appl. 52(2–3), 485–498 (2011)
5. Ercelebi, E., Batakci, L.: Audio watermarking scheme based on embedding strategy in low frequency components with a binary image. Digit. Signal. Process. 19(2), 265–277 (2009)
6. Unoki, M., Hamada, D.: Method of digital-audio watermarking based on cochlear delay characteristics. Int. J. Innov. Comput. I. 6(3), 1325–1346 (2010)
7. Bhat, V., Sengupta, I., Das, A.: A new audio watermarking scheme based on singular value decomposition and quantization. Circ. Syst. Signal. Pr. 30(5), 915–927 (2011)
8. Özer, H., Sankur, B., Memon, N.: An SVD-based audio watermarking technique. In: 7th Workshop on Multimedia and Security, pp. 51–56. IEEE Press, New York (2005)
9. El-Samie, F.: An efficient singular value decomposition algorithm for digital audio watermarking. Int. J. Speech. Technol. 12(1), 27–45 (2009)
10. Vongpraphip, S., Ketcham, M.: An intelligence audio watermarking based on DWT-SVD using ATS. In: WRI Global Conference on Intelligence Systems, pp. 150–154. IEEE Press, New York (2009)
11. Lamarche, L., Liu, Y., Zhao, J.: Flaw in SVD-based watermarking. In: Canadian Conference on Electrical and Computer Engineering, pp. 2082–2085. IEEE Press, New York (2006)
12. Al-Haj, A., Twal, C., Mohammad, A.: Hybrid DWT-SVD audio watermarking. In: 5th International Conference on Digital Information Management, pp. 525–529. IEEE Press, New York (2010)
13. Al-Haj, A., Mohammad, A.: Digital audio watermarking based on the discrete wavelets transform and singular value decomposition. Eur. J. Sci. Res. 39(1), 6–21 (2010)
14. Al-Yaman, M., Al-Taee, M., Alshammas, H.: Audio-watermarking based ownership verification system using en-hanced DWT-SVD technique. International Multi-Conference on Systems, Signals and Devices, pp. 1–5. IEEE Press, New York (2012)
15. Bhat, V., Sengupta, I., Das, A.: An audio watermarking scheme using singular value decomposition and dither-modulation quantization. J. Multimed. Tools. Appl. 52(2–3), 269–283 (2011)
16. Zhang, J.: Analysis on audio watermarking algorithm based on SVD. In: 2nd International Conference on Computer Science and Network Technology, pp. 1986–1989. IEEE Press, New York (2012)

17. Singhal, A., Chaubey, A., Prakkash, C.: Audio watermarking using combination of multilevel wavelet decomposition, DCT and SVD. In: International Conference on Emerging Trends in Networks and Computer Communications, pp. 239–243. IEEE Press, New York (2011)

18. Dhar, P., Shimamura, T.: Audio watermarking in transform domain based on singular value decomposition and quantization. In: 18th Asia-Pacific Conference on Communications, pp. 516–521. IEEE Press, New York (2012)

19. Dhar, P., Shimamura, T.: An audio watermarking scheme using discrete fourier transformation and singular value decomposition. In: 35th International Conference on Telecommunications and Signal Processing, pp. 789–794. IEEE Press, New York (2012)

20. Dhar, P., Shimamura, T.: A DWT-DCT-based audio watermarking method using singular value decomposition and quantization. J. Signal. Process. **17**(3), 69–79 (2013)

21. Suresh, G.: An efficient and simple audio watermarking using DCT-SVD. In: International Conference on Devices, Circuits and System, pp. 177–181. IEEE Press, New York (2012)

22. Karimimehr, S., Samavi, S., Kaviani, H., Mahdavi, M.: Robust audio watermarking based on HWD and SVD. In: 20th Iranian Conference on Electrical Engineering, pp. 1363–1367. IEEE Press, New York (2012)

23. Jiang, W.: Fragile audio watermarking algorithm based on SVD and DWT. In: International Conference on Intelligence Computing and Integrated Systems, pp. 83–86. IEEE Press, New York (2010)

24. Golyandina, N., Nekrutkin, V., Zhigljavsky, A.: Analysis of Time Series Structure: SSA and related techniques. Chapman and Hall/CRC, United States (2001)

25. Information Hiding and its Criteria for evaluation. http://www.ieice.org/emm/ihc/en/

26. RWC Music Database. https://staff.aist.go.jp/m.goto/RWC-MDB/

27. Wu, S., Huang, J.: Efficiently self-synchronized audio watermarking for assured audio data transmission. IEEE Trans. Broadcast. **51**(1), 69–76 (2005)

28. Lei, B.: Robust SVD-based audio watermarking scheme with differential evolution optimization. IEEE Trans. Audio, Speech, Language Process **21**(11), 2368–2378 (2013)

Superpixel-Based Watermarking Scheme for Image Authentication and Recovery

Xiumei Qiao, Rongrong Ni[✉], and Yao Zhao[✉]

Institute of Information Science,
Beijing Key Laboratory of Advanced Information Science
and Network Technology, Beijing Jiaotong University, Beijing 100044, China
{12120347, rrni, yzhao}@bjtu.edu.cn

Abstract. Based on the superpixel segmentation mechanism, a novel fragile watermarking scheme for image authentication and recovery is proposed. For each superpixel region, the authentication watermark is generated by putting the pixels into a feedback-based chaotic system and embedded into the region itself. The content of each superpixel is compressed to construct the recovery watermark, which is embedded into another selected superpixel. To extract the authentication and recovery watermark properly, the superpixel boundaries are marked. The reliability of a superpixel is first determined by its authentication watermark. To improve detection accuracy, the recovery watermark extracted from authentic superpixels is utilized for precise detection. Moreover, the recovery information extracted from authentic superpixels is decompressed to recover the tampered regions. Experimental results demonstrate that the proposed method can not only resist general counterfeiting attacks, especially vector quantization (VQ) attack, but also has an excellent performance on location accuracy and self-recovery.

Keywords: Superpixels · Chaotic system · Precise detection · Authentication · Self-recovery · VQ attack · Watermarking

1 Introduction

Along with the rapid development of public powerful image processing software packages and digital technologies, it becomes difficult to check the authenticity of an image. When a part of the original content is changed by malicious tampers, it is desirable to detect the modified regions. At present, many researchers use watermarking techniques to leave detectable traces in host images to protect the integrity and authenticity of digital images [1].

To locate the tamper position, fragile watermarking strategies often divide a host image into blocks of the same size. In Wong's scheme [2], the messages of the most significant bits of an image block are embedded into the least significant bits of the same block by a public key. Nevertheless, block-wise independence makes most block-wise methods vulnerable to the vector quantization (VQ) attack [3], which can construct a counterfeit image by using a VQ codebook. Since the reliability of each image block is determined by itself, these schemes are so susceptible to the counterfeiting attack that they fail to detect and locate the genuine tampered blocks.

© Springer International Publishing Switzerland 2015
Y.-Q. Shi et al. (Eds.): IWDW 2014, LNCS 9023, pp. 160–173, 2015.
DOI: 10.1007/978-3-319-19321-2_12

To cope with such a counterfeit attack problem, as pointed in Ref. [3], the key is to remove the block-wise independence property by making the watermark related with a set of blocks in the image. So, some schemes are proposed to build a relationship between blocks. Celik et al. [4] proposed a method which used the hierarchical structure to divide the image into a multilevel hierarchy to locate tampered region. Suthaharan proposed a watermarking scheme with the properties of gradient image and bits distribution [5]. Besides, Chen et al. [6] applied the fuzzy c-means (FCM) clustering technique to cluster all the image blocks to create the relationship between image blocks.

Another concern is the quality of recovered images. In 2005, a hierarchical digital watermarking method for detection and recovery was proposed by Lin et al. [7]. They produced a one-to-one block mapping sequence by a secret key and the recovery watermark was generated by encoding the average of block. Li et al. [8] proposed a method based on dual-redundant-ring structure, which could form a block train and utilize redundant insertion to improve the security and the restoration.

To improve the tamper detection accuracy and the recovery quality, He et al. [9] combined average encoding with VQ encoding. This method employed a secret key to obtain two mapping block sequences [7] and the binary random sequence to encrypt average code and VQ code. However, because its VQ watermark is only based on high-frequency component, this scheme is not resistant enough to VQ attack, especially for smooth images.

In summary, these schemes mentioned above usually employ the regular square blocks as embedding units. Sometimes, the detection and localization results are ambiguous because of the relationship between these blocks. Even though the block mapping can improve security, miss-matches unavoidably happen, which results in the decrease of detection performance. To overcome the main drawbacks of such methods, we fall back on superpixels [10–14], which represent small regions with homogeneous appearance and a restricted form of local image segmentation. To the best of our knowledge, however, almost no one has used superpixels to protect the integrity and authenticity of image in the field of watermarking.

Most existing fragile watermark methods usually divide an image into some regular square blocks of the same size, which ignores the image content. On the contrary, the superpixel is superior to single pixel and prior regular block, because it can develop irregular regions by grouping a series of pixels with adjacent position and similar features. Thus, local appearance characteristics and spatial relations can be captured.

In our work, a novel authentication and recovery watermarking scheme based on superpixels is proposed. Using the superpixel segmentation technique, a host image is segmented into appropriate number of irregular regions with approximately uniform size and shape in order to remove the block-wise independence. Then, the authentication watermark is generated on the basis of contents within each superpixel, and is embedded in itself to detect the malicious manipulations. Meanwhile, the compressed content of the superpixel is regarded as the recovery watermark which is used for fine localization and the recovery of the tampered regions. Besides, the superpixel boundaries are marked as a portion of watermark to re-segment the image during extraction and recovery. The authentication watermark is used to detect tampered superpixels, and the recovery watermark is extracted from authentic superpixels to conduct precise detection of tampered superpixels and then recover the tampered regions. Experimental results are presented to demonstrate that our scheme not only optimizes the performance of tamper detection, but also obtains the recovered image with a good quality.

The outline of this paper is organized as follows. In Sect. 2, we describe the watermarking scheme, including watermark generation and embedding procedure. Then, the tamper detection and self-recovery process are explained in Sect. 3. Subsequently, in Sect. 4, some experimental results are given, followed by the conclusion in Sect. 5.

2   Watermark Generation and Embedding Procedure

Denote an original 8-bit gray image as X, whose size is $m \times n$. The flow chart of watermark embedding procedure is shown in Fig. 1.

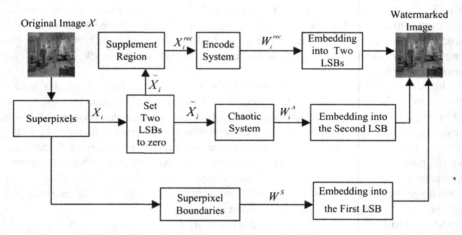

Fig. 1. Flow chart of watermarking embedding procedure

Different from most existing fragile watermarking schemes, in this paper, the watermark data are made up of three parts that will be used respectively: one is for the superpixel boundaries, another is for tampered superpixels localization, and the last one is for precise detection and content recovery. At first, the original image is segmented into some superpixel regions. Next, the superpixel boundaries are marked in the first least significant bit (LSB) plane, and the marked locations are used to generate the superpixel boundary watermark W^S. Then, for each superpixel X_i, after the two LSBs are set as zero, the pixels are fed into a chaotic system to generate authentication watermark W_i^A, which is embedded in the second LSB of the superpixel itself. Finally, the content of X_i is compressed to produce recovery watermark W_i^{rec}, which is embedded into another selected superpixel. Note that the two least significant bits (LSBs) of the pixels are replaced by the watermark data while the original image data in the six most significant bit (MSB) layers are kept unchanged.

2.1   Image Segmentation Based on Superpixels

In the proposed scheme, we would like to obtain the superpixels with approximately uniform size and shape to embed data beneficially. Thereby, we adopt TurboPixels, a geometric-flow-based algorithm proposed by Levinshtein et al. in [14]. On one hand, it limits under-segmentation through a compactness constraint; on the other hand, it respects local boundaries, as shown in Fig. 2. Furthermore, it is fast and allows the user to control the superpixel's shape and density. The algorithm starts from initial seeds regularly placed onto the image, and employs the level set method for superpixels' evolution. The detailed steps of generating superpixels refer to Ref. [14].

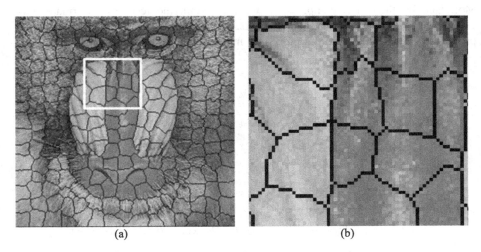

(a)   (b)

Fig. 2. Superpixel segmentation of image "Baboon": (a) The segmentation obtained by TurboPixels, (b) The zooms in on the regions defined by the white rectangle.

Denote the number of seeds is M, that is to say the original image will be divided into M superpixel regions. Then the original image X is segmented into M superpixels by TurboPixels method, and each superpixel is labeled by X_i, $1 \le i \le M$. In addition, the superpixel boundaries are marked and the marked locations are used to generate W^S, which needs to be embedded into the LSB plane.

Note that each pixel on the superpixel boundary is connected with those boundary pixels in its 3×3 neighborhood, as shown in Fig. 2(b). This connectivity [16] characteristic can help identify the superpixel boundary in watermark extraction.

2.2   Construction of Authentication Watermark

Considering the reliability of tamper detection, we utilize a blend optical bi-stable chaotic system with feedback [15] to generate a pseudorandom sequence. Because the chaotic system is sensitive to the initial input value, small content change can make a great difference to the output, which improves the security. In the superpixel X_i, suppose there are K_i pixels within it and S_i pixels on its superpixel boundary, so the total number of pixels in X_i is $L = (K_i + S_i)$. After the two LSBs are set to zero, these L pixels enter the chaotic system in turn. For each pixel, the chaotic system will run iterations for T times and the feedback value is used to compute the initial value for the first iteration of the next pixel. In this way, a sequence values are generated when the last pixel is dealt with, and they are converted to binary values, from which the last 10 bits are selected as the authentication watermark W_i^A.

2.3   Construction of Recovery Watermark

Motivated by the JPEG compression, we can obtain the recovery information by compressing the important DCT coefficients. In Fig. 3, the recovery data construction procedure is presented. And the procedure mainly includes the following two steps.

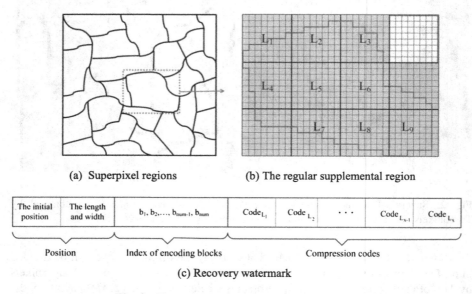

(a) Superpixel regions   (b) The regular supplemental region

(c) Recovery watermark

Fig. 3. The recovery data construction procedure

Step 1. Switching Superpixels' Shape. Since the superpixel regions are irregular before encoding operation, it is necessary to switch their shapes to regular ones. Suppose a host image is divided into 8×8 non-overlapping blocks, and denoted as $B = \{B_j \mid j = 1, 2,\ldots, m \times n/64\}$.

As shown in Fig. 3(b), the red line represents the boundary of X_i and each small lattice represents a pixel. Firstly, the number of pixels, which are included in both X_i and B_j, is computed by,

$$c_{i,j} = count(X_i \cap B_j)\ i \in \{1, 2, \ldots, M\}, j \in \{1, 2, \ldots, m \times n/64\} \qquad (1)$$

where *count (.)* is the cardinality of the set. If $c_{i,j}$ is not equal to zero, X_i' as the extended version of X_i will include the block B_j. In Fig. 3(b), the extended region X_i' is shown in yellow. Then, if X_i' is not a rectangle, it needs to be supplemented to a rectangular region X_i^{rec}, which is a minimum external rectangle of X_i'. In Fig. 3(b), the region with blue border line is X_i^{rec}. Secondly, taking into account the capacity of recovery information, we would like to compress each block B_j for only once. However, the B_j including the pixels on the superpixel boundary may be contained in more than one superpixel's rectangular region. Under this situation, block B_j only belongs to a specific rectangular region X_i^{rec}, if $c_{i,j}$ referring to X_i^{rec} and B_j satisfies the formula (2).

$$c_{i,j} > c_{i',j} \quad i, i' \in \{1, \ldots, M\} \text{ and } \quad i' \neq i \tag{2}$$

Thus, these blocks along the superpixel boundary are guaranteed to be compressed only once. In Fig. 3(b), the final selected blocks to be compressed are $L_1 \sim L_9$ in X_i^{rec}. The position of the selected blocks is recorded in recovery information.

Step.2 Recovery Information Encoding. As shown in Fig. 3(c), the recovery information to be embedded includes three portions: the position information, the index of selected blocks and the compression codes. For each corresponding rectangular region of superpixel, the position information is composed of two parts: the position of the 8×8 block at top-left and the region's height and width measured by 8×8 blocks. The index of a selected block indicates whether the block needs to be encoded, where '1' represents the block needs to be encoded and '0' is opposite. The length of indexes *num* is the number of 8×8 blocks in the rectangular region, while the order of indexes is arranged from left to right, top to bottom. For example, as presented in Fig. 3(b), the height is 3, the width is 4, and the indexes are '1 1 1 0 1 1 1 0 0 1 1 1'. The compression codes are followed. In Fig. 3(c), *x* is the number of selected blocks of X_i^{rec}, and each selected block is transformed into 64 DCT coefficients after their two LSBs are set to zero. These coefficients are quantized according to a predefined quantization table of acceptable quality. And Huffman encoding method is used to generate the recovery data stream. Hence, the recovery watermark W_i^{rec} of superpixel X_i is generated.

In the process of switching the superpixels' shape to the regular one, the length of recovery information may increase because of adding a small part of inhomogeneous content. However, it has a subtle effect on the watermark embedding.

2.4 Watermark Embedding

The resulting watermark covers three portions: the authentication watermark, the superpixel boundary watermark and the recovery watermark. They will be embedded into appropriate places in sequence.

At first, for superpixel X_i, the authentication watermark W_i^A is embedded into its second LSBs. And the rest of the second LSBs are available to embed the recovery watermark W_i^{rec}. Secondly, the first LSBs of the pixels on the superpixel boundary are set to one, that is to say, the watermark W_i^S has been embedded in the first LSBs, as shown in Fig. 4. Thirdly, the available first LSBs are selected to embed the recovery watermark W_i^{rec} as well.

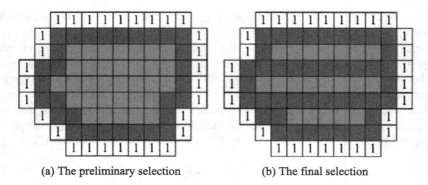

(a) The preliminary selection   (b) The final selection

Fig. 4. The procedure of selecting the available first LSB, in which superpixel boundary labeled as '1', available LSBs marked in red and unavailable LSBs marked in blue (Colour figure online)

Since the superpixel boundaries have been marked in the first LSB plane of the image, the recovery information is embedded without affecting the extraction of original superpixel boundary. The pixels within superpixels and on the superpixel boundary have connectivity characteristic [16]: the boundaries of the superpixel X_i are 8-connected and the pixels within X_i are 4-connected. With the purpose of identifying the superpixel boundary from the embedded watermark, for each pixel on the superpixel boundary, the pixels in the 3 × 3 neighborhood are unavailable, which are labeled in blue. Those pixels labeled in red are preliminary selections, as presented in Fig. 4(a). In addition, to prevent confusing with the superpixel boundary, the embedded watermark cannot compose a closed region. Therefore, the available LSBs are selected every other line. Thus, the available LSBs to embed information are obtained, which are labeled in red, as shown in Fig. 4(b). Those unavailable LSBs labeled in blue are set to zero to distinguish superpixel boundary and prevent the embedding data enclosed. Those available first LSBs combine the available second LSBs to compose embedding capacity for recovery information.

Finally, the recovery watermark of superpixel is embedded into another selected superpixel. To make sure the recovery watermark can be embedded as completely as possible, two superpixel sequences are created. The first one is sorted in descending order by the length of compressed recovery information, while the second one is sorted in the same way according to the embedding capacity. Then, superpixels in the first sequence are mapped to those in the second sequence with the same descending order. As a result, the one-to-one mapping correspondence has been constructed. If a superpixel X_i is just mapped to itself, we exchange X_i and its adjacent superpixel to avoid this case happening. The recovery watermark W_i^{rec} is preferentially embedded into the available first LSB, then into the available second LSBs of its mapping superpixel region.

It is possible that some recovery data cannot be embedded completely if the recovery data are too large. However, the lost data are a small part of the image region, so the recovery quality of tampered image is still good.

3   Tamper Detection and Recovery

Suppose an attacker may only change the content of a watermarked image without altering the image size. Denote the suspicious image as Y. As shown in Fig. 5, the tamper detection and recovery procedure is composed of the following steps.

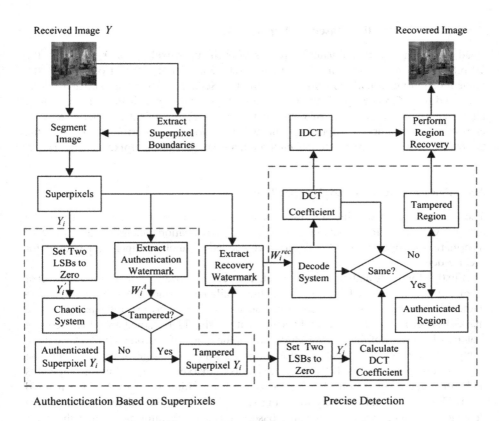

Fig. 5. The tamper detection and recovery procedure

3.1   Extraction of the Superpixel Boundaries

In order to resynchronize the authentication and recovery watermark with those in the embedding procedure, the superpixel boundary should be extracted firstly.

Firstly, read the first least significant bit-plane (*LSBP*) of the image Y. Since the LSBs of pixels on the superpixel boundary are set as '1' during embedding. It needs to identify which pixels with '1' in the LSB are on the superpixel boundary. Secondly, the pixels whose value is zero in *LSBP* are merged into several connected components based on 4-connected rule. At the same time, different labels are assigned to these connected components. Thirdly, for each pixel whose LSB is '1', it is considered to be on the superpixel boundary if those zeros in its 3 × 3 neighborhood have more than one label. This is because the LSBs of those pixels adjacent to superpixel boundaries have been set as zero in the embedding procedure, and these pixels don't come from the same superpixel. As a result, those pixels which have different labels of '0' in the 3 × 3 neighborhood are on the superpixel boundary. Then, the image can be segmented into superpixels by the superpixel boundary.

3.2   Tamper Detection Based on Superpixels

Read the second least significant bit-planes of each superpixel region Y_i to extract the 10 bits authentication watermark. We can produce a reference signal of Y_i using the authentication watermark construction method in Sect. 2.2. Then the extracted watermark and the reference signal are compared to decide whether Y_i is tampered or not. If all elements of the two sets of data are the same, Y_i is authentic; otherwise, Y_i is considered as a tampered superpixel and will be marked as an error. As a result, the tampered superpixels are marked, even though a small part of superpixels are tampered.

3.3   Precise Detection and Tamper Recovery

The marked superpixels include not only the genuine tampered regions, but also the regions without being tampered. To improve the location accuracy, the recovery information of one tampered superpixel embedded in another superpixel is used for precise detection.

Firstly, for each authentic superpixel, the recovery watermark is prior extracted from the available first LSBs and then the available second LSBs. Secondly, each authentic superpixels is inspected to decide whether the recovery information of the marked superpixels has been embedded in it. It should be noted that the recovery watermark consists of the position information, the index of compressed blocks and the compression codes. The position information indicates the range of region where the original superpixel locates. If there are the pixels of marked superpixel in the range, this authentic superpixel is considered as a recovery matching superpixel of the marked ones. Thirdly, after all recovery matching superpixels have been detected, the precise detection and recovery are conducted based on the index information and the compression codes. For each recovery matching superpixel, the index is utilized to identify which blocks have been encoded in the range of region indicated by the position information. In addition, the compression codes are decoded into DCT coefficients which are arranged according to the index. In the suspicious image Y, after the two LSBs are set to zero, each 8 × 8 block containing the pixels within the marked superpixels is transformed into 64 DCT coefficients which will be quantized according to the predefined quantization table. Then, for each block, these quantitative DCT coefficients are compared with the corresponding decoded ones to decide whether the marked pixels in the block are tampered. If the two set of DCT coefficients are the same, the marked pixels in the block are authentic and their marks will be removed; otherwise, they are regarded as genuine tampered pixels. To recover the tampered pixels, IDCT operation will be performed on the relevant decoded DCT coefficients to generate 8 × 8 block whose pixels will replace the corresponding marked pixels.

Thus, the precise detection to the suspicious image is completed and the recovered image of good quality is achieved.

4 Experimental Results

We perform a series of experiments to demonstrate the efficiency of the proposed scheme. Some 256×256 gray images are used as our test images.

To evaluate the performance, the probability of false acceptance (PFA) and the probability of false rejection (PFR) are introduced. They are defined as

$$\text{PFA}: \quad P_{fa} = \left(1 - N_{tp}/N_t\right) \times 100\% \tag{3}$$

$$\text{PFR}: \quad P_{fr} = N_{ft}/(N - N_t) \times 100\% \tag{4}$$

where N denotes the number of image pixels in the test image, N_t is the number of actually tampered pixels, N_{tp} is the number of tampered pixels which are correctly detected, and N_{ft} is the number of pixels which are falsely detected as tampered.

An image "House" is used to demonstrate our scheme can resist general collage attack effectively. Before watermark is embedded, an original image is segmented into superpixels, which is displayed in Fig. 6(a). Since we only use the two least significant bits to embed watermark, the watermarked image is visually almost the same with the original one. After the watermark has been embedded, the watermarked image whose PSNR is 45.74 dB, is shown in Fig. 6(b). The attacker removes the person of the test

(a) Segmentation of original image   (b) Watermarked image   (c) Tampered image

(d) Authentication based on superpixels   (e) Tamper detection   (f) Recovered image

Fig. 6. The authenticated and recovered image for "House"

image to another place and uses its surrounding content to fill this region, as is presented in Fig. 6(c). When detecting the modified image, the superpixel boundaries are extracted to segment the image into superpixels. These superpixels are authenticated and the tampered ones are marked in white, as shown in Fig. 6(d). Then, recovery information is used to conduct precise detection, as we can see in Fig. 6(e). Finally, the tampered regions are recovered with PSNR 42.91 dB in Fig. 6(f).

Another two images "Lena" and "Couple" are tested to further certify our scheme's superior performance on resisting conventional VQ attack. An attacker can forge an image by selecting some blocks from a code book to replace the original blocks. Figure 7 shows the tampered results and the recovered images for "Lena", and Fig. 8 for "Couple". Figure 7(a) presents a watermarked image for "Lena", whose PSNR is

Fig. 7. Original image and tampered detection for "Lena". (a) Watermarked image, (b) The tampered image under VQ attack, (c) Tamper detection results and (d) Recovered image by He's method [9], (e) The authentication based on superpixels, (f) Precise detection and (g) the recovered image by the proposed method

44.16 dB in He's method and 46.00 dB in our method. Figure 8(a) shows a water-marked image for "Couple", whose PSNR is 44.19 dB in He's method and 45.57 dB in our method. Figures 7(b) and 8(b) show the tampered image under conventional VQ attack, in which the region surrounded by a red line is replaced by several 4 × 4 blocks from the code book based on the watermarked image itself. The results of tamper detection are presented by He's [9] method in Figs. 7(c) and 8(c) and by our method in Figs. 7(f) and 8(f). Obviously, the proposed method has a better performance of resisting conventional VQ attack.

The performance comparison of tamper detection and recovery under conventional VQ attack is surveyed on the watermarked images "Lena" and "Couple". Table 1 presents the results in terms of PFA, PFR, and PSNR. He's method cannot effectively

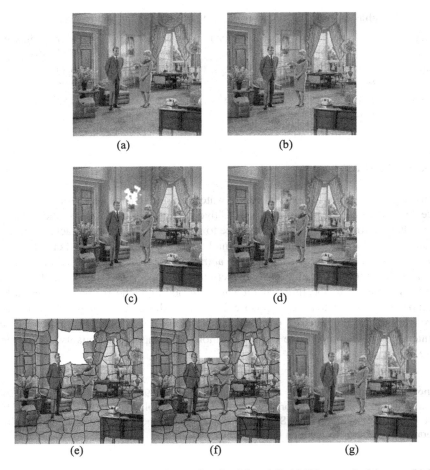

(a)   (b)

(c)   (d)

(e)   (f)   (g)

Fig. 8. Original image and tampered detection for "Couple". (a) Watermarked image, (b) The tampered image under VQ attack, (c) Tamper detection results and (d) Recovered image by He's method [9], (e) The authentication based on superpixel, (f) Precise detection and (g) the recovered image by the proposed method

resist conventional VQ attack for smooth images, indicated by the higher PFA of 70.75 % and 60.25 %. In contrast, our scheme can effectively resist conventional VQ attack, evidenced by the lower PFA 0 %. In addition, the quality of recovered image by the proposed scheme is higher than He's method. This is because He's method only employs high-frequency component of image to form the watermark, which makes it vulnerable to VQ attack in smooth regions. Even though He's method uses a secret key to generate two block mapping sequences to build the relationship between blocks, miss-matches are inevitable and their PFA and PFR are larger than zero. The proposed scheme can resist conventional VQ attack in both smooth regions and texture regions effectively. In addition, because the superpixel shape is not regular and the size is not same, it is very difficult to form a VQ code book.

Table 1. Performance comparison of tamper detection and recovery

Image	Methods	PFA (%)	PFR (%)	Watermarked image PSNR (dB)	Recovery image PSNR (dB)
Lena	He [9]	70.75	1.25	44.16	40.24
	Proposed	0	0.11	46.00	42.76
Couple	He [9]	60.25	0.241	44.19	38.85
	Proposed	0	0.14	45.57	41.40

5   Conclusions

In this paper, we propose a novel fragile watermarking scheme based on superpixels. Since the superpixel segmentation is sensitive to image modifications, the proposed scheme has a strong capability of resistance to general counterfeiting attacks, especially VQ attack. The superpixel boundaries are marked for the extraction of authentication and recovery watermark properly. Besides, the authentication watermark based on a chaotic system with feedback can effectively detect tampered superpixels, because the chaotic system is sensitive to the initial input value. In addition, the recovery watermark is decompressed not only to conduct precise detection of the tampered superpixels, but also to recover the tampered regions when the tamper rate is not too large. In future research, we intend to apply compressive sensing technology to improve the quality of recovered image.

Acknowledgements. This work is supported in part by 973 Program (2011CB302204), National Natural Science Funds for Distinguished Young Scholar (61025013), National NSF of China (61332012, 61272355), PCSIRT (IRT 201206), and Open Projects Program of National Laboratory of Pattern Recognition (201306309).

References

1. Haouzia, A., Noumeir, R.: Methods for image authentication: a survey. Multimed Tools Appl. **39**, 1–46 (2008)
2. Wong, P.W.: A public key watermark for image verication and authentication. In: Proceedings of the IEEE International Conference on Image Processing, Chicago, IL, pp. 425–429, October 1998
3. Holliman, M., Memon, N.: Counterfeiting attacks on oblivious block-wise independent invisible watermarking schemes. IEEE Trans. Image Process. **9**(3), 432–441 (2000)
4. Celik, M.U., Sharma, G., Saber, E., Tekalp, A.M.: Hierarchical watermarking for secure image authentication with localization. IEEE Trans. Image Process. **11**(6), 585–595 (2002)
5. Suthaharan, S., Kim, S.: A gradient image dependent fragile watermarking for improved security and localization. In: Proceedings of the IEEE Southeast Con, pp. 343–348 (2004)
6. Chen, W.C., Wang, M.S.: A fuzzy c-means clustering-based fragile watermarking scheme for image authentication. Expert Syst. Appl. **36**(2), 1300–1307 (2009)
7. Lin, P.L., Hsieh, C.K., Huang, P.W.: A hierarchical digital watermarking method for image tamper detection and recovery. Pattern Recogn. **38**(12), 2519–2529 (2005)
8. Li, C., Wang, Y., Ma, B., Zhang, Z.: A novel self-recovery fragile watermarking scheme based on dual-redundant-ring structure. Comput. Electr. Eng. **37**, 927–940 (2011)
9. He, H., Chen, F., Huo, Y.: Self-embedding fragile watermarking scheme combined average with VQ encoding. In: Shi, Y.Q., Kim, H.-J., Pérez-González, F. (eds.) IWDW 2012. LNCS, vol. 7809, pp. 120–134. Springer, Heidelberg (2013)
10. Ren, X., Malik, J.: Learning a classifacation model for segmentation. In: ICCV 2003, pp. 10–17. IEEE Computer Society (2003)
11. Fulkerson, B., Vedali, A., Soatto, S.: Class segmentation and object localization with superpixel neighborhoods. In: ICCV 2009, pp. 670–677. IEEE (2009)
12. Wang, Z., Feng, J., Xi, H.: Image classification via object-aware holistic superpixel selection. IEEE Trans. Image Process. **22**(11), 4341–4352 (2013)
13. Yang, F., Lu, H., Yang, M.-H.: Robust superpixel tracking. IEEE Trans. Image Process. **23**(4), 1639–1651 (2014)
14. Levinshtein, A.S., Kutulakos, K.N., Fleet, D.J., Dickinson, S.J., Siddiqi, K.: Turbopixels: fast superpixels using geometric flows. IEEE Trans. Pattern Anal. Mach. Intell. **31**(12), 2290–2297 (2009)
15. Ni, R., Ruan, Q.: Neighbor-aided authentication watermarking based on a chaotic system with feedback. IEICE Trans. Inf. Syst. **E91-D**(8), 2196–2198 (2008)
16. Braga-Neto, U., Goutsias, J.: A theoretical tour of connectivity in image processing and analysis. J. Math. Image Vis. **19**(1), 5–31 (2003)

Effects of Fragile and Semi-fragile Watermarking on Iris Recognition System

Zairan Wang[1,2], Jing Dong[1(✉)], Wei Wang[1], and Tieniu Tan[1]

[1] National Laboratory of Pattern Recognition, Center for Research
on Intelligent Perception and Computing, Institute of Automation,
Chinese Academy of Sciences, Beijing, China
{zairan.wang,jdong,wwang,tnt}@nlpr.ia.ac.cn
[2] College of Engineering and Information Technology, University of Chinese
Academy of Sciences, Beijing, China

Abstract. Security is an important issue in biometric recognition systems. In recent years, many researchers proposed to use watermarking to improve the security of biometric systems, but some people concern whether the embedded watermarks will influence recognition results. In this paper, we investigate the effects of several fragile and semi-fragile watermarking methods on the iris recognition performance. Experimental results demonstrate that, even images are fully embedded, fragile watermarking methods nearly have no effects on the recognition performance, while semi-fragile watermarking methods which embed watermark in the visually important components of images have larger effects on the recognition performance than the semi-fragile watermarking methods that embed watermark in the visually unimportant components of images. And embedding parameters, such as embedding strength and watermark length, also have some influences on the recognition results.

Keywords: Fragile watermarking · Semi-fragile watermarking · Iris recognition systems

1 Introduction

Biometric based personal identification techniques have become more and more popular. That is because biometrics technology offers many advantages, compared to traditional token-based or knowledge-based techniques such as PINs, passwords, smart-cards etc. Traditional authentication techniques are prone to human errors since smart-cards can be lost and passwords can be forgotten. Besides, these techniques cannot guarantee that this is a legitimate user in the authentication stage and cannot be reliably used in large-scale applications. Biometric features are any human physiological or behavior characteristics that can be used to verify the identity of an individual. Popular biometric features include face, iris, fingerprint, voice, etc. These features usually belong to one specific person and cannot be lost or forgotten. In addition, biometrics provide the same level of security to all users, and they are impossible to be shared and difficult

© Springer International Publishing Switzerland 2015
Y.-Q. Shi et al. (Eds.): IWDW 2014, LNCS 9023, pp. 174–186, 2015.
DOI: 10.1007/978-3-319-19321-2_13

to be reproduced. Hence, biometric recognition systems do not have most of the issues of the traditional authentication techniques. While biometrics have many advantages, the problem of ensuring the security and integrity of the biometric data is critical [1]. For example, biometric features of an authorized user can be intercepted when the features are transmitted via a communication channel or stored in a database, and biometrics can be reused to spoof the biometric recognition systems. Furthermore, fingerprints can be left on every surface she touches and face images can be easily captured using a camera.

Schneier [2] pointed out that biometrics work well only if the verifier can verify that the biometric came from the person at the time of verification. Ratha et al. [3] introduced eight basic sources of attacks on general biometric systems. With the rapid progress of computer technology, biometric recognition systems are being developed for remote applications, such as e-banking, e-commerce and e-government, or applications in mobile terminals. In such remote applications, resisting the channel attacks, such as resubmission of old digitally stored biometrics or attacking the channel between stored templates and the matcher, is becoming increasingly important. In recent years, some researchers have combined watermarking methods to solve this problem. More specifically, watermarking is used to provide integrity or tampering authentication of the biometric data when they are transmitted in the channel or stored in databases. Watermarking is a technique that embeds some information into digital multimedia and then the embedded information can be extracted for different purposes, such as integrity verification, tampering authentication and copyright protection. Correspondingly, watermarking can be classified into three categories: fragile watermarking, semi-fragile watermarking and robust watermarking. Fragile watermarking is mainly used to verify the integrity of the host signals and detect any modification of the host signals. Semi-fragile watermarking is mainly used for tampering authentication of the host signals. It can tolerate the allowed signal processing, such as lossy compression, and deny signal processing that can change the signal contents. Robust watermarking is mainly used for copyright protection, because it attempts to extract the embedded information no matter what kinds of processing is applied on the host signals. In general, robust watermarking methods have bigger modifications to the watermarked images compared with fragile and semi-fragile watermarking techniques. In this paper, we investigate the effects of fragile and semi-fragile watermarking on the performance of iris recognition system, and what kinds of watermarking methods are more appropriate to be used in an iris recognition system.

The rest of this paper is structured as follows. Section 2 introduces related work in biometric watermarking and explains why we select fragile and semi-fragile watermarking for investigation. In Sect. 3, we introduce the iris recognition system. In Sect. 4, the applied watermarking methods are introduced. In Sect. 5, we do some experiments and study the impacts of several typical fragile and semi-fragile watermarking on the iris recognition performance. In Sect. 6, we discuss the results and conclude the paper.

2   Related Work

The main objectives of watermarking in biometric recognition systems include preventing resubmission of stored images, checking the validity of the transmitted data, reducing transmission bandwidth, etc. Numerous work has been done on biometric watermarking in recent years, which is described as follows.

Ratha [4] et al. described a robust watermarking algorithm, which embedded verification string in wavelet compressed fingerprint images to prevent stored or synthetic fingerprint images from being fraudulently transmitted in the communication channel. They argued that the quality of fingerprint images was not substantially affected, but the effects of watermarking on the recognition performance were not shown in their paper. In [5], Jain et al. hid fingerprint minutiae data in host images by a robust watermarking to increase the security of biometric data exchange and user authentication. Vatsa et al. [6] embedded iris template into face images using a robust watermarking method to verify any individual and protect the biometric template simultaneously. However, they did not show the effects of watermarking on recognition performance in detail. Zebbiche et al. [7] introduced an application of a robust wavelet based watermarking method to hide the fingerprint minutiae data in fingerprint images. The robustness of the watermarking against several attacks had been tested, whereas the effects of watermarking on recognition accuracy were not pointed out. Park et al. [8] embedded iris feature into face data with a robust watermarking method to obtain three objectives: increasing the authentication accuracy, checking the validity of the face image and transmitting iris feature covertly. The change of face recognition accuracy due to watermarking and the accuracy of iris recognition under several attacks were tested in their paper. Tuan et al. [9] embedded fingerprint minutiae in facial images using a bit priority-based fragile watermarking. The effects of priority-based watermarking method and non-priority based watermarking on recognition performance were compared. Kim et al. [10] proposed a blind and robust spread spectrum watermarking algorithm to embed face template into fingerprint sample for safe authentication of the multimodal biometrics data. Fingerprint image recognition accuracy of several watermarking methods under WSQ compression was compared. In [11], Ma et al. proposed a novel robust watermarking scheme to embed fingerprint minutiae into face images for multimodal biometric authentication. The influences of different watermarking strategies to different face recognition methods are illustrated and they argued that different watermarking and recognition methods had different influences on the recognition results. Wang et al. [12] presented a biometric watermarking algorithm to augment remote multimodal recognition by embedding voice characteristics into face images. Experimental results demonstrated that watermarking had some influences on the verification results.

Although there are many watermarking methods that have been used in biometric systems, the authors remain rather vague about the actual aim and required property of the employed watermarking system [13]. Most of the watermarking methods used in biometric systems are robust watermarking, but the author did not explain why they selected robust watermarking methods and ignored different properties of fragile, semi-fragile and robust watermarking. In [14], Hämmerle et al. pointed out that robust watermarking affected the iris recognition, and he also stated that robust watermarking which was used for embedding templates in the context of multimodal biometric systems was not suited to act as the sole means of security in [15]. In fact, modifications of the host images which result from watermarking may have some influences on the biometric recognition performance. In the past several years, several researchers have investigated the effects of robust watermarking on biometric recognition accuracy. Dong et al. [17] investigated effects of the robust QIM watermarking on iris recognition performance. Hämmerle et al. [14] applied a set of blind robust watermarking schemes on the iris images to investigate their impacts on the recognition performance. What is more, they pointed that robust watermarking affected the iris recognition performance, because robust watermarking methods will result in big modifications to images in general. However, as mentioned above, fragile or semi-fragile watermarking have smaller modifications to the images. Moreover, Ma et al. [16] and Hämmerle et al. [13] pointed that fragile or semi-fragile watermarking can satisfy the requirements of the biometric systems in most application scenarios. Therefore, fragile and semi-fragile watermarking methods are more appropriate in biometric systems. To the best of our knowledge, no work has been done to study their effects on the biometric recognition performance. Hence, in this paper, we select several typical fragile and semi-fragile watermarking algorithms and compare their interferences on the iris recognition system.

3   Iris Recognition System

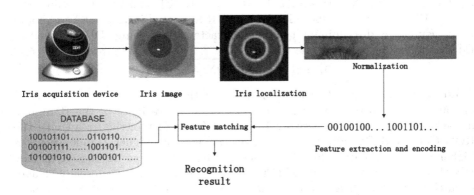

Fig. 1. Flowchart of iris recognition system

In order to better investigate and experiment our idea, we take iris recognition as a typical biometric system. The flowchart of iris recognition system is schematically shown in Fig. 1. Iris recognition system primarily consists of four steps: image acquisition, pre-processing, feature extraction and encoding, matching and recognition [18].

The iris image is first acquired using a special iris camera. This is a very important step, because the following stages are highly depended on the quality of the acquired iris image. The second step can be further divided into iris localization, normalization and image enhancement. The purpose of iris localization is to accurately determine the inner and outer boundaries of an iris and to ensure the iris area in which features are extracted. In the process of iris image acquisition, many human and environmental factors such as focal length, eye rotation, and pupil contraction may result in captured images differing in size, orientation, and translation. Hence, iris localization is performed and iris images are normalized to the same size and position as the template image so as to eliminate interferences of translation, contraction or enlargement, rotation and so on. After that, distinctive features are extracted from the normalized image. The distinctiveness of the extracted features has a direct effect to the accuracy rate of the iris recognition system. From the point of feature extraction, methods now available can be divided into three types: phase analysis based methods such as Daugman's phase encoding method, zero crossing detection based methods such as Boles' 1D wavelet zero-crossing encoding method, and texture analysis based methods such as ordinal measures [19]. In the matcher module, the iris features are compared with a large number of templates in the database to determine if the two irises belong to the same person. Matching algorithms are closely related to feature extraction algorithms, common matching methods include Hamming distance and Euclidean distance. At last, decision is made.

ROC (Receiver Operating Characteristics) curves, equal error rate (EER) and discriminating index (DI) are common metrics used to illustrate the iris recognition performance. In the ROC graphs, the False-Accept-Rate (FAR) is plotted against the X-axis while False-Reject-Rate (FRR) is plotted against the Y-axis. EER is the rate where FAR and FRR are equal in the ROC curve and DI measures the discriminability of the extracted iris features. DI is defined as Eq. 1 as follow:

$$DI = |m_1 + m_2|/\sqrt{(\delta_1^2 + \delta_2^2)/2}. \tag{1}$$

where m_1 and m_2 denote the mean value of the Hamming distance of class one and class two respectively, δ_1^2 and δ_2^2 mean the variance of the Hamming distance of two classes respectively. In general, lower EER or the Area Under the ROC Curve (AUC) indicates better performance, and higher D-index denotes higher discriminability. There are several public iris image databases, include UBath [20], CASIA [21], and ICE2005 [22]. In this paper, a subset of images from the newest CASIA iris image database from the Institute of Automation, Chinese Academy of science [21] are selected. 3963 images of 100 persons are chosen from the IrisV4-Lamp subset, which contain left and right eyes of each person. All the selected iris images are normalized with size of 80 × 512. OM features [19] are extracted from the iris images, because of its good trade-off between distinctiveness and robustness. And linear programming is used for feature selection and matching [23].

4   Watermarking Algorithms

We select two typical fragile watermarking methods and five typical semi-fragile watermarking methods in different domains. Only blind watermarking methods are applied in this paper, because non-blind watermarking is impractical.

Fragile watermarking is very sensitive to any modifications of the host signal, and the extraction algorithm should fail if any changes are made to the host signal. It is usually used for integrity detection of the host data. Hence, if the extracted watermark is different from the embedded watermark, we should doubt about that the transmission channel is not secure or the transmitted iris image is a faked one. We choose two typical fragile watermarking methods, LSB (Least Significant Bit) and Yeung's method (Short for "Yeung" in the following) [24], which are described as follows.

- LSB: LSB is the best known watermarking method that works in the spatial domain, which replaces the least significant bits of pixels to hide information. One pixel can embed one watermark bit.
- Yeung: A look-up-table (LUT) is generated by using a pseudo-random-number generator. The pixel value in spatial domain is modified until the pixel value is equal to the desired value in LUT according to the embedded watermark. The embedding rate is also one bit per pixel.

Semi-fragile watermarking is moderately robust to small modifications, and protects that host signal can undergo normal signal processing operations while it is still possible to detect malevolent alterations and to locate the regions that have been altered. In the mobile applications, the captured iris images may be undergone some image processing to save bandwidth and decrease transmission time. This type of watermarking can tolerate this kind of image processing, but fails to malevolent alterations, such as changing the content of the iris images. We select five typical semi-fragile watermarking methods in different domains, which were proposed by Lin [25], Zhu [26], Qi [27], Inoue [28], and Sun [29] respectively (Short for "Lin", "Zhu", "Qi", "Inoue" and "Sun" in the following). The five selected watermarking methods can be classified into two groups. In the first group, watermark is embedded in the visually unimportant components of images, such as mid or high frequency coefficients in DWT or DCT domain. In the second group, watermark is embedded in the visually important components of images, such as low frequency coefficients in DWT or DCT domain and the largest singular values of the image. We investigate their different impacts on the biometric systems.

- Lin: Embedding is done in DCT domain. DCT is applied on the 8×8 blocks of the image, and the relationships of the coefficients between two blocks are quantized to embed watermark. The embedding rate is 3/128 bit per pixel.
- Zhu: Embedding is done in the three finest wavelet detail subbands. The coefficients are split into blocks, and the block-mean is quantized to embed watermark. The embedding rate is 1/16 bit per pixel.

- Qi: The approximation wavelet subband is selected for watermark embedding. The approximation subband is segmented into small sub-blocks, and one coefficient is selected pseudo-randomly which is quantized according to a watermark bit. The embedding rate is also 1/16 bit per pixel.
- Inoue: Embedding is done in the approximation wavelet subband. The lowest subband is segmented into small sub-blocks, and the mean value of each block is quantized to embed watermark. The embedding rate is also 1/16 bit per pixel.
- Sun: Watermark is embedded in the SVD domain. SVD is applied on the 8×8 blocks of the image, and the largest singular value is quantized to embed watermark. The embedding rate is 1/64 bit per pixel.

Lin and Zhu watermarking methods belong to the first group, and the other three methods belong to the second group. Generally, there are several parameters in watermarking technique, such as embedding strength and watermark length. Larger embedding strength means larger modifications of images. PSNR (peak signal to noise ratio) is a commonly used metric to measure the degree of modifications of the watermarked images. The larger the PSNR value, the smaller the modifications of the images, and vice verse. For semi-fragile watermarking, we can adjust the embedding strength to tune the modifications and PSNR of the images. The largest allowable watermark length of a watermarking algorithm is the product of its embedding rate and the number of pixels of an image. Larger watermark length means more image parts are modified. In experiments, watermark is generated pseudo-randomly by using a secret key and embedded in the normalized iris images, where iris features are extracted. At first, all the methods are fully embedded, which means watermark with the largest allowable watermark length is embedded. We adjust the embedding strength of the semi-fragile watermarking methods so that the PSNR values of all the watermarked iris images are higher than 38 dB and the mean PSNR value of the watermarked iris images is about 44.5 dB. Then we test the effects of different watermark lengths and embedding strengths on the recognition results.

5   Experiments

Figure 2 shows an original iris image and its seven watermarked iris images using different watermarking methods. From the figure, we can see that no visual difference can be detected by human and the modifications which result from watermarking are very small.

Figure 3 shows the comparison of ROC curves of two fragile watermarking methods. In the figure, the 'no watermark' curve denotes the recognition performance without watermark embedded on the iris images. The mean PSNR values of the watermarked iris images using LSB and Yeung watermarking methods are 49.9 dB and 45.51 dB, respectively. From the figure, it can be seen that fragile watermarking methods almost have no effects on the iris recognition performance, even the iris images are fully embedded. The reason may be that the

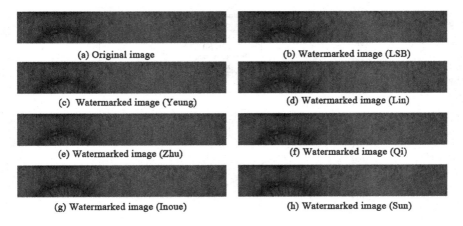

Fig. 2. Perceptibility of the watermarked iris images

fragile watermarking methods are applied on the spatial domain and only very small modifications are made on the iris images.

Figure 4 shows the comparison of ROC curves of two semi-fragile watermarking methods in the first group. In this kind of semi-fragile watermarking, watermark is embedded in the visually unimportant components of the image. Zhu watermarking method is applied on the three finest wavelet detail subbands, and Lin watermarking method embeds watermark in the middle frequency DCT coefficients. The mean PSNR value of the watermarked iris images is about 44.5 dB. From the figure, we can observe that this kind of semi-fragile watermarking almost has no effects on the iris recognition performance at this embedding strength. This indicates that small modifications in the visually unimportant components of iris image has very small effects on the recognition performance.

The effects of three semi-fragile watermarking methods in the second group are shown in Fig. 5. The mean PSNR value of the watermarked iris images in this group is the same with that in the first group, so the embedding strengths of the watermarking methods in both groups are approximately identical. It can be seen that the results are different, although the three semi-fragile watermarking methods all embed watermark in the visually important components of the iris image. Qi and Inoue watermarking methods embed watermark on the approximation wavelet subband, and Sun watermarking method uses the largest singular values to embed watermark. Qi method has very small impacts on the iris recognition performance, while Inoue and Sun methods have larger effects on the systems. The reason could be that only a portion of approximation coefficients are modified in Qi watermarking, however, Inoue and Sun methods spread watermark on the full image. Therefore, compared with Fig. 4, we can say that at the same embedding strength modifications in the visually important components of iris image have larger effects on the recognition performance, but the effects can be decreased by decreasing the number of coefficients which are modified to embed watermark. To verify it, we implement Inoue method with smaller watermark

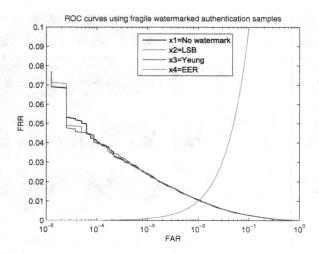

Fig. 3. ROC of iris recognition using fragile watermarked authentication samples

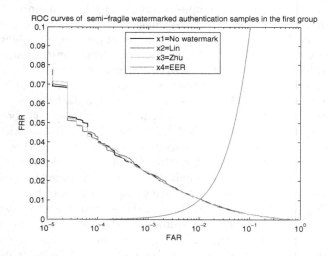

Fig. 4. ROC of iris recognition using semi-fragile watermarked authentication samples

length and maintain the same quantization step at the same time. The results are shown in Fig. 6. "Inoue(1)" means that Inoue method is implemented with the largest allowable watermark length, and "Inoue(0.75)" denotes that Inoue method is implemented with 0.75 multiple of the largest allowable watermark length. We can see that the effects are decreased as we decreased the watermark length.

At last, watermarking methods with different embedding strengths are implemented to test their effects on the recognition results, as shown in Fig. 7. Due to space restrictions, only the results of Inoue method are depicted. In the figure,

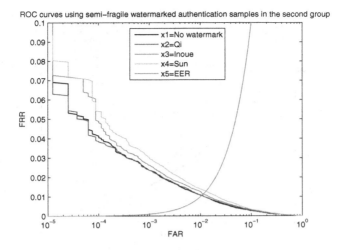

Fig. 5. ROC of iris recognition using semi-fragile watermarked authentication samples

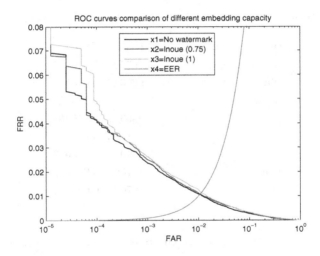

Fig. 6. ROC curves comparison of different embedding capacity

smaller PSNR value means larger embedding strength. It can be observed that EER changes larger as the PSNR value decreases. This indicates that larger watermarking strength has larger effects on the iris recognition performance.

Table 1 depicts DI and EER of different watermarking methods. The results are basically consistent to the ROC curves shown above. The fragile watermarking methods and semi-fragile watermarking methods in the first group nearly have no degradation on the iris recognition performance, while semi-fragile watermarking methods in the second group have slight effects on the recognition performance. This is plausible, since visually important components

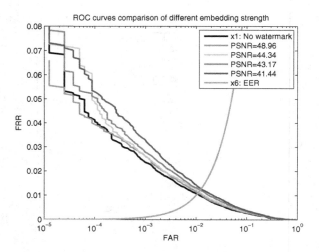

Fig. 7. ROC of iris recognition under different embedding strengths

Table 1. DI and EER of different watermarking methods

watermarking methods	DI	EER
No watermark	3.965512	0.010515
LSB	3.960642	0.010553
Yeung	3.960368	0.010603
Lin	3.966962	0.010608
Zhu	3.961110	0.010641
Qi	3.934939	0.010653
Inoue	3.867693	0.011332
Sun	3.797678	0.012676

contain most energy of the image, which are damaged may affect the extraction of iris features.

6   Conclusions

In this paper, we investigate the effects of fragile and semi-fragile watermarking on the iris recognition performance. Several fragile watermarking and semi-fragile watermarking methods are applied to investigate the effects. From the experiments, we have observed certain trends. Even iris images are fully embedded, fragile watermarking almost has no impacts on the recognition results. For semi-fragile watermarking, at the same embedding strengths, methods that embed watermark in the visually important components have larger effects on the recognition results than methods that embed watermark in the visually unimportant components of images. Embedding parameters, such as embedding strength and watermark length, have some influences on the experimental results. Specifically, smaller watermark length and embedding strength have smaller effects on the recognition results. In other words, we can adjust embedding strength or watermark length to control the effects of semi-fragile watermarking on biometric recognition results. Moreover, fragile and semi-fragile watermarking can also meet the requirement of the biometric systems. In conclusion, fragile and semi-fragile watermarking methods are more appropriate to enhance the security of the iris recognition system we studied in this paper. In the future work, we will extend our study to other recognition algorithms and more biometric modalities, and investigate which watermarking algorithm should be used in each case.

Acknowledgments. This work is funded by the National Basic Research Program of China (Grant No. 2012CB316300), the National Nature Science Foundation of China (Grant No.61303262), and the National Key Technology R&D Program (Grant No.2012BAH04F02).

References

1. Jain, A.K., Uludag, U.: Hiding biometric data. IEEE Trans. Pattern Anal. Mach. Intell. **25**, 1494–1498 (2003)
2. Schneier, B.: The uses and abuses of biometrics. Commun. ACM **42**(8), 136 (1999)
3. Ratha, N.K., Connell, J.H., Bolle, R.M.: Enhancing security and privacy in biometrics-based authentication systems. IBM Syst. J. **40**, 614–634 (2001)
4. Ratha, N.K., Connell, J.H., Bolle, R.M.: Secure data hiding in wavelet compressed fingerprint images. In: ACM Multimedia Conference, pp. 127–130 (2000)
5. Jain, A.K., Uludag, U.: Hiding Fingerprint Minutiae in Images. In: Proceedings of 3rd Workshop on Automatic Identification Advanced Technologies (2002)
6. Vatsa, M., Singh, R., Mitra, P., Noore, A.: Digital watermarking based secure multimodal biometric system. IEEE Int. Conf. Syst. Man Cybern. **3**, 2983–2987 (2004)
7. Zebbiche, K., Ghouti, L., Khelifi, F., Bouridane, A.: Protecting fingerprint data using watermarking, In: First NASA/ESA Conference on Adaptive Hardware and Systems, AHS 2006. pp. 451–456, June 2006
8. Park, K.R., Jeong, D.S., Kang, B.J., Lee, E.C.: A study on iris feature watermarking on face data. In: Beliczynski, B., Dzielinski, A., Iwanowski, M., Ribeiro, B. (eds.) ICANNGA 2007. LNCS, vol. 4432, pp. 415–423. Springer, Heidelberg (2007)
9. Hoang, T., Tran, D., Sharma, D.: Remote multimodal biometric authentication using bit priority-based fragile watermarking. In: International Conference on Pattern Recognition, pp. 1–4 (2008)
10. Kim, W., Lee, H.: Multimodal biometric image watermarking using two-stage integrity verification. Sig. Process. **89**, 2385–2399 (2009)
11. Ma, B., Li, C., Wang, Y., Zhang, Z., Wang, Y.: Block pyramid based adaptive quantization watermarking for multimodal biometric authentication. In: International Conference on Pattern Recognition, pp. 1277–1280 (2010)
12. Wang, S., Hu, R., Yu, H., Zheng, X., Damper, R.I.: Augmenting remote multimodal person verification by embedding voice characteristics into face images. In: IEEE International Conference on Multimedia and Expo Workshops (ICMEW) 2013, pp. 1–6, July 2013

13. Hämmerle-Uhl, J., Raab, K., Uhl, A.: Watermarking as a means to enhance biometric systems: a critical survey. In: Filler, T., Pevný, T., Craver, S., Ker, A. (eds.) IH 2011. LNCS, vol. 6958, pp. 238–254. Springer, Heidelberg (2011)
14. Hämmerle-Uhl, J., Raab, K., Uhl, A.: Experimental study on the impact of robust watermarking on iris recognition accuracy. In: ACM Symposium on Applied Computing, pp. 1479–1484 (2010)
15. Hämmerle-Uhl, J., Raab, K., Uhl, A.: Attack against robust watermarking-based multimodal biometric recognition systems. In: Vielhauer, C., Dittmann, J., Drygajlo, A., Juul, N.C., Fairhurst, M.C. (eds.) BioID 2011. LNCS, vol. 6583, pp. 25–36. Springer, Heidelberg (2011)
16. Ma, B., Li, C., Zhang, Z., Wang, Y.: Biometric information hiding: promoting multimedia security with content and identity authentication. In: IEEE China Summit International Conference on Signal and Information Processing (ChinaSIP), 2013, pp. 442–446, July 2013
17. Dong,. J., Tan, T.: Effects of watermarking on iris recognition performance. In: 10th International Conference on Control, Automation, Robotics and Vision, 2008. ICARCV 2008. pp. 1156–1161, Dec 2008
18. Iris Recognition Technology. http://en.techshino.com/tech/detail.html?id=3. Accessed on June 2014
19. Sun, Z., Tan, T.: Ordinal Measures for Iris Recognition. IEEE Trans. Pattern Anal. Mach. Intell. **31**(12), 2211–2226 (2009)
20. University of Bath Iris Image Database (2009). http://www.bath.ac.uk/elec-eng/pages/sipg/irisweb/
21. Chinese Academy of Sciences Institute of Automation. http://biometrics.idealtest.org/dbDetailForUser.do?id=4. Accessed on June 2014
22. Iris Challenge Evaluation (2009). http://iris.nist.gov/ice/
23. Wang, L., Sun, Z., Tan, T.: Robust regularized feature selection for iris recognition via linear programming. In: 21st International Conference on Pattern Recognition (ICPR), 2012, pp. 3358–3361, 11–15 November 2012
24. Yeung, M.M., Mintzer, F.: An invisible watermarking technique for image verification. In: International Conference on Image Processing, pp. 680–683 (1997)
25. Lin, C.-Y., Chang, S.-F.: Semifragile watermarking for authenticating JPEG visual content. Storage and Retrieval for Image and Video Databases **3971**, 140–151 (2000)
26. Zhu, Y., Li, C.-T., Zhao, H.-J.: Structural digital signature and semi-fragile fingerprinting for image authentication in wavelet domain (2007)
27. Qi, X., Xin, X.: A quantization-based semi-fragile watermarking scheme for image content authentication. J. Vis. Commun. Image Represent. **22**, 187–200 (2011)
28. Inoue, H., Miyazaki, A., Katsura, T.: A digital watermark for images using the wavelet transform. Integr. Comput. C Aided Eng. **7**(2), 105–115 (2000)
29. Sun, R., Sun, H., Yao, T.: A SVD and quantization based semi-fragile watermarking technique for image authentication. In: International Conference on Signal Processing Proceedings (2002)

Zero-Watermarking Based on Improved ORB Features Against Print-cam Attack

Jianfeng Lu[1], Qianru Huang[1], Meng Wang[1], Li Li[1(✉)], Junping Dai[2], and Chin-Chen Chang[3,4]

[1] Institute of Graphics and Image, Hangzhou Dianzi University, Hangzhou Zhejiang, China
lili2008@hdu.edu.cn
[2] Institute of Digital Media, Hangzhou Dianzi University, Hangzhou Zhejiang, China
[3] Department of Information Engineering Computer and Science, Feng Chia University,
No. 100, Wenhwa Rd., Seatwen, Taichung 40724, Taiwan
[4] Department of Computer Science and Information Engineering, Asia University,
No. 500, Lioufeng Rd., Wufeng, Taichung 41354, Taiwan
alan3c@gmail.com

Abstract. Traditional digital image watermarking schemes have the inherent conflicts between imperceptibility and robustness because the insertion of watermarks into the host image inevitably introduces some perceptible quality degradation. Image zero-watermark techniques resolve this dilemma by extracting invariant features from its host image. At present, most zero-watermark schemes are more robust to geometric attacks and the common signal process. But they are not robust to print-cam attack, where the image is first printed and then captured with a mobile phone. To solve the problem, this paper addresses a novel zero-watermarking scheme based on improved ORB (Oriented FAST and Rotated BRIEF) features. Firstly, we increase the initial ORB matching points to improve the matching rate and add color information as another feature. So the added color features can remove the false-positive matches which the color correspondence is wrong. Then, ORB keypoints, ORB descriptors and color descriptors are the zero-watermark to be registered. Finally, we perform outlier filtration using the RANSAC (random sample consensus) method and obtain the final inliers during the zero-watermark detection. Then the original image match the one captured with a mobile phone by the zero-watermark. Experimental results show that the proposed image zero-watermark scheme is robust to geometric attacks, signal processing attacks and print-cam attack.

Keywords: Zero-watermark · Feature match · ORB · Color features · Random sample consensus

1 Introduction

Since digital media can be duplicated easily, digital watermarking technology [1] plays an important role in the domain of digital multimedia copyright protection. Most digital image watermarking schemes are based on embedding watermarks into the host image,

Y.-Q. Shi et al. (Eds.): IWDW 2014, LNCS 9023, pp. 187–198, 2015.
DOI: 10.1007/978-3-319-19321-2_14

which leads to some quality degradations inevitably. To solve the conflicts between imperceptibility and robustness, the zero-watermarking has been proposed in [2]. The scheme proposed that the inherent feature of the host image is extracted as the zero-watermark and the host image is not modified. The feature is saved in the third party for copyright protection.

Image zero-watermark methods are mainly based on the image frequency coefficients, image moment, local invariant image feature and so on. Kou [3] proposed a zero-watermarking algorithm based on piecewise logistic chaotic map and chaotic sequences that is sensitive to initial value. The wavelet coefficients of the third level detail part is selected to be the zero-watermark by the chaotic sequences, which does not make any changes to the original data of the image. Jie [4] proposed an image zero-watermark scheme based on visual attention regions of images. In the proposed scheme visual attention model carefully selects top-N salient areas, where a set of selected Scale Invariant Feature transform (SIFT) descriptors are extracted as a watermark. The distance of each pair of SIFT descriptors from the reference and test images are calculated by Kullback-Leibler (KL) divergence after mapping into the high dimensional space respectively. The final distance of two sets of SIFT descriptor are determined by ensemble similarity. Based on the characteristic of invariant moments, Gao [5] proposed a zero-watermarking algorithm that defines the Tchebichef invariant moments in Cartesian coordinate space and the complex chaotic optimization SVR. And a zero-watermark with Bessel-Fourier moment feature vector in the polar coordinate space is constructed.

The abovec watermarking algorithms are not robust to the print-cam attack. ORB [6] is a robust image detector and descriptor, first presented by Ethan Rublee et al. in 2011. It is at two orders of magnitude faster than SIFT(Scale-invariant feature transform) [7], while performing as well against different image transformations like rotation, scaling and so on. In this paper, we propose an improved ORB feature extraction scheme and add color features to ORB keypoints. ORB keypoints, ORB descriptors and color descriptors are combined into the zero-watermark. During the zero-watermarking detecting process, we employ k-cross-match to get the initial matching points, and then remove the false-positive matches which the color correspondence is wrong by color descriptors. Then we perform outlier filtration using the RANSAC [8] method to get the inliers and the final matching rate. The proposed scheme is robust to rotation, scaling, cropping and signal processing attacks, especially the print-cam attacks.

2   Related Work

The closest system to ORB is described in [6], which contains oFAST (Orientation FAST) and rBRIEF (Rotation Brief).

2.1   oFAST: FAST Keypoint Orientation

Many keypoint detectors include orientation information, but Features from Accelerated Segment Test (FAST) [9, 10] does not. oFAST adds an efficiently computed orientation to FAST. There are many ways to describe the orientation of a keypoint. Rosin [11] proposed the centroid technique to add an orientation in the corners. He defined the moments of a patch as:

$$m_{pq} = \sum_{x,y} x^p y^q I(x, y), \quad where \; p, q = 0, 1, 2, \dots, \tag{1}$$

where $I(x,y)$ is the value of pixel in the location (x,y). The orientation of the patch then simply is:

$$\theta = \mathrm{atan2} \left(m_{01}, m_{10} \right), \tag{2}$$

where atan2 is the quadrant-aware version of arctan.

2.2 rBRIEF: Rotation-Aware Brief

rBRIEF (rotation-aware Binary Robust Independent Elementary Features descriptor [12]) is a efficient feature descriptor with orientation information. The final rBRIEF consists of the 256 new features which have high variance and low correlationship obtained by the greedy algorithm. The similarity degree of the two ORB feature descriptors is presented by the sum of the XOR Hamming distance, which is represented by $D(K_1,K_2)$. Assume two 256-bit binary descriptors depicted as $K_1 = x_0 x_1 \dots x_{255}$ and $K_2 = y_0 y_1 \dots y_{255}$. The $D(K_1,K_2)$ is defined as follow:

$$D \left(K_1, K_2 \right) = \sum_{i=0}^{255} x_i \oplus y_i . \tag{3}$$

2.3 Binary Features Matching

In this section, we demonstrate ORB matching algorithm over the large databases of images in nearest-neighbor. The cross-match technique is applied to reject wrong correspondences. The whole process contains two steps. In first round, the detected feature descriptors are compared with the descriptors of the images in the dataset. And in the next round, the descriptors of each image in the dataset are compared with the detected ones. Only the ones matched correctly in two rounds are returned. Such techniques usually produce the best results with a minimal number of outliers when there are enough candidates. But in some cases, false-positive matches can be produced. To improve our matching results, we can perform outlier filtration using the RANSAC [8] method. Since we're working with an image (a planar object) and we expect it to be rigid, it's acceptable to find the homography transformation between feature points on the pattern image and feature points on the query image. Homography transformation will make the features are compared in the same coordinate system. It uses RANSAC method to calculate the best homography matrix by probing subsets of input points. As a side effect, this function marks each correspondence as either inlier or outlier, depending on the reprojection error for the calculated homography matrix.

3   The Proposed Improvement of ORB Detect and Match

3.1   Increase Initial ORB Features Match Points

Within the existing ORB matching process, the performance depends on the amount of wrong matching points. There are noises, geometric deformation, and pixel distortion on photos because they are obtained with different times, resolution, illumination, and poses. Especially in the case of symmetrical images which contain less rich texture details and rich self-similar structures, the cross-match technique will miss the correct points in the matching process.

To reduce the error-matching rate, a more fitting method is the k-cross-match technique instead of the cross-match technique. We increase the number of candidate points from one to k in the matching process.

Another problem is found when the correct matches are not sufficient; in this case, the matrix obtained by RANSAC is wrong. To solve this problem, we reduce the value of the threshold and increase the number of feature points detected from the image. Then the error rate is controlled to the low value by this mothod. In the experiment, we increase the maximum number of ORB feature points detected from the image to 1000 and reduce the Fast threshold to 15. Then we remove the matching points for Hamming distance of greater than 50 and set k to 5. The comparison result between the original matching and improved matching is shown in Fig. 1. From the figures we can see that the homography matrix in (a2) is not correct and so the transformed image is also wrong. The image is correct in (b3)because its homography matrix is correct in (b2).

3.2   Add Color Information to Feature Descriptor

The existing descriptor of ORB feature points doesn't contain color information. The computation of the descriptor is performed in the gray blocks around the feature points. As a result, an image block might match another with different colors and similar structure. Apparently, the matching result is wrong. Figure 2 shows the examples of two image blocks with different colors and similar structures.

The color feature extraction algorithm is based on the coordinate system and the scale of the ORB feature points, and then the corresponding feature block is extracted. We normalize the orientation of the corresponding feature block according to the orientation information of feature points. Cluster colors of feature blocks are shown after normalizing with the k-mean algorithm. In the experiment, we find that the k value is set to 6 will bring good results. Thus, we quantify the image blocks using six colors. We reduce the size of the image block to 7×7. This is shown in Fig. 3, which is the color matching process based on normalized orientation and color cluster.

In addition, the color feature matching process is described as follows. Firstly, the center point (from color block in the query image) is compared to its 8 neighbors in the 3×3 regions at the color block of the train image, and the minimal Euclidean distance is calculated as the result. We repeat this process in each point of the color block which belongs to the feature point on the photo. We then add up all minimum Euclidean distances. If the result is greater than threshold value 2500, the two color blocks are

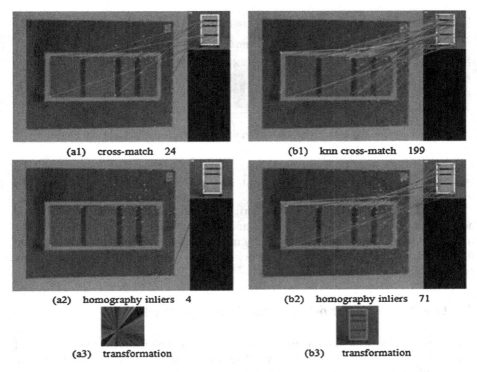

(a1)   cross-match   24

(b1)   knn cross-match   199

(a2)   homography inliers   4

(b2)   homography inliers   71

(a3)   transformation

(b3)   transformation

Fig. 1. (a1) shows that the result of the cross-match technique with the number of matching points is 24; (a2) shows that the homography matrix with the number of inliers is 4; (a3) shows the result of the homography transformation in the photo; (b1) shows that the result of the k-cross-match technique with the number of matching points is 199; (b2) shows that the homography matrix with the number of inliers is 71; and (b3) shows the result of the homography transformation in the photo

(a)   (b)

Fig. 2. (a) presents the horizontal part of the cabinet in the photo, and (b) presents a wheel of cabinets in the original image

different; otherwise they are same. We can get the sum of the minimum Euclidean distance through the formula as Eq. 4:

$$sumdiff = \sum_{1 \leq i \leq 7, 1 \leq j \leq 7} \min(|C'(i,j) - C(i+n, j+m)|), \qquad (4)$$

where $n, m = \{-1, 0, 1\}, 1 \leq i + n \leq 7, 1 \leq j + m \leq 7$, and C' is the color block, which belongs to the feature point on the photo. C is the color block which belongs to the

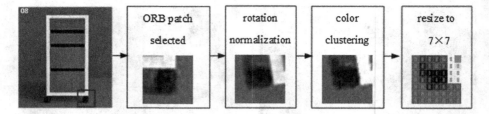

Fig. 3. Color matching process based on normalized orientation and color cluster

matching feature point on the original image. The size of the color block is 7 × 7. C' (i,j) is the vector (R,G,B) on the location (i,j) of C'. C(i + n,j + m) is the vector (R,G,B) on the location (i + n,j + m) of C.

The comparison result between the original matching process and new method adding color features is shown in Figs. 4 and 5. From the figures we can see that the image is correct in c3 and the homography matrix is also correct in c2. And the count of inliers minus the number of matching points which filtered by knn cross-match and color features is increased.

4   The Proposed Zero-Watermarking Approach

A new image zero-watermark is proposed in this paper. The features are consisting of color information and the ORB features. The features are robust to resisting rotation, scaling, illumination change, affine transform, noise and so on.

4.1   Watermark Registering

In our method, The ORB keypoint descriptors of the host image is selected. Keypoint set F is presented as:

$$F = \{F_i | F_i = ((x_i, y_i), s_i, \theta_i), i \in [0, N]\}, \tag{5}$$

where (x_i, y_i) are the location of keypoint in the Cartesian coordinate. The top left corner of the image is origin in the Cartesian coordinate. S_i is the scale of keypoints, θ_i is the main orientation of keypoints and N is the number of keypoints in the original image.

The ORB descriptor set is D and the color descriptor set is C as follow:

$$D = \left\{ D_i \mid D_i = (d_i, \dots, d_{256}), i \in [0, N] \right\}, \tag{6}$$

$$\text{and } C = \left\{ C_i \mid C_i = ((r, g, b)_1, \dots, (r, g, b)_{49}), i \in [0, N] \right\}, \tag{7}$$

where D_i is the corresponding ORB descriptors and C_i is color descriptors of every keypoint F_i in the set F.

The zero-watermark W is generated by combining F, D and C as follows:

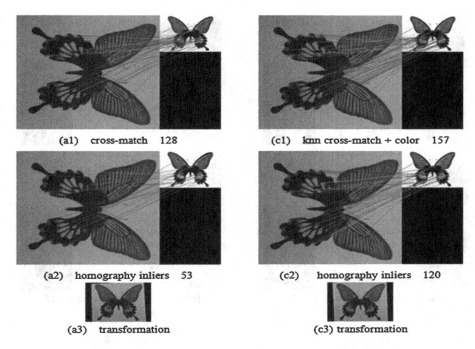

(a1)   cross-match   128   (c1)   knn cross-match + color   157

(a2)   homography inliers   53   (c2)   homography inliers   120

(a3)   transformation   (c3) transformation

Fig. 4. (a1) shows that the result of the cross-match technique with the number of matching points is 128; (a2) shows that the homography matrix with the number of inliers is 53; (a3) shows the result of the homography transformation in the photo; (c1) shows that the result of the k-cross-match and color features technique with the number of matching points is 157; (c2) shows that the homography matrix with the number of inliers is 120; and (c3) shows the result of the homography transformation in the photo

$$W = \{F, D, C\}. \tag{8}$$

Then W register in the third database. Figure 6 shows the whole registering process.

4.2   Watermark Detecting

We first extract the ORB keypoint set F', ORB descriptor set D' and color photo as follow:

$$F' = \left\{ F'_i \mid F'_i = \left((x_i, y_i), s_i, \theta_i \right), i \in [0, M] \right\}, \tag{9}$$

$$D' = \left\{ D' \mid D'_i = \left(d_1, \cdots, d_{256} \right), i \in [0, M] \right\}, \tag{10}$$

$$\text{and } \left\{ C' = C'_i \mid C'_i = \left((r, g, b)_1, \ldots, (r, g, b)_{49} \right), i \in [0, M] \right\}, \tag{11}$$

where M is the number of keypoints in the test photo. Figure 7 shows the whole detecting process.

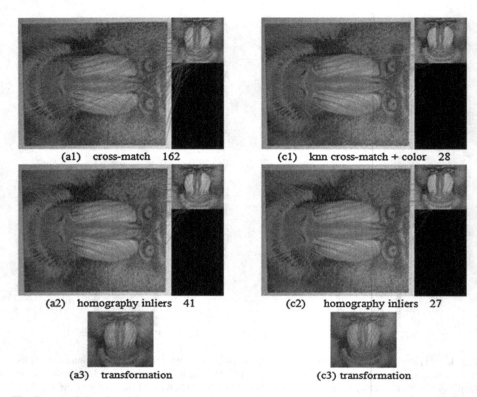

Fig. 5. (a1) shows that the result of the cross-match technique with the number of matching points is 162; (a2) shows that the homography matrix with the number of inliers is 41; (a3) shows the result of the homography transformation in the photo; (c1) shows that the result of the k-cross-match and color features technique with the number of matching points is 28; (c2) shows that the homography matrix with the number of inliers is 27; and (c3) shows the result of the homography transformation in the photo

Retrieving $W_j = \{F_j, D_j, C_j\}$ from the third database, using k-cross-match to remove some mismatches. After that, Adding color descriptor to remove the False-positive matches for which the feature-point correspondence is wrong, then we get the final matches. At last, we perform outlier filtration using the RANSAC method. If the count of final matches is S1, and the count of inliers is S2, the degree of similarity could be defined as: Sim = S2/S1.

Whether the camera image is protected based on the sim compared with a threshold T1 and S2 compared with a threshold T2.

Sim > T1 and S2 > T2 => photo is protected. Else => photo is not protected.

Figure 7 shows the whole zero-watermarking detecting process.

Compared 6 original images with corresponding photos taken by a HTC G12 camera phone, From Table 1, we can see when T1 is 25 % and T2 is 20, the photo is enough to be identified the protected image.

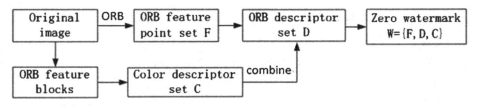

Fig. 6. The whole zero-watermarking registering process

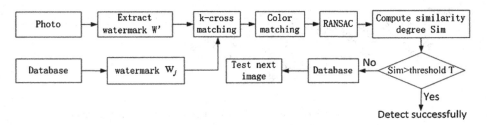

Fig. 7. The whole zero-watermarking detecting process

Table 1. The conparison of the similarity and inliers for each photo and each original image

sim/inliers	Img1	Img2	Img3	Img4	Img5	Img6
Test1	0.377/26	0/0	0/0	0/0	0/0	0/0
Test2	0/0	0.516/32	0/0	0/0	0/0	0/0
Test3	0/0	0/0	0.829/34	0/0	0/0	0/0
Test4	0/0	0/0	0/0	0.764/120	0/0	0/0
Test5	0/0	0/0	0/0	0/0	0.970/33	0/0
Test6	0/0	0/0	0/0	0/0	0/0	0.832/109

5   Experiments and Results

To demonstrate the robustness of our scheme, we applied most of the attacks listed in Stirmark 4.0, including global translation and local distortion. Some simulation results are shown in Fig. 8, from which we can see our method is robustness to signal process and geometrical distortion, such as Affine transformation, JPEG compression, Median filtering, PSNR, rescale, row-column removal, small random distortions, rotation-scaling, rotation-cropping. The degree of the similarity (SIM) and inliers under signal process and geometric distortion are greater than the threshold. We test the proposed scheme in many images. Only the results obtained from Lena and Baboon image are presented due to space limitation.

We also use the images from The Stanford Mobile Visual Search Data Set [13] to test whether our proposed method is robust to print-cam attacks. We test 24 images

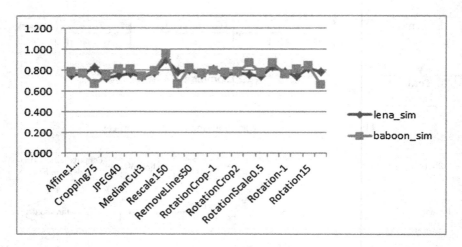

Fig. 8. The degree of similarity (sim) under signal process and geometric distortion

from the business_cards set shown in Fig. 9, and the dvd_covers set shown in Fig. 10, the results are shown in Figs. 11 and 12. From Figs. 11 and 12, we can see the the degrees of similarity (sim) of most images are greater than the threshold. The Failures are mainly photo images not on the focus and the images are captured on Complex background.

Fig. 9. The 24 original images from the "business_cards" sets

Fig. 10. The 24 original images from the "dvd_covers" sets

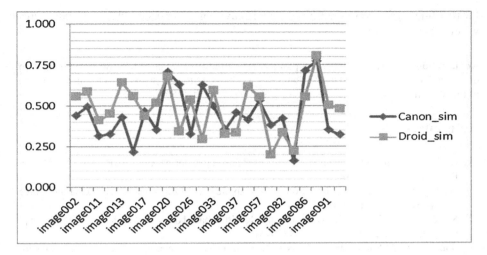

Fig. 11. The degree of similarity (sim) of 24 images from "business_cards" under print-cam attacks

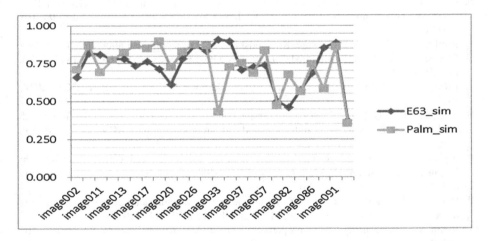

Fig. 12. The degree of similarity (sim) of 24 images from "dvd_covers" under print-cam attacks

6   Conclusion

In this paper, we have proposed a new zero-watermarking scheme based on robust feature match. The experimental results show that our proposed method can resist geometric attacks, signal processing attacks and print-cam attacks. Its robustness to a wide variety of attacks is suitable for many applications requiring high watermarking reliability and imperceptibility, but it imposes a large computational burden, especially for real-time systems. In the future, we will investigate a faster and more robust zero-watermarking algorithm.

Acknowledgements. This work was partially supported by National Natural Science Foundation of China (No. 61370218) and the National Key Technology Research and Development Program of the Ministry of Science and Technology of China (No. 2012BAH91F03).

References

1. Cox, I.J., Miller, M.L.: The first 50 years of electronic watermarking. EURASIP J. Appl. Sig. Process. **2**, 126–132 (2002)
2. Wen, Q., Sun, T.F., Wang, S.X.: Concept and application of zero-watermark. Acta Electronica Sinica. **31**(2), 214–216 (2003)
3. Kou, J.K., Wei, L.X.: Zero-watermarking algorithm based on piecewise logistic chaotic map. Comput. Eng. Des. **34**(2), 464–468 (2013)
4. Shi, J., Yan, Q., Shi, H., Wang, Y.: Visual attention based image zero watermark scheme with ensemble similarity. In: 2013 IEEE International Conference on Wireless Communications and Signal Processing (WCSP), pp. 1–5 (2013)
5. Gao, G.Y., Jiang, G.P.: Zero-bit watermarking resisting geometric attacks based on composite-chaos optimized SVR model. J. China Univ. Posts Telecommun. **18**(2), 94–101 (2011)
6. Rublee, E., Rabaud, V., Konolige, K., Bradski, G.: ORB: an efficient alternative to SIFT or SURF. In: 2011 IEEE International Conference on Proceedings of Computer Vision (ICCV), pp. 2564–2571 (2011)
7. Lowe, D.G.: Distinctive image features from scale-invariant keypoints. Proc. IJCV. **2**(60), 91–110 (2004)
8. Fischler, M.A., Bolles, R.C.: Random sample consensus: a paradigm for model fitting with applications to image analysis and automated cartography. Commun. ACM. **24**(6), 381–395 (1981)
9. Rosten, E., Drummond, T.W.: Machine learning for high-speed corner detection. In: Leonardis, A., Bischof, H., Pinz, A. (eds.) ECCV 2006, Part I. LNCS, vol. 3951, pp. 430–443. Springer, Heidelberg (2006)
10. Rosten, E., Porter, R., Drummond, T.: Faster and better: a machine learning approach to corner detection. IEEE Trans. Pattern Anal. Mach. Intell. **32**(1), 105–119 (2010)
11. Rosin, P.L.: Measuring corner properties. Comput. Vis. Image Underst. **73**(2), 291–307 (1999)
12. Calonder, M., Lepetit, V., Strecha, C., Fua, P.: BRIEF: binary robust independent elementary features. In: Daniilidis, K., Maragos, P., Paragios, N. (eds.) ECCV 2010, Part IV. LNCS, vol. 6314, pp. 778–792. Springer, Heidelberg (2010)
13. Chandrasekhar, V. R., Chen, D. M., Tsai, S. S., Cheung, N. M., Chen, H., Takacs, G., Girod, B.: The stanford mobile visual search data set. In: Proceedings of the second annual ACM Conference on Multimedia Systems, pp. 117–122 (2011)

Reversible Data Hiding

Stereo Image Coding with Histogram-Pair Based Reversible Data Hiding

Xuefeng Tong[1], Guangce Shen[1(✉)], Guorong Xuan[1], Shumeng Li[1],
Zhiqiang Yang[1], Jian Li[3], and Yun-Qing Shi[2]

[1] Department of Computer Science, Tongji University, Shanghai, China
sgcskytt@163.com
[2] ECE, New Jersey Institute of Technology, Newark, NJ, USA
[3] College of Computer Science,
Nanjing University of Information Science and Technology, Nanjing, China

Abstract. This paper presents a stereo image coding method using reversible data hiding technique so that the right frame can be recovered losslessly and the left frame can be reconstructed with high visual quality. Utilizing the similarity between two frames in a stereo image pair the required size of storage and transmission bandwidth for the stereo image pair can be reduced to 50 %. A residual error matrix with a dynamic range of $[-255, 255]$ is obtained by applying a frame-wise disparity algorithm which first shifts the left frame horizontally by a certain amount and then computes its difference to the right frame. Next, thus the generated residual error image with gray levels $[0, 255]$ is obtained losslessly by a proposed labeling scheme. JPEG2000 lossy compression is then applied to the residual error image. The histogram-pair based reversible data hiding scheme is then utilized to embed the JPEG2000 lossy compressed data into the right frame. Compared with the prior art, which uses a block-based disparity estimation algorithm and a location map based reversible data hiding, the proposed method has demonstrated that the stereo image can be reconstructed with higher visual quality and with faster processing speed. Specifically, the experiments have demonstrated that both the PSNR and visual quality of the reconstructed stereo image pair are higher than those achieved by the prior arts.

Keywords: Stereo image coding · Histogram-pair based image reversible data hiding · Frame-wise algorithm · Labeling scheme

1 Introduction

With the rapid development of information technology, especially unprecedented computing capacity, stereo vision technology has made considerable progress and been applied widely in the fields like 3d TV etc. More and more vivid visual experiences are brought to people. But one stereo image pair is composed of two 2-D similar images,

This research is largely supported by Shanghai City Board of education scientific research innovation projects (12ZZ033) and National Natural Science Foundation of China (NSFC) on project (90304017).

© Springer International Publishing Switzerland 2015
Y.-Q. Shi et al. (Eds.): IWDW 2014, LNCS 9023, pp. 201–214, 2015.
DOI: 10.1007/978-3-319-19321-2_15

its storage space and transmission bandwidth required may be twice larger than the traditional image applications. So it is important to develop efficient stereo image coding techniques to decrease the cost of the storing and transmitting stereo images.

Coltuc and Caciula proposed a method in [4] to solve this problem. Using the relation between two frames of a stereo image pair, they first achieved a residual error image by predicting the left frame using the right frame. Then the residual error image was applied lossy compression, and then reversibly embedded into the right frame. So only the marked right frame needed to be saved or transmitted as it contained the information of the whole stereo image. In the decoding end, the compressed residual error image can be losslessly retrieved from the right frame. With the retrieved error image and the right frame, the left frame can be reconstructed approximately. If the residual error image was embedded without going through the lossy compression, the left frame can be recovered losslessly as well. However, the capacity of reversible data hiding is usually unable to satisfy the requirement of saving all the information of the residual error image. Hence, the distortion to the left frame is unavoidable in [4].

In order to reduce the distortion, Coltuc [6] further proposed a dense disparity compensation scheme to decrease the information of the residual error image. This scheme calculates the disparity of every left frame point with SAD (sum of absolute differences). In consequence, better relevant information can be achieved and the quality of reconstructed left frame was enhanced. However, this way needs to record too much disparity information and hence leads to high computational complexity.

After that, Ellinas [5] and Chen [3] proposed the block-based disparity estimation and compensation schemes by. They divided the image into non-overlapping but connected blocks, and obtained the relevant information by searching the right frame for the matched block in the left frame. The SAD is used to evaluate the matching precision. The calculated relevant information is comprised of a disparity vector field and a residual error matrix. Although this method reduces the record information and computational complexity, the improvement is not obviously.

If every pixel of a frame is presented by an 8 bits number, the value range of the residual error matrix is [−255, 255]. And for the convenience of data compression, the residual error matrix should be preprocessed to generate a residual error image with value range constrained in [0, 255]. For instance, in [4–6], every pixel of the residual error matrix is first added by 255 and then divided by 2, followed by a ceiling operation to obtain the integer pixel value of the residual error image. In recovery, each pixel in the residual error image is multiplied by 2 and then minus by 255. It can be seen that the scheme adopted by [4] will generate distortion. To eliminate the distortion, a conditionally reversible preprocessing algorithm was proposed in [3]. Although the proposed scheme can eliminate distortion in some images, but in other images, the distortion always exits.In this paper we first propose a frame-wise disparity estimation algorithm to calculate residual error matrix. Then the residual error matrix is processed to a residual error image with value range [0, 255]. This process is lossless by means of a labeling scheme. Moreover, a more efficient reversible data hiding method named Histogram-Pair Based Reversible Data Hiding is proposed to increase the embedding capacity and improve the PSNR of the watermarked right frame. The experimental results show that both the PSNR and visual quality of the reconstructed stereo image pair are higher than that achieved by the prior arts [3–6].

2 Block Diagram of Proposed Stereo Image Coding

The stereo image transmission framework proposed in this paper is illustrated in Fig. 1. In the coding process, a stereo image pair is coded as a watermarked 2D image. Specifically it is the right frame with watermark hidden inside which can help us to reconstruct the left-frame approximately. In the receiver, the stereo image pair can be reconstructed if the stereo image decoder is conducted. Concretely, the right frame can be reconstructed exactly, while the left frame can be reconstructed closely to the original left frame. Without the above-mentioned processing at the receiver side, however, only a slightly degraded 2D right frame can be shown. Notations used in this paper are listed below.

L: the left frame of a stereo image pair
R: the right frame of the stereo image pair
M × N: the size of the left and right frame
SAD: sum of absolute differences
P: the frame-wise disparity estimated according to SAD (the detailed definition will be
    given in Sect. 3)
r: residual error matrix of stereo image
r': residual error image obtained from r
cr: compressed residual error image
mr: recovered residual error image at end of decompression
mr': recovered residual error matrix obtained from mr
L': the left matrix reconstructed by mr and R

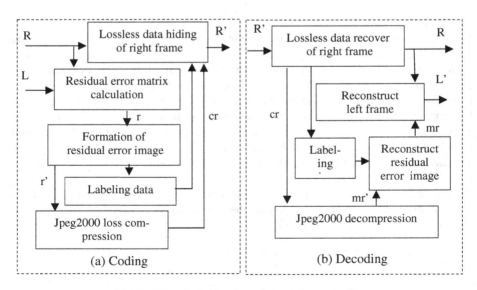

Fig. 1. Flowchart of proposed stereo image coding

3   Residual Information and Sum of Absolute Differences

This paper proposes a frame-wise disparity estimation algorithm, which also employs SAD (sum of absolute differences) to evaluate the similarity between frames. However, unlike the traditional estimation algorithms [3, 5, 6], we compute the SAD between two overall frames instead of a large number of blocks or pixels. Meanwhile, only one shifting offset, the left frame with respect to the right frame, need to be recorded. Apparently, the computational complexity of the estimation of disparity is greatly decreased. And we also note that the effect of the estimation is not obviously degraded because the stereo image pair are rather similar to each other. The detailed description is shown as follows.

Given a stereo image pair with size M × N, the frame-wise disparity can be calculated by:

$$P = \arg\min_{d}(SAD(d)), \quad m \leq d \leq n \tag{1}$$

Where d is the shifting offset of the left frame with respect to the right frame with a predefined value range in [m, n]. Although the offset could be with fraction implemented by image interpolation, we find integer is accurate enough for our disparity estimation. The difference between two frames SAD is calculated as follows,

$$SAD(d) = \sum_{i=1}^{M} \sum_{j=1}^{d} |L(i,j) - R(i,1)|$$
$$+ \sum_{i=1}^{M} \sum_{j=1}^{N-d} |L(i,j+d) - R(i,j)|, \quad m \leq d \leq n \tag{2}$$

Equation (2) consists of two terms. The first one is associated with the part of left frame that is shifted beyond the range of right frame. To obtain the difference between the two frames in this case, we just subtract the first column of the right frame from each column of this part of the left frame. The second term of Eq. (2) is associated with the rest part of the left frame. We compute the difference for the pixels in this part to the ones that are located at the same positions of the right frame. Furthermore, only horizontally shifting needs to be considered in the applications like 3D TV, as the 3D cameras are usually fixed with the same height. So we only add d to the horizontal coordinate of L. For example, if we set m = 1 and n = 9, the minimum SAD will be searched by shifting left frame from 1 to 9 pixels. Assuming it is $d = 6$ we obtain the minimum SAD, the frame-wise disparity P is equal 6.

Figure 2 illustrates our pipeline of calculating residual error matrix as well as disparity estimation. After the frame-wise disparity P has been calculated, the residual error matrix can be calculated by Eq. (3):

$$r(i,j) = \begin{cases} L(i,j+P) - R(i,j) & , \quad 1 \leq i \leq M, \ 1 \leq j \leq N - P \\ L(i,j) - R(i,1) & , \quad 1 \leq i \leq M, \ 1 \leq j \leq P \end{cases} \tag{3}$$

We note again that in left frame the columns which are shifted beyond the right frame (i.e., the column number is smaller than P) should be corresponding to the first

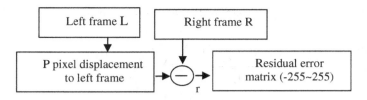

Fig. 2. Residual error matrix calculation

column of the right frame. Similarly, the procedure of reconstruction of the left frame
L' in the decoder end is also performed with two different manners, namely:

$$L'(i,j) = \begin{cases} mr(i,j+P) + R(i,j) & , \quad 1 \le i \le M,\ 1 \le j \le N - P \\ mr(i,j) + R(i,1) & , \quad 1 \le i \le M,\ 1 \le j \le P \end{cases} \quad (4)$$

Where $mr(.)$ is the residual error matrix recovered at decoding end. Because of
JPEG2000 lossy compression performed in the encoding end (introduced in the next
section), $mr(.)$ is not completely equal to r. So if there are pixels in L' beyond the
normal value range [0, 255], we just truncate them to 0 or 255.

4   Residual Error Image and Labeling Scheme

For a stereo image presented on 8 bits, the values in the residual error matrix r obtained
by Eq. (3) lie in [− 255, 255]. For the convenience of data compression, r should be
preprocessed to generate a grayscale residual error image denoted by r′ whose pixel
values are constrained to [0, 255].The scheme adopted by [4–6] are all irreversible and
adopted in [3] also generate distortion in some images. To eliminate distortion, labeling
scheme was proposed in this paper. According to our experimental results on many
stereo images downloaded from http://vision.middlebury.edu/stereo, we find most
points of a residual error matrix are in the range of [-127,127]. So we generate residual
error image by shrinking the histogram of the residual error matrix as illustrated in
Eq. (5) and Fig. 3.

In Eq. (5) the first line is associated with the points of residual matrix r ranging
from −128 to127 (B and C in Fig. 3). The second and third lines are corresponding to
region A and D in Fig. 3, respectively.

$$r'(i,j) = \begin{cases} 128 + r(i,j) & , \quad if\ -128 \le r(i,j) \le +127 \\ -r(i,j) - 129 & , \quad if\ r(i,j) < -128 \\ 128 + abs\{(r(i,j) - 255)\} & , \quad if\ r(i,j) > +127 \end{cases} \quad (5)$$

In order for reversibility, we need to record the positions of the points in A and D
regions of Fig. 3. Namely, if r (i, j) is greater than 127 or smaller than −128, we record
its coordinate (i, j), namely labeling in this paper. Because the frames of a stereo image
pair are rather similar to each other, only a limited amount of information needs to be
recorded. We will also embed this recorded information into right frame after

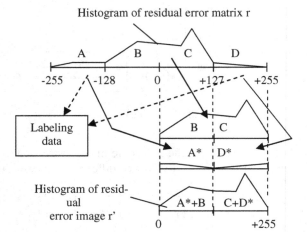

Fig. 3. Formation of residual error image by residual error matrix

compressed labeling data losslessly by using the adaptive arithmetic coding (AAC) algorithm [7].

Using the labeling scheme given in Eq. (5) and Fig. 3, we are able to losslessly transfer the residual error matrix to the residual error image, making it convenient to compress the residual via mature image coding method like JPEG2000. Our proposed labeling scheme consists of two functions, namely position recording and histogram shrinking. We note that in Fig. 3 and Eq. (5) the points in region A and D of the histogram are not simply shifted as shown in Fig. 4 and Eq. (6). Instead, we first invert A and D left to right before shifting them to merge with B and C.

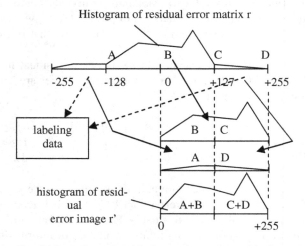

Fig. 4. Simple formation of residual error image by residual error matrix

The motivation reduces the change in pixel and maintains the spatial correlation between pixels in the residual error image. And experimental results show that using the shrinking method of Eq. (5) can improve the PSNR about 0.5 dB comparing that given by Eq. (6).

$$r'(i,j)_{Simple} = \begin{cases} 128 + r(i,j) & , & if \quad -128 \leq r(i,j) \leq +127 \\ r(i,j) + 255 & , & if \quad r(i,j) < -128 \\ r(i,j) & , & if \quad r(i,j) > +127 \end{cases} \tag{6}$$

Because the lossy JPEG2000 compression and decompression, the recover residual error matrix mr' will have some digression from r'. Equation (7) shows how to recover the residual error matrix from the residual error image in the decoding end. The first line is at [0 ~ −+255] or B and C in lower of Fig. 3. The second line is at [0 ~ +127] (before JPEG2000, the pixel gray level with labeling is only at the range [0 ~ +126]) or A* (reverse rank) in lower of Fig. 3. The third line is at [+128 ~ −+255] or D* (reverse rank) in lower of Fig. 3.

$$mr(i,j) = \begin{cases} -128 + mr'(i,j) & , & if\ no\ labeling\ and\ 0 \leq mr'(i,j) \leq +255 \\ -255 + abs\{(mr'(i,j) - 126)\} & , & if\ with\ labeling\ and\ mr'(i,j) < +128 \\ 128 + abs\{(mr'(i,j) - 255)\} & , & if\ with\ labeling\ and\ mr'(i,j) \geq +128 \end{cases}$$

$$\tag{7}$$

From Eqs. (5) and (7) and Fig. 3, we can see that the residual error image can be recovered with small distortion by lossy JPEG2000 compression and decompression only.

5 Large Payload Optimal Histogram-Pair Image Reversible Data Hiding

The data hiding approach employed in this paper is an extension of the one given in [2], namely our proposed Optimal Histogram-pair and Prediction-error based Image Reversible data hiding approach. The major improvement made here is that using multiple circles embedding scheme in order for large capacity of data hiding. The output image of each pass of circle embedding is the input image of the next pass (refer to Fig. 5 and Tables 1 and 2). The embedding capacity of the approach in [2] is 0.7bpp, which is satisfying for authentication. But it is not large enough for stereo image coding, because we cannot accomplish the coding unless the compression ratio on the left frame is smaller than 0.1 (0.7/8). In order to guarantee the high quality of recovery a data hiding approach with large capacity is required. With our newly proposed multiple circle embedding the embedding capacity is clearly improved, say, to 2.6bpp (5 pass) and 1.6 bpp (4 pass) for Baby and Tsukuba, respectively. The detailed setting of the data hiding approach used in this paper is given in Tables 1 and 2. In our implementation we employ the numbers of circle 4 and 6 for the two stereo images.

In order to explain the parameters involved in Tables 1 and 2, we simply introduce the process of our proposed histogram-pair based reversible data hiding approach.

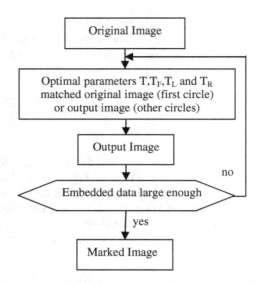

Fig. 5. Large payload by histogram-pair reversible data hiding using multi-circles

Table 1. Image Tsukuba embedding by histogram-pair based reversible data hiding

Circle	Payload (bpp)	PSNR (dB)	T	T_F	T_L	T_R	Image (original)	Δ Payload (bpp)	Image (marked)
1	0.8	37.71	4	350	7	5	Tsukuba	0.8	Tsukuba1
2	1.2	30.39	6	2500	6	6	Tsukuba1	0.4	Tsukuba2
3	1.5	24.48	14	6000	14	14	Tsukuba2	0.3	Tsukuba3
4	1.6	20.01	8	14000	8	9	Tsukuba3	0.1	Tsukuba4

Table 2. Image Baby embedding by histogram-pair based reversible data hiding

Circle	Payload (bpp)	PSNR (dB)	T	T_F	T_L	T_R	Image (original)	Δ Payload (bpp)	Image (marked)
1	1.0	41.51	−3	100	0	0	Baby	1.0	Baby1
2	1.6	33.98	6	800	0	0	Baby1	0.6	Baby2
3	2.0	28.88	12	3000	6	8	Baby2	0.4	Baby3
4	2.3	26.38	−4	5000	0	4	Baby3	0.3	Baby4
5	2.5	24.79	40	5000	0	12	Baby4	0.2	Baby5
6	2.6	23.76	10	3000	0	3	Baby5	0.1	Baby6

This data hiding approach was first proposed by our group in 2007 [9] where the readers may find some detailed introductions. The data, a binary sequence, is hided in the image by modifying the magnitude in the transform domain.

When hiding the data, we first define a threshold T. Then from the beginning of the image, say the top left, each magnitude x is modified as follows.

$$x = \begin{cases} x & , \quad \textit{if } x < T \\ x + b & , \quad \textit{if } x = T \\ x + 1 & , \quad \textit{if } x > T \end{cases} \quad (8)$$

Where b is one of the information bit to be hided. If there are still data bits left when all the magnitudes have been scanned, we enlarge the threshold T and perform the data hiding process again. This iteration may be repeated until all the data bits can embedded into the image.

Now let's introduce the four optimal threshold parameters in Tables 1 and 2, namely T, TF, TL and TR. In the multiple circles embedding scheme the input image is different in each pass. So we need to re-choose the four parameters during new the data hiding process.

(a) The optimal magnitude threshold T: the threshold that is corresponding to the highest PSNR given the data to be embedded.

(b) The optimal fluctuation threshold T_F, defining the image regions by surrounding neighbors, which are comparatively smoother than the others. Hiding data into the smooth image region will make the highest PSNR. The optimal context threshold

(c) The optimal left and right grayscale threshold T_L and T_R: Before data hiding, we shrink the histogram of image, such that the grayscale range is within after data hiding. In consequence, not only optimal result is obtained, but also the overflow/underflow problem can be effectively relieved.

From Fig. 6 it can be observed that our employed lossless data hiding method is able to embed more data bits, and meanwhile the PSNR is much larger than the prior arts [3, 6].

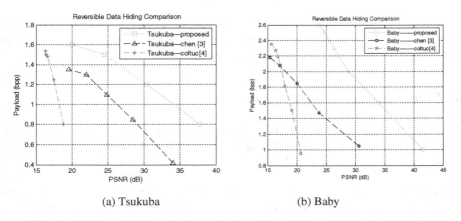

(a) Tsukuba   (b) Baby

Fig. 6. PSNR vs. Payload for the test images of Tsukuba and Baby (see Fig. 7).

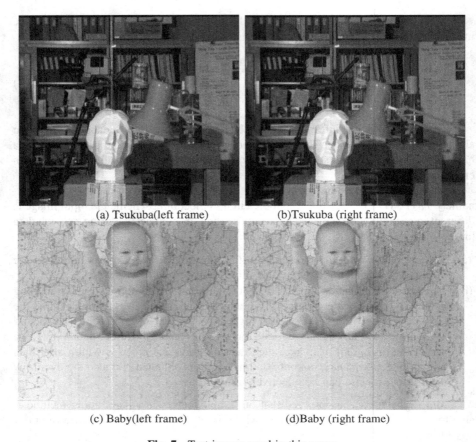

(a) Tsukuba(left frame)   (b)Tsukuba (right frame)

(c) Baby(left frame)   (d)Baby (right frame)

Fig. 7. Test images used in this paper

The marked stereo image with high visual quality is favorable for the applications that stereo image decoding is unavailable. For instance, the users of 3D television can watch the 2D video directly when they lack of the decoder for 3D signal.

6 Stereo Image Reconstruction

As shown in Fig. 1, if decoder is available users can obtain the stereo image by decoding (otherwise, they can only watch the marked two-dimensional image). The decoding process is given as follows:

- Step 1: Using the data extracting method provided by [2], we obtain the compressed residual image cr, record information and visual difference value P. In addition, the original right frame R is also recovered meanwhile.
- Step 2: Decompress cr by means of JPEG2000 to obtain the residual image mr'. Decoding the record information by mean of Arithmetic coding algorithm in [7].

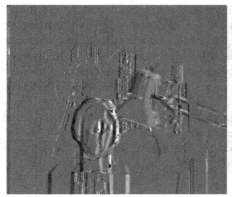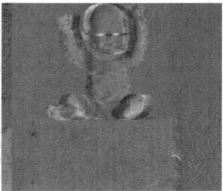

Fig. 8. The Residual Image

(a) Proposed reconstructed left frame   (b) Proposed embedded right frame

(c) Coltuc [6] reconstructed left frame   (d) Coltuc[6] embedded right frame

Fig. 9. Test results of Tsukuba

- Step 3: Modifying mr' to obtain correlation matrix mr. According to Eq. (7), for the pixels in mr' the coordinates of which are not given in record information, we subtract 128 from their values. For the pixels in mr' the coordinates of which are given in record information and its gray value less than 128, we multiply their values by −1 and minus 129. For the pixels in mr' the coordinates of which are given in record information and its gray value more than 128, we use 255 minus its gray value and add 128.
- Step 4: Reconstructing the right frame L' via the right frame R and the correlation information mr. According to Eq. (4), before adding with the right frame R, we left translate the correlation information with and offset of P pixel. The columns translated beyond the frame are added to the first column of R.

7   Experimental Results

We test our proposed method by means of two standard stereo images, namely Tsukuba (384 × 288 in size) and Baby (413 × 370 in size) as shown in Fig. 3.

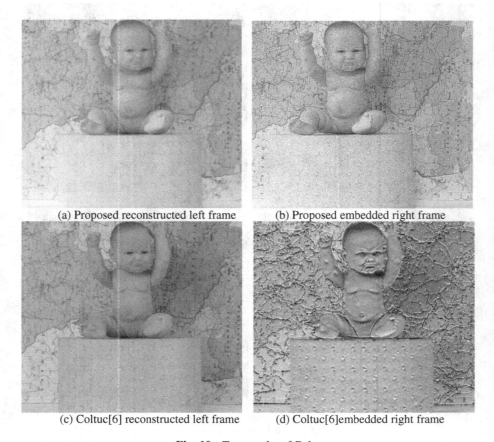

(a) Proposed reconstructed left frame   (b) Proposed embedded right frame

(c) Coltuc[6] reconstructed left frame   (d) Coltuc[6]embedded right frame

Fig. 10.   Test results of Baby

The residual images of Tsukuba and Baby derived from the disparity of two frames (refer to Sect. 2) are given in Fig. 8.

In order for good visual quality of the reconstructed image, we wish the loss JPEG2000 compression performed on residual image could be as slightly as possible. And hence, the data hiding capacity should be large enough to store the compressed residual image. As presented in Fig. 6, the employed reversible data hiding method is able to embed more data under the same PSNR in comparison with the method in [1, 8].

Figures 9 and 10 present the frames at the decoding end of Tsukuba and Baby, respectively. Each figure includes the marked right frame and the reconstructed left frame. In addition, the results of Coltuc's method are also given. It is easy to observe the advantage of our proposed coding method in visual quality.

Table 3 presents the comparison result of the proposed stereo image coding method with three state-of-the-art ones in terms of payload vs. PSNR. It can be observed that the proposed method is able to reconstruct the left frames of the both stereo images with the largest PSNR. This result can also explain the good visual quality of the decoded stereo images illustrated in Figs. 9 and 10.

Table 3. Comparisons of stereo image coding methods on Payload vs. PSNR

Method	Tsukuba			Baby		
	Payload (bpp)	Embedded right frame PSNR (dB)	Reconstructed left frame PSNR (dB)	Payload (bpp)	Embedded right frame PSNR (dB)	Reconstructed left frame PSNR (dB)
Proposed	1.6	20.01	44.63	2.56	23.76	49.96
Chen [3]	1.35	19.59	42.72	2.18	15.44	48.96
Coltuc [4]	1.55	16.3	38.5	2.4	15.8	39.0
Coltuc [6]	1.55	16.3	44	2.4	15.8	41.5

8 Discussions and Conclusions

1. This paper proposed a stereo image encoding/decoding method, which is able to hide the stereo information into one frame and only this frame needs to be transmitted. As a result, the transmission efficiency is doubled and the storage cost is saved greatly. In addition, the visual quality of the marked image is improved in comparison with the prior arts. Because to watch the marked image directly without decoding is visually acceptable, the stereo image playback system is compatible with the 2D image system.
2. The right frame can be recovered losslessly and the left frame can be reconstructed with high quality. For example, the PSNR of reconstructed of left frame in proposed method reaches either 44.63 dB (Tsukuba) or 49.96 dB (Baby) respectively. It is about 2 dB (Tsukuba) or 1 dB (Baby) proposed higher than that of prior-arts, see Table 3.
3. We conclude as follows why our decoded stereo image is with better visual quality than the prior arts:

(a) The compressed residual image is embedded by means of histogram-pair based data hiding algorithm. Comparing with Tian's DE-based algorithm [1], the histogram-pair based algorithm is with higher PSNR and larger embedding capacity. Refer to Table 3, the embedding capacity is 1.6 bpp when PSNR is 20.01 dB for the proposed method marking Tsukuba image, which improves 0.25 bpp comparing the best prior art under similar PSNR value. And the improvement for Baby image is even more obvious. Furthermore, owing to the advantage of the proposed histogram-pair based data hiding method, we can obtain the better visual quality than the prior arts under the same PSNR value (refer to Fig. 10(a) and (c)).

(b) The residual error image [0, 255] is generated by labeling scheme proposed from residual error matrix lossless (before JPEG2000 loss compression). The residual error matrix [−255,255] is obtained lossless in proposed scheme instead of obtained loss by downsize images with gray level [−127, 127] in prior-arts.

4. The proposed method is with higher stereo image coding speed than the prior arts owing to the use of frame-wise disparity algorithm. The algorithm simplifies the computation and satisfies the requirement of real time applications. And, more important, higher quality of left frame than that in prior-arts.

References

1. Tian, J.: Reversible data embedding using a difference expansion. IEEE Trans. Circ. Syst. Video Technol. **13**, 890–896 (2003)
2. Xuan, G., Tong, X., Teng, J., Zhang, X., Shi, Y.Q.: Optimal histogram-pair and prediction-error based image reversible data hiding. In: Shi, Y.Q., Kim, H.-J., Pérez-González, F. (eds.) IWDW 2012. LNCS, vol. 7809, pp. 368–383. Springer, Heidelberg (2013)
3. Chen, H.: An effective stereo image coding method with reversible watermarking. J. Comput. Inf. Syst. **8**(7), 2761–2768 (2012)
4. Coltuc, D., Caciula, I.: Stereo embedding by reversible watermarking: further results. In: Proceedings of the International Symposium on Signals, Circuits and Systems, pp. 1–4 (2009)
5. Ellinas, J.N.: Reversible watermarking on stereo image sequences. Int. J. Sign. Proces. **5**(3), 210–215 (2009)
6. Coltuc, D.: On stereo embedding by reversible watermarking. In: Proceedings. of International. Symposium on Signals, Circuits and Systems, pp. 1–4 (2007)
7. Fred, W.: An adaptive arithmetic coding library. http://www.cipr.rpi.edu/swheeler/ac
8. Coltuc, D.: Improved capacity reversible watermarking. In: IEEE International Conference on Image Processing (ICIP 2007), San Antonio, Texas, USA, vol. 3, pp. 249–252, (2007)
9. Xuan, G., Shi, Y.Q., Chai, P., Cui, X., Ni, Z., Tong, X.: Optimum histogram pair based image lossless data embedding. In: Shi, Y.Q., Kim, H.-J., Katzenbeisser, S. (eds.) IWDW 2007. LNCS, vol. 5041, pp. 264–278. Springer, Heidelberg (2008)

Reversible and Robust Audio Watermarking Based on Spread Spectrum and Amplitude Expansion

Akira Nishimura[✉]

Department of Informatics, Faculty of Informatics, Tokyo University of Information
Sciences, 4-1 Onaridai, Wakaba, Chiba, Chiba 265-8501, Japan
akira@rsch.tuis.ac.jp

Abstract. Recently, a technique that uses quantization index modulation and amplitude expansion has been proposed for reversible and robust audio watermarking. However, when applied to modified stego audio, the technique is not reversible. Here, a novel technique that is both reversible and robust is proposed for hiding data in audio. It is perfectly reversible for unmodified stego signals and is semi-reversible for perceptually coded stego signals. A robust payload is embedded by direct-sequence spread-spectrum modulation, with the sequence determined from the amplitude expansion in time and frequency of integer modified discrete cosine transform (MDCT) coefficients. Simultaneously, a reversible payload is embedded into the apertures in the amplitude histogram that result from amplitude expansion of the integer MDCT coefficients. The robustness and size of the reversible payload were evaluated by simulation for 20 music pieces. The reversible-payload capacity was approximately 4.8 kilobits per second. Encoding the stego signals into MP3, tandem MP3, and MPEG4AAC, and applying an additive single delay to the stego signals, revealed a maximum bit error rate of less than 6.5 % with a robust payload of 7.2-bits per second. Measurement of the objective quality of the stego audio and audio recovered from the modified stego signal was done by using software based on the perceptual evaluation of audio quality algorithm. The results showed that the mean objective difference grade (ODG) was better than 'perceptible, but not annoying' for the stego audio. Semi-recovery from the perceptually coded stego signals was realized in terms of small differences in ODG between the recovered and coded signals.

Keywords: Audio coding · Robustness · Acoustic signal processing · Information hiding · Objective audio quality

1 Introduction

Reversible data hiding is a technique to embed a payload into host data in such a way that the consistency of the host is perfectly preserved and the host data can be restored during extraction of the payload [22]. Conventional techniques

© Springer International Publishing Switzerland 2015
Y.-Q. Shi et al. (Eds.): IWDW 2014, LNCS 9023, pp. 215–229, 2015.
DOI: 10.1007/978-3-319-19321-2_16

for reversible data hiding include histogram expansion [27], histogram-based difference expansion [12], and lossless compression [6]. Reversible data hiding in audio can be classified into three categories of technique according to the domain of the embedded data: the waveform domain [17,20,23,26], spectral domain [13], or compressed data domain [16].

Reversible data hiding in audio is useful for archiving, transmitting, and authenticating high-quality audio data that contains any of metadata, secret data, and forensic tampering-detection data. Hiding techniques should include the ability to remove and rehide these data. For most applications, a reversible payload capacity of more than several kilobits per second is needed. However, all existing techniques for reversible data hiding in audio are so fragile that any modification to the stego signal, such as the application of perceptual codecs, additive noise, or low-pass filtering, completely corrupts the payload. Such techniques are therefore not suitable for use in conjunction with copyright protection schemes, for which the payload should survive after modifying the stego signal.

Robust audio watermarking technology intended for copyright protection is typically designed to make it difficult to separate the identification code from the audio signal after embedding. Watermarking is expected to be robust and secure against audio coding [21] and intentional attacks [7] on the stego signal. In addition, the quality degradation of the stego signal relative to the host signal should be minimized to maintain the commercial value of the underlying host signal.

Several reversible and robust watermarking techniques have been proposed for video [2] and still images [3,4,24]. However, the methods applied to visual data cannot be applied directly to audio data without compromising the audibility of the data and robustness of the watermarking. For example, a high-pass filtering attack with a low cut-off frequency (e.g., 20 Hz) and amplification/attenuation attacks easily modify the histogram rotation [3,24] of the waveform's amplitude without degrading the sound quality of the stego audio.

Recently, a robust and reversible audio watermarking has been proposed [20]. In the technique, a robust payload is embedded by quantization index modulation (QIM) of the averaged power levels of the segmented stego waveforms. Simultaneously, a reversible payload is embedded into the apertures in the amplitude histogram that result from amplitude expansion by QIM. Extraction of the reversible payload and robust payload and reconstruction of the host audio are achievable so long as no modification is applied to the stego audio. The robust payload can be extracted after only non-intentional modification to the stego signal. However, semi-reversibility, that is, moderate recovery of the host signal from the modified stego signal, such as can be done with MP3-coded stego audio, is not possible.

In this paper, a novel technique for reversible and robust audio watermarking is proposed. By combining a spread-spectrum technique with amplitude expansion, semi-reversibility is achieved, in addition to the features of the previously mentioned technique. In other words, a robust watermark can be removed from the modified stego audio so that moderate recovery of the host sound quality is achieved.

2   Encoding

Techniques for reversible hiding of audio data in the frequency domain first convert segmented waveform signals into spectral data by using an integer conversion, such as an integer discrete cosine transform (intDCT) [13] or an integer modified-DCT (intMDCT) [18]. These techniques amplify the spectral coefficients in the high-frequency region by shifting the coefficients 1 bit toward the most significant bit position, which allows adding payload data to the least significant bit (LSB) position. Subsequent application of the inverse transform to the modified spectral data generates the stego waveform data. Unfortunately, these techniques are so fragile that no data can be extracted after modification of the stego audio [13] and extraction of a robust payload was limited at best [18].

In this section, a direct-sequence spread-spectrum modulation technique based on expansion (i.e., amplification) of intMDCT spectra is proposed. The amount of phase shift of a pseudorandom number (PN) sequence is used as a robust watermark. A reversible payload is embedded into apertures in the amplitude histogram that result from amplitude expansion; this is described in Sect. 2.2.

2.1   Embedding a Robust Payload Using Direct-Sequence Spread-Spectrum Modulation

The host signal waveform is segmented and fed into an N-point intMDCT. IntMDCT is implemented as intDCT type IV [11] with a lifting scheme that uses a half-overlapped sine window [9]. The intMDCT sends the ith frame of an N-sample waveform x_i into the $N/2$-sample frequency data $H(f, i)$, where $f(1 \leq f \leq N/2)$ is a discrete frequency and $1 \leq i \leq M$. IntMDCT and inverse intMDCT are perfectly reconstructive conversions across the entire frequency domain. A robust payload is embedded into an M-frame data segment frames; that is, one data frame consists of $(M + 1)N/2$ samples of a host signal, which corresponds to a duration of T_f s. Thus, an $M \times N/2$ time and frequency mapping of intMDCT coefficients is constructed to embed payload data.

The PN sequence $P(i)$ of length M is determined pseudorandomly by choosing entry as 1 or α with equal probability, where $(1 < \alpha \leq 2)$. The sequence is generated by a known secret key and specifies the discrete temporal positions at which to expand the coefficients of the frequency channel indicated by α. The PN sequence therefore forms the amplitude expansion map $A_e(f, i)$.

Figure 1 shows a schematic diagram of the two-dimensional expansion map $A_e(f, i)$ in time and frequency space, where a temporal PN sequence $P(i)$ indicates the coefficients to amplify; these are marked by filled squares in the figure. Robust payload bits are embedded into the relative phase difference between the pilot subbands and the payload subbands. The pilot subbands and the payload subbands are selected with equal probability by the known secret key. The coefficients of the lowest frequency are not used in order to maintain sound quality. In the left part of Fig. 1, the first payload subbands are circularly shifted by one frame, and the second payload subbands are shifted by four frames. The sifting width can be selected from among 0 to $M - 1$ in each data segment, so that

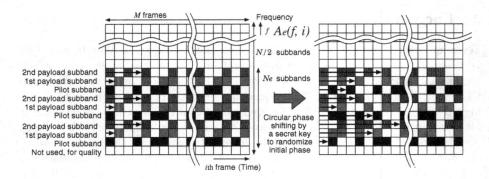

Fig. 1. Schematic two-dimensional representation in time and frequency space, with the PN sequence and embedding robust payload indicated. Filled squares represent an expansion factor of α.

the amount of payload bits that can be represented by one subband group is $\lfloor \log_2 M \rfloor$. Robust payload bits are Gray coded to reduce error bits in the extraction process. After that, the PN sequences for all subbands are circularly shifted by the secret key to randomize the initial phases. This constructs $A_e(f, i)$.

2.2   Reversible Data Hiding Based on Amplitude Expansion

Linear amplitude expansion and rounding for the intMDCT spectrum, that is, $H(f, i)$ multiplied by $A_e(f, i)$, creates apertures in the amplitude histogram of the spectra. A binary reversible payload $b(k) \in \{0, 1\}$ can be embedded in these apertures. Letting k represent the index for the kth bit of the reversible payload, the embedding operation that yields the stego spectra $S(f, i)$ is as follows:

$$
S(f, i) = \begin{cases} \text{round}(A_e(f, i)H(f, i)) - b(k) & \text{if round}(A_e(f, i)H(f, i) + 1) \neq \\ & \text{round}(A_e(f, i)H(f, i)) + 1 \text{ and } H(f, i) > 0, \\ \text{round}(A_e(f, i)H(f, i)) + b(k) & \text{if round}(A_e(f, i)H(f, i) - 1) \neq \\ & \text{round}(A_e(f, i)H(f, i)) - 1 \text{ and } H(f, i) < 0, \\ \text{round}(A_e(f, i)H(f, i)) & \text{otherwise.} \end{cases} \tag{1}
$$

The inverse intMDCT generates the stego waveform from the resultant stego spectral data. If amplitude overflow or underflow occurs in the stego signal, amplification is canceled in that frame. Since successive frames are overlapped by $N/2$ samples, amplification is canceled in the previous frames if the overflow/underflow is still observed. Those frames in which amplification was canceled are recorded in a location map represented as M bits, with each frame represented by 1 bit with the value of 1 (canceled) or 0 (not canceled). The location map is embedded into the LSBs at the end of the data frame; this is described in Sect. 2.3.

2.3   LSB Synchronization in Encoding Stage

To detect a payload and recover the host signal, MDCT frames created during the embedding process should perfectly match those recovered during the detection process. For this reason, precise frame synchronization should be implemented. Two methods of synchronization are used: a fast LSB synchronization for unmodified stego signals [20] and a relatively slow stepwise MDCT synchronization for modified stego signals.

An LSB synchronization method [20] that preserves the stego signal is as follows. Signature bits are generated by applying bitwise-XOR operations to the K ($K \geq 32$) bits of the synchronization code and to masking bits selected from the LSBs of the stego samples at locations predetermined from the secret key.

The signature bits are put into the stego samples in place of the LSBs at the determined locations. Before substitution, the to-be-replaced LSBs of the stego samples are embedded into the reserved frame. The same masking and replacement procedures are conducted to embed the location map.

3   Decoding

The decoding process begins the LSB synchronization. The decoder must know the secret key and embedding parameters used by the encoder. A flow diagram of the decoding process is shown in Fig. 2.

3.1   LSB Synchronization in Decoding Stage

Finding the signature bits that have been substituted for the LSBs of the stego samples accomplishes frame synchronization. To do this, the detector performs bitwise-XOR operations on the LSBs of the stego sample, which constitute the masking bits, using the signature bits. This is possible because the relative positions of the masking bits and the signature bits are known from the secret key. The resultant bits will be identical to the synchronization bits if the selected positions are synchronized with those used in the embedding process. A stepwise search by shifting the selected positions achieves frame synchronization with a low computational load.

3.2   MDCT Synchronization

Failure to find the signature bits in a stego segment longer than the length of a data frame implies that the stego signal in the frame has been tampered with. In such cases, another synchronization technique is used, which consists of stepwise MDCT trials conducted by shifting the initial sample of the frame. This synchronization method is shown in the upper right part of Fig. 2 and is described next.

Let $\boldsymbol{y}_j(t)$ be a stego signal starting at the jth sample, with $t = 0, 1, ..., (M + 1)N/2 - 1$. IntMDCT operations are applied to $\boldsymbol{y}_j(t)$ segmented by N-sampling to obtain the MDCT coefficient vectors $\boldsymbol{F}(i)$, where $i = 1, 2, ..., M$ is the frame number. This generates an $M \times N/2$ time and frequency map of MDCT coefficients. The initial phases of the temporal series of the pilot subbands are aligned by using the secret key, and then the absolute values of the coefficients in all pilot subbands are summed to obtain $F_p(i)$ (SyncSum procedure in Fig. 2). The function $X_p(i)$ gives the cross-correlation between the PN sequence $P(i)$ and $F_p(i)$ (XCorr procedure in Fig. 2). The output of $X_p(i)$ exhibits a distinct peak at frame number $T_p(j)$, which is offset from the initial frame of the target data frame. These transform operations are repeated while increment from $j = 1$ to $j \leq N/2$. The sample t_s that exhibits the largest peak among $X_p(T_p(j)), j = 1, 2, ..., N/2$ is chosen as the initial sample of the frame for MDCT, and $T_p(t_s)$ is the initial frame number of the target data frame.

3.3 Decoding Robust Payload

After frame synchronization, the robust payload is extracted. The lower right part of Fig. 2 shows the extraction of the robust payload.

IntMDCT operations are successively applied to the stego signal frames y_{t_s} beginning with the t_sth sample to build the coefficient map $S'(f, i)$. The phase differences among each subband are aligned by using the secret key. The absolute value of the MDCT coefficients belonging to the gth payload subbands are summed to create a temporal subband envelope $F_g(i)$. The cross-correlation between $F_g(i)$ and $P(i)$ will exhibit a distinct peak at the T_gth frame. The robust payload bits are extracted from this by decoding the Gray coding of T_g.

3.4 Decoding Reversible Payload

When LSB synchronization is accomplished, the stego signal is known to be unmodified, and so the host signal can be perfectly recovered. The location map that indexes the unexpanded frames is extracted at the beginning of decoding. A two-dimensional (time and frequency) expansion map $A_e(f, i)$ is perfectly reconstructed by using the extracted robust payload data, the location map extracted from the reserved LSBs of the stego signal, and the secret key. This is done by the method described in Sect. 2.1. In addition, the stego spectra $S(f, i)$ can be perfectly derived from the stego signal. Equation 2 extracts the reversible payload $b(k)$. The condition $b(k) = null$ indicates cases where no payload was embedded.

$$b(k) = \begin{cases} 0 & \text{if round(round}((S(f, i) \pm 1)/A_e(f, i))A_e(f, i)) \neq S(f, i) \pm 1 \\ 1 & \text{if round(round}(S(f, i)/A_e(f, i))A_e(f, i)) \neq S(f, i) \\ null & \text{otherwise.} \end{cases} \qquad (2)$$

3.5 Recovery of the Host Signal

If the stego signal has been modified, that is, if LSB synchronization fails, or if the robust payload could not be correctly extracted, then perfect recovery of the host signal is not possible. However, moderate recovery (semi-recovery) of the

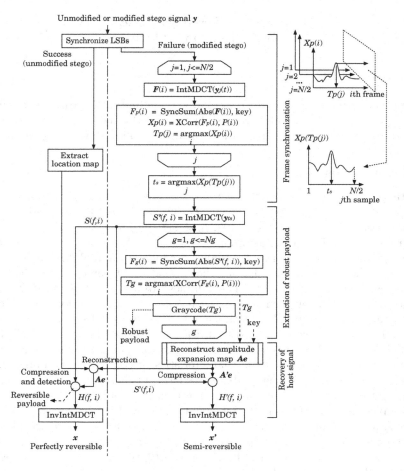

Fig. 2. Flow diagram of frame synchronization, payload detection, and recovery of the host signal.

host sound quality is possible. Equation (3) realizes semi-recovery of the host MDCT spectra $H'(f, i)$.

$$H'(f, i) = \text{round}(S'(f, i)/A'_e(f, i)), \qquad (3)$$

where $A'_e(f, i)$ is an expansion map reconstruceted from the extracted robust payload data.

When decoding the reversible payload from the spectra of unmodified stego audio is possible, Eq. (4) will perfectly recover the host MDCT spectra $H(f, i)$. When $b(k) = null$, the equality $b(k) = 0$ is substituted for Eq. (4). This gives

$$H(f, i) = \begin{cases} \text{round}((S(f, i) + b(k))/A_e(f, i)) & (S(f, i) \geq 0), \\ \text{round}((S(f, i) - b(k))/A_e(f, i)) & (S(f, i) < 0). \end{cases} \qquad (4)$$

Inverse intMDCT and inverse half-overlapped sine windowing are applied to $H'(f, i)$ (resp. $H(f, i)$) to obtain the recovered host signal $\boldsymbol{x}'$ (resp. $\boldsymbol{x}$).

4   Evaluation

Computer simulation was used to evaluate reversibility, the objective quality of the stego audio, the amount of reversible payload that could be embedded, and robustness against several types of modification applied to the stego audio.

4.1   Conditions

The target host signals consisted of 8 tracks from the sound quality assessment material (SQAM) collection [8] (tracks 27, 32, 35, 40, 65, 66, 69, and 70), each of which was played for 60 s. These host signals are also used in the Japan Electronics and Information Technology Industries Association technical report entitled 'The designation of audio quality for memory audio' [5]. The collection includes audio materials suitable for the evaluation of perceptual audio codecs and is distributed freely online. The samples are also recommended for use in testing robust audio watermarking technology [14]. In addition to the above tracks, the initial 60 s of 12 musical samples (tracks 1, 7, 13, 28, 37, 49, 54, 67, 64, 85, 91, and 100) were selected from the music genre database (RWC-MDB-G-2001) [10], which covers various music genres. These samples were chosen as representative of the acoustic characteristics of contemporary music pieces. These 20 pieces of music have also served the purpose of exploring common criteria for evaluating audio watermarking technologies [21]. These host signals are sampled at 44.1 kHz, with 16-bit quantization and stereo format.

Both a robust and a reversible payload were simultaneously embedded into each host signal. The robust payload consisted of random binary data, which was distributed at a rate of 108 bits over 15 s (7.2 bps). The size of the robust payload, which is defined by the parameter values shown in Table 1, was not tested as a parameter in the simulation since a rate of 6 bps is sufficient for storing a copyright management payload [1]. The reversible payload was in the form of random binary data.

The simulation was separated into four series of evaluations for different measures: amount of embeddable reversible payload, bit error rate (BER) of the robust payload after several types of modifications to the stego signal, objective sound quality degradation of the stego signals, and objective sound quality degradation of the recovered perceptually coded stego signals.

Because the reversible payload cannot be extracted from modified stego signals, the BER was measured for only the robust payload.

4.2   Amount of Embeddable Reversible Payload

Perfect recovery of the host signal from the stego signal and detection of a reversible payload require perfect detection of the robust payload. The robust payload was perfectly detected from all unmodified stego signals, which means that perfect recovery of the host signal was achieved.

Table 1. Parameter values for embedding.

Parameter	Symbol	Value
Expansion factor	α	1.26
Number of samples per frame	N	512
Number of subbands to embed	N_e	112
Number of groups	N_g	2
Length of synchronization code	K	32 bits
Length of data frame	M	860 frames
Duration of data frame	T_f	5.0 s
Sampling frequency	F_s	44.1 kHz

The average bitrate of the amount of reversible payload in 60 s of each host audio sample is shown in Fig. 3. The bitrate of the reversible payload depends on the expansion factor. Statistically, the bitrate of the reversible payload, excluding the M-bit location map and K-bit synchronization code, in every T_f-s period is $N_e(\alpha - 1)F_s/(N_f/2) - (M + K)/T_f = 4838$ bps.

Figure 3 shows that the contemporary music pieces from the RWC database maintain a relatively constant bitrate that is quite close to the theoretical value. The bitrates for SQAM tracks differ widely among the tracks. The amount of reversible payload depends mainly on the amplitude of the host signals. Signal frames that exhibit small amplitudes result in a large number of zeros in the MDCT domain. The reversible payload cannot be embedded into coefficients with a value of zero. In SQAM tracks 27, 66, and 70, from 18 % to 22 % frames have a root mean square (RMS) level below –80 dBFS.

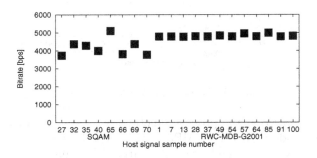

Fig. 3. Averaged bitrate of reversible payload.

4.3 Robustness Against Modifications

Robustness was tested by extracting the robust payload from the modified stego signal. From each sample, 45 s of the modified stego audio were chosen by beginning at a randomly chosen point in the initial 15 s, which simulates a clipping attack on the stego audio. The BER was measured for the 216 bits embedded

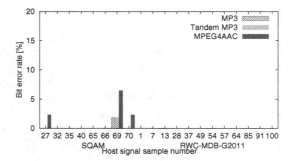

Fig. 4. BER for 216-bit robust payload after encoding and decoding using the perceptual codec.

in the interval from 15 to 45 s of the attacked (or coded) stego audio. The above evaluation method is recommended as part of the IHC evaluation criteria [14].

The results for testing with 128-kbps MP3 in joint-stereo mode, tandem 128-kbps MP3 in joint-stereo mode, and 96-kbps MPEG4AAC are shown in Fig. 4. The results with additive Gaussian noise included at an overall signal-to-noise ratio of 36 dB; bandpass filtering for the frequencies between 100 and 6000 Hz, –12 dB/oct.; and an additive single 100-ms delay of –6 dB are shown in Fig. 5.

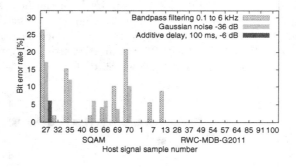

Fig. 5. BER for 216-bit robust payload.

The results show that the proposed method is robust against additive delay and perceptual codecs, including MP3, tandem MP3, and MPEG4AAC. However, SQAM tracks 27, 35, and 70 exhibit large BERs under additive Gaussian noise and bandpass filtering conditions. These SQAM tracks contain many frames with an RMS level below –80 dBFS. These frames resulted in a high BER when Gaussian noise was added or the bandpass filter was applied.

4.4   Objective Quality of Stego Audio

The perceptual evaluation of audio quality (PEAQ) algorithm uses a number of psycho-acoustical measures that are combined to provide a measure of the quality difference between two instances of a signal (a reference and a test signal).

The PEAQ measurement is produced as an objective difference grade (ODG), which corresponds to the subjective difference grade (SDG) likely to be obtained from the procedure of subjective quality evaluation (ITU-R BS.1116-1).

A basic implementation of the PEAQ algorithm based on ITU-R BS.1387 implemented by Kabal [15] (PQevalAudio v2r0) was used to calculate the ODGs of the 20 music signals. The reference signal was the CD-quality host signal. The test signals were the stego signal, the stego signal encoded in MP3 in joint stereo mode at 128 kbps, tandem MP3 in joint stereo mode at 128 kbps, and MPEG4AAC HE-AAC format at 96 kbps. For comparison with these watermarking conditions, the ODGs of perceptually coded host signals were also measured.

The ODGs of raw stego signals and MP3-coded stego signals are shown in Fig. 6. The averaged ODG for the raw stego signals is –0.49, which is better than the ODG of 'perceptible, but not annoying'. The IHC evaluation criteria [14] recommends that the lowest ODG among the eight SQAM tracks be above –2.5 and that the mean ODG among the eight MP3-coded SQAM tracks be above –2.0. The current results fulfill these IHC evaluation criteria.

4.5 Recovery from Perceptual Coded Stego Signals

Figure 7 shows recovery of the host signals from MP3-encoded stego signals; additionally, the ODGs of coded host signals, coded stego signals, and recovered signals from the coded stego signals are shown. Figs. 8 and 9 show recovery of the host signal from tandem MP3-encoded stego signals and MP4-encoded stego signals, respectively.

The average ODG for the recovered MP3-encoded stego signals is –1.06, which is slightly inferior to the average ODG of –0.92 for the MP3-encoded host signal. This implies that the watermark expressed by random amplification has been almost removed. The average ODG for the recovered tandem MP3-encoded stego signals is –2.00, which is slightly inferior to the average ODG of –1.85 for the tandem MP3-encoded host signal. The average ODG for the recovered MPEG4AAC-encoded stego signals is –1.47, which is slightly inferior to the average ODG of –1.28 for the MPEG4AAC-encoded host signal.

In summary, semi-recovery from the perceptually coded stego signals is realized in terms of small differences in ODG between recovered and coded signals. In other words, the watermark can be almost removed from perceptually coded stego signals.

5 Discussion

The robustness of the present implementation of watermarking may be inferior to state-of-the-art watermarking technologies [25, 28], especially against additive Gaussian noise, frequency conversion, and malicious attacks such as temporal conversion and collusion attacks, which are not considered in this paper. However, a strict comparison between the proposed method and those of previous studies is not possible because the previous studies have not examined various types of music excerpts with respect to cropping attacks. Compared with the

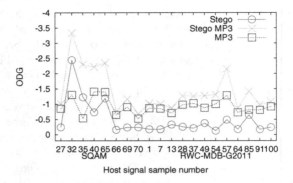

Fig. 6. ODGs for the raw stego signals (Stego), MP3-coded host signals (MP3), and MP3-coded stego signals (Stego MP3).

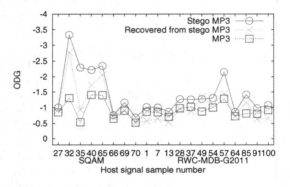

Fig. 7. Recovery of the host signal from the MP3-encoded stego signals. ODGs of coded host signals, coded stego signals, and recovered signals from the coded stego signals are shown.

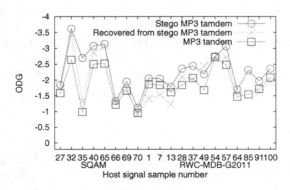

Fig. 8. Recovery of the host signal from the tandem MP3-encoded stego signals. ODGS of coded host signals, coded stego signals, and recovered signals from the coded stego signals are shown.

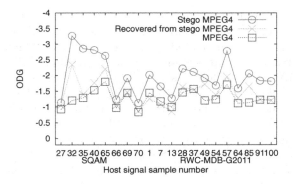

Fig. 9. Recovery of the host signal from the MPEG4AAC-encoded stego signals. ODGs of coded host signals, coded stego signals, and recovered signals from the coded stego signals are shown.

results of previous studies that used the same host signals [19, 20], the current results show higher robustness against perceptual codecs.

The proposed watermarking is known to be fragile to digital-to-analog and analog-to-digital (DA/AD) conversion. DA/AD conversion often causes a slight sampling frequency difference between a DA converter and an AD converter. This mismatch in sampling frequency results in slightly distorted time and frequency mapping of the MDCT coefficients. MDCT is sensitive to the phase of the input waveform, so that the magnitude of the MDCT coefficients are dynamically changed by DA/AD conversion. Despite the disadvantages in terms of robustness, the proposed framework for audio watermarking, which takes into account both reversibility and robustness, is expected to result in greater availability and applicability of data hiding in audio signals for applications such as commercial distribution of high-quality music audio via the Internet. This is because the proposed method can remove watermarking from not only raw stego signals but also perceptually coded stego signals.

The proposed technique of expanding MDCT coefficients may be applicable to the coded domain, such as is present in MP3 and MPEG4AAC. These perceptual codings compress MDCT coefficients of the framed audio waveform. Expansion and compression of the coefficients can be achieved by directly rewriting the scale factors of the coded domain. Removing and rewriting watermark from the coded domain are targets for future research.

6   Summary

The present study proposes a novel technique for reversibly and robustly hiding data in audio. It is perfectly reversible for unmodified stego signals and is semi-reversible for perceptually coded stego signals. A robust payload is embedded by direct-sequence spread-spectrum modulation, with the sequence encoded within amplitude expansion. Simultaneously, a reversible payload is embedded into the apertures in the amplitude histogram that result from amplitude expansion.

Simulation was used to evaluate reversibility, the objective quality of the stego audio, the amount of embeddable reversible payload, and robustness against several types of modification applied to the stego audio for 20 music pieces. The bitrate for reversible payload was approximately 4.8 kbps. MP3, tandem MP3 coding, MPEG4AAC, and additive single delay of the stego signals each induced a maximum BER of less than 6.5 % in a 7.2 bps robust payload. Objective quality measurements of the stego audio and recovered audio from modified stego signal were taken by software that implements the PEAQ algorithm.

The results showed that the mean ODG of the raw stego audio was better than 'perceptible, but not annoying'. Semi-recovery from the perceptually coded stego signals was realized as small differences in ODG between recovered and coded signals. In other words, the watermark could be almost removed from perceptually coded stego signals.

Acknowledgments. This work was supported by JSPS KAKENHI Grant Number 24500128.

References

1. 4C Entity: 4C 12 BIT watermark specification (1999). http://www.4centity.com/technologies.aspx
2. Alavianmehr, M., Rezaei, M., Helfroush, M., Tashk, A.: A lossless data hiding scheme on video raw data robust against H.264/AVC compression. In: Proceeding of the 2nd International Conference on Computer and Knowledge Engineering, pp. 194–198 (2012)
3. An, L., Gao, X., Deng, C.: Reliable embedding for robust reversible watermarking. In: Proceedings of the Second International Conference on Internet Multimedia Computing and Service, pp. 57–60 (2010)
4. An, L., Gao, X., Li, X., Tao, D., Deng, C., Li, J.: Robust reversible watermarking via clustering and enhanced pixel-wise masking. IEEE Trans. Image Process. **21**(8), 3598–3611 (2012)
5. AV & IT Equipment Standardization Committee: JEITA CPR-2601 the designation of audio quality for memory audio (2010). http://www.jeita.or.jp/japanese/standard/book/CPR-2601/
6. Celik, M., Sharma, G., Tekalp, A., Saber, E.: Lossless generalized-LSB data embedding. IEEE Trans. Image Process. **14**(2), 253–266 (2005)
7. Cvejic, N., Seppänen, T.: Introduction to digital audio watermarking. In: Cvejic, N., Seppänen, T. (eds.) Digital Audio Watermarking Techniques and Technologies, Applications and Benchmarks, pp. 1–10. Information Science Reference, New York (2008)
8. EBU Committee: Sound quality assessment material recordings for subjective tests. http://tech.ebu.ch/webdav/site/tech/shared/tech/tech3253.pdf
9. Geiger, R., Sporer, T., Koller, J., Brandenburg, K.: Audio coding based on integer transforms. In: Proceedings of the 111th AES Convention, No. 5471 (2001)
10. Goto, M., Hashiguchi, H., Nishimura, T., Oka, R.: RWC music database: music genre database and musical instrument sound database. In: Proceedings of the 4th International Conference on Music Information Retrieval (ISMIR 2003), pp. 229–230 (2003)

11. HaiBin, H., Susanto, R., Rongshan, Y., Xiao, L.: A fast algorithm of integer mdct for lossless audio coding. In: Proceedings of ICASSP 2004 IV, pp. 177–180 (2004)

12. Huang, H.C., Fang, W.C., Tsai, I.T.: Reversible data hiding using histogram-based difference expansion. In: IEEE International Symposium on Circuits and Systems, pp. 1661–1664 (2009)

13. Huang, X., Nishimura, A., Echizen, I.: A reversible acoustic steganography for integrity verification. In: Kim, H.-J., Shi, Y.Q., Barni, M. (eds.) IWDW 2010. LNCS, vol. 6526, pp. 305–316. Springer, Heidelberg (2011)

14. IHC Committee: IHC evaluation criteria (2014). http://www.ieice.org/iss/emm/ ihc/IHC_criteriaVer3.pdf

15. Kabal, P.: An examination and interpretation of ITU-R BS.1387: Perceptual evaluation of audio quality. TSP Lab Technical Report, Dept. Electrical & Computer Engineering, McGill University, pp. 1–89 (2002)

16. Li, M., Jiao, Y., Niu, X.: Reversible watermarking for compressed speech. In: Proceedings of Eighth International Conference on Intelligent System Design and Applications, pp. 197–201 (2008)

17. Nishimura, A.: Reversible audio data hiding using linear prediction and error expansion. In: Proceedings of IIHMSP2011, pp. 318–321 (2011)

18. Nishimura, A.: Reversible audio data hiding in spectral and time domains. In: Kondo, K. (ed.) Multimedia Information Hiding Technologies and Methodologies for Controlling Data, pp. 19–41. IGI Global, New York (2012)

19. Nishimura, A.: Audio watermarking based on amplitude modulation and modulation masking. In: Proceeding of the 1st International Workshop on Information Hiding and its Criteria for Evaluation, pp. 49–55. ACM (2014)

20. Nishimura, A.: Reversible and robust audio watermarking based on quantization index modulation and amplitude expansion. In: Shi, Y.Q., Kim, H.-J., Pérez-González, F. (eds.) IWDW 2013. LNCS, vol. 8389, pp. 275–287. Springer, Heidelberg (2014)

21. Nishimura, A., Unoki, M., Ogiwara, A., Kondo, K.: Objective evaluation of sound quality for attacks on robust audio watermarking. In: International Congress on Acoustics 2013, POMA, vol. 19 (2013)

22. Shi, Y.Q.: Reversible data hiding. In: Cox, I.J., Kalker, T., Lee, H.-K. (eds.) Digital Watermarking. LNCS, vol. 3304, pp. 1–12. Springer, Heidelberg (2005)

23. van der Veen, M., van Leest, A., Bruekers, F.: Reversible audio watermarking. In: Proceedings of the 114th AES Convention, No. 5818 (2003)

24. Vleeschouwer, C.D., Delaigle, J., Macq, B.: Circular interpretation of bijective transformations in lossless watermarking for media asset management. IEEE Trans. Multimedia **5**(1), 97–105 (2003)

25. Xiang, S., Huang, J.: Histogram-based audio watermarking against time-scale modification and cropping attacks. IEEE Trans. Multimedia **9**(7), 1357–1372 (2007)

26. Yan, D., Wang, R.: Reversible data hiding for audio based on prediction error expansion. In: Proceedings of IIHMSP 2008, pp. 249–252 (2008)

27. Yang, B., Schmucker, M., Busch, C., Niu, X., Sun, S.: Approaching optimal value expansion for reversible watermarking. Proc. Multimedia Secur. Workshop **2005**, 95–101 (2005)

28. Zhao, X., Guo, Y., Liu, J., Yan, Y.: Quantization index modulation audio watermarking system using a psychoacoustic model. In: Proceedings of IEEE International Conference on Information, Communications and Signal Processing, pp. 1–4 (2011)

Reversible Data Hiding in Encrypted Images Using Interpolation and Histogram Shifting

Dawen Xu[1,2(✉)] and Rangding Wang[3]

[1] School of Electronics and Information Engineering,
Ningbo University of Technology, Ningbo 315016, China
xdw@nbut.edu.cn
[2] Shanghai Key Laboratory of Integrate Administration Technologies
for Information Security, Shanghai 200240, China
[3] CKC Software Lab, Ningbo University, Ningbo 315211, China

Abstract. Due to the security and privacy-preserving requirements from cloud data management, it is sometimes desired that the image content is accessible in encrypted form. Reversible data hiding in the encrypted domain is an emerging technology, as it can perform data hiding in encrypted images without decryption which preserves the confidentiality of the content. In this paper, a reversible data hiding scheme in encrypted images based on interpolation technique is proposed. Before encryption, the down-sampled pixels are utilized to obtain the estimations of the rest non-sample pixels. Then, the down-sampled pixels are encrypted using a standard stream cipher. The data-hider, who does not know the original image content, may reversibly embed secret data into interpolation-error using a modified version of histogram shifting technique. With an encrypted image containing hidden data, data extraction can be carried out either in encrypted or decrypted domain. In addition, real reversibility is realized, that is, data extraction and image recovery are free of any error. Experimental results demonstrate the feasibility and efficiency of the proposed scheme.

Keywords: Image encryption · Reversible data hiding · Privacy protection · Interpolation · Histogram shifting

1 Introduction

With the rapid development of mobile internet and cloud storage, privacy and security of personal data has gained significant attention nowadays. Several surveys also show that a majority of potential cloud consumers are worried about the privacy of their data. Under this specific circumstance, multimedia data are often encrypted to avoid unauthorized viewing as well as to protect privacy. The cloud service provider (who stores the data) is not authorized to access the original content (i.e., plaintext). However, in many scenarios, the cloud servers or database managers need to embed some additional messages, such as labeling or authentication data, origin information, and owner identity information, directly into an encrypted data for tamper detection or ownership declaration or copyright management purposes. For example, patient's information can be embedded into his/her encrypted medical image to avoid unwanted exposure of confidential information.

© Springer International Publishing Switzerland 2015
Y.-Q. Shi et al. (Eds.): IWDW 2014, LNCS 9023, pp. 230–242, 2015.
DOI: 10.1007/978-3-319-19321-2_17

The capability of performing data hiding directly in encrypted images would avoid the leakage of image content, which can help address the security and privacy concerns with cloud computing. In [1], a novel technique is proposed to embed a robust watermark in the compressed and encrypted JPEG2000 images using three different existing watermarking schemes. A Walsh- Hadamard transform based image watermarking algorithm in the encrypted domain using Paillier cryptosystem is presented in [2]. However, due to the constraints of the Paillier cryptosystem, the encryption of an original image results in a high overhead in storage and computation. Recently, a novel unified data embedding-scrambling technique is proposed to achieve high payload and adaptive scalable quality degradation [3]. In [4], data hiding in the encrypted version of H.264/AVC video stream is proposed. Intra-prediction modes, motion vector differences, and residual coefficients are encrypted with stream ciphers. Then, a data-hider may embed additional data in the encrypted domain by using codeword substituting technique. However, within the aforementioned schemes [1–4], the host image/video is permanently distorted caused by data embedding. In general, the cloud service provider has no right to introduce permanent distortion during data embedding in encrypted data. To solve this problem, reversible data hiding (RDH) in encrypted domain, which can restore the original image without any distortion after data extraction and image decryption, is preferred.

RDH in encrypted domain is gaining more attention in recent years. In [5], Zhang divided the encrypted image into blocks, and each block carries one bit by flipping 3 Least Significant Bits (LSB) of each encrypted pixel in a set. Hong et al. [6] improved Zhang's method by adopting new smooth evaluation function and side-match mechanism to decrease the error rate of extracted bits. In both [5] and [6], the encrypted image containing hidden data should be first decrypted before data extraction, which is a major limitation to practical application. To separate data extraction from image decryption, the method in [7] compressed the LSB of encrypted pixels to create a space for accommodating the addition data. The embedding capacity of these methods [5–7] is relatively small and some errors occur during data extraction and/or image recovery. In [8], Ma et al. provided a RDH idea in encrypted images by reserving room before encryption. This method first empties out room by embedding LSBs of some pixels into other pixels with a traditional RDH method and then encrypts the image, so the positions of these LSBs in the encrypted image can be used for data hiding. Although the embedding capacity of this method is greatly improved, an additional RDH has to be implemented. Zhang et al. [9] proposed a reversibility improved RDH method in encrypted images. Prior to encrypting the image, room for data hiding is vacated by shifting the histogram of estimating errors.

Different from previous schemes, this paper proposes an efficient scheme of reversible data hiding in encrypted images based on interpolation technique. Before encryption and data embedding, an interpolation technique is adopted to generate interpolation-error. Sample pixels, which are sampled to form the low-resolution image, are encrypted using a standard stream cipher. The additional data can be embedded in the encrypted image by modifying the histogram of interpolation-error. In contrast to the existing technologies [5–7] discussed above, the proposed scheme can achieve excellent performance in the following prospects.

- The proposed method can achieve complete reversibility, i.e., no errors occur in data extraction and image recovery.
- The scheme can be applied to two different application scenarios by extracting the hidden data either from the encrypted image or from the decrypted image.

The rest of the paper is organized as follows. In Sect. 2, we describe the proposed scheme, which includes image encryption, data embedding in encrypted image, data extraction and original image recovery. Experimental results and analysis are presented in Sect. 3. Finally in Sect. 4, conclusion and future work are drawn.

2 Proposed Scheme

In this section, a reversible data hiding method in encrypted version of images is illustrated, which is made up of image encryption, data embedding in encrypted image, data extraction and image recovery phases. The content owner encrypts the original image using standard stream cipher with encryption key to produce an encrypted image. Then, the data-hider without knowing the actual contents of the original images can embed some additional data into the encrypted image. Here, the data-hider can be a third party, e.g., a database manager or a cloud provider, who is not authorized to access the original content of the signal (i.e., plaintext). At the receiving end, maybe the content owner himself or an authorized third party can extract the embedded data either in encrypted or decrypted image. Based on this observation, the framework of the proposed scheme is shown in Fig. 1, where image encryption and data embedding are depicted in part (a), data extraction and image decryption are shown in part (b).

2.1 Generation of Interpolation-Error

Assume the original image is an 8 bit gray-scale image with its size $N \times M$ and pixels $X(i,j) \in [0, 255]$, $1 \leq i \leq N$, $1 \leq j \leq M$. In particular, we classify all pixels in an image into two categories, namely, (a) sample pixels (SP) and, (b) non-sample pixels (NSP). Here, the set of SP consists of the pixels in every other column and row as depicted in Fig. 2 (a), which is sampled to form the low-resolution image. Those sample pixels are utilized as the reference points to estimate the missing pixels of high resolution image. Correspondingly, NSP refers to the pixels in the original image except sample pixels. Many prediction methods have been proposed to estimate pixel values in spatial domain [3]. The operator here for generating residual values is an interpolation technique [10]. The estimation of the missing high-resolution pixels $X(i,j) \in NSP$ can be obtained in two steps. In the first step, those missing pixels marked as '①' in Fig. 2 (b) are interpolated. Next, the other missing pixels marked as '②' in Fig. 2 (c) are interpolated with the help of the already estimated pixels. In fact, the proposed RDH scheme does not rely on the specific interpolation algorithm. The details of interpolation can refer to [10] and [11]. After the interpolating operation, the interpolation-error of pixels belonging to NSP, denoted by $E(i,j)$, can be obtained via calculating the difference between the interpolated pixel values and the original pixel values.

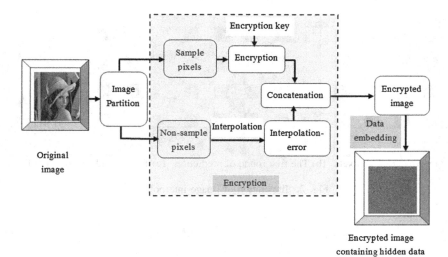

(a) Image encryption and data embedding

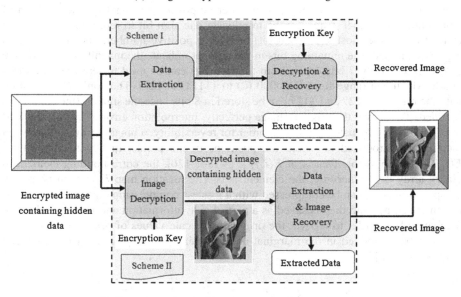

(b) Data extraction and image recovery in two scenarios

Fig. 1. The framework of proposed scheme

The next step is to replace the gray value with its interpolation error for the pixels belonging to NSP. Each pixel with gray value falling into [0, 255] can be represented by 8 bits, $b_{(i,j)}(0)$, $b_{(i,j)}(1)$,..., $b_{(i,j)}(7)$, such that

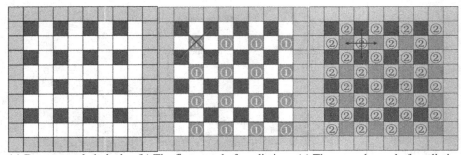

(a) Down-sampled pixels   (b) The first round of prediction   (c) The second round of prediction

Fig. 2. Illustration of image interpolation

$$b_{(i,j)}(k) = \left\lfloor \frac{X(i,j)}{2^k} \right\rfloor \mod 2, \quad k = 0,1,\ldots,7 \tag{1}$$

where $\lfloor \bullet \rfloor$ is a floor function that maps a real number to the largest previous integer. Since the interpolation error $E(i,j)$ can either be positive or negative, the problem of representing a number's sign can be to allocate one sign bit to represent the sign: set that bit (often the most significant bit) to 0 for a positive number, and set to 1 for a negative number. The remaining bits in the number indicate the magnitude (or absolute value). Hence only 7 bits (apart from the sign bit) can be used to represent the magnitude which can range from 0000000 (0) to 1111111 (127). Thus only $E(i,j)$ falling with the range of -127 and $+127$ can be stored in 8 bits once the sign bit (the eighth bit) is added. To recover the original image perfectly, interpolation error $E(i,j)$ is truncated into $[-126, 126]$ by using Eq. (2). In order for reversibility, a binary array, i.e., location map L_1, is introduced to record the positions of the points, in which error values $E(i,j) \notin [-126, 126]$. That is, if $E(i,j) \notin [-126, 126]$, the corresponding element in binary array is 1; otherwise, the element is 0. The location map L_1, which is mainly composed of zero, can be compressed with a lossless compression algorithm (e.g., run-length encoding) and then is saved as a part of side information and transmitted to the receiver side in order to recover the original grayscale values of pixels. As known, it can also be embedded in the marginal area by using LSB replacement just like Luo et al.'s method [10].

$$E(i,j) = \begin{cases} E(i,j) + 126 & \text{if } E(i,j) \leq -127 \\ E(i,j) - 126 & \text{if } E(i,j) \geq 127 \end{cases} \tag{2}$$

After applying the above interpolation method, the rearranged image $\overline{X}(i,j)$ consists of two parts: SP and interpolation-error of NSP.

2.2 Image Encryption

In general, image encryption is executed by the content owner. Since the reference points (i.e., SP) are stored directly without prediction, they can be encrypted using a standard stream algorithm. First, each pixel belonging to SP can be represented by 8 bits as Eq. (1). Then, the bitwise exclusive-or (XOR) operation is performed on the original bits $b_{(i,j)}(k)$ and pseudo-random bits $r_{(i,j)}(k)$ as follows:

$$B_{en(i,j)}(k) = b_{i,j}(k) \oplus r_{i,j}(k) \tag{3}$$

Pseudo-random bits are generated via a standard stream cipher determined by the encryption key En_{key_1}. In the next step, $B_{en(i,j)}(k)$ are concatenated orderly as the encrypted SP, i.e., $\sum_{k=0}^{7} B_{en(i,j)}(k).2^k$. In addition to SP, interpolation-error of NSP can also be encrypted to further improve the scrambling performance. The content owner may select $q\%$ interpolation-error randomly, denoted by E_{IN}, according to the encryption key En_{key_2}. In the following, the encrypted interpolation-error, denoted by $\hat{E}(i,j)$, can be obtained via the encryption process which is the same as SP's encryption process. However, for simplicity, in this paper, we only consider the encryption of SP, i.e., parameter q is set to 0. Finally, the encrypted image, denoted by $X_{en}(i,j)$, is formulated by combining encryption version of SP with interpolation-error of NSP. Anyone without the encryption key, such as a potential attacker or the data hider, cannot access the content of original image, thus privacy of the content owner is being protected in a trustworthy fashion. The main advantage of this encryption algorithm is that it is simple and can operate at a high speed, as this operation only includes an XOR operation.

2.3   Data Embedding in Encrypted Image

Once the data hider receives the encrypted image, he can embed some information into it for the purpose of content notation, integrity authentication, or transaction tracking, etc. Here, the data hider does not have the key to decrypt and get the plain image.

Up till now, a large number of researches, e.g., histogram modification based [12], difference expansion based [13], have been carried out in the field of RDH. A latest review of recent research in this field is presented in [14]. Ni et al.'s histogram shifting-based algorithm [12] is an important work of reversible data hiding, in which the peak of image histogram is utilized to embed data. In this paper, a bidirectional histogram shifting algorithm [15], which is a modified version of Ni et al.'s method, is adopted to embed additional data into interpolation-error of NSP. The detailed procedure of data embedding is described as follows.

Step 1: Generate the histogram of interpolation-error.

Step 2: In the histogram, find two highest bins in the histogram denoted by T_p and T_n, respectively. That is,

$$T_p = \arg \max_{h_x \in H} num(h_x) \tag{4}$$

and

$$T_n = \underset{h_x \in H, h_x \neq T_p}{\arg \max} \; num(h_x) \tag{5}$$

where h_x is the number of occurrence when the interpolation-error is equal to x and H denotes the set of interpolation-error. Without loss of generality, assume $T_n < T_p$.

Step 3: The embedding operation is formulated as

$$\tilde{E}(i,j) = \begin{cases} E(i,j) + \mathrm{sgn}(E(i,j)) \times w & \text{if } E(i,j) = T_p \text{ or } T_n \\ E(i,j) + \mathrm{sgn}(E(i,j)) \times 1 & \text{if } E(i,j) \in (T_{lz}, T_n) \cup (T_p, T_{rz}) \\ E(i,j) & \text{otherwise} \end{cases} \tag{6}$$

where $\tilde{E}(i,j)$ represents the marked interpolation-error, $w \in \{0, 1\}$ is the to-be-embedded message bit, T_{lz} and T_{rz} denote two zero points, and $\mathrm{sgn}(\bullet)$ is a sign function specified as

$$\mathrm{sgn}(E(i,j)) = \begin{cases} 1 & \text{if } E(i,j) \geq T_p \\ -1 & \text{if } E(i,j) \leq T_n \end{cases} \tag{7}$$

Note that the original interpolation-error $E(i,j)$ has been truncated to $[-126, 126]$, so even after histogram shifting, the interpolation-error $\tilde{E}(i,j)$ is still within the range $[-127, 127]$. Overflow/underflow does not occur here. Four parameters (T_p, T_n, T_{lz} and T_{rz}) should also be transmitted to the receiver side. After data embedding, the data hider can construct the marked encrypted image, denoted by $\overline{X_{en}}(i,j)$, by combining encryption version of SP with marked interpolation-error of NSP.

2.4   Data Extraction and Original Image Recovery

In this scheme, the hidden data can be extracted either in encrypted or decrypted domain, as shown in Fig. 1 (b). Besides, our method is also reversible, where the hidden data could be removed to obtain the original image.

A. Scheme I: Encrypted Domain Extraction. In order to protect the users' privacy, the database manager does not have sufficient permissions to access original video content due to the absence of encryption key. But the manager sometimes need to note and mark the personal information in corresponding encrypted videos as well as to verify images' integrity. In this case, both data embedding and extraction should be manipulated in encrypted domain.

Once T_p, T_n, T_{lz} and T_{rz} are obtained, the embedded data $\tilde{w}$ can be extracted as

$$\tilde{w} = \begin{cases} 0 & \text{if } \tilde{E}(i,j) = T_p \text{ or } T_n \\ 1 & \text{if } \tilde{E}(i,j) = T_p + 1 \text{ or } T_n - 1 \end{cases} \tag{8}$$

The original interpolation-error $E(i,j)$ can be further recovered by

$$E(i,j) = \begin{cases} \tilde{E}(i,j) - \mathrm{sgn}\big(\tilde{E}(i,j)\big) \times \tilde{w} & \text{if } \tilde{E}(i,j) \in \{T_p,\ T_p+1,\ T_n-1,\ \text{or } T_n\} \\ \tilde{E}(i,j) - \mathrm{sgn}\big(\tilde{E}(i,j)\big) \times 1 & \text{if } \tilde{E}(i,j) \in [T_p+1,\ T_{rz}] \cup [T_{lz},\ T_n-1] \\ \tilde{E}(i,j) & \text{otherwise} \end{cases}$$

(9)

Since the whole process is entirely performed in the encrypted domain, it avoids the leakage of original content. Furthermore, because the embedding and extraction rules are reversible, both the host encrypted image and the hidden message can be recovered losslessly when the marked image is not attacked. With the encryption key, the content owner can further decrypt the image to get the original cover image.

B. Scheme II: Decrypted Domain Extraction. In scheme I, both data embedding and extraction are performed in encrypted domain. However, in some cases, users want to decrypt the image first and then extract the hidden data from the decrypted image when it is needed. For example, with the encryption key, an authorized user wants to achieve the decrypted image containing the hidden data, which can be used to trace the source of the data. In this case, data extraction after image decryption is suitable. The entire process is comprised of the following steps.

(a) Generating the marked decrypted image. To form the marked decrypted image X'' which is made up of SP and NSP, the following steps should be done.

Step 1: With the encryption key En_{key_1}, the original pixels $X(i,j) \in SP$ can be obtained. Because of the symmetry of the XOR operation, the decryption operation is symmetric to the encryption operation. That is, the encrypted data can be decrypted by performing XOR operation with generated pseudorandom bits, and then two XOR operations cancel each other out. Since the pseudorandom bits depend on the encryption key, the decryption is possible only for the authorized users.

Step 2: Once $X(i,j) \in SP$ is obtained, the estimation of $X(i,j) \in NSP$, denoted by $X'(i,j) \in NSP$, can be calculated using the above-mentioned interpolation technology as discussed in Sect. 2.1. As long as at extraction one has the same interpolation-error, the reversibility of the scheme is ensured.

Step 3: According to Eq. (2), interpolation error $E(i,j)$ ranging out of $[-126, 126]$ has been truncated. To restore the pixels $X''(i,j) \in NSP$, the following inverse operation should be done on the interpolation error according to the location map L_1.

$$\tilde{E}(i,j) = \begin{cases} \tilde{E}(i,j) - 126 & \text{if } \tilde{E}(i,j) < 0\ \&\ (i,j) \in L_1 \\ \tilde{E}(i,j) + 126 & \text{if } \tilde{E}(i,j) > 0\ \&\ (i,j) \in L_1 \end{cases}$$

(10)

Step 4: The marked pixels $X''(i,j) \in NSP$ can be further obtained via

$$X''(i,j) = X'(i,j) + \tilde{E}(i,j)$$

(11)

Since $\tilde{E}(i,j)$ is the modified interpolation error value, overflow/underflow may occur when $X'(i,j)$ are changed from 255 to 256 or from 0 to -1. To restore the original image perfectly, the positions (i,j) such that $X''(i,j) = 256\ or\ -1$ should also be recorded in a location map L_2. At the same time, $X''(i,j)$ is adjusted from 256 to 255 or from -1 to 0.

Step 5: The marked decrypted image can finally be formulated by substituting $\tilde{E}(i,j)$ with $X''(i,j)$. No visible distortions can be observed in the marked decrypted images, as show in later experimental results.

(b) Data extraction and image recovery. After generating the marked decrypted image, the authorized user can further extract the hidden data and recover the original image. The corresponding extracting and recovering process is described as follows.

Step 1: Generating the estimation of pixels belonging to NSP, i.e., $X'(i,j) \in NSP$, using the same interpolation technology as given in Sect. 2.1.

Step 2: The interpolation errors are calculated by

$$\tilde{E}(i,j) = X''(i,j) - X'(i,j) \tag{12}$$

Note that some errors whose positions belong to the location map L_2 should be further adjusted as follows.

$$\tilde{E}(i,j) = \begin{cases} \tilde{E}(i,j) - 1 & if\ X''(i,j) == 0 \\ \tilde{E}(i,j) + 1 & if\ X''(i,j) == 255 \end{cases} \tag{13}$$

Step 3: The hidden data bit $\tilde{w}$ can be extracted from $\tilde{E}(i,j)$ using Eq. (8), and the original interpolation-error $E(i,j)$ can be recovered using Eq. (9).

Step 4: The original pixels of $X(i,j) \in NSP$ can be recovered via

$$X(i,j) = X'(i,j) + E(i,j) \tag{14}$$

Step 5: The original image can be recovered successfully by replacing the marked pixel $X''(i,j) \in NSP$ with its original value $X(i,j) \in NSP$.

3   Experimental Results

Four well-known standard images, i.e., *Lena, Baboon, Barbara, and Peppers*, are considered for experimental purposes. The size of all images is $512 \times 512 \times 8$. To investigate the scrambling effect, the original images are given in Fig. 3, and their corresponding encrypted results are shown in Fig. 4. The results are obtained with the setting $q = 0$. In general, PSNR values of encrypted images are below 9 dB, as shown in Fig. 4. With the increase of p, the scrambling effect is also improved. Due to space limitations, we do not list the results of all images.

Obviously, the embedding capacity in each image is determined by the number of T_p and T_n, i.e., $C = num(T_n) + num(T_p)$, which depends on the quality of the interpolation. For *Lena, Baboon, Barbara, and Peppers*, the embedding rate is 0.21, 0.06, 0.13, and 0.14 bit per pixel (bpp), respectively. We can observe that the embedding capacity of the proposed scheme depends strongly on the characteristics of the original cover image, as each image has a different number of interpolation errors associated

Fig. 3. Original images

(a) *Lena*, PSNR = 7.20 dB,   (b) *Baboon*, PSNR = 7.95 dB,(c) *Barbara*, PSNR = 6.52 dB, (d) *Peppers*, PSNR = 8.04 dB

Fig. 4. Encrypted images

(a) *Lena*, PSNR = 50.06 dB, (b) *Baboon*, PSNR = 49.58 dB,(c) *Barbara*, PSNR = 49.82 dB,(d) *Peppers*, PSNR = 49.85 dB

Fig. 5. Decrypted images containing hidden data

with the peak point. As expected, for image of higher spatial activity (e.g., *Baboon*), the prediction accuracy decreases and hence low embedding rete is achieved. On the other hand, image of lower spatial activity (e.g., *Lena*) achieves higher embedding rate due to higher pixel prediction accuracy. In addition, higher capacities can be achieved by applying multiple-layer embedding strategy.

With an encrypted image containing hidden data, we could extract the hidden data either in encrypted domain or decrypted domain. If we directly decrypted the encrypted image containing hidden data using the encryption key, PSNR values of decrypted images are 50.06, 49.58, 49.82 and 49.85 dB. It is almost impossible to detect the degradation in image quality caused by data embedding. As illustrated in Fig. 5, no visible artifacts can be observed in all of the decrypted images containing hidden data.

Since the embedding scheme is reversible, the original cover content can be perfectly recovered after extraction of the hidden data. In addition, from experiments, we observe that computation is fast and efficient.

Besides four standard images, i.e., *Lena, Baboon, Barbara, and Peppers*, another 50 images are randomly selected from a popular gray-scale image database [16] for testing. The embedding rates of 50 test images are shown in Fig. 6, and the corresponding PSNR values of decrypted images are given in Fig. 7. It is observed that for all images, PSNR is greater than 49.5 dB.

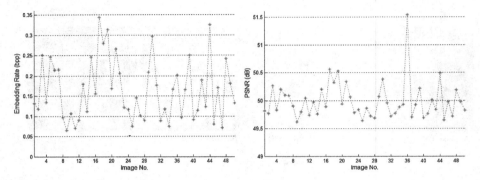

Fig. 6. Embedding rates of 50 test images   **Fig. 7.** PSNR values of decrypted images

Limited research has been carried out on reversible data hiding in encrypted image. As mentioned in Sect. 1, all methods in [5–7] may introduce some errors on data extraction and/or image recovery, while the complete reversibility can be achieved in the proposed method. More importantly, these methods are designed to carry only small payloads. Take Zhang's method [5] as instance, the embedding rate is 0.0156 bpp associated with block size 8×8. If error correction mechanism is introduced, the actual embedding rate will be further decreased. It can be observed that our method achieves significantly higher embedding rate. For methods such as [8, 9], completely error-free data extraction and image recovery can be obtained. But in [9], a large portion of pixels are utilized to estimate the rest $p\%$ pixels. The cost is considerably expensive because p is usually smaller than 20. But in our proposed scheme, only 25 % of the pixels are stored to predict the remaining 75 %, which promises a larger embedding capacity. This has also been demonstrated in the light of the experimental results.

4   Conclusion and Future Work

In this paper, an algorithm to reversibly embed secret data in encrypted images is presented, which consists of image encryption, data embedding and data extraction three phases. The data-hider can embed the secret data into the encrypted image using the histogram-shifting method, even though he does not know the original image content. Since the embedding is done on encrypted data, our scheme preserves the confidentiality of content. Data extraction is separable from image decryption, i.e., the additional data can be extracted either in encrypted domain or decrypted domain. Furthermore, this algorithm can achieve real reversibility, and high quality of marked decrypted images. One of the possible applications of this method is image annotation in cloud computing where high image quality and reversibility are greatly desired.

Although reversible data hiding and cryptography have been studied extensively and many techniques are available, but reversible data hiding in encrypted domain is a highly interdisciplinary area of research. Technical research in this field has only just begun, and there is still an open space for research in this interdisciplinary research area. In future, considerable more effort is needed to design more efficient reversible data hiding scheme in homomorphic encrypted domain.

Acknowledgements. This work is supported by the National Natural Science Foundation of China (61301247, 61170137), Zhejiang Provincial Natural Science Foundation of China (LY13F020013), Ningbo Natural Science Foundation (2013A610059), and the Opening Project of Shanghai Key Laboratory of Integrate Administration Technologies for Information Security (AGK2013004).

References

1. Subramanyam, A.V., Emmanuel, S., Kankanhalli, M.S.: Robust watermarking of compressed and encrypted JPEG2000 images. IEEE Trans. Multimed. **14**(3), 703–716 (2012)
2. Zheng, P., Huang, J.: Walsh-hadamard transform in the homomorphic encrypted domain and its application in image watermarking. In: Kirchner, M., Ghosal, D. (eds.) IH 2012. LNCS, vol. 7692, pp. 240–254. Springer, Heidelberg (2013)
3. Rad, R.M., Wong, K.S., Guo, J.M.: A unified data embedding and scrambling method. IEEE Trans. Image Process. **23**(4), 1463–1475 (2014)
4. Xu, D.W., Wang, R.D., Shi, Y.Q.: Data hiding in encrypted H.264/AVC video streams by codeword substitution. IEEE Trans. Inf. Forensics Secur. **9**(4), 596–606 (2014)
5. Zhang, X.P.: Reversible data hiding in encrypted image. IEEE Signal Process. Lett. **18**(4), 255–258 (2011)
6. Hong, W., Chen, T.S., Wu, H.Y.: An improved reversible data hiding in encrypted images using side match. IEEE Signal Process. Lett. **19**(4), 199–202 (2012)
7. Zhang, X.P.: Separable reversible data hiding in encrypted image. IEEE Trans. Inf. Forensics Secur. **7**(2), 826–832 (2012)
8. Ma, K.D., Zhang, W.M., Zhao, X.F., et al.: Reversible data hiding in encrypted images by reserving room before encryption. IEEE Trans. Inf. Forensics Secur. **8**(3), 553–562 (2013)
9. Zhang, W.M., Ma, K.D., Yu, N.H.: Reversibility improved data hiding in encrypted images. Sig. Process. **94**, 118–127 (2014)
10. Luo, L.X., Chen, Z.Y., Chen, M.: Reversible image watermarking using interpolation technique. IEEE Trans. Inf. Forensics Secur. **5**(1), 187–193 (2010)
11. Zhang, L., Wu, X.: An edge-guided image interpolation algorithm via directional filtering and data fusion. IEEE Trans. Image Process. **15**(8), 2226–2238 (2006)
12. Ni, Z.C., Shi, Y.Q., Ansari, N., Su, W.: Reversible data hiding. IEEE Trans. Circuits Syst. Video Technol. **16**(3), 354–362 (2006)
13. Tian, J.: Reversible data embedding using a difference expansion. IEEE Trans. Circ. Syst. Video Technol. **13**(8), 890–896 (2003)

14. Khan, A., Siddiqa, A., Mubib, S., Malik, S.A.: A recent survey of reversible watermarking techniques. Inf. Sci. **279**, 251–272 (2014)
15. Xu, D.W., Wang, R.D., Shi, Y.Q.: An improved reversible data hiding-based approach for intra-frame error concealment in H.264/AVC. J. Vis. Commun. Image Represent. **25**(2), 410–422 (2014)
16. Miscelaneous gray level images. http://decsai.ugr.es/cvg/dbimagenes/g512.php

High-Dimensional Histogram Utilization for Reversible Data Hiding

Xinlu Gui, Xiaolong Li, and Bin Yang[✉]

Institute of Computer Science and Technology, Peking University,
Beijing 100871, China
{guixinlu,lixiaolong,yang_bin}@pku.edu.cn

Abstract. Histogram-shifting (HS) is an efficient technique for reversible data hiding (RDH). In this paper, in contrast to previous HS-based RDH works that utilize one or two dimensional histogram, we propose a new RDH scheme exploring three-dimensional histogram. Referred to the recently proposed general framework of HS-based RDH, we first divide the host image into non-overlapping pixel triples to generate a three-dimensional histogram, and then utilize each triple for embedding or shifting based on an applicable triple classification. To further exploit the image redundancy to enhance the embedding performance, we apply the pixel-selection technique in our scheme such that smooth pixel triples are priorly embedded. Experimental results have verified the superiority of the proposed scheme over some state-of-the-art RDH works.

Keywords: Reversible data hiding (RDH) · Three-dimensional histogram · Pixel-selection (PS)

1 Introduction

Reversible data hiding (RDH) is a technique to embed useful information into the digital image such that the intended recipient can extract the embedded data as well as recover the host medium [1–5]. This technique has been widely applied to many sensitive applications, such as law forensics, medical image processing, and military image processing. To achieve the best performance of RDH in such applications, it is necessary to minimize the embedding distortion given the certain embedding capacity (EC).

Previous studies have proposed many efficient RDH methods, especially those based on difference expansion (DE) and histogram-shifting (HS). On one hand, DE-based RDH is first proposed by Tian [3] and can provide a high EC with low distortion. This method is applied on pixel pairs and one bit is embedded into each selected pixel pair by expanding its difference, in which the storage of the location map yields a negative influence. Afterwards, the DE technique has been widely investigated and well-developed in many aspects such as integer transform generalization [6–10], location map reduction [11–14], and prediction-error expansion (PEE) [15–21], etc.

© Springer International Publishing Switzerland 2015
Y.-Q. Shi et al. (Eds.): IWDW 2014, LNCS 9023, pp. 243–253, 2015.
DOI: 10.1007/978-3-319-19321-2_18

On the other hand, HS-based RDH is implemented by modifying host image's histogram of a certain dimension [4, 22–29]. This kind of method is first proposed by Ni *et al.* [4], which takes advantage of the peak point of the pixel-intensity-histogram for data embedding. In this method, each pixel value is modified at most by 1, and thus the marked image quality is well guaranteed with a PSNR larger than 48.13 dB. Later on, the HS technique is applied to the difference histogram (equivalent to the two-dimensional histogram) in Lee *et al.*'s work [22]. Compared with the ordinary one-dimensional histogram utilized in [4], the difference histogram in [22] is better for RDH since it is regular in shape and has a much higher peak point.

Note that, conventional RDH schemes such as [15, 16, 26] treat all image pixels equally and sequentially embed data into pixels one by one. However, it is widely recognized that embedding in noisy pixels may cause larger distortion than that in smooth ones with identical embedded data size. To remedy this drawback, Li *et al.* proposed adaptive embedding based on the pixel-selection (PS) strategy in a recent work [30]. This method guarantees that more data is embedded into a smoother pixel according to a local complexity measurement. The adaptive embedding using PS has been proved efficient in enhancing the embedding performance of RDH.

The feasibility of RDH is mainly due to the lossless compressibility of natural images, and one can usually get a better performance by fully exploiting the image redundancy. Furthermore, our previous work [31] has pointed out that, by using HS, it is more desirable to take high-dimensional histogram to design RDH. Accordingly, in contrast to previous HS-based RDH methods that leverage one or two dimensional histogram, we propose an efficient RDH scheme based on three-dimensional histogram modification. In particular, we first generate a three-dimensional histogram by counting non-overlapping pixel triples. Then, according to the general framework of HS-based RDH proposed in [31], we make use of each triple for embedding or shifting based on an applicable triple classification. Moreover, inspired by adaptive embedding in [30], we employ the PS strategy such that smooth pixel triples are priorly embedded to obtain better marked image quality. Experimental results show that the proposed scheme outperforms some state-of-the-art RDH methods in terms of capacity-distortion performance.

The rest of this paper is organized as follows. The general framework of HS-based RDH is introduced in Sect. 2. Then, Sect. 3 presents the proposed RDH scheme in details. Experimental results and further comparison are presented in Sect. 4. Finally, we conclude our work in the last section.

2   General Framework of HS-based RDH

In this section, we briefly describe the general framework of HS-based RDH proposed by Li *et al.* [31]. In particular, in this framework, the host image is first divided into non-overlapping blocks such that each block contains n pixels. Then, the n-dimensional histogram is generated by counting the frequency of divided blocks. Finally, data embedding is implemented by modifying the resulting

n-dimensional histogram. Notice that, since the pixel block is represented as an element of $\mathbb{Z}^n$, it is necessary to divide $\mathbb{Z}^n$ into two disjointed sets, such that one set is used to carry hidden data by expansion embedding, while the other set is simply shifted to create vacant space to ensure the reversibility.

Let S and T be a partition of $\mathbb{Z}^n$: $S \cup T = \mathbb{Z}^n$ and $S \cap T = \emptyset$. Suppose that three functions $g : T \to \mathbb{Z}^n$, $f_0 : S \to \mathbb{Z}^n$, and $f_1 : S \to \mathbb{Z}^n$ satisfy the following two conditions:

$C1$: The functions g, f_0, and f_1 are injective.
$C2$: The sets $g(T)$, $f_0(S)$, and $f_1(S)$ are disjointed with each other.

Here, g is called "shifting function" and will be used to shift pixel values, f_0 and f_1 are called "embedding functions" and will be used to embed data. More specifically, each block with value $\mathbf{x} \in T$ will be shifted to $g(\mathbf{x})$, and the block with value $\mathbf{x} \in S$ will be expanded to either $f_0(\mathbf{x})$ or $f_1(\mathbf{x})$ to carry one data bit. The shifting and embedding functions will give a HS-based RDH scheme whose reversibility is guaranteed by those two conditions, $C1$ and $C2$.

The underflow/overflow is an inevitable problem of RDH, i.e., for a gray-scale image, the shifted and expanded values should be restricted in the range of $[0, 255]$. To deal with this, the above defined sets S and T need be further processed. Particularly, we denote the set of all pixel-value-arrays of length n of a gray-scale image as

$$A_n = \{\mathbf{x} = (x_1, ..., x_n) \in \mathbb{Z}^n : 0 \le x_i \le 255\} \tag{1}$$

Then, we define

$$\begin{cases} T_s = A_n \cap g^{-1}(A_n) \\ S_e = A_n \cap f_0^{-1}(A_n) \cap f_1^{-1}(A_n) \\ T_{u,o} = A_n \cap T - T_s \\ S_{u,o} = A_n \cap S - S_e. \end{cases} \tag{2}$$

Here, the sub-indices "s", "e", and "u, o" denote "shift", "embed", and "underflow/overflow", respectively. It is obvious that, the four sets, i.e., T_s, S_e, $T_{u,o}$, and $S_{u,o}$, are disjointed with each other and constitute a partition of A_n, i.e., $A_n = T_s \cup S_e \cup T_{u,o} \cup S_{u,o}$. Moreover, the sets $g(T_s)$, $f_0(S_e)$, and $f_1(S_e)$ are included in A_n and the condition $C2$ ensures that they are also disjointed.

According to (2), each block with value $\mathbf{x} \in T_s$ will be shifted, each block with value $\mathbf{x} \in S_e$ will be expanded to carry one data bit, and the block with value $\mathbf{x} \in T_{u,o} \cup S_{u,o}$ will remain unchanged since it cannot be shifted or expanded due to undeflow/overflow. The data embedding procedure based on this general framework is illustrated in Fig. 1. After data embedding, the sets $g(T_s)$, $f_0(S_e)$ and $f_1(S_e)$ are disjointed with each other, but the two sets $TS_u \triangleq T_{u,o} \cup S_{u,o}$ and $g(T_s) \cup f_0(S_e) \cup f_1(S_e)$ may be overlapped, and a location map will be used to record the locations of pixel blocks whose values belong to TS_u.

By using this framework, the two-dimensional-histogram-based RDH schemes can be analyzed in a simple way. For these methods, since two adjacent pixels are embedded or shifted as a pixel pair, it can be represented by a red or black point

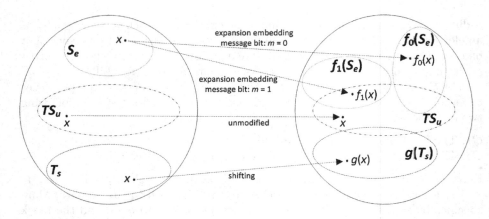

Fig. 1. Data embedding using shifting and embedding functions.

in the plane grid, respectively, and the embedding procedure can be demonstrated by a pixel pair mapping (PPM). For example, Lee *et al.*'s method [22] modifies the pixel pairs with difference 1 or -1 to carry data. Concretely, for data embedding, the marked pixel pair can be obtained as

$$(p^*, q^*) = \begin{cases} (p,q) & \text{if } p-q = 0 \\ (p, q-m) & \text{if } p-q = 1 \\ (p, q+m) & \text{if } p-q = -1 \\ (p, q-1) & \text{if } p-q > 1 \\ (p, q+1) & \text{if } p-q < -1 \end{cases} \tag{3}$$

where (p,q) is a cover pixel pair and $m \in \{0,1\}$ is a data bit to be embedded. The corresponding sets (S,T) can be defined as $S = \{(x,y) \in \mathbb{Z}^2 : |x-y| = 1\}$ and $T = \mathbb{Z}^2 - S$, and the PPM is shown as the left figure in Fig. 2. In this way, for each red point, it goes to its mapping point if the to-be-embedded bit is 1 and otherwise keeps unchanged, while each black point is simply shifted to its mapping point. Finally, we remark that, based on PPM, new RDH scheme can be easily designed. For example, as illustrated in the right figure of Fig. 2, for any $a < b$, one can get a new RDH scheme by taking $S = \{(x,y) \in \mathbb{Z}^2 : x-y \in \{a,b\}\}$ and $T = \mathbb{Z}^2 - S$.

3   Proposed Scheme

Compared with [4] which is based on one-dimensional histogram, Lee *et al.*'s method [22] is better for RDH by using the two-dimensional one. Since pixel pairs contain more redundant information than single pixels, high-dimensional histogram yields significant benefit to RDH. Inspired by this, we take advantage of the general framework of HS-based RDH and propose a new RDH scheme based on three-dimensional histogram by setting $n = 3$ and designing corresponding sets (S,T) and functions (g, f_0, f_1). In general, after dividing the host

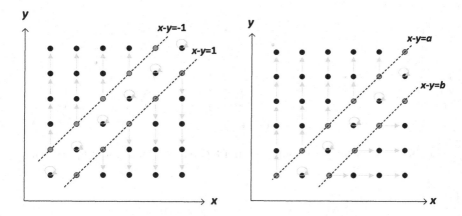

Fig. 2. Pixel pair mappings for Lee *et al.*'s method [22] and its analogue with $a < b$. Here, (a, b) is taken as $(0, 2)$ for illustration.

image into non-overlapping pixel triples, all the triples will be decomposed into several sets, each of which will be embedded using an analogue of Lee *et al.*'s method as shown in the right figure of Fig. 2.

In particular, for each integer k, we first define

$$\Gamma_k = \{(x, y, z) \in \mathbb{Z}^3 : \min\{x, y, z\} = k\}. \tag{4}$$

Then, Γ_k is further decomposed into three subsets as

$$\begin{cases} \Gamma_k^1 = \{(x, y, z) \in \Gamma_k : x = k\} \\ \Gamma_k^2 = \{(x, y, z) \in \Gamma_k - \Gamma_k^1 : y = k\} \\ \Gamma_k^3 = \Gamma_k - \Gamma_k^1 - \Gamma_k^2. \end{cases} \tag{5}$$

As a result, we have a partition of $\mathbb{Z}^3$: $\mathbb{Z}^3 = \cup_{k \in \mathbb{Z}}(\Gamma_k^1 \cup \Gamma_k^2 \cup \Gamma_k^3)$.

Note that, the sets Γ_k^i can be represented as

$$\begin{cases} \Gamma_k^1 = \{(x, y, z) \in \mathbb{Z}^3 : x = k, y \geq k, z \geq k\} \\ \Gamma_k^2 = \{(x, y, z) \in \mathbb{Z}^3 : x > k, y = k, z \geq k\} \\ \Gamma_k^3 = \{(x, y, z) \in \mathbb{Z}^3 : x > k, y > k, z = k\}. \end{cases} \tag{6}$$

This represents that, each Γ_k^i is a "quarter" of $\mathbb{Z}^2$ and, clearly, the three-dimensional histogram counting pixel triples is somewhat regular on Γ_k^i. For example, for Γ_k^1, one can expect that the most frequent histogram bins are located in the lines where $|y - z|$ is small. Then for each Γ_k^i, we can use the method described in the right figure of Fig. 2 to embed data into it.

We define the sets S and T as

$$\begin{cases} S = \underset{k \in \mathbb{Z}}{\cup}(S_k^1 \cup S_k^2 \cup S_k^3) \\ T = \underset{k \in \mathbb{Z}}{\cup}(T_k^1 \cup T_k^2 \cup T_k^3) \end{cases} \tag{7}$$

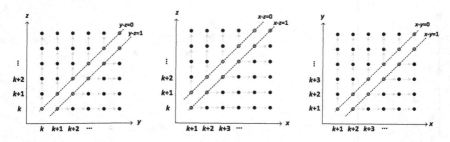

Fig. 3. Pixel pair mappings for the sets Γ_k^1 (left), Γ_k^2 (center) and Γ_k^3 (right).

where

$$\begin{cases} S_k^1 = \{(x, y, z) \in \Gamma_k^1 : y - z = 0 \text{ or } 1\} \\ S_k^2 = \{(x, y, z) \in \Gamma_k^2 : x - z = 0 \text{ or } 1\} \\ S_k^3 = \{(x, y, z) \in \Gamma_k^3 : x - y = 0 \text{ or } 1\} \end{cases} \qquad (8)$$

and, for each k and i, $T_k^i = \Gamma_k^i - S_k^i$.

For each triple $(x, y, z) \in \Gamma_k^1$, x is a constant and our embedding operation is conducted on the two-dimensional histogram of (y, z). Among these triples, the ones satisfying $y - z = 0$ or $y - z = 1$ are embedded with data while others are shifted. In other words, in Γ_k^1, its subset S_k^1 will be used for carrying data, and the complementary set of S_k^1, T_k^1, will be shifted. More specifically, for each $(x, y, z) \in S_k^1$, the embedding functions f_0 and f_1 on S_k^1 are defined as

$$\begin{cases} f_0(x, y, z) = (x, y, z) \\ f_1(x, y, z) = \begin{cases} (x, y + 1, z), \text{ if } y - z = 1 \\ (x, y, z + 1), \text{ if } y - z = 0. \end{cases} \end{cases} \qquad (9)$$

And, for each $(x, y, z) \in T_k^1$, the shifting function g on T_k^1 is defined as

$$g(x, y, z) = \begin{cases} (x, y + 1, z), \text{ if } y - z > 1 \\ (x, y, z + 1), \text{ if } y - z < 0. \end{cases} \qquad (10)$$

With these definitions, one can verify that $f_0(S_k^1), f_1(S_k^1), g(T_k^1) \subset \Gamma_k^1$, that is, Γ_k^1 is invariant after data embedding. Moreover, since the embedding operation is conducted on the two-dimensional histogram of (y, z), it can be illustrated as a PPM. According to (9) and (10), the expansion and shifting rules in the form of PPM are illustrated in the left figure of Fig. 3.

The definitions of (g, f_0, f_1) on Γ_k^2 and Γ_k^3 can be formed in the similar way. Instead of providing the detailed formulations, we simply demonstrate the embedding rules on Γ_k^2 and Γ_k^3 using PPM, in the center and right figure of Fig. 3, respectively. Furthermore, it is easy to verify that the conditions $C1$ and $C2$ are satisfied in our case, and thus, (S, T) and (g, f_0, f_1) defined above lead to a RDH scheme. Due to the limited space, please refer to [31] for the details about data embedding and extraction procedures including the treatment of underflow/overflow.

To better understand the proposed scheme, we illustrate some examples of data embedding in the following. For a triple $(x, y, z) = (10, 11, 11)$, its minimum is $x = 10$ and it belongs to Γ_{10}^1. Since $y - z = 0$, we can see that $(x, y, z) \in S_{10}^1$ and it will be used for carrying data. According to the left PPM of Fig. 3, the marked pixel triple is $(10, 11, 11)$ if the to-be-embedded data bit m is 0 and $(10, 11, 12)$ if $m = 1$. For another triple $(x, y, z) = (15, 12, 10)$, we see that $(x, y, z) \in \Gamma_{10}^3$ since $x > z$ and $y > z$ hold. Then, as $x - y = 3$, according to the right PPM of Fig. 3, the triple is shifted and its marked values are $(16, 12, 10)$.

The partition of pixel triples in our scheme is shown in Fig. 4 where the pixels with the same number are collected as a triple. Considering that the three pixels in a triple in Fig. 4 are more highly connected with each other than the ones consisting of three consecutive pixels in a vertical or horizontal line, we then divide pixel triples in this way to generate the three-dimensional histogram.

In the rest of this section, we will describe how to utilize the PS strategy in our scheme. First, we define a measurement for the noise level of each pixel triple according to its context. More specifically, for a triple (x, y, z), its noise level is computed as the sum of absolute differences of every two consecutive pixels, in both vertical and horizontal directions, within its context that contains five pixels $\{a, b, c, d, e\}$ (see Fig. 5). Then, given a threshold T, only the triples with noise level less than T will be embedded while other triples are ignored. Note that, to incorporate the PS strategy into the general framework of HS-based RDH, it is straightforward to count the triples with noise level less than T to generate the three-dimensional histogram. Finally, given a certain EC, the threshold T is iteratively determined as the smallest integer such that the payload can be embedded. In this way, the payload is always priorly embedded into the relatively smoother regions such that the marked image quality can be enhanced.

1	1	2	3	3	4	⋯
1	2	2	3	4	4	⋯
5	5	6	7	7	8	⋯
5	6	6	7	8	8	⋯
⋮	⋮	⋮	⋮	⋮	⋮	⋯

Fig. 4. Pixel triples partition.

4   Experimental Results

To illustrate the effectiveness of our proposed scheme with PS, we compare it with the methods of Lee et al. [22], D2 algorithm of Thodi and Rodriguez [15], Hu et al. [16], Sachnev et al. [17], Luo et al. [18] and Qin et al. [32]. This comparison is conducted on four 512×512 sized gray-scale images including Lena, Barbara, Airplane and Elaine.

Fig. 5. Pixel triple (x, y, z) and its corresponding context.

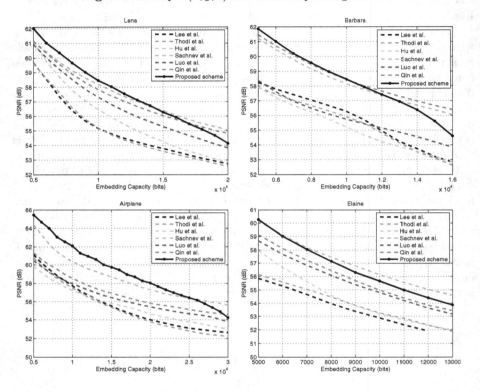

Fig. 6. Performance comparison between our scheme and some state-of-the-art RDH works.

It can be observed from Fig. 6 that our scheme shows significant superiority over all the other methods except [17] and [32], especially for low EC cases. As the methods [22] and [15] are based on two-dimensional histogram modification, the proposed scheme has the advantage of utilizing more redundant information by exploring three-dimensional histogram. Our proposed scheme outperforms Hu *et al.*'s and Luo *et al.*'s PEE-based methods [16,18] as well, which indicates the effectiveness of designing RDH based on high-dimensional histogram.

As for the comparison with the well-designed methods [17,32], the proposed scheme is comparable in low EC cases while it is inferior to them in high EC cases as the PS strategy fails to work very well. However, for the relatively smooth image such as Airplane, the proposed scheme yields an obvious advantage over

[17,32] when EC is less than 25,000 bits. In addition, Table 1 illustrates the comparison of PSNR in dB between our proposed scheme and those state-of-the-art methods. From this table, we can observe that, for an EC of 10,000 bits, our proposed method can significantly raise the PSNR over that of [17] and [32] by 0.47 dB and 1.22 dB in average, respectively, which further verifies the superiority of our method on the whole.

In summary, compared with a couple of previous works, our proposed scheme can achieve a better capacity-distortion performance, proving the advantage of high-dimensional histogram utilization in RDH.

Table 1. Comparison of PSNR (in dB) between our scheme and some state-of-the-art RDH works, for an EC of 10,000 bits.

Method	Lena	Barbara	Airplane	Elaine	Average
Lee et al. [22]	55.16	56.28	57.73	52.87	**55.51**
Thodi et al. [15]	55.19	55.92	57.50	53.25	**55.47**
Hu et al. [16]	56.46	55.21	57.24	53.19	**55.53**
Sachnev et al. [17]	58.19	58.15	60.34	56.12	**58.20**
Luo et al. [18]	57.31	55.74	57.97	54.80	**56.46**
Qin et al. [32]	57.83	58.44	58.54	54.98	**57.45**
Proposed scheme	58.45	58.46	62.10	55.66	**58.67**

5   Conclusion

To the best knowledge of the authors, existing HS-based RDH methods are mainly based on one or two dimensional histogram. To leverage the redundant information existed in higher-dimensional histogram, in this paper, we followed the general framework of HS-based RDH and proposed an efficient RDH scheme based on three-dimensional histogram. Experimental results showed the superiority of the proposed scheme over a couple of previous works [15–18,22,32] and reveal the effectiveness of designing RDH based on high-dimensional histogram.

Despite of low EC, it is indeed valuable to explore constructing RDH schemes with effective mapping of high-dimensional histogram. In the future, we will design better RDH schemes by taking advantage of high-dimensional histogram and further exploiting the image redundancy. Moreover, we remark that, the performance of the proposed scheme can be enhanced if the PPMs of Fig. 3 could be updated by better ones (e.g., the image-content-dependent ones), which is another direction for future work.

Acknowledgement. The authors would like to thank Dr. Chuan Qin of University of Shanghai for Science and Technology (Shanghai 200093, China) and Dr. Ying-Hsuan Huang of National Chung Hsing University (Taichung 40227, Taiwan), for providing us the experimental results of their work [32].

References

1. Shi, Y.Q.: Reversible data hiding. In: Cox, I., Kalker, T., Lee, H.-K. (eds.) IWDW 2004. LNCS, vol. 3304, pp. 1–12. Springer, Heidelberg (2005)
2. Shi, Y.Q., Ni, Z., Zou, D., Liang, C., Xuan, G.: Lossless data hiding: fundamentals, algorithms and applications. In: Proceedinds of IEEE ISCAS, vol. 2, pp. 33–36 (2004)
3. Tian, J.: Reversible data embedding using a difference expansion. IEEE Trans. Circ. Syst. Video Technol. 13(8), 890–896 (2003)
4. Ni, Z., Shi, Y., Ansari, N., Su, W.: Reversible data hiding. IEEE Trans. Circ. Syst. Video Technol. 16(3), 354–362 (2006)
5. Caldelli, R., Filippini, F., Becarelli, R.: Reversible watermarking techniques: an overview and a classification. EURASIP J. Inf. Secur. 2010, Article ID 134546, 2:1–2:19 (2010)
6. Alattar, A.: Reversible watermark using the difference expansion of a generalized integer transform. IEEE Trans. Image Process. 13(8), 1147–1156 (2004)
7. Wang, X., Li, X., Yang, B., Guo, Z.: Efficient generalized integer transform for reversible watermarking. IEEE Signal Process. Lett. 17(6), 567–570 (2010)
8. Peng, F., Li, X., Yang, B.: Adaptive reversible data hiding scheme based on integer transform. Signal Proc. 92(1), 54–62 (2012)
9. Coltuc, D.: Low distortion transform for reversible watermarking. IEEE Trans. Image Process 21(1), 412–417 (2012)
10. Gui, X., Li, X., Yang, B.: A novel integer transform for efficient reversible watermarking. In: Proceedings of ICPR, pp. 947–950 (2012)
11. Kamstra, L., Heijmans, H.J.A.M.: Reversible data embedding into images using wavelet techniques and sorting. IEEE Trans. Image Process. 14(12), 2082–2090 (2005)
12. Weng, S., Zhao, Y., Pan, J., Ni, R.: Reversible watermarking based on invariability and adjustment on pixel pairs. IEEE Signal Process. Lett. 15, 721–724 (2008)
13. Kim, H.J., Sachnev, V., Shi, Y.Q., Nam, J., Choo, H.G.: A novel difference expansion transform for reversible data embedding. IEEE Trans. Inf. Forens. Secur. 4(3), 456–465 (2008)
14. Liu, M., Seah, H.S., Zhu, C., Lin, W., Tian, F.: Reducing location map in prediction-based difference expansion for reversible image data embedding. Signal Proc. 92(3), 819–828 (2012)
15. Thodi, D., Rodriguez, J.: Expansion embedding techniques for reversible watermarking. IEEE Trans. Image Process. 16(3), 721–730 (2007)
16. Hu, Y., Lee, H., Li, J.: DE-based reversible data hiding with improved overflow location map. IEEE Trans. Circ. Syst. Video Technol. 19(2), 250–260 (2009)
17. Sachnev, V., Kim, H.J., Nam, J., Suresh, S., Shi, Y.Q.: Reversible watermarking algorithm using sorting and prediction. IEEE Trans. Circ. Syst. Video Technol. 19(7), 989–999 (2009)
18. Luo, L., Chen, Z., Chen, M., Zeng, X., Xiong, Z.: Reversible image watermarking using interpolation technique. IEEE Trans. Inf. Forens. Secur. 5(1), 187–193 (2010)
19. Wu, H.T., Huang, J.: Reversible image watermarking on prediction errors by efficient histogram modification. Signal Proc. 92(12), 3000–3009 (2012)
20. Ou, B., Li, X., Zhao, Y., Ni, R., Shi, Y.Q.: Pairwise prediction-error expansion for efficient reversible data hiding. IEEE Trans. Image Process 22(12), 5010–5021 (2013)

21. Dragoi, I.C., Coltuc, D.: Local-prediction-based difference expansion reversible watermarking. IEEE Trans. Image Process **23**(4), 1779–1790 (2014)
22. Lee, S.K., Suh, Y.H., Ho, Y.S.: Reversible image authentication based on watermarking. In: Proceedings of IEEE ICME, pp. 1321–1324 (2006)
23. Hwang, J.H., Kim, J., Choi, J.: A reversible watermarking based on histogram shifting. In: Shi, Y.Q., Jeon, B. (eds.) IWDW 2006. LNCS, vol. 4283, pp. 348–361. Springer, Heidelberg (2006)
24. Fallahpour, M.: Reversible image data hiding based on gradient adjusted prediction. IEICE Electron. Express **5**(20), 870–876 (2008)
25. Tai, W.L., Yeh, C.M., Chang, C.C.: Reversible data hiding based on histogram modification of pixel differences. IEEE Trans. Circ. Syst. Video Technol. **19**(6), 906–910 (2009)
26. Hong, W., Chen, T., Shiu, C.: Reversible data hiding for high quality images using modification of prediction errors. J. Syst. Softw. **82**(11), 1833–1842 (2009)
27. Gao, X., An, L., Yuan, Y., Tao, D., Li, X.: Lossless data embedding using generalized statistical quantity histogram. IEEE Trans. Circ. Syst. Video Technol. **21**(8), 1061–1070 (2011)
28. Xuan, G., Shi, Y.Q., Teng, J., Tong, X., Chai, P.: Double-threshold reversible data hiding. In: Proceedings of IEEE ISCAS, pp. 1129–1132 (2010)
29. Xuan, G., Tong, X., Teng, J., Zhang, X., Shi, Y.Q.: Optimal histogram-pair and prediction-error based image reversible data hiding. In: Shi, Y.Q., Kim, H.-J., Pérez-González, F. (eds.) IWDW 2012. LNCS, vol. 7809, pp. 368–383. Springer, Heidelberg (2013)
30. Li, X., Yang, B., Zeng, T.: Efficient reversible watermarking based on adaptive prediction-error expansion and pixel selection. IEEE Trans. Image Process. **20**(12), 3524–3533 (2011)
31. Li, X., Li, B., Yang, B., Zeng, T.: General framework to histogram-shifting-based reversible data hiding. IEEE Trans. Image Process. **22**(6), 2181–2191 (2013)
32. Qin, C., Chang, C.C., Huang, Y.H., Liao, L.T.: An inpainting-assisted reversible steganographic scheme using a histogram shifting mechanism. IEEE Trans. Circ. Syst. Video Technol. **23**(7), 1109–1118 (2013)

Reversible Data Hiding Based on Combined Predictor and Prediction Error Expansion

Xiaochao Qu[1], Suah Kim[1], Run Cui[1], Fangjun Huang[2],
and Hyoung Joong Kim[1(✉)]

[1] Graduate School of Information Security and Management,
Korea University, Seoul 136-701, Korea
{quxiaochao,suahnkim}@gmail.com, {cuirun,khj-}@korea.ac.kr
[2] School of Information Science and Technology, Sun Yat-Sen University,
Guangdong 510-006, China
huangfj@mail.sysu.edu.cn

Abstract. This paper presents a novel reversible data hiding method which uses a combined predictor. The proposed combined predictor combines five base predictors according to their global and local predicting performance. The weights to combine the base predictors are calculated with a pixel by pixel manner that they adjust to the local image patch characteristics. The proposed predictor is shown to have high prediction precision which is beneficial for the following prediction error expansion (PEE). Observing that our predictor performs well even for images with complex textures, a novel pixel selection criterion that bases on the prediction errors is proposed, which can accurately select the pixels that have small prediction errors to use. Extensive experiments are conducted to verify the superior performance of the proposed method.

Keywords: Reversible data hiding · Combined predictor · Pixel selection · Prediction error expansion

1 Introduction

Reversible data hiding is a technique that can embed data into host image and the data can be extracted from the marked image. After the extraction of data, the host image can be recovered perfectly. The ability of recovering the original host image is required in applications such as military and medical image processing where any distortion can not be tolerated.

Many reversible data hiding methods have been proposed that can be categorized as lossless compression based [5], integer transform based [15,22], histogram shifting based [12,13,19] and difference expansion based [21]. Among the above mentioned methods, difference expansion based method is the most popular one due to its high embedding capacity and low embedding distortion.

Difference expansion (DE) was first proposed by Tian [21] which expands the difference value between a pair of pixels to embed 1 bit data. Later on,

© Springer International Publishing Switzerland 2015
Y.-Q. Shi et al. (Eds.): IWDW 2014, LNCS 9023, pp. 254–265, 2015.
DOI: 10.1007/978-3-319-19321-2_19

DE was improved in various different ways. The first way is to generalize DE where $n-1$ bits can be embedded into a n pixel vector [1]. The second way is to reduce the size of the location map. Kamastra [8] proposed sorting to make the location map more compressible. Kim [9] proposed a novel difference expansion transform with a simplified location map. The location map in their method has a better compression ratio thus the true capacity of their method is increased. Hu [7] constructs a payload-dependent overflow location map which reduces unnecessary alteration to image and has a better compressibility. Thodi [20] uses histogram shifting to separate the embedded pixel and the un-embedded pixel such that the location map size is significantly reduced. The third way is to use prediction error expansion (PEE) proposed by Thodi [20] instead of DE. PEE has two advantages over DE: larger embedding capacity and smaller distortion. Predictors used in PEE can better utilize the correlation of pixels and the obtained prediction error is usually smaller compared with pixel difference. Many predictors are proposed such as rhombus predictor [18], orthogonal projection [6], gradient adjusted predictor (GAP) [11], pixel value ordering based predictor [10,16], partial differential equation based predictor [14], edge based difference expansion [17] and local predictor [4]. Recently, a novel improvement of DE called context embedding was proposed [2,3]. Context embedding distributes the embedding distortion to the context pixels which reduces the overall embedding distortion.

In this paper, we propose a high performance reversible data hiding method using a novel combined predictor and a new pixel selection criterion. Five base predictors are linearly combined into a final predictor. The weights for combining those five base predictors are determined by the base predictor's global performance and local performance. The base predictor is texture selective that it performs well when certain texture appears. By adjusting the weight pixel by pixel, the proposed combined predictor performs well with different textures, including very complex textures. To realize the full potential of the combined predictor, a novel pixel selection criterion is used. The new criterion is based on the characteristics of the combined predictor's prediction errors. It selects the image regions with small prediction errors to use such that the texture regions can be utilized. In the experiment, the proposed method is compared with the methods in [11,18], and it is shown that our method has the best performance.

The rest of the paper is organized as follows. The reversible data hiding based on PEE is introduced in Sect. 2. Section 3 describes the proposed combined predictor, the new pixel selection method and the way to avoid overflow and underflow problems. The experiment result is shown in Sect. 4. Finally, Sect. 5 is the conclusion.

2   Reversible Data Hiding Based on Prediction Error Expansion

Without loss of generality, the predictor in [18] is used in this section (Fig. 1). Assume the current pixel is x and it's four context pixels are x_1, x_2, x_3 and x_4.

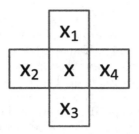

Fig. 1. The four context pixels of the pixel x.

The prediction of x is calculated as:

$$\hat{x} = \left\lfloor \frac{(x_1 + x_2 + x_3 + x_4)}{4} + 0.5 \right\rfloor \tag{1}$$

where the $\lfloor . \rfloor$ is the floor operation which rounds down the value to the next lowest integer value. The prediction error is calculated as:

$$e = x - \hat{x} \tag{2}$$

The prediction error can be expanded to embed a bit $b \in \{0, 1\}$ as:

$$\hat{e} = 2 \times e + b \tag{3}$$

The marked pixel is obtained after the embedding as:

$$X = \hat{x} + \hat{e} \tag{4}$$

To control the embedding capacity and distortion, a pair of threshold $T_p \in [0, +\infty)$ and $T_n \in (-\infty, 0)$ determines which pixel to use. The pixels where $e > T_p$ or $e < T_n$ are shifted as:

$$X = \begin{cases} x + T_p + 1, \text{ if } e > T_p \\ x + T_n, \quad\quad \text{if } e < T_n. \end{cases} \tag{5}$$

At data extraction, the same prediction $\hat{x}$ is calculated and $\hat{e}$ is obtained as $X - \hat{x}$. If $\hat{e} \in [2 \times T_n, 2 \times T_p + 1]$, the extracted data can be calculated as:

$$b = \hat{e} - 2 \times \left\lfloor \frac{\hat{e}}{2} \right\rfloor \tag{6}$$

The original pixel value x can be recovered as:

$$x = \hat{x} + \left\lfloor \frac{\hat{e}}{2} \right\rfloor \tag{7}$$

If $\hat{e} \in (-\infty, 2 \times T_n) \cup (2 \times T_p + 1, \infty)$, no data can be extracted and the original pixel value is recovered as:

$$x = \begin{cases} X - T_p - 1, \text{ if } \hat{e} > 2 \times T_p + 1 \\ X - T_n, \quad\quad \text{if } \hat{e} < 2 \times T_n. \end{cases} \tag{8}$$

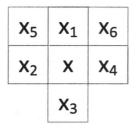

Fig. 2. The proposed six context pixels of the pixel x.

3 Proposed Method

3.1 Combined Predictor

The proposed predictor uses the nearest six context pixels to predict the center pixel x as shown in Fig. 2. x_5 and x_6 can not be used in the predictor of [18] due to the sorting operation. Pixel selection is used instead of sorting in our method which allows x_5 and x_6 to be included into the context pixels. When extracting data from the current pixel x, all it's context pixels have been recovered which guarantees the predictions of the x in the extracting process and embedding process have the same value.

Using those context pixels, five base predictors can be defined as:

$$
\begin{aligned}
p_1 &= \frac{x_1+x_2+x_3+x_4}{4} \\
p_2 &= \frac{x_2+x_4}{2} \\
p_3 &= \frac{x_1+x_3}{2} \\
p_4 &= x_5 \\
p_5 &= x_6
\end{aligned}
\tag{9}
$$

The performance of these five base predictors are different for different kinds of textures. For example, p_2 performs well when encountering an horizontal edge in the image. Therefore, it is not optimal to select one of these five base predictors to use for the whole image since there are different textures in different regions of the image. It is better to assign weights to these five base predictors and linearly combine them. Higher weights are assigned to the predictors that are proper for the current image texture.

For determining the weights, the global and the local performance of the base predictors are considered together. The global performance of the base predictors are measured by the prediction errors of the whole host image. Assume the accumulated absolute prediction error of the base predictor p_i for the host image I is E_i^{global} (the summation of all the absolute prediction errors for a host image), the global weight assigned to base predictor p_i is calculated as:

$$
w_i^{global} = \frac{\frac{1}{E_i^{global}}}{\sum_{i=1}^{5} \frac{1}{E_i^{global}}}
\tag{10}
$$

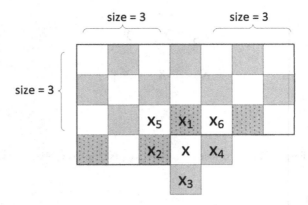

Fig. 3. The local region with red border is used to evaluate the predictor's local performance. The pixels with red dots are not included due to incomplete context pixels.

Clearly, the base predictor with small global prediction error will be assigned with large global weight. However, the global weight itself is not enough to capture the local texture characteristics. Image texture varies from region to region, therefore, local performance of each base predictor should also be considered. The local performance is measured by the prediction error of this base predictor in a small local region. Figure 3 shows an example of the small region with size equals to three. Notice that the pixels with red dots can not be used due to incomplete context pixels, which guarantees that the embedding process and the extracting process has the same pixel information. The current pixel x is white pixel so that all gray pixels are available, and all white pixels that above x are also available. x_1 and x_2 hve incomplete context pixel because of x is not available. The other two red dot pixels have incomplete context pixel because of the lower vertical pixels are not available Assume the accumulated absolute prediction error in the local region is E_i^{local} for the base predictor p_i, the local weight assigned to base predictor p_i is calculated as:

$$w_i^{local} = \frac{\frac{1}{E_i^{local}}}{\sum_{i=1}^{5} \frac{1}{E_i^{local}}} \qquad (11)$$

Notice that if the pixel in the local region does not have full context available, it will be ignored when computing the accumulated absolute error. The base predictor with small local prediction errors will be assigned with large local weight. With the global weight and local weight at hand, the next step is to combine these two weights into the final weights as:

$$w_i = \frac{w_i^{local} \times w_i^{global}}{\sum_{i=1}^{5} w_i^{local} \times w_i^{global}} \qquad (12)$$

The rationale of the proposed predictor can also be explained with Bayes' theorem. The weight reflects the probability of selecting each base predictor.

The global weight can be regarded as the prior of each base predictor and the local weight is the likelihood of each base predictor. If there is no local region pixels available, the prior (global weight) will be used directly. By observing the local region prediction errors, the likelihood is estimated and it transforms the prior into the posteriori.

The proposed combined predictor can be calculated as:

$$p = \left\lfloor \sum_{i=1}^{5} w_i \times p_i + 0.5 \right\rfloor \tag{13}$$

3.2 Pixel Selection Using Prediction Errors

Pixel selection separates the host image into two parts: usable part and unusable part. The prediction errors in the usable part tends to be smaller than that in the unusable part. For each pixel, a pixel selection measurement can be calculated. Then, a proper pixel selection threshold T is determined given a certain payload. The pixels with the pixel selection measurement smaller than T are used to embed data, and all other pixels are skipped.

Conventionally, pixel selection uses neighboring pixel value variance or difference as the metric. The assumption behind is that predictor performs well in smooth regions and those regions should be embedded with priority. However, with the proposed combined predictor, this assumption is not true any more. The proposed predictor adaptively assigns weights to the five base predictors such that it performs well in complex texture regions (e.g., strong edges).

In order to use the texture region as well (which is skipped when using pixel value variance), a new pixel selection metric is proposed. The new metric considers the prediction error values instead of the pixel values. The idea is that the prediction error in the small local region near the current pixel can reflect the performance of the combined predictor to some extent. We can assume that the performance of the combined predictor is similar for the current pixel and it's neighbor pixels. Hence, the prediction errors in the small local region can be used to decide whether to use the current pixel to embed data. Assume the absolute prediction errors in the small local region are grouped into one vector denoted as PE, the pixel selection metric is calculated as $\max(\text{PE}) - \min(\text{PE})$, where $\max()$ and $\min()$ compute the maximum and minimum value of PE, respectively. The advantage of the new metric is that it predicts the predictor's performance using that predictor's historic predicting performance, which can better utilize those pixels in texture but easy to predict region.

3.3 Overflow and Underflow Prevention and Side Information Construction

In the embedding process, some modifications to original pixels may occur overflow and underflow problems that the modified pixel value may be out of the intensity level, for example, $[0, 255]$ for eight-bit grayscale image. Usually, a binary location map with the same size of the host image is needed to record such locations and transmitted to the decoder side. Due to the large size of the location map, compression is needed to reduce the location map's size. The usage of compression makes the algorithm complex and the determination of parameters for the embedding algorithm is hard. We use a strategy to construct a location map that compression is avoided as in [11].

Before embedding, all pixels should be checked if an overflow or underflow problem may occur, if it is possible to have such problems, then the location of this pixel needs to be recoded and this pixel is not used to embed data. For a $W \times H$ grayscale image, each location needs $\lfloor log_2(W \times H) \rfloor + 1$ bits. Besides the location map, some other side information should also be recorded:

1. Compressed location map size ($\lfloor log_2(W \times H) \rfloor + 1$).
2. Global weights for five base predictors (16 bits for each weight).
3. Local region size (8 bits).
4. Embedding threshold T (8 bits).
5. Pixel selection threshold T_{ps} (16 bits).

All the side information concatenated with the location map is embedded using least significant bit (LSB) substitution as in [11].

4   Experiment

The test images used in our experiment have the size of 512×512, namely *Lena*, *F*16, *Baboon*, *Barbara*, *Sailboat* and *Elaine* which can be downloaded from SIPI image database (*sipi.usc.edu/database/*) except *Barbara*. Capacity-distortion performance is used to evaluate the performance of reversible data hiding method. The embedding capacity is measured with bits per pixel (bpp) and distortion is measured with peak signal-to-noise ratio (PSNR).

The performance of the PEE based reversible data hiding is highly dependent on the predictor's performance. An accurate predictor produces small prediction errors which can achieve large embedding capacity with low distortion. The performance of the predictor can be measured by the entropy of the prediction errors which is calculated as:

$$entropy = -\sum_{i=1}^{N} p_i log_2(p_i) \tag{14}$$

where p_i is the probability of of the ith prediction error and N is the total number of possible values of the prediction error. A small entropy means that the prediction errors are more concentrated which is beneficial for the following expansion operation. The entropy comparison of the proposed combined predictor with other predictors is shown in Table. 1. The window size is set to 3 since we found that the window size of 3 has the best trade-off of prediction performance and computation complexity. Henceforth, all the window size used is 3.

Table 1. Comparisons in terms of entropy for different predictors.

Image	MED [20]	GAP [11]	Rhombus [18]	Combined predictor
Lena	4.55	4.39	4.10	3.99
F16	4.18	4.12	3.86	3.80
Baboon	6.27	6.21	5.96	5.82
Barbara	5.48	5.38	5.14	4.75
Sailboat	5.38	5.25	4.97	4.92
Elaine	5.34	5.15	4.89	4.77
Average	5.20	5.08	4.82	4.67

To show the capacity-distortion performance of the proposed reversible data hiding method, we conduct two separate experiments for small size payload and large size payload. The experiment for small size payload can also show the performance of the proposed new pixel selection method.

Pixel selection is more important with small size payload than with large size payload. With large size payload, pixel selection has to select most pixels to use. While with small size payload, the pixel selection has more freedom to decide which pixel to use. The proposed pixel selection based on prediction error distribution is compared with pixel section based on pixel variance as in [18]. The capacity-distortion performance comparison with small size payload is shown in Fig. 4. The embedding capacity tested is from 0.01 bpp to 0.1 bpp. *Proposed* 1 utilizes the combined predictor and the pixel selection based on prediction error distribution. *Proposed* 2 utilizes the combined predictor and the pixel selection based on pixel variance. The only difference of *Proposed* 1 and *Proposed* 2 is the pixel selection method, hence, the performance difference of these two methods can reflect the effectiveness of the respective pixel selection method. As can be seen, *Proposed* 1 performs better than *Proposed* 2 for all the test images. Compared with other two methods in [11] and [18], *Proposed* 1 and *Proposed* 2 both performs better.

With large embedding capacity, we compare the proposed method (combined predictor + pixel selection based on prediction error) with [11] and [18] given the payload size from 0.1 bpp to the maximum embedding capacity. The proposed method outperforms [11] and [18] for all the test images. However, the performance gap between the proposed method with [11] and [18] is different from image to image. For the relatively smooth images, e.g., *F*16, the performance gain of the proposed method is not significant. The reason is that the advantage of the proposed combined predictor is less with smooth images. Given the images with complex texture patterns, e.g., *Barbara*, the proposed combined predictor performs well, therefore, the overall performance of the proposed reversible data hiding method is excellent (Fig. 5).

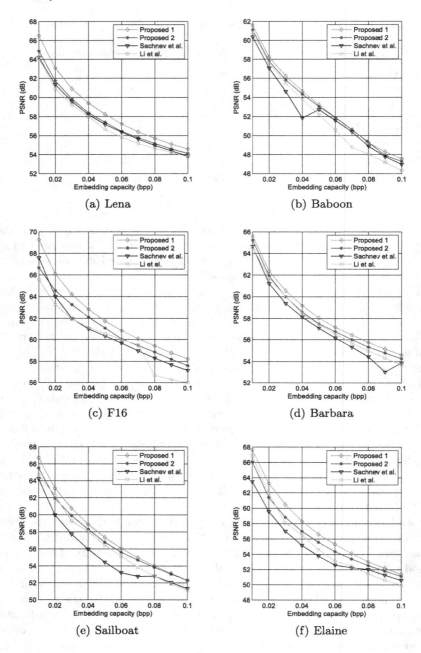

(a) Lena

(b) Baboon

(c) F16

(d) Barbara

(e) Sailboat

(f) Elaine

Fig. 4. The capacity-distortion performance of the proposed method compared with the methods of Li et al. [11] and Sachnev et al. [18] with low payload size.

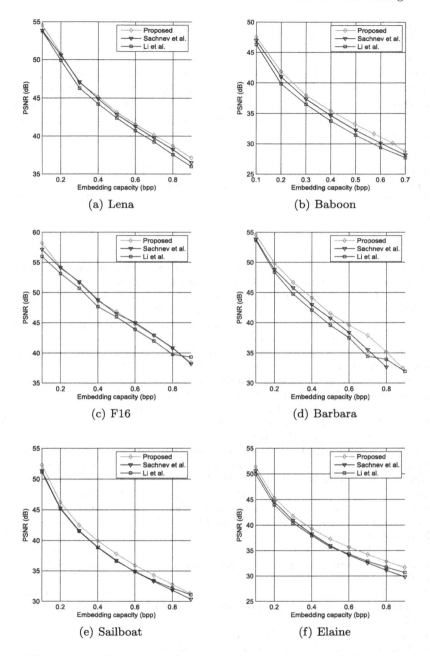

(a) Lena

(b) Baboon

(c) F16

(d) Barbara

(e) Sailboat

(f) Elaine

Fig. 5. The capacity-distortion performance of the proposed method compared with the methods of Li et al. [11] and Sachnev et al. [18] with large payload size.

5   Conclusion

In this paper, a high performance combined predictor and a novel pixel selection method is proposed. It is shown that the proposed combined predictor performs well especially for complex textured images and the proposed pixel selection can better choose the proper pixel to use. Combining the combined predictor and the proposed pixel selection together, the proposed reversible data hiding method achieves excellent result.

Acknowledgments. This work was supported by the National Research Foundation of Korea (NRF) grant funded by the Korea government (MEST) (No. 2012015587), and the National Natural Science Foundation of China (no. 61173147).

References

1. Alattar, A.M.: Reversible watermark using the difference expansion of a generalized integer transform. IEEE Trans. Image Process **13**(8), 1147–1156 (2004)
2. Coltuc, D.: Improved embedding for prediction-based reversible watermarking. IEEE Trans. Inf. Forensics Secur. **6**(3), 873–882 (2011)
3. Coltuc, D.: Low distortion transform for reversible watermarking. IEEE Trans. Image Process **21**(1), 412–417 (2012)
4. Dragoi, I., Coltuc, D.: Local prediction based difference expansion reversible watermarking. IEEE Trans. Image Process **23**(4), 1779–1790 (2014)
5. Fridrich, J., Goljan, M., Du, R.: Lossless data embeddingnew paradigm in digital watermarking. EURASIP J. Adv. Sig. Process. **2002**(2), 185–196 (1900)
6. Hong, W., Chen, T.S., Chang, Y.P., Shiu, C.W.: A high capacity reversible data hiding scheme using orthogonal projection and prediction error modification. Sig. Process. **90**(11), 2911–2922 (2010)
7. Hu, Y., Lee, H.K., Li, J.: De-based reversible data hiding with improved overflow location map. IEEE Trans. Circ. Syst. Video Technol. **19**(2), 250–260 (2009)
8. Kamstra, L., Heijmans, H.J.: Reversible data embedding into images using wavelet techniques and sorting. IEEE Trans. Image Process **14**(12), 2082–2090 (2005)
9. Kim, H.J., Sachnev, V., Shi, Y.Q., Nam, J., Choo, H.G.: A novel difference expansion transform for reversible data embedding. IEEE Trans. Inf. Forensics Secur. **3**(3), 456–465 (2008)
10. Li, X., Li, J., Li, B., Yang, B.: High-fidelity reversible data hiding scheme based on pixel-value-ordering and prediction-error expansion. Sig. process. **93**(1), 198–205 (2013)
11. Li, X., Yang, B., Zeng, T.: Efficient reversible watermarking based on adaptive prediction-error expansion and pixel selection. IEEE Trans. Image Process **20**(12), 3524–3533 (2011)
12. Li, X., Zhang, W., Gui, X., Yang, B.: A novel reversible data hiding scheme based on two-dimensional difference-histogram modification. IEEE Trans. Inf. Forensics Secur. **8**(7), 1091–1100 (2013)
13. Ni, Z., Shi, Y.Q., Ansari, N., Su, W.: Reversible data hiding. IEEE Trans. Circ. Syst. Video Technol. **16**(3), 354–362 (2006)
14. Ou, B., Li, X., Zhao, Y., Ni, R.: Reversible data hiding based on pde predictor. J. Syst. Softw. **86**(10), 2700–2709 (2013)

15. Peng, F., Li, X., Yang, B.: Adaptive reversible data hiding scheme based on integer transform. Sig. Process. **92**(1), 54–62 (2012)
16. Peng, F., Li, X., Yang, B.: Improved pvo-based reversible data hiding. Digit. Sig. Process. **25**, 255–265 (2014)
17. Qu, X., Kim, S., Kim, H.: Reversible watermarking using edge based difference modification. In: Fifth International Conference on Graphic and Image Processing. pp. 90690Q–90690Q. International Society for Optics and Photonics (2014)
18. Sachnev, V., Kim, H.J., Nam, J., Suresh, S., Shi, Y.Q.: Reversible watermarking algorithm using sorting and prediction. IEEE Trans. Circ. Syst. Video Technol. **19**(7), 989–999 (2009)
19. Tai, W.L., Yeh, C.M., Chang, C.C.: Reversible data hiding based on histogram modification of pixel differences. IEEE Trans. Circ. Syst. Video Technol. **19**(6), 906–910 (2009)
20. Thodi, D.M., Rodríguez, J.J.: Expansion embedding techniques for reversible watermarking. IEEE Trans. Image Process. **16**(3), 721–730 (2007)
21. Tian, J.: Reversible data embedding using a difference expansion. IEEE Trans. Circ. Syst. Video Technol. **13**(8), 890–896 (2003)
22. Weng, S., Zhao, Y., Pan, J.S., Ni, R.: A novel reversible watermarking based on an integer transform. In: IEEE International Conference on Image Processing, 2007, ICIP 2007, vol. 3, pp. III-241–III-244. IEEE (2007)

Reversible Shared Data Hiding Based on Modified Signed Digit EMD

Wen-Chung Kuo[1]([✉]), Chun-Cheng Wang[2], Hong-Ching Hou[3], and Chen-Tsun Chuang[3]

[1] Department of Computer Science and Information Engineering, National Yunlin University of Science and Technology, Douliu, Taiwan, R.O.C.
simonkuo@yuntech.edu.tw
[2] Graduate School of Engineering Science and Technology Doctoral Program, National Yunlin University of Science and Technology, Douliu, Taiwan, R.O.C.
[3] Department of Computer Science and Information Engineering, National Formosa University, Huwei, Taiwan, R.O.C.

Abstract. The reversible data hiding schemes not only extract the embedded secret data from the stego-image but also recover the original cover image. This can be extended for use with multiple parties where the embedded secret data is undecipherable unless all members contribute. Recently, Chang *et al.* [2] proposed a reversible data hiding scheme based on EMD (Exploiting Modification Direction) which can be used for this purpose. However, the capacity of EMD decreases quickly with the increased number of stego-images. To address this disadvantage, we will propose a reversible data hiding scheme based on modified signed digit EMD in this paper. According to our experiments, this scheme achieves the requirement of reversible shared data hiding and keeping good image quality but also maintains embedding capacity of least 1 bpp (bits per pixel).

Keywords: Reversible data hiding · EMD (Exploiting Modification Direction) · Signed digit · Embedding capacity

1 Introduction

Steganography embeds messages into cover multimedia without adversely affecting the quality of multimedia. However, we need to consider the capacity of the cover multimedia in the process of data hiding. Secret information may span several cover multimedia and transferring the multimedia costs much time. Therefore, how to increase the capacity and maintain the security without affecting the quality of multimedia is an open issue.

In 2006, Zhang and Wang [8] proposed the Exploiting Modification Direction (EMD) data hiding scheme. Their scheme used n adjacent pixels for a pixel group and only adjusted one pixel in each pixel group. They also defined a function to extract the secret message easily. According to our analysis, their embedding capacity decreases quickly with increasing number of pixels in pixel group.

© Springer International Publishing Switzerland 2015
Y.-Q. Shi et al. (Eds.): IWDW 2014, LNCS 9023, pp. 266–275, 2015.
DOI: 10.1007/978-3-319-19321-2_20

In 2013, Kuo and Wang [5] proposed the Generalized Exploiting Modification Direction (GEMD) scheme. This scheme overcame the issue in Lee *et al.* [7] scheme proposed in 2007, IEMD (Improving Exploiting Modification Direction), where only $n = 2$ is allowed. In addition, the GEMD scheme is suitable for binary data stream. In the same year, Kuo *et al.* [6] proposed another EMD scheme based on binary coefficient. This scheme improved the capacity decreasing problem of EMD effectively. This scheme maintained 1 bpp capacity and did not adjust adjacent pixels at the same time.

How we create a reversible shared data hiding scheme. Recently, Chang *et al.* [2] proposed a similar visual secret sharing scheme (CHL scheme) which used EMD. Their scheme disperses secret messages over several identical cover images randomly and is reversible. However, the embedding capacity of the CHL scheme decreased quickly with the increasing number of cover images. In order to overcome this disadvantage, we propose a reversible shared data scheme based on modified signed digit EMD (MSD scheme). According to our experiments and analysis, we demonstrate our proposed scheme achieves reversible shared data hiding and keeping good image quality but also maintaining the embedding capacity at least 1 bpp.

This paper is organized as follows. The EMD, MSD and CHL schemes are reviewed briefly in Sect. 2. The proposed data hiding scheme and our experimental results are described in Sects. 3 and 4, respectively. We give some conclusions in Sect. 5.

2   Review Some Data Hiding Schemes

2.1   EMD Scheme

In 2006, Zhang and Wang [8] proposed the EMD data hiding scheme. In their scheme, they collect n pixels for each pixel group. Then, according to the defined extraction function (Eq. (1)), they adjust one pixel in each pixel group ± 1 to embed $(2n+1)$-ary secret message. The extraction function of Zhang and Wang's scheme is:

$$f_{EMD}(x_1, x_2, \ldots, x_n) = \sum_{i=1}^{n} i \times x_i \bmod (2n + 1) \tag{1}$$

where n is the number of pixels in the pixel group, and x_i is the i-th pixel value.

Algorithm 1. The EMD embedding algorithm
Input: cover image and secret message s
Output: stego-image

Step 1. Choose n and then divide the cover image to pixel groups having n pixels and convert secret message s to $(2n + 1)$-ary.
Step 2. Compute $f_{EMD}(x_1, x_2, \ldots, x_n)$ with the pixel groups.
Step 3. Compute the difference $d = (s - f_{EMD}) \bmod (2n + 1)$.

Step 4. If $d = 0$, do not adjust pixels and go to Step 6.
Step 5. If $d \leq n$, adjust the d-th pixel in pixel group by $+1$, otherwise adjust the $((2n + 1) - d)$-th pixel in pixel group by -1.
Step 6. Repeat the above steps until secret message is embedded.

Example 1. Let the cover pixels value s be $(22, 23, 24, 25)$ with two pixels per group. Stego-pixels $(23, 23, 23, 25)$ are obtained from secret message $(10111)_2$ by the following steps:

Step 1. Covert secret message $(10111)_2$ to $(43)_5$.
Step 2. Compute $f_{EMD}(x_1, x_2, \ldots, x_n)$ with $(22, 23)$ and $(24, 25)$ for $(3, 4)$.
Step 3. Compute differences $(d_1, d_2) = (1, 4)_5$.
Step 4. The resulting stego-pixel values are $(23, 23, 23, 25)$.

2.2 Signed Digit EMD

Recently, Kuo *et al.* [6] proposed an improved embedding capacity data hiding scheme named the MSD scheme. There are two major contributions of their scheme. One is embedding capacity is at least 1 bpp and the other is the adjacent pixels are never both adjusted. The MSD extraction function and the modulus are shown as Eqs. (2) and (3).

$$f_b(x_1, x_2, \ldots, x_n) = \sum_{i=1}^{n} 2^{i-1} \times x_i \bmod t \tag{2}$$

$$t = 2^{2-(n \bmod 2)} \times \left(\frac{4^{\lfloor \frac{(n+1)}{2} \rfloor} - 1}{3}\right) + 1 \tag{3}$$

Algorithm 2. Signed Digit EMD embedding algorithm
Input: cover image and secret message s
Output: stego-image

Step 1. Select n and compute the modulus t.
Step 2. Convert the secret message s to t-ary.
Step 3. Compute $f_b(x_1, x_2, \ldots, x_n)$.
Step 4. Compute the difference $d = s - f_b(x_1, x_2, \ldots, x_n) \bmod t$.
Step 5. Adjust the difference expressions $d = (d_1, d_2, \ldots, d_n)$ by using the Modified Signed Digit algorithm [3].
Step 6. Compute stego-pixels $(y_1, y_2, \ldots, y_n) = (x_1 + d_1, x_2 + d_2, \ldots, x_n + d_n)$.
Step 7. Repeat the above steps until secret message is embedded.

Algorithm 2 is demonstrated in the following example:

Example 2. Let $n = 3$, $s = 5$ with cover pixels $(23, 26, 27)$. Then, the stego-pixels $(23, 25, 27)$ are obtained by using Algorithm 2:

Step 1. Compute the modulus $t = 2 \times (\frac{4^2-1}{3}) + 1 = 11$.
Step 2. Compute $f_b(23, 26, 27) \bmod 11 = 7$.
Step 3. Compute the difference $d = 5 - 7 = -2$ and then use Modified Signed Digit to convert to $(0(-1)0)_2$.
Step 4. Get the stego-pixels $(y_1, y_2, y_3) = (23, 25, 27)$.

2.3   Secret Sharing Scheme Based on EMD

In 2012, Chang *et al.* [2] proposed a similar visual secret sharing scheme based on EMD (CHL-scheme). There are three major contributions in the CHL-scheme: (a) random dispersion of secret messages into the several copies of the same cover image; (b) the embedding process only adjusts one pixel value and (c) reversible data hiding. The CHL scheme will be briefly described. For more detail, we encourage readers to reference [2].

Algorithm 3. The Embedding steps of CHL-scheme
Input: cover image, random key k, secret message s
Output: stego-image

Step 1. Convert secret message s to $(2n + 1)$-ary.
Step 2. Use k to generate n digit sequence, i.e., the length equal to the pixel number of the cover image. Then generate the $(n-1)$ identical cover images.
Step 3. Choose the same pixel from each cover image and according to the digit in k, choose the pixel in the corresponding image for marking pixel. Then use the remaining pixels for pixel group and use EMD to embed secret message.
Step 4. Repeat the above steps until the secret message is embedded.

3   The Proposed Scheme

CHL-scheme is reversible. However, the shortcoming of the original EMD scheme also exists in the CHL scheme where the embedding capacity is quickly decreased when the number of sharing images increases. Therefore, this work proposes a high capacity shared data hiding scheme in this section.

3.1   Adjacent Pixel Difference Adjustment (APDA)

From the MSD scheme, we find a very special characteristic; the adjacent pixels are not adjusted at the same time. However, it does not use this advantage directly because it has adjacent pixel difference adjustment (APDA). The four modified cases of $01010\ldots10$, $0\bar{1}0\bar{1}0\ldots\bar{1}0$, $10101\ldots01$, $\bar{1}0\bar{1}0\bar{1}\ldots0\bar{1}$ are called the APDA state. For example, in Table 1, the pixel group is $(5, 5, 5)$ and $n = 3$. The adjusted value 2 modifies the stego-pixel group to be $(5, 6, 5)$ and the adjusted value 6 makes stego-pixel group be $(4, 5, 4)$. The receiver does not know whether the original pixel is 5 or 4. This is the same case in stego-pixel group with $(6, 5, 6)$ and $(5, 4, 5)$.

Due to conflicting results when the cover image is recovered, we must perform some adaptive modifications. When n is odd, we change $01010\ldots10$ and $0\bar{1}0\bar{1}0\ldots\bar{1}0$ to $01010...02$ and $0\bar{1}0\bar{1}0...0\bar{2}$, respectively. For example, in Table 1, the two pixel groups having conflict are $(5, 6, 5)$ and $(5, 4, 5)$ are changed to $(5, 5, 7)$ and $(5, 5, 3)$. When n is even, we change $10101\cdots10$ and $\bar{1}0\bar{1}0\bar{1}\cdots\bar{1}0$ to $10101\cdots02$ and $\bar{1}0\bar{1}0\bar{1}\cdots0\bar{2}$.

The embedding algorithm is shown as following:

Table 1. The adjustment value for pixel group $= (5, 5, 5)$

Adjustment value	Stego-pixel group	Changed case
0	5 5 5	—
1	5 5 6	—
2	5 6 5	$(5, 5, 7)$
3	6 5 4	—
4	6 5 5	—
5	5 6 5	—
6	4 5 4	—
7	4 5 5	—
8	4 5 6	—
9	5 4 5	$(5, 5, 3)$
10	5 5 4	—

Algorithm 4. The embedding algorithm

Input: cover image, secret message s
Output: stego-image

Step 1. Select n and compute t.
Step 2. Convert the secret message s to t-ary.
Step 3. Compute $f_b(x_1, x_2, \ldots, x_n)$.
Step 4. Compute the difference between s and $f_b(x_1, x_2, \ldots, x_n)$, i.e. $d = s - f_b(x_1, x_2, \ldots, x_n) \bmod t$.
Step 5. Adjust the difference expressions $d = (d_1, d_2, \ldots, d_n)$ by using the Modified Signed Digit algorithm.
Step 6. If the d's type belongs to ADPA, go to Step 7. Otherwise, use Signed Digit EMD to embed and go to Step 8.
Step 7. If n is odd, then we will change $01010\cdots10$ and $0\bar{1}0\bar{1}0\cdots\bar{1}0$ to $01010\cdots02$ and $0\bar{1}0\bar{1}0\cdots0\bar{2}$, respectively; Otherwise, we will modify $10101\cdots10$ and $\bar{1}0\bar{1}0\bar{1}\cdots\bar{1}0$ to $10101\cdots02$ and $\bar{1}0\bar{1}0\bar{1}\cdots0\bar{2}$ when n is even.
Step 8. Combine the changed MSD and stego-pixel group.
Step 9. Repeat the above steps until secret message is embedded.

Where x_i is the value of the same position pixel x in the i-th share image for $i \in \{1, 2, \cdots, n\}$.

3.2 The Reversible Rule

According to above analysis, we generalize following three recovery rules:

Rule 1. If all pixel value $(x_1, x_2, \ldots, x_n)$ are the same, then the original pixel is x_1.
Rule 2. If $|x_i - x_{i-1}| = 2$, then x_{i-1} is the original pixel value.

Rule 3. If $(x_i - x_{i+1})(x_{i+1} - x_{i+2}) = 1$ or $(x_i - x_{i+1})(x_{i+1} - x_{i+2}) = 0$, then the x_{i+1} is the original pixel value for $i = 1, 2, \cdots, n - 2$.

The extraction and recovery algorithm are shown as:

Algorithm 5. Extraction and recovery algorithm
Input: stego-image
Output: cover image, secret message s

Step 1. Group pixels into pixel groups $x_1, x_2, x_3, \ldots, x_{n-1}, x_n$ having n pixels.
Step 2. Use the reversible rules (Rules 1–3) to recover the original pixel and extract the secret message.
Step 3. Repeat the above steps until all secret messages are extracted and the cover image is found.

3.3   The Proposed Method

Algorithm 6. Generating n shared stego-images
Input: cover image, secret message, n
Output: n stego-images

Step 1. Compute the modulus t.
Step 2. Generate n cover images and convert the secret message to t-ary.
Step 3. Choose the same position pixels in the cover images to form the pixel group.
Step 4. Use embedding the Algorithm 4 to embed secret message.
Step 5. Repeat the step 3 and step 4 until all secret messages are embedded.

Algorithm 7. The recover cover image algorithm for n shared stego-images
Input: n stego-images
Output: cover image and secret messages

Step 1. Choose the same position pixels in the stego-images from the pixel group.
Step 2. Use Algorithm 5 to extract the secret message and recover the original pixel.
Step 3. Repeat the above step until all secret messages are extracted and the cover image is recovered.

3.4   Overflow Problem

Location map are used to solve the overflow problem in our proposed scheme. First, we record the locations of pixel values 0, 1, 254 and 255 to form the location map and compress it. Then we turn the pixel value of 0, 1 to 2 and 254, 255 to 253. Finally, we put the compressed location map in front of the secret message and embed it. When the receiver gets the stego-image, he can extract the secret message and recover the adjusted image and use the location map to recover the original image.

(a). The first stego-image of Lena and upper-left pixels

(b). The second stego-image of Lena and upper-left pixels

(c). The third stego-image of Lena and upper-left pixels

Fig. 1. The stego image for Lena

4　Experimental Results and Analysis

In this paper, we use the grayscale cover image Lena as the simulation example with image size 512×512.

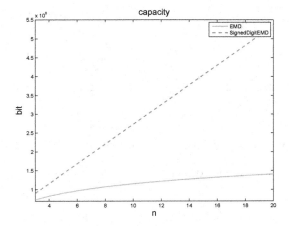

Fig. 2. Embedding capacity of reversible EMD and Signed Digit EMD

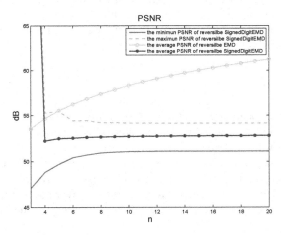

Fig. 3. PSNR values of reversible EMD and Signed Digit EMD

4.1 Experimental Results

The simulation results are shown Fig. 1(a)–(c) for reversible Signed Digit EMD scheme with $n = 3$. The stego-image and the upper-left pixels of stego-image are shown in Fig. 1.

4.2 Experimental Analysis

According to the experimental results, the capacity of reversible Sign Digital EMD is larger than reversible EMD [2]. Although the stego-image quality of our scheme is not better than reversible EMD, the average quality maintains 52 dB and is indiscernible to the naked eye. The average image quality is very

d	d_3	d_2	d_1
0	0	0	0
1	0	0	1
2	0	1	0
3	1	0	-1
4	1	0	0
5	1	0	1
6	-1	0	-1
7	-1	0	0
8	-1	0	1
9	0	-1	0
10	0	0	-1

d	d_3	d_2	d_1
0	0	0	0
1	0	0	1
2	0	0	2
3	1	0	-1
4	1	0	0
5	1	0	1
6	-1	0	-1
7	-1	0	0
8	-1	0	1
9	0	0	-2
10	0	0	-1

(a) The original MSD adjusted   The modified MSD adjusted

Fig. 4. The MSD modified table when $n = 3$

good when $n = 3$, since the middle pixels are not changed. To solve the conflict problem of Signed Digit EMD, it will be adjusted and the reason is described in the Sect. 3. Figure 4(a) shows the original MSD adjusted and Fig. 4(b) shows the MSD adjusted value method to solve the conflict problem. Therefore, in special case(when $n = 3$), the MSE value is 0 and PSNR is infinity for the second stego-image, respectively (Figs. 2 and 3).

5   Conclusions

Chang *et al.* [2] proposed the reversible data hiding scheme, though the embedding capacity decreases quickly when the shared cover images increase. So, the scheme is not suitable for transferring large secret messages or for large number of shares. In this paper, we have proposed a reversible Signed Digit EMD scheme to improve on the problem. According to the experimental results, our scheme not only provides 1 bpp capacity, but also maintains average image quality above 50 dB. In addition, capacity in our scheme is not affected by the number of cover images.

Acknowledgment. This work was supported by MOST 103-2221-E-224 -046.

References

1. Abdulla, A.A., Jassimand, S.A., Sellahewa, H.: Efficient high-capacity steganography technique. In: Proceedings of SPIE8755, Mobile Multimedia/Image Processing, Security, and Applications (2013)
2. Chang, C.C., Huynh, N.T., Lin, C.C.: Strong tamper-localization, visual secret sharing scheme based on exploiting modification direction. In: 2012 Seventh Asia Joint Conference Information Security (Asia JCIS), pp. 10–16, August 2012
3. Jedwab, J., Mitchell, C.J.: Minimum weight modified signed-digit representation and fast exponentiation. Electron. Lett. **25**(17), 1171–1173 (1989)

4. Kuo, W.C., Wuu, L.C., Shyi, C.N., Kuo, S.H.: A data hiding scheme with high embedding capacity based on general improving exploiting modification direction method. In: The Ninth International Conference on Hybrid Intelligent Systems (HIS2009), pp. 69–73, August 2009
5. Kuo, W.C., Wang, C.C.: Data hiding based on generalised exploiting modification direction method. J. Imaging Sci. **61**(6), 484–490 (2013)
6. Kuo, W.C., Hou, H.C., Chuang, C.T.: Data hiding scheme based on binary coefficient EMD. In: NCS 2013, 13–14 December 2013
7. Lee, F.C., Wang, Y.R., Chang, C.C.: A steganographic method with high embedding capacity by improving exploiting modification direction. In: Proceedings of the Third International Conference on Intelligent Information Hiding and Multimedia Signal Processing (IIHMSP 2007), pp. 497–500 (2007)
8. Zhang, X., Wang, S.: Efficient steganographic embedding by exploiting modification direction. IEEE Commun. Lett. **10**(11), 1–3 (2006)

Adaptive Predictor Structure Based Interpolation for Reversible Data Hiding

Sunil Prasad Jaiswal[1]([✉]), Oscar Au[1], Vinit Jakhetiya[1],
Andy Yuanfang Guo[1], and Anil K. Tiwari[2]

[1] The Hong Kong University of Science and Technology, Kowloon, Hong Kong
{spjaiswal,eeau,vjakhetiya,eeandyguo}@ust.hk
[2] Indian Institute of Technology, Rajasthan, India
akt@iitj.ac.in

Abstract. In this paper, we present an additive prediction error expansion (PEE) based reversible data hiding scheme that gives overall low distortion and relatively high embedding capacity. Recently reported interpolation based PEE method uses fixed order predictor that fails to exploit the correlation between the neighborhood pixels and the unknown pixel (to be interpolated). We observed that embedding capacity and distortion of PEE based algorithm depends on the prediction accuracy of the predictor. In view of this observation, we propose an interpolation based method that predicts pixels using predictors of different structure and order. Moreover, we use only original pixels for interpolation. Experimental results demonstrate that the proposed algorithm outperforms the state-of-the-art algorithms both in terms of embedding capacity and Peak Signal to Noise Ratio.

Keywords: Reversible image watermarking · Predictor order · Embedding capacity · Interpolation

1 Introduction

Reversible watermarking receives much popularity in recent years because of copyright protection of data. Reversible image watermarking means embedding a specific information into an image in such a way that the original image can be recovered at the decoder. Reversible watermarking is also useful in other applications such as image/video coding [1].

Reversible image watermarking (RIW) can be divided into two categories [2]: histogram shifting methods based data hiding [3–5], and difference expansion (DE) based reversible data hiding (RDH) methods [6–8]. Algorithms based on DE method have achieved better embedding capacity with low computation cost as compared to other methods. Algorithms in [9–11] have extended DE based methods by prediction error expansion (PEE) method i.e. by embedding watermarking data into prediction error sample instead of difference between paired pixels as done in DE schemes and leads to achieve improved embedding capacity. Luo et al. [11] proposed an interpolation based PEE (IPEE) method and embedded data into interpolation error instead of prediction error.

© Springer International Publishing Switzerland 2015
Y.-Q. Shi et al. (Eds.): IWDW 2014, LNCS 9023, pp. 276–288, 2015.
DOI: 10.1007/978-3-319-19321-2_21

1. Though the interpolation technique used in [11] is adaptive to edges but uses a fixed 4th order predictor and hence fails to exploit correlation between the neighborhood pixels and the unknown pixel.
2. Moreover, the interpolation algorithm used in [11] is a two pass process. In first pass, $(1/4)^{th}$ of total missing samples are interpolated using the original pixels and in second pass, rest of the missing samples are interpolated using both original pixels and interpolated pixels. Thus use of the interpolated pixels in the second pass causes error propagation from first pass to second pass and hence decreases the prediction accuracy.

In view of the above mentioned problems, main contributions of proposed algorithm are as follows:

1. We propose a prediction method that uses only original pixels for interpolation in both the passes and thus no error propagation occurs from first pass to second pass which increases the prediction accuracy.
2. Also, we propose a higher order predictor as against of 4th order proposed by IPEE [11].

The rest of paper is organized as follows. In Sect. 2, additive PEE based data hiding is explained. Existing interpolation based PEE algorithm is discussed in Sect. 3 while proposed method is given in Sect. 4. Section 5 includes simulation results and concluding remarks are given in Sect. 6.

2   Additive Prediction Error Expansion

Watermark data (0 or 1) is embedded by using the prediction error expansion (PEE) method [9–11] as discussed below:

2.1   Encoder

Suppose a prediction method is applied on the original pixel $I(n)$ and prediction value $P(n)$ is obtained. For prediction use causal pixels as decoder do not have information of non-causal pixel. Then prediction error is obtained as,

$$e(n) = I(n) - P(n). \tag{1}$$

Thus after getting the prediction error, additive PEE-based embedding is performed as given in (2).

$$e_w(n) = \begin{cases} e(n) - b.sign(e(n)).Q & -Q \leq e(n) < Q \\ e(n) - Q & e(n) < -Q \\ e(n) + Q & e(n) >= Q \end{cases} \tag{2}$$

Here b is the to-be-embedded watermark bit (0 or 1), $sign(e(n))$ implies $+1$ if $e(n)$ is positive and (-1) if negative and Q is the capacity parameters. In (2), embedding of bit (b) is done in prediction error samples $(e(n))$ in the range of

$[-Q, Q)$ only. Other value of $e(n)$ gets shifted so as to avoid overlapping and no watermark information is embedded. Thus after additive PEE, watermarked pixels can be given by,

$$I_w(n) = P(n) + e_w(n) \tag{3}$$

Additive PEE based embedding algorithms involve error expansion and shifting operations which may cause overflow/underflow problems i.e. some pixels may go outside the range of $[0, 255]$ for an 8 bit image. This may result ambiguity and thus perfect reconstruction at decoder will not be possible. To deal such problem a location map is generated, at encoder, to keep record of location of pixels and embedding operation is not done on such pixels to avoid ambiguity. These location map needs to be send to decoder losslessly to ensure reversibility.

2.2   Decoder

In a reverse order, we can restore the original image ($\mathbf{I}$) from the watermarked image ($\mathbf{I_w}$).

At first, check whether the current pixel location is recorded in location map. If recorded, then the given pixel is the original pixel itself and thus no watermark bit is extracted. Else, the decoding process can be described as follows:

1. First, prediction value $P(n)$ is estimated (as it is obtained at encoder) and thus $e_w(n)$ can be calculated via, $e_w(n) = I_w(n) - P(n)$.
2. Once we get $e_w(n)$, the prediction error pixel ($e(n)$) and the hidden bit (b) can be obtained using (4) given below.

$$e(n) = \begin{cases} e_w(n) \text{ and b} = 0 \\ \quad \text{if } -Q \leq e_w(n) < Q \\ \\ e_w(n) - sign(e_w(n)) \times -Q \text{ and b=1} \\ \quad \text{if } -2 \times Q \leq e_w(n) < -Q \\ \quad \text{or } Q \leq e_w(n) < 2 \times Q \\ \\ e_w(n) - sign(e_w(n)) \times Q \\ \quad \text{otherwise} \end{cases} \tag{4}$$

3. Then original pixel is estimated by, $I(n) = P(n) + e(n)$.

Thus, we can recover both the original image ($\mathbf{I}$) and the watermarked data (b) at the decoder.

The relationship between $e(n)$ and $e_w(n)$ is discussed in method [10] and is given as follows: When an original pixel undergoes watermarking processes by (2), the distortion caused be the process is $I(n) - I_w(n) = (P(n) + e(n)) - (P(n) + e_w(n)) = e(n) - e_w(n) \leq Q$. Thus, distortion is small and changes in the watermarked image is imperceptible for smaller values of Q. From (2), we observe that bits (b) are embedded into residue samples ($e(n)$) having values in the range of $[-Q, Q]$. Thus, better the accuracy of the predictor, more will be the embedding capacity.

3   Existing Interpolation Based PEE Algorithm

In [11], original image **I** of dimension $W \times H$ is down sampled by a factor of two; row wise and column wise. Due to direct down sampling operation, a low resolution (**LR**) version image of dimension $W/2 \times H/2$ is obtained. The low resolution image (**LR**) is then interpolated to High Resolution Image (**P**) using a two pass algorithm. The odd-odd positioned pixels denoted by black dots in Fig. 1 are copied from LR image as shown in (5).

$$P(2i - 1, 2j - 1) = LR(i, j) \quad \forall\ (i, j) \in LR \tag{5}$$

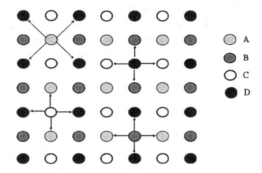

Fig. 1. Black dots represent original pixel of LR image. Rest of the pixel are to be interpolated (Color figure online).

Based on the co-ordinate position of the pixels to be interpolated, we label the pixels of **P** by four symbols; $A(n)$, $B(n)$, $C(n)$, $D(n)$. **A**, **B**, **C** are symbols for the unknown pixels (to be interpolated) located at even-even positions, even-odd positions, odd-even positions respectively while symbols D are the original pixels located at odd-odd positions. Without loss of generality, consider first pixel of the image to be at odd-odd position i.e., (1, 1). By using these symbols, a part of given image is shown in Fig. 1. The working procedure of [11] can be divided into two phase as follows:

3.1   First Phase: Watermarking Process of $(3/4)^{th}$ of Total Pixels

1. In first pass, all the even-even positioned pixels (type **A**) denoted by gray dots in Fig. 1 are predicted using its 4 diagonal neighboring pixels i.e. the predictor order is 4. Thus in first pass, it uses only original pixels for prediction.
2. In second pass, all the pixels denoted by **B** and **C** (denoted by blue and white dots respectively) in Fig. 1 are predicted using four closest neighboring pixels. It involves two original pixels (black dots) and two interpolated pixels (gray dots) for prediction.

It is clear that prediction accuracy decreases in second pass due to involvement of interpolated pixels. Thus two-pass method can propagate errors from first pass to second pass. After predicting $(3/4)^{th}$ of the total pixels in **P** and finding its corresponding $e(n)$, additive PEE method is used to obtain the corresponding watermarked pixels.

3.2   Second Phase: Watermarking Process of Remaining Pixels

By the above phase, only $(3/4)^{th}$ pixels of **I** undergo watermarking process. The watermarking process for remaining original $(1/4)^{th}$ pixels (type **D**) can be described as follows:

The odd-odd positioned pixels ($(1/4)^{th}$ pixel of **I**) can be predicted using watermarked samples along two orthogonal directions as shown in Fig. 1. Thus after predicting each pixel of odd-odd position, find its corresponding $e(n)$, and apply additive PEE method to get corresponding watermarked pixels. Thus final watermarked image ($\mathbf{I_w}$) is obtained and then sent to decoder.

At decoder, in a reverse order of watermarking algorithm (performed at encoder), we can recover the original image (**I**) and the watermark data (b) easily [11].

4   Proposed Algorithm

For PEE based embedding algorithm, embedding capacity and distortion of an algorithm depends on the prediction accuracy of the predictor. Thus the aim of proposed algorithm is to increase the prediction accuracy so as to achieve higher embedding capacity.

4.1   First Phase: Watermarking Process of $(3/4)^{th}$ Pixels of I

In the first phase, we interpolate the LR image to a high resolution image (**P**) using proposed prediction algorithm as described below.

Prediction of Even-Even Positioned Pixels (A Type). In first pass, we predict pixels denoted by **A**. However the proposed predictor structure is different from IPEE [11]. Proposed predictor structure consist of 6 original pixels and is shown in Fig. 2(a). We define the linear predictor for $A(n)$ as $\hat{A}(n)$ and is given in (6).

$$\hat{A}(n) = \boldsymbol{a}^T \boldsymbol{\phi}_i = \sum_{k=1}^{6} a_k \phi_i(k) \tag{6}$$

Here $\boldsymbol{a} = [a_1, a_2, a_3, a_4, a_5, a_6]^T$ are prediction coefficients and $\boldsymbol{\phi}_i = [D(n-4), C(n-3), D(n-2), B(n-1), D(n+2), D(n+4)]$ is a vector consisting of neighboring pixels of $A(n)$. Note that the prediction is based on the four odd-odd positioned pixels (**D** type) and two causal pixels. Hence, decoder can obtain the same prediction without any ambiguity.

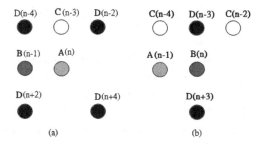

D(n-4) C(n-3) D(n-2)   C(n-4) D(n-3) C(n-2)

B(n-1) A(n)   A(n-1) B(n)

D(n+2)   D(n+4)   D(n+3)

(a)   (b)

Fig. 2. (a) Predictor structure of A(n) consists of 4 D-type pixels (black dots) and 2 causal pixels, (b) Predictor structure of B(n) consists of 2 D-type pixels (black dots) and 3 causal pixels.

For finding prediction coefficients (a), we propose to adopt method given in [13]. However, predictor structure of [13] consists of only causal pixels whereas proposed predictor structure consists of both causal and non-causal pixels and is described as below:

We first find gradients at the unknown pixel ($A(n)$) in horizontal direction (D_H) and in vertical direction (D_V) and then find relative variation as,

$$S = D_H - D_V \tag{7}$$

where $D_V = |D(n-4) - B(n-1)| + |B(n-1) - D(n+2)| + |D(n-2) - D(n+4)|$ and $D_H = |D(n-4) - C(n-3)| + |C(n-3) - D(n-2)| + |D(n+2) - D(n+4)|$.

After finding gradients, slope S is classified into 7 bins and its description is given Table 1. The bin boundaries given in Table 1 are chosen in such a way that there are approximately same number of pixels in each bin. By doing so, we are doing equal treatment to pixels belonging to various bins [13].

1. We classify the pixels of type A ($(1/4)^{th}$ pixels of **I**) in 7 bins as per the bin boundaries given in Table 1. Each bin consists of pixels which have similar edge structure (Table 1) and thus Least Square (LS) based prediction coefficient is most suitable for precise prediction [12–16].
2. For each bin, LS based prediction coefficients (a) is estimated by minimizing the following cost function.

$$J(\boldsymbol{a}) = \sum_{n=1}^{Z} (A(n) - \boldsymbol{a}^T \phi_i)^2 \tag{8}$$

where, Z is the total number of pixels in corresponding bin. Hence, we obtain optimal the LS based weights $\boldsymbol{a}$ by differentiating (9) with respect to the parameters i.e.

$$\boldsymbol{a}^* = \min_{a} \ J(\boldsymbol{a}) \tag{9}$$

It is well-known that the LS optimization has a closed-form solution and is given by

$$\boldsymbol{a}^* = (\boldsymbol{\Phi}^T \boldsymbol{\Phi})^{-1} (\boldsymbol{\Phi}^T \boldsymbol{y}) \tag{10}$$

Table 1. Classification of Slope (S) into bins.

Slope S	Bin	Description
$S > 40$	Bin 1	Sharp edge along vertical direction
$40 \geq S > 20$	Bin 2	Edge along vertical direction
$20 \geq S > 8$	Bin 3	Weak edge along vertical direction
$8 \geq S > -8$	Bin 4	No edge
$-8 \geq S > -20$	Bin 5	Weak edge along horizontal direction
$-20 \geq S > -40$	Bin 6	Edge along horizontal direction
$S \geq -40$	Bin 7	Sharp edge along horizontal direction

Here $\boldsymbol{\Phi} = [\phi_1 \, \phi_2 \, \phi_k \ldots \phi_Z]^T$ and $\boldsymbol{y} = [A(1) \, A(2) \, A(3) \, \ldots \, A(Z)]^T$. Hence for each bin, we find a 6th order prediction coefficient ($\boldsymbol{a}$) and thus predict all the pixels of that bin using the same prediction coefficients.

3. Repeat step 2 to find prediction coefficients for each bin.

Thus for 7 bins, seven set of prediction coefficients of 6th order are estimated. In this way, all pixels of type **A** are predicted efficiently.

Prediction of Even-Odd Positioned Pixels (B Type). In this pass, we predict pixels denoted by **B**. The proposed algorithm again uses original pixels for prediction and the predictor structure for prediction is shown in Fig. 2(b). Proposed predictor structure consist of 5 pixels: two odd-odd positioned pixels and three causal pixels. Hence, decoder can obtain the same prediction and thus no ambiguity occurs.

Here again relative variation S is estimated and is given in (7) with $D_H = |C(n-4) - D(n-3)| + |C(n-2) - D(n-3)| + |A(n-1) - ((D(n-3) + (D(n+3))/2|$ and $D_V = |C(n-4) - A(n-1)| + |D(n-3) - D(n+3)| + |C(n-2) - D(n+3)|$.

As previously, we classify the pixels into 7 bins by classifying S with the bin boundaries given in Table 1. For each bin, we estimate LS based prediction coefficient of 5th order and predict the pixels denoted by **B** as given below.

$$\hat{B}(n) = \boldsymbol{a}^T \boldsymbol{\phi}_i = \sum_{k=1}^{5} a_k \phi_i(k) \qquad (11)$$

Here $\boldsymbol{a} = [a_1, a_2, a_3, a_4, a_5]^T$ is a vector of prediction coefficients and $\boldsymbol{\phi}_i = [C(n-4), D(n-3), C(n-2), A(n-1), D(n+3)]$ is neighboring pixels of $B(n)$. Hence in order to predict all the pixels denoted by **B**, we need seven set of prediction coefficients of order 5.

Prediction of Odd-Even Positioned Pixels (C Type). Similar to previous pass, the predictor structure consist of 5 original pixels and it is shown in Fig. 3(a). In this case, relative variation S given in (7) is estimated using

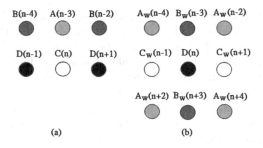

Fig. 3. (a) Predictor structure of C(n): 2 D-type pixels (black dots) and 3 causal pixels, (b) Predictor structure of D(n) consist of watermarked pixels (obtained from First phase)

$D_H = |B(n-4)-A(n-3)|+|B(n-2)-A(n-3)|+|D(n-1)-D(n+1)|$ and $D_V = |B(n-4) - D(n-1)| + |B(n-2) - D(n+1)| + |A(-3) - (D(n-1) + D(n+1))/2|$.

Prediction of **C** typed pixels is done exactly the same way as it is done for previous cases. Predictor structure in this pass is different and is shown in Fig. 3(a). Again, in order to predict all the pixels denoted by **C**, we need seven set of LS based prediction coefficients of order 5.

Unlike [11], the proposed algorithm interpolates the LR image i.e., predicts pixels of even-even, even-odd and odd-even positioned pixels by using original pixels only. Thus, no error propagation occurs from one pass to other pass during prediction. After predicting $(3/4)^{th}$ of the total pixels of **I** and finding corresponding $e(n)$, we can apply additive PEE method to get corresponding watermarked pixels.

4.2 Second Phase: Watermarking Process of Remaining $(1/4)^{th}$ Pixels - Type D Pixels

In this phase, pixels denoted by **D** are predicted and then undergoes watermarking process. Prediction is done by using only watermarked samples as decoder does not have the information of neighboring original pixels. The proposed predictor structure is shown in Fig. 3(b).

Similar to the previous case, we classify pixels in 7 bins and find predictors of order 4 for each of the classes. However, relative variation S, given in (7), is estimated using $D_H = |A_w(n - 4) - B_w(n - 3)| + |C_w(n - 1) - C_w(n + 1)| + |A_w(n + 2) - A_w(n + 4)|$ and $D_V = |A_w(n - 4) - A_w(n + 2)| + |B_w(n - 3) - B_w(n+3)| + |A_w(n-2) - A_w(n+4)|$. Prediction of pixels denoted by D is given by $\hat{D}(n)$ as below

$$\hat{D}(n) = a^T \phi_i = \sum_{k=1}^{4} a_k \phi_i(k) \qquad (12)$$

Here $a = [a_1, a_2, a_3, a_4]^T$ denotes the prediction coefficients and $\phi_i = [B_w(n - 3), B_w(n + 3), C_w(n - 1), C_w(n + 1)]$ denotes the neighboring pixels of $D(n)$.

Hence in order to predict all the pixels denoted by **D**, we need seven LS based optimized predictor of order 4. After prediction remaining $(1/4)^{th}$ pixels of type D, apply additive PEE method to get corresponding watermarked pixels.

Thus in first phase, for interpolation of LR image to high resolution image (**P**), we need 21 set of prediction coefficients i.e. 7 set of 6th order predictor (for **A** type), 7 set of 5th order predictor (for **B** type), 7 set of 5th order predictor (for **C** type). For second phase, we need 7 set of 4th order predictor (for **D** type). These coefficients estimated at encoder is sent to decoder as an overhead with final watermarked image ($\mathbf{I_w}$). Thus decoder does not need to estimate any coefficients.

4.3   Decoder of Proposed Algorithm

At the decoder side, we have watermarked image ($\mathbf{I_w}$) and 28 set of prediction parameters (sent from encoder). The decoder of proposed algorithm works as follows:

1. For each pixel of type **D**, estimate the slope S, and based on the value of S given in (7), corresponding 4th order coefficients are used to predict the pixels using (12). Then apply inverse PEE using (4) to get the secret bits and original pixels. Thus odd-odd position of the image can be recovered easily.
2. Then follow raster scan order for rest of the pixels. After reconstruction of type **D** pixels, our proposed algorithm formulate the predictor structure for each pixel with the help of its causal neighboring original pixels and neighboring type **D** pixels.
3. From this predictor structure (consists of original causal neighboring pixels and original type **D** pixels), slope S is estimated and based upon the value of S corresponding prediction coefficient are used for prediction of pixels. Then apply inverse PEE method using (4) to get secret bits and original pixels.
4. Repeat steps 2 and 3 until all the pixels in the entire image are recovered. Recovering is done in raster scan order.

5   Simulation Result

We implemented our proposed reversible data hiding algorithm and compared its performance with existing methods. For this purpose, we use standard test images of 8 bit resolution and of 512×512 dimension.

We compared the predictor order of proposed algorithm with IPEE [11] and is shown in Table 2. From Table 2, we can say that proposed algorithm uses higher order predictor and is adaptive as well. Moreover, our prediction algorithm uses only original pixels for interpolation (first phase) and thus prediction accuracy increases as compared to IPEE. We compared the prediction performance of proposed algorithm with IPEE after interpolating LR image to high resolution image (i.e. after predicting pixels of type **A**, type **B** and type **C** respectively). Visual quality obtained by both the algorithms are shown in Fig. 4. We can find

Table 2. Predictor Order (PO) comparison

Methods	Type A	Type B	Type C	Type D
IPEE [11]	4	4	4	4
Proposed	6	5	5	4

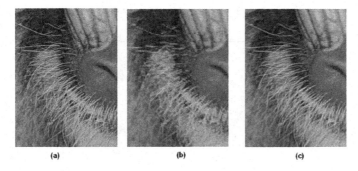

(a)   (b)   (c)

Fig. 4. Portions of (a) Original Baboon Image, (b) Interpolated image by IPEE [11] (c) Interpolated image by Proposed Method

that IPEE produces blurred image as compared to original image where edges are more preserved by proposed algorithm. It is because proposed algorithm uses only original pixels for prediction. Moreover proposed algorithm obtains a higher order predictor as against the fixed 4th order in IPEE (shown in Table 2).

Table 3. Performance comparison of Proposed Algorithm with various other methods - Embedding Capacity (number of bits)

Schemes	Lena	Baboon	Sailboat	Plane
Ni [3]	5,460	5,421	7,301	16,171
Lin [4]	59,900	19,130	37,644	80,006
Hu [8]	60,241	21,411	28,259	77,254
SJ [10]	66,512	22,685	42,241	91,890
IPEE [11]	71,674	22,696	38,734	84,050
Proposed	**74,412**	**25,341**	**45,651**	**95,890**

We also compared our results with other algorithms to check the effectiveness of proposed algorithm. The overhead required for sending the location map as well as prediction parameters to decoder has been taken account. In Table 3, we consider the case when capacity parameter is one ($Q = 1$). It can be noticed that in all the four images, we achieve higher embedding capacity as compared to existing algorithms. We performed an experiment and is shown in Table 4.

Table 4. E_C refers to embedding capacity in bits and PSNR in dB for plane image

Methods		Q = 1	Q = 2	Q = 3	Q = 4
IPEE [11]	E_C	84,050	117,500	164,100	198,450
	PSNR	48.94	43.60	40.5	38.01
Proposed	E_C	95,890	145,667	185,840	211,510
	PSNR	49.03	43.68	40.60	38.36

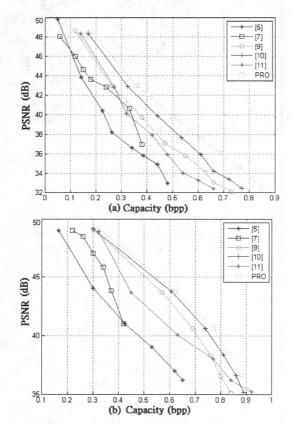

Fig. 5. For higher capacity parameters ($Q >= 1$): (a) Sailboat (b) Plane. Here PRO refers to proposed algorithm and bpp refers to bits per pixel.

We can see that for fixed Q, proposed algorithm has better embedding capacity with less distortion as compared to IPEE.

To show effectiveness of our method for capacity parameters $Q >= 1$, we compared our results with existing algorithms and is shown in Fig. 5. It can be observed that proposed algorithm outperforms the existing algorithms for high capacity parameters ($Q >= 1$) as well.

The encoder of proposed algorithm requires more computational power as compared to IPEE [11]. It is because, proposed algorithm needs to estimate 28 set of LS based prediction coefficients which requires addition, multiplication and matrix inversion. These estimated LS based coefficients are quantized and then tagged with the watermarked image and is sent to decoder. Thus, decoder of proposed algorithm remains more simple as it needs not to estimate any prediction coefficients.

6 Conclusion

In this paper, we proposed a novel reversible data hiding algorithm based on additive PEE. We observed that interpolation method based on fixed order predictor fails to exploit the neighborhood pixels effectively for interpolation. In view of this, we developed an efficient interpolation method based on adaptive predictor structure that exploits correlation between the neighborhood pixels and the unknown pixels (to be interpolated) effectively. Moreover we proposed to use only original pixels for interpolation. Experimental results proves that the proposed algorithm results in a better performance than the existing methods.

References

1. Li, R., Au, O.C., Yuk, C.K.M., Yip, S., Chan, T.: Enhanced image trans-coding using reversible data hiding. In: IEEE International Symposium on Circuits and Systems ISCAS 2007, pp. 1273–1276
2. Feng, J.B., Lin, I.C., Tsai, C.S., Chu, Y.P.: Reversible watermarking: current status and key issues. Int. J. Netw. Secur. **2**(3), 161–171 (2006)
3. Ni, Z., Shi, Y.Q., Ansari, N., Wei, S.: Reversible data hiding. IEEE Trans. Circuits Syst. Video Technol. **16**(3), 354–362 (2006)
4. Lin, C.C., Hsueh, N.L.: Lossless data hiding scheme based on three-pixel block differences. Pattern Recogn. **41**(4), 1415–1425 (2008)
5. Kim, K.-S., Leea, M.-J., Leeb, H.-Y., Leea, H.-K.: Reversible data hiding exploiting spatial correlation between sub-sampled images. Pattern Recogn. (2009). doi:10.1016/j.patcog.2009.04.004
6. Tian, J.: Reversible data embedding using a difference expansion. IEEE Trans. Circuits Syst. Video Technol. **13**(8), 890–896 (2003)
7. Kim, H.-J., Sachnev, V., Shi, Y.Q., Nam, J., Choo, H.-G.: A novel difference expansion transform for reversible data embedding. IEEE Trans. Inf. Forensic Secur. **3**(3), 456–465 (2008)
8. Hu, Y., Lee, H.-K., Li, J.: DE-based reversible data hiding with improved overflow location map. IEEE Trans. Circuits Syst. Video Technol. **19**(2), 250–260 (2009)
9. Chen, M., Chen, Z., Zeng, X., Xiong, Z.: Reversible image watermarking based on full context prediction. In: International Conference on Image Processing (ICIP), pp. 4253–4256. IEEE (2009)
10. Jaiswal, S.P., Au, O.C., Jakhetiya, V., Guo, Y., Tiwari, A., Yue, K.: Efficient adaptive prediction based reversible image watermarking. In: IEEE International Conference on Image Processing (ICIP) (2013)

11. Luo, L., Chen, Z., Chenm, M., Zeng, X., Zhang, X.: Reversible image watermarking using interpolation technique. IEEE Trans. Inf. Forensic Secur. 5(1), 187–193 (2010)
12. Tsai, J., Hang, H.M.: Modeling of pattern based block motion estimation and its application. IEEE Trans. Circuits Syst. Video Technol. 19(1), 108–113 (2009)
13. Tiwari, A.K., Kumar, R.V.: Least squares based optimal switched predictor for lossless compression of images. In: 2008 IEEE International Conference on Multimedia and Expo, 26 April 2008
14. Jaiswal, S.P., Jakhetiya, V., Tiwari, A.K.: A lossless image prediction algorithm using slope estimation and least square optimization. In: 2012 IEEE International Instrumentation and Measurement Technology Conference (I2MTC), pp. 1567–1570, May 2012
15. Jakhetiya, V., Jaiswal, S.P., Tiwari, A.K.: Interpolation based symmetrical predictor structure for lossless image coding. In: 2012 IEEE International Symposium on Circuits and Systems (ISCAS), pp. 2913–2916, May 2012
16. Jaiswal, S.P., Mittal, G., Jakhetiya, V., Tiwari, A.K.: An efficient two pass lossless invisible watermarking algorithm for natural images. In: 2012 19th International Conference on Systems, Signals and Image Processing (IWSSIP), April 2012

Reversible Data Hiding by Median-Preserving Histogram Modification for Image Contrast Enhancement

Hao-Tian Wu[1]([✉]), Yuan Liu[1], and Yun-Qing Shi[2]

[1] School of Digital Media, Jiangnan University,
Wuxi 214122, Jiangsu, People's Republic of China
htwu@jiangnan.edu.cn, lyuan1800@sina.com
[2] Department of Electrical and Computer Engineering,
New Jersey Institute of Technology, Newark, NJ 07103, USA
shi@njit.edu

Abstract. A new image reversible data hiding algorithm is proposed in this paper based on histogram modification. Instead of trying to keep the image PSNR value high after data hiding, the proposed algorithm aims at enhancing the image contrast for better visual effect. To make the hidden data blindly extractable, the median point in the histogram is preserved after modifying two selected bins in a special way. Multiple pairs of histogram bins are further selected to be modified in sequence to achieve the effect of contrast enhancement. To avoid overflow and underflow, pre-process is performed on the pixel values and a location map is generated. By embedding the side information along with the message bits, the original image can be completely recovered without additional information. The proposed algorithm was applied to two sets of test images and the experimental results have shown that the better effect of contrast enhancement can be achieved than the previous works. In addition to reversibility, the evaluation results show that the visual quality of test images has been preserved after data hiding, even better than three specific MATLAB functions.

Keywords: Reversible data hiding · Image contrast enhancement · Visual quality · Histogram modification · Median point

1 Introduction

Reversible data hiding (RDH) has been extensively studied in the community over the past decade (e.g. [1–13]). Also referred as reversible watermarking, lossless data hiding or reversible data embedding, RDH is to embed a piece of information into a host signal to generate the marked one, from which the original signal can be exactly recovered after extracting the embedded data. In general, a RDH algorithm should satisfy the requirement of *reversibility* without using any parameter dependent on the host signal in both data extraction and recovering the original signal. There also exists the requirement of embedding capacity,

© Springer International Publishing Switzerland 2015
Y.-Q. Shi et al. (Eds.): IWDW 2014, LNCS 9023, pp. 289–301, 2015.
DOI: 10.1007/978-3-319-19321-2_22

and it is preferred that data hiding does not degrade the perceptual quality. The technique of RDH is especially useful in some sensitive applications where no permanent change is allowed on the host signal. In the literature, most of the proposed reversible algorithms are designed for digital images (e.g. [1–10]), while the others are for audio (e.g. [11]) and video signal (e.g. [12]), as well as 3D models (e.g. [13]).

To evaluate the performance of an image RDH algorithm, the hiding rate and the marked image quality are two important metrics. It has been observed that a trade-off exists between them because increasing the hiding rate often causes more distortion in image content. To measure the distortion, the peak signal-to-noise ratio (PSNR) of the marked image is calculated by comparing with the original version. Generally speaking, direct modification of image histogram [3] provides less embedding capacity because the distribution of pixel values is not concentrated for most images. In contrast, the more recent image RDH algorithms (e.g. [6–8]) manipulate the prediction errors generated from the host image by exploiting the correlations among the neighboring pixels. In this category of algorithms, the pixel values are modified to change the more centrally distributed prediction errors so that less changes can be made to reversibly embed a certain amount of message bits. Although the PSNR of a marked image generated with a prediction error based algorithm is relatively high, the visual quality can hardly be improved because more or less distortion has been introduced into the image content. In some applications (e.g. for those images acquired with poor illumination), keeping the PSNR as high as possible is not so important as improving the visual quality. For the better visual effect, contrast enhancement is often performed to improve visibility of image details but the PSNR value of the enhanced image is low. For instance, contrast enhancement of medical or satellite images is important to show the details for visual inspection. To enhance the image contrast instead of trying to keep the PSNR of the marked image high, a RDH algorithm is firstly proposed in [10] so that a considerable amount of data can be reversibly embedded into the contrast-enhanced image, from which the original image can be exactly recovered. In this paper, a new RDH algorithm is further proposed to achieve the effect of contrast enhancement in addition to fulfilling the requirements of reversibility and blind extraction.

In principle, image contrast enhancement can be achieved by the process of histogram equalization [14]. Like the algorithm in [10], the algorithm proposed in this paper is performed in the spatial domain by modifying the histogram of pixel values. To make the hidden data blindly extractable, data embedding is performed by selecting two histogram bins according to the defined median point and splitting each of them into two adjacent bins, respectively. A strategy is further proposed to select multiple pairs of histogram bins to be split so as to achieve the satisfactory effect of histogram equalization. To avoid the overflows and underflows due to histogram modification, the bounding pixel values are pre-processed and a location map is generated to memorize their locations. The location map is compressed and embedded with other side information into the host image so that its original version can be blindly and exactly recovered without additional information. The proposed algorithm was applied to two sets of images to show its efficiency. We compare the performance with the algorithm in [10] and three specific MATLAB functions used for image contrast enhancement. The experimental results have shown that the better effect of contrast enhancement than [10] has been achieved. In addition to reversibility, the evaluation results show that the visual quality of test images has been preserved after data hiding, even better than the three specific MATLAB functions.

The rest of this paper is organized as follows. Section 2 presents the details of the proposed RDH algorithm featured by blind data extraction and image contrast enhancement. The experimental results are given and analyzed in Sect. 3. Finally, a conclusion is drawn in Sect. 4.

2   RDH Algorithm for Image Contrast Enhancement

2.1   Data Embedding by Median-Preserving Histogram Modification

The algorithm to be presented is primarily for gray-level images and can be extended to color images if needed. For a 8-bit gray-scale image I, we can easily calculate the histogram by counting the number of pixels with the same value j where $j \in \{0, 1, \cdots, 254, 255\}$. We use h_I to denote the image histogram so that $h_I(j)$ represents the number of pixels with a value j. Suppose that there are N different pixel values in I. N is much greater than 1 and no larger than 256 for natural images. The median point M_L in the histogram is defined as the $\lfloor \frac{N+1}{2} \rfloor$-th bin value after sorting the N bins in ascending order from the left to the right, while the value of the $(\lfloor \frac{N+1}{2} \rfloor + 1)$-th bin after sorting is defined as the other median point and denoted by M_R. The two histogram bins are accordingly selected for data embedding.

For a pixel P_i in I with value M_i, the embedding operation is given by

$$M_i' = \begin{cases} M_i - 1, & \text{if } M_i < M_L \\ M_L - b_k, & \text{if } M_i = M_L \\ M_R + b_k, & \text{if } M_i = M_R \\ M_i + 1, & \text{if } M_i > M_R \end{cases}, \tag{1}$$

where M_i' is the modified pixel value, and b_k is the k-th binary value (0 or 1) to be hidden. It is required that there are equal (or almost so) numbers of 0's and 1s in the binary values to be embedded. After applying Eq. (1) to all pixels counted in h_I, there will be $N + 2$ different pixel values in the modified histogram if there is no underflow or overflow. Figure 1 illustrates an example of the aforementioned median-preserving histogram modification. In the modified histogram, the median point M_L is the value of the $\lfloor \frac{(N+2)+1}{2} \rfloor$-th bin after sorting the $N + 2$ pixel values (i.e. gray scales) in ascending order. So the median point in the histogram is preserved by Eq. (1) because the $\lfloor \frac{(N+2)+1}{2} \rfloor$-th bin value in the modified histogram is just the $\lfloor \frac{N+1}{2} \rfloor$-th one in the original histogram.

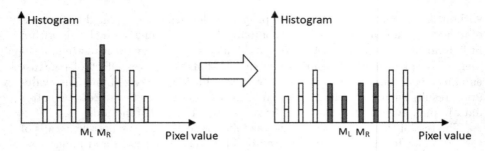

Fig. 1. An example of median-preserving histogram modification.

For a pixel value M_i' in the modified histogram, the extraction operation is performed by

$$b_k' = \begin{cases} 1, \text{ if } M_i' = M_L - 1 \\ 0, \text{ if } M_i' = M_L \\ 0, \text{ if } M_i' = M_R \\ 1, \text{ if } M_i' = M_R + 1 \end{cases}, \qquad (2)$$

where b_k' is the k-th extracted binary value (0 or 1). According to Eq. (1), the recovery operation is performed by

$$M_i = \begin{cases} M_i' + 1, \text{ if } M_i' < M_L - 1 \\ M_L, \quad \text{ if } M_i' = M_L - 1 \text{ or } M_i' = M_L \\ M_R, \quad \text{ if } M_i' = M_R \text{ or } M_i' = M_R + 1 \\ M_i' - 1, \text{ if } M_i' > M_R + 1 \end{cases}. \qquad (3)$$

Since the median points M_L and M_R can be directly obtained from the modified histogram, all the embedded binary values can be correctly extracted while the original pixel values can be recovered.

2.2   Pre-process to Prevent the Overflow and Underflow

In the aforementioned algorithm, the values of M_L and M_R are preserved if there is no overflow or underflow of pixel values. If there is any bounding pixel value (0 or 255) in h_I, overflow or underflow will be caused. To avoid it, the histogram needs to be pre-processed. Specifically, the pixel values of 0 and 255 are modified to 1 and 254, respectively. Therefore, no overflow or underflow will happen because the possible change of each pixel value caused by Eq. (1) is ± 1. To memorize the pre-processed pixels, a location map with the same size as the original image is generated by assigning 1 to the location of a modified pixel, and 0 to that of an unchanged one. The location map can be pre-computed and compressed with the lossless JBIG2 [15]. By embedding the bitstream of the compressed location map together with the message bits to be hidden, it can be obtained from the data extracted from the modified histogram so that the pixels modified in the pre-process can be identified. By restoring the original values of those pixels accordingly, the original image can be completely recovered.

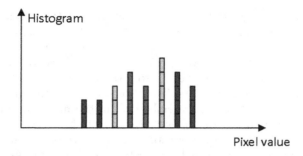

Fig. 2. Multiple pairs of histogram bins can be employed for data embedding.

2.3   Multi-pair Embedding and Contrast Enhancement

In Sect. 2.1, only one pair of histogram bins (with the values of M_L and M_R) are utilized for data embedding. To increase the embedding rate and enhance the contrast, multiple pairs of histogram bins can be selected to be modified while the data embedded with them can still be blindly extracted.

Multi-Pair Embedding. A conventional way is to choose multiple pairs of histogram bins around the median points M_L and M_R. Since the histogram bins corresponding to M_L and M_R are the $\lfloor \frac{N+1}{2} \rfloor$-th and $(\lfloor \frac{N+1}{2} \rfloor + 1)$-th ones, the $(\lfloor \frac{N+1}{2} \rfloor - 1)$-th and $(\lfloor \frac{N+1}{2} \rfloor + 2)$-th bins, as well as the $(\lfloor \frac{N+1}{2} \rfloor - 2)$-th and $(\lfloor \frac{N+1}{2} \rfloor + 3)$-th, and so on, can be adopted to make up the histogram bin pair for data embedding. Given that the number of the chosen histogram bin pairs is L, the range of pixel values from 0 to $L-1$ are added by L while the pixels from $256 - L$ to 255 are subtracted by L in the pre-process (noting L is a positive integer). The location map can be generated and compressed before modifying the histogram for data embedding, as discussed in Sect. 2.2.

An example of the proposed multi-pair embedding strategy is shown in Fig. 2, where 4 histogram bin pairs are used for data embedding in the descending order of their distances to the median points. Firstly, the most outer pair are modified, then the second outer pair, and so on, until the most inner pair which are corresponding to the median points. Suppose the values of a histogram bin pair selected to be modified are denoted by M_S and M_B with $M_S < M_B$. For a pixel value M_i which is no more than M_S or no less than M_B, the embedding operation can be performed by replacing M_L and M_R in Eq. (1) with M_S and M_B, while the pixel values between M_S and M_B are unchanged. Data extraction and histogram restoration are performed in the converse order. Firstly, the most inner four bins are used to restore the most inner pair by Eq. (3) while the data embedded within them can be extracted by Eq. (2). Then the four bins closest to the restored histogram bin pair are used to restore the second inner pair, and so on until the most outer pair adopted for data embedding are restored. Meanwhile, the data embedded within these pairs of histogram bins can be extracted by turn after each time of histogram restoration. By knowing the values of the histogram bin pair to be restored (denoted by M_S and M_B), data extraction and histogram restoration can be performed by replacing M_L, M_R, M_L-1 and M_R+1 in Eq. (2) and Eq. (3) with M_S, M_B, $M_S - 1$ and $M_B + 1$, respectively.

It should be noted that the bitstream of the compressed location map is embedded at first, which can be divided into several parts if needed to be embedded with several histogram bin pairs. The value of L, and the bitstream length of the compressed location map, are embedded in the most inner pair (i.e. the histogram bins corresponding to M_L and M_R) so as to be firstly extracted. After data extraction and histogram restoration from inner to outer, the bitstream of the compressed location map can be collected and decompressed so that the pixel values modified in the pre-process can be identified.

Image Contrast Enhancement. In the proposed algorithm, the numbers of 0 s and 1 s in the binary values to be hidden are required to be equal (or almost so). Otherwise, some extra bits can be appended and the whole string is scrambled to make the uniform distribution of 0 s and 1 s. By applying Eq. (1) to every pixel counted in the histogram, each of the two histogram bins corresponding to M_L and M_R is modified into two adjacent bins with the similar or same heights. In the aforementioned multi-pair embedding strategy, multiple pairs of histogram bins are used for data embedding so that each of the selected histogram bins is modified into two adjacent bins with the similar heights. Since the selected histogram bins are around the median points and each of them is modified once, the satisfactory effect of *contrast enhancement* can be achieved by increasing the number of the selected histogram pairs. In other words, both reversible data hiding and image contrast enhancement can be performed by choosing the appropriate number of histogram bin pairs to be modified. In Sect. 3, we will further evaluate the performance of the multi-pair embedding strategy for image contrast enhancement.

2.4   Procedure of the Proposed Algorithm

The procedure of the proposed algorithm is illustrated in Fig. 3. Given that totally L histogram bin pairs are used for data embedding, the **embedding** procedure includes the following steps:

(1) Pre-process: For the original image I, the pixels in the range of $[0, L-1]$ are added by L while those in the range of $[256 - L, 255]$ are subtracted by L. A location map is generated to record the locations of the modified pixels and compressed by the JBIG2 standard [15].
(2) The histogram of the pixel values in the pre-processed image is calculated.
(3) The median points M_L and M_R in the obtained histogram are calculated.
(4) The median-preserving histogram modification is performed by applying Eq. (1) to every pixel counted in the histogram if $L = 1$ or by applying the multi-pair strategy in Sect. 2.3 if $L > 1$.

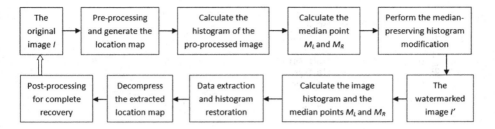

Fig. 3. Procedure of the proposed RDH algorithm.

- In the case of $L = 1$, the value of L, the bitstream of the compressed location map and its length, together with the message bits, are embedded by modifying the histogram bins with the values of M_L and M_R, respectively.
- In the case of multi-pair embedding, the bitstream of the compressed location map is embedded at first, followed by the message bits, while the value of L and the length of the compressed location map are embedded at last by modifying the histogram bins with the values of M_L and M_R, respectively.

The **extraction** and **recovery** process include the following steps:

(1) The histogram of the watermarked image I' is calculated.
(2) The median points M_L and M_R in the obtained histogram are calculated.
(3) With the obtained values of M_L, M_R, $M_L - 1$ and $M_R + 1$, the data embedded within the corresponding bins are extracted with Eq. (2) so that the value of L and the length of the compressed location map are known, as well as the bitstream of the compressed location map if $L = 1$. Meanwhile, the histogram bin pair corresponding to M_L and M_R are restored with Eq. (3). The data extraction and histogram restoration process is repeated from inner to outer until the last pair of histogram bins modified for data embedding.
(4) The compressed location map is obtained from the extracted data and decompressed to the image size. For those positions with value 1 in the location map, a pixel value is subtracted by L if it is less than 128, or increased by L otherwise (To comply with this rule, the maximum value of L is 64 to avoid ambiguity). Consequently, the original image I is completely recovered.

3   Experimental Results

In the experiments, 8 test images in USC-SIPI Image Database [16] and 24 test images in Kodak Lossless True Color Image Suite [17] were employed and converted into grey-level images. The USC-SIPI images are with the size of 512×512, while the Kodak images are with the size of 768×512. The message bits to be hidden can be any string of binary values in which the numbers of 0 s and 1 s are almost equal, otherwise some extra bits can be appended to make so. The only parameter in the proposed algorithm is L, i.e. the number of histogram

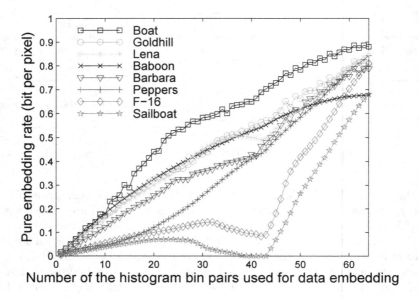

Fig. 4. The hiding rates change with the number of histogram bins used for data embedding in the proposed algorithm.

bin pairs selected for data embedding, and the multi-pair embedding strategy was tested on both image sets. For any test image in the USC-SIPI set, the watermarked image can be generated for any $L \in [1, 64]$. For the Kodak set, the watermarked image can be generated in most cases but when the value of L is small, the embedding capacity is less than the size of side information for several test images. Nevertheless, the experimental results show that both blind data extraction and complete recovery of the original images have been achieved for every of the marked images.

As shown in Fig. 4, the hiding rates change with the number of the histogram bin pairs used for data embedding in the proposed algorithm. For $L \in [1, 64]$, the highest hiding rate was 0.810 bit per pixel (bpp) for F-16, 0.880 bpp for Boat, 0.677 bpp for Baboon, and averagely 0.794 bpp for the 8 USC-SIPI images. The embedding capacity varied from image to image, and the average of the highest hiding rates for the 24 Kodak images is 0.800 bpp. For the test images "F-16" and "Sailboat", the curve drops in the middle because the amount of side information (the majority is the bitstream of the compressed location map) is increased by using more histogram bin pairs for data embedding, faster than the gain in embedding capacity. It should be noted that all hiding rates given in this paper were calculated by subtracting the bit number of the side information for recovery (including the bitstream of the compressed location map) from the total amount of the embedded bits.

For visual inspection of the contrast enhancement effect, the original and marked versions of the test images "Lena" and "Goldhill" are shown in Fig. 5 and

(a) Original image of "Lena"   (b) Proposed: L=15, PSNR=25.39 dB

(c) Proposed: L=20, PSNR=23.14 dB   (d) *imadjust*: PSNR=21.89 dB

(e) *histeq*: PSNR=19.09 dB   (f) *adapthisteq*: PSNR=18.84 dB

Fig. 5. Experimental results with the proposed algorithm and three matlab functions: (a) Original image of "Lena"; (b) Proposed algorithm with L=15: PSNR=25.39 dB; (c) Proposed algorithm with L=20: PSNR=23.14 dB; (d) *imadjust* with the default setting: PSNR=21.89 dB; (e) *histeq* with the default setting: PSNR=19.09 dB; (f) *adapthisteq* with the default setting: PSNR=18.84 dB.

(a) Original image of "Goldhill"   (b) Proposed: L=15, PSNR=25.42 dB

(c) Proposed: L=20, PSNR=23.19 dB   (d) *imadjust*: PSNR=24.79 dB

(e) *histeq*: PSNR=17.55 dB   (f) *adapthisteq*: PSNR=17.89 dB

Fig. 6. Experimental results with the proposed algorithm and three matlab functions: (a) Original image of "Goldhill"; (b) Proposed algorithm with L=15: PSNR=25.42 dB; (c) Proposed algorithm with L=20: PSNR=23.19 dB; (d) *imadjust* with the default setting: PSNR=24.79 dB; (e) *histeq* with the default setting: PSNR=17.55 dB; (f) *adapthisteq* with the default setting: PSNR=17.89 dB.

Table 1. Statistical Evaluation (Mean) of 8 USC-SIPI images

Algorithm	RCE	REE	RMBE	RSS	PSNR (dB)	Payload (bpp)
Prop.10p	0.5317	0.5062	0.9910	0.9625	28.53	0.115
Prop.15p	0.5470	0.5092	0.9874	0.9453	25.25	0.178
Prop.20p	0.5618	0.5123	0.9843	0.9292	23.00	0.243
[10].*10p*	0.5253	0.5155	0.9926	0.9694	30.34	0.270
[10].*15p*	0.5367	0.5210	0.9891	0.9561	27.20	0.370
[10].*20p*	0.5477	0.5255	0.9887	0.9438	25.05	0.458
imadjust	0.5631	0.4958	0.9643	0.9223	22.37	null
histeq	0.5941	0.4182	0.9539	0.8728	18.62	null
adapthisteq	0.5475	0.5383	0.9689	0.8820	18.62	null

Fig. 6, respectively. The marked images were obtained by using 15 and 20 pairs of histogram bins for data embedding in the proposed algorithm, respectively.

We further compare the proposed algorithm with three MATLAB functions used for contrast enhancement, i.e. *imadjust*, *histeq*, and *adapthisteq*. The MATLAB routines were applied on each test image with the default settings, respectively. As shown in Figs. 5 and 6, it can be seen that the comparable effect of contrast enhancement has been achieved with the proposed algorithm. Although a considerable amount of message bits have been embedded, the visual quality of the two test images was preserved by the proposed algorithm.

To further compare the proposed algorithms with the three MATLAB functions by evaluating the enhancement effect and image quality, the relative contrast error (RCE), relative entropy error (REE), relative mean brightness error (RMBE) and relative structural similarity (RSS) used in [18] were calculated between the original and enhanced images. The RCE and REE values greater than 0.5 indicate the enhanced contrast and increased image data, respectively. The less difference in mean brightness from the original image, the closer RMBE is to 1. The greater the structural similarity between two images, the closer RSS is to 1. Five evaluation values (including RCE, REE, RMBE, RSS, and PSNR) were calculated from every of the enhanced images generated with the proposed algorithm, *imadjust*, *histeq* or *adapthisteq* for performance comparison.

Tables 1 and 2 show the statistical results of two image sets, respectively. Each item listed in the two tables is the mean of 8 or 24 test images. In the two tables, the proposed algorithm using 10, 15 and 20 pairs of histogram bins are denoted by *Prop.10p*, *Prop.15p* and *Prop.20p*, while the algorithm in [10] using 10, 15 and 20 pairs of histogram bins are denoted by [10].*10p*, [10].*15p* and [10].*20p* respectively. It can be seen that the contrast of test images were gradually enhanced (indicated by the increased RCE values) by using more histogram bins for data embedding in the proposed algorithm while more differences were introduced in brightness and structural similarity (indicated by the decreased RMBE and RSS values). Compared with [10], the mean RCE values obtained by

Table 2. Statistical Evaluation (Mean) of 24 Kodak images

Algorithm	RCE	REE	RMBE	RSS	PSNR (dB)	Payload (bpp)
Prop.10p	0.5265	0.5086	0.9827	0.9619	28.70	0.130
Prop.15p	0.5376	0.5105	0.9751	0.9466	25.46	0.187
Prop.20p	0.5485	0.5126	0.9679	0.9313	23.28	0.239
[10].*10p*	0.5159	0.5144	0.9947	0.9781	30.38	0.313
[10].*15p*	0.5331	0.5239	0.9889	0.9556	27.19	0.420
[10].*20p*	0.5435	0.5281	0.9852	0.9418	24.89	0.511
imadjust	0.5451	0.4956	0.9529	0.9310	24.09	null
histeq	0.6074	0.4217	0.9027	0.8248	15.49	null
adapthisteq	0.5408	0.5356	0.9377	0.8664	17.67	null

using the same number of histogram bins in the proposed algorithm are higher, indicating that better contrast enhancement effect has been achieved. Compared with the three MATLAB functions, the RCEs obtained with *Prop.20p* are less than those of *histeq*, but higher or close to *imadjust* and *adapthisteq*, indicating that image contrast were enhanced more or close to *imadjust* and *adapthisteq*. Meanwhile, the REE values listed in the tables indicate that image data were increased by *Prop.20p* and *adapthisteq*, but decreased by *imadjust* and *histeq*. As for the RMBE and RSS values, *Prop.20p* outperformed the three MATLAB functions, indicating that less changes were made to the image brightness and structural similarity. Besides the higher PSNR values than those obtained with the three MATLAB functions, the original image can be blindly recovered from the enhanced image with the proposed algorithm. So it is more advantageous to use it for image contrast enhancement than the three MATLAB functions.

4   Conclusion

In this paper, a new reversible data hiding algorithm has been proposed for the purpose of image contrast enhancement. For blind extraction of the hidden data, the median points in the histogram are preserved after modifying the selected histogram bins. A strategy has been proposed to sequentially modify multiple pairs of histogram bins so that the effect of image contrast enhancement can be achieved. The experimental results have shown that better effect of contrast enhancement has been achieved with the proposed algorithm than the previous work in [10] if the same number of histogram bins are used. Compared with three specific MATLAB functions, the image visual quality has been better preserved. With the proposed algorithm, the original image can be blindly and exactly recovered from the enhanced image. Applying it to the medical and satellite images to improve the visibility of region of interest will be our future work.

Acknowledgment. This work was supported by the National Natural Science Foundation of China (No.61100169), the Fundamental Research Funds for the Central Universities of China (No.JUSRP1047) and China Scholarship Council (No. 201208440173). The authors would like to thank Mr. Shu Hong at Columbia University in the City of New York, Fu Foundation School of Engineering and Applied Science, IEOR Department, for conducting part of the experiments.

References

1. Xuan, G., Zhu, J., Chen, J., Shi, Y.Q., Ni, Z., Su, W.: Distortionless data hiding based on integer wavelet transform. IEE Electron. Lett. **38**(25), 1646–1648 (2002)
2. Tian, J.: Reversible data embedding using a difference expansion. IEEE Trans. Circ. Syst. Video Technol. **13**(8), 890–896 (2003)
3. Ni, Z., Shi, Y.Q., Ansari, N., Su, W.: Reversible data hiding. IEEE Trans. Circ. Syst. Video Technol. **16**(3), 354–362 (2006)
4. Thodi, D.M., Rodriguez, J.J.: Expansion embedding techniques for reversible watermarking. IEEE Trans. Image Process. **16**(3), 721–730 (2007)
5. Hu, Y., Lee, H.K., Li, J.: DE-based reversible data hiding with improved overflow location map. IEEE Trans. Circ. Syst. Video Technol. **19**(2), 250–260 (2009)
6. Sachnev, V., Kim, H.J., Nam, J., Suresh, S., Shi, Y.Q.: Reversible watermarking algorithm using sorting and prediction. IEEE Trans. Circ. Syst. Video Technol. **19**(7), 989–999 (2009)
7. Li, X., Yang, B., Zeng, T.: Efficient reversible watermarking based on adaptive prediction-error expansion and pixel selection. IEEE Trans. Image Process. **20**(12), 3524–3533 (2011)
8. Wu, H.T., Huang, J.: Reversible image watermarking on prediction error by efficient histogram modification. Signal Process. **92**(12), 3000–3009 (2012)
9. Zhao, Z., Luo, H., Lu, Z.M., Pan, J.S.: Reversible data hiding based on multilevel histogram modification and sequential recovery. Int. J. Electron. Commun. (AEÜ) **65**, 814–826 (2011)
10. Wu, H.T., Dugelay, J.L., Shi, Y.Q.: Reversible image data hiding with contrast enhancement. IEEE Signal Process. Lett. **22**(1), 81–85 (2015)
11. Veen, M., Bruekers, F., Leest, A., Cavin, S.: High capacity reversible watermarking for audio. In: SPIE, Security, Steganography, and Watermarking of Multimedia Content, pp. 1–11 (2003)
12. Fridrich J., Du, R.: Lossless authentication of MPEG-2 video. In: The International Conference on Image Processing, pp. 893–896. IEEE Press (2002)
13. Wu, H.T., Dugelay, J.L.: Reversible watermarking of 3D mesh models by prediction-error expansion. In: The International Workshop on Multimedia Signal Processing, pp. 797–802. IEEE Press (2008)
14. Stark, J.A.: Adaptive image contrast enhancement using generalizations of histogram equalization. IEEE Trans. Image Process. **9**(5), 889–896 (2000)
15. Howard, P.G., Kossentini, F., Martins, B., Forchhammer, S., Rucklidge, W.J.: The emerging JBIG2 standard. IEEE Trans. Circ. Syst. Video Technol. **8**(7), 838–848 (1998)
16. The USC-SIPI Image Database. http://sipi.usc.edu/database/
17. Kodak Lossless True Color Image Suite. http://www.r0k.us/graphics/kodak/
18. Gao, M.Z., Wu, Z.G., Wang, L.: Comprehensive evaluation for he based contrast enhancement techniques. Adv. Intell. Syst. Appl. **2**, 331–338 (2013)

Visual Cryptography

Two-in-One Image Secret Sharing Scheme Based on Boolean Operations

Peng Li[1(✉)], Ching-Nung Yang[2], and Qian Kong[1]

[1] Department of Mathematics and Physics,
North China Electric Power University, Baoding, Hebei, China
lphit@163.com, qiankongkong@126.com
[2] Department of CSIE, National Dong Hwa University, Hualien, Taiwan
cnyang@mail.ndhu.edu.tw

Abstract. Two-in-one image secret sharing (TiOISS) scheme shares a secret image into n multiple shadows. In the revealing process, stacking any k ($k \leq n$) shadows can decode a vague secret image in the first stage. It also can reveal the original secret image by computation in the second stage. Many TiOISS schemes have proposed based on visual cryptography scheme (VCS) and polynomial-based image secret sharing (PISS). Since PISS reveals the secret image by Lagrange's interpolation, it needs complicated computation. In this paper, we combine perfect black VCS with image secret sharing based on Boolean operations, and propose a new TiOISS scheme. Compared with existing TiOISS schemes, our scheme only needs few XOR operations to reveal the secret image in the second-stage reconstruction phase.

Keywords: Image secret sharing · Visual cryptography · Boolean operation · Gray mixing model

1 Introduction

The secure protection of secret image has attracted many researches in the multimedia community. Image secret sharing (ISS) is technique to divide the secret image into multiple shadows, if and only if qualified subset of shadows can reveal the secret image. A special case is (k, n)-ISS, by which a secret image is shared into n shadows, and only k or more shadows together can reveal the secret image.

One category of ISS is polynomial-based ISS (PISS) scheme. In 1979, Shamir first introduced (k, n) threshold secret sharing scheme [1]. The secret is embedded into constant coefficient of a randomly generated $(k{-}1)$-degree polynomial. Based on Shamir's scheme, Thien and Lin reduced the shadow size by using all coefficients of the $(k{-}1)$-degree polynomial to embed secret image pixels [2]. Hence the shadow size is $1/k$ times of the secret. In the revealing process, the secret image can be reveal with any k shadows by Lagrange's interpolation. Many PISS schemes were proposed for different application [3–5].

Another category of ISS is visual cryptography scheme (VCS). Naor and Shamir first introduced the concept of VCS [7]. In a (k, n)-VCS, a binary secret image is shared into n shadows. Each shadow is printed on a transparency. In the revealing process, the

© Springer International Publishing Switzerland 2015
Y.-Q. Shi et al. (Eds.): IWDW 2014, LNCS 9023, pp. 305–318, 2015.
DOI: 10.1007/978-3-319-19321-2_23

secret image is decoded by stacking any k shadows with human eyes. Compared with PISS, VCS has the advantage of low computation in the revealing process. There are also many VCSs with special feathers, such as VCS with meaningful shadows [7, 8], sharing gray and color images [9–11].

Two-in-one ISS (TiOISS) scheme is a special kind of ISS scheme with two decoding options. One is revealing the secret image by stacking shadows, and another is by computation. TiOISS scheme can be also explained as an ISS scheme sharing two secret images: one is binary secret image revealed by stacking shadows, and another is a grayscale image revealed by computation. Lin and Lin introduced a TiOISS scheme by combining VCS and TiOISS scheme [12]. Yang and Ciou improved Lin and Lin's scheme with smaller shadow size [13]. Li et al.'s further improved Yang and Ciou's scheme to get better visual quality of the revealed image by stacking shadows [14]. Recently, Li et al. introduced the concept of general gray visual cryptography scheme (GVCS), which can be also considered as TiOISS scheme [15]. All above TiOISS schemes [12–15] are based on PISS, which means the grayscale image is revealed by complicated computation.

ISS scheme based on Boolean operation can also share grayscale secret image, and it can reveal the secret image without distortion. Moreover, it only needs simple bits operations rather than complicated interpolating computation. Some researchers also proposed ISS scheme based on Boolean operations [16, 17]. In this paper, we propose a TiOISS scheme based on Boolean operations. The grayscale image can be revealed by fewer computations than traditional PISS based TiOISS schemes. The following sections are organized as follows. Section 2 reviews the related VCS and ISS based on Boolean operation. The proposed scheme is introduced in Sect. 3. Experimental results and comparison are given in Sect. 4. Finally, conclusions are drawn in Sect. 5.

2   Related Works

2.1   VCS

The first concept of (k, n)-VCS was introduced by Naor and Shamir [6]. Generally, a VCS can be designed by a pair of collections of $n \times m$ Boolean matrices (C_0, C_1) with entries '1' and '0' denoting black and white sub-pixel, respectively. The matrices in the collections (C_0, C_1) are called share matrices. Usually, the collection of share matrices C_0 (resp. C_1) can be constructed from a basis matrix B_0 (resp. B_1) by permuting the columns of B_0 (resp. B_1), where B_0 and B_1 are $n \times m$ Boolean matrices. If the secret pixel is white (resp. black), randomly choose a share matrix in C_0 (resp. C_1) and distribute each row of the share matrix to corresponding shadows as a block of sub-pixels. Therefore, one secret pixel is represented by an m-pixel block. Let $OR(D|r)$ denote the 'OR'-ed vector of any r rows of D, and $H(v)$ be the Hamming weight of vector v. Let l and h be nonnegative integers satisfying $0 \leq l < h \leq m$. For a (k, n)-VCS, the basis matrices B_0 and B_1 should satisfy the following conditions:

(1-i) (Contrast condition) $H(OR(B_0|k)) \leq l$, and $H(OR(B_1|k)) \geq h$;
(1-ii) (Security condition) For any $i_1 < i_2 < \ldots < it$ in $\{1, 2, \ldots, n\}$ with $t < k$, the two
       collections of $t \times m$ matrices F_j for $j \in \{0, 1\}$, obtained by restricting each

$n \times m$ matrix in C_j to rows $i_1, i_2, \ldots, it$, are indistinguishable in the sense that they contain the same matrices with the same frequencies.

The contrast condition ensures any k shadows will be able to distinguish the black and white pixels. Usually, the visual quality of the revealed image is evaluated by contrast, which is defined by $(h-l)/m$. The security condition ensures any $k-1$ or fewer shadows cannot get any content of the secret image.

Specifically, VCS is also called perfect black VCS if $h = m$, which means the 'OR'-ed vector of any k rows of B_1 consists of all '1'. Therefore, in perfect black VCS, a black secret pixel is revealed as a block of m black pixels. In practice, the OR-ed operation can be simulated by stacking operation on printed binary transparences. Each shadow should be printed on a transparence at first. In the revealing process, stacking any k transparences can visually decode the secret image.

For example, a perfect black (2, 3)-VCS can be constructed using following basis matrices.

$$B_0 = \begin{bmatrix} 1 & 1 & 0 \\ 1 & 1 & 0 \\ 1 & 1 & 0 \end{bmatrix}, B_1 = \begin{bmatrix} 1 & 1 & 0 \\ 0 & 1 & 1 \\ 1 & 0 & 1 \end{bmatrix} \tag{1}$$

With these two basis matrices of (2, 3)-PBVCS, a secret image can be shared into three shadows, where stacking any two shadows can perfectly reveal the black secret pixels. Figure 1 shows an experiment of (2, 3)-PBVCS.

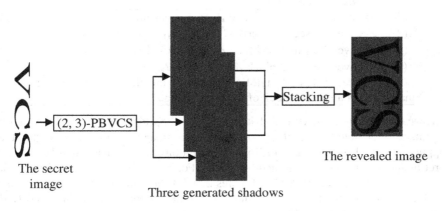

The secret image

Three generated shadows

The revealed image

Fig. 1. An experiment of (2, 3)-PBVCS.

2.2 Pixel Processing with Boolean Operations in Chao and Lin's ISS

Usually, traditional VCS cannot reveal perfect grayscale image. Although PISS has the advantage of perfect revealing for grayscale secret image, it needs complicated computation. It is desirable to design an image secret sharing method with the benefits of perfect revealing and low computational load. In Chao and Lin's image secret sharing scheme, they proposed a novel method to encrypt secret image based on Boolean operation [17]. To restore a secret pixel, it only needs three bit-by-bit XOR operations, and each XOR is between a pair of 8-bit values if image is grayscale. In this paper, we briefly introduce the pixel processing with Boolean operations in Chao and Lin's ISS.

Algorithm 1. The encryption process with Boolean operations in Chao and Lin's ISS.

Input: Grayscale secret image S.

Output: $2m$ pixels $S_1, S_2, ..., S_{2m}$.

(1-1) Read-in un-processed m gray secret pixels as a block A.

(1-2) Randomly generate block B_1 with m grayscale values $B_{11}, B_{12}, ..., B_{1m}$. Generate block $B_2 = B_1 \oplus A$ using XOR operation in bit-by-bit manner to obtain m values $B_{21}, B_{22}, ..., B_{2m}$.

(1-3) Compute the security mask C^* by XOR operation.
$$C^* = B_{11} \oplus B_{12} \oplus ... \oplus B_{1m}$$

(1-4) Shift each B_{2i} to C_{2i} by $C_{2i} = B_{2i} \oplus C^*$ for security reason, and obtain block C_2.

(1-5) Physically attaching C_{2i} to B_{1i} to obtain S^* as the corresponding pixels of $S_1, S_2, ..., S_{2m}$.

(1-6) Repeat Step 1-Step 5 until all pixels in S are processed. Finally, we have $2m$ pixels $S_1, S_2, ..., S_{2m}$.

Algorithm 2. The decoding process with Boolean operations in Chao and Lin's ISS.

Input: $2m$ pixels $S_1, S_2, ..., S_{2m}$.

Output: Grayscale secret image S.

(2-1) Extract a pair blocks C_2 and B_1 from m shadows.

(2-2) Recover the security mask C^* by $C^* = B_{11} \oplus B_{12} \oplus ... \oplus B_{1m}$.

(2-3) Recover the values in block B_2 by $B_{2i} = C_{2i} \oplus C^*$.

(2-4) Recover the secret block A by $A = B_1 \oplus B_2$.

(2-5) Repeat (1-1)-(1-4) until all blocks of the shadows are processed. Finally we get all secret block of the secret image S.

If we concatenate all generated shadows $S_1, S_2, ..., S_m$ together, we get a new noise-like image with double-size of the original secret image. From the view point of mapping, the pixel processing with Boolean operations in Chao and Lin's ISS maps a secret image S to image SI consisted by blocks. For each block of SI with $2m$ pixels, we can reveal an m-pixel block of S. Figures 2 and 3 show the encryption process and decoding process of the pixel processing with Boolean operations in Chao and Lin's ISS, where $m = 3$, respectively.

3   The Proposed TiOISS Scheme Based on PBVCS and Boolean Operation

In this section, we propose a new (k, n)-TiOISS scheme based on PBVCS and Boolean operation. A grayscale secret image and its halftone image are shared in our TiOISS scheme. In the revealing process, stacking any k shadows can visually reveal the

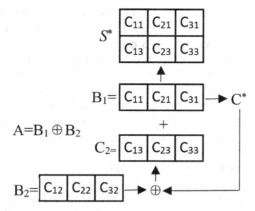

Fig. 2. A flowchart showing encryption process of the pixel processing with Boolean operations in Chao and Lin's ISS, where $m = 3$.

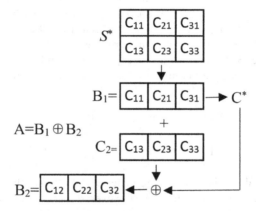

Fig. 3. A flowchart showing the decoding process of the pixel processing with Boolean operations in Chao and Lin's ISS, where $m = 3$.

previewed secret image with low visual quality. It also can decode the original grayscale secret image by computation with any k shadows.

3.1 Main Idea

First, we process every m grayscale secret pixels of S using the pixel processing with Boolean operations in Chao and Lin's ISS, and get $2m$ processed pixels. Then, expand the pixel expansion of (k, n)-PBVCS from m to $2m$. Finally, the processed $2m$ pixels are embedded into (k, n)-PBVCS with pixel expansion $2m$ when sharing a black secret pixel of the halftone image H. Finally, we have n grayscale shadows. In the revealing process, a vague secret image can be revealed by stacking any k shadows in the first stage. In the second stage, we can extract the processed pixels from k shadows, and then decode the grayscale secret image S using Algorithm 2.

As we mentioned before, in (k, n)-PBVCS, a black secret pixels can be revealed as a block with all black sub-pixels. In another word, if we select any k rows of basis matrix B_1 to form a new matrix, it is clear that each column of the new matrix has at least one '1'. Obviously, if we all the columns in each basis matrix of (k, n)-PBVCS with pixel expansion m are chose twice, we can construct a corresponding (k, n)-PBVCS with pixel expansion $2 m$. In the proposed TiOISS scheme, the black sub-pixels '1' in share matrix D_1 are replaced by gray values, where D_1 (referred as black share matrix) is generated by permuting columns of B_1. It should be noted that all black sub-pixels in the same column of D_1 are replaced by the same gray value. Since (k, n)-PBVCS with size expansion $2 m$ is employed, we can embed $2 m$ gray values in a black share matrix D_1 to form grayscale share matrix G_1. In addition, the white sub-pixels ('0') in D_1 are changed as gray value 255 in G_1. For the security consideration, each share matrix D_0 (referred as white share matrix) generated by permuting columns of B_0 also need to embed gray values in the same way to form gray share matrix G_0. In our TiOISS scheme, the gray values embedded in gray share matrix G_1 are come from processed pixels with Boolean operation in Chao and Lin's ISS, while the gray values embedded in gray share matrix G_0 are randomly generated.

For example, a $(2, 3)$-PBVCS with size expansion 6 can be constructed from $(2, 3)$-PBVCS by double choosing all columns of each basis matrix. The new basis matrices are shown as follows.

$$
B_0 = \begin{bmatrix} 1 & 1 & 1 & 1 & 0 & 0 \\ 1 & 1 & 1 & 1 & 0 & 0 \\ 1 & 1 & 1 & 1 & 0 & 0 \end{bmatrix}, B_1 = \begin{bmatrix} 1 & 1 & 1 & 1 & 0 & 0 \\ 0 & 0 & 1 & 1 & 1 & 1 \\ 1 & 1 & 0 & 0 & 1 & 1 \end{bmatrix} \tag{2}
$$

Then, the grayscale basis matrices are generated. Note that the grayscale values g_j $(j = 1,\ldots,4)$ in G_0 are randomly generated. However, the grayscale values g_j $(j = 1,\ldots,6)$ in G_1 are coming from the processed pixels C_{i1} and C_{i3} $(i = 1,2,3)$, respectively, and '0's are replaced by 255. The grayscale basis matrices G_0 and G_1 are shown as follows.

$$
G_0 = \begin{bmatrix} g_1 & g_2 & g_3 & g_4 & 0 & 0 \\ g_1 & g_2 & g_3 & g_4 & 0 & 0 \\ g_1 & g_2 & g_3 & g_4 & 0 & 0 \end{bmatrix} \; G_1 = \begin{bmatrix} g_1 & g_2 & g_3 & g_4 & 255 & 255 \\ 255 & 255 & g_3 & g_4 & g_5 & g_6 \\ g_1 & g_2 & 255 & 255 & g_5 & g_6 \end{bmatrix} \tag{3}
$$

In the extracting process, any k rows of G_1 can retrieve $2 m$ embedded gray values by ignoring the white sub-pixels (255) in each column. A diagram of embedding and retrieving gray values in gray share matrix G_1 of $(2, 3)$-PBVCS is shown in Fig. 4.

In order to distinguish G_0 and G_1 by any k rows in the second stage of revealing process, the gray values embedded in G_0 and G_1 should be smaller than 255 (<255). Otherwise, the embedded gray value 255 may be confused with the white sub-pixels. Therefore, in the decoding process, for each sub-pixel in a block of the k involved

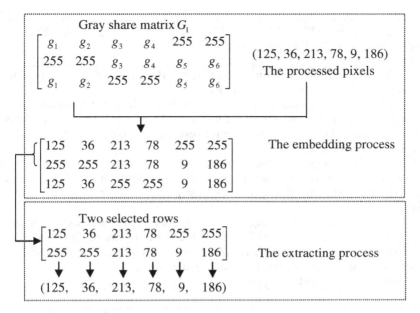

Fig. 4. A diagram of embedding and retrieving gray values in black share matrix of (2, 3)-PBVCS.

shadows, if there is at least one gray value smaller than 255 in the same position, then this block refers a black pixel. Hence m embedded grayscale values can be extracted from k involved shadows.

As described in Sub-sect. 2.2, the size of the processed image SI are two times of the secret image I. In addition, all gray values in SI equaled to 255 should be modified to avoid confusion with white pixel for security consideration. The confusion problem is similar to the first weakness of Yang et al.'s scheme [13] pointed by Li et al. [14]. A possible solution to avoid confusion is that to divide the gray value larger than or equal to 254 into two values: 254 and the gray value minus to 254. That is, 254 is divided into 254 and 0, and 255 is divided into 254 and 1. The transformation process and the inverse transformation process are the same as Algorithm 1 and 2 in Li et al.' scheme, respectively. The final SI after transformation is denoted as SI'. Since each pixel with gray values larger than 253 in SI is replaced as two pixels in SI', the size of SI' is a little larger than SI.

Let the size of S be $M \times N$, then the size of SI is $2M \times N$. The size of SI' would be little larger than $2M \times N$. Suppose SI' has Num pixels. Since sharing each black pixel by our scheme can embed $2\,m$ grayscale values, there should be at least $Num/2\,m$ black pixels in H. Hence, the size of grayscale secret image S may need to be resized, to make sure the halftone image H of S has enough black secret pixels.

The sharing and revealing processes of the proposed scheme can be described by the following two algorithms.

Algorithm 3. The sharing process of the proposed (k, n)-TiOISS scheme.

Input: Grayscale secret image S with $M \times N$ pixels.

Output: n shadows $P_1, P_2, ..., P_n$.

(3-1) Determine the basis matrices of (k, n)-PBVCS with the size expansion m, and then expand the size expansion to $2m$.

(3-2) Processing pixels of the secret image S with Boolean operations in Chao and Lin's ISS to get processed image SI. Then transform SI to SI' using by Algorithm 1 in Li et al.'s scheme for resisting all pixels smaller than 255. Suppose SI' has Num pixels.

(3-3) Dither S to get halftone image H.

(3-4) If the number of black pixels in H is smaller than $Num/2m$, enlarge the size of secret image S, and go back to step (3-3). Otherwise, go to step (3-5).

(3-5) Share the halftone image H by (k, n)-PBVCS with size expansion $2m$. All pixels in SI' are embedded into the black sub-pixels of shadows when sharing black pixels of H, while the black sub-pixels of shadows when sharing white pixels of H are replaced by random grayscale values.

(3-6) Finally, we get n grayscale shadows $P_1, P_2, ..., P_n$.

Algorithm 4. The revealing process of the proposed (k, n)-TiOISS scheme

Input: k shadows $P_1, P_2, ..., P_k$.

Output: Previewed image P and the secret image S.

(4-1) Stack k shadows $P_1, P_2, ..., P_k$ can visually decode a previewed image P.

(4-2) Extract each un-processed $2m$-pixel-block of $P_1, P_2, ..., P_k$ to form a $k \times 2m$ matrix R, where each $2m$-pixel-block is served as a row of R.

(4-3) If each column of R has at least one value smaller than 255, then R is regarded as black-pixel block, and the gray values embedded in R can be extracted as the corresponding values of SI'.

(4-4) Repeat steps (4-2) and (4-3) until all blocks of $P_1, P_2, ..., P_k$ are processed.

(4-5) Inversely transform SI' to SI by using Algorithm 2 in Li et al.'s scheme.

(4-6) Decrypt SI to get the secret image S by Algorithm 2.

3.2   Security and Performance Analysis

In the proposed scheme, we need stacking operation on grayscale values. Usually, a gray mixing model is employed to simulate the stacking operation. A formal definition of gray mixing model is shown as follows.

Definition 1. Let g_1 and g_2 be two grayscale values. Two transparencies with colors g_1 and g_2 are stacked. The resulting grayscale value g_3 can be approximately expressed as:

$$g_3 = MX(g_1, g_2) = \text{int}(g_1 \times g_2/255).$$

where the int($\cdot$) function approximates its argument to the nearest integer, and $MX(\cdot)$ represents the gray-mixed result of its arguments.

Obviously, stacking three grayscale values can be represented by stacking two grayscale values twice. In general, we have

$$MX\,(g_1,\ g_2,\ \ldots,g_n)\ =\ MX(MX(g_1,\ \ldots,g_{n-1}),\ g_n)$$

Since the stacking results of gray values are still gray, our scheme is also a gray visual cryptography scheme (GVCS). Therefore, our scheme should satisfy the security condition in probabilistic sense. Let $GM(G_i|k)$ be the gray-mixed vector of gray share matrix G_i restricted to any k rows, where $i = 0, 1$. Let $Avg(v)$ be the average expected gray value of all elements in vector v. In the first stage of revealing process, our scheme can reveal the secret by stacking k shadows, and any k–1 or fewer shadows can not reveal any information about secret image. Therefore, it should satisfy the following conditions for GVCS.

(2-i) (Contrast condition) $Avg(GM(G_1|k)) > Avg(GM(G_0|k))$
(2-ii) (Security condition) $Avg(GM(G_0|t)) = Avg(GM(G_1|t))$, for any $0 < t < k$.

In the second stage of revealing process, any k shadows can extract enough information to reveal the secret image by computation, while any k–1 or few shadows can get no information about the secret image. Therefore, the proposed scheme also should satisfy the following conditions for image secret sharing.

(3-i) (Threshold condition) Any k shadows can extract enough information to decode the secret image.
(3-ii) (Security condition) Any k–1 or fewer shadows cannot reveal the secret image.

As described in Sect. 3.1, the secret image S is processed by Chao and Lin's ISS scheme with Boolean operation, which means m secret pixels are encrypted into $2\,m$ pixels. Then $2\,m$ encrypted pixels are embedded into a gray share matrix G_1 and shared into n shadows when sharing a black pixel. In the revealing process, if and only if when k or more shadows together, it can extract $2\,m$ encrypted pixels, and then decrypt them to get m secret pixels. With k–1 or fewer shadows, we can get less than $2\,m$ encrypted pixels, and then we cannot decrypt the secret pixels. Chao and Lin have proved the recoverability and security of their ISS scheme with Boolean operation.

Now, we need to prove the proposed scheme satisfy condition (2-ii).

Theorem 1. The proposed scheme satisfies the security condition (2-ii).

Proof: As described in Sect. 3.1, G_0 and G_1 are generated from D_0 and D_1, respectively, where D_0 and D_1 are the share matrix of (k, n)-PBVCS. Both G_0 and G_1 are generated by changing '1' in D_0 and D_1 to random gray values in 0-254, and '0' to 255, respectively. Since D_0 and D_1 should satisfy the security condition (1-ii) of VCS, D_0 and D_1 have the same columns if we restrict them to any t rows, $t < k$. Therefore, if we restrict G_0 and G_1 to any t rows, $G_0|t$ and $G_1|t$ have columns with the same structure. Here, two columns have the same structure means they have the same number of white sub-pixels (255) and the same number of gray sub-pixels (0-254). Since all gray sub-pixels are pseudo-random integers in (0-254), the expected value of each gray sub-pixel is 127. Therefore, the expected gray-mixed values of two columns are the same if they have the same structure. Finally, the average of the gray-mixed values of all columns in $G_0|t$ is equal to that in $G_1|t$, which means $Avg(GM(G_0|t)) = Avg(GM(G_1|t))$, for any $0 < t < k$.

For the contrast condition (2-i), it is hard to prove that theoretically. However, it is easy to evaluate the average expected gray values in the revealed black area and white area. In the proposed scheme, we also take the contrast definition defined in Li et al.'s scheme.

Definition 2. Let α be the contrast of the revealed image by stacking shadows, it is defined as follows.

$$\alpha = Avg(GM(G_1|k)) - Avg(GM(G_0|k))$$

For a pair of basis matrices of the corresponding (k, n)-PBVCS, it is easy to evaluate the contrast. For example, for a proposed $(2, 3)$-TiOISS scheme with basis matrices of $(2, 3)$-PBVCS as shown in Eq. (1), the expected gray value of each grayscale sub-pixel is 127, and the expected gray-mixed value of two grayscale sub-pixels with the same gray value is 85. So the contrast of $(2, 3)$-TiOISS is 0.11.

3.3   Some Special Cases for the Construction of PBVCS

PBVCS is a special kind of VCS. The main difference between PBVCS to VCS is that the OR-ed vector of any k row of B_1 in PBVCS is consisted of all '1'. Most researchers studied the construction of the basis matrices of general VCS. Some of them are also belong to PBVCS. For example, the (n, n)-VCS constructed by Naor and Shamir's scheme is also a (n, n)-PBVCS.

For $(2, n)$-VCS constructed by Naor and Shamir's scheme, the basis matrices is constructed as the pair of following $n \times n$ matrices $B0$ and $B1$.

$$B_0 = \begin{bmatrix} 100 \cdots 0 \\ 100 \cdots 0 \\ \cdots \\ 100 \cdots 0 \end{bmatrix}, B_1 = \begin{bmatrix} 100 \cdots 0 \\ 010 \cdots 0 \\ \cdots \\ 000 \cdots 1 \end{bmatrix}$$

Actually, it is easy to modify a $(2, n)$-VCS to a $(2, n)$-PBVCS by replacing all '0' (resp. '1') by '1' (resp. '0'). Then we have the basis matrices of $(2, n)$-PBVCS as follows.

$$B_0 = \begin{bmatrix} 011 \cdots 1 \\ 011 \cdots 1 \\ \cdots \\ 011 \cdots 1 \end{bmatrix}, B_1 = \begin{bmatrix} 011 \cdots 1 \\ 101 \cdots 1 \\ \cdots \\ 111 \cdots 0 \end{bmatrix}$$

For PBVCS with general access structure, we can use Viet and Kurosawa's scheme to generate the basis matrices [18].

4 Experimental Results and Comparison

In this section, we show the experimental result of the proposed scheme. A (2, 3)-TiOISS scheme is conducted with basis matrices of the corresponding (2, 3)-PBVCS as shown in Eq. (1). The secret image I is image 'Lena' with 256 × 256 pixels as shown in Fig. 5(a). On one hand, I is encrypted into SI with 256 × 512 pixels by (3, 3)-ISS based on Boolean operation as shown in Fig. 5(b). Then translate SI to SI' such that all pixels' values in SI' are smaller than 255. Finally we have SI' with 132107 pixels. On the other hand, a halftone version H of I should be shared by (2, 3)-PBVCS. In order to embed SI' into the final shadows, H must have enough black pixels. Otherwise, the secret image I should be enlarged and then dithered to H. In this experiment, share each black secret pixel in H can embed 6 grayscale values of SI', hence H should have at least 22018 black pixels. The final halftone image H is generated with 350 × 125 pixels, including 22471 black pixels. After share generation process, we get three grayscale shadows as shown in Fig. 6(a)–(c). In the first stage of the decoding process, stacking any two shadows can visually reveal the secret image with low visual quality. Figure 6(d) shows the result by stacking Fig. 6(a) and (b). In the second stage, we can extract the embedded values in two shadows, and decode the original secret image I by computation.

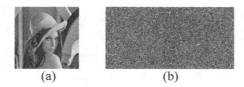

(a)   (b)

Fig. 5. The secret image and the encrypted image. (a) the secret image Lena with 256 × 256 pixels. (b) the encrypted image SI with 256 × 512 pixels.

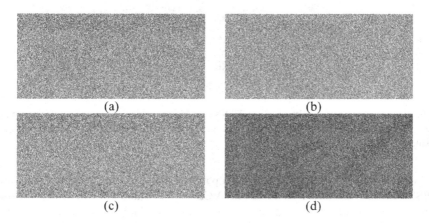

(a)   (b)

(c)   (d)

Fig. 6. The experimental results of the proposed (2, 3)-TiOISS scheme. (a)–(c) three generated shadows with 350 × 750 pixels. (d) the revealed image by stacking (a) and (b).

Actually, our scheme can also share two secret images: one is a binary image, and another is a grayscale image. We also show the experimental result of the proposed (2, 3)-TiOISS scheme when sharing two secret images. The binary secret image H is chosen as the inverse version of the text-image as shown in Fig. 2. And the grayscale secret image I is also the image Lena with 256×256 pixels. As shown before, in order to embed all information in SI', H should have enough black pixels. In this experiment, the resized binary image H is shown in Fig. 7(a) with the size of 210×140 pixels, including 22199 black pixels. Finally, we have three generated shadows as shown in Fig. 7(b)–(d) and the revealed image by stacking two shadows is shown in Fig. 7(e). In addition, the embedded information can be extracted from any two shadows and then decode the image I by computation.

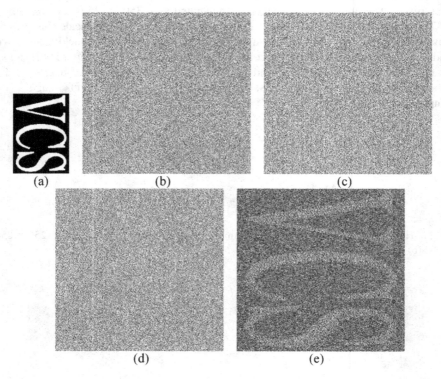

Fig. 7. The experimental results of (2, 3)-TiOISS on binary secret image. (a) the resized binary secret image (420×140 pixels), (b)-(d) three generated shadows, (e) the revealed image by stacking (b) and (c).

TiOISS scheme has the distinctive property of two decoding options. Traditional TiOISS schemes are based on PISS and VCS, or PISS and GVCS. However, these schemes need complicated computation to reveal the original grayscale secret image in the second stage of revealing process. Since these schemes use PISS to share the secret image, the revealing process needs employ Lagrange's interpolation. The time complexity of Lagrange's interpolation is $O(\log^2 k)$ mathematical operation. The proposed TiOISS scheme is based on XOR operation and GVCS. In the second stage of revealing process, it only need three times of XOR operation to decode a secret pixel. Obviously, the time complexity is smaller than traditional schemes. Although the visual quality of the revealed image by stacking shadows is poor, we can improve the contrast with the cost of enlarged shadow size by using general GVCS introduced by Li et al. in [15]. Table 1 shows the comparison between the traditional schemes and the proposed TiOISS scheme.

Table 1. The comparisons between literature schemes and the proposed TiOISS scheme

Schemes	Construction method	Decoding by stacking or computation	Time complexity of decoding by computation
Naor and Shamir's VCS [7]	VCS	Stacking	–
Thien and Lin's ISS scheme [2]	PISS	Computation	$O(\log^2 k)$ (math operation)
Lin and Lin's TiOISS scheme [12]	PISS + VCS	Both	$O(\log^2 k)$ (math operation)
Yang and Ciou's TiOISS scheme [13]	PISS + GVCS	Both	$O(\log^2 k)$ (math operation)
Li et al.'s TiOISS scheme [14]	PISS + GVCS	Both	$O(\log^2 k)$ (math operation)
Li et al.'s GVCS [15]	PISS + GVCS	Both	$O(\log^2 k)$ (math operation)
The proposed TiOISS scheme	PBVCS + ISS based on Boolean operation	Both	3 (XOR operation)

5 Conclusion

In this paper, we propose a TiOISS scheme based on PBVCS and Boolean operation. The grayscale secret image is first processed by Chao and Lin's ISS with Boolean operation and then embedded into shadows of PBVCS. In the revealing process, our scheme can not only reveal a vague secret image by stacking shadows, but also decode the grayscale secret image by fewer computations. The main contribution of the proposed scheme is that we dexterously combine PBVCS and Chao and Lin's ISS with Boolean operation, which is faster than traditional TiOISS schemes based on PISS in decoding process.

Acknowledgments. This work was supported by the Natural Science Funds of Hebei (Grant No: F2015502014).

References

1. Shamir, A.: How to share a secret. Commun. Assoc. Comput. Mach. **22**, 612–613 (1979)
2. Thien, C.C., Lin, J.C.: Secret image sharing. Comput. Graphics **26**, 765–770 (2002)
3. Yang, C.N., Chen, T.S., Yu, K.H., Wang, C.C.: Improvements of image sharing with steganography and authentication. J. Syst. Softw. **80**, 1070–1076 (2007)
4. Wang, R.Z., Shyu, S.J.: Scalable secret image sharing. Sig. Process. Image Commun. **22**, 363–373 (2007)
5. Yang, C.N., Huang, S.M.: Constructions and properties of k out of n scalable secret image sharing. Optics Communications 2831750–1762 (2010)
6. Naor, Moni, Shamir, Adi: Visual Cryptography. In: De Santis, Alfredo (ed.) EUROCRYPT 1994. LNCS, vol. 950, pp. 1–12. Springer, Heidelberg (1995)
7. Yang, C.N., Chen, T.S.: Extended visual secret sharing schemes: improving the shadow image quality. Int. J. Pattern Recogn. Artif. Intell. **21**, 879–898 (2007)
8. Liu, F., Wu, C.K.: Embedded extended visual cryptography schemes. IEEE Trans. Inf. Forensics Secur. **6**, 307–322 (2011)
9. Yang, C.N., Chen, T.S.: Colored visual cryptography scheme based on additive color mixing. Pattern Recogn. **41**, 3114–3129 (2008)
10. Shyu, S.J.: Efficient visual secret sharing scheme for color images. Pattern Recogn. **39**, 866–880 (2006)
11. Liu, F., Wu, C.K., Lin, X.J.: Color visual cryptography schemes. IET Inf. Secur. **2**, 151–165 (2008)
12. Lin, S.J., Lin, J.C.: VCPSS: a two-in-one two-decoding-options image sharing method combining visual cryptography (VC) and polynomial-style sharing (PSS) approaches. Pattern Recogn. **40**, 3652–3666 (2007)
13. Yang, C.N., Ciou, C.B.: Image secret sharing method with two-decoding-options: lossless recovery and previewing capability. Image Vis. Comput. **28**, 1600–1610 (2010)
14. Li, P., Ma, P.J., Su, X.H., Yang, C.N.: Improvements of a two-in-one image secret sharing scheme based on gray mixing model. J. Vis. Commun. Image Represent. **23**, 441–453 (2012)
15. Li, P., Yang, C.N., Kong, Q., Ma, Y., Liu, Z.: Sharing more information in gray visual cryptography scheme. J. Vis. Commun. Image Represent. **24**, 1380–1393 (2013)
16. Wang, D., Zhang, L., Ma, N., Li, X.: Two secret sharing schemes based on Boolean operations. Patt. Recogn. **40**, 2776–2785 (2007)
17. Chao, K.Y., Lin, J.C.: Secret image sharing: a boolean-operations-based approach combining benefits of polynomial-based and fast approaches. Int. J. Pattern Recogn. Artif. Intell. **23**, 263–285 (2009)
18. Viet, Duong Quang, Kurosawa, Kaoru: almost ideal contrast visual cryptography with reversing. In: Okamoto, Tatsuaki (ed.) CT-RSA 2004. LNCS, vol. 2964, pp. 353–365. Springer, Heidelberg (2004)

Random Girds-Based Threshold Visual Secret Sharing with Improved Contrast by Boolean Operations

Xuehu Yan[1]([✉]), Guohui Chen[2], Ching-Nung Yang[3], and Song-Ruei Cai[3]

[1] School of Computer Science and Technology, Harbin Institute of Technology,
Harbin 150080, China
`xuehu.yan@ict.hit.edu.cn`
[2] Hebei University of Science and Technology, Shi Jiazhuang 050018, China
[3] Department of CSIE, National Dong Hwa University, Hualien 974, Taiwan

Abstract. In recent years, visual secret sharing (VSS) by random grids (RG) has gained much attention since it can avoid pixel expansion problem as well as has no codebook needed, which has acceptable visual quality based on the internal structure of the designed scheme. Till now, the previous schemes still suffer from low visual quality, from our point of view, and visual quality decreases fast when n increases. In this paper, a new RG-based VSS with improved visual quality based on Boolean operations is proposed, based on two different quality-improved approaches and gaining both advantages. The proposed scheme has several features such as (k, n) threshold, no codebook design, and no pixel expansion. Moreover, it has higher contrast compared with related schemes.

Keywords: Visual cryptography · Visual secret sharing · Boolean operations · Random grid

1 Introduction

User secret data covered by one single carrier may be easily lost. Secret image sharing has solved this problem since the method shares the user data into different shares (also called shadows) and distributes them to multiple participants. It has attracted more attention from scientists and engineers. Visual secret sharing (VSS) [1–4] is one branch in secret sharing with simple decryption.

Naor and Shamir [1] first proposed the threshold-based visual cryptography scheme (VCS). In their scheme, a binary secret image is shared by generating corresponding n noise-like shadow images. And any k or more noise-like shadow images are stacking to recover the secret image visually based on human visual system (HVS) and probability. While less than k participants cannot reveal any information of the secret image by inspecting their shares. However, the scheme suffers from codebook (basic matrices) design and pixel expansion [4].

Since VSS by random grids (RG) could avoid pixel expansion and has no codebook design, some researchers have paid more attention to RG-based VSS.

© Springer International Publishing Switzerland 2015
Y.-Q. Shi et al. (Eds.): IWDW 2014, LNCS 9023, pp. 319–332, 2015.
DOI: 10.1007/978-3-319-19321-2_24

Encryption of binary secret images based on RG is first presented by Kafri and Keren [5], each of which is generated into two noise-like RGs (shadow images or share images) that have the same size as the original secret image. The decryption operation is the same as VCS. However, traditional image encryption by RG [5] satisfies no pixel expansion but no (k, n) threshold.

Chen and Tsao [6] have proposed a (k, n) RG-based VSS scheme based on Boolean operations. In [6], the same $(2, 2)$ RG-based VSS approach is extended to (k, n) threshold scheme by applying $(2, 2)$ RG-based VSS repeatedly for the first k bits and generating the last $n - k$ bits randomly.

Recently, motivated by [6], Wu and Sun [7] have improved the visual quality of reconstructed secret image through changing the last $n - k$ bits from randomly selecting to be equal to the k th bit. The advantage of Wu and Sun's scheme is, significantly improving the visual quality when $n - k$ is smaller. However, the visual quality decreases more rapidly when $n - k$ increases.

Quite recently, Guo et al. [8] improve the visual quality of Chen and Tsao's scheme [6] through computing every k bits by applying Chen and Tsao's scheme [8] for $N_k = \lfloor n/k \rfloor$ times, and setting the last $n - N_k \times k$ bits randomly. The advantage of Guo et al.'s [8] scheme is, the visual quality decreases more slowly when $n - k$ increases. However, the visual quality also increases more slowly when $n - k$ is smaller.

As observed from Wu and Sun's scheme [7] and Guo et al.'s scheme [8], they improve the visual quality of Chen and Tsao's scheme [6] trough utilizing the random bits to increase the correct decryption probability, in different approaches and with different advantages or disadvantages.

In this paper, we propose a new (k, n) threshold VSS scheme based on RG and Boolean operations which improves visual quality by combining the advantages of both Wu and Sun's scheme and Guo et al.'s scheme The core idea of the proposed scheme is: Selecting random bits in the n bits, the random bits could be utilized to gain better properties under security condition, such as improving the visual quality. The recovery is also based on stacking (Boolean OR operation) and HVS. Additionally, the proposed scheme has several other features such as (k, n) threshold, no codebook design, and avoiding the pixel expansion problem Experimental results and security analyses show the effectiveness of the proposed scheme. Comparisons with previous approaches show the advantages of the proposed scheme.

The rest of the paper is organized as follows. Section 2 introduces the related works and preliminary techniques as the basis for the proposed scheme. In Sect. 3, the proposed scheme is presented in detail. Section 4 is devoted to experimental results. Finally, Sect. 5 concludes this paper.

2   Related Works and Preliminaries

In this section, we give some preliminaries and the related work, RG-based [6–8] VSS, as the basis for the proposed scheme. In what follows, symbols $\oplus$ and $\otimes$ denote the Boolean XOR and OR operations. $\bar{b}$ is a bit-wise complementary operation of any bit b. The binary secret image S is shared among n shadow images, while the reconstructed secret image S' is reconstructed from t $(2 \leq t \leq n, t \in \mathbb{Z}^+)$ shadow images. Here 0 denotes white pixels, 1 denotes black pixels.

For a certain pixel s in binary image S with size of $M \times N$, the probability of pixel color is transparent or white () say $(s = 0)$ and the same for the probability of pixel color is opaque or black (1). Besides $(S = 0) = 1 - \frac{1}{MN} \sum_{i=1}^{M} \sum_{j=1}^{N} S(i,j), 1 \leq i \leq M, 1 \leq j \leq N$.

$AS0$ (resp., $AS1$) is the white (resp., black) area of original secret image S defined as $S0 = \{(i,j)|S(i,j) = 0, 1 \leq i \leq M, 1 \leq j \leq N\}$ (resp., $S1 = \{(i,j)|S(i,j) = 1, 1 \leq i \leq M, 1 \leq j \leq N\}$).

Definition 1 (Contrast): The visual quality, which will decide how well human eyes could recognize the recovered image, of the recovered secret image S' corresponding to the original secret image S is evaluated by contrast defined as follows [6,9]:

$$\alpha = \frac{P_0 - P_1}{1 + P_1} = \frac{P(S'[AS0] = 0) - P(S'[AS1] = 0)}{1 + P(S'[AS1] = 0)} \tag{1}$$

Where α denotes contrast, P_0 (resp., P_1) is the appearance probability of white pixels in the recovered image S' in the corresponding white (resp., black) area of original secret image S, that is, P_0 is the correctly decrypted probability corresponding to the white area of original secret image S, and P_1 is the wrongly decrypted probability corresponding to the black area of original secret image S.

Definition 2 (Visually Recognizable) [1,6]**:** The recovered secret image S' could be recognized as the corresponding original secret image S if $\alpha > 0$ when $t \geq k$.

Definition 3 (Security) [1,6]**:** The scheme is secure if $\alpha = 0$ when $t < k$, which means no information of S could be recognized through S'.

In RG-based VSS [6], the shadow images covered secret after sharing are denoted as SC_p. The generation and recovery phases of original (2, 2) RG-based [6] VSS are described below.

Step 1: Randomly generate 1 RG SC_1
Step 2: Compute SC_2 as in Eq. (2)

Recovery: $S' = SC_1 \otimes SC_2$ as in Eq. (3). If a certain secret pixel $s = S(i,j)$ is 1, the recovery result $SC_1 \otimes SC_2 = 1$ is always black. If a certain secret pixel s is 0, the recovery result $SC_1 \otimes SC_2 = SC_1(i,j) \otimes SC_1(i,j)$ has half chance to be black or white since SC_1 is generated randomly.

$$SC_2(i,j) = \begin{cases} SC_1(i,j) & if \ S = 0 \\ \overline{SC_1(i,j)} & if \ S = 1 \end{cases} \tag{2}$$

$$\begin{aligned} S'(i,j) &= SC_1(i,j) \otimes SC_2(i,j) \\ &= \begin{cases} SC_1(i,j) \otimes SC_1(i,j) & if \ S(i,j) = 0 \\ SC_1(i,j) \otimes \overline{SC_1(i,j)} = 1 & if \ S(i,j) = 1 \end{cases} \end{aligned} \tag{3}$$

Equation (2) is equal to $sc_2 = sc_1 \oplus s$ or $s = sc_1 \oplus sc_2$. Since if $s = 0 \Rightarrow$ $sc_2 = sc_1 \oplus 0 \Rightarrow sc_2 = sc_1$, and if $s = 1 \Rightarrow sc_2 = sc_1 \oplus 1 \Rightarrow sc_2 = \overline{sc_1}$.

The same equation could be extended to $s = sc_1 \oplus sc_2 \oplus \cdots \oplus sc_k$, meanwhile the same approach can be extended to (k, n) threshold scheme by applying the above process repeatedly for the first k bits and generating the last n-k bits randomly.

In addition Wu and Sun's scheme [7] improves the contrast of the scheme [6] by change the last $n - k$ bits to be equal to the kth bit in step 5 of Chen and Tsao's (k, n) RG-based VSS.

Guo et al. [8] improve the visual quality of Chen and Tsao's scheme [6] in another way, i.e., computing every k bits by applying Chen and Tsao's scheme for $N_k = \lfloor n/k \rfloor$ times, and setting the last $n - N_k \times k$ bits randomly.

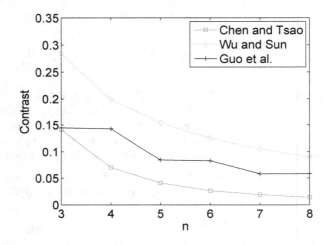

Fig. 1. Average contrast of secret image reconstructed by $t = 2$ shadow images in Wu and Sun's scheme and Guo et al.'s scheme with different n when $k = 2$

Based on the above three RG-based VSS schemes, there are random bits in the corresponding n bits. The random bits are utilized in Wu and Sun's scheme and Guo et al.'s scheme to improve the visual quality in different methods. The comparison between the two schemes is shown in Fig. 1, which shows the average contrast of secret image reconstructed by $t = 2$ shadow images, with different n when $k = 2$. We can find that Wu and Sun's scheme has a better improved effect than Guo et al.'s scheme, while the contrast of Guo et al.'s scheme decreases more slowly when $n - k$ increases.

Here we aim to overcome the above disadvantages and improve the visual quality of the secret image. Precisely, we combine the advantages of both Wu and Sun's scheme and Guo et al.'s scheme by utilizing the random bits. Prior to the detail of the proposed scheme, the diagrammatic design concepts comparison between the proposed scheme and related schemes is shown in Fig. 2. There are some random bits, such as the middle $(N_k - 1) \times k$ bits and the last $n - k$ bits in the previous schemes [6–8], which are applied for improving the visual quality in the proposed scheme. Thus the proposed scheme can enhance the contrast.

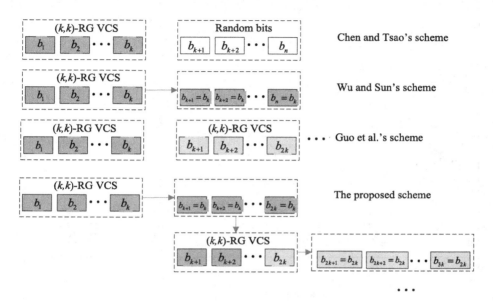

Fig. 2. The design concepts comparison between the proposed scheme and related schemes

3   The Proposed Scheme

In this section, we propose a novel (k, n) (generally $n, k \in \mathbf{Z}^+, 2 \le k \le n$) VSS based on RG to improve the visual quality through utilizing the random bits in the n bits corresponding to n shares Here "1" denotes black pixel, "0" denotes white pixel.

3.1   Scheme: RG-based VSS with Improved Visual Quality

The shadow images generation architecture of the proposed scheme is illustrated in Fig. 3, the corresponding algorithmic steps are described in detail in Algorithm 1.

The secret recovery of the proposed scheme is also based on stacking ($\otimes$) or HVS

From the above steps, in step 3, Guo *et al.*'s scheme is utilized in the proposed scheme to gain threshold Steps 4–6 combine Wu's and Sun's scheme to improve

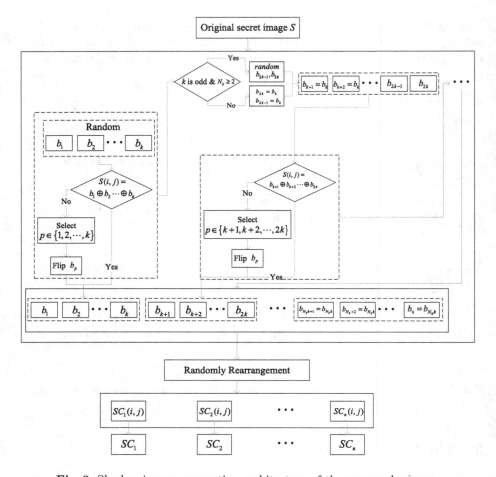

Fig. 3. Shadow images generation architecture of the proposed scheme

the visual quality and security condition. In such a way, the proposed scheme combines the two schemes to gain the advantages from the two schemes.

Step 5 sets some random bits aiming to satisfy the security condition. We take the second k bits as an example to show the reason. When k is odd, step 3 requires $S(i,j) = b_{k+1} \oplus b_{k+2} \cdots \oplus b_{2k}$, if $b_{k+1} = b_k, b_{k+2} = b_k, \cdots b_{2k} = b_k$, then $S(i,j) = b_k \oplus b_k \cdots \oplus b_k = b_k$ hence there will be secret leakage.

In step 7, aiming to make all the shadow images be equal to each other, the generated n bits are randomly rearranged to corresponding n shadow images bits.

3.2   Extension

The proposed scheme can be extended to share grayscale/color images [6,7,10] To share a grayscale image, halftone technologies such as error diffusion [11] are

Algorithm 1. The proposed scheme
Input: A $M \times N$ binary secret image S , the threshold parameters (k, n)
Output: n shadow images $SC_1, SC_2, \cdots SC_n$
Step 1: For each position $(i, j) \in \{(i, j)\|1 \leq i \leq M, 1 \leq j \leq N\}$, repeat Steps 2-7
Step 2: Select $b_1, b_2, \cdots b_k \in \{0, 1\}$ randomly, repeat Steps 37 for $w = 1, 2, \cdots, N_k$,
where $N_k = \lfloor n/k \rfloor$ denotes the repeated times, $b_i(i = 1, 2, \cdots n)$ is the temporary variable
Step 3: If $S(i, j) \neq b_{(w-1)k+1} \oplus b_{(w-1)k+2} \cdots \oplus b_{(w-1)k+k}$, randomly select $p \in \{(w-1)k+1, (w-1)k+2, \cdots, (w-1)k+k\}$ flip $b_p = \overline{b_p}$ (that is $0 \rightarrow 1$ or $1 \rightarrow 0$).
Step 4: Set $b_{wk+1} = b_{wk}, b_{wk+2} = b_{wk}, \cdots b_{(w+1)k-2} = b_{wk}$.
Step 5: If k is odd and $N_k \geq 2$, set $b_{(w+1)k-1}, b_{(w+1)k} \in \{0, 1\}$ randomly; else $b_{(w+1)k-1} = b_{(w+1)k} = b_{wk}$
Step 6: Set $b_{N_k \times k+1} = b_{N_k \times k+2} = \cdots b_n = b_{N_k \times k}$
Step 7: Randomly rearrange $b_1, b_2, \cdots b_n$ to $SC_1(i, j), SC_2(i, j), \cdots SC_n(i, j)$
Step 8: Output the n shadow images $SC_1, SC_2, \cdots SC_n$

applied to convert the grayscale image into binary image, and then the proposed scheme could be used.

For sharing a color image, color decomposition, halftone technologies and color composition are applied. A color image can be described by color model. Here, CMY (cyan–magenta–yellow) model will be applied, which is subtractive color model, and displays a color by reflecting light from a surface of an object. Based on the color model, a color image can be processed by three grayscale images(R, G, B) with the same extension methods for sharing grayscale images.

4   Experimental Results and Analyses

In this section, we conduct experiments and analyses to evaluate the effectiveness of the proposed scheme. In the experiments, several secret images are used: original binary secret image1 as shown in Fig. 4 (a), original binary secret image2 as shown in Fig. 5 (a), and original color secret image3 as shown in Fig. 6 (a) are used as the binary secret images, with size of 512×512, to test the efficiency of the proposed scheme.

4.1   Image Illustration

In our experiments, (2, 5) (i.e. $k = 2$, $n = 5$) threshold with secret image1, (3, 4) threshold with secret image2, (2, 3) threshold with color secret image3 are used to do the test of the proposed scheme.

Figure 4 (b-f) show the 5 shadow images SC_1, SC_2, SC_3, SC_4 and SC_5, which are random noise-like. Figure 4 (g-j) show the reconstructed binary secret image with any $t(2 \leq t \leq 5)$ (taking the first t shadow images as an example) with stacking (OR) recovery, from which better visual of the reconstructed secret will be gained by stacking more shadow images.

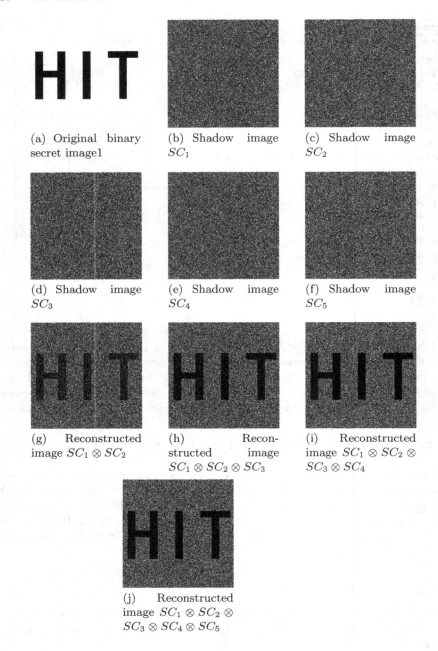

(a) Original binary secret image1

(b) Shadow image SC_1

(c) Shadow image SC_2

(d) Shadow image SC_3

(e) Shadow image SC_4

(f) Shadow image SC_5

(g) Reconstructed image $SC_1 \otimes SC_2$

(h) Reconstructed image $SC_1 \otimes SC_2 \otimes SC_3$

(i) Reconstructed image $SC_1 \otimes SC_2 \otimes SC_3 \otimes SC_4$

(j) Reconstructed image $SC_1 \otimes SC_2 \otimes SC_3 \otimes SC_4 \otimes SC_5$

Fig. 4. Experimental example of the proposed (2, 5) scheme for binary secret image1

Figure 5 (b-e) show the 4 shadow images SC_1, SC_2, SC_3 and SC_4, which are random noise-like. Figure 5 (f-g) show the reconstructed secret image with

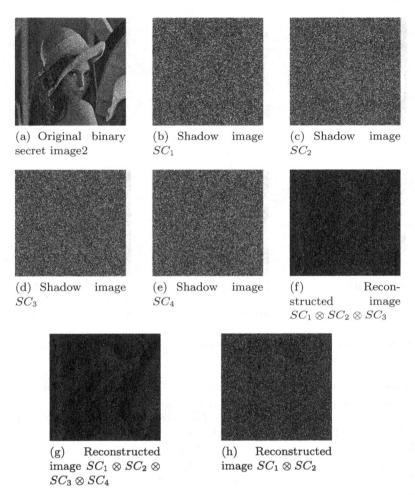

(a) Original binary secret image2

(b) Shadow image SC_1

(c) Shadow image SC_2

(d) Shadow image SC_3

(e) Shadow image SC_4

(f) Reconstructed image $SC_1 \otimes SC_2 \otimes SC_3$

(g) Reconstructed image $SC_1 \otimes SC_2 \otimes SC_3 \otimes SC_4$

(h) Reconstructed image $SC_1 \otimes SC_2$

Fig. 5. Experimental example of the proposed (3, 4) scheme for binary secret image2

any 3(taking 1, 2, 3 as an example) or 4 shadow images with OR recovery, from which the secret image reconstructed from $t = k = 3$ shadow images could be recognized based on OR. Figure 5 (h) shows the reconstructed secret image with any less than k shadow images based on OR recovery, from which there is no information could be recognized.

Figure 6 (b-d) show the 3 shadow images $HCSC_1$, $HCSC_2$ and $HCSC_3$ for color secret image 3, which are random noise-like. Figure 6 (e-f) show the reconstructed secret image with any 2 (taking 1,2 as an example) or 3 shadow images with OR recovery, from which, the reconstructed secret image could be recognized and the progressive visual quality will be gained.

Based on the obtained results we can conclude that:

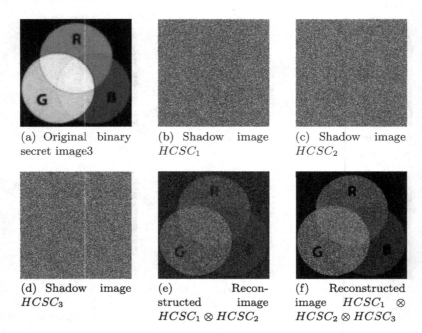

(a) Original binary secret image3

(b) Shadow image $HCSC_1$

(c) Shadow image $HCSC_2$

(d) Shadow image $HCSC_3$

(e) Reconstructed image $HCSC_1 \otimes HCSC_2$

(f) Reconstructed image $HCSC_1 \otimes HCSC_2 \otimes HCSC_3$

Fig. 6. Experimental example of the proposed (2, 3) scheme for color secret image3

- The shadow images are random noise-like, hence the proposed scheme has no cross interference of secret image in the shadow images.
- The progressive visual quality of the reconstructed secret can be gained for the proposed scheme when t is less than 6.
- When $t < k$ shadow images are collected, there is no information of the secret image could be recognized, which shows the security of the proposed scheme.
- When $t(k \leq t \leq n)$ shadow images are reconstructed by stacking, the secret image could be recognized.
- The proposed scheme can also be applied for grayscale and color images.

4.2   Comparisons with Related Schemes

In the section, we compare the proposed scheme with other related schemes especially Chen and Tsao's scheme [6] Wu and Sun's scheme [7], and Guo *et al.*'s scheme [8], since the proposed scheme is a continuous and extension work of the schemes [6–8]. In addition, schemes in [6–8] have good features in VSS, such as no codebook design, no pixel expansion and so on.

Image Illustration Comparison. (2, 5) threshold with $k \leq t \leq n$ is applied as an example shown in Fig. 7. We can see that Wu and Sun's scheme and Guo *et al.*'s scheme both improve the visual quality of Chen and Tsao's scheme.

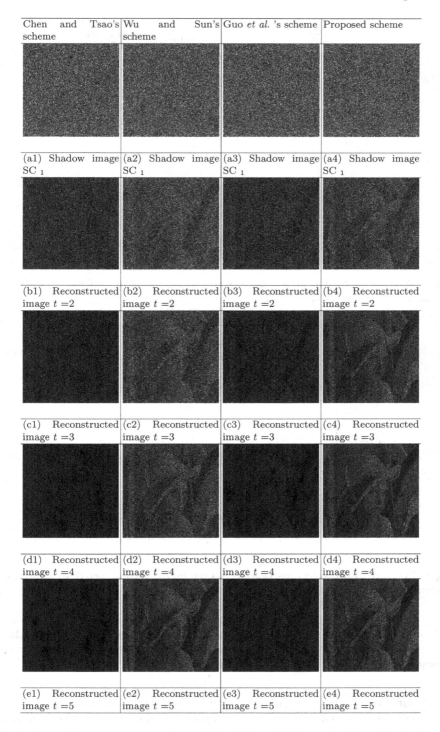

Fig. 7. Image illustration comparison of (2, 5) threshold between the related schemes

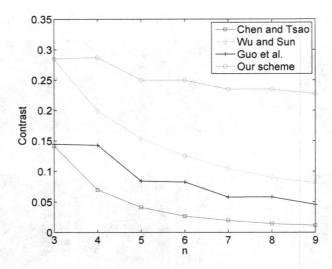

Fig. 8. Average contrast comparisons of secret image reconstructed by $t = 2$ shadow images, with different n when $k = 2$

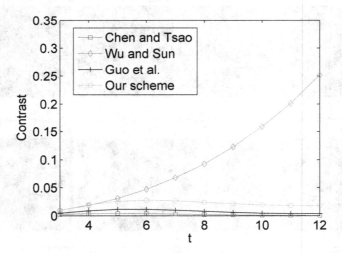

Fig. 9. Average contrast comparisons of secret image reconstructed by different t shadow images when $k = 3$, $n = 12$

The proposed scheme has the best visual quality in comparison with the three schemes. Guo *et al.*'s scheme and Chen and Tsao's scheme are darker, while the darkness of the proposed scheme is acceptable.

Contrast Comparison. Figures 8, 9 and 10 show the contrast comparisons of reconstructed secret images between the proposed scheme and related schemes.

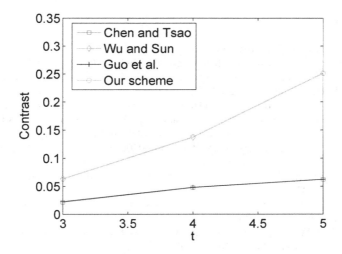

Fig. 10. Average contrast comparisons of secret image reconstructed by different t shadow images when $k =3$, $n =5$

In Fig. 8, secret images are reconstructed by $t = 2$ shadow images, with different n when $k =2$. We can see the proposed scheme gains the advantages of both Guo *et al.*'s scheme and Wu and Sun's scheme, i.e., the contrast improves significantly and decreases slowly. In addition, when k is even, the proposed scheme has better visual quality than the related schemes.

The visual quality relationship between the proposed scheme and related schemes are further shown in Figs. 9 and 10, which indicate that the proposed scheme is similar as Guo *et al.*'s scheme and smaller than Wu and Sun's scheme when k is odd and $N_k \geq 2$, while similar as Wu and Sun's scheme and higher than Guo *et al.*'s scheme when k is odd and $N_k = 1$.

5   Conclusion

This paper proposed a new RG-based VSS with improved visual quality, which combines the advantages of the recently proposed schemes. The main idea of redesign is utilizing the random bits to increase the correct decryption probability of secret pixels under security condition. In such a way, we obtain the better visual quality of reconstructed secrets. The crucial successful points in the proposed scheme lie in: (1) (k,n) threshold, (2) no complex codebook design, (3) avoiding the pixel expansion, (5) higher contrast values than the previous related schemes proposed very recently. The new scheme can be broadly used in several VSS applications.

Acknowledgement. The authors would like to thank the anonymous reviewers for their valuable discussions and comments.

References

1. Naor, M., Shamir, A.: Visual cryptography. In: De Santis, A. (ed.) EUROCRYPT 1994. LNCS, vol. 950, pp. 1–12. Springer, Heidelberg (1995)
2. Yang, C.N.: New visual secret sharing schemes using probabilistic method. Pattern Recogn. Lett. **25**, 481–494 (2004)
3. Yan, X., Wang, S., Niu, X.: Threshold construction from specific cases in visual cryptography without the pixel expansion. Sig. Process. **105**, 389–398 (2014)
4. Weir, J., Yan, W.: A comprehensive study of visual cryptography. In: Shi, Y.Q. (ed.) Transactions on DHMS V. LNCS, vol. 6010, pp. 70–105. Springer, Heidelberg (2010)
5. Kafri, O., Keren, E.: Encryption of pictures and shapes by random grids. Opt. Lett. **12**, 377–379 (1987)
6. Chen, T.H., Tsao, K.H.: Threshold visual secret sharing by random grids. J. Syst. Softw. **84**, 1197–1208 (2011)
7. Wu, X., Sun, W.: Improving the visual quality of random grid-based visual secret sharing. Sig. Process. **93**, 977–995 (2013)
8. Guo, T., Liu, F., Wu, C.: Threshold visual secret sharing by random grids with improved contrast. J. Syst. Softw. **86**, 2094–2109 (2013)
9. Shyu, S.J.: Image encryption by random grids. Pattern Recogn. **40**, 1014–1031 (2007)
10. Hou, Y.C.: Visual cryptography for color images. Pattern Recogn. **36**, 1619–1629 (2003)
11. Wang, Z., Arce, G.R., Di Crescenzo, G.: Halftone visual cryptography via error diffusion. IEEE Trans. Inf. Forensics Secur. **4**, 383–396 (2009)

Optimal XOR Based (2,n)-Visual Cryptography Schemes

Feng Liu [✉] and ChuanKun Wu

State Key Laboratory Of Information Security,
Institute of Information Engineering Chinese Academy of Sciences,
Beijing 100093, China
fengliu.cas@gmail.com

Abstract. A $(2,n)$ Visual Cryptography Scheme (VCS) is a kind of secret sharing scheme, where n participants share a secret image, and any two of them can recover the secret image visually without any cryptographic knowledge and computation devices, but any one of them cannot get any information about the secret image other than the size of the secret image. This paper studies the $(2,n) - VCS_{XOR}$, and shows the smallest (optimal) pixel expansion of such scheme, and the largest possible contrast for the $(2,n) - VCS_{XOR}$ given their optimal pixel expansion. It also shows the largest (optimal) contrast of the $(2,n) - VCS_{XOR}$, and the smallest possible pixel expansion of such schemes given their optimal contrast. The results of this paper show that the $(2,n) - VCS_{XOR}$ can achieve smaller pixel expansion and larger contrast than that of $(2,n) - VCS_{OR}$. It also shows that the construction of the basis matrix of optimal contrast $(2,n) - VCS_{XOR}$ is equivalent to the construction of binary codes when they reach the maximum capability, and the construction of a specific class of optimal contrast $(2,n) - VCS_{XOR}$ for $n = 2^k - 1$ is given.

Keywords: Secret sharing · Visual cryptography scheme · Coding theory

1 Introduction

The basic principle of Visual Cryptography Scheme (VCS) was first introduced by Naor and Shamir. The idea of the visual cryptography model proposed in [26] is to split an image into two random shares (printed on transparencies) which separately reveal no information about the original secret image other than the size of the secret image. The image is composed of black and white pixels. The original image can be reconstructed visually by superimposing the two shares. The underlying operation of such scheme is OR. Similar model of visual cryptography with different underlying operation has been proposed. Such as the

---

A full version of the paper can be found in the "Cryptology ePrint Archive" http://eprint.iacr.org/2010/545.

© Springer International Publishing Switzerland 2015
Y.-Q. Shi et al. (Eds.): IWDW 2014, LNCS 9023, pp. 333–349, 2015.
DOI: 10.1007/978-3-319-19321-2_25

XOR operation studied in [3,19,21,33,34], examples of the visual cryptography system under the XOR operation can be found in [19,20,35,39,42]. Besides, the XOR based VCS can be applied on some state of the art displays, such as multi-layer display [27]. In this paper, we denote VCS_{XOR} and VCS_{OR} as VCS under XOR and OR operations respectively. A simple 2 out of 2 VCS_{XOR} is shown in Fig. 1: denote $\oplus$ as the XOR operation, we have $(d) = (b) \oplus (c)$ in Fig. 1.

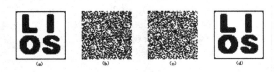

Fig. 1. A 2 out of 2 VCS_{XOR} where (a) is the original image, (b) and (c) are the shares, (d) is the recovered image from (b) and (c).

VCS seems quite primitive, however some of its properties make VCS quite useful. From a practical viewpoint, first, complex encryption techniques may not convince the users for better security, instead the users may feel more worries about those complex techniques they do not understand. For many users, seeing is believing. Second, traditional cryptography highly relies on complex computations, the attackers can not recover the plaintexts in a reasonable time without knowing the key. Hence, for the traditional cryptography, computation devices are necessary for decrypting ciphertexts. However, the computation devices are usually vulnerable to trojan horses and virus. Another possibility of leaking secrets comes from users' incorrect operations. To avoid this, it is usually required that the users know some professional cryptographic knowledge, which is not realistic for ordinary people in many circumstances. As we have already mentioned, VCS outputs a secret image on decrypting, and the users can see the decrypted image directly. Furthermore, the decryption of VCS does not rely on any computation devices and does not require the users to know any cryptographic knowledge. From the above viewpoint, VCS shows some advantages against the traditional cryptography. Many applications of VCS have been proposed by now [14,17,22,25,28,32,41]. Besides, recently, many copyright protection schemes which take Visual Cryptography Schemes (VCS) as building blocks are proposed, for example [5,6,15,23,38,44]. Although some of these copyright protection schemes take the OR based VCS as building blocks, it is clear that, if we change the OR based VCS to the XOR based ones, then the copyright schemes are still valid and can be significantly simplified.

VCS's are mainly characterized by two parameters: the pixel expansion, which is the number of sub-pixels each pixel of the original secret image is encoded into, and the contrast, which measures the clearness of the recovered image. To improve the quality of the recovered image, many schemes have been proposed in [2,9,13,26], but the drawbacks of those schemes are the large value of pixel expansion and that the participants have to take many shares with them. Recent studies show that VCS_{XOR} often has advantages on pixel expansion and contrast properties compared with VCS_{OR}, see examples in [21,34]. In this paper, we focus on optimization of pixel expansion and contrast for VCS_{XOR}.

So far three ways have been found to realize the XOR based visual cryptography scheme. The first was proposed in [19], which realized the XOR operation by using a Mach-Zehnder Interferometer. The second was proposed in [3,33,34], which realized the XOR operation by making use of the polarization property of light where two liquid crystal displays are needed. And the third method, proposed in [36], needs a copy machine with the reversing function. By investigating the above three ways of realizing XOR based VCS, it is easy to find, that the decoding method of these three ways becomes more complicated when decode more shares. Particularly, the first and the second methods need k Mach-Zehnder Interferometers or liquid crystal displays to decode the secret image for the $(k, n) - VCS_{XOR}$, and will inevitably make the cryptography system complicated and cause many difficulties, such as aligning the pixels and signal attenuation. For the third method, it will need many reversing copies to decode the secret image, see examples in [7,36]. In other words, the XOR based VCS is most practical for the $(2, n)$ case. In this paper, we only consider the $(2, n) - VCS_{XOR}$.

Many studies in the literature also focused on $(2, n) - VCS$. Blundo et al. [2,4] studies the contrast and pixel expansion bounds for the $(2, n) - VCS$ only under the OR operation. Santis [30] considers the contrast and pixel expansion bounds for $(2, n) - VCS$ under the combination function f, however, their pixel expansion bound $n < \binom{m}{\lfloor m/2 \rfloor}$ can be improved, and they do not give any explicit constructions for the $(2, n) - VCS$ with regard to the optimal pixel expansion and the optimal contrast. Biham [3] gives a simple construction of the $(2, n) - VCS_{XOR}$ and Tuyls et al. [33,34] presents an simple equivalence relationship between the construction of the $(2, n) - VCS_{XOR}$ and the binary code. However neither of them has given deep discussions on how to construct optimal $(2, n) - VCS_{XOR}$ with regard to the pixel expansion or contrast.

The construction of schemes with both optimal contrast and optimal pixel expansion seems impossible. So, in this paper we construct VCS with optimal pixel expansion and optimal contrast respectively. Without confusion, we sometimes refer the largest contrast as the optimal contrast, and smallest pixel expansion as the optimal pixel expansion. Compared to the studies in the literature, the contribution of this paper can be reflected from the following three aspects:

- We construct the $(2, n) - VCS_{XOR}$ with the optimal pixel expansion $\lceil \log_2 n \rceil$. We also study the contrast property of such schemes, and prove that, the largest possible contrast of the optimal pixel expansion $(2, n) - VCS_{XOR}$ is $\frac{1}{\lceil \log_2 n \rceil}$, and the largest average contrast of such a scheme is $\frac{2\lfloor n/2 \rfloor \lceil n/2 \rceil}{n(n-1)}$.
- We prove that the optimal contrast of $(2, n) - VCS_{XOR}$ is $\frac{2\lfloor n/2 \rfloor \lceil n/2 \rceil}{n(n-1)}$, which is twice better than the optimal contrast for the OR based VCS, and we give explicit constructions for $(2, n) - VCS_{XOR}$ with the optimal contrast. Furthermore we study the pixel expansion property of such $(2, n) - VCS_{XOR}$ and show the smallest possible pixel expansion of the optimal contrast scheme that can be

achieved and show how to construct such schemes. The pixel expansion bound of our scheme is proved to be optimal while the bound in [30] is not optimal.

- We further study the relationship between the $(2, n) - VCS_{XOR}$ and the binary code, in particular, when the scheme has optimal contrast. We find, that for odd n, the rows of the basis matrix of the optimal contrast $(2, n+1) - VCS_{XOR}$ are equivalent to the $(m, \frac{n+1}{2n}m)$ binary code which reaches its maximum capacity, and the rows of the basis matrix of the optimal contrast $(2, n) - VCS_{XOR}$ are equivalent to the $(m, \frac{(n+1)m}{2n}, \frac{(n\pm1)m}{2n})$ constant weight code which reaches its maximum capacity, hence we can use the known construction of maximum capacity binary codes to construct the optimal contrast $(2, n) - VCS_{XOR}$. In addition, we also give a construction of optimal contrast $(2, n) - VCS_{XOR}$ for $n = 2^k - 1$, by using the technique of m-sequences.

The rest of this paper is organized as follows: Sect. 2 gives some definitions of VCS, and in Sect. 3, we study the schemes with smallest (optimal) pixel expansion, in Sect. 4, we study the schemes with largest (optimal) contrast, in Sect. 5, we study the relationship between the construction of optimal contrast VCS and that of binary codes with maximum capacity. The paper is then concluded in Sect. 6.

2   Preliminaries

In this section, we will give some definitions about visual cryptography under the operation •, which can be the OR operation as discussed in [26] or the XOR operation as discussed in [3, 19, 33, 34]. We will restrict ourselves to images only consisting of black and white pixels and encode pixels one at a time, where we denote by 1 for a black pixel and 0 for a white pixel. In order to share a complete image, the scheme has to be applied to all the pixels in the image.

The $(2, n) - VCS_{XOR}$ is a special case of the $(k, n) - VCS_{XOR}$. By a $(k, n) - VCS_{XOR}$ we mean a scheme in which a secret pixel (black or white) is divided into n shares which are distributed to the n users (participants). Any subgroup of k out of these n users, can reconstruct the secret but any subgroup consisting of less than k users does not have any information other than the size about the secret image.

For a vector $v \in GF^m(2)$, we denote by $w(v)$ the number of 1's in the vector v (i.e. $w(v)$ is the Hamming weight of the vector v). A (k, n)-VCS, denoted by (C_0, C_1), consists of two collections of $n \times m$ binary share matrices C_0 and C_1. To share a white (resp. black) pixel, a dealer (the one who sets up the system) randomly chooses one of the matrices in C_0 (resp. C_1) and distributes its rows (shares) to the n participants of the scheme. For convenience, we call a column (resp. row) of a boolean matrix with an even number of 1's *even column (resp. row)* and otherwise *odd column (resp. row)*.

More precisely, we give a formal definition of (k, n)-VCS as follows.

Definition 1 *([12, 34]). Let k, n, m, l and h be nonnegative integers satisfying $2 \leq k \leq n$ and $0 \leq l < h \leq m$. The two collections of $n \times m$ share matrices (C_0, C_1) constitute a threshold Visual Cryptography scheme $(k, n) - VCS$ if the following conditions are satisfied:*

1. *(Contrast)* *For any* $s \in C_0$, *the* "$\bullet$" *operation of any* k *out of* n *rows of* s *satisfies* $w(v) \leq l$.
2. *(Contrast)* *For any* $s \in C_1$, *the* "$\bullet$" *operation of any* k *out of* n *rows of* s *satisfies* $w(v) \geq h$.
3. *(Security)* *For any* $i_1 < i_2 < \cdots < i_t$ *in* $\{1, 2, \cdots, n\}$ *with* $t < k$, *the two collections of* $t \times m$ *matrices* D_j *for* $j \in \{0, 1\}$, *obtained by restricting each* $n \times m$ *matrix in* C_j *to rows* $i_1, i_2, \cdots i_t$, *they are indistinguishable in the sense that they contain the same matrices with the same frequencies.*

In the above definition,

1. v is the result vector of the operation "$\bullet$" operation of the restricted k out of the n rows.
2. h and l are the thresholds of the scheme, h is called *darkness level* and l is called the *whiteness level*.
3. m is called the pixel expansion of the scheme.
4. Define $\alpha = \frac{h-l}{m}$ as the contrast of *VCS*. For underlying operations *OR* and *XOR* we use the notations α_{OR} and α_{XOR} respectively, if necessary.

We notice that the definitions of VCS under *OR* and *XOR* operation are quite similar. Actually when we do the summation of vectors we mean *OR* and *XOR* operation on them respectively, unless we point out explicitly.

The definition of the *average contrast* was already given in [3, 16, 18]. Here we adopt the same definition, i.e. $\bar{\alpha} = \frac{\bar{h}-\bar{l}}{m}$, where $\bar{h}$ is the average value of darkness level in collection C_1 and $\bar{l}$ is the average value of the whiteness level in collection C_0. For the $(2, n) - VCS$, we can calculate the average contrast as follows: Formally, denote r_i, r_j as two rows of an $n \times m$ binary matrix M in C_1 (resp. C_0), and $\bar{h}_M$ (resp. $\bar{l}_M$) be the average value of darkness level (resp. whiteness level) of M, defined as: $\bar{h}_M = \frac{\sum_{1 \leq i < j \leq n} w(r_i \oplus r_j)}{\binom{n}{2}}$ and $\bar{h} = \frac{\sum_{M \in C_1} \bar{h}_M}{|C_1|}$ (resp, $\bar{l}_M = \frac{\sum_{1 \leq i < j \leq n} w(r_i \oplus r_j)}{\binom{n}{2}}$ and $\bar{l} = \frac{\sum_{M \in C_0} \bar{l}_M}{|C_0|}$). Note that, the difference between $\bar{h}_M$ and $\bar{l}_M$ is that, they are computed from the different collections C_1 or C_0 respectively. At this time, we can calculate the average contrast by using the formula $\bar{\alpha} = \frac{\bar{h}-\bar{l}}{m}$.

The average contrast is used to evaluate the clearness of the recovered secret image in an overall viewpoint. But it has the disadvantage in reflecting the clearness of the details in the recovered secret image. i.e. the average contrast is suitable as a criterion of the clearness for the secret images drawn with fairly thick lines (see discussions in [40]). The average contrast is important for the VCS's, especially when their share matrices have different values of $w(r_i \oplus r_j)$ where $1 \leq i < j \leq n$. For such share matrices, the traditional definition of contrast only reflect the smallest (resp. largest) value of the $w(r_i \oplus r_j)$ in the collections C_1 (resp. C_0), while the average contrast reflect the values of $w(r_i \oplus r_j)$ from an overall viewpoint.

Note that $m \geq 1$ and $0 < \alpha, \bar{\alpha} \leq 1$. In general, we are interested in schemes with m being as small as possible and with the contrast α and the average contrast $\bar{\alpha}$ being as large as possible.

As stated in Definition 1, the first two conditions ensure that the participants will be able to distinguish the black and white pixels, and the third condition ensures the security of the scheme.

To simplify the discussion, all of our constructions in this paper will be based on basis matrix as defined in Definition 2. And since we only consider the $(2, n) - VCS_{XOR}$ in this paper, the following definition of basis matrix is only for $(2, n) - VCS_{XOR}$, and hence has a few differences from the general one of Definition 1. One will find that the Definition 2 will simplifies the discussions significantly on analyzing and constructing optimal $(2, n) - VCS_{XOR}$.

Definition 2 (Basis matrix of $(2, n) - VCS_{XOR}$). *Let n, m and h be positive integers satisfying $0 < h \leq m$. An $n \times m$ binary matrix M is called a basis matrix for a $(2, n) - VCS_{XOR}$, if it satisfies the following contrast condition: the weight of the XOR (denoted by $\oplus$) of any 2 out of n rows in M satisfies: $w(j_{i_1} \oplus j_{i_2}) \geq h$, where j_i $(i = 1, \cdots, n)$ is a row of M and $h \geq 1$.*

By using the basis matrix M presented in Definition 2, one can realize an $(2, n) - VCS_{XOR}$ construction under the Definition 1 as follows: Define $M(i)$ be the $n \times m$ matrix obtained by a cyclic shift on the rows of M over i positions, denote by C_1 the collection $C_1 = \{M(0), M(1), \cdots, M(n - 1)\}$. Define $A(\mathbf{r})$ be the $n \times m$ matrix for which each row equals $\mathbf{r}$, and denote by C_0 the collection $C_0 = \{A(j_1), A(j_2), \cdots, A(j_n)\}$, where $j_1, j_2, \cdots, j_n$ are the n rows of M.

Note that in the above definition, the value of the whiteness level $l = 0$, and the contrast $\alpha_{XOR} = h/m$. This approach of the construction of $(2, n) - VCS_{XOR}$ will have small memory requirements (it keeps only a basis matrix) and it is efficient (to choose a matrix in C_1 or C_0) as it only needs to cyclicly shift the rows of the basis matrix, or choose a row from M and generate $A(\mathbf{r})$).

We note that some kinds of sub-matrices always exist in the basis matrix of VCS_{XOR}. For example, the sub-matrices $\begin{bmatrix} 0 \\ 1 \end{bmatrix}$ or $\begin{bmatrix} 1 \\ 0 \end{bmatrix}$ (i.e. the sub-matrix which consists of a 1 and a 0) always exist in any basis matrix of the $(2, n) - VCS_{XOR}$ since they cause of the contrast of the VCS_{XOR}, because the $\oplus$ of the two rows of them is 1, recall that the other patterns $\begin{bmatrix} 0 \\ 0 \end{bmatrix}$ and $\begin{bmatrix} 1 \\ 1 \end{bmatrix}$. do not contribute to the value of $w(v)$ in the Definition 1. In this paper, these kinds of sub-matrices are called *unavoidable patterns*. Note that, the definition of the unavoidable pattern under the XOR operation is different to the definition in [2,4], where the two patterns $\begin{bmatrix} 0 \\ 1 \end{bmatrix}$ and $\begin{bmatrix} 1 \\ 0 \end{bmatrix}$ are called unavoidable patterns respectively, but, here and hereafter, we call the two patterns together as the unavoidable patterns under the XOR operation. i.e. the basis matrix of the Definition 2 contains at least one of the two patterns.

Furthermore, it is easy to verify that any share matrix in the collection C_1 of Definition 1 for a $(2, n) - VCS_{XOR}$ can be a basis matrix of Definition 2 (i.e. given any collections (C_0, C_1) of a $(2, n) - VCS_{XOR}$ of Definition 1, we can construct a basis matrix $(2, n) - VCS_{XOR}$ under the Definition 2, which have the same pixel expansion and an equal or larger contrast), which implies there does not exist a

$(2, n) - VCS_{XOR}$ under Definition 1 that has smaller pixel expansion or larger contrast. And because we study the optimal schemes (smallest pixel expansion and largest contrast) of $(2, n) - VCS_{XOR}$, so in this paper, we can study the $(2, n) - VCS_{XOR}$ only based on the basis matrix defined in the Definition 2.

3 $(2, n) - VCS_{XOR}$ with Optimal Pixel Expansion

In this section, we give the optimal pixel expansion of $(2, n) - VCS_{XOR}$, and show the largest possible contrast and average contrast of the optimal pixel expansion $(2, n) - VCS_{XOR}$. And give a concrete construction of $(2, n) - VCS_{XOR}$ that has largest possible contrast and average contrast given the optimal pixel expansion. It can be easily verified that the bounds here are far better than the one in [30], and the constructions are better than the ones in [34] with regard to the pixel expansion.

First, the following Theorem 1 shows the optimal pixel expansion of $(2, n) - VCS_{XOR}$. Here and hereafter, we denote $\lceil x \rceil$ as the smallest integer larger than or equal to x, and denote m^* as the optimal pixel expansion of $(2, n) - VCS_{XOR}$.

Theorem 1. *The optimal pixel expansion of $(2, n) - VCS_{XOR}$ is $m^* = \lceil \log_2 n \rceil$.*

Given a $(2, n) - VCS_{XOR}$ with optimal pixel expansion, its largest possible contrast should be no larger than the optimal contrast of $(2, n) - VCS_{XOR}$ without the optimal pixel expansion constraint. The following Theorem 2 shows the largest possible contrast of the optimal pixel expansion $(2, n) - VCS_{XOR}$.

Theorem 2. *The largest possible contrast of the $(2, n) - VCS_{XOR}$ given the optimal pixel expansion is $\alpha_{XOR} = \frac{1}{\lceil \log_2 n \rceil}$.*

The largest possible contrast of a $(2, n) - VCS_{XOR}$ is affected by its pixel expansion constraint. However the average contrast is not. We show below that even a $(2, n) - VCS_{XOR}$ has optimal pixel expansion, its average contrast can reach its maximum value.

Theorem 3. *There exists a $(2, n) - VCS_{XOR}$ with the optimal pixel expansion $m^* = \lceil \log_2 n \rceil$ and the largest average contrast $\bar{\alpha}_{XOR} = \frac{2 \lfloor n/2 \rfloor \lceil n/2 \rceil}{n(n-1)}$, and it is achieved if and only if all the rows of the basis matrix are different vectors and all the columns of the basis matrix have Hamming weight $\lfloor n/2 \rfloor$ or $\lceil n/2 \rceil$.*

At this point, we give a concrete construction of $(2, n) - VCS_{XOR}$ that has largest possible contrast and average contrast given the optimal pixel expansion.

Construction 1. *Let M' be the $2^{\lceil \log_2 n \rceil} \times \lceil \log_2 n \rceil$ matrix that its rows contain all the vectors of length $\lceil \log_2 n \rceil$. Denote a row vector of M' as $r = (l_1, l_2, \cdots, l_{\lceil \log_2 n \rceil})$ where $l_1, l_2, \cdots, l_{\lceil \log_2 n \rceil} \in \{0, 1\}$, and denote its complementary row vector as $\bar{r} = (1 - l_1, 1 - l_2, \cdots, 1 - l_{\lceil \log_2 n \rceil})$. r and $\bar{r}$ are called a complementary row vector pair. For an even n, choose $(2^{\lceil \log_2 n \rceil} - n)/2$ complementary row vector pairs* *randomly, and for an odd n, choose $(2^{\lceil \log_2 n \rceil} - (n+1))/2$ complementary row vector pairs and another row vector randomly. Remove these rows from M', then the resulting $n \times \lceil \log_2 n \rceil$ matrix, denoted by M, is a basis matrix of $(2, n) - VCS_{XOR}$ with optimal pixel expansion $m^* = \lceil \log_2 n \rceil$, contrast $\alpha_{XOR} = \frac{1}{\lceil \log_2 n \rceil}$ and largest average contrast $\bar{\alpha}_{XOR} = \frac{2 \lfloor n/2 \rfloor \lceil n/2 \rceil}{n(n-1)}$.*

4 $(2, n) - VCS_{XOR}$ with Optimal Contrast

In this section, we will discuss the $(2, n) - VCS_{XOR}$ with the optimal contrast (not average contrast any more). We will first construct $(2, n) - VCS_{XOR}$ with optimal contrast $\alpha^*_{XOR} = \frac{2 \lfloor n/2 \rfloor \lceil n/2 \rceil}{n(n-1)}$, which is twice of that of $(2, n) - VCS_{OR}$. And then we show the smallest possible pixel expansion of the $(2, n) - VCS_{XOR}$ given the optimal contrast, we will give explicit constructions for such schemes. The result of Theorem 7 shows the smallest possible pixel expansion of the optimal contrast $(2, n) - VCS_{XOR}$ is smaller than that of $(2, n) - VCS_{OR}$ in some cases.

4.1   Optimal Contrast of $(2, n) - VCS_{XOR}$ and Some Structural Properties

The following theorem shows the optimal contrast of the $(2, n) - VCS_{XOR}$.

Theorem 4. *The contrast for a $(2, n) - VCS_{XOR}$ satisfies $\alpha_{XOR} \leq \frac{2 \lfloor n/2 \rfloor \lceil n/2 \rceil}{n(n-1)}$, and equality holds if and only if all the columns have weight $\lfloor n/2 \rfloor$ or $\lceil n/2 \rceil$ and the Hamming weight of the sum of any two rows of the basis matrix is exactly $\frac{2 \lfloor n/2 \rfloor \lceil n/2 \rceil}{n(n-1)} \cdot m$, where m is the pixel expansion of the scheme.*

The optimal contrast for the $(2, n) - VCS_{OR}$ has already been studied in [4]. The following lemma shows the optimal contrast of $(2, n) - VCS_{OR}$ and a structural property of such scheme.

Lemma 1 (Property 2 of Lemma 4.3 in [4]). *For any pair of distinct rows of the basis matrix M of the $(2, n) - VCS_{OR}$ with optimal contrast for the black secret pixel, the unavoidable pattern $\begin{bmatrix} 0 \\ 1 \end{bmatrix}$ (resp. $\begin{bmatrix} 1 \\ 0 \end{bmatrix}$) appears exactly $\alpha^*_{OR} \cdot m$ times, where $\alpha^*_{OR} = \frac{\lfloor n/2 \rfloor \lceil n/2 \rceil}{n(n-1)}$.*

From the Lemma 1, it is clear that the optimal contrasts of $(2, n) - VCS_{XOR}$ and $(2, n) - VCS_{OR}$ satisfy $\alpha^*_{XOR} = 2\alpha^*_{OR}$, the reason is that the unavoidable patterns $\begin{bmatrix} 0 \\ 1 \end{bmatrix}$ and $\begin{bmatrix} 1 \\ 0 \end{bmatrix}$ both cause the contrast in $(2, n) - VCS_{XOR}$, but only one of them causes the contrast in $(2, n) - VCS_{OR}$. Furthermore, we have the following theorem which reveals the relationship between the optimal contrast of $(2, n) - VCS_{XOR}$ and $(2, n) - VCS_{OR}$.

Theorem 5. *The basis matrix of a optimal contrast* $(2, n) - VCS_{OR}$ *for the black secret pixel is also a basis matrix of a optimal contrast* $(2, n) - VCS_{XOR}$. *Hence the smallest pixel expansion for the optimal contrast* $(2, n) - VCS_{XOR}$ *is no larger than that of optimal contrast* $(2, n) - VCS_{OR}$.

We then turn to discuss the lower bounds of the pixel expansion of $(2, n) - VCS_{XOR}$ given the optimal contrast, and such bounds for the $(2, n) - VCS_{OR}$ has been studied in [4] by the following lemma.

Lemma 2 (Theorem 4.9 in [4]). *Denote m as the pixel expansion of* $(2, n) - VCS_{OR}$ *with optimal contrast, then the following equations hold:*

$$m \geq \begin{cases} 2n - 2 & \text{if } n \text{ is even} \\ n & \text{if } n \equiv 3 \bmod 4 \\ 2n & \text{if } n \equiv 1 \bmod 4 \end{cases}$$

the equality holds if the Hadamard Matrix Conjecture is true. (The Hadamard Matrix Conjecture says that Hadamard matrices exist for all orders divisible by four.)

By Theorem 5 and the Lemma 2, and assuming the Hadamard Matrix Conjecture holds, we have the following corollary:

Corollary 1. *Assuming the Hadamard Matrix Conjecture holds, the smallest possible pixel expansion m_c^* of the* $(2, n) - VCS_{XOR}$ *given the optimal contrast are smaller than that of the optimal contrast* $(2, n) - VCS_{OR}$, *i.e.*

$$m_c^* \leq \begin{cases} 2n - 2 & \text{if } n \text{ is even} \\ n & \text{if } n \equiv 3 \bmod 4 \\ 2n & \text{if } n \equiv 1 \bmod 4 \end{cases}$$

Lemma 3 (Structural Properties). *Denote M as the basis matrix of a* $(2, n) - VCS_{XOR}$ *with contrast α_{XOR}.*

1. *Let s be a column vector of M, and $\bar{s}$ be the complementary vector of s. Denote M' as the matrix in which we replace the column s by $\bar{s}$, then M' is also a basis matrix of a* $(2, n) - VCS_{XOR}$ *with contrast α_{XOR}. Hence if there exists a basis matrix of* $(2, n) - VCS_{XOR}$ *with optimal contrast α_{XOR}^*, then there must exist a basis matrix of* $(2, n) - VCS_{XOR}$ *with all the columns have constant weight $\lfloor n/2 \rfloor$ (resp. $\lceil n/2 \rceil$) and optimal contrast α_{XOR}^*.*
2. *Denote $r_1, r_2, \cdots, r_n$ as the row vectors of M, then the matrix M' formed by the row vectors $r_1 + r, r_2 + r, \cdots, r_n + r$, where r is an arbitrary vector of length m, is also a basis matrix of a* $(2, n) - VCS_{XOR}$ *with contrast α_{XOR}. Hence there exist a basis matrix of a* $(2, n) - VCS_{XOR}$ *with one of its rows is the zero vector.*

4.2 Smallest Possible Pixel Expansion of the $(2, n) - VCS_{XOR}$ Given Optimal Contrast and Constructions

When a $(2, n) - VCS_{XOR}$ has the optimal contrast, it may have different pixel expansion properties. In this case, the smallest possible pixel expansion may be larger than in the general case without the optimal contrast constraint. In this section we show the smallest possible pixel expansion of the $(2, n) - VCS_{XOR}$ given its optimal contrast.

First we consider the case when the number of rows of the basis matrix is odd, i.e. the number of participants is odd.

Lemma 4. *For an odd n (≥ 3), if there exist a $(2, n) - VCS_{XOR}$ with optimal contrast α^*_{XOR}, and denote its pixel expansion as m, then we have $n | m$.*

Lemma 5. *For a $(2, n) - VCS_{XOR}$ with $n \equiv 1 \mod 4$ and optimal contrast $\alpha^*_{XOR} = \frac{n+1}{2n}$, the pixel expansion of such scheme satisfies $m \neq n$.*

Lemma 4 implies that $m \geq n$. Together with Lemma 5 we get the smallest pixel expansion for the case $n \equiv 1 \mod 4$ as follows.

Corollary 2. *For $n \equiv 1 \mod 4$, the smallest pixel expansion m^*_c of a $(2, n) - VCS_{XOR}$ given optimal contrast is $2n$.*

Then for an even number of participants, we have

Lemma 6. *Denote by m^*_c the smallest possible pixel expansion for a $(2, n) - VCS_{XOR}$ with odd n given the optimal contrast $\alpha^*_{XOR} = \frac{2\lfloor n/2 \rfloor \lceil n/2 \rceil}{n(n-1)} = \frac{n+1}{2n}$, then the smallest possible pixel expansion for a $(2, n+1) - VCS_{XOR}$ given the optimal contrast $\alpha^*_{XOR} = \frac{2\lfloor (n+1)/2 \rfloor \lceil (n+1)/2 \rceil}{n(n+1)} = \frac{n+1}{2n}$ is at least m^*_c.*

In order to describe the construction of the $(2, n) - VCS$ more clearly, we introduce some basic results of the from the combinatorial mathematics. A (v, k, λ)-BIBD (Balanced Incomplete Block Design [8]) is a pair $(X, \mathcal{B})$, where X is a set of v elements (called points) and $\mathcal{B}$ is a collection of subsets of X (called blocks), such that each block contains exactly k points and each pair of points is a subset of exactly λ blocks. In a (v, k, λ)-BIBD, each point occurs in exactly $r = \lambda(v-1)/(k-1)$ blocks, and the total number of blocks is $b = vr/k = \lambda(v^2 - v)/(k^2 - k)$. The number r is called the *replication number* of the BIBD.

Lemma 7

1. *(Theorem 4.7 of [4]) Assuming that $n \equiv 3 \mod 4$ and there exists a $(2, n) - VCS_{OR}$ with pixel expansion m and contrast $\alpha^*_{OR} = \frac{\lfloor n/2 \rfloor \lceil n/2 \rceil}{n(n-1)}$. Then $m \geq n$ and $m = n$ if and only if there exists a $(n, \frac{n-1}{2}, \frac{n-3}{4})$-BIBD (or, equivalently, a Hadamard matrix of order $n+1$).*
2. *(Theorem 4.8 of [4]) Assuming that $n \equiv 1 \mod 4$ and there exists a $(2, n) - VCS_{OR}$ with pixel expansion m and contrast $\alpha^*_{OR} = \frac{\lfloor n/2 \rfloor \lceil n/2 \rceil}{n(n-1)}$. Then $m \geq 2n$ and $m = 2n$ if and only if there exists a $(n, \frac{n-1}{2}, \frac{n-3}{2})$-BIBD or an $(n + 1, \frac{n+1}{2}, \frac{n-1}{2})$-BIBD.*

The point-block incidence matrix M of the $(X, \mathcal{B})$-BIBD stated above will be the basis matrix of the corresponding $(2, n) - VCS_{OR}$. And the point-block incidence matrix M of the BIBD is defined as follows:

$$m_{xB} = \begin{cases} 1 \ if \ x \in B \\ 0 \ otherwise \end{cases}$$

where x is a point of X and B is a block of $\mathcal{B}$, and m_{xB} is an entry of the matrix M.

By combining the Theorem 5 and the Lemma 7, for an odd n, it is clear that there exist $(2, n) - VCS_{XOR}$ with optimal contrast $\alpha^*_{XOR} = \frac{2\lfloor n/2 \rfloor \lceil n/2 \rceil}{n(n-1)} = \frac{n+1}{2n}$ if the Hadamard Matrix Conjecture holds. And the construction of the $(2, n) - VCS_{XOR}$ can be converted to the construction of the point-block incidence matrix of the corresponding BIBD, more details of such construction can be found in [4].

Second we consider the case when the number of rows of the basis matrix is even, i.e. there are even number of participants. The following lemma is required in our following discussions. (The most important lemma of this paper)

Lemma 8. *Denote M as an $n \times m$ binary matrix which satisfies:*

1. *n is odd*
2. *the minimum Hamming distance of any two rows of M is $\frac{(n+1)m}{2n}$*
3. *each column of M has the same hamming weight $\frac{n-1}{2}$ (or respectively $\frac{n+1}{2}$)*

then the rows of M all have the same hamming weight $\frac{(n-1)m}{2n}$ (or respectively $\frac{(n+1)m}{2n}$)

Theorem 6. *For an odd n, there exists a $(2, n) - VCS_{XOR}$ with the optimal contrast $\alpha^*_{XOR} = \frac{(n+1)}{2n}$ and pixel expansion m if and only if there exists a $(2, n+1) - VCS_{XOR}$ with optimal contrast same as $\alpha^*_{XOR} = \frac{(n+1)}{2n}$ and the same pixel expansion m.*

Note that in the above discussion, it has been assumed that the Hadamard Matrix Conjecture holds. By making the same assumption, we further have:

Theorem 7. *The smallest possible pixel expansion m^*_c of $(2, n) - VCS_{XOR}$ given the optimal contrast $\alpha^*_{XOR} = \frac{2\lfloor n/2 \rfloor \lceil n/2 \rceil}{n(n-1)}$ is as follows:*

$$m^*_c = \begin{cases} 1 & if\ n = 2 \\ n & if\ n \equiv 3\ mod\ 4 \\ n-1 & if\ n \equiv 0\ mod\ 4 \\ 2n & if\ n \equiv 1\ mod\ 4 \\ 2n-2 & if\ n \equiv 2\ mod\ 4\ and\ n \neq 2 \end{cases}$$

The Theorem 7 shows the smallest possible pixel expansion of the scheme given the optimal contrast, which are much smaller than the ones under the OR operation for the cases $n = 2$ and $n \equiv 0\ mod\ 4$. One can find a more clear comparison in Table 1.

At this point, we summarize the constructions of optimal contrast $(2, n) - VCS_{XOR}$ with smallest pixel expansion as follows.

Construction 2. *For $n = 2$ we let the basis matrix $M = \begin{bmatrix} 0 \\ 1 \end{bmatrix}$, it is clear that its contrast is optimal and its pixel expansion is 1.*

We omit the constructions for the cases of $n \equiv 3\ mod\ 4$, $n \equiv 1\ mod\ 4$ and $n \equiv 2\ mod\ 4$ as they are the same as that in [4].

Table 1. Comparison on the smallest pixel expansions of $(2, n) - VCS_{XOR}$ and $(2, n) - VCS_{OR}$ given optimal contrasts.

	OR	XOR
$n = 2$	2	**1**
$n \equiv 3 \bmod 4$	n	n
$n \equiv 0 \bmod 4$	$2n - 2$	**n-1**
$n \equiv 1 \bmod 4$	$2n$	$2n$
$n \equiv 2 \bmod 4$	$2n - 2$	$2n - 2$

For the case $n \equiv 0 \bmod 4$, we first apply Blundo's construction in [4] to generate the basis matrix, denoted by M', of the black secret pixels for the case $n - 1 \equiv 3 \bmod 4$. We have the pixel expansion of M' is $n - 1$. Then we apply properties 1 of Lemma 3 to transform M' into M'' that satisfies all the columns of M'' has constant Hamming weight. We have each row of M'' has constant Hamming weight $(n-2)/2$ or $n/2$. By adding an all 1 row if the Hamming weight of M'' is $(n-2)/2$, or adding an all 0 row if the Hamming weight of M'' is $n/2$. Denote the resulting matrix as M, then M is the basis matrix of $(2, n) - VCS_{XOR}$ with optimal contrast and pixel expansion $n - 1$ for the case $n \equiv 0 \bmod 4$.

5   Relationship with the Constructions of Optimal Contrast $(2, n) - VCS_{XOR}$ and Binary Codes with Maximum Capacity

Tuyls et al. [34] present a simple equivalence relationship between the $(2, n) - VCS_{XOR}$ and the binary code. In this section, we further study the relationship between them, especially when the VCS has optimal contrast. And find that for odd n, the rows of the basis matrix of the optimal contrast $(2, n + 1) - VCS_{XOR}$ is equivalent to the $(m, \frac{n+1}{2n}m)$ binary code which reaches its maximum capacity, and the rows of the basis matrix of the optimal contrast $(2, n) - VCS_{XOR}$ is equivalent to the $(m, \frac{(n+1)m}{2n}, \frac{(n\pm1)m}{2n})$ constant weight code which reaches its maximum capacity, hence we can use the known construction of maximum capacity binary codes to construct the optimal contrast $(2, n) - VCS_{XOR}$. In addition, we give a construction of optimal contrast $(2, n) - VCS_{XOR}$ for $n = 2^k - 1$ is given, by using the technique of m-sequence.

Denote an $n \times m$ binary matrix M as the basis matrix of a $(2, n) - VCS_{XOR}$ with contrast α and the pixel expansion m. According to the first condition of Definition 1, the rows of M comprise an $(m, m\alpha)$ binary code, where m is the length of the codes and $m\alpha$ is the minimum Hamming distance. Hence by constructing an $(m, m\alpha)$ binary code with n codewords (if exists), we can construct a $(2, n) - VCS_{XOR}$ with contrast α and the pixel expansion m.

Denote $A(m, d)$ as the maximum number of codewords in any (linear or nonlinear) binary code of length m and minimum Hamming distance d. and $A(m, d, w)$

as the maximum number of codewords in any binary code of length m, constant weight w and minimum Hamming distance d. The two notations $A(m, d)$ and $A(m, d, w)$ are widely used in coding theory see [1, 24, 29, 31, 37].

In order to make use of some results from coding theory, we hereby interpret some of the previous results in this paper with respect to $A(m, d)$ and $A(m, d, w)$.

First, we talk about the $(2, n) - VCS_{XOR}$ with smallest pixel expansion: The following two equations are from [29],

$$A(m, 1) = 2^m$$

$$A(m, 2) = 2^{m-1}$$

And it is obvious that if $d_1 \leq d_2$, then $A(m, d_1) \geq A(m, d_2)$, simply because the codewords of (m, d_2) can be the codewords of (m, d_1). Therefore, one can find alternative proofs of two of the theorems in Sect. 3 (Theorems 1 and 2) by using the above property. (Interest readers can find explicit proofs in the full paper.)

Second, we discuss the $(2, n) - VCS_{XOR}$ with optimal contrast: We call that a (m, d) binary code reaches its *maximum capacity* if it has $A(m, d)$ codewords, and for binary constant weight code (m, d, w), it reaches its *maximum capacity* if it has $A(m, d, w)$ codewords. The construction of binary code with maximum capacity has been widely studied and one can find some of the constructions in [1, 24, 29, 31, 37]. The following lemmas will be needed in the proof of Theorems 8 and 9 as introduced below:

Lemma 9 *(Plotkin's Bound [24, 37]). Provided certain Hadamard matrices of order n' or less exist, then*
$A(n', 2\delta) = 2\lfloor \frac{2\delta}{4\delta - n'} \rfloor$ *if* $2\delta \leq n' < 4\delta$
$A(4\delta, 2\delta) = 8\delta$
$A(n', 2\delta) = 1$ *if* $n' < 2\delta$

Where here and hereafter $\lfloor x \rfloor$ denotes the largest integer no larger than x.

Lemma 10 *(Johnson's Bound [31]) define $d=2u$, if $n'u > w(n' - w)$ then*
$A(n', d, w) \leq \lfloor \frac{n'u}{n'u - w(n' - w)} \rfloor$

The following theorem shows that, for an odd n, the rows of the basis matrices of the $(2, n + 1) - VCS_{XOR}$ with optimal contrast form a special binary code with maximum capacity.

Theorem 8. *For an odd n, there exists a basis matrix for the $(2, n+1) - VCS_{XOR}$ with optimal contrast $\alpha = \frac{n+1}{2n}$ if and only if there exists a $(m, \alpha m)$ binary code which reaches its maximum capacity, where m is the pixel expansion of the $(2, n + 1) - VCS_{XOR}$.*

At this point, to construct a $(2, n + 1) - VCS_{XOR}$, we only need to construct a $(m, \alpha m)$ binary code which reaches its maximum capacity, and such construction with $m \leq 28$ can be found in [1].

According to Lemma 3, given the $n+1$ rows of the basis matrix of the $(2, n+1)-VCS_{XOR}$, and by adding the first row to all the $n+1$ rows, one get that, the newly generated 2-nd,3-rd,$\cdots$,n-th,$(n+1)$-th rows are all have constant weight $\frac{(n+1)m}{2n}$ and the Hamming distance between them is $\frac{(n+1)m}{2n}$, meanwhile, the complement of the 2-nd,3-rd,$\cdots$,n-th,$(n+1)$-th rows all have constant weight $\frac{(n-1)m}{2n}$ and the Hamming distance between them is $\frac{(n+1)m}{2n}$ too. We give the following theorem to show the relationship between the $(m, \frac{(n+1)m}{2n}, \frac{(n\pm1)m}{2n})$ constant weight code and the rows of the basis matrix of the optimal contrast $(2, n) - VCS_{XOR}$:

Theorem 9. *For odd n, there exist basis matrices for the $(2, n) - VCS_{XOR}$ with optimal contrast $\alpha = \frac{n+1}{2n}$ if and only if there exists a $(m, \frac{(n+1)m}{2n}, \frac{(n\pm1)m}{2n})$ binary constant weight code which reaches its maximum capacity, where m is the pixel expansion of the $(2, n) - VCS_{XOR}$.*

At this point, we get to know that, for an odd n, the construction of a $(2, n) - VCS_{XOR}$ with optimal contrast $\alpha = \frac{n+1}{2n}$ can be converted into the construction of an $(m, \frac{(n+1)m}{2n}, \frac{(n\pm1)m}{2n})$ binary constant weight code which reaches its maximum capacity, and the construction of such binary constant weight codes have been studied in [1, 10, 31].

Particularly, for $n = 2^k - 1$, where k is a positive integer, the construction of $(2, n) - VCS_{XOR}$ and $(2, n + 1) - VCS_{XOR}$ can be realized via m-sequence (maximum length sequence), which is a kind of periodic bit sequences generated using linear feedback shift registers and has maximum length [11]. For any of such n, there exists an m-sequence which has period n and in each period, there are 2^{k-1} 1's. Any cyclic shift of such a sequence is also an m-sequence, and the XOR of an m-sequence and its shift is also an m-sequence (Theorem 15.3.11 in [43]). So let M be the matrix where all its rows are all the possible cyclic shifts of an m-sequence in one period. Then the rows of M form a binary constant weight code which is also linear. Moreover, M is an $n \times n$ matrix with each rows (as well as columns) having 2^{k-1} 1's. By adding the all-zero vector as a new row to the matrix M, it makes a new $(2, n + 1) - VCS_{XOR}$ basis matrix. Hence we have the following theorem:

Theorem 10. *For $n = 2^k - 1$, there exists an m-sequence r which has period n, and the n m-sequences r_i, where $i = 0, 1, \cdots, n - 1$ are generated by cyclic shift i bits of r, form a basis matrix of $(2, n) - VCS_{XOR}$, and this VCS has optimal contrast $\alpha = \frac{n+1}{2n}$, where k is a positive integer.*

6   Conclusions

In this paper, we studied the optimal $(2, n) - VCS_{XOR}$, and have given some new results about the optimal pixel expansion of such schemes and the largest possible contrast for schemes given the optimal pixel expansion. We also studied the optimal contrast of the $(2, n) - VCS_{XOR}$, and the smallest possible pixel expansion of such schemes given the optimal contrast. The results of this paper show the properties of the $(2, n) - VCS_{XOR}$ have some advantages over the $(2, n) - VCS_{OR}$ in the sense of larger contrast and smaller pixel expansion.

It is noted that in the construction of the $(2, n) - VCS_{XOR}$ with the largest contrast and the smallest possible pixel expansion, the Hadamard Matrix Conjecture is assumed to hold. The same assumption was made in [4] as well.

We have shown that, the construction of the basis matrix of optimal contrast $(2, n) - VCS_{XOR}$ is equivalent to the construction of binary codes with specific parameters, which reaches its maximum capacity, hence we can use the known constructions of maximum capacity binary code (constant weight or not constant weight) to construct optimal contrast $(2, n) - VCS_{XOR}$, meanwhile we also give a construction of $(2, n) - VCS_{XOR}$ with optimal contrast for $n = 2^k - 1$, by using the technique of the m-sequence.

Acknowledgements. This work was supported by "Strategic Priority Research Program of the Chinese Academy of Sciences with No.XDA06010701, and the "Youth Innovation Promotion Association Program" of the Chinese Academy of Sciences. We want to thank Dr. Wen Wang for his help on checking this paper. Last but most important, we want to thank an old man in Russia, although we don't know his name until now. He offered a great help on proving the Lemma 8, which is the most difficult part of the paper.

References

1. Sloane, N.J.A., Brouwer, A.E., Shearer, J.B., Warren, D.S.: A new table of constant weight codes. IEEE Trans. Inf. Theory **36**(6), 1334–1380 (1990)
2. Ateniese, G., Blundo, C., De Santis, A., Stinson, D.R.: Visual cryptography for general access structures. Inf. Comput. **129**, 86–106 (1996)
3. Biham, E., Itzkovitz, A.: Visual cryptography with polarization. In: The Dagstuhl Seminar on Cryptography, September 1997, and in the RUMP session of CRYPTO 1998 (1997)
4. Blundo, C., De Santis, A., Stinson, D.R.: On the contrast in visual cryptography schemes. J. Cryptol. **12**(4), 261–289 (1999)
5. Chang, C.C., Chuang, J.C.: An image intellectual property protection scheme for gray-level images using visual secret sharing strategy. Pattern Recogn. Lett. **23**, 931–941 (2002)
6. Chen, T.H., Tsai, D.S.: Owner-customer right protection mechanism using a watermarking scheme and a watermarking protocol. Pattern Recogn. **39**, 1530–1541 (2006)
7. Cimato, S., De Santis, A., Ferrara, A.L., Masucci, B.: Ideal contrast visual cryptography schemes with reversing. Inf. Process. Lett. **93**, 199–206 (2005)
8. Dinitz, J.H., Stinson, D.R.: Chap. 1 in Contemporary Design Theory: A Collection of Surveys. Wiley, New York (1992)
9. Droste, S.: New results on visual cryptography. In: Koblitz, N. (ed.) CRYPTO 1996. LNCS, vol. 1109, pp. 401–415. Springer, Heidelberg (1996)
10. Vardy, A., Agrell, E., Zeger, K.: A table of upper bounds for binary codes. IEEE Trans. Inf. Theory **47**(7), 3004–3006 (2001)

11. Golomb, S.: Shift Register Sequences. Holden-Day, San Francisco (1967)
12. Guo, T., Liu, F., Wu, C.K.: On the equivalence of two definitions of visual cryptography scheme. In: Ryan, M.D., Smyth, B., Wang, G. (eds.) ISPEC 2012. LNCS, vol. 7232, pp. 217–227. Springer, Heidelberg (2012)
13. Guo, T., Liu, F., Wu, C.K.: Threshold visual secret sharing by random grids with improved contrast. J. Syst. Softw. **86**(8), 2094–2109 (2013)
14. Hawkes, L.W., Yasinsac, A., Cline, C.: An application of visual cryptography to financial documents. In: Master thesis of Security and Assurance in Information Technology Laboratory, Computer Science Department, Florida State University (1997)
15. Hsu, C.S., Hou, Y.C.: Copyright protection scheme for digital images using visual cryptography and sampling methods. Opt. Eng. **44**(7), 077003:1–077003:10 (2005)
16. Ito, R., Kuwakado, H., Tanaka, H.: Image size invariant visual cryptography. IEICE Trans. Fundam. Electron. Commun. Comput. Sci. **E82**(A.No.10), 2172–2177 (1999)
17. Kuwakado, H., Morii, M., Tanaka, H.: Visual cryptographic protocols using the trusted initializer. In: Qing, S., Mao, W., López, J., Wang, G. (eds.) ICICS 2005. LNCS, vol. 3783, pp. 112–122. Springer, Heidelberg (2005)
18. Kuwakado, H., Tanaka, H.: Size-reduced visual secret sharing scheme. IEICE Trans. Fundam. **87**, 1193–1197 (2004)
19. Lee, S.S., Na, J.C., Sohn, S.W., Park, C., Seo, D.H., Kim, S.J.: Visual cryptography based on an interferometric encryption technique. ETRI J. **24**(5), 373–380 (2002)
20. Liu, F., Wu, C.K., Lin, X.J.: Some extensions on threshold visual cryptography schemes. Comput. J. **53**(1), 107–119 (2010)
21. Liu, F., Wu, C.K., Lin, X.J.: Step construction of visual cryptography schemes. IEEE Trans. Inf. Forensics Secur. **5**(1), 27–38 (2010)
22. Liu, F., Wu, C.K., Lin, X.J.: Cheating immune visual cryptography scheme. IET Inf. Secur. **5**(1), 51–59 (2011)
23. Lou, D.C., Tso, H.K., Liu, J.L.: A copyright protection scheme for digital images using visual cryptography technique. Comput. Stand. Interfaces **29**, 125–131 (2007)
24. Plotkin, M.: Binary codes with specified minimum distances. IEEE Trans. Inf. Theory **6**, 445–450 (1960)
25. Naor, M., Pinkas, B.: Visual authentication and identification. In: Kaliski Jr, B.S. (ed.) CRYPTO 1997. LNCS, vol. 1294, pp. 322–336. Springer, Heidelberg (1997)
26. Naor, M., Shamir, A.: Visual cryptography. In: De Santis, A. (ed.) EUROCRYPT 1994. LNCS, vol. 950, pp. 1–12. Springer, Heidelberg (1995)
27. PureDepth.: Puredepth multi-layer display. http://www.puredepth.com. Accessed 15 March 2006
28. Revenkar, P.S., Anjum, A., Gandhare, W.Z.: Secure iris authentication using visual cryptography. (IJCSIS) Int. J. Comput. Sci. Inf. Secur. **7**(3), 217–221 (2010)
29. Hamming, R.W.: Error detecting and error correcting codes. Bell Syst. Technol. J. **29**, 147–160 (1950)
30. De Santis, A.: On visual cryptography schemes. In: Proceedings of the Information Theory Workshop 1998, pp. 154–155. IEEE (1998)
31. Johnson, S.: A new upper bound for error correction codes. IRE Trans. **IT–8**, 203–207 (1962)
32. Sudharsanan, S.: Shared key encryption of jpeg color images. IEEE Trans. Consum. Electron. **51**(4), 1204–1211 (2005)
33. Tuyls, P., Hollmann, H.D.L., Lint, H.H.V., Tolhuizen, L.: A polarisation based visual crypto system and its secret sharing schemes (2002). http://eprint.iacr.org
34. Tuyls, P., Hollmann, H.D.L., van Lint, J.H., Tolhuizen, L.: Xor-based visual cryptography schemes. Des. Codes Cryptogr. **37**, 169–186 (2005)

35. Tuyls, P., Kevenaar, T., Schrijen, G.J., Staring, T., van Dijk, M.: Security display-senabling secure communications. In: First International Conference on Pervasive Computing, Boppard, Germany LNCS, vol. 2802, pp. 271–284. Springer, Heidelberg (2004)
36. Viet, D.Q., Kurosawa, K.: Almost ideal contrast visual cryptography with reversing. In: Okamoto, T. (ed.) CT-RSA 2004. LNCS, vol. 2964, pp. 353–365. Springer, Heidelberg (2004)
37. Levenshtein, V.I.: The application of hadamard matrixes to a problem in coding. Probl. Cybern. **5**, 166–184 (1964)
38. Wang, F.H., Yen, K.K., Jain, L.C., Pan, J.S.: Multiuser-based shadow watermark extraction system. Inf. Sci. **177**, 2522–2532 (2007)
39. Patent with International Application No.: PCT/IB2003/000261: Secure Visual Message Communication Method And Device (2003)
40. Yang, C.N.: New visual secret sharing schemes using probabilistic method. Pattern Recogn. Lett. **25**, 481–494 (2004)
41. Yang, C.N., Chen, T.S., Ching, M.H.: Embed additional private information into two-dimensional bar codes by the visual secret sharing scheme. Integr. Comput. Aided Eng. **13**(2), 189–199 (2006)
42. Yang, C.N., Wang, D.: Property analysis of xor based visual cryptography. IEEE Trans. Circuits Syst. Video Technol. **24**(2), 189–197 (2014)
43. Yang, Y.X., Lin, X.D.: Coding and Cryptography (in Chinese). Posts and Telecom Press, Beijing (1992)
44. Liu, F., Wu, C.: A robust visual cryptography based watermarking scheme for multiple cover images and multiple owners. IET Inf. Secur. **5**(2), 121–128 (2010)

Visual Two-Secret Sharing Schemes by Different Superimposition Positions

Yi Hao Li and Shyong Jian Shyu[✉]

Department of Computer Science and Information Engineering,
Ming Chuan University, Taoyuan 33348, Taiwan
john999970@gmail.com, sjshyu@mail.mcu.edu.tw

Abstract. We propose two novel visual two-secret sharing schemes in this paper. The major difference between the previous and our approaches is that the two secrets are revealed by superimposing shares at different distances. In our schemes, two secret images would be encoded into two shares with different sizes, and the two secrets can be revealed by superimposing the two shares at two different superimposition positions. The distant superimposition for decoding enhances the flexibility of the visual cryptographic system.

1 Introduction

As the advancement of technology and the popularity of the Internet, the amount and transformation of digital information increase explosively. The protection of these digital information becomes a critical issue in the cyber space. Conventional cryptography skills have widely been applied to encrypt data and only the private/public key holder(s) can decrypt it. However, the decryption process requires computing power from computers.

Visual cryptography proposed by Noar and Shamir [1] provides another approach for protecting digital information. It utilizes the encoded transparencies, their superimposition and human visual ability to execute the decryption process so that no computational device and cryptographic knowledge are needed. When the cost of installing computers is too high or impossible, visual cryptography becomes an effective solution for protecting the digital information.

In [1], k out of n visual cryptographic schemes (VCSs) were defined and designed, in which one secret image P can be encoded into n transparencies in such a way that any k transparencies can reveal P when superimposed, while any $k-1$ ones cannot. The features in VCSs have attracted much attention from researchers since Noar and Shamir's introduction. Please refer to [2] for a thorough understanding for this research.

There are some innovative studies involving the design of visual multiple secrets sharing schemes [3, 4]. Additional operations such as shifting, rotation, turning and/or

---

This research was supported in part by the Ministry of Science and Technology, Taiwan, under Grants MOST 102-2221-E-130-005 and 103-2221-E-130-002-MY3.

Y.-Q. Shi et al. (Eds.): IWDW 2014, LNCS 9023, pp. 350–363, 2015.
DOI: 10.1007/978-3-319-19321-2_26

flipping may be adopted to reveal more secrets. In this paper, we propose two novel visual two-secret sharing schemes. The major difference between the previous and our approaches is that the two secrets are revealed by superimposing shares at different positions with regard to the decoder's eyes. Specifically, two secret images P_1 and P_2 would be encoded into two shares S_1 and S_2 such that $(S_1, d_1) \otimes (S_2, d_2)$ reveals P_1 when $d_1 = d_2$ and P_2 when $d_2 = 2d_1$ (see Fig. 1) where (S_i, d_i) denotes S_i is placed at distance d_i in front of the decoder's eyes for $i \in \{1, 2\}$ and $\otimes$ is the superimposition operation.

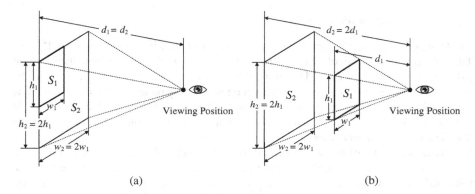

Fig. 1. Relationship of S_1, S_2, d_1, d_2 and $(S_1, d_1) \otimes (S_2, d_2)$ (a) $d_1 = d_2$ (b) $d_2 = 2d_1$

The rest of this paper is organized as follows. Section 2 introduces some informative results in the literature that inspire our study. Sections 3.1 and 3.2 present our two algorithms for visual two-secret sharing schemes by different superimposition positions. Section 4 gives some implementation results of our algorithms. We then provide concluding remarks in Sect. 5.

2 Literature Review

2.1 Naor and Shamir's Visual Cryptographic Scheme

Consider a secret image P that is encrypted into two shares S_1 and S_2. The basic idea of Naor and Shamir's visual cryptographic scheme [1] can be illustrated by Table 1.

Table 1. Basic idea of Naor and Shamir's visual cryptography scheme.

p	probability	s_1	s_2	$s_1 \otimes s_2$
☐	0.5	▮☐	▮☐	▮☐
	0.5	☐▮	☐▮	☐▮
▮	0.5	▮☐	☐▮	▮▮
	0.5	☐▮	▮☐	▮▮

If the secret pixel $p \in P$ is white, one of the first two rows of Table 1 would be randomly chosen to encode $s_1 \in S_1$ and $s_2 \in S_2$. The stacked result $s_1 \otimes s_2$ would be a 1×2 white block consisting of one white pixel and one black pixel. If p is black, one of the last two rows of Table 1 would be randomly chosen to encode s_1 and s_2. The stacked result $s_1 \otimes s_2$ would be a 1×2 black block consisting of two black pixels. Any one who owns S_1 or S_2 individually sees only a random picture and cannot get any information about P. Only when S_1 and S_2 are superimposed can the two participants recognize P from the superimposed result.

2.2 Secure Information Display

The technique of *secure information display* was introduced by Yamamoto et al. [5–10]. They utilized the concept of visual cryptography to protect the information displayed on a display panel (such as an LCD monitor). The encoded two shares are designed to be with different sizes. The larger one is shown on the display panel and the other is used as the decoding mask (maybe a transparency or acrylic sheet). When the decoding mask is placed in front of the display panel at a predefined position, the secret image can be revealed within a limited viewing zone.

Yamamoto et al. discussed secure information display for multi-color or grayscale secret images [6, 7], analyzed and confirmed experimentally of viewing zone with the relationships between the size and the position of the display image and the viewing space [8], developed two limited viewing zones using two decoding masks to reveal two secrets [9, 10]. Shyu et al. designed a novel scheme to securing n secrets in one display and n masks for $n \geq 2$ [11].

The superimposition of the shares in these studies is in the pixel-by-pixel basis. That is, each pixel in one share would be superimposed onto one pixel in another share. In our proposed schemes, each pixel in one share may be superimposed onto several pixels in another. The encoding skills are thus different. Still, our study follows the same requirement that the decoder should be in a limited viewing zone.

3 Visual Two-Secret Sharing Scheme by Different Superimposition Positions

We propose two algorithms to construct visual cryptographic schemes for sharing two secrets, namely P_1 and P_2, by different superimposition positions (VCS-2DSP) in this section. Figure 1 illustrates our techniques for decrypting two secrets by two shares via two different superimposition positions.

As shown in Fig. 1, our schemes share P_1 and P_2 into two encoded shares S_1 and S_2 which ensure that $(S_1, d_1) \otimes (S_2, d_2)$ reveals P_1 to our eyes when $d_1 = d_2$ (see Fig. 1(a)) and P_2 when $d_2 = 2d_1$ (see Fig. 1(b)) where S_1 and S_2 is the encoded shares, (S_i, d_i) means that S_i is placed in front of the viewing position (or decoder's eyes) with a distance of d_i and $\otimes$ denotes the superimposition operation for shares. Let h_i and w_i denote the height and weight, respectively, of S_i for $i \in \{1, 2\}$. Then, $w_2 = 2w_1$ and

$h_2 = 2h_1$ (see Fig. 1). Sections 3.1 and 3.2 presents these two algorithms, which adopt $m_{s1} = 4$ and $m_{s2} = 16$ as well as $m_{s1} = 1$ and $m_{s2} = 4$, respectively.

3.1   Algorithm 1: VCS-2DSP with $M_{s1} = 4$ and $M_{s2} = 16$

Consider $p_1 = P_1(i, j)$ and $p_2 = P_2(i, j)$ as shown in Fig. 2(a) and (b) for $1 \leq i \leq h$ and $1 \leq j \leq w$. We may call them the *corresponding pixels* owing to they have the same coordinates in P_1 and P_2, respectively. For the same reason, $S_1[i, j]$ is called the *corresponding block* of p_1 and p_2 in S_1. Since P_1 (P_2) would be revealed by $T_1 = (S_1, d_1) \otimes (S_2, d_2)$ with $d_1 = d_2$, which is exactly $S_1 \otimes S_2$ by aligning their left upper corners ($T_2 = (S_1, d_1) \otimes (S_2, d_2)$ with $d_2 = 2d_1$), the corresponding block of p_1 and $S_1[i, j]$ (p_2 and $S_1[i, j]$) would be denoted as $S_2{}^1[i, j]$ ($S_2{}^2[i, j]$). We expect that T_1 reveals P_1 and T_2 reveals P_2 to our eyes.

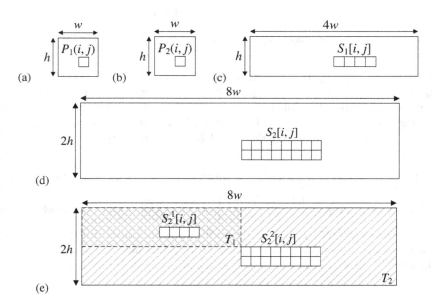

Fig. 2. Related blocks of P_1, P_2, S_1 and S_2 in A1: (a) $P_1(i, j) \in P_1$, (b) $P_2(i, j) \in P_2$, (c) $S_1[i, j] \in S_1$, (d) $S_2[i, j] \in S_2$, (e) $T_1 = (S_1, d_1) \otimes (S_2, d_2)$ with $d_1 = d_2$ and $T_2 = (S_1, d_1) \otimes (S_2, d_2)$ with $d_2 = 2d_1$

To achieve our goal, our first algorithm (A1) adopts $m_{s1} = 4$ and $m_{s2} = 16$ where the size of the encoded shares S_1 is $h \times 4w$ and that of S_2 is $2 h \times 8w$. Specifically, A1 sets $S_1[i, j]$ (= {$S_1(i, 4j)$, $S_1(i, 4j + 1)$, $S_1(i, 4j + 2)$, $S_1(i, 4j + 3)$}; see Fig. 2(c)) and $S_2{}^1[i, j]$ (= {$S_2(i, 4j)$, $S_2(i, 4j + 1)$, $S_2(i, 4j + 2)$, $S_2(i, 4j + 3)$}, see Fig. 2(e)) as two 1×4 blocks as well as $S_2 [i, j] = S_2{}^2[i, j]$ (= {$S_2(2i, 8j)$, $S_2(2i, 8j + 1)$, $S_2(2i, 8j + 2)$, $S_2(2i, 8j + 3)$, $S_2(2i, 8j + 4)$, $S_2(2i, 8j + 5)$, $S_2(2i, 8j + 6)$, $S_2(2i, 8j + 7)$, $S_2(2i + 1, 8j)$, $S_2(2i + 1, 8j + 1)$, $S_2(2i + 1, 8j + 2)$, $S_2(2i + 1, 8j + 3)$, $S_2(2i + 1, 8j + 4)$, $S_2(2i + 1, 8j + 5)$, $S_2(2i + 1, 8j + 6)$, $S_2(2i + 1, 8j + 7)$}; see Fig. 2(d) and (e)) as a 2×8 block. Note that we represent the coordinate (i, j) of a pixel as (i, j); while that of a block as $[i, j]$ in this paper.

Essentially, A1 insists that $S_1[i, j] \otimes S_2{}^1[i, j]$ and $S_1[i, j] \otimes S_2{}^2[i, j]$ should reveal $P_1(i, j)$ and $P_2(i, j)$ when $d_1 = d_2$ and $d_2 = 2d_1$, respectively, for $1 \le j \le h$ and $1 \le j \le w$. To realize these, A1 performs two major steps as shown in Fig. 3: ① After $s_2^1 = S_2{}^1[i, j]$ has been determined, A1 encodes $s_1 = S_1[i, j]$ according to p_1 and s_2^1. ② A1 goes on encoding $s_2 = S_2{}^2[i, j]$ according to p_2 and s_1. We present the realization of these two major steps and the determination of the initial $s_2^1 = S_2{}^1[1,1]$ in the following.

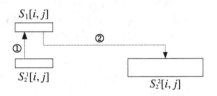

Fig. 3. Two major steps in A1 for encoding $S_1[i, j]$ and $S_2^2[i, j]$

First of all, we prepare some basic blocks needed in A1 as follows. Let $\Omega = \{\blacksquare, \blacksquare, \blacksquare, \blacksquare\}$, which contains all 1×4 blocks of three black and one white pixels. We define $b_W = \square$ and $b_B = \blacksquare$ which are 1×2 blocks consisting of all white and black pixels. Let $\Phi = \{b_W b_B, b_B b_W\} = \{\square\blacksquare, \blacksquare\square\}$, which contains 1×4 blocks merged by one b_W and one b_B horizontally.

Let $\begin{smallmatrix} b_W \\ b_W \end{smallmatrix} (\begin{smallmatrix} b_B \\ b_B \end{smallmatrix})$ denote ($\boxminus$ ($\blacksquare$),), which is a 2×2 block merged by two b_W's (b_B's) vertically. Let $\psi = \left\{ \begin{matrix} b_W b_B & b_B b_W \\ b_W b_B \end{matrix}, \begin{matrix} b_B b_W \end{matrix} \right\} = \{\boxminus, \blacksquare\}$, which contains two 2×8 blocks merged by one {\text{bWbW}} and one {\text{bBbB}} horizontally. A1 shall choose s_1 from Ω, pick up s_2^1 from Φ and determine s_2^1 from Ψ.

In step ①, A1 depends on p_1 and s_2^1 to encode s_1 by the rules in Table 2.

Table 2. Encoding s_1 $(= S_1[i, j])$ according to p_1 $(= P_1(i, j))$ and s_2^1 $(= S_2^1[i, j])$.

p_1	s_2^1	probability	s_1	p_1	s_2^1	probability	s_1
		0.5				0.5	
		0.5				0.5	
		0.5				0.5	
		0.5				0.5	

In step ②, A1 relies on p_2 and the previously determined s_1 to decide S_2^2 using the rules in Table 3.

Table 3. Encoding s_2^2 ($= S_2^2[i, j]$) according to p_2 ($= P_2(i, j)$) and s_1 ($= S_1[i, j]$).

p_2	s_1	probability	s_2^2	p_2	s_1	probability	s_2^2
		0.5				0.5	
		0.5				0.5	
		0.5				0.5	
		0.5				0.5	
		0.5				0.5	
		0.5				0.5	
		0.5				0.5	
		0.5				0.5	

We now explain how would $S_2^2[1, 1]$, $S_1[1, 1]$ and $S_2^1[1, 1]$ be generated in A1. Note that at the very beginning concerning $p_1 = P_1(1, 1)$ and $p_2 = P_2(1, 1)$, the four pixels in the left-upper corner of $S_2^2 = S_2^2[1, 1]$ coincide with the four pixels of $s_2^1 = S_2^1[1, 1]$. The determination of S_2^2 determines s_2^1; thus, we simply ignore the generation of the latter. We may design several approaches to encode $s_1 = S_1[1, 1]$ and $S_2^2 = S_2^2[1, 1]$ in A1. A simple one is to choose s_1 from Ω randomly, then encode S_2^2 relying on p_2 and the chosen s_1 using the rules in Table 3. In this way, p_2 could be revealed via $(s_1, d_1) \otimes (s_1, d_2)$ when $d_2 = 2d_1$ (but, there is no guarantee for p_1 to be revealed). On the other hand, we could choose s_2 randomly from $\prod = \{B_L B_L, \ B_L B_R, \ B_R B_L, \ B_R B_R\} = \{$, , , $\}$, then encode s_1 depending on p_1 and the 1×4 block in the left-upper area of the chosen s_2 (denoted as s_2^1, i.e. the corresponding block of p_1 and s_1 in S_2 by the rules in Table 2). Hence, p_1 could be revealed via $(s_1, d_1) \otimes (s_2, d_2)$ when $d_1 = d_2$ (but, there is no guarantee for p_2 to be revealed). In fact, randomly choosing one the two approaches would be applicable, too. We encapsulate the process of the determination of S_2^2 and s_1 depending on p_1 and p_2 as procedure $(s_1, S_2^2) = initialization(p_1, p_2)$.

Our A1 is now clear.

Algorithm: A1

Input: $h \times w$ secret images P_1 and P_2
Output: encoded shares S_1 and S_2 such that $(S_1, d_1) \otimes (S_2, d_2)$
         reveals P_1 when $d_1 = d_2$ and P_2 when $d_2 = 2d_1$
1. $(S_1[1,1], S_2^2[1,1]) = initialization(P_1(1,1), P_2(1,1))$
2.   for (each coordinate $(i,j) \in \{(1,2)-(h,w)\}$) do
2.1   { $p_1 = P_1(i,j)$; $s_2^1 = S_2^1[i,j]$
2.2 $S_1[i,j] = encode\_s_1(p_1, s_2^1)$ // Table 2
2.3 $p_2 = P_2(i,j)$; $s_1 = S_1[i,j]$
2.4 $S_2^2[i,j] = encode\_s_2(p_2, s_1)$ // Table 3
      }
3.   output (S_1, S_2)

Suppose that the secret P_1 and P_2 are completely white images. Figure 4 illustrates the encoding process of A1. For all pairs of corresponding pixels $p_1 \in P_1(i, j)$ and $p_2 \in P_2(i, j)$ one by one. Regarding the initialization stage, choose $S_1[1, 1]$ (or $S_2^2[1, 1]$) from Ω (or Π) randomly, then encode $S_2^2[1, 1]$ (or $S_1[1, 1]$) relying on $P_2(1, 1)$ (or $P_1(1, 1)$) and the chosen $S_1[1, 1]$ (or $S_2^1[1, 1]$) using the rules in Table 3 (or Table 2) (see Fig. 4(a), In step ①, A1 iteratively determines $S_1[i, j]$ according to $S_2^1[i, j]$ and $P_1(i, j)$ (see Fig. 4(b)), In step ②, A1 iteratively determines $S_2^2[i, j]$ according to $S_1[i, j]$ and $P_2(i, j)$ (see Fig. 4(c)).

3.2   Algorithm 2: VCS-2DSP with $M_{s1} = 1$ and $M_{s2} = 4$

The encoding skill of our second algorithm (A2) is similar to that of A1. A2 adopts $m_{s1} = 1$ and $m_{s2} = 4$. The size of the encoded shares S_1 is $h \times w$ and that of S_2 is $2h \times 2w$. Assume that $h = w$ (that is, the height and the weight of P_1 (P_2) are the same). As mentioned in the previous section, $p_1 = P_1(i, j)$ and $p_2 = P_2(i, j)$ are referred to as corresponding pixels as shown in Fig. 5(a) and (b) for $1 \leq i \leq h$ and $1 \leq j \leq w$. Their corresponding block in S_1, denoted as $s_1 = S_1[i, j]$, is exactly pixel $S_1(i, j)$ (see Fig. 5 (c)). The corresponding block of p_1 and s_1 in S_2 would be $s_2^1 = S_2^1[i, j]$, which is actually pixel $S_2(i, j)$ (see Fig. 5(e)) and that of p_2 and s_1 is $S_2^2 = S_2^2[i, j]$, which is a 2×2 block containing pixels: $S_2(2i, 2j)$, $S_2(2i, 2j + 1)$, $S_2(2i + 1, 2j)$, $S_2(2i + 1, 2j + 1)$ (see Fig. 5(d) and (e)).

First of all, A2 decomposes P_1, P_2, S_1 and S_2 into $\lambda = \lceil \log_2(w + 1) \rceil$ regions, namely $R_1, R_2, ..., R_\lambda$, as shown in Fig. 6(a)–(d) where $(i, j) \in R_k$ if and only if $w/2^k \leq i \leq w/2^{k-1}$ or $h/2^k \leq j \leq h/2^{k-1}$ for $1 \leq k \leq \lambda$. Note that the size of R_k in S_1 is 1/4 smaller than that in S_2 for $1 \leq k \leq \lambda$.

Let $U = \{$ $\}$, $V = \{$ $\}$ and $W = U \cup V$. We define $h(w)$ to be

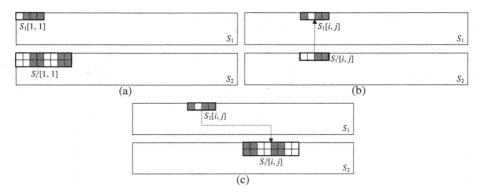

Fig. 4. Illustrating the first three steps of A1. (a) Choose $S_1[1, 1]$ (or $S_2[1, 1]$) randomly, then encode $S_2^2[1, 1]$ (or $S_1[1, 1]$) according to $P_2(1, 1)$ (or $P_1(1, 1)$) and the chosen $S_1[1, 1]$ (or $S_2^1[1, 1]$), (b) Encode $S_1[i, j]$ according to $S_2^1[i, j]$ and $P_1(i, j)$, (c) Encode $S_2^2[i, j]$ according to $S_1[i, j]$ and $P_2(i, j)$

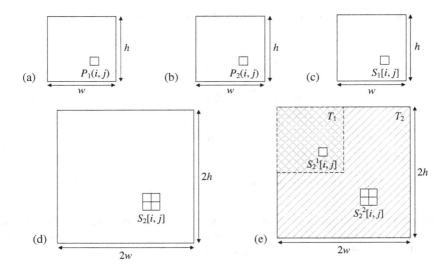

Fig. 5. Related blocks of P_1, P_2, S_1 and S_2 in A2: (a) $P_1(i, j) \in P_1$, (b) $P_2(i, j) \in P_2$, (c) $S_1[i, j] \in S_1$, (d) $S_2[i, j] \in S_2$, (e) $T_1 = (S_1, d_1) \otimes (S_2, d_2)$ with $d_1 = d_2$ and $T_2 = (S_1, d_1) \otimes (S_2, d_2)$ with $d_2 = 2d_1$

the number of black pixels in block $w \in W$. Therefore, $W = \{w \mid w$ is a 2×2 block and $0 \leq h(w) \leq 4 \}$, that is, W contains all combinations of 2×2 blocks.

A2 involves three stages: (1) initialization, (2) encoding, and (3) adjusting. (Note that A1 involves no adjusting stage.) In the encoding stage, A2 performs two major steps region by region as shown in Fig. 7: ① After $S_2^2 = S_2^2[i, j]$ has been determined, A2 encodes $s_1 = S_1[i, j]$ according to $p_2 = P_2(i, j)$ and S_2^2. ② A2 goes on encoding $s_2^1 = S_2^1[i, j]$ according to $p_1 = P_1(i, j)$ and $s_1 = S_1[i, j]$. These two steps are similar as those in A1; yet, A2 encodes regions $R_1, R_2, \ldots, R_\lambda$ in sequence (while A1 treats P_1 (P_2, S_1 and S_2) as one single region only).

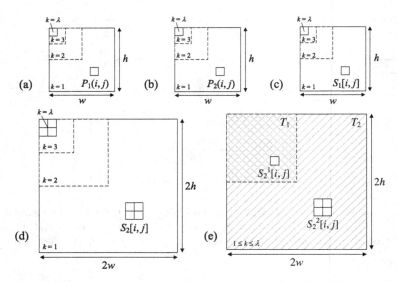

Fig. 6. Decomposition of P_1, P_2, S_1 and S_2 into $\lambda = \lceil \log_2(w+1) \rceil$ regions

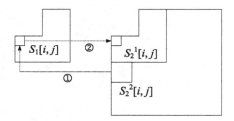

Fig. 7. Two major steps in A2 for encoding $S_1[i, j]$ and $S_2^1[i, j]$

For step ① in iteration k, since S_2^2 would be previously chosen from W, A2 determines s_1 according to this S_2^2 and p_2 using the rules in Table 4, in which t is a threshold value such that $t = 2$ (1.5) for $1 \le k < \lambda$ ($k = \lambda$).

Table 4. Encoding s_1 according to s_2^2 and p_2.

p_2	s_2^2	probability	s_1
	$\{s_2^2 \mid h(s_2^2) < t\}$	1	☐
☐	$\{s_2^2 \mid h(s_2^2) > t\}$	1	■
	$\{s_2^2 \mid h(s_2^2) = t\}$	0.5	☐
		0.5	■
	$\{s_2^2 \mid h(s_2^2) < t\}$	1	■
■	$\{s_2^2 \mid h(s_2^2) > t\}$	1	☐
	$\{s_2^2 \mid h(s_2^2) = t\}$	0.5	☐
		0.5	■

In step ②, A2 relies on p_1 and the previously determined s_1 to decide s_2^1 using the rules in Table 5.

Table 5. Encoding s_2^1 according to s_1 and p_1.

p_1	s_1	s_2^1
□	□	□
	■	■
■	□	■
	■	□

Regarding the initialization stage, A2 simply chooses $S_2^2 = S_2^2[i, j]$ in region R_1, from $\{w \mid h(w) = 0 \text{ or } h(w) = 4 \} (= \{ \boxplus,\ \blacksquare \})$ randomly.

Suppose that we apply A2 involving stages (1) and (2) (without stage (3)) only. The encoded S_2 would not look constantly random (see Fig. 10(b) in Sect. 4) and the superimposed results are not constantly clear (see Fig. 10(c) and (d)), either. Applying stage (3) could resolve such a problem. Particularly, in stage (3) A2 adjusts $S_2^2 = \{w \mid h(w) = 0 \}(\{w \mid h(w) = 4 \})$ in region R_1 to $\{w \mid h(w) = 0 \text{ or } h(w) = 1 \}(\{w \mid h(w) = 3 \text{ or } h(w) = 4 \})$ using the rules in Table 6. The adjusted S_2^2 is denoted as $\hat{s}_2$.

Further, A2 adjusts $S_2^2 = \{w \mid h(w) = 2 \}$ in region R_k to $\{w \mid 0 \le h(w) \le 4 \}$ for $1 < k \le \lambda$, complements $S_2(2i, 2j)$ ($S_2(2i, 2j + 1)$, $S_2(2i + 1, 2j)$, $S_2(2i + 1, 2j + 1)$) = □ (■) to ■ (□) with probability = 0.2, and adjusts S_2^2 to $\{w \mid h(w) = 0 \}$ ($\{w \mid h(w) = 4 \}$) with probability = 0.1 as shown in Table 7.

Table 6. Adjusting s_2^2 in region R_1

s_2^2	probability	$\hat{s}_2$	s_2^2	probability	$\hat{s}_2$
⊞	0.2	⊞	■	0.2	■
	0.2	▛		0.2	▟
	0.2	▙		0.2	▜
	0.2	▟		0.2	▛
	0.2	▜		0.2	▙

Below illustrates our A2.

Algorithm: A2

Input: $h \times w$ secret images P_1 and P_2

Output: encoded shares S_1 and S_2 such that $(S_1, d_1) \otimes (S_2, d_2)$
       reveals P_1 when $d_1 = d_2$ and P_2 when $d_2 = 2d_1$

```
1.      for (each coordinate (i,j)∈R₁) do
        // h/2 < i ≤ h or w/2 < j ≤ w
            S₂²[i, j] = random({ ⊞ , ■ })
2.      for (each region 1 ≤ k ≤ λ)    // λ = ⌈log₂(w+1)⌉
        {   for (each coordinate (i,j)∈Rₖ)
                // h/2ᵏ < i ≤ h/2ᵏ⁻¹ or w/2ᵏ < j ≤ w/2ᵏ⁻¹
            {   p₂ = P₂(i,j);  s₂² = S₂²[i,j];
                if (k < λ) t = 2
                else t = 1.5
                S₁[i,j] = encode_s₁_A2(p₂,s₂²,t)   // Table 4
                p₁= P₁(i,j);  s₁ = S₁[i, j];
                s₂¹[i,j] = encode_s₂_A2(p₁,s₁)      // Table 5
            }
        }
3.      for (each coordinate (i, j))
            S₂²[i, j] = adjust_s₂²(s₂²)   // Tables 6 and 7
4.      output(S₁, S₂)
```

Table 7. Adjusting s_2^2 in region R_k

s_2^2	probability	$\hat{s}_2$	s_2^2	probability	$\hat{s}_2$	s_2^2	probability	$\hat{s}_2$
	0.1			0.1			0.1	
	0.2			0.2			0.2	
	0.2			0.2			0.2	
	0.2			0.2			0.2	
	0.2			0.2			0.2	
	0.1			0.1			0.1	
	0.1			0.1			0.1	
	0.2			0.2			0.2	
	0.2			0.2			0.2	
	0.2			0.2			0.2	
	0.2			0.2			0.2	
	0.1			0.1			0.1	

Figure 8 illustrates the encoding process of A2. Regarding the initialization stage, A2 determines $S_2^2[i, j]$ in region R_1 from $\{w \mid h(w) = 0 \text{ or } h(w) = 4\}$ randomly (see Fig. 8(a)). In step ①, A2 iteratively determines $S_1[i, j]$ according to $S_2^2[i, j]$ (if $k = \lambda$ then $S_2^2[i, j] = \{S_2(1, 2), S_2(2, 1), S_2(2, 2)\}$, see Fig. 8(d)) and $P_2(i, j)$ (see Fig. 8(b)). In step ②, A2 iteratively determines $S_2^1[i, j]$ (if $k = \lambda$ then $S_2^1[i, j]$ is actually pixel $S_2(1, 1)$, see Fig. 8(e)) according to $S_1[i, j]$ and $P_1(i, j)$ (see Fig. 8(c)), and in stage (3), A2 adjusts S_2^2 in region R_1 and R_k by using Tables 6 and 7, respectively.

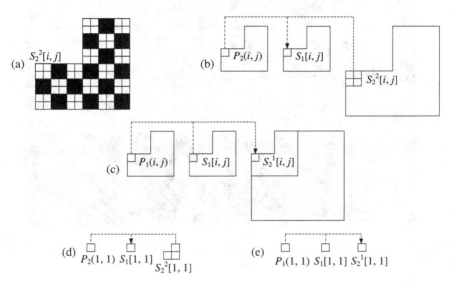

Fig. 8. Illustrating the first three steps of A2. (a) Determine $S_2^2[i, j]$ in region R_1 randomly, (b) Encode $S_1[i, j]$ according to $S_2^2[i, j]$ and $P_2(i, j)$, (c) Encode $S_2^1[i, j]$ according to $S_1[i, j]$ and $P_1(i, j)$, (d)(e) for steps ① and ② when $k = \lambda$.

4 Experimental Result and Discussion

We conducted two experiments to test A1 and A2, respectively, by computer programs coded in C# and run in a personal computer with Microsoft Windows 7. The experimental results are summarized as follows.

Experiment 1. Figure 9 presents the results of an implementation of A1. Figure 9(a) and (b) give the 128 × 128 secret images P_1 and P_2, (c) and (d) are shares S_1 and S_2 generated by A1, (e) is $(S_1, d_1) \otimes (S_2, d_2)$ when $d_1 = d_2$, which reveals P_1 and (f) is $(S_1, d_1) \otimes (S_2, d_2)$ when $d_2 = 2d_1$, which reveals P_2.

Experiment 2. Figure 10 presents the results of an implementation of A2 using the same secret image P_1 and P_2 as in Experiment 1. Figure 10(a)–(d) are S_1, S_2, $(S_1, d_1) \otimes (S_2, d_2)$ when $d_1 = d_2$ and $d_2 = 2d_1$, respectively, which are generated by A2 using stages (1) and (2) only (without stage (3)). The phenomenon (that S_2 is not a constantly random-looking share mentioned in Sect. 3.2) exists. Figure 10(e)–(h) are the corresponding

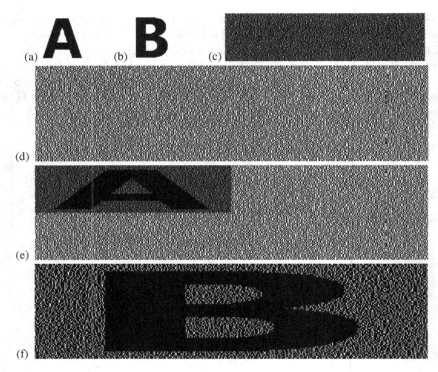

Fig. 9. Implementation results of A1 (a) P_1, (b) P_2, (c) S_1, (d) S_2, (e) $(S_1, d_1) \otimes (S_2, d_2)$ when $d_1 = d_2$ (f) $(S_1, d_1) \otimes (S_2, d_2)$ when $d_2 = 2d_1$.

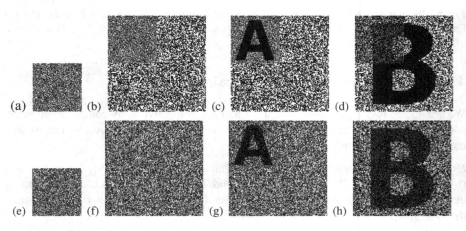

Fig. 10. Implementation results of A2 involves stage (1) and (2): (a) S_1, (b) S_2, (c) $(S_1, d_1) \otimes (S_2, d_2)$ reveals P_1 when $d_1 = d_2$, (d) $(S_1, d_1) \otimes (S_2, d_2)$ reveals P_2 when $d_2 = 2d_1$, A2 involves stage (1)-(3): (e) S_1, (f) S_2, (g) $(S_1, d_1) \otimes (S_2, d_2)$ reveals P_1 when $d_1 = d_2$, (h) $(S_1, d_1) \otimes (S_2, d_2)$ reveals P_2 when $d_2 = 2d_1$.

results generated by A2 using all stages (1)-(3), which demonstrate that A2 is a feasible VCS-2DSP.

The experimental results above demonstrate the effectiveness of our A1 and A2 for being feasible VCS-2DSP. The reconstructed contrast of A1 looks better than that of A2. On the other hand, the pixel expansion of A1 is larger than that of A2.

5 Conclusions and Future Works

We propose two algorithms to construct VCS-2DSP. The relationship of the corresponding blocks in the secret images and encoded shares are thoughtfully considered. This makes our study different from those of secure information display and MVCSs relying rotation, shifting, or flipping/flopping operations, whose corresponding blocks are with the same size. Our Algorithm 1 requires larger pixel expansions than Algorithm 2. However, the recognition to the reconstructed results in the former is better than those in the latter.

This study has many future works including a formal analysis on the contrast in the reconstructed results, an improved VCS-2DSP that takes less pixel expansion or larger contrast in the reconstructed results, an enhanced VCS-DSP for more than two secret images, more shares, or more flexible superimposition positions, just to name a few.

References

1. Naor, M., Shamir, A.: Visual cryptography. In: De Santis, A. (ed.) EUROCRYPT 1994. LNCS, vol. 950, pp. 1–12. Springer, Heidelberg (1995)
2. Cimato, S., Yang, C.N.: Visual Cryptography and Secret Image Sharing. Taylor & Francis/ CRC Press, Boca Raton (2011)
3. Shyu, S.J., Chen, K.: Visual multiple secret sharing based upon turning and flipping. Inf. Sci. 181(15), 3246–3266 (2011)
4. Shyu, S.J., Huang, S.-Y., Lee, Y.-L., Wang, R.-Z., Chen, K.: Sharing multiple secrets in visual cryptography. Pattern Recogn. 40(12), 3633–3651 (2007)
5. Yamamoto, H., Hayasaki, Y., Nishida, N.: Securing information display by use of visual cryptography. Opt. Lett. 28, 1564–1566 (2003)
6. Yamamoto, H., Hayasaki, Y., Nishida, N.: Secure information display with limited viewing zone by use of multi-color visual cryptography. Opt. Express 12, 1258–1270 (2004)
7. Yamamoto, H., Hayasaki, Y., Nishida, N.: Securing display of grayscale and multicolored images by use of visual cryptography. In: Proceedings of the SPIE, vol. 5306, pp. 716–724 (2004)
8. Yamamoto, H., Hayasaki, Y.: Secure display that limits the viewing space by use of optically decodable encryption. In: Proceedings of the SPIE, vol. 6482, p. 64820C (2007)
9. Yamamoto, H., Hayasaki, Y., Nishida, N.: Secure information display with two limited viewing zones using two decoding masks based on visual secret sharing scheme. Jpn. J. Appl. Phys. Part 1 44, 1803–1807 (2005)
10. Yamamoto, H., Hayasaki, Y., Nishida, N.: Secure information display by use of multiple decoding masks. In: Proceedings of the SPIE, vol. 5600, pp. 192–199 (2011)
11. Shyu, S.J., Chen, M.-C., Chao, K.-M.: Securing information display for multiple secrets. Opt. Eng. 48(5), 057005-1-057005-12 (2009)

Visual Cryptography Scheme
with Autostereogram

Dao-Shun Wang[1(✉)], Feng Yi[1], and Ching-Nung Yang[2]

[1] Department of Computer Science and Technology,
Tsinghua University, Beijing, China
daoshun@mail.tsinghua.edu.cn, yifeng137@gmail.com
[2] Department of Computer Science and Information Engineering,
National Dong Hwa University, Shoufeng, Taiwan
cnyang@mail.ndhu.edu.tw

Abstract. Visual cryptography scheme (VCS) is an encryption technique that utilizes the human visual system in recovering of the secret image and does not require any cryptographic computation. Autostereogram is a single two dimensional image which becomes a virtual three dimensional image when viewed with proper eye convergence or divergence. Combing the two technologies via human vision, this paper presents a new scheme called (k, n)-VCS with autostereogram. In the scheme, a secret image is encrypted into n images called shares, each of which can function as an autostereogram. By stacking any k shares, the secret image is recovered visually without any equipment, whereas no secret information is obtained with less than k shares.

Keywords: Visual cryptography · Visual secret sharing · Autostereogram

1 Introduction

Naor and Shamir [1] firstly introduced visual cryptography scheme (VCS), also called visual secret sharing scheme, and constructed (k, n) - VCS which conceals the original data into n images called shares. The original data is recovered from the overlap of at least k shares through the human vision without any knowledge of cryptography or cryptographic computations. With the development of the field, Alteniese et al. [2] proposed an extended VCS to share a secret image. The minimum pixel expansion is obtained by using the hypergraph coloring method. Wang et al. [3] gave a general construction method for extended VCSs by concatenating an extended matrix to each basis matrix. Among these schemes, some groups of shares can reconstruct the original secret image, but each share cannot conceal any information without any operation.

Another interesting research based on the properties of human visual system is autostereogram (also known as single image stereogram), which is derived from stereopair or stereogram. As early as 1838, Wheatstone [4, 5] discovered the stereoscopic phenomenon which allows a person to see a three dimensional (3D) image from two dimensional (2D) pictures with a special contraption. Julesz [6] invented the random-dot stereogram by using two slightly different images. Based on the wallpaper effect discovered by Brewster, Tyler et al. [7] designed the single image random-dot

© Springer International Publishing Switzerland 2015
Y.-Q. Shi et al. (Eds.): IWDW 2014, LNCS 9023, pp. 364–375, 2015.
DOI: 10.1007/978-3-319-19321-2_27

stereogram in which the 3D scene can be viewed by unaided eyes. After that, Thimble [8] provided a simple and symmetric algorithm for autostereogram. Desmedt et al. [9] proposed a cerebral cryptography in which the decryption is done not use the sub-tractive properties of light, but use the perceived 3D properties of the human visual system. Minh et al. [10] introduced a new way to detect hidden surfaces in a 3D scene and extended the algorithm to moving objects. With respect to these previous schemes, the autostereograms conceal 3D images independently, but they are unable to hide a secret image together. Papas et al. [11] proposed an automatic approach to design and manufacture passive display device based on optical hidden image decoding. Tsai et al. [12] proposed a new visual cryptography scheme with the stereoscopic display which showed and accurately decrypted the hidden information for gray images. Yamamoto et al. [13] proposed a new visual cryptography by utilizing a recently reported depth perception illusion.

To sum up, both VCS and autostereograms are based on the properties of the human vision. The simplicities of the secret image decryption in a VCS and the 3D image display in an autostereogram may bring an interesting work designing a cryptography system which possesses the characteristics of both VCS and autostereogram. This combinational system can encode a secret image into n shares, acting as an autostereogram which shows 3D effect, and the original secret image can be visually recovered by stacking any k shares. Such a combinational scheme is presented in this paper. The proposed (k, n) scheme encodes an original secret image and n original grayscale images which are n depth maps of the virtual 3D scenes revealed in the n autostereograms. The output is n shares that show 3D effects related to n original grayscale images. Printing the n shares on transparencies and overlapping any k of them, we can "see" the original secret image, whereas we are not able to obtain any secret information by any means through less than k shares.

2 Background

2.1 A Binary (k, n)-VCS

In a binary VCS, the secret image consists of a collection of black-and-white pixels and each pixel is subdivided into a collection of m black-and-white sub-pixels in each of the n shares. The collection of sub-pixels can be represented by a $n \times m$ Boolean matrix $S = [s_{ij}]$, where the element s_{ij} represents the j-th sub-pixel in the i-th share. A white pixel is represented as a 0, and a black pixel is represented as a 1. When we Xerox a share onto a transparency, using an overhead projector, white sub-pixels allow light to pass through while black sub-pixels stop light. $s_{ij} = 1$ if and only if the j-th pixel in the i-th share is black. Stacking shares $i_1, \cdots, i_r$ together, the grey-level of each pixel (m sub-pixels) of the combined share is proportional to the Hamming weight (the number of 1's in the vector V) $H(V)$ of the OR-ed ("OR" operation) m-vector $V = OR(i_1, \cdots, i_r)$ where $i_1, \cdots, i_r$ are the rows of S associated with the shares we stack. The following definition is the formal definition for the visual cryptography scheme.

Definition 1[1]. A solution to the k out of n visual cryptography scheme consists of two collections of $n \times m$ Boolean matrices C_0 and C_1. To share a white pixel, the dealer randomly chooses one of the matrices in C_0, and to share a black pixel, the dealer randomly chooses one of the matrices in C_1. The chosen matrix defines the color of the m subpixels in each one of n transparencies. The solution is considered valid if the following three conditions are met.

1. For any S in C_0, the OR V of any k of the n rows satisfies $H(V) \leq d - \alpha \cdot m$.
2. For any S in C_1, the OR V of any k of the n rows satisfies $H(V) \geq d$.
3. For any subset $\{i_1, \cdots, i_q\}$ of $\{1, \cdots, n\}$ with $q < k$, the two collections of $q \times m$ matrices C_0 for $t \in \{0, 1\}$ obtained by restricting each $n \times m$ matrix in C_t (where $t = 0, 1$) to rows $i_1, \cdots, i_q$ are indistinguishable in the sense that they contain the same matrices with the same frequencies.

For a visual cryptography scheme (VCS) to be valid, the three conditions must be met. The first two conditions of this definition are called *contrast* and the third condition is called *security*. The pixel expansion m represents the loss in resolution from the original image to the recovered one. The relative difference α refers to the difference in weight between recovered black original pixel and recovered white original pixel. We would like m to be as small as possible and α to be as large as possible.

From Definition 1, a binary $(k, n)-$ VCS can be realized by the two Boolean matrices C_0 and C_1. The collection B_0 (resp. B_1) can be obtained by permuting the columns of the corresponding Boolean matrix C_0 (resp. C_1) in all possible ways. B_0 and B_1 are called *basis matrices*, and hence each collection has $m!$ matrices.

Example 1. This is an example of a (2, 2)-VCS.

Figure 1 depicts a (2, 2)-VCS, which has the following basis matrices:

(a)   (b)

(c)   (d)

Fig. 1. A (2, 2)-VCS, (a) Secret image, (b) Share 1, (c) Share 2, (d) Recovered secret image.

$$B_0 = \begin{bmatrix} 0 & 1 \\ 0 & 1 \end{bmatrix}, \quad B_1 = \begin{bmatrix} 0 & 1 \\ 1 & 0 \end{bmatrix}$$

An original secret image is encoded to two shares. Through stacking the two shares, the original secret image is recovered.

2.2   Autostereogram

Stereoscopic images provide a method to describe 3D objects based on the depth perception principle which is discovered through binocular vision. Both of the eyes view two slightly different 2D pictures which are put together in the human brain by matching two equivalent points in the two pictures, and thus the distance of the object is perceived by the brain.

There are two view techniques, wall-eyes (Fig. 2) and cross-eyed (Fig. 3). Actually, it is a more natural function to converge than diverge. Therefore, in this paper, all autostereograms are encoded for wall-eyed viewing.

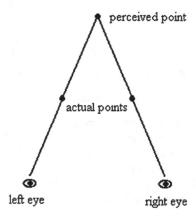

Fig. 2. Wall-eyed viewing

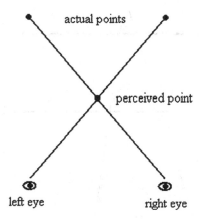

Fig. 3. Cross-eyed viewing

The basis of autostereogram is the wallpaper effect. If some repeating patterns are arranged horizontally, the brain will be tricked into matching the equivalent points and thereby perceiving a virtual plane behind or in front of the physical plane with the eyes converged or diverged. Next Fig. 4. shows the wallpaper effect.

Fig. 4. Wallpaper effect

Looking at these repeating patterns, we notice that the red leaves are nearer to us than the green trees, because the interval of the red leaves is less than that of the green trees. The principle is that the closer these icons are arranged horizontally, the higher they are lifted from the background plane.

Based on wallpaper effect, single image stereogram was invented. Timbleby et al. [8] analyzed the geometry form of the autostereogram, as shown in Fig. 5.

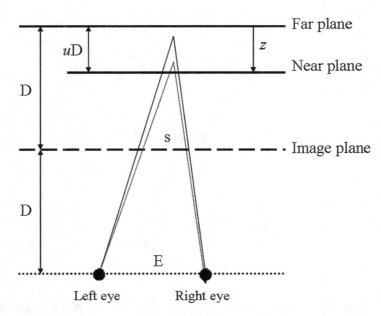

Fig. 5. The geometry form of autostereogram with wall-eyed viewing

Timbleby et al. [8] also provided an equation to describe the relationship between the object's depth z and the distance s between a pair of pixels that corresponds to the same virtual point.

$$s = \frac{(1 - uz)}{2 - uz} \cdot E \tag{1}$$

Here, s is the stereo separation for a point, and z is a vector from the far plane to the near plane, ranging from 0 to 1. E is the distance between two pupils and u is a fixed number which is chosen to be 1/3. The equation indicates that the smaller distance s produces the larger z, so the virtual point is nearer to the eyes.

3 The Proposed Scheme

Our proposed scheme is a (k, n)-VCS which functions as both VCS and autostereo-grams. In the scheme, a secret image is shared among n participants. Each participant holds an image called share which can be viewed as an autostereogram, showing a virtual 3D scene when viewed with proper eye convergence or divergence. By printing the shares on transparencies and stacking them, only k or more participants can recover the original secret image. With less than k participants, nothing can be obtained even with infinite power.

Our scheme satisfies perfect security and also has pixel expansion. Therefore, further discussion is necessary to the distance parameter s between two equivalent actual points that converge to a virtual point.

Suppose an original autostereogram with distance s_0. If each original pixel p_0 is replaced by a row vector $V = (p_0, r_1, \cdots, r_{v-1})$, r_1 is a random numbers, and v is a positive integer, $1 \leq i \leq v - 1$, $v \geq 1$. The new distance s_1 between two equivalent pixels is v times larger than s_0, thus we need to reduce the distance s_1 to s_1/v, namely s_0 (Table 1).

3.1 Construction Method

To construct an autostereogram, a depth map of the original 3D scene can be showed in a grayscale image in which the larger grayscale value represents the smaller distance between two equivalent points. 0 represents black and 255 represents white. The following is an algorithm of a (k, n)-VCS with autostereogram.

Note that the subpixel arrangement of our scheme is different from that of previous VCS. In our scheme, the blocks in the same row of a share need to satisfy some conditions to realize the effect of an autostereogram.

Let $R_i = (p_1, \cdots, p_x)$ be the i-th row of the original secret image. To share an original secret pixel $p_{j+y \cdot s}$, we construct the basis matrix $D_{j+y \cdot s}$ by using the above Construction, $j = 1, \cdots, s$, $y = 0, 1, \cdots, \lfloor x/s \rfloor$.

Table 1. The algorithm to generate the basis matrix of a (k, n)-VCS with autostereogram

---

Input:

1. The basis matrices B_0 and B_1 of a -VCS with pixel expansion m

2. The color $k_0 \in \{0, 1\}$ of the pixels of the original secret image, here 1 represents black, and 0 represents white.

3. The color $k_0, \cdots, k_n \in \{0, \cdots, 255\}$ of the pixels in the n grayscale images (depth maps).

Generation of the n shares:

1. Calculate the new pixel expansion $m' = m + m_A$. Here, m_A is a positive integer. (In next Sect. 3.4, we will verify the minimum $m_A = \lceil n/(k-1) \rceil$)

2. Let $m' = (m'/v) \times v$, which means each block has m'/v rows and v columns.

3. Construct n autostereograms according to the n grayscale images by using any previous autostereogram algorithm. The distance parameter of the autostereogram algorithm is reduced to $1/v$.

4. Construct a matrix A with n rows and m_A columns. In the j-th column of A, the i-th element equals to k_i, the other elements in A are 1's, $(j-1) \times k \le i \le j \times k - 1$, $1 \le j \le m_A$.

5. Construct new basis matrices $D_0 = A \circ B_0$, $D_1 = A \circ B_1$. The symbol "$\circ$" represents the concatenation of two matrices.

Output:

The new basis matrices D_0 and D_1.

$$D_{j+y \cdot s} = A_{j+y \cdot s} \circ T_{j+y \cdot s}.$$

Here, $T_{j+y \cdot s} \in \{B_0, B_1\}$. Suppose the matrix $D'_{j+y \cdot s}$ is used to set the m' subpixels of the n blocks which are corresponding to the n shares respectively.

$$D'_{j+y \cdot s} = P'(A_{j+y \cdot s}) \circ P(B_{j+y \cdot s}) \tag{2}$$

The symbol "P'" be a kind of permutation, and "P" be a random permutation to permute the columns of $B_{j+y \cdot s}$ to the residual columns. Formula (2) means that the matrix $D'_{j+y \cdot s}$ is obtained by permuting the columns of basis matrix $D_{j+y \cdot s}$. The part "A" of $D_j, D_{j+s}, D_{j+2 \cdot s}, \ldots$ must according to a uniform permutation. The purpose is to make the subpixels which show the content of the $l - th$ autostereogram in the same row of the $l - th$ share, $1 \le l \le n$.

3.2   Example

Example 2. In Fig. 6,(a) and (b) are two original 3D scenes. Encoding them to autostereograms with distance $s_1 = 90$ pixels and $s_2 = 90$ pixels, we get (c) and (d).

In the following, we will construct a (2, 2)-VCS with autostereogram by using the results from example 1 and 2.

Suppose a (2, 2)-VCS, the basis matrices are $B_0 = \begin{bmatrix} 0 & 1 \\ 0 & 1 \end{bmatrix}$ and $B_1 = \begin{bmatrix} 0 & 1 \\ 1 & 0 \end{bmatrix}$. The corresponding (2, 2)-VCS with autostereograms has pixel expansion $m' = 4$.

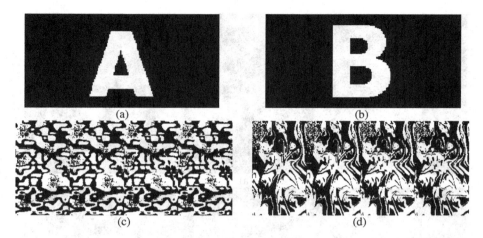

Fig. 6. Autostereogram, (a) Original 3D scene O_1, (b) Original 3D scene O_2, (c) Autostereogram G_1, (d) Autostereogram G_2.

We arrange the four sbupixels in a block with 2 rows and 2 columns. Because the distance in an original autostereogram is $s = 90$, we construct the two new autostereograms G_1 and G_2 with new distance $s'_1 = s'_2 = 90/2 = 45$.

For an original pixel of the original secret image, assume the corresponding pixels in autostereograms S_1 and S_2 are p_1 and p_2. Let $A = \begin{bmatrix} p_1 & 1 \\ 1 & p_2 \end{bmatrix}$. Thus, $D_0 = A \circ B_0$ and $D_1 = A \circ B_1$ are basis matrices for a valid (2, 2)-VCS with autostereograms. Here, the symbol "∘" denotes the concatenation of two matrices. The experiment results are shown in Fig. 7.

We verify the validity of the above scheme as follows. Since each autostereogram is independent of the secret image, the security of the proposed scheme follows directly from that of the old scheme. The contrast condition is satisfied, because the Hamming weight of the OR of the two rows in the new basis matrix D_0 is 3, but the Hamming weight of the OR of the two rows in D_1 is 4.

3.3 Discussion

To combine a VCS and autostereogram, there are two possible ways. One is to add some 3D information into shares of a VCS, and the difficulty is how to maintain the 3D effect of each share. This method has introduced in Sect. 3.2. Another method is to establish the relationship among n shares and n autostereograms. Now, we discuss the latter method.

Suppose $S_1, \ldots, S_n$ are the n shares of an original (k, n)-VCS, $G_1, \ldots, G_n$ are the n original autostereograms, and $S'_1, \ldots, S'_n$ are the n shares of the proposed scheme. $S_1, \ldots, S_n$ are the same size. Assume the pixel expansion of the original VCS is m. To keep the contrast of the reconstructed secret image, $m_A - 1$ black pixels have to add to each block. Therefore, the pixel expansion of the proposed VCS with

Fig. 7. A (2, 2)-VCS with autostereogram, (a) Share 1, (b) Share 2, (c) Recovered secret image from share1 and share2.

autostereograms is $m' = m + 1 + m_A - 1 = m + m_A$. We compress each original share and original autostereogram into $m'/(m_A + 1)$ of the size of the original share.

Let $q_1, \cdots, q_n$ be the $ij - th$ element of the autostereograms $G_1, \cdots, G_n$. According to the step 4 of the Construction above, we get the matrix A. Let $p_1, \cdots, p_n$ be the $ij - th$ element of the shares $S_1, \cdots, S_n$. The new basis matrix $D = A \circ (p_1, \cdots, p_n)^T$, here T represents transpose operation.

Thus, the n shares of the (k, n)-VCS and that of the (k, n)-VCS with autostereogram are the same size, namely $S_1, \cdots, S_n$ and $S'_1, \ldots, S'_n$ are the same size, because $(m'/(m_A + 1)) \times (m_A + 1) = m'$.

3.4 A (k, n)-VCS with Autostereogram

In Ref. [2, 3], the authors extended the Naor and Shamir's VCS [1] with the pixel expansion m and construct an extended VCS(EVCS) in which each share is a meaningful image. The optimal pixel expansion is $m + \lceil n/(k - 1) \rceil$.

Lemma 1[2, 3]. Let m be the pixel expansion of a binary (k, n)-VCS, there exists a (k, n)-EVCS with pixel expansion $m + \lceil n/(k - 1) \rceil$.

Next, we will construct a (k, n)-VCS with autostereogram. Suppose B_0 and B_1 are basis matrix of a (k, n)-VCS. Assume A is a matrix called extended matrix collection which has the following properties:

The $i - th$ row in A has an only element to represent the pixel in the $i - th$ autostereogram, $i = 1, \cdots, n$. Each column in A has at most $k - 1$ elements could be used to represent the pixels of the autostereograms. All the other elements in A are all 1's. Here, 1 represents black.

The next theorem proves that $D_0 = A \circ B_0$ and $D_1 = A \circ B_1$ are basis matrices of a (k, n)-VCS with autostereograms, and the extended matrix collection A has the minimum pixel expansion $m_A \geq \lceil n/(k - 1) \rceil$. The symbol $\circ$ represents the concatenation of two matrices.

Theorem 1. A (k, n)-VCS with autostereograms can be constructed by pixel expansion $m' = m + m_A$ and $m_A \geq \lceil n/(k - 1) \rceil$. Here, m is the pixel expansion of a previous (k, n)-VCS, and m_A is the pixel expansion of the extended matrix collection. The relative difference of the recovered secret image is $\alpha' = \alpha \cdot m/m'$.

Proof: From the lemma 1 above, $D_0 = A \circ B_0$ and $D_1 = A \circ B_1$ satisfies the security of the secret image. The contrast condition is verified as follows. Randomly select k rows $i_1, \cdots, i_k$. From the properties of the extended matrix collection A, the OR V_A of the k rows in A has the Hamming weight (the number of 1's in the V) $H(V) = m_A$ A. From the definition 1, suppose a (k, n)-VCS with pixel expansion m and relative difference α. The OR V_{B_0} and V_{B_1} of the k rows $i_1, \cdots, i_k$ in the basis matrices B_0 and B_1 satisfies $H(V_{B_0}) \leq d - \alpha \cdot m$ and $H(V_{B_1}) \geq d$. Thus we have:

$$H(V_{D_0}) = H(V_{B_0}) + H(V_A) \leq d - \alpha \cdot m + m_A$$

$$H(V_{D_1}) = H(V_{B_1}) + H(V_A) \geq d + m_A$$

Therefore, the new scheme satisfies $\alpha' \cdot m' = H(V_{D_1}) - H(V_{D_0}) = \alpha \cdot m$, namely $\alpha' = \alpha \cdot m/m'$.

Next, we verify the minimum pixel expansion m_A of the extended matrices collection. From the properties of the extended matrix collection A, The $i - th$ row in A has an only element to represent the pixel in the $i - th$ autostereogram, $i = 1, \cdots, n$. Thus at most n elements in A can be used to represent the pixels of autostereograms.

According to the properties, each column in A has at most $k - 1$ elements could be used to represent the pixels of the autostereograms. Assume m_A be the number of columns of the extended matrix collection A. Thus $m_A \times (k - 1) \geq n$, namely $m_A \geq \lceil n_i'(k - 1) \rceil$. ∎

4 Conclusion

In our (k, n) scheme, overlapping any k of n shares, we can visual view the original secret image, whereas we are not able to obtain any secret information by any means through less than k shares. Each share is autostereogram which shows 3D effect. A shortage of our scheme is that the reconstructed 3D scene in each share is not clear. One solution is to combine the 3D surface reconstruction. Each share of our (k, n)-VCS with autostereogram is also an autostereogram, so the previous reconstruction method can be implemented directly.

Acknowledgements. This research was supported in part by the National Natural Science Foundation of China (Grant Nos. 61170032 and 61373020), and was also supported by the Testbed@TWISC, National Science Council under the Grant NSC 100-2219-E-006-001.

References

1. Naor, M., Shamir, A.: Visual Cryptography. In: De Santis, A. (ed.) EUROCRYPT 1994. LNCS, vol. 950, pp. 1–12. Springer, Heidelberg (1995)
2. Alteniese, G., Blundo, C., De Santis, A., Sinson, D.R.: Extended capabilities for visual cryptography. Theoret. Comput. Sci. **250**, 143–161 (2001)
3. Wang, D.S., Yi, F., Li, X.: On general construction for extended visual cryptography schemes. Pattern Recogn. **42**(11), 3071–3082 (2009)
4. Wheastone, C.: contributions to the physiology of vision, part i: on some remarkable and hitherto unobserved, phenomena of binocular vision. Philos. Trans. R. Soc. Lond. **128**, 371–394 (1838)
5. Wheastone, C.: Contributions to the physiology of vision, Part II: On some remarkable and hitherto unobserved, phenomena of binocular vision (continued). The London, Edinburgh and Dublin Phil. Mag. J. Sci. **4**(3), 504–523 (1852)
6. Julesz, B.: Binocular depth perception of computer generated patterns. The Bell Syst. Tech. J. **39**, 1125–1162 (1960)
7. Tyler, C.W., Clarke, M.B.: The autostereogram. SPIE Stereoscopic Displays Appl. **1256**, 182–196 (1990)
8. Thimbleby, H.W., Inglis, S., Witten, I.H.: Displaying 3D images: algorithms for single-image random-dot stereograms. COMPUTER **27**(10), 38–48 (1994)
9. Desmedt, Y.G., Hou, S., Quisquater, J.-J.: Cerebral cryptography. In: Aucsmith, D. (ed.) IH 1998. LNCS, vol. 1525, pp. 62–72. Springer, Heidelberg (1998)
10. Minh, S.T., Fazekas, K., Gschwindt, A.: The presentation of three-dimensional objects with single image stereogram. IEEE Trans. Instrum. Meas. **51**(5), 955–961 (2002)
11. Papas, M., Houit, T., Nowrouzezahrai, D., Gross, M., Jarosz, Wo.: The magic lens: refractive steganography. ACM SIGGRANPH Asia 2012. (2012) Available at http://www.disneyresearch.com/wp-content/uploads/project_magiclens_paper.pdf

12. Tsai, S.-L., Wen, C.-H.: Towards a design guideline of visual cryptography on stereoscopic displays. In: Kurosu, M. (ed.) HCII/HCI 2013, Part III. LNCS, vol. 8006, pp. 78–84. Springer, Heidelberg (2013)
13. Yamamoto H., Tada S., Suyama S.: Use of DFD (depth-fused 3-D) perception for visual cryptography. Available at http://www.perceptionweb.com/abstract.cgi?id=v110728

Progressive Visual Secret Sharing with Multiple Decryptions and Unexpanded Shares

Guohui Chen[1], Chunying Wang[2], Xuehu Yan[3]([✉]), and Peng Li[4]

[1] Hebei University of Science and Technology, Shi Jiazhuang 050018, China
[2] Hebei Sailhero Environmental Protection Hi-teeh Co.Ltd.,
Shi Jiazhuang 050035, China
[3] School of Computer Science and Technology, Harbin Institute of Technology,
Harbin 150080, China
xuehu.yan@ict.hit.edu.cn
[4] Department of Mathematics and Physics, North China Electric Power University,
Baoding 071003, China

Abstract. Differently from traditional secret sharing, progressive and perceptual secret sharing can gain clearer recovered secret image with more shares. Recently, Hou and Quan proposed a progressive visual secret sharing (PVSS) scheme that solves the pixel expansion problem of previous research. However, Hou and Quan's scheme suffers from some problems, such as different color representation from ordinary digital images, and lossy recovery. Aiming to solve the problems, in this paper, one PVSS scheme is proposed, which has the abilities of stacking and additive decryptions. If a light-weight device is not available, the secret could be reconstructed by stacking. On the other hand, if a light-weight device is available, the secret will be reconstructed losslessly by additive operation. In addition, the proposed scheme has no the pixel expansion as well as supports different image formats. Experiments are conducted to evaluate the efficiency of the proposed scheme.

Keywords: Progressive visual secret sharing · Perceptual visual secret sharing · Multiple decryptions · Lossless recovery

1 Introduction

Along with the wide application and development of internet and multimedia technology, digital images are easily obtained, transmitted and manipulated. Security of digital images protects the sensitive information from the malicious behavior in transmission. An alternative method to ensure the confidentiality and high level of security is cryptography [1]. Cryptography deals with the techniques that transform the data between comprehensible and incomprehensible forms by encryption/decryption operations under the control of key(s). It provides the content confidentiality and access control [1]. Even if one bit of the data is destroyed and the whole secret information isn't leaked, the data is not available in cryptography. Therefore, retrieving the original data without any distortion is a matter of importance in case of a certain amount of data is lost in the transmission.

© Springer International Publishing Switzerland 2015
Y.-Q. Shi et al. (Eds.): IWDW 2014, LNCS 9023, pp. 376–386, 2015.
DOI: 10.1007/978-3-319-19321-2_28

Secret image sharing has solved the problem since the method shares the user data into different secret shadows and distributes them to multiple participants. Therefore, it has attracted more attention from scientist and engineers. Visual secret sharing (VSS) [2–4], is one of the primary branches in secret sharing.

Naor and Shamir [2] firstly propose the threshold-based VSS. In their scheme, a binary secret image is shared by generating corresponding n noise-like shadow images (shares). And any k or more noise-like shadow images are superposed to recover the secret image visually based on human visual system (HVS) and probability. Furthermore, less than k participants cannot reveal any information of the secret image by inspecting their shares, which is called "All-or-Nothing". Main properties of the VSS are simple recovered method and alternative order of the shadow images. Simple recovered method means that the decryption of secret image is completely based on HVS without any cryptographic computation. However, it also suffers from pixel expansion [5], since pixel expansion will increase storage and transmission bandwidth.

In addition, since multimedia is different from data, "All-or-Nothing" of traditional VSS maybe limited in some multimedia applications. Differently from traditional VSS, "progressive VSS" not only has the same property of recovering by staking at least k shares but also improves the clarity of a secret image progressively by stacking more and more shares [6–8]. However, they overall have drawbacks such as pixel expansion problem and poor visual quality of the recovered secret image.

In order to solve the pixel expansion problem, Hou and Quan [9] propose a $(2, n)$ progressive visual secret sharing (PVSS) with unexpanded shares by designing two basic sharing matrices. In Hou and Quan's scheme, the possibility of either black or white pixels to appear as black pixels on the shares is equal to $1/n$. And when more shares are stacking (Boolean OR operation), clearer secret will be gained. Unfortunately, Hou and Quan's scheme has several weaknesses such as lossy recovery, and incompatible with color representation of ordinary digital images [3,10]. In most digital image formats like BMP and JPEG, and common digital image processing related software, such as Matlab and Photoshop, 0 denotes black or opaque pixel value and 1 denotes white or transparent pixel value. Different color representations will increase computation time for reversing or complementing operations (that is $0 \rightarrow 1$ or $1 \rightarrow 0$).

In this paper, we propose one efficient PVSS scheme(progressive and perceptual secret sharing [11]), which has two kinds of decryption methods, respectively. The proposed scheme improves Hou and Quan's scheme to be the same color representation as digital images, which is very important for various digital applications. In addition, it has the abilities of two decryptions. If a light-weight device is not available, the secret could be recovered by HVS with no pixel expansion and the same visual quality as Hou and Quan's scheme. On the other hand, if a light-weight device is available, the secret will be recovered losslessly by only additive operation. Experimental results demonstrate the effectiveness of the proposed scheme.

The rest of the paper is organized as follows. In Sect. 2, the proposed scheme is presented in detail. Section 3 gives the performance analyses of the proposed scheme. Section 4 is devoted to experimental results. Finally, Sect. 5 concludes this paper.

2 The Proposed Scheme

In this section, we propose one PVSS. Here "1" denotes white pixels, "0" denotes black pixels, which are the same as color representation of digital images.

2.1 Improved Progressive Visual Cryptography with Unexpanded Shares

Aiming to improve Hou and Quan's scheme to be the same color representation as digital images, and to have the abilities of two decryptions, i.e. if a light-weight device is not available the secret could be recovered by stacking ($\&$) with the same visual quality and no pixel expansion as Hou and Quan's scheme, otherwise, the secret will be recovered losslessly based on addition, we design two $n \times n$ matrices denoted by C^0 and C^1 as shown in Table 1 for the proposed scheme.

Table 1. Two $n \times n$ secret sharing basic matrices of the proposed scheme

Secret pixel	Basic matrices	Matrix collections				Probability	Shadow images 1	2	$\cdots$	n	Recovery method
▫(1)	$C^I = \begin{pmatrix} 0 & 0 & \cdots & 0 \\ 1 & 1 & \cdots & 1 \\ \vdots & \vdots & \vdots & \vdots \\ 1 & 1 & \cdots & 1 \end{pmatrix}_{n\times n}$	0	0	$\cdots$	0	$1/n$			$\cdots$		
		1	1	$\cdots$	1	$1/n$			$\cdots$		
		$\vdots$	$\vdots$	$\vdots$	$\vdots$	$\vdots$	$\vdots$	$\vdots$	$\vdots$	$\vdots$	1.Stacking ($\&$)
		1	1	$\cdots$	1	$1/n$			$\cdots$		2.Addtion
▪(0)	$C^0 = \begin{pmatrix} 0 & 1 & \cdots & 1 \\ 1 & 0 & \cdots & 1 \\ \vdots & \vdots & \ddots & \vdots \\ 1 & 1 & \cdots & 0 \end{pmatrix}_{n\times n}$	0	1	$\cdots$	1	$1/n$			$\cdots$		
		1	0	$\cdots$	1	$1/n$			$\cdots$		
		$\vdots$	$\vdots$	$\ddots$	$\vdots$	$\vdots$	$\vdots$	$\vdots$	$\ddots$	$\vdots$	
		1	1	$\cdots$	0	$1/n$			$\cdots$		

The algorithmic steps are described in detail in Algorithm 1. First, the two basic matrices are generated according to Table 1. Second, for every position (i, j) of S, select L from $1, 2, \cdots, n$ randomly and choose the current basic matrix depending on $S(i, j)$. Finally, attribute the Lth row of the chosen basic matrix to the corresponding n pixels of the n shadow images.

The secret recovery algorithmic steps are described in detail in Algorithm 2. There are two decryptions for the recovery of the proposed scheme. The recovery method 1 is based on stacking (Boolean $\&$ operation) if no light-weight device available. When a light-weight computation device is available, the recovery method 2 is addition and comparison, and the secret can be recovered losslessly, since different sum of Lth row for the two basic matrices (C^1 is 0 or n while C^0 is $[1, n-1]$).

Algorithm 1. The proposed scheme.

Input: A $M \times N$ binary secret image S, the threshold parameter n

Output: n shadow images $SC_1, SC_2, \cdots SC_n$

Step 1: Generate two basic matrices C^0 and C^1.

Step 2: For each position $(i,j) \in \{(i,j)|1 \leq i \leq M, 1 \leq j \leq N\}$, repeat Steps 3-4.

Step 3: Select $L \in \{1, 2, \cdots, n\}$ randomly.

Step 4: If $S(i,j) = 0$, $SC_m(i,j) = C^0(L,m)$. Else $SC_m(i,j) = C^1(L,m)$, $m = 1, 2, \cdots, n$.

Step 5: Output the n shadow images $SC_1, SC_2, \cdots SC_n$.

Algorithm 2. Secret image recovery of the proposed scheme.

Input: t shadow images $SC_{j_1}, SC_{j_2}, \cdots SC_{j_t}$, the threshold parameter n

Output: A $M \times N$ binary secret image S'

Step 1: If no light-weight computation device, $S' = SC_{j_1} \& SC_{j_2} \& \cdots SC_{j_t}$, go to Step 5; else go to Step 2.

Step 2: For each position $(i,j) \in \{(i,j)|1 \leq i \leq M, 1 \leq j \leq N\}$, repeat Steps 3-4.

Step 3: Compute $num = SC_{j_1}(i,j) + SC_{j_2}(i,j) + \cdots + SC_{j_t}(i,j)$.

Step 4: If $num = 0 \, or \, n$, $S'(i,j) = 1$; else $S'(i,j) = 0$.

Step 5: Output the binary secret image S'.

It is noted that, the proposed scheme, perceptual secret sharing [11] which has better properties than PVSS, maintains good security and performance as Hou and Quan's scheme, progressive VSS. Besides, it complies with the color representation of digital images and flexible decryption methods, which outperforms Hou and Quan's scheme.

Since researchers in this field follow the scenario of Naor and Shamir's paper [2], though flipping operation is a trivial operation, we explain why the recovery of the proposed scheme with the same color representation as digital images is also stacking or HVS.

Visual cryptography is a secret sharing technique that allows a "visual" reconstruction of the secret. That is, participants have to be able to simply stack the shares (printed on transparencies) to recover the secret. And the HVS could be performed after the stacking operation with no cryptographic operation. Different stacking results and probabilities will lead to the contrast. The secret could be revealed by HVS when contrast is greater than 0. Thus, if the secret image could be recovered with contrast by stacking the two or more shadow images together, then, the secret image will be revealed by HVS with no cryptographic operation.

Remark that, the results of the stacking operation in Hou and Quan's scheme [9] as shown in Table 1 of [9], where 1 represents black pixels and 0 represents white pixels, are the same as Boolean OR operation of 0 or 1. Thus, in Hou and Quan's scheme, the stacking is corresponding to Boolean OR operation

The color representation idea of the proposed scheme is presented in Table 1, where 1 denotes white pixels, 0 denotes black pixels, which are the same as color representation method of digital images. When stacking the two or more shadow images, the opaque (black) pixels will also cover the transparent (white) pixels. The probability of black secret pixel is decoded into black pixel, is greater than that of white secret pixel into white pixel, thus the contrast is also introduced. So, the secret image will be revealed by HVS with no cryptographic operation. While, the stacking operation results of the proposed scheme is the same as Boolean AND operation of 0 or 1. Thus, the stacking operation in the proposed scheme is corresponding to Boolean AND operation. Based on the above discussion, both Hou and Quan's scheme and the proposed scheme is based on stacking. The proposed scheme uses the AND operation for the recovery, the recovery also can be performed by the stacking or HVS. Hence the proposed scheme in fact is visual.

2.2   Extension for Grayscale/Color Images

The proposed scheme can be extended to share grayscale/color images [12]. To share a grayscale image, halftone technologies such as error diffusion [3,13] are applied to convert the grayscale image into binary image, then the proposed scheme could be used.

For sharing a color image, color decomposition, halftone technologies and color composition are applied. A color image can be described by color model, such as CMY (cyan–magenta–yellow) model. CMY is a subtractive color model which displays a color by reflecting light from a surface of an object.

3   Performance Analyses of the Proposed Scheme

This section introduces the performances of the proposed scheme by theoretically analyzing the security and the visual quality.

Definition 1 (Contrast): The visual quality, which will decide how well human eyes could recognize the recovered image, of the recovered secret image S' corresponding to the original secret image S is evaluated by contrast defined as follows [10, 14–16]:

$$\alpha = \frac{P_1 - P_0}{1 + P_0} = \frac{P\left(S'\left[AS1\right] = 1\right) - P\left(S'\left[AS0\right] = 1\right)}{1 + P\left(S'\left[AS0\right] = 1\right)} \tag{1}$$

where α denotes contrast, P_0 (resp., P_1) is the appearance probability of white pixels in the recovered image S' in the corresponding black (resp., white) area of original secret image S, that is, P_1 is the correctly decrypted probability corresponding to the white area of original secret image S, and P_0 is the wrongly decrypted probability corresponding to the black area of original secret image S . $AS0$ (resp., $AS1$) is the black (resp., white) area of original secret image S, $AS0 = \{(i,j) \,|\, S\,(i,j) = 0, 1 \leq i \leq M, 1 \leq j \leq N\}$

Definition 2 (Visually Recognizable) [2,10,15,16]: The recovered secret image S' could be recognized as the corresponding original secret image S, if $\alpha > 0$ when $k \leq t$.

In addition, α will increase as t increases in PVSS.

Definition 3 (Security) [2,10,15,16]: The scheme is secure if $\alpha = 0$ when $k > t$, which means no information of S could be recognized through S'.

We note that, definition 1 on the contrast partially borrowed from [16], has been widely accepted and used in some reported RG-based VSS scheme [17–19][15].

The other definition on contrast used in traditional VSS [9] and probabilistic VSS [20] is given by $\frac{P_1 - P_0}{m}$.

Where m is referred to the pixel expansion. It merely evaluates the absolute difference rate between the secret and background.

From HVS, when the same difference is achieved, better image quality is obtained when P_0 becomes smaller [16]. Hence, Definition 1 is adopted in this paper for evaluating the contrast.

For conventional VSS, the security can be determined by the contrast. Such definitions are the same as Definitions 2 and 3, since the contrast is bigger than zero or equal to zero if and only if the difference is bigger than zero or equal to zero.

Theorem 1: The proposed scheme is secure and visually recognizable. The contrast of the recovered secret image recovered by any $t(2 \leq t \leq n)$ shadow images, which are generated by the proposed scheme, is computed as follows:

$$\alpha = \begin{cases} 1, & Additive\ recovery \\ \frac{t-1}{2n-t}, & Stacking\ recovery \end{cases} \tag{2}$$

Proof: From Algorithms 1 and 2, except for the color representation and decryption methods, other parts are the same as Hou and Quan's scheme. Hence, the proposed scheme is secure, which means a single could reveal nothing about the secret, and visually recognizable when $t(2 \leq t \leq n)$ shadow images are stacking.

If $t(2 \leq t \leq n)$ and light-weight device is not available, when t shadow images are stacking, the probability for the white part of the secret image to appear as black remains $1/n$, while for the black part, the probability increases to t/n. Based on Definition 1, we have:

$$\frac{P_1 - P_0}{1 + P_0} = \frac{\frac{n-1}{n} - \frac{n-t}{n}}{1 + \frac{n-t}{n}} = \frac{t-1}{2n-t}$$

If a light-weight device is available, the secret can be recovered losslessly based on addition, since different sum of Lth row for the two basic matrices, i.e., sum of Lth row for C^1 is 0 or n while that of C^0 is $[1, n-1]$.

4   Experimental Results and Analyses

In this section, we conducted experiments and analyses to evaluate the effectiveness of the proposed scheme. In the experiments, several secret images, of size 512×512, are used: original binary secret image1 as shown in Fig. 1 (a), and original grayscale secret image2 as shown in Fig. 2 are used as the secret images to test the efficiency of the proposed scheme.

4.1   Image Illustration

In our experiments, (2, 5) (i.e. $k = 2$, $n = 5$) threshold of scheme with secret image1, and (2, 4) threshold of scheme with grayscale secret image2 are used to test the proposed scheme.

Figure 1 (b-f) show the five shadow images SC_1, SC_2, SC_3, SC_4 and SC_5, which are random noise-like. Figure 1 (g-j) show the recovered binary secret image with any $t\,(2 \leq t \leq 5)$ (taking the first tth shadow images as an example) with stacking (AND) recovery, from which better visual of the recovered secret will be gained by stacking more shadow images. The secret image recovered from $t = 2$ or more shadow images is lossless when a light-weight device is available.

Figure 2(b-f) show the halftone secret image and 4 shadow images SC_1, SC_2, SC_3 and SC_4 for grayscale secret image 3, the shadow images are random noise-like. Figure 2 (g-i) show the recovered secret image with any $t\,(2 \leq t \leq 4)$ (taking the first t shadow images as an example) with stacking(AND) recovery, from which the progressive visual quality will be gained. The secret image recovered by $t = 2$ or more shadow images with available light-compute device is the same as the halftone secret image.

From the results shown in Figs. 1, 2:

- The shadow images are random noise-like, hence the proposed scheme have no cross interference of secret image in the shadow images.
- The progressive visual quality of the recovered secret can be gained for the proposed scheme.
- The proposed scheme has decryption flexibility depending on the light-weight device. When a light-weight device is available, the secret could be recovered losslessly for the proposed scheme.
- The proposed scheme can also be applied for grayscale and color images.

4.2   Visual Quality of the Recovered Secret Images

In this section, the visual quality of the recovered secret images is evaluated by contrast in Definition 1. The same original binary secret image as shown in Fig. 1 (a) is used to perform the experiments of contrast.

Average contrast of the proposed $(2, n)$ scheme whether a light-weight device is available or not is shown in Table 2. From Table 2, the progressive visual quality can be achieved and the secret can be recovered losslessly when collecting all shadow images with light-weight device. In addition, the experimental results are close to the theoretical results.

4.3   Comparisons with Related Scheme

In the section, we compare the proposed scheme with other related scheme especially [9], since the proposed scheme is continuous and extensive work of the scheme [9].

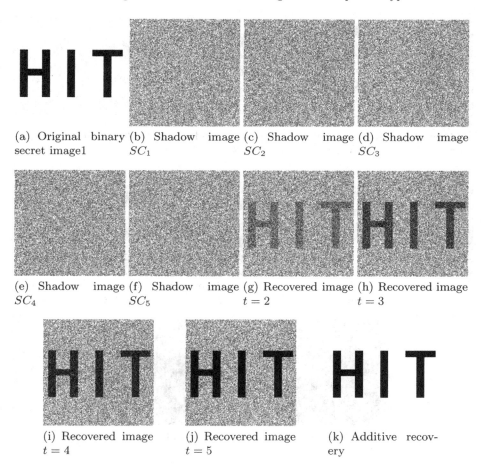

(a) Original binary secret image1

(b) Shadow image SC_1

(c) Shadow image SC_2

(d) Shadow image SC_3

(e) Shadow image SC_4

(f) Shadow image SC_5

(g) Recovered image $t = 2$

(h) Recovered image $t = 3$

(i) Recovered image $t = 4$

(j) Recovered image $t = 5$

(k) Additive recovery

Fig. 1. Experimental example of the proposed $(2, 5)$ scheme for binary secret image1

Table 2. Average contrast of the proposed scheme

	light-weight device not available				light-weight device available			
$(2, n)$	$t = 2$	$t = 3$	$t = 4$	$t = 5$	$t = 2$	$t = 3$	$t = 4$	$t = 5$
$(2, 2)$	0.5005				1			
$(2, 3)$	0.2492	0.6656			1	1		
$(2, 4)$	0.16731	0.40077	0.75097		1	1	1	
$(2, 5)$	0.12457	0.28522	0.49943	0.79931	1	1	1	1

Contrast Comparison. Except the color representation and decryption methods, other parts are the same as Hou and Quan's scheme, such as the security and visual quality. Hence, the contrast of the proposed scheme is the same as Hou and Quan's scheme if a light-weight device is not available. In addition,

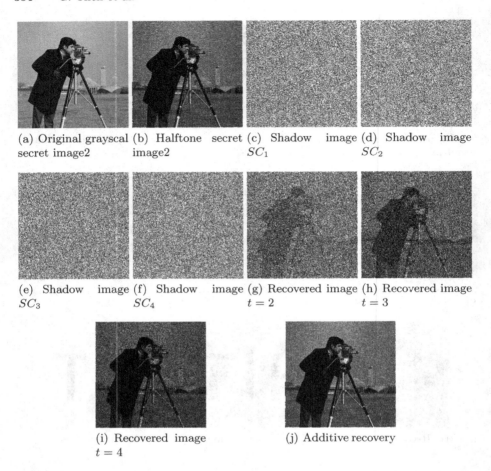

(a) Original grayscal secret image2

(b) Halftone secret image2

(c) Shadow image SC_1

(d) Shadow image SC_2

(e) Shadow image SC_3

(f) Shadow image SC_4

(g) Recovered image $t = 2$

(h) Recovered image $t = 3$

(i) Recovered image $t = 4$

(j) Additive recovery

Fig. 2. Experimental example of the proposed (2, 4) scheme for grayscale secret image2

for the proposed scheme, the secret will be lossless if a light-weight device is available, which means the contrast of the proposed scheme is greater than Hou and Quan's scheme.

Functionality Comparison. In this section, we highlight the main advantages of the proposed scheme and compare them with the relative scheme as shown in Table 3. From Table 3, the proposed scheme has more good properties than other competitive scheme.

Compared with Hou and Quan's scheme [9], the proposed scheme has the same color representation as digital images and two decryptions, based on which the secret can be recovered losslessly.

Table 3. Properties comparison with relative schemes

Scheme	Progressive	(k, n) threshold	Recovering measure	$m = 1$	Lossless	Digital color
Ref. [13]	×	✓	Stacking	×	×	×
Ref. [21]	×	✓	Boolean	✓	✓	×
Ref. [2]	×	✓	Stacking	×	×	×
Ref. [15]	✓	✓	Stacking	✓	×	×
Ref. [20]	×	✓	Stacking	✓	×	×
Ref. [9]	✓	$(2, n)$	Stacking(OR)	✓	×	×
Ours	✓	$(2, n)$	Stacking(AND)/Addition	✓	✓	✓

5   Conclusion

An efficient visual secret image sharing threshold scheme with two decryptions, progressive and perceptual sharing scheme, has been proposed. The proposed scheme is an improvement of Hou and Quan's scheme. It solves the problems of color representation and lossy recovery. The proposed scheme has no pixel expansion and two decryptions. We have performed several experimental results and analyses to evaluate the security and efficiency of the proposed scheme. Comparisons with previous approaches suggest that the proposed scheme has several merits. The idea applied in this paper can be extended in other VCSs. Supporting (k, n) threshold will be the future work.

Acknowledgement. The authors would like to thank the anonymous reviewers for their valuable discussions and comments.

References

1. Li, L., El-Latif, A.A.A., Shi, Z., Niu, X.: A new loss-tolerant image encryption scheme based on secret sharing and two chaotic systems. Res. J. Appl. Sci. Eng. Technol. **4**, 877–883 (2012)
2. Naor, M., Shamir, A.: Visual cryptography. In: De Santis, A. (ed.) EUROCRYPT 1994. LNCS, vol. 950, pp. 1–12. Springer, Heidelberg (1995)
3. Wang, Z., Arce, G.R., Di Crescenzo, G.: Halftone visual cryptography via error diffusion. IEEE Trans. Inf. Forensics Security. **4**, 383–396 (2009)
4. Yan, X., Wang, S., Niu, X.: Threshold construction from specific cases in visual cryptography without the pixel expansion. Sig. Process. **105**, 389–398 (2014)
5. Weir, J., Yan, W.Q.: A comprehensive study of visual cryptography. In: Shi, Y.Q. (ed.) Transactions on DHMS V. LNCS, vol. 6010, pp. 70–105. Springer, Heidelberg (2010)
6. Jin, D., Yan, W.Q., Kankanhalli, M.S.: Progressive color visual cryptography. J. Electron. Imaging **14**, 033019-1–033019-13 (2005)
7. Hou, Y.C., Quan, Z.Y., Tsai, C.F., Tseng, A.Y.: Block-based progressive visual secret sharing. Inf. Sci. **233**, 290–304 (2013)
8. Fang, W.P., Lin, J.C.: Progressive viewing and sharing of sensitive images. Pattern Recogn. Image Anal. **16**, 632–636 (2006)

9. Hou, Y.C., Quan, Z.Y.: Progressive visual cryptography with unexpanded shares. IEEE Trans. Circ. Sys. Video Tech. **21**, 1760–1764 (2011)

10. Yan, X., Wang, S., El-Latif, A.A.A., Niu, X.: Visual secret sharing based on random grids with abilities of a AND and XOR lossless recovery. Multimedia Tools Appl. **74**, 1–22 (2013)

11. Yan, X., Wang, S., El-Latif, A.A.A., Sang, J., Niu, X.: A novel perceptual secret sharing scheme. In: Shi, Y.Q., Liu, F., Yan, W. (eds.) Transactions on Data Hiding and Multimedia Security IX. LNCS, vol. 8363, pp. 68–90. Springer, Heidelberg (2014)

12. Hou, Y.C.: Visual cryptography for color images. Pattern Recogn. **36**, 1619–1629 (2003)

13. Zhou, Z., Arce, G.R., Di Crescenzo, G.: Halftone visual cryptography. IEEE Trans. Image Process. **15**, 2441–2453 (2006)

14. Shyu, S.J.: Image encryption by random grids. Pattern Recogn. **40**, 1014–1031 (2007)

15. Chen, T.H., Tsao, K.H.: Threshold visual secret sharing by random grids. J. Syst. Softw. **84**, 1197–1208 (2011)

16. Wu, X., Sun, W.: Random grid-based visual secret sharing with abilities of or and xor decryptions. J. Vis. Commun. Image Represent. **24**, 48–62 (2013)

17. Shyu, S.J.: Image encryption by multiple random grids. Pattern Recogn. **42**, 1582–1596 (2009)

18. Chen, T.H., Tsao, K.H.: Image encryption by (n, n) random grids. In: Proceedings of 18th Information Security Conference, Hualien, IEEE (2008)

19. Chen, T.H., Tsao, K.H.: Visual secret sharing by random grids revisited. Pattern Recogn. **42**, 2203–2217 (2009)

20. Yang, C.N.: New visual secret sharing schemes using probabilistic method. Pattern Recognit. Lett. **25**, 481–494 (2004)

21. Wang, D., Zhang, L., Ma, N., Li, X.: Two secret sharing schemese based on boolean operations. Pattern Recognit. **40**, 2776–2785 (2007)

Poster Session

Content-Adaptive Residual for Steganalysis

Xu Lin[1], Bingwen Feng[1], Wei Lu[1](✉), and Wei Sun[2]

[1] School of Information Science and Technology, Sun Yat-sen University,
Guangzhou 510006, China
linx37@mail2.sysu.edu.cn, bingwfeng@gmail.com, luwei3@mail.sysu.edu.cn
[2] School of Software, Sun Yat-sen University, Guangzhou 510006, China
sunwei@mail.sysu.edu.cn

Abstract. This paper employs the concept of the content-adaptive residual and presents a low-dimensional feature set for detecting the grayscale steganography in spatial domain. The testing image is first segmented into three kinds of areas, that is, the smooth, edge, and textural areas. Then, different pixel predictors are used to calculate the residuals responded to different areas. The yielded different co-occurrence matrices are finally collected as the steganalytic features. Experiments reported show that the proposed method is effective and yields good performances when detecting popular steganographic algorithms such as LSB matching, EA, and HUGO.

Keywords: Steganalysis · Content-adaptive residual · Co-occurrence matrices

1 Introduction

Steganography embeds secret messages into multimedia, such as image, audio, and video, to guarantee the secret communication. In contrast, steganalysis aims to detect the existence of the hidden information given some multimedia. A stego system is considered unsafe if there is a steganalytic method that can correctly judge the given multimedia with a much higher probability than the random guessing. Recently, a lot of steganographic algorithms have been proposed for the multimedia, or especially, the images, among which, the least-significant-bit (LSB) replacement is the simplest approach and thus commonly employed in image steganography. It replaces the LSBs of image pixels with the secret message bits to be hidden. Due to the anomaly of pixel distribution, LSB replacement can be easily detected, even the embedded message length can be accurately estimated by, for example, the RS attacker [4]. Another method referred as LSB matching (LSBM) or ± 1 embedding increases or decreases the selected pixels by one according to the secret message bits to be hidden. LSBM is more difficult to be detected because it removes the anomaly in the LSB replacement. Subsequently, LSBM becomes the basic tool for other popular steganographic methods.

© Springer International Publishing Switzerland 2015
Y.-Q. Shi et al. (Eds.): IWDW 2014, LNCS 9023, pp. 389–398, 2015.
DOI: 10.1007/978-3-319-19321-2_29

In [13], Luo et al. proposed an Edge-Adaptive (EA) steganographic method which selects those pixels in edge areas to hidden secret messages. Instead of using the simple standard LSB matching, it introduces the concept of pair-wise containing two adjacent pixels around the image edges based on LSB matching revisited (LSBMR) [14] method. Only sharper edge areas will be modified after embedding messages in lower embedding rates. In recent years, a lot of papers have been devoted to design a robust distortion function caused by embedding to create a higher undetectable steganographic system. Pevný et al. proposed a Highly-Undetectable steGO (HUGO) [16] steganographic system for real digital media. Given a payload, HUGO intends to minimize the embedding distortion between the cover and its corresponding stego image. Moreover, HUGO utilize the concept of Syndrome-Trellis Code (STC) [3] to reduce the number of pixels to be modified which would allow HUGO embed $7\times$ longer messages with the same secure level compared to LSB matching. More recently, a much more undetectable steganogrophic method WOW (Wavelet Obtained Weights) [10] was designed by Holub et al. using the Haar and Daubechies 8-tap wavelets to compute its embedding distortions. WOW also employs STC to embed messages likely into the textural areas that are much harder to model for steganalysis. It's much more security than all the methods mentioned above due to its texture-adaptive property.

Since the arts of steganography are springing up, more and more steganalytic systems have been proposed against them as well. In terms of the LSB matching embedding, Zhang et al. discovered in [17] that the local maxima values of the histogram of images decrease and the local minima values increase after embedding. The sum of the absolute differences between local extreme values and their neighbors in the histogram of cover images would be larger than stego images. This property would be adopted directly to detect images without any machine learning methods. Harmsen et al. [8] proposed a method based on the context of additive noises. It assumes that the hidden messages are independent of the original image and the histogram of stego image is a convolution of the noise probability mass function (PMF) and the histogram of cover image. In frequency domain, the convolution is deemed to a multiplication of the noise feature function and the histogram characteristic function (HCF). The HCF center of mass (HCF COM) will decrease after data embedding which could be used to classify the testing images. In [15], Pevný et al. proposed a steganalytic method referred as SPAM (Steganalysis by Subtractive Pixel Adjacent Matrix). The SPAM method firstly computes differences between adjacent pixels in eight directions, then it uses first-order and second-order Markov chains to model final features to classify given images with Support Vector Machine (SVM). SPAM has high performance results when detecting images embedded by LSB matching.

All the steganalytic methods above just employ a single-model to extract features for image steganalysis. They either exploit the variation between the cover and stego images or the certain specified thresholds to determine their classes or present a low-dimensional feature set to identify them with machine learning methods. Since HUGO, WOW etc. minimize the distortion caused by data embedding and use STC to reduce the number of pixels to be changed, just using a single model may not capture enough variations to divide the testing images into two classes accurately especially in those textural images. Fridrich et al. provided spatial rich models (SRM) [5] to increase feature diversity which would yield a good performance that a single model could not achieve. As a result directly, the feature set will possess such a high dimension (up to 34,761) that it uses an efficient machine learning method, that is, ensemble classifier [12], for classification. The purpose of this paper is not to exploit another rich models to yield better performances than SRM but to introduce a novel low-dimensional set of features for steganalysis based on content-adaptive residual model (CARM) and co-occurrence matrices too. After extracting features from a given image database, we use SVM to train features and classify the testing images.

The rest of this paper is organized as follows. Section 2 introduces the motivation and process of implementation of the proposed method in detail. The experiment results of our proposed approach as well as the comparison with other schemes are shown in Sect. 3. The conclusions are drawn in Sect. 4.

2   The Proposed Method

2.1   Motivation

In recent years, a lot of papers have been devoted to design a good distortion function or find high frequency areas such as the edge or textural regions directly to embed messages. As a result, those pixels are too hard to model accurately that will worsen the final classification performance. A popular approach for steganalysis is to compute differences of an input image firstly, then it uses the first-order histogram features or higher-order co-occurrence features to train classifiers. The residual R [5] of the image I can be defined as

$$R_{ij} = \frac{1}{c}\hat{I}_{ij}(\mathcal{N}_{ij}) - I_{ij}, \tag{1}$$

where c is a nonzero integer representing the residual order. $I_{ij} \in \{0, \cdots, 255\}$, where $i \in [0, n_1)$ and $j \in [0, n_2)$, represents the pixels in the $n_1 \times n_2$ size grayscale image I. $\mathcal{N}_{ij}$ stands for the local neighborhoods of pixel I_{ij}, $I_{ij} \notin \mathcal{N}_{ij}$. $\hat{I}_{ij}(\cdot)$ is a predictor of I_{ij}. In order to avoid the curse of dimensionality of features, each residual is truncated and quantized into smaller values by

$$R_{ij} = \text{trunc}_T\left(\text{round}\left(\frac{R_{ij}}{q}\right)\right), \tag{2}$$

where $\text{trunc}_T(x) = x$ when $x \in [-T, -T+1, \cdots, T]$ and $\text{trunc}_T(x) = T\text{sign}(x)$ otherwise. $\text{round}(x)$ represents the operation of rounding to an integer. $q > 0$ is a quantization step and T is a threshold.

Since many content-adaptive steganographic approaches tend to embed secret messages in those high frequency areas whose absolute values of computed residual samples are larger than the appointed T, the residuals after truncation have almost the same values between a cover image and its corresponding stego image at the same coordinates, which may cause loss of a lot of important information. These two approximate residuals will increase the difficulty to detect stego images. Moreover, since differences among those pixels in regions with complex textures or edges have such a strong gradient that they are hardly to estimate, more accurate predictors with higher-orders are usually utilized [6]. Subsequently, those predictors will have a larger dynamic range which calls for a larger threshold T. Thus, before truncating the residuals into $[-T, -T + 1, \cdots, T]$, the residual samples may be quantized by (2) with q to decrease their values as well. Apparently, this operation will also cause loss of much information if $q > 1$. The quantized residual with $q = 2$ may be interpreted as right shift of the residual values, which will lost about 50 % of all embedding changes [6]. The larger the quantization step q is, the more embedding changes are lost. At the same time, the averaging caused by more sophisticated filters may distort the statistics of the stego noise, which results in worse detection accuracy [15].

In order to reduce the loss of useful information after truncation and quantization on residuals, a content-adaptive residual is necessary. For pixels of different areas, using suitable filters to calculate residuals from images is presented in this paper. We try to suppress as more values of the residual matrix into $[-T, -T + 1, \cdots, T]$ naturally as possible to adapt the original difference distribution of images rather than pure truncation and quantization. It's a trade-off between the sophisticated predictors with high order and the threshold T. This method is described in detail as follows.

2.2 Features Based on Content-Adaptive Residual

In this subsection, the whole framework of the proposed method is presented, then detailed description of each part.

Algorithm Framework. The framework of the proposed approach is shown in Fig. 1. We divide a given testing image into three kinds of areas, that is, the smooth areas, edge areas and textured areas. In different areas, we utilize adaptive filters to model them. The features based on co-occurrence matrix are extracted in the horizontal, vertical, diagonal and minor diagonal directions and we finally present a low-dimensional feature set for every image. Instead of simple filters to get residual, our method is aimed at providing a better way to model different pixels in three kinds of areas. At last, we utilize the supervised classifier to evaluate the proposed approach.

Image Segmentation. Generally, a testing image I is considered as consisting of the smooth areas S, edge areas E and textural areas TEX in spatial domain that the smooth areas are usually described as low frequency domains while the others are considered as high frequency domains in turn. The adjacent pixels in high frequency domains have larger variance than the smooth areas. These three kinds of areas can be identified following the steps below.

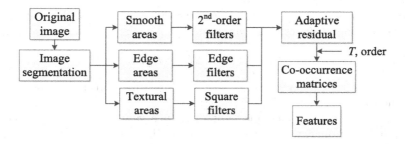

Fig. 1. The proposed algorithm framework.

For a given image, since the absolute pixel differences around edges may be the largest with respect to the rest areas, we firstly extract edges E from the image using a popular edge detector such as Sobel detector.

Secondly, for $\forall I_{ij} \notin E$, we firstly extract a 3×3 size block of pixels from the nearest eight adjacent neighbors of I_{ij} (x_5 in Fig. 2). I_{ij} is a pixel located in the textured areas [7] that is $I_{ij} \in TEX$ if and only if,

(a) The four pixels of block $B \in \{B_{lu}, B_{ru}, B_{lb}, B_{rb}\}$ shown in Fig. 2 have three different values at least.
(b) All the four blocks are satisfied with the condition (a) above.

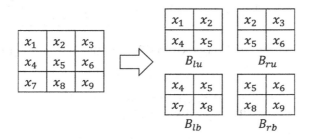

Fig. 2. A 3×3 block and its sub-blocks

Finally, because of $I = S \cup E \cup TEX$ and $S \cap E = E \cap TEX = TEX \cap S = \emptyset$, the rest pixels are among smooth areas apparently.

The input image I is divided into different areas following these steps above which would contribute to the next operations of feature extraction.

Adaptive Filtering. After image segmentation, we employ different filters to calculate the residual values respectively by the operation of convolution, which is the other form to calculate pixel differences. For any finite set $X \subset \mathbb{R}$, where $\mathbb{R}$ represents all real numbers, $x = \Theta(X)$ denotes the function that x is equal to the number who has the minimum absolute value in X. The approach to compute noise residual is presented as follows.

For those pixels among smooth areas, the difference $r^{(\mathrm{h})}$ of the central pixel along the horizontal direction is computed by

$$r^{(\mathrm{h})} = I_{i,j-1} - 2I_{ij} + I_{i,j+1}. \tag{3}$$

The differences $r^{(\mathrm{v})}, r^{(\mathrm{d})}, r^{(\mathrm{m})}$ along another three directions are defined analogically, then $R_{ij} = \Theta([r^{(\mathrm{h})}, r^{(\mathrm{v})}, r^{(\mathrm{d})}, r^{(\mathrm{m})}])$.

As shown in Fig. 3, calculate eight difference values $r_1, \cdots, r_8$ at pixel I_{ij} using eight directional edge filters in edge areas. Similarly, $R_{ij} = \Theta([r_1, \cdots, r_8])$.

Finally, since textural areas are hard to model by a filter with small size, we predict the difference of central pixel using the large square kernel (4) presented in [11] from its 5×5 neighborhoods. Note that the predictor was obtained as a result of optimizing the coefficients of a circularly symmetrical kernel using the Nelder-Mead algorithm to minimize the detection error for the embedding algorithm HUGO [16], which may decrease the detection error [5].

-1	2	-1
2	-4	2
0	0	0

0	0	0
2	-4	2
-1	2	-1

-1	2	0
2	-4	0
-1	2	0

0	2	-1
0	-4	2
0	2	-1

-1	0	0
2	-1	0
-1	2	-1

-1	2	-1
0	-1	2
0	0	-1

-1	2	-1
2	-1	0
-1	0	0

0	0	-1
0	-1	2
-1	2	-1

Fig. 3. Eight directional predictors used to calculate the differences of pixels in edge areas.

In each operation of convolution, the yielded residual sample R_{ij} is truncated and quantized by (2) respectively with $q = 1$, which may give us the best performance [6].

$$K_{5 \times 5} = \begin{pmatrix} -1 & 2 & -2 & 2 & -1 \\ 2 & -6 & 8 & -6 & 2 \\ -2 & 8 & -12 & 8 & -2 \\ 2 & -6 & 8 & -6 & 2 \\ -1 & 2 & -2 & 2 & -1 \end{pmatrix} \tag{4}$$

Co-Occurrence Matrix. By the way of the adaptive filters to residual, the construction of the final features for images continues with computing four co-occurrence matrices of neighborhood samples along the horizontal, vertical, diagonal and minor diagonal directions. The dimensionality of the co-occurrence matrix grows exponentially with the increase of T or the order of co-occurrence matrix just by one. In order to keep the co-occurrences populated and reduce the loss of information caused by truncation and quantization, we choose the third-order co-occurrences and set $T = 3$. We denote the number of elements in a given set by $|\cdot|$, then the horizontal co-occurrence matrix can be defined as

$$C^{(h)}_{u,v,w} = \left|(R_{ij}, R_{i,j+1}, R_{i,j+2})|R_{ij} = u, R_{i,j+1} = v, R_{i,j+2} = w\right| \quad (5)$$

where $u, v, w \in [-T, -T+1, \cdots, T]$. The vertical $C^{(v)}_{u,v,w}$, diagonal $C^{(d)}_{u,v,w}$ and minor diagonal $C^{(m)}_{u,v,w}$ are defined analogically. The final features $F_{1,\cdots,2k}$ consist of two parts that are $F_{1,\cdots,k} = \frac{1}{2}[C^{(h)} + C^{(v)}]$ and $F_{k+1,\cdots,2k} = \frac{1}{2}[C^{(d)} + C^{(m)}]$, where $k = (2T + 1)^3$. For the fixed T and co-occurrence order, we would finally obtain a set of 686-dimensional features of each image in spatial domain, the same as the 2nd-order SPAM.

3   Experiments

In this section, we conduct several experiments to evaluate the proposed approach on the BOSSBase v1.01 cover database from the Break Our Steganographic System (BOSS) contest [1] consisting of 10,000 grayscale images with no compression. Two sets of stego images are created with payloads 0.5 bits per pixel (bpp) and 0.25 bpp from the whole images of BOSS using steganographic methods respectively. These two payloads were also used in [15] which are already difficult to detect reliably. Before all experiments, we divide the cover and stego images into a training and testing set of equal size randomly. Ensure that the cover images and the stego images in the training set are not used in the testing set repeatedly. The comparisons between the proposed approach and prior arts appear next.

Support Vector Machine (SVM) with a Gaussian kernel is utilized to classify the covers and stegos in our experiments. Before training the classifier, the values of the penalization parameter C and the Gaussian kernel parameter γ are adjusted to get optimal experimental results. These two values should be chosen to give the classifier the ability to generalize. They are set through a grid-search method using the LIBSVM [2] by the five-fold cross-validation on the training set. The group of those two values possessing the lowest decision error are selected to train the model of SVM. In the experiments, all the stego images are labeled as +1 (positive) while the cover images are labeled as −1 (negative). We repeat the random half split of BOSSbase for 10 times and evaluate the performance using the detection error on the testing set

$$P_E = \min_{P_{FA}} \frac{1}{2}(P_{FA} + P_{MD}(P_{FA})) \quad (6)$$

as a function of the payload expressed in bpp, where P_{FA} and P_{MD} are the probabilities of false alarm and missed detection.

The results of the proposed CARM, SPAM [15] and SQUARE [11], which was also taken in SRM [5], are shown in Table 1. Note that the SQUARE features are obtained simply by using (4) to calculate the noise residual image

Table 1. Detection error P_E for three steganalytic algorithms to detect three steganographic schemes for payload 0.50 and 0.25 bpp.

Steganography	bpp	SPAM [15]	SQAURE [11]	CARM(proposed)
LSBM	0.25	0.0900	**0.0439**	0.0775
	0.50	0.0448	**0.0219**	0.0302
EA [13]	0.25	0.2917	0.2164	**0.2114**
	0.50	0.1188	0.0922	**0.0910**
HUGO [16]	0.25	0.4582	**0.3292**	0.3486
	0.50	0.3282	**0.1601**	0.1922

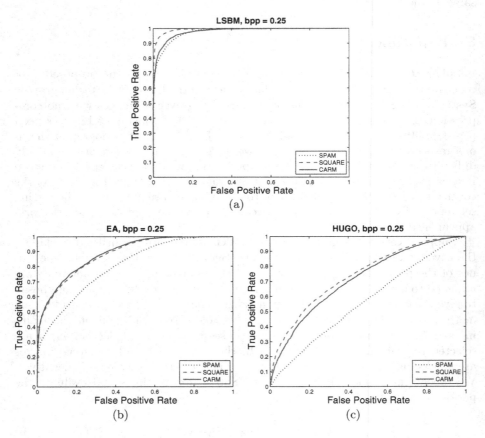

Fig. 4. ROC curves of the proposed approach (CARM), SPAM and SQUARE to detect LSBM, EA and HUGO (default parameters presented in [16]) respectively.

for the co-occurrence matrix. For fair comparison, the threshold T and the co-occurrence order are also equal to 3 respectively while the sign-symmetry are not employed to decrease the dimensionality of features. We use the simple LSBM steganography and two other adaptive methods namely EA [13] and HUGO [16] to compare their performances respectively. To compare the proposed approach with SPAM visually, the Receiver Operating Characteristic (ROC) curves for each set of stego images are also depicted in Fig. 4. It can be seen from Table 1 and Fig. 4 apparently that the proposed approach is better than SPAM in terms of all the testing steganographic systems especially for those adaptive ones. At the same time, it's also comparable to SQUARE that the SQUARE features seem to perform better about $1\% - 3\%$ when detecting LSBM and HUGO. This is likely due to the fact that the adaptive filters to different regions "distorts" the coefficients' optimization of the SQUARE kernel in minimizing the detection error for HUGO. In spite of this, the proposed approach, however, yields almost the same, even slightly better, performances when detecting the EA algorithm. The results are consistent with our former intuition that adaptive residual would decrease the detection error by capturing much more useful distortions in stego images caused by information embedding. In short, these experiments show that the proposed method is effective in blind steganalysis.

4   Conclusion

The modern steganographic schemes are tend to exploit those pixels of image in textured or edge areas to carry secret messages. As a result, a single model for steganalysis seems hardly to detect stego images because of the high adaptivity of steganographic methods. This paper tries to provide a single model for blind steganalysis using an adaptive residual. The two statical models that co-occurrence matrix and histogram are widely utilized by many steganalyzers while they will, however, lost much important information because of truncation or quantization. To reduce the loss of useful information, we extract features based on co-occurrence matrix too from a single adaptive model. The approach proposed in this paper suppresses the difference values as small as possible to locate between the appointed positive threshold and its opposite number. This approach is more practical than rich models in real-time applications as its low dimensionality. As shown in the experiments, the new steganalyzer yields good performances in steganlysis for those content adaptive steganographic tools.

For the future work, more accurate approach for image segmentation will be exploited. What's more, we would like to mine other adaptive predictors that they can provide better estimates at different areas respectively. For instance, we can employ the optimization method presented in [9] to generate a better predictor by minimizing the detection error for the embedding algorithm EA, which would be utilized to estimate those pixels in edge areas then.

References

1. Bas, P., Filler, T., Pevný, T.: Break our steganographic system: the ins and outs of organizing BOSS. In: Filler, T., Pevný, T., Craver, S., Ker, A. (eds.) IH 2011. LNCS, vol. 6958, pp. 59–70. Springer, Heidelberg (2011)

2. Chang, C.C., Lin, C.J.: LIBSVM: a library for support vector machine (2012). Software available at http://www.csie.ntu.edu.tw/cjlin/libsvm

3. Filler, T., Judas, J., Fridrich, J.: Minimizing embedding impact in steganography using trellis-coded quantization. In: Proceedings of SPIE, Electronic Imaging, Media Watermarking, Security II, vol. 754105 (2010)

4. Fridrich, J., Goljan, M., Du, R.: Detecting LSB steganography in color, and grayscale images. IEEE Multimed. **8**(4), 22–28 (2001)

5. Fridrich, J., Kodovský, J.: Rich models for steganalysis of digital images. IEEE Trans. Inf. Forensics Secur. **7**(3), 868–882 (2012)

6. Fridrich, J., Kodovský, J., Holub, V., Goljan, M.: Steganalysis of content-adaptive steganography in spatial domain. In: Filler, T., Pevný, T., Craver, S., Ker, A. (eds.) IH 2011. LNCS, vol. 6958, pp. 102–117. Springer, Heidelberg (2011)

7. Fridrich, J., Du, R.: Secure steganographic methods for palette images. In: Pfitzmann, A. (ed.) IH 1999. LNCS, vol. 1768, pp. 47–60. Springer, Heidelberg (2000)

8. Harmsen, J.J., Pearlman, W.A.: Steganalysis of additive-noise modelable information hiding. In: Proceedings of SPIE-IS&T Electronic Imaging, pp. 131–142 (2003)

9. Holub, V., Fridrich, J.: Optimizing pixel predictors for steganalysis. In: Proceedings of SPIE, Electronic Imaging, Media Watermarking, Security and Forensics, vol. 830309 (2012)

10. Holub, V., Fridrich, J.J.: Designing steganographic distortion using directional filters. In: IEEE International Workshop on Information Forensics and Security, pp. 234–239 (2012)

11. Kodovský, J., Fridrich, J., Holub, V.: On dangers of overtraining steganography to incomplete cover model. In: Proceedings of the 13th ACM Multimedia Workshop on Multimedia and Security, pp. 69–76 (2011)

12. Kodovský, J., Fridrich, J., Holub, V.: Ensemble classifiers for steganalysis of digital media. IEEE Trans. Inf. Forensics Secur. **7**(2), 432–444 (2012)

13. Luo, W., Huang, F., Huang, J.: Edge adaptive image steganography based on LSB matching revisited. IEEE Trans. Inf. Forensics Secur. **5**(2), 201–214 (2010)

14. Mielikainen, J.: LSB matching revisited. IEEE Signal Process. Lett. **13**(5), 285–287 (2006)

15. Pevný, T., Bas, P., Fridrich, J.: Steganalysis by subtractive pixel adjacency matrix. IEEE Trans. Inf. Forensics Secur. **5**(2), 215–224 (2010)

16. Pevný, T., Filler, T., Bas, P.: Using high-dimensional image models to perform highly undetectable steganography. In: Böhme, R., Fong, P.W.L., Safavi-Naini, R. (eds.) IH 2010. LNCS, vol. 6387, pp. 161–177. Springer, Heidelberg (2010)

17. Zhang, J., Cox, I.J., Doërr, G.: Steganalysis for LSB matching in images with high-frequency noise. In: IEEE 9th Workshop on Multimedia Signal Processing, pp. 385–388 (2007)

Improved Spread Transform Dither Modulation: A New Modulation Technique for Secure Watermarking

Jian Cao[✉]

Shenzhen Graduate School, Harbin Institute of Technology, Shenzhen, China
phdcaojian@163.com

Abstract. It is well known that Spread Transform Dither Modulation (STDM) is more robust to re-quantization such as JPEG compression than regular Quantization Index Modulation (QIM). However, we will show that the attacker can remove the watermark of STDM with low distortion. The approach is to firstly estimate the projection vector used at the encoder by Principal Component Analysis (PCA), and then nullify the watermarked signal's projection onto the estimated projection vector. This paper introduces a new watermarking modulation technique, which we call Improved Spread Transform Dither Modulation (ISTDM). The ISTDM's projection vector is random but can be estimated by the decoder for correct decoding. The experimental results show that the ISTDM achieves the security against the estimation of projection vector at the cost of slightly lower robustness ...

Keywords: QIM watermarking · PCA · Watermarking security

1 Introduction

In the past few years, it has been found that it is wrong to claim a watermarking technique to be secure just because a secret key is used at the encoder. The reason is that if the same secret key is reused, it is possible that the observation of several watermarked signals can provide sufficient information for an attacker to estimate the secret key. For example, in [1–3], it has already been shown that the secret carriers of additive spread spectrum (SS) watermarking [4] and improved spread spectrum (ISS) watermarking [5] can be estimated, e.g. by the blind source separation technique such as Principal Component Analysis (PCA) and Independent Component Analysis (ICA)[6]; in [7], it has already been shown that the set-membership estimation techniques can successfully provide accurate estimates of the dither signal used in quantization index modulation (QIM)[8]. According to the definitions proposed in [9], the notions of security and robustness are very different in essence. Specifically, the goal of the security attack is to gain knowledge about the secret key of encoding process and/or decoding process, while the goal of the robustness attack is to increase the bit error probability of the watermarking channel. However, the notions of security

© Springer International Publishing Switzerland 2015
Y.-Q. Shi et al. (Eds.): IWDW 2014, LNCS 9023, pp. 399–409, 2015.
DOI: 10.1007/978-3-319-19321-2_30

and robustness are also close. This is because the attacker can design more powerful robustness attacks if he can gain enough knowledge about the secret key.

Many recent efforts have focused on designing secure SS watermarking techniques. One example is the circular extension of ISS (CW-ISS) [10], which randomly spreads the clusters of ISS on the whole decoding regions such that the projection of watermarked signal onto the embedding subspace after the embedding has an invariant distribution under rotations. The CW-ISS can resist against the unauthorized embedding attack since the attacker can estimate the secret carriers only up to the embedding subspace. The other example is the natural watermarking (NW)[11], which can keep the distribution of host signal's projection onto the embedding subspace invariant during embedding. The NW can resist against both the unauthorized embedding attack and the unauthorized removal attack at the cost of relatively low robustness.

The QIM is another very popular watermarking technique, which is based on the framework of communications with side information [12], and can reduce or even eliminate the interference from the host signal, achieving a much higher robustness to additive noise than SS. Spread transform dither modulation (STDM) is a variant of the basic QIM. STDM differs from regular QIM in that the host signal is first projected onto the projection vector $\mathbf{u}$, and the resulting scalar value is then quantized for embedding the watermark message. The same as regular QIM, STDM can also reduce or even eliminate the interference from the host signal, achieving a very high robustness to additive noise attack. However, as we will see, the attacker can estimate the projection vector $\mathbf{u}$ very accurate by PCA such that he can completely remove the watermark of STDM with low distortion, e.g., by nullifying the watermarked signal's projection onto the estimated projection vector.

In this paper, we propose a new but simple watermarking modulation technique, which we call improved spread transform dither modulation (ISTDM). The projection vector used in the encoder is random but can be estimated by the decoder for correct decoding. Specifically, the host signal space is divided into two mutually orthogonal subspaces with the same dimension. One is called as the reference subspace, and the other is called as the embedding subspace. We use the STDM algorithm for embedding watermark message only in the embedding subspace, in which the projection vector $\mathbf{u}$ is the normalized host signal's projection onto the reference subspace. Since we modify the host signal only in the embedding subspace, the decoder can estimate the projection vector $\mathbf{u}$ used in the embedding subspace, and so can correctly decode the watermark message. The experimental results show that at the cost of slightly lower robustness, the ISTDM achieves the security against the unauthorized removal attack where the attacker firstly estimates the projection vector at the encoder and then nullifies the watermarked signal's projection onto the estimated projection vector.

The remainder of the paper is organized as follows. In Sect. 2, we set up the notations used later. In Sect. 3, we review traditional STDM watermarking and show that the attacker can remove the watermark of STDM with low distortion. The approach is to firstly estimate the projection vector used at the encoder by

PCA, and then nullify the watermarked signal's projection onto the estimated projection vector. In Sect. 4, we present our ISTDM watermarking technique. In Sect. 5, we compare the performance of the STDM and the ISTDM in terms of their robustness and security. Finally, in Sect. 6, we draw our conclusions.

2   Notations

We use an upper case and bold English letter for a matrix, a lower case and bold English letter for a vector, and a lower case and italic English letter for a scalar variable. This paper assumes that the host signal $\mathbf{x} \in \mathcal{R}^{N_v}$ is Gaussian-distributed with mean vector $\mathbf{0}$ and covariance matrix $\sigma_x^2 \mathbf{I}_{N_v}$, i.e., $\mathbf{x} \sim \mathcal{N}(\mathbf{0}, \sigma_x^2 \mathbf{I}_{N_v})$, where $\mathbf{I}_{N_v}$ denotes the identity matrix of size $N_v \times N_v$.

The watermark embedding is to add the watermark signal $\mathbf{w}$ to the host signal $\mathbf{x}$, resulting in a watermarked signal $\mathbf{s}$, i.e.,

$$\mathbf{s} = \mathbf{x} + \mathbf{w}. \tag{1}$$

We measure the embedding distortion by using the watermark-to-content ratio (WCR):

$$\mathrm{WCR}_{[\mathrm{dB}]} = 10 \log_{10} \left(\frac{\sigma_w^2}{\sigma_x^2} \right), \tag{2}$$

where σ_w^2 denotes the variance of the watermark signal, and σ_x^2 denotes the variance of the host signal. The robustness attacks are modeled as additive noise, resulting in an attacked signal $\mathbf{y}$, i.e.,

$$\mathbf{y} = \mathbf{s} + \mathbf{n}, \tag{3}$$

where the noise $\mathbf{n}$ is Gaussian-distributed with mean vector $\mathbf{0}$ and covariance matrix $\sigma_n^2 \mathbf{I}_{N_v}$, i.e., $\mathbf{n} \sim \mathcal{N}(\mathbf{0}, \sigma_n^2 \mathbf{I}_{N_v})$. Following [5], we assess the strength of robustness attacks by means of the signal-to-noise ratio (SNR):

$$\mathrm{SNR}_{[\mathrm{dB}]} = 10 \log_{10} \left(\frac{\sigma_x^2}{\sigma_n^2} \right). \tag{4}$$

The performance of decoding is measured by means of the bit error probability P_e:

$$P_e = Pr\{\hat{m} \neq m\}, \tag{5}$$

where $m \in \{0, 1\}$ denotes the watermark message, and $\hat{m}$ denotes the estimation of m.

3   Traditional Spread Transform Dither Modulation

The basic QIM watermarking algorithm quantizes each signal sample, x, using a quantizer, $Q(.)$, that is chosen from a family of quantizers based on the message bit, m, that is to be embedded. The watermarked signal sample, s, is given by:

$$s = Q(x, \triangle, m, \delta), \quad m \in \{0, 1\} \tag{6}$$

where $\triangle$ is a fixed quantization step size and δ a random dither signal. The quantizer $Q(:)$ is defined as follows:

$$Q(x, \triangle, m, \delta) = \triangle.\text{round}\left(\frac{x - \delta - m\frac{\triangle}{2}}{\triangle}\right) + \delta + m\frac{\triangle}{2}, \tag{7}$$

where the round(.) function returns the value of a number rounded to the nearest integer.

At the detector, the received signal sample, y, a corrupted version of s, is re-quantized using the family of quantizers to determine the embedded message bit, i.e.,

$$\hat{m} = \arg \min_{b \in \{0,1\}} |y - Q(y, \triangle, b, \delta)|. \tag{8}$$

The STDM differs from the regular QIM in that the host signal, $\mathbf{x}$, is first projected onto the projection vector, $\mathbf{u}$. the resulting scalar value is then quantized before being added to the components of the signal that are orthogonal to $\mathbf{u}$. The equation for embedding is thus

$$\mathbf{s} = \mathbf{x} + \left(Q(\mathbf{x}^T\mathbf{u}, \triangle, m, \delta) - \mathbf{x}^T\mathbf{u}\right)\mathbf{u}, \tag{9}$$

and the corresponding detection is given by:

$$\hat{m} = \arg \min_{b \in \{0,1\}} |\mathbf{y}^T\mathbf{u} - Q(\mathbf{y}^T\mathbf{u}, \triangle, b, \delta)|. \tag{10}$$

The dither signal δ, the quantization step $\triangle$, and the projection vector $\mathbf{u}$ can be considered as the secret key of traditional STDM, without which, detection is not possible. However, since the watermark energy is focused in the projection vector after the STDM embedding, principal components analysis (PCA) can be used for accurately estimating the projection vector. The goal of PCA is to search the direction on which the projection of watermarked signal has the maximum variance. In other words, the estimator of the projection vector by PCA is simply given by

$$\hat{\mathbf{u}} = \arg \max_{\mathbf{r}} \text{var}(\mathbf{s}^T\mathbf{r}), \quad s.t., \mathbf{r}^T\mathbf{r} = 1. \tag{11}$$

This implies that the attacker can remove the watermark with low distortion, by first estimating the projection vector used at the encoder by Principal Components Analysis (PCA), and then nullifying the watermarked signal's projection onto the estimated projection vector $\hat{\mathbf{u}}$. Figure 1 compares the bit error probability that the decoder decodes the watermark message after the watermark removal attack with PCA to that after the watermark removal attack with additive Gaussian noise for the same SNR. As we can see, with the same SNR, the watermark removal attack with PCA can completely remove the watermark of STDM, while additive Gaussian noise cannot remove the watermark at all.

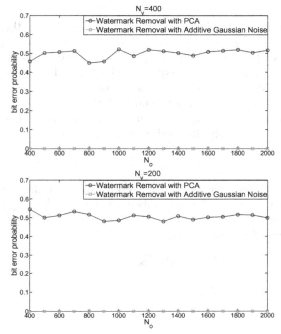

Fig. 1. The bit error probability that the decoder decodes the watermark message after the watermark removal attack with PCA and that after the watermark removal attack with additive Gaussian noise for the same SNR. $\sigma_x^2 = 1$, $\triangle = 5$, and $\delta = 0$

4   Improved Spread Transform Dither Modulation

A simple approach for improving the traditional STDM's security is to use random projection vector at embedding the watermark. However, it will lead to a problem that the decoder can not correctly decode the watermark message since he doesn't know the used projection vector at the encoder. Improved Spread Transform Dither Modulation(ISTDM) is a new but simple watermarking modulation technique whose projection vector is random but can be estimated by the decoder for correct decoding.

4.1   Embedding

In particular, the ISTDM divides the host signal space into two mutually orthogonal subspaces with the same dimension (for simplicity, we assume that the length of host signal is even number). One is called as the reference subspace, and the other is called as the embedding subspace. Assume that the column vectors of the matrix $\mathbf{A}$ form an orthogonal basis of the embedding subspace, and the column vectors of the matrix $\mathbf{B}$ form an orthogonal basis of the reference subspace:

$$\mathbf{A}^T\mathbf{A} = \mathbf{I}_{N_v/2}, \mathbf{B}^T\mathbf{B} = \mathbf{I}_{N_v/2}, \mathbf{A}^T\mathbf{B} = \mathbf{0}_{N_v/2} \tag{12}$$

in which $\mathbf{I}_{N_v/2}$ denotes the identity matrix of size $N_v/2$, and $\mathbf{0}_{N_v/2}$ denotes the square matrix of size $N_v/2$ with all zeros. Then, the host signal's projection onto the embedding subspace $\mathbf{x}_A$ is equal to $\mathbf{A}^T\mathbf{x}$, and the host signal's projection onto the reference subspace $\mathbf{x}_B$ is equal to $\mathbf{B}^T\mathbf{x}$. The ISTDM uses the STDM algorithm for embedding watermark message only in the embedding subspace, in which the projection vector $\mathbf{u}$ is the normalized host signal's projection onto the reference subspace. Formally, the watermarked signal's projection onto the embedding subspace after the ISTDM embedding is given by

$$\mathbf{s}_A = \mathbf{x}_A + \left(Q(\mathbf{x}_A^T\mathbf{u}, \Delta, m, \delta) - \mathbf{x}_A^T\mathbf{u}\right)\mathbf{u} \tag{13}$$

in which the used projection vector $\mathbf{u}$ is equal to the unit vector of the host signal's projection on the reference subspace, i.e., $\mathbf{x_B}/\|\mathbf{x_B}\|_2$. Note that the ISTDM embeds watermark message only in the embedding subspace. So, the watermarked signa after the ISTDM embedding is given by

$$\mathbf{s} = \mathbf{B}\mathbf{B}^T\mathbf{x} + \mathbf{A}\mathbf{s}_A \tag{14}$$

in which $\mathbf{s}_A$ is given by the Eq. 13.

4.2 Decoding

The first step of decoding is to estimate the projection vector at the encoder as the attacked signal $\mathbf{y}$'s projection onto the reference subspace:

$$\hat{\mathbf{u}} = \frac{\mathbf{y}_B}{\|\mathbf{y}_B\|_2}, \tag{15}$$

in which $\mathbf{y}_B = \mathbf{B}^T\mathbf{y}$. From the Eq. 14, it is easy to show

$$\hat{\mathbf{u}} = \frac{\mathbf{x}_B + \mathbf{n}_B}{\|\mathbf{x}_B + \mathbf{n}_B\|_2}. \tag{16}$$

This implies that the decoder can correctly estimate the projection vector at the encoder without error under the attack-free context. After the estimation of the projection vector at the encoder, the detection process is given by:

$$\hat{m} = \arg\min_{b\in\{0,1\}} |\mathbf{y}_A^T\hat{\mathbf{u}} - Q(\mathbf{y}_A^T\hat{\mathbf{u}}, \Delta, b, \delta)|. \tag{17}$$

5 Simulation Results and Analysis

This section is devoted to comparing the performance of the STDM watermarking and the ISTDM watermarking in terms of security and robustness for the same embedding distortion. For the STDM watermarking and the ISTDM watermarking, the same embedding parameters: the length of host signal, The dither signal, and the quantization step, results in the same embedding distortion (please refer to Fig. 2).

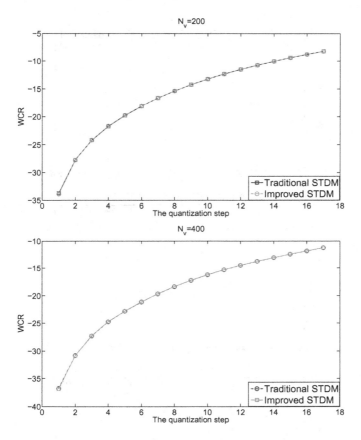

Fig. 2. The comparison of WCR for the STDM watermarking and the ISTDM watermarking in which the variance of host signal is equal to one and the dither signal is equal to zero.

5.1   Security

We measure the security by the bit error probability that the decoder decodes the watermark message after the attacker carries out the unauthorized removal attack, i.e., firstly estimating the projection vector used at the encoder by the PCA, and then nullifying the watermarked signal's projection onto the estimated projection vector. The more accurate estimation of the projection vector, the higher the bit error probability that the decoder decodes the watermark message after the attacker carries out the above-mentioned unauthorized removal attack, and the more insecure the corresponding watermarking algorithm is. From Fig. 3, we can see that the traditional STDM watermarking is very insecure and the above-mentioned unauthorized removal attack can completely remove the watermark message of traditional STDM, i.e., the bit error probability is close to that of random guess, 0.5. From Fig. 3, we can also see that

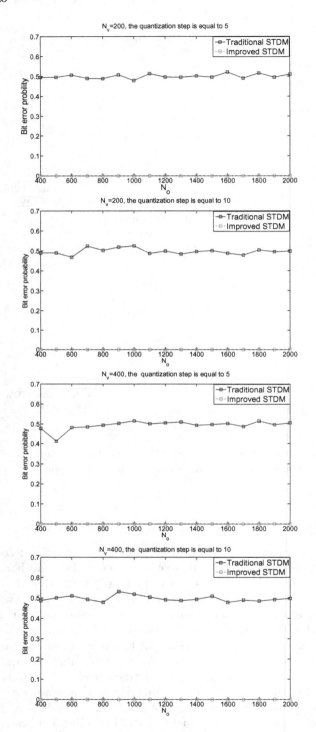

Fig. 3. The comparison of security for the STDM and the ISTDM in which $\sigma_x^2 = 1$ and $\delta = 0$

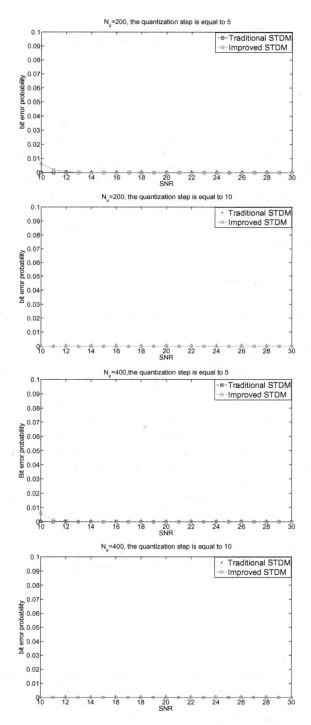

Fig. 4. The comparison of robustness for the STDM and the ISTDM in which $\sigma_x^2 = 1$ and $\delta = 0$

the above-mentioned unauthorized removal attack cannot remove the watermark message of the ISTDM at all, the decoder can decode the watermark message without error.

5.2 Robustness

We measure the robustness by the bit error probability that the decoder decodes the watermark message from the watermarked signal corrupted by additive white Gaussian noise. The more robust the watermarking algorithm is, the lower the bit error probability that the decoder decodes the watermark message from the watermarked signal corrupted by additive white Gaussian noise. From Fig. 4, we can see that the ISTDM watermarking is robust in which the decoder can decode the watermark message without error in most cases, while the traditional STDM is very robust since the decoder can decode the watermark message without error in all considered cases.

6   Concluding Remarks

In this paper, we have studied a new watermarking scheme under the WOA framework, which we refer to as improved spread transform dither modulation (ISTDM). Unlike the traditional STDM watermarking, the ISTDM watermarking scheme uses the random rather than fixed projection vector at the encoder for security. Further, the random projection vector used at the encoder can be estimated by the decoder for correct decoding. The experimental results show that at the cost of slightly lower robustness, the ISTDM achieves the security against the unauthorized removal attack that the attacker firstly estimates the projection vector used at the encoder and then nullifies the watermarked signal's projection onto the estimated projection vector. Further research directions include the further improvement of the traditional STDM watermarking scheme such that it can not only assist against the above-mentioned unauthorized removal attack but also assist against scaling of the signal, i.e., a simple change in the scale of the watermarked signal.

Acknowledgements. The work was supported by NSFC (61300208), China Postdoctoral Science Foundation funded project (2012M520734), and the Shenzhen Municipal Science and Technology Innovation Council under Grant JCYJ20130329154017293.

References

1. Pérez-Freire, L., Pérez-González, F.: Spread-spectrum watermarking security. IEEE Trans. Inf. Forensics Secur. **4**(1), 2–24 (2009)
2. Cayre, F., Bas, P.: Kerckhoffs-based embedding security classes for WOA data hiding. IEEE Trans. Inf. Forensics Secur. **3**(1), 1–15 (2008)
3. Cayre, F., Fontaine, C., Furon, T.: Watermarking security: theory and practice. IEEE Trans. Signal Process. **53**(10), 3976–3987 (2005)

4. Cox, I.J., Kilian, J., Leighton, F.T., Shamoon, T.: Secure spread spectrum watermarking for multimedia. IEEE Trans. Image Process. **6**(12), 1673–1687 (1997)
5. Malvar, H.S., Florencio, D.A.F.: Improved spread spectrum: a new modulation technique for robust watermarking. IEEE Trans. Signal Process. **51**(4), 898–905 (2003)
6. Hyvarinen, A.: Fast and robust fixed-point algorithms for independent component analysis. IEEE Trans. Neural Netw. **10**(3), 626–634 (1999)
7. Pérez-Freire, L., Pérez-González, F., Furon, T., Comesana, P.: Security of lattice based data hiding against the known message attack. IEEE Trans. Inf. Forensics Secur. **1**(4), 421–439 (2006)
8. Chen, B., Wornell, G.W.: Quantization index modulation: a class of provably good methods for digital watermarking and information embedding. IEEE Trans. Inform. Theory **47**, 1423–1443 (2001)
9. Pérez-Freire, L., Comesaña, P., Pérez-González, F.: Information-theoretic analysis of security in side-informed data hiding. In: Barni, M., Herrera-Joancomartí, J., Katzenbeisser, S., Pérez-González, F. (eds.) IH 2005. LNCS, vol. 3727, pp. 131–145. Springer, Heidelberg (2005)
10. Bas, P., Cayre, F.: Achieving subspace or key security for woa using natural or circular watermarking. In: Proceedings of the 8th ACM Workshop on Multimedia and Security (MM&Sec 2006), Geneva, Switzerland, pp. 80–88, September 2006
11. Bas, P., Cayre, F.: Natural watermarking: a secure spread spectrum technique for WOA. In: Camenisch, J.L., Collberg, C.S., Johnson, N.F., Sallee, P. (eds.) IH 2006. LNCS, vol. 4437, pp. 1–14. Springer, Heidelberg (2007)
12. Cox, I., Miller, M., McKellips, A.: Watermarking as communications with side information. Proc. IEEE **87**, 1127–1141 (1999)

Cloning Localization Based on Feature Extraction and K-means Clustering

Areej S. Alfraih$^{(\boxtimes)}$, Johann A. Briffa, and Stephan Wesemeyer

Department of Computing, University of Surrey, Guildford Gu2 7xh, UK
a.alfraih@surrey.ac.uk

Abstract. The field of image forensics is expanding rapidly. Many passive image tamper detection techniques have been presented. Some of these techniques use feature extraction methods for tamper detection and localization. This work is based on extracting Maximally Stable Extremal Regions (MSER) features for cloning detection, followed by k-means clustering for cloning localization. Then for comparison purposes, we implement the same approach using Speeded Up Robust Features (SURF) and Scale-Invariant Feature Transform (SIFT). Experimental results show that we can detect and localize cloning in tampered images with an accuracy reaching 97 % using MSER features. The usability and efficacy of our approach is verified by comparing with recent state-of-the-art approaches.

Keywords: Cloning localization · MSER features · SIFT · SURF · K-means clustering

1 Introduction

Multimedia validity is a major issue of concern nowadays due to the ease with which one can modify media using readily available software. As a result, the field of image forensics is targeted towards studying and analyzing multimedia to confirm authenticity or tampering. Image forensic tools can be classified into two main categories: active and passive. Watermarking, for example, is a well-known active image forensic tool where data is embedded into an image during the acquisition process. On the other hand, passive forensic tools do not depend on any prior data at all. Therefore, the analysis is performed on a blind basis.

Many algorithms based on feature detection and extraction have been presented. Feature detectors are either keypoint-based or block-based. Keypoint-based detectors extract keypoint features from a whole image, where block-based detectors extract features from image blocks. Christlein *et al.* [6] compare the performance of keypoint-based and block-based detectors. Experiments were performed to measure both image-level and pixel level performance. Results show that keypoint-based detectors such as SURF and SIFT perform really well in terms of forgery detection in addition to having very low computational cost. Block-based detectors, on the other hand, have a higher computational cost,

© Springer International Publishing Switzerland 2015
Y.-Q. Shi et al. (Eds.): IWDW 2014, LNCS 9023, pp. 410–419, 2015.
DOI: 10.1007/978-3-319-19321-2_31

but they can improve results when the image contains low contrast regions. The following review sheds some light on techniques that use keypoint detectors, followed by techniques that use block detectors.

Amerini et al. [1] present a method for copy-move detection based on Scale-Invariant Feature Transform (SIFT) feature extraction. The method uses agglomerative hierarchical clustering to localize the cloned areas in an image. This step is then followed by geometric transformation estimation. The same authors also present an improved version of their detection method in [2]. The improved method uses the J-Linkage algorithm to perform robust clustering in the space of the geometric transformation. Experimental results show that the method is reliable in detecting forgery with precise localization.

In [5] Bo et al. use Speed Up Robust Features (SURF) for copy-move detection. The method performs well in cases of rotation and scaling. No quantitative measures were provided about the detection rate. Rather, detection results were presented visually since the algorithm was solely based on feature matching. Similarly, Shivakumar and Baboo [4] use SURF and a KD-tree for copy-move detection. Overall, the method performs well but fails in detecting very small sized regions.

Li et al. [9] present a method for detecting copy-move forgery based on circular pattern matching. A Polar Harmonic Transform (PHT) is used to extract rotation and scale invariant features from circular image blocks. Feature vectors are then sorted lexicographically. Similar block pairs indicate the presence of forgery.

Zhao and Zhao [17] use Harris Feature Points and local binary patterns (LBP) for extracting feature vectors from circle patches. They use the best-bin-first (BBF) algorithm for duplicate region detection. Results show that this method can detect rotation, flipping and blurring. However, Harris corners and LBP are sensitive to scaling which minimizes duplication detection.

In another work, YunJie et al. [16] present a method for copy-rotate-move forgery detection. The method is based on decomposing overlapping blocks using dual tree complex wavelet transform (DTCWT). Afterwards, rotationally invariant features are extracted using Fourier transform. Finally, lexicographical sorting is used for forgery detection. Results show good detection rates for blocks of different sizes.

Davarzani et al. [7] present a technique that relies on block feature extraction using Multiresolution Local Binary Patterns (MLBP) for copy-move forgery detection. Their technique can efficiently detect duplicated regions even if they were rotated, scaled, blurred or compressed.

Ryu et al. [15] present a method for detecting copy-rotate-move forgery using Zernike moments. The image is divided into overlapping blocks. The Zernike moments are caluculated for each block. All computed moments are vectorized. The complete set of vectors is then lexicographically sorted. The Euclidean distance is computed between adjacent pairs of vectors. If the distance is less than the specified threshold, then the two blocks are suspected to be forged. The same authors improved their technique in [14] by extracting the magnitudes of Zernike moments from image blocks and using them as features. Afterwrds, locality sensitive hashing (LSH) is used for removing falsely matched block pairs.

For this paper we chose to use key-point detection and clustering as first introduced by Armerini *et al.* in [1,2]. Experimental results in these papers showed that clustering is effective when used for tamper localization. For this reason, we wanted to implement another type of clustering (k-means) to be able to compare with hierarchical clustering. The reason for choosing k-means is that it is less computationally intensive than hierarchical clustering. Furthermore, we ideally expect to have 2 clusters representing tampered and original matches. Therefore, we can specify the number of clusters beforehand.

This paper is organized as follows: Sect. 2 explains our proposed method. Section 3 gives experimental results. Finally, we provide our conclusion and future work in Sect. 4.

2   Proposed Method

Our proposed method is composed of four main steps. The first step is based on feature extraction and keypoint matching. The second step computes two metrics (slope and length) which will then be used in the clustering phase. The third step uses k-means clustering. Finally, the last step is making a decision on the image.

First we start by choosing three different sets of features. The two most commonly used features for cloning detection are (SIFT) [10], (SURF) [3]. The third set of features is Maximally Stable Extremal Regions (MSER) [8]. The reason behind choosing MSER features is that they were proven to be useful in a wide range of applications such as image segmentation [12] and video stabilization [13]. Furthermore, MSER can detect regions in various image conditions such as blur and dense textures. Mikolajczyk *et al.* [11] compared the performance of six different region detectors including MSER. They found that MSER outperforms the other five region detectors in detecting regions with different view points. In this analysis, MSER also comes second after Hessian detectors in detection regions after changes in scale. In addition, MSER consistently resulted in the highest score through many tests such as light change, viewpoint change, and scale change. We compare with SIFT and SURF as they are the two most well known robust features used for cloning detection in images.

We start by extracting a collection of keypoints depending on the specified feature detection algorithm (i.e. SURF, SIFT, or MSER). Each keypoint will have a corresponding feature vector containing multiple elements called descriptors. In order to find matches between keypoints, we compute the Euclidean distance between keypoint descriptors. If the Euclidean distance between descriptors is less than the threshold we specified based on image heuristics, then it is considered a match.

After finding all the matches we compute length and slope of the line connecting each pair of matches (i.e. between 2 keypoints). The length of the line, or distance between matching features, is computed as follows:

$$d(p,q) = \sqrt{\sum_{i=1}^{n}(p_i - q_i)^2},$$

where p and q are points in the Euclidean space, and p_i and q_i is the ith element in the Euclidean vector of points p and q respectively. The angle is the inverse tangent function and is computed for the line connecting two matched keypoints. It is defined as the principal value θ in the range $(-\pi, \pi)$ of the argument function applied to the complex number $x + iy$:

$$\theta = \text{atan2}(y, x)$$

, where θ is the angle in radians between the positive x-axis and the line between the point (x, y) and the origin. We are using this measurement to find out if there is a similarity in the directions of the lines connecting two regions in an image. After computing the slopes and lengths of all the lines connecting matched keypoints, we use k-means clustering to group similar keypoint matches together. We start by setting the number of clusters to two. One cluster would contain the matches between original regions in the image and the other cluster would contain matches between original and cloned regions. Original images will have two clusters of matches that are original (i.e. matches between original regions in the image).

To distinguish between clusters of tampered matches and clusters of original matches (i.e. matches between similar original textures), we compute the standard deviation for the lengths in each cluster. In cases of cloning we will usually have a set of lines with similar slopes and lengths. Therefore, the standard deviation of the lengths in the tampered matches cluster will be smaller than the original matches cluster. The final step in the algorithm is to make a decision on the image based on the standard deviation of the lengths in each cluster. We generated histograms of standard deviations of tampered clusters in tampered images in order to find a threshold for making the final decision on an image. We are currently using a fixed threshold for decision making. If the image is tampered the algorithm will specify which cluster represents cloning. Fig. 1 shows the algorithm's flowchart and Fig. 2 shows an example of the algorithm's final output.

3   Experimental Results

The images used in our experiments are from the MICC-F2000 dataset [1], containing 1300 original and 700 tampered images. All tampered regions are rectangular shaped, and on average occupy 1.12 % of the whole image. Tampered images were obtained by cloning another part of the same image; translation, rotation, scaling, or a combination was applied to the cloned region.

We ran separate experiments for each feature detection algorithm (MSER, SURF and SIFT), and compare with two state-of-the-art techniques by Amerini

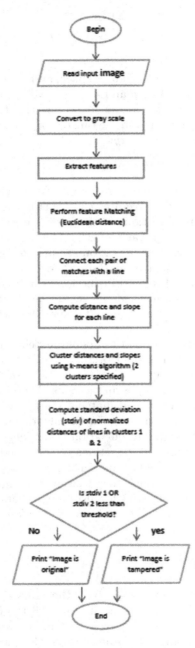

Fig. 1. Algorithm flowchart

Fig. 2. Tamper Detection and Cloning Localization: Cyan lines represent cloning (Color figure online)

Table 1. Comparison of cloning detection and localization results

	MSER	SURF	SIFT	[1]	[2]
TPR(%)	97	93	88	93.42	94.86
TNR(%)	92	90	93	88.39	90.85

MSER   SURF   SIFT

Fig. 3. Detection of features within cloned regions with asymmetric downscaling and rotation; yellow lines represent matches identified as cloning (Color figure online)

et al. [1,2]. Overall true positive rate (TPR) and true negative rate (TNR) results can be found in Table 1. It is clear that MSER is better than SIFT and SURF when combined with our clustering method. We observed that MSER was more successful than SURF and SIFT in detecting features within the cloned region when the it underwent asymmetric scaling and rotation. An example of this can be seen in Fig. 3. We can also see that SIFT has the lowest TPR, because SIFT is more sensitive to asymmetric scaling.

To confirm this hypothesis we repeated the experiment for subsets with the following transformations: (a) translation, (b) 90° rotation, (c) symmetric upscaling ×1.2, (d) symmetric downscaling ×0.2, (e) asymmetric upscaling ×1.1x, 1.6y and 40° rotation, and (f) asymmetric downscaling ×0.7x, 0.9y and 30° rotation. Each subset contains 50 tampered and 50 original images, with the originals being the same for all subsets. We were limited to such a small subset because there are only 50 tampered images for each geometric transformation

Table 2. TPR(%) Results for different geometric transformations

	Translation	Rotation	Upscale	Downscale	Upscale+Rot.	Downscale+Rot.
MSER	94	94	96	88	82	74
SURF	100	98	96	94	80	86
SIFT	100	100	88	58	18	18

(a)　　　　　　　　　　　　　　　　(b)

Fig. 4. 90° rotation: changing the number of clusters from (a) 2 to (b) 4 improves detection results: cyan represents matches identified as cloning (Color figure online)

available. Results can be found in Table 2. We can see that MSER marginally outperforms SURF in cases of upscaling+rotation, and outperforms SIFT in all cases except pure translation and rotation. On the other hand, SURF is as good as or better than MSER in all other cases. All three algorithms perform worse with combined asymmetric scaling and rotation.

There are three main challenges for our proposed method. The first involves the use of a fixed threshold on the standard deviation of distances in a cluster to decide whether an image is tampered. SIFT and SURF extract far more features than MSER, generating clusters with smaller standard deviation. This decreases the TPR for SIFT and SURF. The second involves a decrease in performance when the cloned region is rotated by 90°. An example is given in Fig. 4. In this case, matches within the cloned region will have more varied angles to account for the rotation. If these matches are in the same cluster, the standard deviation increases. If it is higher than the threshold, the cluster is marked as untampered, giving a false indication of authenticity. Furthermore, when the cloned region has a combination of asymmetric scaling and rotation the algorithm finds it harder to detect matches. The third challenge involves the nature of the K-means algorithm, which has to assign every match to a cluster. If any matches that are not due to

Table 3. TPR (%) Results for different geometric transformations and different # of clusters

Clusters	Rotation			Upscale			Downscale		
	MSER	SURF	SIFT	MSER	SURF	SIFT	MSER	SURF	SIFT
3	96	100	100	98	98	90	90	96	60
4	98	100	100	98	100	92	90	96	60
5	98	100	100	98	100	92	90	96	60
6	98	100	100	98	100	92	90	96	60

Table 4. Average processing times in seconds

	Ours	Amerini [1]
Tampered images	0.61318	6.2940
Original images	0.78664	5.8921

cloning are assigned to the cluster with cloning matches, the standard deviation of the cluster will increase. Again, if it is higher than the threshold, the cluster is marked as untampered, giving a false indication of authenticity.

In order to improve performance in these cases, we tried increasing the number of clusters used from 2 through 6. Results can be found in Table 3. We can see that there is an improvement in the TPR when the number of clusters is increased from 2 to 3. We can see further improvements when we use 4 clusters. Increasing the number of clusters further does not seem to make a difference, with the results for 5 and 6 clusters being consistent with the use of 4 clusters. With 7 clusters, K-means started generating empty clusters for some images in the dataset.

Finally, we measured the processing time for cloning detection and localization. The processing time was measured for 20 JPEG images (10 original and 10 tampered) of size 2048×1536 pixels. We used Matlab R2013a on a machine with and Intel Core 2 Duo E8400 CPU and Ubuntu 12.04 LTS. Average processing times are given in Table 4. Our method is faster because we the MSER algorithm generates far fewer keypoints than SIFT and SURF, speeding up feature matching and clustering. When we measured the speed of MSER and SURF on the 200 dataset that we used we were able to obtain detection results for MSER in 30 min while it took triple the time for SURF.

4   Conclusion

The objective of this work was to evaluate the performance of MSER features for cloning detection and use k-means clustering for cloning localization. MSER features generated good results with a TPR of 97 %. We also compared the performance of MSER features against the two most well known and used features for cloning detection SIFT and SURF. Results show that MSER features are robust and can be used in the field of image forensics. However, the performance of MSER features is slightly lower than SURF in some cases of geometric transformations. We also found that SIFT is more sensitive than MSER and SURF to asymmetric geometric transformations. Our technique compares favorably with two other state of the art techniques that implemented SIFT extraction and hierarchical clustering, in addition to a significant improvement in the processing time. In further work, we intend to investigate an adaptive method for decision making. We also intend to test using a combination of features. However, there will be a trade-off between detection performance and computational complexity.

References

1. Amerini, I., Ballan, L., Caldelli, R., Bimbo, A.D., Serra, G.: A sift-based forensic method for copy-move attack detection and transformation recovery. IEEE Trans. Inf. Forensics Secur. **6**(3), 1099–1110 (2011)
2. Amerini, I., Ballan, L., Caldelli, R., Bimbo, A.D., Tongo, L.D., Serra, G.: Copy-move forgery detection and localization by means of robust clustering with j-linkage. Signal Process. Image Commun. **28**, 659–669 (2013)
3. Bay, H., Tuytelaars, T., van Gool, L.: Surf: speed up robust features. In: Proceedings of Computer Vision-ECCV, pp. 404–417 (2006)
4. Shivakumar, B.L., Baboo, L.D.S.: Detection of region duplication forgery in digital images using surf. Int. J. Comput. Sci. Issues **8**(4), 1 199–205 (2011)
5. Bo, X., Junwen, W., Guangjie, L., Yuewei, D.: Image copy-move forgery detection based on surf. In: International Conference on Multimedia Information Networking and Security (2010)
6. Christlein, V., Riess, C., Jordan, J., Angelopoulou, E.: An evaluation of popular copy-move forgery detection approaches. IEEE Trans. Inf. Forensics Secur. **7**(6), 1841–1854 (2012)
7. Davarzani, R., Yaghmaie, K., Mozaffari, S., Tapak, M.: Copy-move forgery detection using multiresolution local binary patterns. Forensic Sci. Int. **231**, 61–72 (2013)
8. Kimmel, R., Zhang, C., Bronstein, A., Bronstein, M.: Are MSER features really interesting? IEEE Trans. PAMI **33**(11), 2316–2320 (2010)
9. Li, L., Li, S., Zhu, H., Wu, X.: Detecting copy-move forgery under affine transforms for image forensics. Comput. Electr. Eng. **40**(6), 1951–1956 (2013)
10. Lowe, D.G.: Distinctive image feature from scale-invariant keypoints. Int. J. Comput. Vis. **60**(2), 91–110 (2004)
11. Mikolajczyk, K., Tuytelaars, T., Schmid, C., Zisserman, A., Kadir, T., Gool, L.V.: A comparison of affine region detectors. Int. J. Comput. Vis. **65**, 43–72 (2005)
12. Oh, I.-S., Lee, J., Majumder, A.: Multi-scale image segmentation using MSER. In: Wilson, R., Hancock, E., Bors, A., Smith, W. (eds.) CAIP 2013, Part II. LNCS, vol. 8048, pp. 201–208. Springer, Heidelberg (2013)
13. Okade, M., Biswas, P.K.: Video stabilization using maximally stable extremal region features. Multimedia Tools Appl. **68**(3), 947–968 (2012)
14. Ryu, S.J., Kirchner, M., Lee, M.J., Lee, H.K.: Rotation invariant localization of duplicated image regions based on Zernike moments. IEEE Trans. Inf. Forensics Secur. **8**(8), 1355–1370 (2013)

15. Ryu, S.-J., Lee, M.-J., Lee, H.-K.: Detection of copy-rotate-move forgery using Zernike moments. In: Böhme, R., Fong, P.W.L., Safavi-Naini, R. (eds.) IH 2010. LNCS, vol. 6387, pp. 51–65. Springer, Heidelberg (2010)
16. YunJie, W., Yu, D., HaiBin, D., LinNa, Z.: Dual tree complex wavelet transform approach to copy-rotate-move forgery detection. Inf. Sci. **57**(1), 1–12 (2014)
17. Zhao, J., Zhao, W.: Passive forensic for region duplication image forgery based on harris feature points and local binary patterns. Sci. World J. **2013**, 1 (2013)

A Reversible Image Watermarking Scheme Based on Modified Integer-to-Integer Discrete Wavelet Transform and CDMA Algorithm

Bin Ma[1(✉)] and Yun Qing Shi[2]

[1] Key Laboratory of Evidence-Identifying in Universities of Shandong,
Shandong University of Political Science and Law, Jinan, China
mab@sdupsl.edu.cn
[2] New Jersey Institute of Technology, Newark, NJ, USA
shi@njit.edu

Abstract. This paper presents a secure and large capacity reversible water-marking scheme based on modified integer-to-integer discrete wavelet transform (iDWT) and code division multiple access (CDMA) algorithms. In this scheme, the watermark data are spread by orthogonal spreading sequence and then embedded into wavelet domain, which can only be extracted with same spreading codes and be removed after extraction to recover the original image exactly. The iDWT is modified with the method of exchanging the positions of nearby pixels to generate positive wavelet coefficients, through which the length of the spreading sequence is cut down and the embedding capacity enhanced effectively. The influence of the length of different spreading sequences on watermark capacity is discussed and optimal length of orthogonal spreading sequence is obtained to achieve balance between the watermark capacity and image distortion. Performance comparison with some state-of-art reversible watermarking schemes shows that the proposed scheme achieves higher embedding capacity while maintaining image distortion at lower level.

Keywords: Integer-to-integer discrete wavelet transform (iDWT) · Code division multiple access (CDMA) · Reversible image watermarking · Spreading sequence

1 Introduction

Digital watermarking is an effective method aiming at copyright protection, content security and authentication. The watermark embedding usually introduces permanently distortion to the original image, even though the distortion may be very small. In some sensitive applications, such as military or medical imagery, the original image is so crucial that even a slight degradation is not acceptable, therefore, it is required that the watermarking system have the ability of recovering the original image after watermark is extracted out. The reversible watermarking system can not only extract the embedded data, but also recover the original image without any distortion, and thus becomes a very active research area in recent years.

© Springer International Publishing Switzerland 2015
Y.-Q. Shi et al. (Eds.): IWDW 2014, LNCS 9023, pp. 420–432, 2015.
DOI: 10.1007/978-3-319-19321-2_32

Since the introduction of the concept of reversible watermarking in Barton's patent [1], several methods have been proposed. Among them, three major approaches for image reversible watermarking have received more attention, they are reversible watermarking based on lossless compression, on histogram shifting and on difference expansion. The lossless compression based approach substitutes the least significant bits of host image pixels with the compressed codes of substituted part and the watermarks, this scheme can only achieve rather low embedding ratio and get very small watermark capacity [2]. Histogram shifting approach is a more efficient approach for reversible watermarking proposed by Ni, et al. [3]. Since data embedding is achieved by shifting the selected histogram bins of image, the embedding capacity generally limited by the maximum value bin. Although the higher capacity can achieved through shift more bins, the host image distortion also increased simultaneously. The Difference-Expansion (DE) reversible watermarking is another active research direction introduced by Tian [4]. It expands two times the difference between adjacent pairs of pixels, and then one bit of data is added to the expanded difference. At detection, the embedded bits are recovered as the LSBs of the pixel differences and the original pixels are recovered correspondingly. The improvement on DE scheme includes applying DE to triple or quads of adjacent pixels for reversible embedding [5], the median edge detector for prediction-error expansion (MED) [6], the gradient-adjusted prediction (GAP) [7], prediction on the rhombus context [8], local-prediction based predictor and adaptive Prediction-error Expansion [9] et al.; these scheme raise the embedding capacity and keep the watermarked image in good quality. Furthermore, some reversible watermarking schemes in transform domain are proposed. Yang et al. proposed a reversible watermarking scheme based on discrete cosine transform (DCT) [10]; Xuan et al. reversibly embedded the watermark bits into the middle and high frequency integer wavelet coefficients [11]; Arsalin et al. proposed an intelligent reversible watermarking in integer wavelet domain for medical images [12]; Samee et al. presented a CDMA based blind watermarking scheme, in which the watermarks are represented by CDMA vectors and added to frequency coefficients in discrete wavelet domain, and the spread watermark can only be extracted with same code. However, since the real wavelet transform adopted in this scheme is not lossless, the recovered image is not the same as original one, therefore, the scheme cannot be used for reversible watermarking; it's another disadvantage is none–zero bit error rate (BER) even if the watermarked image has not been attacked. Besides, duo to the fact that coefficients of the real discrete wavelet transform (DWT) are quit small, the embedding of the watermark degrades the quality of the image largely. Furthermore, whether the embedded watermark induce overflow/underflow is not discussed [13].

Although most of current reversible watermarking schemes could embed many watermark data into the image with low distortion, the performance of reversible watermarking still can be enhanced. In this paper a novel reversible watermarking scheme based on the code division multiple access (CDMA) and modified integer-to-integer discrete wavelet transformer (iDWT) is presented. The watermark is spread through orthogonal sequence and arithmetically added to the wavelet coefficients of original image, it can only be extracted with the same spreading codes, and the original image can be recovered exactly after watermark removal. An modified iDWT algorithm is designed to assure that the wavelet coefficients are positive and image transform is loss-less, through which the length of spreading sequence can be cut down and the capacity of reversible watermarking scheme can be enhanced effectively.

The rest of the paper is organized as follows. The algorithm of CDMA based reversible watermarking is discussed in Sect. 2. The modified integer to integer lifting wavelet transform is introduced in Sect. 3. In Sect. 4, the performance of the proposed scheme and comparisons with the classical schemes are studied. Concluding remarks are given in the last section.

2   The Algorithm of CDMA Based Reversible Watermarking

In the modified iDWT and CDMA based reversible watermarking system, the bits of the watermark signals are spread by orthogonal sequence and embedded into the image similar to add integer white noise. Extraction of the watermark is achieved by de-correlation of wavelet coefficients with spreading sequence, the original image is recovered by the watermark sequence removal [13, 14]. The algorithm of the scheme is shown as follows:

2.1   Watermark Embedding

Let ω_{in} be a binary watermark which is changed to antipodal bits (simply replacing the bits with the equation $b_i = 1 - 2\omega_{in}$) to form a watermark representation $\omega = [b_1, b_2, b_3, \ldots, b_n]$, where $b_i \in \{-1, 1\}$, Design "K" mutually orthogonal pseudo spreading sequences as $S_i = [s_1, s_2, s_3, \ldots, s_l]$, l as the length of the sequence will be discussed below. The spreading sequence is required to have zero mean and follow the necessary conditions. $s_i \in \{-1, 1\}$, and $\sum_{i=1}^{l} s_i = 0$. Then:

$$\langle S_i, S_j \rangle = S_i \cdot S_j^T = 0; \quad if \ i \neq j \tag{1}$$

Supposed X is an image of size $N \times N$. In order to improve the robustness of the watermarking scheme, the image is transformed into wavelet domain with integer-to-integer discrete wavelet transform(iDWT) algorithm. The watermarks are embedded into the medium frequency band in wavelet domain. The transform expression is:

$$Y = iDWT(X) \tag{2}$$

The coefficients in medium frequency band can be expressed in vector form $i_j = [i_1, i_2, i_3, \ldots, i_l]$. The Length l of i_j must be the same as the length of orthogonal spreading sequence S_i. When different watermarks are embedded into the image, the expression becomes:

$$i_j' = i_j + [\alpha_1 \cdot b_{w1} S_1 + \alpha_2 \cdot b_{w2} S_2 + \cdots + \alpha_k \cdot b_{wk} S_k] \tag{3}$$

Here, b_{Wk} is the specific bit belongs to watermarks, S_k is spreading sequence for different watermark. α is the gain factor, which controls the intensity of watermark. The larger the value of α, the stronger the watermark and the noisier the watermarked image would be. "k" groups of watermark data can be embedded with different spreading sequence i_j. Replacing all i_j vectors with i'_j to form Y', the watermarked image X' can be achieved by applying inverse integer-to-integer Discrete Wavelet Transform (iiDWT).

$$X' = iiDWT\left(Y'\right) \tag{4}$$

The capacity of the watermarking system would be enhanced effectively if different spreading sequences are used together to embed watermarks. In addition, the robustness of the watermark can also be modified efficiently if the same watermark is embedded repeatedly with different spreading sequences.

2.2 Watermark Extraction

The extraction of the watermark is achieved with following algorithm. Suppose X'' is a watermarked image, its wavelet coefficient matrix can be obtained by iDWT:

$$Y'' = iDWT\left(X''\right) \tag{5}$$

If we choose the same i_j in the medium frequency band of the wavelet domain as before, which be expressed as i''_j now, every bit can be extracted by calculating cross correlation between i''_j and spreading code S_i.

$$\left\langle i''_j \cdot S_i \right\rangle = i''_j \cdot S_i^T = i_j \cdot S_i^T + [\alpha_1 \cdot b_{W1}S_1 + \alpha_2 \cdot b_{W2}S_2 + \cdots + \alpha_k \cdot b_{Wk}S_k] \cdot S_i^T \tag{6}$$

According to the orthogonal characteristic of the spreading sequence, the Eq. (6) simplified as:

$$\left\langle i''_j \cdot S_i \right\rangle = i''_j \cdot S_i^T = i_j \cdot S_i^T + \alpha_i \cdot b_{Wi}S_i \cdot S_i^T \tag{7}$$

where, α is a positive quantity and $S_i \cdot S_i^T$ is always positive, so the sign of $\alpha_i \cdot b_{Wi}S_i \cdot S_i^T$ is determined by b_i. Therefore,

$$b_{Wi} = sign\left\langle i''_j \cdot S_i \right\rangle \ if \ \left| i_j \cdot S_i^T \right| < \left| \alpha_i \cdot S_i \cdot S_i^T \right| \tag{8}$$

where, b_{Wi} is the bit of watermark Wi extracted from the received image. According to this approach, every embedded bit can be extracted and form the watermark $W' = [b_{W11}, b_{W12}, b_{W13}, \ldots, b_{W14}]$. b_{Wij} is the jth bit of watermark Wi.

The expression (8) shows that as long as $\left|i_j \cdot S_i^T\right| < \left|\alpha_i \cdot S_i \cdot S_i^T\right|$ is satisfied, the watermark can be embedded/extracted correctly. Since S_i is a zero mean spreading sequence and the elements of i_j are mutually correlated in an image, the magnitude of $\left|i_j \cdot S_i^T\right|$ would be small if the length of the spreading codes is long. Generally, the coefficients in medium frequency band of the wavelet domain are quite small and similar in an image. So if the coefficients of medium frequency band (such as *LH, HL*) are used to embed watermark, it would be easy to satisfy the Expression (8).

2.3 Original Image Recovery

Once the watermark is extracted correctly, the original image can be obtained by removing the watermark spreading sequence from the watermarked image. The result is:

$$i_j^0 = i_j'' - [\alpha_1 \cdot b_{W1}S_1 + \alpha_2 \cdot b_{W2}S_2 + \cdots + \alpha_k \cdot b_{Wk}S_k] \tag{9}$$

If the wavelet transform is lossless and the image has not been attacked in the transmission period, we will get $i_j^0 = i_j$; the original image can be recovered with all i_j'' be replaced by i_j^0.

3   Modified Integer-to-Integer Wavelet Transform Algorithm

The wavelet transform has the merits of multiple resolution analysis that match human visual system (HVS) as well as robustness. Thus, it has been widely used in image processing. Conventional wavelet transform is not suitable for reversible watermarking system because it cannot reconstruct the original image exactly. When an image with integer pixel values is transformed to wavelet domain with float-point wavelet transform, the wavelet coefficients would be decimals. Truncation of the floating-point pixels values may result in the loss of information and ultimately leads to the failure of the reversible watermark scheme [14, 15].

The integer-to-integer discrete wavelet transform can maps the image pixels from integer to integer and does not cause any information loss in forward and inverse transform. The canonical 5/3 integer-to-integer discrete wavelet transform has the merits of high transform efficiency and exact-revertible ability. It has been adopted as a standard algorithm in Jpeg2000. In this work, we adopt 5/3 integer-to-integer discrete wavelet transform (iDWT) and modify it for the reversible watermarking system. The algorithm of 5/3 iDWT is shown as follows:

In the forward transform:

$$
\begin{aligned}
&split: &&c_i = x_{2i} \; d_i = x_{2i+1}; \\
&predict: &&d_{1,n} = c_{0,2n+1} - \left\lfloor \frac{1}{2}\left(c_{0,2n} + c_{0,2n+2}\right) + \frac{1}{2} \right\rfloor; \\
&update: &&c_{1,n} = c_{0,2n} + \left\lfloor \frac{1}{4}\left(d_{1,n-1} + d_{1,n}\right) + \frac{1}{2} \right\rfloor
\end{aligned}
\tag{10}
$$

In the reverse transform:

$$reverse\ update:\ c_{0,2n} = c_{1,n} - \left\lfloor \frac{1}{4}\left(d_{1,n-1} + d_{1,n}\right) + \frac{1}{2} \right\rfloor;$$

$$reverse\ predict:\ c_{0,2n+1} = d_{1,n} + \left\lfloor \frac{1}{2}\left(c_{0,2n} + c_{0,2n+2}\right) + \frac{1}{2} \right\rfloor; \tag{11}$$

$$reverse\ split:\quad x_{2i} = c_i \quad x_{2i+1} = d_i$$

where, $c_{i,n}$ and $d_{i,n}$ are the *nth* low-frequency and high-frequency wavelet coefficients at *ith* level. In this way, an image can be transformed into wavelet domain with integer coefficients and lossless recovered.

One problem with this integer-to-integer discrete wavelet transform algorithm when used for our reversible watermarking system is that there is no guarantee that all the wavelet coefficients are positive or negative. Since the spreading sequence S has the zero mean and the number of "1"and "-1" are the same in it. The product of $\left| i_j \cdot S_i^T \right|$ would be minimized when the elements of i_j are all positive or all negative and similar to each other. If this condition is not satisfied, the length of S would be too long to embed watermarks.

For example, for a 8 levels random matrix,

$$P = \begin{bmatrix} 64 & 2 & 3 & 61 & 60 & 6 & 7 & 57 \\ 9 & 55 & 54 & 12 & 13 & 51 & 50 & 16 \\ 17 & 47 & 46 & 20 & 21 & 43 & 42 & 24 \\ 40 & 26 & 27 & 37 & 36 & 30 & 31 & 33 \\ 32 & 34 & 35 & 29 & 28 & 38 & 39 & 25 \\ 41 & 23 & 22 & 44 & 45 & 19 & 18 & 48 \\ 49 & 15 & 14 & 52 & 53 & 11 & 10 & 56 \\ 8 & 58 & 59 & 5 & 4 & 62 & 63 & 1 \end{bmatrix} \tag{12}$$

When the 5/3 iDWT is applied on it, the result is:

$$P_{wo} = \begin{bmatrix} 50 & 11 & 54 & 20 & -23 & 23 & -20 & 45 \\ 18 & 51 & 17 & 50 & 20 & -17 & 16 & -3 \\ 35 & 31 & 33 & 39 & -3 & 2 & 1 & 12 \\ 43 & 28 & 49 & 30 & -8 & 11 & -11 & 40 \\ -23 & 30 & -28 & 23 & 32 & -29 & 28 & -37 \\ 12 & -14 & 12 & -9 & -15 & 14 & -11 & 14 \\ 1 & -2 & 4 & -5 & 0 & 3 & -4 & 11 \\ -8 & 52 & -21 & 54 & 33 & -35 & 39 & -55 \end{bmatrix} \tag{13}$$

If we choose the *LH* band of the matrix P_{wo} to embed watermark data, supposed the spreading sequence $S = [1, -1, 1, -1]$, the negative coefficients in the matrix will expand the product value as follows.

$$R = \begin{bmatrix} -23 & 23 & -20 & 45 \\ 20 & -17 & 16 & -3 \\ -3 & 2 & 1 & 12 \\ -8 & 11 & -11 & 40 \end{bmatrix} * \begin{bmatrix} 1 \\ -1 \\ 1 \\ -1 \end{bmatrix} = \begin{bmatrix} -111 \\ 56 \\ -16 \\ -70 \end{bmatrix} \tag{14}$$

Apparently, the value of $\left| i_j \cdot S_i^T \right|$ in R is too large to suit the CDMA based reversible watermarking scheme. The integer-to-integer method needs to be modified to fit in the proposed scheme. According to the Eq. (10), we can know that the results of d_{in} will be positive and all the wavelet coefficients would be positive, only if the value of $c_{0,2n+1}$ satisfy the follow expression:

$$c_{0,2n+1} \geq \left\lfloor \frac{1}{2} \left(c_{0,2n} + c_{0,2n+2} \right) + \frac{1}{2} \right\rfloor \tag{15}$$

According to the Eq. (15), we only need compare the value of $c_{0,2n}, c_{0,2n+1}, c_{0,2n+2}$ and make sure that $c_{0,2n+1}$ is the largest one in the group before iDWT is performed to fulfill the requirement. The modified wavelet matrix is:

$$P_{wt} = \begin{bmatrix} 53 & 50 & 45 & 48 & 19 & 33 & 33 & 35 \\ 27 & 22 & 17 & 26 & 24 & 34 & 34 & 37 \\ 16 & 17 & 22 & 33 & 32 & 33 & 33 & 35 \\ 36 & 42 & 44 & 55 & 26 & 37 & 37 & 37 \\ 33 & 32 & 33 & 24 & 5 & 1 & 1 & 2 \\ 20 & 19 & 12 & 8 & 9 & 2 & 2 & 2 \\ 23 & 26 & 23 & 19 & 6 & 1 & 1 & 2 \\ 44 & 42 & 48 & 43 & 14 & 17 & 17 & 17 \end{bmatrix} \tag{16}$$

The dot product of $S = [1, -1, 1, -1]$ and the row vector in LH area of the matrix is:

$$R = \begin{bmatrix} 19 & 33 & 33 & 35 \\ 24 & 34 & 34 & 37 \\ 32 & 33 & 33 & 35 \\ 26 & 37 & 37 & 37 \end{bmatrix} * \begin{bmatrix} 1 \\ -1 \\ 1 \\ -1 \end{bmatrix} = \begin{bmatrix} 16 \\ 13 \\ 3 \\ 11 \end{bmatrix} \tag{17}$$

It is apparent that the values of $\left| i_j \cdot S_i^T \right|$ in R are very small so that Expression (8) can be satisfied with quite short spreading sequence. Therefore the watermark embedding and extraction algorithm based on CDMA and modified iDWT can be realized efficiently.

4 Experimental Results and Discussion

In the experiment, the grayscale images with size of 512×512 from the USC-SIPI database are used to test the proposed scheme. The modified 5/3 iDWT is adopted for image transform. The embedding capacity and the quality of the watermarked image are

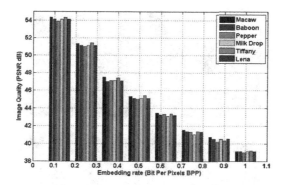

Fig. 1. The correlation of image quality in PSNR (vertical axis) and embedding rate in BPP (Horizontal axis)

evaluated by Bit Per Pixel (BPP) and Peak Signal to Noise Ratio (PSNR) respectively. According to the robustness of the watermark and visual quality of the watermarked image, the *LH* and *HL* area are chosen to embed watermark data. The location map marks the position of pixels change for modified iDWT is embedded into image concatenate with the watermarks. Since the watermarks can be embedded with different orthogonal spreading sequence S_i, and the vector i_j formed with coefficients in medium frequency band can be constructed differently by shifting ahead one coefficient every times, accordingly, the embedding capacity can reach almost "$k/2$" BPP theoretically (k is the length of vector i_j).

4.1 Performance Test of Proposed Scheme

The images including Macaw, Baboon, Pepper, Milk drop, Tiffany and Lena are chosen to test the performance of the proposed scheme. The length of the spreading sequence is 32 bits and the embedding coefficient $\alpha = 1$. The embedding capacity and the quality of the watermarked image are represented in the units of BPP and PSNR respectively, respectively. The watermark bits are randomly generated by a matlab function. The Haar wavelet basis is used as spreading sequence for data embedding. The correlation of image quality in PSNR and embedding capacity in BPP is shown in Fig. 1. The result shows that the proposed scheme achieves high capacity at low distortion when embed watermark into the image. When the BPP rate is 0.1, the PSNR value of water-marked image is around 54 dB, and the PSNR value is about 39 dB when the BPP rate reaches 1.0. Generally, nothing is visible if the noise is evenly spread over the whole image when the PSNR value of the watermarked image is above 38 dB, which means that the watermarked image has high visual quality even at high embedding capacity. It has also been discovered from the Fig. 1 that the capacity-distortion only has slight variation for different images. The reason is that the proposed scheme changes the values of the wavelet coefficients equally every time, so that the Mean Square Error between the original and watermarked image is quite similar. Therefore, the difference in PSNR is small.

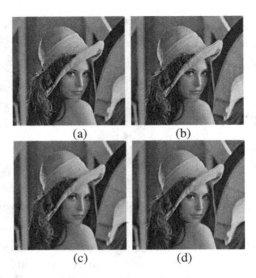

(a)   (b)

(c)   (d)

Fig. 2. Original image Lena (a) and watermarked image with proposed scheme. (b) 0.25 BPP with PSNR 50.36 dB; (c) 0.5 BPP with PSNR 44.82 dB; (d)1.0 BPP with PSNR 38.89 dB.

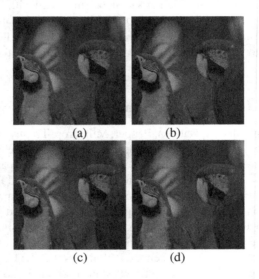

(a)   (b)

(c)   (d)

Fig. 3. Original image Macaw (a) and watermarked image with proposed scheme. (b) 0.25 BPP with PSNR 51.22 dB; (c) 0.5 BPP with PSNR 45.11 dB; (d) 1.0 BPP with PSNR 39.02 dB.

The proposed scheme achieves high subjective visual quality after watermark embedding. Figures 2 and 3 shows the original and watermarked image at different embedding capacity for grayscale Lena and Macaw respectively. As shown in the figures, the visual quality of the watermarked image is quite well preserved especially when the capacity is low or moderate, even when embedding rate is 1.0 bpp, the PSNR value is still above 38 dB and the quality is completely acceptable.

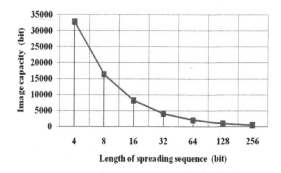

Fig. 4. The watermark capacity in bits versus the length of vector

4.2 Optimal Length of Spreading Sequence

In the proposed scheme, the length of the spreading sequence can be adjusted to meet different requirements. As for a grayscale images with size of 512×512, Fig. 4 shows how the capacity of the proposed scheme changes with different spreading sequence of lengths 4, 8, 16, 64, 128 and 256 bits. We find that with the increase of the spreading sequence length, the watermark capacity of the image decreases monotonically. As shown in Fig. 4, the capacity is 32768 when the spreading sequence length is 4 bits, but when the length is 256 bits, the watermark capacity of the image declines to 512 (for one-time watermark embedding). Hence, we can conclude that the longer the spreading sequence is, the smaller the amount of watermark data can be embedded.

The performance of reversible watermarking scheme based on iDWT and CDMA algorithms is tested with different images at different length of spreading sequence (The watermarks embed once and $\alpha = 1$). Results of modified scheme compared with non-modified watermarking scheme are shown as follows.

Figure 5 shows that when the condition of conventional iDWT is used, the positions of nearby pixels are not exchanged and the image wavelet coefficients cannot be always positive. The least spreading sequence length need to be 256 bits or more to assure that all watermarks are extracted correctly (BER = 0), i.e. $\left| i_j \cdot S_i^T \right| < \left| \alpha_i \cdot S_i \cdot S_i^T \right| (\alpha_i = 1)$ be satisfied. Figure 6 is the result when the positions of pixels in a group are exchanged to satisfy Expression (15), under this circumstance, all the wavelet coefficients would be positive. The watermark can be extracted correctly in all tested image only if when the spreading sequence length is 32 or longer. The watermark capacity is 8 times of the un-exchanged one after we adopt modified the iDWT. The performance of the proposed scheme is greatly enhanced.

4.3 Performance Comparison with Existing Schemes

In this section, performance of the proposed scheme is compared with existing reversible watermarking schemes. Figure 7 shows the image quality in PSNR versus to the embedding capacity in BPP for grayscale Lena with those of the exiting reversible schemes at different embedding capacity. As shown in the figure, the difference-expanding (DE)

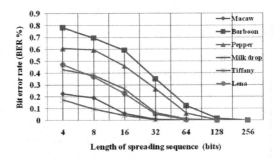

Fig. 5. The bit error rate (BER) versus length of spreading sequence of non-modified algorithm for different images.

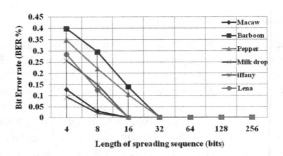

Fig. 6. The bit error rate (BER) versus length of spreading sequence of modified algorithm for different images.

based reversible watermarking scheme has low image quality when embedded watermarks, whose PSNR value is already under 38 dB when the BPP rate is only 0.3 [4]. The reason is that the difference expansion brings large distortion to the host image, which induces the scheme to have low capacity. Image quality after embedding with The int-DCT based scheme also declines rapidly when the BPP grows. Its PSNR value is lower than 38 dB when the BPP rate is 0.5 [10]. The iDWT based scheme presented by Xuan and the block iDWT based scheme presented by Lee have comparatively better performance [11, 15], however, the PSNR values is still under 38 dB when embedding rate reaches 0.7 bpp. One important reason that their performance is superior to those previous two is that they both adopt iDWT technology, which generates small degradation in visual quality after data embedding. Unlike our proposed approach, Xuan embed data into the image by increase the wavelet coefficients, which would generate larger distortion to the image apparently. In the scheme proposed by Lee, blocks with different size are used, some blocks embed additional information, and other blocks embed watermark data with bit-shifting technology. Although only blocks with small coefficient values are chosen to embed data, the distortion is still apparent. In the proposed scheme, only 1 bit of the wavelet coefficients is changed once a time when watermark embedded. Thus the influence of the embedded data on the original image would be trivial comparing with previous arts. As shown in the Fig. 7, the PSNR Value is still above 39 dB when the BPP is 1.0; the quality of the watermarked image has an improvement of 5.2 dB when the same amounts of secret data were embedded. In other words, the proposed scheme achieves high embedding capacity ability with low image distortion than other schemes.

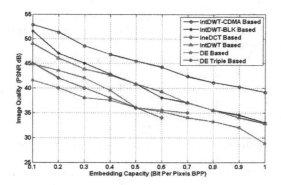

Fig. 7. The performance of proposed scheme compare with existing schemes.

5   Conclusion

A modified integer-to-integer discrete wavelet transform and CDMA based secure and large capacity reversible watermarking scheme is presented in this paper. The watermark is spread by orthogonal sequence and arithmetically added to the wavelet coefficients of original image. The original image could be recovered without distortion after the embedded data be extracted and removed with same spreading codes. The integer-to-integer wavelet transform is modified with the method of exchanging the positions of nearby pixels to generate positive wavelet coefficients, thereby reducing the product of wavelet coefficients and spreading sequence effectively. Hence, the watermark can be embedded/extracted with short spreading sequence and the capacity of the image enhanced. Experimental results comparing with some state-of-the-art reversible watermarking schemes have shown that the proposed scheme has achieved better performance in terms of embedding capacity versus quality of watermarked image measured by PSNR. It can be applied to military or medical imagery authentication and some other applications.

Acknowledgements. This paper is sponsored by the natural science foundation of Shandong Provence (No. ZR2012F014); the natural science foundation of China (No. 41202206); Jinan university & institutes innovation program (JN201402005); Science and Technology Project of Colleges and universities in Shandong Province (J14LN11).

References

1. Barton, J.M.: Method and apparatus for embedding authentication information within digital data. Patent, no. US5646997 A (1997)
2. Fridrich, J., Goljan, M., Du, R.: Invertible authentication. In: Proceedings of the SPIE Photonics West, Califonia, vol. 3971, pp. 197–208, January 2001
3. Ni, Z., Shi, Y.Q., Ansari, N., Su, W.: Reversible data hiding. IEEE Trans. Circ. Syst. Video Technol. **16**(3), 354–362 (2006)
4. Tian, J.: Reversible data embedding using a difference expansion. IEEE Trans. Circ. Syst. Video Technol. **13**(8), 890–896 (2003)
5. Alattar, A.M.: Reversible watermark using difference expansion of a generalized integer transform. IEEE Trans. Image Process. **13**(8), 1147–1156 (2004)
6. Thodi, D.M., Rodriguez, J.J.: Expansion embedding techniques for reversible watermarking. IEEE Trans. Image Process. **16**(3), 721–730 (2007)
7. Coltuc, D.: Low distortion transform for reversible watermarking. IEEE Trans. Image Process. **21**(1), 412–417 (2012)
8. Coatrieux, G., Pan, W., Cuppens, F.: Reversible watermarking based on invariant image classification and dynamic histogram shifting. IEEE Trans. Inf. Process. Secur. **8**(1) 2013
9. Dragoi, I., Coltuc, D.: Local-predication based difference expansion reversible watermarking. IEEE Trans. Image Process. **23**(4), 1779–1790 (2014)
10. Yang, B., Schmucker, M., Funk, W., Busch, C., Sun, S.: Integer DCT-based reversible watermarking for image using companding technique. In: Proceedings of the SPIE, SSWMC, San Jose, CA, pp. 405–415, January 2004
11. Xuan, G., Yao, Q., Yang, C., Gao, J., Chai, P., Shi, Y.Q., Ni, Z.: Lossless data hiding using histogram shifting method based on integer wavelets. In: Shi, Y.Q., Jeon, B. (eds.) IWDW 2006. LNCS, vol. 4283, pp. 323–332. Springer, Heidelberg (2006)
12. Asalan, M., Malik, S.A., Khan, A.: Intelligent reversible watermarking in integer wavelet domain for medical images. J. Syst. Softw. **85**(4), 883–894 (2012)
13. Samee, M.K., Gotze, J.: CAMA based blind and reversible watermarking scheme for image in wavelet domain. In: Proceedings of the IWSSIP, Vienna, Austria, pp. 11–13, April 2012
14. Samee, M.K., Geldmacher, J., Gotze, J.: Authentication and scrambling of radiofrequency signals using reversible watermarking. In: Proceedings of the IEEE ISCCSP, Roma, Italy, pp. 322–326, May 2012
15. Lee, S., Yoo, C.D., Kaller, T.: Reversible image watermarking based on integer-to-integer wavelet transform. IEEE Trans. Inf. Forenstics Secur. **2**(3), 321–330 (2007)

A Novel Hybrid Image Authentication Scheme for AMBTC-Compressed Images

Chia-Chen Lin[1(✉)], Yuehong Huang[1], and Wei-Liang Tai[2]

[1] Department of Computer Science and Information Management, Providence University, Taichung, Taiwan
{ally.cclin,fulva.hyh}@gmail.com
[2] Department of Information Communications, Chinese Culture University, Taipei, Taiwan
tai.wei.liang@gmail.com

Abstract. A novel hybrid image authentication scheme is proposed in this paper to protect the integrity of images that are compressed by absolute moment block truncation coding (AMBTC). In this proposed scheme, all blocks of a compressed image are classified into two groups. For smooth blocks, the authentication code for each block will be embedded into the bitmap of each block. For complex blocks, the authentication code will be embedded into quantization levels of each block according to a reference table. The experimental results show that this proposed scheme achieves high image quality of the embedded image and almost 100 % detection precision when eb = 3.

Keywords: Image authentication · Tamper detection · Absolute moment block truncation coding · Complex block · Smooth block

1 Introduction

In recent decades, many image authentication methods have been proposed. In 2001, Lin and Chang proposed a new scheme [2] that can protect images from malicious manipulations, but allow the manipulations made by JPEG lossy compression. In the same year, Wong and Memon [3] extended the Wong schemes [4, 5] to optimize the original algorithm for resisting the VQ attack. In 2006, a new watermarking scheme was proposed by Lie et al. [6] to provide dual protection of JPEG images. In 2008, an effective dual scheme was proposed by Lee and Lin [7] for image tamper detection and recovery. In 2010, a hash-based image authentication scheme [8] that provided both security and robustness was proposed by Ahmed and Siyal for image authentication. In 2011, a novel quantization-based semi-fragile watermarking scheme [9] was proposed by Qi and Xin for image content authentication with the capacity of tampering localization. In the same year, an adaptive image authentication scheme was proposed by Chung and Hu [10] to detect illegal modifications for images that were compressed by vector quantization. In 2013, Hu et al. proposed a novel image authentication method [11] to protect AMBTC-compressed images. In the same year, another group led by Hu proposed a new scheme [12] for AMBTC-compressed images for better image quality of watermarked AMBTC-compressed images. In these two schemes, images are compressed into block trios, and

© Springer International Publishing Switzerland 2015
Y.-Q. Shi et al. (Eds.): IWDW 2014, LNCS 9023, pp. 433–443, 2015.
DOI: 10.1007/978-3-319-19321-2_33

the authentication code of each block is embedded into bitmap and quantization levels, respectively.

To further improve the image quality and detection performance for AMBTC-compressed images, in this paper, a new image authentication scheme is proposed. The rest of this paper is organized as follows. Section 2 reviews AMBTC. Section 3 demonstrates our proposed scheme. Section 4 presents and discusses the experimental results. Finally, Sect. 5 gives conclusions.

2   Absolute Moment Block Truncation Coding

In 1984, Lema and Mitchell [1] designed a new technique called absolute moment block truncation coding (AMBTC) based on BTC to enhance the image quality of the reconstructed image. In AMBTC, an image sized $W \times H$ is partitioned into $w \times h$ non-overlapping blocks and the size of each block is $n \times n$ ($w = W/n$, $h = H/n$). Each pixel block is treated as a vector and the size of each vector is k where $k = n \times n$. Pixels of a block are arranged in a vector follow the order from left-to-right and from top-to-down.

Let $x_1, x_2, x_3, \ldots, x_k$ be values of pixels of each vector, the mean value $\bar{x}$ of values of each vector can be computed using Eq. (1):

$$\bar{x} = \frac{1}{k} \sum_{i=1}^{k} x_i. \tag{1}$$

Here, k is the number of pixels in a pixel block, x_i is the ith value in a vector, where $i = 1, 2, \ldots, k$. $\bar{x}$ is a threshold that classifies pixels in a block into two groups. The classification rule is:

$$x_i \in \begin{cases} G_0, \ when \ x_i < \bar{x} \\ G_1, \ Otherwise \end{cases} \tag{2}$$

G_0 is a group that contains pixels whose values are smaller than the mean value $\bar{x}$. G_1 is a group that contains pixels whose values are larger or equal to the mean value $\bar{x}$, $i = 1, 2, \cdots k$. Two quantization levels a and b can be calculated using Eqs. (3) and (4), respectively:

$$a = \frac{1}{k - m} \sum_{x_i < \bar{x}} x_i, \tag{3}$$

$$b = \frac{1}{m} \sum_{x_i \geq \bar{x}} x_i \tag{4}$$

Here, a is the lower level of the quantizer of a block, b is the higher level of the quantizer of a block, k is the number of pixels in a block, m is the size of group G_1, k-m is the size of G_0, x_i is the ith value of a pixel block, $i = 1, 2, \cdots k$, $\bar{x}$ is the mean value of a pixel block. Finally, an AMBTC-compressed block can be presented as a compressed trio (a, b, BM). Bitmap (BM) of each block records which group (G_0 or G_1) each pixel in a block belongs to. BM is sized $n \times n$ bits and it is defined as $\{bm_1, bm_2 \cdots bm_k\}$.

If x_i belongs to G_0, its corresponding value bm_i is set as 0, otherwise, the corresponding value bm_i is set as 1.

Decoding procedure of AMBTC is very simple. Let $r_1, r_2, \cdots r_k$ be the values of pixels of a reconstructed image block. The decoding rule is:

$$r_i = \begin{cases} a, when\ bm_i\ equals\ 0 \\ b, otherwise \end{cases} \tag{5}$$

Here, bm_i is the ith value of BM, r_i is the value of ith pixel of reconstructed image block, a and b are two quantization levels in a block trio, $i = 1, 2, \cdots k$.

3 Proposed Scheme

After we carefully studied two image authentication schemes proposed by Hu et al. [11, 12] and compared those two schemes. We have the following observations: their first scheme embedded authentication code into the BM of a compressed trio, and the second scheme embedded authentication code into the quantization levels of a compressed trio. They both have their advantages and disadvantages. When the difference value between two quantization levels of a block is very large, if the bitmap is changed, the reconstructed image will be obviously damaged and human visual system can tell it easily. When the size of a block is large, if the quantization levels are changed, it may cause more distortion than change which is made in the BM of this compressed trio. In other words, different blocks may suit different embedding methods. Based on above observations, in this paper, we proposed a new scheme that embeds authentication code into either quantization levels or BM based on each block's characteristics.

This proposed scheme is consistent of four procedures: (1) authentication code generation procedure, (2) classifications of smooth and complex blocks, (3) authentication code embedding procedure, and (4) tamper detection procedure.

3.1 The Authentication Code Generation Procedure

Suppose an AMBTC-compressed image has $W \times H$ pixels, and the size of each pixel block is $n \times n$; this compressed image thus has $w \times h$ compressed trios, $w = W/w$, $h = H/h$. Let (a, b, BM) be a compressed trio and eb be the number of bits of an authentication code.

Every compressed trio needs an authentication code, the pseudo random number generator (PRNG), and a user-defined seed employed to generate $w \times h$ random values; authentication codes are converted from random values using Eq. (6):

$$ac = rv \, mod \, 2^{eb} \tag{6}$$

where ac is the authentication code, rv is the random value, and eb is the number of bits of authentication code. The generated authentication code will be embedded into a compressed trio. Before the embedding procedure, the authentication code needs to be transformed into binary mode, and the binary sequence is presented as $ac_1, ac_2, \cdots, ac_{eb}$.

3.2   Classifications of Smooth and Complex Blocks

Our proposed scheme designs different embedding strategies for different types of blocks. Therefore, blocks of an image need to be classified into two groups using Eqs. (7) and (8):

$$dv = b - a \tag{7}$$

$$block \in \begin{cases} smooth\ one,\ when\ dv\ <\ threshold \\ complex\ one,\ otherwise \end{cases} \tag{8}$$

Here, dv is the difference value between two quantization levels, so it is obvious that the classification rule depends on the difference value of two quantization levels. When the difference value is lower than the predefined threshold value, the block is defined as smooth; otherwise the block is defined as complex. The value of the threshold cannot be defined optionally. In Sect. 4, detailed discussions regarding threshold will be given.

3.3   The Authentication Code Embedding Procedure

Before embedding, some processing work should be done. First, if BM is full of 1, quantization level a must be set as quantization level b and BM must be changed into 01010101 ⋯ 0101 to make sure the decompression procedure works well later. After all the preprocessing work is done, the embedding phases are processed according to the flowchart shown in Fig. 1.

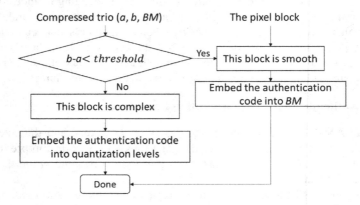

Fig. 1. Flowchart of authentication code embedding procedure

For Smooth Blocks. As Fig. 1 shows, for smooth blocks, authentication code is embedded into BM. Figure 2 shows the flowchart of the authentication code embedding procedure designed for smooth blocks. As Fig. 2 shows, the BM is subdivided into eb sub-blocks, and each sub-block carries a 1-bit authentication code.

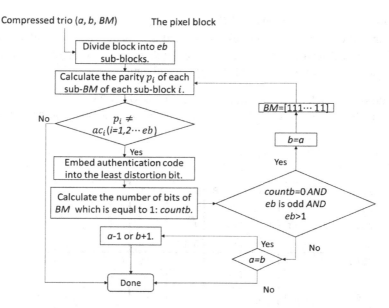

Fig. 2. Flowchart of authentication code embedding procedure for smooth blocks

A BM has $n \times n$ elements; these elements can be presented as $BM = [bm_1, bm_2, \cdots, bm_{n \times n}]$. The subdivided block is presented as $SDBM_i = [sdbm_1, sdbm_2, \cdots, sdbm_g]$, where $1 \leq i \leq eb$ and g is the size of $SDBM_i$. The division rule is shown below:

$$sdbm_j = bm_{h * eb + i} \tag{9}$$

Where $1 \leq j \leq g$, $sdbm_j$ is the jth element in $SDBM_i$; $0 \leq h \leq n \times n/eb - 1$, i is the number of subdivided BM, and $(h * eb + i))$ should stay no larger than $n \times n$.

Take a 4×4 block for example. When eb equals 1, there is only one subdivided block; $SDBM_1$. If eb equals 2, $bm_1, bm_3, bm_5, \cdots, bm_{15}$ are subdivided into $SDBM_1$, and $bm_2, bm_4, bm_6, \cdots, bm_{16}$ are subdivided into $SDBM_2$.

The parity of every subdivided BM is calculated using Eq. (10):

$$p_i = (sdbm_1 + sdbm_2 + \cdots + sdbm_g) \ mod2. \tag{10}$$

Here, p_i is the parity of the subdivided BM $SDBM_i$ and $sdbm_i$ is the ith element of $SDBM_i$. If $p_i = ac_i$, the embedding operation of $SDBM_i$ is completed; otherwise, if $p_i \neq ac_i$, the least distortion bit of the subdivided BM should be found. The distortion of each bit of $SDBM_i$ is calculated using Eq. (11):

$$dist_j = \begin{cases} \left[x_{j + (i-1) \times n \times n/eb} - b\right]^2, when \ sdbm_j \ equals \ 0 \\ \left[x_{j + (i-1) \times n \times n/eb} - a\right]^2, otherwise \end{cases} \tag{11}$$

Here, $sdbm_j$ is the jth element of $SDBM_i$, $x_{j+(i-1) \times n \times n/eb}$ $sdbm_j$ points to, a and b are two quantization levels in a compressed trio, and $dist_j$ is the distortion value if $sdbm_j$ is changed. After distortions of all the bits are obtained, the least distortion bit is found and its value needs to be changed for carrying authentication code.

For Complex Blocks. It is noted, a reference table sized 256×256 shown in Fig. 3 based on 16 Sudoku tables is used for authentication code embedding for complex blocks.

b	0	1	2	3	4	5	6	7	8	9	⋯	251	252	253	254	255	
255	1	6	4	9	7	2	5	B	3	E	⋯	C	A	8	F	G	
254	7	D	F	A	8	3	9	C	1	6	⋯	G	5	B	E	4	
253	E	2	G	B	4	D	A	6	7	F	⋯	5	1	9	3	C	
252	3	8	5	C	F	E	G	1	B	A	⋯	4	7	2	6	D	
251	F	G	8	7	9	6	B	E	5	2	⋯	3	C	D	1	A	
⋮	⋮	⋮	⋮	⋮	⋮	⋮	⋮	⋮	⋮	⋮	⋮	⋮	⋮	⋮	⋮	⋮	
9	2	C	1	D	3	4	7	5	E	9	⋯	F	B	6	G	8	
8	6	5	A	3	C	F	2	8	G	B	⋯	D	E	4	7	9	
7	9	1	6	E	B	8	3	F	4	7	⋯	A	D	C	2	5	
6	4	F	7	2	6	C	E	D	9	3	⋯	8	G	A	B	1	
5	A	B	D	G	2	5	1	9	F	C	⋯	E	8	3	4	7	
4	8	3	C	5	G	7	4	A	D	1	⋯	2	6	E	9	F	
3	D	7	B	1	5	9	8	3	A	4	⋯	6	2	G	C	E	
2	G	4	9	6	A	B	C	2	8	5	⋯	1	F	7	D	3	
1	C	E	3	8	D	1	F	4	2	G	⋯	B	9	5	A	6	
0	5	A	2	F	E	G	6	7	C	D	⋯	9	4	1	8	B	a
	0	1	2	3	4	5	6	7	8	9	⋮	251	252	253	254	255	

Fig. 3. 256×256 Reference table

Each compressed trio (a, b, BM) has two quantization levels (a, b). Here, quantization levels are used to locate the value $r_{a,b}$ from reference table R at the position (a, b). Reference code $rc_{a,b}$ can be derived using Eq. (12):

$$rc_{a,b} = r_{a,b} \bmod 2^{eb} \tag{12}$$

Here, eb is the number of bits of authentication code, and r reference code $rc_{a,b}$ is used to compare with the corresponding authentication code.

If $rc_{a,b} = ac$, the embedding work is done; otherwise, find two modified quantization levels (a', b') which not only causes the least distortion but also satisfies $rc_{a',b'} = ac$ and $b' - a' \geq threshold$.

3.4 The Tamper Detection Procedure

The tamper detection procedure detects whether the AMBTC-compressed image has been tampered and identifies which parts of the AMBTC-compressed image have been tampered with. Several parameters must be known, such as W, H, eb, authentication seed, reference table R, and the size of compressed block is $n \times n$.

Our proposed tamper detection procedure is quite straightforward. Receivers just extract the authentication code eac from the received image and compare the extracted authentication code with the authentication code generated by PRNG with the received authentication seed. If they are not identical, the received AMBTC-compressed image is determined as tampered one. Many refine strategies can be used to enhance the tamper detection performance. An iterative tamper refinement mechanism adopted in [11, 12] is used to perform further refinement and make our tamper detection accurate.

4 Experimental Results

In this section, experimental results are presented and discussed in detail to prove our performance on image quality of decompressed image and tamper detection performance. The testing algorithms are written in Java. Six grayscale images of 512×512 pixels are served as test images as shown in Fig. 4, which are "Airplane," "Boat," "Girl," "Goldhill," "Lena," and "Peppers."

(a) "Airplane"   (b) "Boat"   (c) "Girl"

(d) "Goldhill"   (e) "Lena"   (f) "Peppers"

Fig. 4. Six test images

To measure the image quality of decompressed image, Peak signal-to-noise ratio (PSNR) is used:

$$PSNR = 10 \times 10g_{10} \left(\frac{255^2}{MSE} \right).$$ (13)

Mean squared error (MSE) is defined as:

$$MSE = \frac{1}{H \times W} \sum_{i=1}^{H} \sum_{j=1}^{W} \left(x_{ij} - x'_{ij} \right)^2.$$ (14)

$H \times W$ is the size of an image, and x_{ij} is a pixel value in row i and column j before an image undergoes any lossy image processing. x'_{ij} is the pixel value in row i and column j after lossy image processing.

When the block size is 2×2, the average image quality of AMBTC scheme is 40.947 dB. When the block size increases to 4×4, the average image quality decreases to 33.604 dB; and when the block size increases to 8×8, the average image quality decreases to 30.176 dB. It is obvious that when the size of compressed block increases, the quality of the reconstructed image will be decreased (Table 1).

Table 1. Image quality of AMBTC-compressed images

Block size	2×2	4×4	8×8
Airplane	40.768	33.286	30.156
Boat	39.459	31.97	28.987
Girl	41.935	34.803	31.077
Goldhill	41.346	33.728	30.310
Lena	40.683	33.724	30.264
Peppers	41.492	33.103	30.264
AVG	40.947	33.604	30.176

In our experiments, the average value of best threshold of eight images as the default threshold. Under the threshold defined in Table 2, image quality comparisons among our proposed scheme and two existing schemes are shown in Table 3.

The comparisons shown in Table 3 are under different sizes of block and different values of eb. However, no matter which condition, the proposed scheme achieves the best performance.

To demonstrate our tamper detection performance, Fig. 5 shows the tampered "Goldhill" when the block size is 4×4. From Fig. 5(a) and (d) we can see, when a white wall is pasted over a dark edifice to create an instance of tampering with the embedded image, the tampered part is found with our proposed scheme and is highlighted by red lines.

Table 2. The definite values of threshold for different values of *eb* and different sizes of block

Size of block \ eb	1	2	3
2×2	2	0	0
4×4	11	7	7
8×8	116	87	57

Table 3. Comparison of average PSNRs among our scheme and two existing schemes (Unit: dB)

Block sizes \ Schemes \ eb		1	2	3
2×2	Hu's 1th scheme [11]	37.039	34.436	33.156
	Hu's 2th scheme [12]	40.729	40.531	39.695
	Our scheme	40.763	40.543	40.193
4×4	Hu's 1th scheme [11]	33.400	32.677	31.864
	Hu's 2th scheme [12]	33.565	33.526	33.368
	Our scheme	33.580	33.544	33.489
8×8	Hu's 1th scheme [11]	30.204	30.117	29.980
	Hu's 2th scheme [12]	30.159	30.142	30.071
	Our scheme	30.206	30.200	30.167

From Table 4, we can see there are 71.2 % tampered blocks have been detected out when $eb = 2$ without using refine mechanism. When $eb = 3$, 87.5 % of tampered blocks can be detected out without using refine mechanism. It is noted that detection ratio is up to 99.4 % after working with refine mechanism when $eb = 3$.

Table 4. Analysis of detection performance of embedded "Goldhill" when the size of block is 4×4

eb \ Factors	Number of tampered pixels	Number of tampered blocks	Before refine: detected blocks	After refine: detected blocks
1	8054	537	263	503
2	8051	541	387	526
3	8049	539	472	536

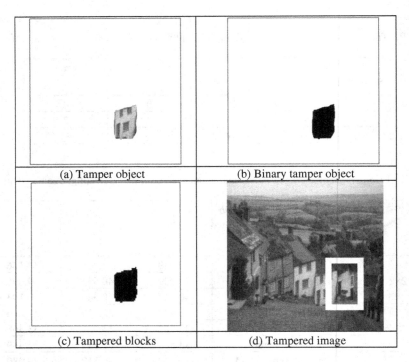

(a) Tamper object	(b) Binary tamper object
(c) Tampered blocks	(d) Tampered image

Fig. 5. Tampered "Goldhill" when the block size is 4×4 (Color figure online).

5 Conclusions

An image authentication scheme for AMBTC-compressed images based on blocks' characteristics is proposed in this paper. Experimental results confirm that our proposed scheme achieves both high image quality and high detection precision compared with two existing schemes. Especially, when $eb = 3$, the detection ratio is almost up to 100 % with our proposed scheme while maintaining good visual quality.

References

1. Lema, M.D., Mitchell, O.R.: Absolute moment block truncation coding and its application to color image. IEEE Trans. Commun. **32**(10), 1148–1157 (1984)
2. Lin, C.Y., Chang, S.F.: A robust image authentication method distinguish JPEG compression from malicious manipulation. IEEE Trans. Circ. Syst. Video Technol. **11**(2), 153–168 (2001)
3. Wong, P.W., Memon, N.: Secret and public key image watermarking schemes for image authentication and ownership verification. IEEE Trans. Image Process. **10**(10), 1593–1601 (2001)
4. Wong, P.W.: A watermark for image integrity and ownership verification. In: Proceedings of IS&T PIC Conference, Portland, OR, May 1998
5. Wong, P.W.: A public key watermark for image verification and authentication. In: Proceedings of ICIP, Chicago, IL, October 1998

6. Lie, W.N., Lin, G.S., Chen, S.L.: Dual protection of JPEG images based on informed embedding and two-stage watermark extraction techniques. IEEE Trans. Inf. Forensics. Sec. **1**(3), 330–341 (2006)
7. Lee, T.Y., Lin, S.D.: Dual watermark for image tamper detection and recovery. Pattern Recognit. **41**(11), 3497–3506 (2008)
8. Ahmed, F., Siyal, M.Y.: A secure and robust hash-based scheme for image authentication. Sig. Process. **90**, 1456–1470 (2010)
9. Qi, X., Xin, X.: A quantization-based semi-fragile watermarking scheme for image content authentication. J. Vis. Commun. Image Represent. **22**(2), 187–200 (2011)
10. Chuang, J.C., Hu, Y.C.: An adaptive image authentication scheme for vector quantization compressed image. J. Vis. Commun. Image Represent. **22**(5), 440–449 (2011)
11. Hu, Y.C., Lo, C.C., Chen, W.L., Wen, C.H.: Joint image coding and image authentication based on absolute moment block truncation coding. J. Electron. Imaging **22**(1), 013012 (2013)
12. Hu, Y.C., Lo, C.C., Wu, C.M., Chen, W.L., Wen, C.H.: Probability-based tamper detection scheme for BTC-compressed images based on quantization levels modification. Int. J. Secur. Appl. **7**(3), 11–32 (2013)

An Improved Visual Cryptography
with Cheating Prevention

Yu-Chi Chen[1], Kunhan Lu[2], Raylin Tso[2(✉)], and Mu-En Wu[3]

[1] Institute of Information Science, Academia Sinica,
Taipei, Taiwan
wycchen@ieee.org
[2] Department of Computer Science,
National Chengchi University, Taipei, Taiwan
101753018@nccu.edu.tw, raylin@cs.nccu.edu.tw
[3] Department of Mathematics, Soochow University,
Taipei, Taiwan
mn@scu.edu.tw

Abstract. Visual cryptography was firstly proposed by Naor and Shamir in 1994, which has been extended into many applications, including image encryption, information hiding, visual authentication, and visual identification. One important security issue in visual cryptography is the cheating prevention. However, in 2006, Horng et al. introduced the cheating problem in visual cryptography, where some dishonest participants, cheaters, can deceive other participants, victims, using forged transparencies. Since that, many cheating prevention works have been done in this area. In this paper, we introduce a new cheating prevention scheme which is secure and more efficient than previous schemes.

Keywords: Cheating prevention · Visual cryptography

1 Introduction

Visual cryptography is a field of cryptography proposed by Naor and Shamir in 1994 [15] to realize secret sharing without any computation, and therefore it is also called visual secret sharing (VSS). In a VSS scheme, participants only need to overlap image transparencies with each other to generate a reconstructed image that can be found by using the human vision's natural ability to perceive incomplete pictures and reveal a secret image. Compared to traditional secret sharing [1, 8], VSS does not require a computer to calculate any complex cryptographic operation. However, it only depends on stacking the transparencies with each other to decrypt the message. Based on this concept, many different research studies have been introduced, such as image encryption [6, 12], visual authentication and identification [14], steganography [4, 21], or some non-binary secret images, i.e. gray-scale images [2, 13] and color images [8, 17]. On the other hand, some studies focus on enhancing the contrast of the reorganization image and improving the pixel expansion [3, 19].

In addition to the above relative studies, in 2006, Horng et al. first showed how visual secret images can be forged [9]. The scenario is like that some dishonest

© Springer International Publishing Switzerland 2015
Y.-Q. Shi et al. (Eds.): IWDW 2014, LNCS 9023, pp. 444–454, 2015.
DOI: 10.1007/978-3-319-19321-2_34

participants collude together, and then they can calculate the shared images of other honest participants. Finally, they are able to generate forged shared images to deceive the others. Since then, how to prevent the cheating problem in visual secret sharing has attracted lots amount of attention. Therefore, cheating prevention visual secret-sharing (CPVSS) schemes have come into limelight [5, 7, 10, 11, 16, 20, 22]. In this paper, we focus on cheating prevention in VSS. Recently, [5] pointed out that the method in [10] was insecure, and put forward a proposal to improve this fault. However, this proposal requires a significant amount of pixel expansion which significantly reduces the clarity of the secret image. Therefore, [11] proposed a new improvement method to minimize pixel expansion. However, it still has some problems so we introduce a new scheme to remedy.

2   Visual Cryptography

2.1   Model

In 1994, visual cryptography techniques were proposed by Naor and Shamir [15]. This technique used a VSS mechanism to encrypt a secret image into n shared images. If the shared images are superimposed over at least k pieces, it is possible to decrypt the original secret information. This is the so called k out of n scheme. For example, a two out of two mechanism encrypts a secret image into two shared images, and by superimposing the two shared images, secret information can be obtained (Fig. 1).

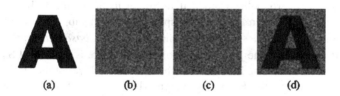

(a)   (b)   (c)   (d)

Fig. 1. Two out of two scheme: (a) secret image, (b) shared image 1, (c) shared image 2, and (d) stacked result

In a VSS scheme, first the input secret image is encrypted. The conventional process of encryption uses pixel expansion. Assuming a pixel of the secret image is white, then one row from the white section of Fig. 2 is randomly selected, and the 2×2 blocks of pixels are written to shared images 1 and 2, respectively, such that an image of two black and two white pixels results after superimposition. Conversely, for a black pixel of the secret image, one row from the black section of Fig. 2 is randomly selected, and the 2×2 pixel blocks are written to shared images 1 and 2, respectively, such that an all-black image results after superimposition. Based on human visual characteristics, the block of two black and two white pixels will appear gray, and have 50 % chromatic aberration with respect to the all-black blocks. Hence, the original secret information can be obtained after the images being superimposed.

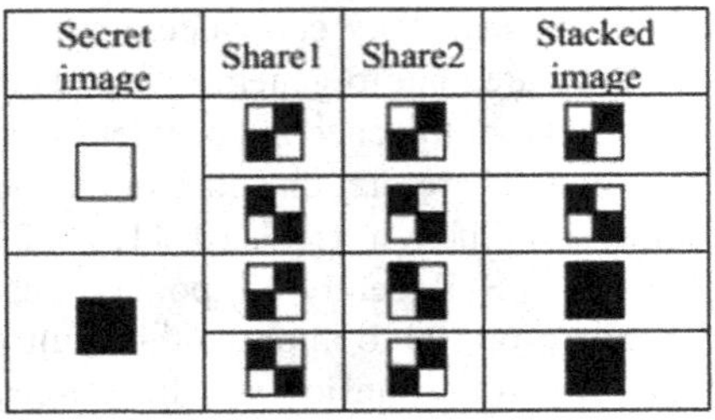

Fig. 2. Sharing and stacking scheme of black and white pixels.

Given a secret image, pixel expansion can be used to generate n shared images that are given to n secret participants, and as long as there are k or more participants to superimpose the shared images, hidden secrets will be recovered. The above mechanism is called a (k, n)-threshold VSS mechanism (or scheme) [15].

A VSS scheme is a special variant of a k-out-of-n secret-sharing scheme, where the shares given to participants are copied onto transparencies. Therefore, a share is also called a transparency. If X is a qualified subset of participants, then the participants in X can visually recover the secret image by stacking their transparencies without performing any cryptographic computation. Usually, the secret is an image. To create the transparencies, each pixel, either black or white, of the secret image is separately handled. It appears as a collection of m black and white subpixels in each of the n transparencies. We say that these m subpixels together form a block. This block is referred to as a black (or white) block if the pixel to be shared is black (or white). Therefore, a pixel of the secret image corresponds to n × m subpixels. We can describe the n × m subpixels by an n × m Boolean matrix, called a *base matrix*, $S = [S_{ij}]$ such that $S_{ij} = 1$ if and only if the j-th subpixel of the i-th share is black and $S_{ij} = 0$ if and only if the j-th subpixel of the i-th share is white. The gray level of the stack of k-shared blocks is determined by the Hamming weight H(V) of the ORed m-vector V of the corresponding k rows in S. This gray level is interpreted by the visual system of the participants as black if $H(V) \geq d$ and as white if $H(V) \leq d - \alpha \times m$ for some fixed threshold d and relative difference α. Usually, m and α are referred to as the pixel expansion factor and the scheme contrast, respectively. We would like m to be as small as possible and α to be as large as possible.

More formally, a solution to a k-out-of-n VSS scheme consists of two collections C^0 and C^1 of n × m base matrices. To share a white pixel, the dealer randomly chooses one of the matrices from C^0, and to share a black pixel, the dealer randomly chooses one of the matrices from C^1. The chosen matrix determines the m subpixels in each one of the n transparencies. The solution is considered valid if the two conditions are met.

Contrast conditions:

1. For any matrix S^0 in C^0, V of any k of the n rows satisfies $H(V) \leq d - \alpha \times m$.
2. For any matrix S^1 in C^1, V of any k of the n rows satisfies $H(V) \geq d$.

Security condition:

3. For any subset $\{i_1, i_2, \ldots, i_q\}$ of $\{1, 2, \ldots, n\}$ with $q < k$, the two collections D^0 and D^1 of $q \times m$ matrices obtained by restricting each $n \times m$ matrix in C^0 and C^1 to rows $i_1, i_2, \ldots, i_q$ are indistinguishable, in the sense that they contain the same matrices with the same frequencies.

In the black-and-white VSS mechanism, first we assume that S^0 and S^1 are the two fundamental matrices of size $n \times m$ used to generate the shared image, where S^0 represents a white point and S^1 represents a black point. For example, in a (k, n)-threshold VSS mechanism, dealer assume that the secret image at each pixel in an image share S_i (where $i = 1, 2, 3, \ldots, n$) is a pixel expansion of m points, where S^0 and S^1 are defined as follows.

$$S^0 = \begin{bmatrix} 1 & 0 & 0 \\ 1 & 0 & 0 \\ 1 & 0 & 0 \end{bmatrix},$$

$$S^1 = \begin{bmatrix} 1 & 0 & 0 \\ 0 & 1 & 0 \\ 0 & 0 & 1 \end{bmatrix}.$$

In this case, $n = m = 3$, $k = 2$, and S_i is generated as follows:

Step 1: If the pixel of secret image is white, three bits of S^0 are put into the i-th row into S_i.

Step 2: If the pixel of secret image is black, three bits of S^1 are put into i-th row into S_i.

2.2   Cheating

The issue of cheating is well studied and understood in secret-sharing schemes [18]. Since Visual Cryptography (VC) is a variant of secret sharing, it is natural to also consider this issue. Most cheating attacks in VC are known plaintext attacks where the cheaters know the secret image and are able to infer the blocks of the victim's transparency based on the base matrices. Let us consider a 2-out-of-3 VSS scheme as an example. Assume Alice, Bob, and Carol are three participants in a 2-out-of-3 VSS scheme. In the following, we refer to an image as a message since each image represents a password. A secret message is transformed into three distinct shared images, denoted by S_A, S_B, and S_C. They are then delivered to Alice, Bob, and Carol, respectively. Stacking two of the three shares will reveal the secret message. Figure 3 shows the overall cheating process.

Alice and Bob are assumed to be the collusive cheaters who intend to deceive the victim Carol. The related parameters used are $B_v = 2$, $W_v = 1$, $H(S^0) = 1$, $H(S^1) = 1$, and $m = 3$, where:

m: the number of subpixels in a block.

B_V: the number of black subpixels in a block that represents a single black pixel of the reconstructed secret image.

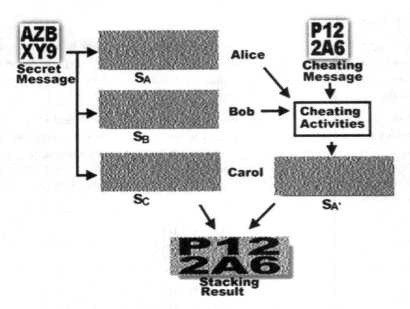

Fig. 3. Horng et al. in 2006 [9]: cheating in a visual cryptographic scheme.

W_V: the number of black subpixels in a block that represents a single white pixel of the reconstructed secret image.

$H(S^0)$: the number of black subpixels of any block in C^0.

$H(S^1)$: the number of black subpixels of any block in C^1.

Let

$$C^0 = \begin{bmatrix} C_1^0 \\ C_2^0 \\ C_3^0 \end{bmatrix}$$

$$= \left\{ \text{all the matrices obtained by permuting the columns of } \begin{bmatrix} 1 & 0 & 0 \\ 1 & 0 & 0 \\ 1 & 0 & 0 \end{bmatrix} \right\}$$

$$C^1 = \begin{bmatrix} C_1^1 \\ C_2^1 \\ C_3^1 \end{bmatrix}$$

$$= \left\{ \text{all the matrices obtained by permuting the columns of } \begin{bmatrix} 1 & 0 & 0 \\ 0 & 1 & 0 \\ 0 & 0 & 1 \end{bmatrix} \right\}$$

Based on C^0 and C^1, it produces three shares S_A, S_B, and S_C. If the i-th pixel in the secret message is white, a matrix M^0 is chosen randomly from C^0 and M_1^0, M_2^0, and M_3^0 are assigned to S_{Ai}, S_{Bi}, and S_{Ci}, respectively. Conversely, if the i-th pixel is black, a matrix M^1 is chosen randomly from C^1 and M_1^1, M_2^1, and M_3^1 are assigned to S_{Ai}, S_{Bi}, and S_{Ci}, respectively. This operation will repeat until every pixel of the secret message is encoded. Intuitively, collusive cheaters can derive the exact values from their shares. The secret message is composed of many white or black blocks. If the cheaters intend to cheat someone, it is necessary for them to change the construction of their shares. First, they predict the positions of black and white subpixels in the victim's share. Then, based on this prediction, they change the positions of the black and white subpixels in the forged shares. Finally, after stacking the forged shares with the victim's shares, the forged message will be revealed instead of the real secret message. The main problems for cheaters are how to predict the positions of black and white subpixels in the victim's share and rearrange the new positions of black and white subpixels in the cheaters' shares. There are four possible cases, as listed in Table 1.

Table 1. Horng et al. [9]: the basic concept of cheating in 2-out-of-3 VSS.

	Pixel in Secret message	Block in Share S_A	Block in Share S_B	Block in Share S_C	Pixel in Cheating message	Block in Share S'_A	Block in Share S'_B
Case 1	white	[1 0 0]	[1 0 0]	[1 0 0]	white	[1 0 0]	[1 0 0]
Case 2	white	[1 0 0]	[1 0 0]	[1 0 0]	black	[0 1 0]	[0 0 1]
Case 3	black	[1 0 0]	[0 1 0]	[0 0 1]	white	[0 0 1]	[0 0 1]
Case 4	black	[1 0 0]	[0 1 0]	[0 0 1]	black	[1 0 0]	[0 1 0]

3 The Proposed Cheating Prevention Scheme

The cheating prevention scheme proposed by Hu et al. [10] seems to be secure until 2012. In the year Chen et al. found a new attack technique [5]. Chen et al. also introduced a new scheme as a remedy. However, the pixel has been expanded to twice its original width, hence in order to reduce the required space, Liu et al. proposed an improved scheme [11] that requires minimal pixel expansion to prevent the attack. However, we found that in Liu et al.'s scheme, malicious participants can generate a forged shared image to cheat on honest participants using the black regions of the secret image. In order to solve this problem such that malicious participants cannot generate a forged shared image, we propose a new scheme.

Let S^0 and S^1 be the $n \times m$-sized basic matrices for shared image generation in a VSS method, where S^0 and S^1 are for white and black pixels, respectively. Furthermore, each participant P_i holds shared image S_i ($i = 1, 2, ..., n$) and a pixel in a secret image is expanded to m subpixels in a shared image.

First, dealer create five $n \times (m + 3)$-sized basic matrices T^0, T^1, R^0, R^1, and R^2 as follows:

$$T^0 = \begin{bmatrix} \begin{matrix} 1 & 0 & 0 \\ & \vdots & \\ 1 & 0 & 0 \end{matrix} & S^0 \end{bmatrix},$$

$$T^1 = \begin{bmatrix} \begin{matrix} 1 & 0 & 0 \\ & \vdots & \\ 1 & 0 & 0 \end{matrix} & S^1 \end{bmatrix}, \qquad R^0 = \begin{bmatrix} \begin{matrix} 1 & 0 & 0 \\ & \vdots & \\ 1 & 0 & 0 \end{matrix} & 0 \end{bmatrix},$$

$$R^1 = \begin{bmatrix} \begin{matrix} 0 & 1 & 0 \\ & \vdots & \\ 0 & 1 & 0 \end{matrix} & 0 \end{bmatrix}, \qquad R^2 = \begin{bmatrix} \begin{matrix} 0 & 0 & 1 \\ & \vdots & \\ 0 & 0 & 1 \end{matrix} & 0 \end{bmatrix},$$

where, T^0 and T^1 are used to generate shared image S_i, as in [10]. In our scheme, participants can choose their desired verification image. The generation of verification shared-image is divided into four cases:

Case 1: The focal pixels in the secret and verification images are white.

Case 2: The focal pixels in the secret and verification images are black and white, respectively.

Case 3: The focal pixels in the secret and verification images are white and black, respectively.

Case 4: The focal pixels in the secret and verification images are black.

Furthermore, each $(m + 3)$-length subpixel in the verification shared image V_i is generated as follows:

Case 1: As in [11], r_i^0 is put into V_i. In addition, where party-dependent $(m + 3)$-length row vector r_i^0 is obtained from t_i^0, the i-th row of T^0 (where $i = 1, 2, \ldots, n$), and t_i^0 is defined by the following formula

$$t_i^0 = [1 0 0 | s_i^0],$$

where s_i^0 is the i-th row of S^0, the number of ones in s_i^0 is x (where $0 < x < m$), and the number of ones in t_i^0 is $(x + 1)$. The position of a one is randomly chosen from the $(x + 1)$ existing ones, and other ones are set to zero to obtain a new $(m + 3)$-length row vector r_i^0. For example, when $t_i^0 = [1 0 0 1 0 0]$, $r_i^0 = [1 0 0 0 0 0]$ or $r_i^0 = [0 0 0 1 0 0]$.

Case 2: As in [16], the i-th row of R^0 is put into V_i as $(m + 3)$-length subpixels.

Case 3: First, dealer randomly select a V_i from V_1 to V_n. If the point happens to be in case 3, then dealer put the i-th row of R^1 into V_i as in [10]. For other participants $P_j (j \neq i)$ and V_j is in case 3, then dealer put the j-th row of R^2 into V_j. In other words, only one participant's V is generated by R^1, all the other participants' Vs are generated by R^2. For example, if there are five participants with verification images V_1 to V_5, respectively. First, assume dealer randomly selected V_2 from V_1 to V_5. In addition, assume V_1, V_2, and V_4 happened to be in case 3. As a result, dealer would put the 2-nd row of R^1 into V_2, and put the 1-st row of R^2 into V_1 and the put 4-th row of R^2 into V_4.

Case 4: The procedure for case 4 is the same as for case 3. First, dealer randomly select a V_i from V_1 to V_n. If that point happens to be in case 4, then dealer put the i-th row of R^1 into V_i as in [10]. For other participants $P_j (j \neq i)$ and V_j is in case 4, then dealer put the j-th row of R^2 into V_j. In other words, only one participant's V is generated by R^1, all the other participants' Vs are generated by R^2. For example, if there are five participants with verification images V_1 to V_5, respectively. First, assume dealer randomly selected V_2 from V_1 to V_5. In addition, assume V_1, V_2, and V_4 happened to be in case 4. As a result, dealer would put the 2-nd row of R^1 into V_2, and put the 1-st row of R^2 into V_1 and the put 4-th row of R^2 into V_4.

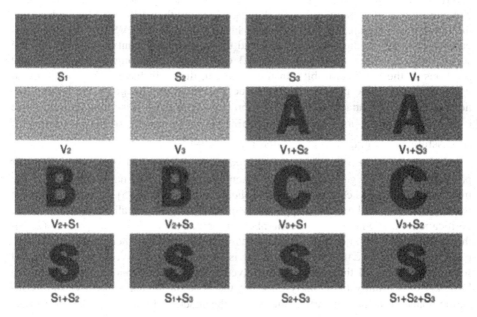

Fig. 4. Example of our proposed scheme 2 on a (2, 3)-threshold VSS method.

Figure 4 is an example of our proposed scheme 2 on a (2, 3)-threshold VSS method. Three participants P_1, P_2, and P_3 have their own verification images A, B, and C, respectively. For P_1, if S_2 and S_3 are stacked with V_1, respectively, and verification image A appears, then it can be guaranteed that S_2 and S_3 are the correct shared images. Similarly, P_2 and P_3 can also use the same method to confirm whether they have the correct shared image. All the verification pixels cannot be accurately estimated, so it is impossible to generate a forged shared image.

4 Security

Here, we analyze the security of our scheme in four cases.

Case 1: In this case, there is no difference between our scheme and the scheme [11]. If the malicious participants wish to cheat together to lead a honest participant into believing that the secret image is black, they will have $1/2$ opportunity of wrongly guessing the position having value 1 in the verification image of the honest participant. Assuming an image size is $X \times Y$, and each pixel has $1/4$ probability to be in case 1, so the probability of successfully generating a forged shared image is $\left(\frac{1}{2}\right)^{\frac{XY}{4}}$.

Case 2: As scheme 2 slightly expands the verification bit and allows only one participant's V to be generated by R^1, where all the other participants' Vs are generated by R^2 when the verification image is black. If the malicious participants choose inverted verification images as in [5] to attack the honest participants, they will have $1/n$ opportunity of wrongly guessing all the positions of the verification bits (where n is the number of participants). For example, in a (2, 3)-threshold VSS, if the malicious participants wish to cheat together and lead the honest participants to believe that the secret image is white, they will have $1/3$ opportunity of wrongly guessing all the positions of the verification bits. In this situation, they will have $1/2$ opportunity of wrongly guessing the position having value 1 in the share image of the honest participant. Hence, the attack will fail with a probability of $\frac{1}{3} \times \frac{1}{2}$. Assuming an image size is $X \times Y$, and each pixel has $1/4$ probability to be in case 2, so the probability of successfully generating a forged shared image is $\left(\frac{5}{6}\right)^{\frac{XY}{4}}$.

Case 3: As in case 2, only one participant's V is generated by R^1, and all other participants' Vs are generated by R^2 when the verification image is black. If the malicious participants choose inverted verification images as in [5] to attack the honest participants, they will have $1/n$ opportunity of wrongly guessing all the positions of the verification bits (where n is the number of participants). For example, in (2, 3)-threshold VSS, if the malicious participants wish to cheat together to lead the honest participants to believe that the secret image is black, they will have $1/3$ opportunity of wrongly guessing all the positions of the verification bits. In this situation, they will have $2/3$ opportunity of wrongly guessing the position having value 1 in the verification image of the honest participant. Hence, the attack will fail with probability $\frac{1}{3} \times \frac{2}{3}$. Assuming an image size is $X \times Y$, and each pixel has $1/4$ probability to be in case 3, so the probability of successfully generating a forged shared image is $\left(\frac{7}{9}\right)^{\frac{XY}{4}}$.

Case 4: As in case 2, scheme 2 slightly expands the verification bits, and only one participant's V is generated by R^1, where and all the other participants' Vs are generated by R^2 when the verification image is black. If the malicious participants choose inverted verification images as in [5] to attack the honest participants, they will have $1/n$ opportunity of wrongly guessing all the positions of the verification bits (where n is the number of participants). For example, in (2, 3)-threshold VSS, if the malicious participants wish to cheat together to lead the honest participants to believe that the secret image is white, they will have $1/3$ opportunity of wrongly guessing all the positions of the verification bits. In this situation, they will have $1/2$ opportunity of wrongly guessing the position having value 1 in the share image of the honest participant. Hence, the attack will fail with a probability of $\frac{1}{3} \times \frac{1}{2}$. Assuming an image size is X × Y, and each pixel has $1/4$ probability to be in case 4, so the probability of successfully generating a forged shared image is $\left(\frac{5}{6}\right)^{\frac{XY}{4}}$.

The report in [7] mentions two kinds of cheating, meaningful cheating and meaningful deterministic cheating. We now discuss these types of cheating with respect to schemes 1 and 2. In scheme 1, for any single point, malicious participants cannot completely construct a forged share point, so the scheme can resist meaningful deterministic cheating. In scheme 2, for any single point, malicious participants in some situations can completely generate a forged share point, so the scheme cannot resist meaningful deterministic cheating. However, for the whole image, malicious participants cannot generate a complete forged shared image, so the scheme can resist meaningful cheating (Table 2).

Table 2. Performance comparison

Scheme	Pixel expansion	Security
De Prisco and De Santis [16]	m + 2	Insecure
Wang et al. [21]	m + (n + 1)	Secure
Liu et al. [11]	m + 2	Insecure
Our scheme	m + 3	Secure

ps: m is the number of bits required for presenting a pixel in any VSS scheme without cheating prevention

5   Conclusions

Visual cryptography was proposed by Naor and Shamir in 1994. Cheating is a well-known security issue. In this paper, we have introduced a new CPVSS scheme. As a result, our scheme is secure and more efficient than the existing schemes.

Acknowledgment. This research is supported by the National Science Council of the Republic of China under Contract no. MOST 103-2221-E-004-009 and MOST 103-2218-E-031-001.

References

1. Blakley, G.: Safeguarding cryptographic keys. In: Proceedings. AFIPS National Conference, p. 313 (1979)
2. Blundo, C., De Santis, A., Naor, M.: Visual cryptography for grey level images. Inf. Process. Lett. **75**(6), 255–259 (2000)
3. Blundo, C., D'Arco, P., De Santis, A., Stinson, D.R.: Contrast optimal threshold visual cryptography schemes. SIAM J. Discrete Math. **16**(2), 224–261 (2003)

4. Chang, C.C., Chuang, J.C.: An image intellectual property protection scheme for gray-level image using visual secret sharing strategy. Pattern Recog. Lett. **23**(8), 931–941 (2002)
5. Chen, Y.C., Horng, G., Tsai, D.S.: Comment on 'cheating prevention in visual cryptography'. IEEE Trans. Image Process. **21**(7), 3319–3323 (2012)
6. Chen, T.H., Tsai, D.S.: Owner-customer right protection mechanism using a watermarking scheme and a watermarking protocol. Pattern Recog. **39**(8), 1530–1541 (2006)
7. Chen, Y.C., Tsai, D.S., Horng, G.: Visual secret sharing with cheating prevention revisited. Digit. Signal Proc. **23**(5), 1496–1504 (2013)
8. Hou, Y.C.: Visual cryptography for color images. Pattern Recog. **36**(7), 1619–1629 (2003)
9. Horng, G., Chen, T.H., Tsai, D.S.: Cheating in visual cryptography. Des. Codes Crypt. **38** (2), 219–236 (2006)
10. Hu, C.M., Tzeng, W.G.: Cheating prevention in visual cryptography. IEEE Trans. Image Process. **16**(1), 36–45 (2007)
11. Liu, S.C., Fujiyoshi, M., Kiya, H.: A cheat-prevention visual secret sharing scheme with efficient pixel expansion. IEICE Trans. Fundam. Electron. Commun. Comput. Sci. **E96-A** (11), 2134–2141 (2013)
12. Lukac, R., Plataniotis, K.N.: Bit-level based secret sharing for image encryption. Pattern Recog. **38**(5), 767–772 (2005)
13. Lin, C.C., Tsai, W.H.: Visual cryptography for gray-level images by dithering techniques. Pattern Recog. Lett. **24**(1–3), 349–358 (2003)
14. Naor, M., Pinkas, B.: Visual authentication and identification. In: Kaliski Jr., B.S. (ed.) CRYPTO 1997. LNCS, vol. 1294, pp. 322–336. Springer, Heidelberg (1997)
15. Naor, M., Shamir, A.: Visual cryptography. In: De Santis, A. (ed.) EUROCRYPT 1994. LNCS, vol. 950, pp. 1–12. Springer, Heidelberg (1995)
16. De Prisco, R., De Santis, A.: Cheating immune threshold visual secret sharing. Comput. J. **53**(9), 1485–1496 (2009)
17. Rijmen, V., Preneel, B.: Efficient colour visual encryption for shared colors of Benetton. In: Proceedings of the Rump Session of EUROCRYPTO, Berlin, Germany (1996)
18. Shamir, A.: How to share a secret. Comm. ACM **22**(11), 612–613 (1979)
19. Shamir, A., Naor, M.: Visual cryptography II. In: Lomas, M. (ed.) Security Protocols. LNCS, vol. 1189, pp. 1–12. Springer, Heidelberg (1996)
20. Tsai, D.S., Chen, T.H., Horng, G.: A cheating prevention scheme for binary visual cryptography with homogeneous secret images. Pattern Recog. **40**(8), 2356–2366 (2007)
21. Wang, C.C., Tai, S.C., Yu, C.S.: Repeating image watermarking technique by the visual cryptography. IEICE Trans. Fundam. Electron. Commun. Comput. Sci. **E83-A**(8), 1589–1598 (2000)
22. Yan, H., Gan, Z., Chen, Z.: Acheater detectable visual cryptography scheme. J Shanghai Jiaotong Univ. **38**(1), 179–196 (2004)

Efficient Reversible Data Hiding Based on Prefix Matching and Directed LSB Embedding

Hanzhou Wu[1], Hongxia Wang[1(✉)], Yi Hu[2], and Linna Zhou[3]

[1] School of Information Science and Technology,
Southwest Jiaotong University, Chengdu, China
hxwang@home.swjtu.edu.cn
[2] Computer Science Department,
Northern Kentucky University, Highland Heights, USA
[3] University of International Relations, Beijing, China

Abstract. This paper presents a novel reversible data hiding method, which can recover the original image content without distortion from the stego images after the secret data have been extracted. The method utilizes the original cover image to finally generate two visually similar stego images by embedding additional data. During the data embedding process, the pixels in the first stego image are utilized to embed secret data by applying the proposed prefix matching technique, which exploits each of the gray values to carry one or two bits only with ± 1 operation. Pixels in the second stego image are adaptively modified to carry rest secret data by referring to the first stego image using the directed LSB embedding. For the recipient, the additional data can be extracted from the two stego images with the DH key, and the original cover image can be recovered with the location map. If the cover image has no boundary gray-values, one can always recover the cover image from the two stego images without the aid of any extra information. Experiments show that the proposed method can achieve desirable embedding capacity and maintain a high level of image quality.

Keywords: Reversible data hiding · Prefix matching · LSB · Embedding capacity

1 Introduction

Data hiding (DH) [1–3] is the art of embedding secret data into common digital media, e.g., images, and concealing the existence of hidden information to achieve covert communication. Many existing data hiding techniques [4–8] embed secret data by altering the insignificant components of cover signals. However, these DH techniques always result in different levels of distortion in the cover signals. Although the distortion may be imperceptible to human visual system (HVS), it is unacceptable to some sensitive application scenarios such as military, medical images, etc. Reversible data hiding (RDH) is then of increasing concerns to researchers.

Reversibility allows original cover signals to be completely recovered without any loss from stego signals after the embedded data has been successfully extracted.

© Springer International Publishing Switzerland 2015
Y.-Q. Shi et al. (Eds.): IWDW 2014, LNCS 9023, pp. 455–469, 2015.
DOI: 10.1007/978-3-319-19321-2_35

Many RDH techniques [1–3, 9–21] have been reported in the literature. Early RDH techniques mainly use lossless compression [13–15] to reserve extra space for embedding additional data. Later on, more efficient techniques have been proposed to emphasize on increasing the embedding capacity and keeping the distortion low. For example, Tian [1] presented a difference expansion (DE) technique, which discovers extra storage space by exploring the redundancy in cover content. Alattar [16] extended Tian's method by using difference expansion of pixel-vectors, instead of pixel-pairs, to increase the payloads and computational efficiency. Kamstra and Heijmans [17] improved Tian's method by utilizing correlations among neighboring pixels. In the method, the location map size is reduced by sorting pairs according to correlation measures to facilitate message compression. In 2006, Ni et al. [2] introduced a novel RDH method based on histogram shifting (HS). The method utilizes the zero or minimum histogram-points of an image and slightly modifies the gray-values to embed secret data into the cover image. Hwang et al. [18] extended Ni et al's method and employed location map to recover the original image without the knowledge of the peak point and zero point. Tsai et al. [19] explored the similarity of neighboring pixels by using prediction technique and the residual histogram of the predicted errors of the cover image to embed data. The embedding capacity is increased by using the over-lapping between peak and zero pairs. Thodi and Rodríguez [3] introduced a novel RDH method utilizing prediction error expansion (PEE). This new technique significantly exploits the correlation inherent in the neighborhood of a pixel than the DE method. The PEE and the HS are combined to form an effective method for embedding, which provide a better performance compared to Tian's [1] method. In 2009, Sachnev et al. [11] applied the prediction error (PE) to embed data and used a sorting method to record the PE using magnitude of local variance. Their method can embed more data with less distortion compared to previous methods, e.g. [3, 17, 20, 22].

Recently, Qin et al. [23] propose a novel RDH method based on exploiting modification direction (EMD) [5]. The method uses an image to generate two visually similar stego images. During embedding process, the pixels in the first stego image are modified to carry data by using the traditional EMD method, while the pixels in the second one are adaptively modified. On the receiver side, the hidden data in both two stego images can be successfully extracted. Meanwhile, according to the two stego images, the original image can be perfectly recovered. Experiments show the method can achieve high capacity and desirable visual quality. In this paper, we propose a novel technique called the prefix matching (PM) and utilize a directed LSB embedding method to embed data. We also use a cover image to generate two visually similar stego images. During the data embedding process, we utilize the PM method to embed secret data in the first stego image, while the pixels in the second one are modified according to the directed LSB embedding by referring to the first stego image. For the recipient, the hidden data can be successfully extracted and the original image can be perfectly recovered according to the two stego images and the DH key. Furthermore, if the original image has no boundary gray-values, the recipient can recover the original image without the aid of any extra information according to the two stego images, which may be desirable in some applications. Experimental results show that the proposed method can achieve high embedding capacity. Moreover, the proposed method can maintain a high level of image quality, comparing with Qin et al.'s method.

The remainder of this paper is organized as follows. In Sect. 2, both the EMD method and Qin *et al.*'s method are briefly reviewed. The detailed data embedding, data extraction and image recovery methods are presented in Sect. 3. Experiments are given in Sect. 4. Finally, conclusions are drawn in Sect. 5.

2 Related Works

2.1 EMD-Based Method

Zhang and Wang [5] presented an effective data embedding method that utilizes n cover pixels to carry a secret digit in $(2n + 1)$-ary notational system. In the method, the secret bit stream is firstly represented in $(2n + 1)$-ary notational system, namely the values of secret digits are in the range of $[0, 2n]$. All the cover pixels are pseudo-randomly permuted and divided into a number of pixel groups, each of which contains n pixels. Let the gray values for each pixel group be $p_1, p_2, \ldots, p_n$. Then the data extraction function f for the pixel group is defined as a weighted sum module $(2n + 1)$:

$$f(p_1, p_2, \ldots, p_n) = [\sum_{i=1}^{n} (i \times p_i)] \bmod (2n + 1). \tag{1}$$

During the data embedding process, if the current secret digit d equals f calculated from the current pixel group based on Eq. (1), then no modification is needed. Otherwise, the module difference between the secret digit d and f is computed as:

$$r = (d - f) \bmod (2n + 1), \, (1 \le r \le 2n). \tag{2}$$

If r is no more than n, p_r will be increased by 1; otherwise, p_{2n+1-r} will be decreased by 1. Therefore, the secret digit d can be embedded into the pixel group. On the receiver side, one can correctly extract the secret digit from the stego pixel group.

2.2 Qin *et al.*'s Method

Qin *et al.*'s method [23] uses a cover image O to generate two similar stego images. The pixels in the first image S are modified by using the EMD embedding, while the pixels in the second image T are modified by referring to S. Clearly, the gray values in the range of $[0, 2n]$ and $[255-2n, 255]$ $(n = 2)$ in O are firstly set to $2n + 1$ and $254-2n$, respectively. It is to avoid the gray overflow during the data embedding process. The original gray values and coordinates of modified pixels are all recorded for image recovery and compressed by arithmetic coding to form the location map, which will be embedded into the cover pixels together with the secret message. Let C denote the preprocessed cover image derived from O. The two stego images S and T are set the same as C initially. The pixels in S and T are divided into non-overlapping pixel-pairs using the same key. During the data embedding process, let (s_1, s_2) denote the gray values of the current processing pixel-pair in S. And (t_1, t_2) and (c_1, c_2) are the corresponding gray-pairs of (s_1, s_2) in T and C, respectively. We have $s_1 = t_1 = c_1$ and $s_2 = t_2 = c_2$ initially. We compute the value f_s for (s_1, s_2) based on Eq. (1). If the current secret digit d_s equals f_s, no modification is needed. Otherwise, we compute $r_s = (d_s - f_s)$ mod 5 and compare it with n. Then we modify (s_1, s_2) as follows:

$$(s_1, s_2) = \begin{cases} (s_1 + 1, s_2), & (r_s = 1) \\ (s_1, s_2 + 1), & (r_s = 2) \\ (s_1, s_2 - 1), & (r_s = 3) \\ (s_1 - 1, s_2), & (r_s = 4) \end{cases} \qquad (3)$$

By performing the EMD method, we can embed additional data into S. In order to embed rest data and ensure image recovery, T is also adaptively generated. Based on Eq. (3), there are only three cases for (s_1, s_2) and (c_1, c_2) after data embedding, namely

Case 1: $(s_1, s_2) = (c_1, c_2)$
Case 2: $(s_1, s_2) = (c_1, c_2 \pm 1)$
Case 3: $(s_1, s_2) = (c_1 \pm 1, c_2)$

For the current processing gray-pair (t_1, t_2) in T, which corresponds to (s_1, s_2) and (c_1, c_2), if the Case 1 is satisfied, if the secret digit d_t to be embedded is equal to f_t for (t_1, t_2) based on Eq. (1), then no modification is needed for (t_1, t_2). Otherwise, we further compute $r_t = (d_t - f_t)$ mod 5 and modify (t_1, t_2) as follows:

$$(t_1, t_2) = \begin{cases} (t_1 + 1, t_2), & (r_t = 1) \\ (t_1, t_2 + 1), & (r_t = 2) \\ (t_1, t_2 - 1), & (r_t = 3) \\ (t_1 - 1, t_2), & (r_t = 4) \end{cases} \qquad (4)$$

If the Case 2 is satisfied, a proper integer k will be found to meet Eq. (5):

$$(t_1, t_2) = (t_1, t_2 - k \cdot \mu(s_2 - t_2)), (1 \leq k \leq 2n + 1). \qquad (5)$$

Here, $\mu(x)$ returns 1 and -1 for a positive x and a negative x, respectively.
If the Case 3 is satisfied, a proper integer k will be found to meet Eq. (6):

$$(t_1, t_2) = (t_1 - k \cdot \mu(s_1 - t_1), t_2), (1 \leq k \leq 2n + 1). \qquad (6)$$

This way, T can be also generated. For the recipient, based on Eq. (1), he can extract the hidden data from S and T. In order to perfectly recover C, the data recipient should calculate the difference of the two corresponding pixel-pairs:

$$D = |(s_1 - t_1) + (s_2 - t_2)|. \qquad (7)$$

If D is equal to 0 or 1, it means that the original gray-pair (c_1, c_2) is equal to (s_1, s_2). Under the condition $D > 1$, if $s_1 = t_1$ is satisfied, then the original gray-pair must be:

$$(c_1, c_2) = (s_1, s_2 - \mu(s_2 - t_2)). \qquad (8)$$

$$(c_1, c_2) = (s_1 - \mu(s_1 - t_1), s_2). \qquad (9)$$

Otherwise, the original gray-pair can be determined as Eq. (9). By performing the above recovery operation, we can recover the preprocessed cover image C. With the location map, we can further recover the original image O.

3 Proposed Method

The proposed method utilizes a cover image O to finally generate two stego images S and T. As the cover pixel values are modified with ±1 operation, the original pixels with a value of 0 or 255 in O are set to 1 or 254 in order to avoid the overflow operation. The gray values and coordinates of modified pixels in O are recorded and compressed by entropy coding to form the location map, which should be embedded into the cover pixels together with the secret data. Let C denote the preprocessed cover image derived from O. S and T are set the same as C initially. During the data embedding process, S is modified to embed secret data with the prefix matching (PM) method, while T is altered to carry rest secret data using directed LSB embedding. By utilizing S and T, on the receiver side, the recipient can extract the hidden information and recover C. With the aid of the location map, the recipient can further recover O. Furthermore, if O has no boundary gray-values, one can always recover O from S and T without any extra information, which is desirable in some applications. Figure 1 shows the sketch for the proposed method. In the following, we will introduce the proposed PM method, data embedding, data extraction and image recovery in detail.

3.1 Proposed PM Method

The proposed prefix matching (PM) method uses gray-level images. Gray values are assigned to one bit stream before data embedding. The data embedding process is performed for one pixel at a time. Let p denote the pixel with a gray value of x, and $y = f(x)$ be the bit stream embedded by x. During the data embedding process, if y is a prefix of the secret bit stream M, i.e. the secret message, then x is kept unchanged. Otherwise, x is modified as $(x + 1)$ or $(x - 1)$ so that $f(x + 1)$ or $f(x - 1)$ is a prefix of M. Let $(x, x + 1, x + 2)$ be a triple of consecutive gray values. In the well-known LSB replacement, all values in $(x, x + 1, x + 2)$ are used to represent one secret bit, namely

$$\begin{cases} f(x + 1) = \text{LSB}(x + 1) \\ f(x) = f(x + 2) = 1 - \text{LSB}(x + 1) \end{cases} \qquad (10)$$

For the proposed PM method, the mapping function f for the triple $(x, x + 1, x + 2)$ is

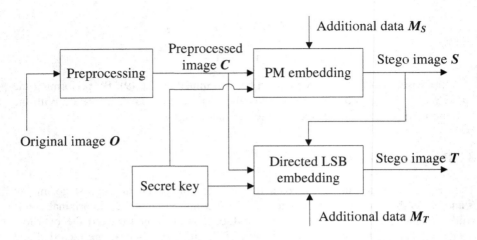

(a) data embedding

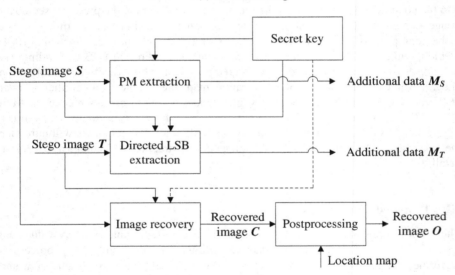

(b) data extraction and image recovery

Fig. 1. Sketch for the proposed data hiding scheme

$$\begin{cases} f(u) = \overline{b} \\ f(v) = b\overline{b}, f(w) = bb \end{cases}, (b \in \{0, 1\}, \overline{b} = 1 - b). \tag{11}$$

where $\{x, x + 1, x + 2\} = \{u\} \cup \{v\} \cup \{w\}$.

For example, for the triple (171, 172, 173), we can construct the mapping function as $f(171) = 10, f(172) = 0$, and $f(173) = 11$. During the data embedding process, let the current pixel value be 172. If the secret bit stream M starts with "0", the pixel is kept unchanged. Otherwise, either "10" or "11" must be a prefix of M, which means either 171 or 173 can be used to replace 172 to carry "10" or "11". Moreover, the new pixel value can carry two secret bits. Generally, let the gray values of a given cover image be integers that range from 0 to $(2^n - 1)$, e.g. $n = 8$. The proposed PM assignment is

$$
f(x) = \begin{cases} b, & \text{if } x = 0 \text{ or } x = (2^n - 2) \\ \bar{b}, & \text{if } x = 1 \text{ or } x = (2^n - 1) \\ b\bar{b}, & \text{if } 2 \leq x \leq (2^n - 3) \text{ and } x = 0 \ (\text{mod } 3) \\ \bar{b}, & \text{if } 2 \leq x \leq (2^n - 3) \text{ and } x = 1 \ (\text{mod } 3) \\ bb, & \text{if } 2 \leq x \leq (2^n - 3) \text{ and } x = 2 \ (\text{mod } 3) \end{cases} \tag{12}
$$

where $b \in \{0, 1\}$ and $\bar{b}$ is an opposite value to b.

Table 1 shows the actual bit stream values due to different bit-parameters. It is obvious that two-thirds the gray-levels can carry two secret bits and the others carry one secret bit. For the boundary-triples, e.g., (0, 1, 2), they do not satisfy Eq. (11) as the boundary-values $\{0, 2^n - 1\}$ should be assigned to only one secret bit so that all the gray-levels can carry bits. As shown in Eq. (12), for the proposed PM method, according to random ± 1 operation, each of the gray-levels except $\{0, 1, 2^n - 2, 2^n - 1\}$ can be used to embed 1.5-bit, approximately. It implies that the proposed PM method can achieve higher embedding capacity, comparing with both the LSB replacement method and the LSB matching method.

Table 1. Actual bit stream values due to different bit-parameters.

x	0	1	2	3	4	5	...	$2^n - 2$	$2^n - 1$
$f(x), (b = 1)$	1	0	11	10	0	11	...	1	0
$f(x), (b = 0)$	0	1	00	01	1	00	...	0	1

3.2 Data Embedding

As the cover pixel values are only modified with ± 1 operation, the original pixels with a value of 0 or 255 in O are set to 1 or 254 to form the preprocessed cover image C to avoid overflow operation. The original gray values and coordinates of the modified pixels are then recorded for image recovery and compressed by entropy coding to form the location map, which will be embedded into the cover pixels together with the secret message. Moreover, as the original gray values must be 0 or 255, we can only use one bit value "0" and "1" to represent the original values 0 and 255 respectively, to form the location map. The proposed data embedding process utilizes the preprocessed cover image C to generate two stego images S and T. The proposed PM technique is used to embed secret data for image S. The pixels in the second stego image T are then modified to carry rest secret data by using directed LSB embedding by referring to S. Figure 1(a) shows the sketch for the proposed data embedding process. Based on Fig. 1(a), in the PM embedding process, the cases $b = 0$ and $b = 1$ shown in Table 1 are utilized to embed secret data. Let $h(0, x)$ and $h(1, x)$ denote the values of $f(x)$ in the cases $b = 0$ and $b = 1$, respectively. During the data embedding process, for the current processing pixel p with a gray-level value of x, an integer r is randomly generated by using a pseudo-random number-generation (PRNG) function R_r, namely $r = R_r(k)$ where k is the secret key (shared between the data hider and recipient). No modification is need if $h(\text{LSB}(r), x)$ matches one prefix of the secret bit stream M_S; otherwise, x is modified as either $(x + 1)$ or $(x - 1)$ so that $h(\text{LSB}(r), x + 1)$ or $h(\text{LSB}(r), x - 1)$ matches one prefix of M_S. Steps of the data embedding process for generating S are as follows.

Step (1)   Set S the same as the preprocessed cover image C.

Step (2)   Let $P = [p_1 p_2 p_3 ... p_l]$ and $M_S = [b_1 b_2 b_3 ... b_L]$ denote the cover pixel sequence and the secret bit streamrespectively. The proposed bit stream assignment is completed according to Eq. (12), initially. To protect the secret data securely, both the cryptographic method and random permutation are used before embedding. It means that P is always a random permutation for the cover image pixels and M_S is always been encrypted.

Step (3)   For each cover pixel p_j ($1 \leq j \leq l$) in Pcompute $r_j = R_r(k_j)$, where k_j is the secret key. The gray-level value of p_j is x_j. p_j is kept unchanged if $h(\text{LSB}(r_j), x_j)$ is a prefix of M_S; otherwise, either $(x_j + 1)$ or $(x_j - 1)$ is used to replace x_j so that either $h(\text{LSB}(r_j), x_j + 1)$ or $h(\text{LSB}(r_j), x_j - 1)$ is a prefix of M_S. Therefore the new pixel value always matches one prefix of M_S. Then remove the prefix of M_S, and repeat the current step until M_S has a length of zero. Finally, we can construct the stego pixel sequence $P_S = [s_1 s_2 ... s_l]$, where s_j corresponds to p_j ($1 \leq j \leq l$).

Step (4)   According to the inverse-permutationthe data hider can use the pixel carrying the secret message to form the corresponding stego image S.

For instance, let the gray-level values of the permuted pixel-sequence and the secret message be $X = [4, 4, 2, 6, 5, 3, 4]$ and $M_S = [101100111000]$, respectively. With LSB ($[r_1, r_2, ..., r_7]) = [0, 0, 1, 0, 1, 0, 1]$, the new gray-level values carrying bits are $Y = [4, 3, 3, 6, 5, 2, 4]$. This way, seven pixels are used to carry 12 secret bits.

As the first stego image S has been generated, we then embed more secret message M_T into the second stego image T. As shown in Fig. 1(a), we apply the directed LSB embedding to embed data by referring to S. The detailed steps of the data embedding process for generating the second stego image T are as follows.

Step (1)   Set T the same as the preprocessed cover image C.

Step (2)   Let $Q = [q_1 q_2 q_3 ... q_l]$ and $M_T = [d_1 d_2 d_3 ... d_N]$ denote the cover pixel sequence and the secret bit stream, respectively. To protect the secret data securely, both the cryptographic method and random permutation are used before embedding. It means that Q is always a random permutation for the cover image pixels and M_T is always been encrypted. Moreover, Q is generated by the same secret key as used for generating P, which means that we have $Q = P$ initially. (P has been defined in the processing for the stego image S.).

Step (3)   For each cover pixel q_j ($1 \leq j \leq l$) in Q, let x_j and y_j denote the gray-level of $q_j \in Q$ and $s_j \in P_S$ respectively. No modification is needed if x_j is equal to

y_j, which means that x_j does not carry secret data. Under the condition $x_j < y_j$, x_j is kept unchanged if LSB(x_j) matches the current secret bit d_k ($1 \leq k \leq N$) in M_T; otherwise, x_j is modified as (x_j-1) as LSB(x_j-1) = d_k. Under the condition $x_j > y_j$, x_j is kept unchanged if we have that LSB(x_j) = d_k; otherwise x_j is modified as (x_j + 1) in order to match d_k. Repeat the current step until all the secret bits are embedded into the cover pixels and finally we can construct the stego pixel sequence $Q_T = [t_1 t_2 ... t_l]$, where t_j corresponds to q_j ($1 \leq j \leq l$).

Step (4)   According to the inverse-permutation, the data hider can use the pixel carrying the secret message to form the corresponding stego image T.

Therefore, by performing the PM embedding process and the directed LSB embedding process, we can successfully embed additional data into the two visually similar stego images S and T. Finally, the two stego images can be sent to the data recipient according to the public channel.

3.3   Data Extraction and Image Recovery

On the receiver side, as shown in Fig. 1(b), the recipient can successfully extract secret data from the two stego images S and T with the DH key, respectively. Clearly, for the first stego image S, the recipient can reconstruct $P_S = [s_1 s_2 ... s_l]$ with the secret key at first. For each s_j ($1 \leq j \leq l$) in P_S, $r_j = R_r(k_j)$ is computed and the stream embedded by s_j can be easily obtained based on Eq. (12). This way, the recipient can concatenate all the secret bit streams to form $M_S = [b_1 b_2 b_3 ... b_L]$. For the stego image T, the recipient can also extract the secret data M_T from T by referring to S. Therefore, the secret information embedded into the stego images can be obtained. During the data extraction, the original image O can be further recovered without any distortion. The detailed steps of data extraction and image recovery are as follows.

Step (1)   According to the secret permutation key, the recipient firstly reconstruct the two stego pixel sequences $P_S = [s_1 s_2 ... s_l]$ and $Q_T = [t_1 t_2 ... t_l]$. Let M_S and M_T be empty initially and $C_P = [c_1 c_2 ... c_l]$ denote the cover pixel sequence of C.

Step (2)   For each stego pixel s_j ($1 \leq j \leq l$) in P_S, the recipient computes $r_j = R_r(k_j)$, where k_j is the secret key. Let x_j, y_j and z_j denote the gray-level values of s_j, t_j and c_j, respectively. By computing $h(\text{LSB}(r_j), x_j)$, the recipient can easily extract the data embedded by x_j and append the embedded bit stream to the end of M_S. Then we perform the next step.

Step (3)   The recipient then compares y_j with x_j in order to extract secret data from y_j. If y_j is equal to x_j, it means that no secret data is embedded into y_j and the original pixel value z_j must be x_j. Therefore, z_j will be set to be x_j. Otherwise, we append the embedded secret bit LSB(y_j) to the end of M_T. At the same time, we set z_j as ($x_j - 1$) if $y_j < x_j$, otherwise, we set z_j as ($x_j + 1$) if $y_j > x_j$. If all the secret data are extracted, we perform the next step; otherwise, we perform **Step 2)**.

Step (4)   Finally, we can obtain the hidden information M_S and M_T. With the aid of the permutation key, we can use $C_P = [c_1c_2...c_l]$ to form the original preprocessed cover image C without any distortion. Based on the location map retrieved from M_S and M_T, we can further recover the original cover image O without any loss.

Actually, if O has no boundary gray-values, it means that the preprocessed image C should be the same as O. This way, one can always recover O from the two stego images without the aid of any extra information. Clearly, let $S_{i,j}$ and $T_{i,j}$ denote the gray values in S and T at the pixel position (i, j), respectively. If $S_{i,j}$ equals $T_{i,j}$, it means the corresponding pixel value $O_{i,j}$ in O must be equal to $S_{i,j}$. Otherwise, $O_{i,j}$ must equal $(S_{i,j} - 1)$ if $S_{i,j} > T_{i,j}$, or $(S_{i,j} + 1)$ if $S_{i,j} < T_{i,j}$. Therefore, it can be inferred that the recipient can always recover O without the aid of any extra information. In some application scenarios, it may be necessary that the original content should be successfully recovered without loss though the recipient does not know the data hiding key.

4   Experiments and Analysis

We present some experiments and results to evaluate the performance of our proposed method in this section. The Peak Signal-to-Noise Ratio (PSNR) was used to evaluate the image quality of stego images. The formula of PSNR is defined as:

$$\text{PSNR} = 10 \times \log_{10}\frac{255^2}{\text{MSE}}\,(\text{dB}). \tag{13}$$

$$\text{MSE} = \frac{1}{W \times H} \cdot \sum_{i=1}^{W}\sum_{j=1}^{H}(I_{i,j} - J_{i,j})^2 \tag{14}$$

Here $I_{i,j}$ and $J_{i,j}$ denote the original gray value and the processed gray value at the pixel position (i, j) respectively. Typically, the higher the PSNR value is, the better image quality can be achieved.

We firstly take the well-known Lena image with a size of 512 × 512 (256-gray), shown in Fig. 2(a), to demonstrate the feasibility of the proposed method. As the Lena image used in our experiment has no boundary-values, it means the location map size is extremely low, which can be ignored for the embedding capacity. Figures 2(b) and (c) shows the stego image S using the PM method and the stego image T using directed LSB embedding. Experiments show that the embedding capacity for S is 1.50 bpp, while the embedding capacity for T is 0.67 bpp. Meanwhile, the PSNR value for S is 49.89 dB, and the PSNR value for T is 52.89 dB. It can be seen from Fig. 2 that both the two resultant images do not introduce any noticeable artifacts. With the aid of the location map, the original image can be perfectly recovered without loss, as shown in Fig. 2(d). Actually, as the Lena image has no boundary-values, the original image can be recovered from the two stego images without the aid of any extra information.

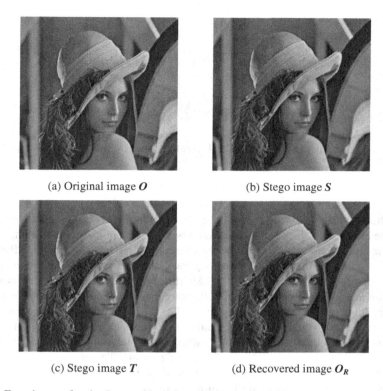

(a) Original image O

(b) Stego image S

(c) Stego image T

(d) Recovered image O_R

Fig. 2. Experiments for the Lena with a size of 512×512 (256-gray): (a) the original Lena image O, (b) the stego image S using the proposed PM method (1.50 bpp), (c) the stego image T based on directed LSB embedding (0.67 bpp), (d) the recovered image O_R without any loss.

We analyze the average MSE of the proposed PM method so that the stego image quality can be theoretically measured. Let $\alpha = L/(W \times H)$ denote the embedding rate for the proposed PM method, where L is the length of secret bit stream. For the proposed PM method, there will be $\alpha/1.5$ of the total pixels carrying secret bits as each pixel can be utilized to embed 1.5-bit averagely. For any pixel value with k, the probability of keeping unchanged is $2^{-l(k)}$, where $l(k)$ denotes the length of $f(k)$ (here, $f(k)$ has been defined in Eq. (11)). According to Eq. (14), we have

$$\text{MSE}_{PM} = \frac{1}{W \times H} \cdot \sum_{k=0}^{2^n-1} \left[h(k) \cdot \frac{\alpha}{1.5} \cdot (1 - 2^{-l(k)}) \right] \quad (15)$$

Here, $h(k)$ denotes the frequency of the gray value k, and $l(k) \in \{1, 2\}$, $n = 8$. Let β denote the rate of gray-levels carrying two secret bits, i.e.

$$\beta = \frac{\sum_{k=0, l(k)=2}^{2^n-1} h(k)}{W \times H} \quad (16)$$

Then we have

$$\sum_{k=0}^{2^n-1} [h(k) \cdot (1 - 2^{-l(k)})] = W \cdot H \cdot (\frac{1}{2} + \frac{\beta}{4}) \qquad (17)$$

$$\text{MSE}_{\text{PM}} = (\frac{1}{3} + \frac{\beta}{6}) \cdot \alpha \qquad (18)$$

Generally, we always have $\beta \approx 2/3$ for nature images, namely we always have

$$\text{MSE}_{\text{PM}} \approx \frac{4}{9} \alpha \qquad (19)$$

As shown in Eq. (12), for the proposed PM method, each of the gray-level values except the boundary-values can be used to embed 1.5-bit, approximately. It implies that the PM method can achieve a maximum embedding payload of 1.5 bpp. Based on Eq. (19), under the maximum embedding rate, the average MSE is equal to 2/3, resulting in a high PSNR value of 49.89 dB. Furthermore, under the maximum embedding rate for the proposed method, the maximum embedding rate for the directed LSB embedding method is 0.67 bpp as only 2/3 of the cover pixels will carry secret bits to generate the stego image T. At the same time, for each pixel to be used for data embedding, the probability of keeping unchanged is 1/2, which means the average MSE equals 1/3, resulting in a high PSNR of 52.90 dB. Therefore, for the proposed method, the maximum embedding rates for the stego image S and T are 1.50 bpp and 0.67 bpp, respectively. Under the maximum embedding rates, the theoretical PSNR values for the stego images S and T are 49.89 dB and 52.90 dB, respectively. Our experimental results for the Lena image show our theoretical analysis.

In the experiments, we compared the performance of our method with that of Qin et al.'s method [23] as Qin et al. proposed a novel reversible data hiding method based on the EMD technique [5] to also generate two visually similar stego images, denoted by S and T. During the data embedding process, both Qin et al's method and the proposed method have to construct the location map, which is compressed and then embedded together with the secret message. In order to compare the proposed method with Qin et al.'s method under the same compression condition, we also utilized the arithmetic coding [24] to compress the location map for the proposed method. In the experiments, we use eight standard test images: Airplane, Baboon, Bridge, Couple, Hair, Lake, Man and Peppers, as shown in Fig. 3, to demonstrate the feasibility of the proposed method. The methods in [2] and [22] were also compared to evaluate the performance of the proposed method. As shown in Table 2, it can be seen that the proposed method can achieve a maximum embedding payload of 1.08 bpp, while Qin et al.'s method can achieve a maximum embedding payload of 1.16 bpp, which is slightly higher than that of the proposed method. The proposed method can provide significantly more embedding capacity than that of [2, 22]. It can be also seen from some of the test images (e.g. the Bridge, Couple and Hair images) that Qin et al.'s method needs more embedding space for the location map. Furthermore, as shown in Table 2, though the PSNR values for the stego image S of the proposed method are slightly lower than that of Qin *et al.*'s method, the PSNR values for the stego image *T* of the proposed method are around 11 dB higher than that of Qin *et al.*'s method. And, the proposed method has higher PSNRs compared to the methods in [2, 22]. Moreover, the average PSNR value of the proposed method is 4.5 dB higher than that of Qin *et al.*'s method, which means the proposed method can maintain a high level of image quality.

| (a) Airplane | (b) Baboon | (c) Bridge | (d) Couple |
| (e) Hair | (f) Lake | (g) Man | (h) Peppers |

Fig. 3. Eight standard test images all with a size of 512×512 (256-gray)

Table 2. Comparsion results between [2, 22, 23] and the proposed method: Pure P. denotes the pure embedding payload (bpp); $PSNR_S$ and $PSNR_T$ denote the PSNRs (dB) for the stego images *S* and *T*; Entire P_S and Entire P_T denote the entire payload for *S* and *T*, respectively.

Images		Airplane	Baboon	Bridge	Couple	Hair	Lake	Man	Peppers
[2]	PSNR	48.26	48.18	48.19	48.35	48.28	48.19	48.40	49.25
	Pure P.	0.06	0.02	0.01	0.03	0.06	0.03	0.05	0.09
[22]	PSNR	48.73	48.55	48.34	48.45	48.87	48.43	48.56	49.23
	Pure P.	0.26	0.10	0.09	0.14	0.31	0.13	0.19	0.36
[23]	$PSNR_S$	52.11	52.12	51.71	51.71	51.66	52.11	52.12	52.08
	Entire P_S	1.16	1.16	1.16	1.16	1.16	1.16	1.16	1.16
	$PSNR_T$	41.65	41.66	41.63	41.62	41.62	41.66	41.66	41.66
	Entire P_T	1.16	1.16	1.16	1.16	1.16	1.16	1.16	1.16
	Pure P.	1.16	1.16	1.13	1.12	1.12	1.16	1.16	1.16
Our method	$PSNR_S$	49.89	49.89	49.89	49.89	49.89	49.89	49.88	49.84
	Entire P_S	1.50	1.50	1.50	1.50	1.50	1.50	1.50	1.50
	$PSNR_T$	52.94	52.92	52.90	52.88	52.91	52.90	52.87	52.86
	Entire P_T	0.67	0.67	0.67	0.67	0.67	0.67	0.67	0.67
	Pure P.	1.08	1.08	1.07	1.07	1.08	1.08	1.08	1.08

5 Conclusions

This paper presents a novel RDH method based on prefix matching and directed LSB embedding. The proposed method utilizes a cover image to generate two visually similar stego images. During the data embedding process, the first stego image is generated by applying the proposed PM method, resulting in a high level of embedding payload of 1.50 bpp. The pixels in the second stego image are modified to carry secret message by using directed LSB embedding by referring to the first stego image, resulting in an embedding rate of 0.67 bpp. On the receiver side, the data recipient can correctly extract the secret data with the DH key and further recover the original image with the aid of the location map. Furthermore, if the original image has no boundary-values, one can always recover the original image from the stego images without the aid of any extra information. Experimental results show our proposed method can carry high embedding payload and maintain a high level of image quality.

Acknowledgement. This work is supported in part by the National Natural Science Foundation of China (NSFC) under the grant Nos. 61170226, 61170175, the Young Innovative Research Team of Sichuan Province under the grant No. 2011JTD0007, and Chengdu Science and Technology program under the grant No. 12DXYB214JH-002.

References

1. Tian, J.: Reversible data embedding using a difference expansion. IEEE Trans. Circuits Syst. Video Technol. **13**(8), 890–896 (2003)
2. Ni, Z., Shi, Y., Ansari, N., Su, W.: Reversible data hiding. IEEE Trans. Circuits Syst. Video Technol. **16**(3), 354–362 (2006)
3. Thodi, D.M., Rodríguez, J.J.: Expansion embedding techniques for reversible watermarking. IEEE Trans. Image Process. **16**(3), 721–730 (2007)
4. Li, X., Yang, B., Zeng, T.: Efficient reversible watermarking based on adaptive prediction-error expansion and pixel selection. IEEE Trans. Image Process. **20**(12), 3524–3533 (2011)
5. Zhang, X., Wang, S.: Efficient steganography embedding by exploiting modification direction. IEEE Commun. Lett. **10**(11), 781–783 (2006)
6. Wang, J., Sun, Y., Xu, H., Chen, K., Kim, H.J., Joo, S.: An improved section-wise exploiting modification direction method. Signal Process. **90**(11), 2954–2964 (2010)
7. Wu, H., Huang, J.: Reversible image watermarking on prediction errors by efficient histogram modification. Signal Process. **92**(12), 3000–3009 (2012)
8. Hong, W., Chen, T.: A novel data hiding embedding method using adaptive pixel pair matching. IEEE Trans. Inf. Forensics Secur. **7**(1), 176–184 (2012)
9. Zhang, X.: Reversible data hiding with optimal value transfer. IEEE Trans. Multimedia **15**(2), 316–325 (2013)
10. Ou, B., Li, X., Zhao, Y., Ni, R., Shi, Y.: Pairwise predication-error expansion for efficient reversible data hiding. IEEE Trans. Image Process. **22**(12), 5010–5021 (2013)
11. Sachnev, V., Kim, H.J., Nam, J., Suresh, S., Shi, Y.: Reversible watermarking algorithm using sorting and prediction. IEEE Trans. Circuits Syst. Video Technol. **19**(7), 989–999 (2009)

12. Hu, Y., Lee, H., Li, J.: DE-based reversible data hiding with improved overflow location map. IEEE Trans. Circuits Syst. Video Technol. **19**(2), 250–260 (2009)
13. Fridrich, J., Goljan, M., Du, R.: Invertible authentication. In: Proceedings of SPIE Photonics West, Security and Watermarking of Multimedia Contests III, vol. 3971, pp. 197–208. San Jose, CA (2001)
14. Fridrich, J., Goljan, M., Du, R.: Lossless data embedding: new paradigm in digital watermarking. EURASIP J. Adv. Signal Process. **2**, 185–196 (2002)
15. Celik, M.U., Sharma, G., Tekalp, A.M.: Lossless watermarking for image authentication: a new framework and an implementation. IEEE Trans. Image Process. **15**(4), 1042–1049 (2006)
16. Alattar, A.M.: Reversible watermarking using the difference expansion of a generalized integer transform. IEEE Trans. Image Process. **13**(8), 1147–1156 (2004)
17. Kamstra, L., Heijmans, H.J.A.M.: Reversible data embedding into images using wavelet techniques and sorting. IEEE Trans. Image Process. **14**(12), 2082–2090 (2005)
18. Hwang, J., Kim, J., Choi, J.,: A reversible watermarking based on histogram shifting. In: Shi, Y.Q., Jeon, B. (eds.) IWDW 2006. LNCS, vol. 4283, pp. 348–361. Springer, Heidelberg (2006)
19. Tsai, P., Hu, Y., Yeh, H.: Reversible image hiding scheme using predictive coding and histogram shifting. Sig. Process. **89**(6), 1129–1143 (2009)
20. Lee, S., Yoo, C.D., Kalker, T.: Reversible image watermarking based on integer-to-integer wavelet transform. IEEE Trans. Inf. Forensics Secur. **2**(3), 321–330 (2007)
21. Luo, L., Chen, Z., Chen, M., Zeng, X., Xiong, Z.: Reversible image watermarking using interpolation technique. IEEE Trans. Inf. Forensics Secur. **5**(1), 187–193 (2010)
22. Li, Y., Yeh, C., Chang, C.: Data hiding based on the similarity between neighboring pixels with reversibility. Digit. Signal Proc. **20**(4), 1116–1128 (2010)
23. Qin, C., Chang, C., Hsu, T.: Reversible data hiding scheme based on exploiting modification direction with two steganographic images. Multimedia Tools Appl. (2014). http://link. springer.com/article/10.1007/s11042-014-1894-5
24. Eric Bodden (2003). http://www.bodden.de/legacy/arithmetic-coding/

Multi-class JPEG Image Steganalysis by Ensemble Linear SVM Classifier

Jie Zhu, Qingxiao Guan$^{(\boxtimes)}$, and Xianfeng Zhao

State Key Laboratory of Information Security,
Institute of Information Engineering, Chinese Academy of Sciences,
89A, Minzhuang Rd., Beijing 100093, People's Republic of China
{zhujie,guanqingxiao,zhaoxianfeng}@iie.ac.cn

Abstract. Multi-class steganalysis utilizes multi-class classification methods to predict the category of steganographic schemes used for generating stego files. In this paper we propose a novel multi-class approach towards more efficiently classifying JPEG stego-images with CC-JRM features. Because CC-JRM has successfully cooperates with ensemble classifier in detecting the presence of stego images, we modified ensemble classifier for multi-class steganalysis. The ideas of performing ensemble in different steps results in two schemes in our proposed method. These two schemes are based on different multi-class ensemble strategies, and utilize linear SVM as base classifier. The experimental results shows our methods received better results with less computing cost compared to other multi-class steganalysis method.

Keywords: Multi-class steganalysis · Steganography · Ensemble classifier

1 Introduction

Steganography can hide secret message in innocent-looking media. It is a covert communication method via public channel, which can be used for some vicious purposes such as illegal information transmission. Digital image is a popular cover media file format for steganographers. As a countering method, image steganalysis was developed to distinguish between cover and stego objects. Since many steganographic methods for image have been proposed, it is necessary to detect the category of steganographic methods for stego images. Multi-class steganalysis has been developed to deal with this problem [1–5]. For a stego-image, multi-class steganalysis adopts the image feature and the multi-class classifier to predict which steganographic method had been used in generating the stego image. It can provide useful information for further analysis such as quantitative steganalysis or modification position locating. For these reasons, multi-class steganalysis became an important part in steganalysis system.

Previous works on multi-class steganalysis concentrated on using traditional steganalysis feature and multi-class classifier. Pevný and Fridrich [2] use PEV-274 feature and multi-class Kernel SVM to detect multi-class JPEG stego images. Experimental results on JPEG stego images of different categories proved this method effective. Similarly, Dong et al. apply run-length feature for multi-class steganalysis in [3]. Lubenko and Ker [5] use SPAM feature and Logistic Regression for multi-class

© Springer International Publishing Switzerland 2015
Y.-Q. Shi et al. (Eds.): IWDW 2014, LNCS 9023, pp. 470–484, 2015.
DOI: 10.1007/978-3-319-19321-2_36

steganalysis on spatial images. They also compared logistic regression with SVM and the result showed logistic regression has comparable accuracy to SVM methods.

In recent years, Fridrich et al. [6–9] proposed rich model feature for steganalysis in. Unlike traditional steganalysis feature, the dimensionality of rich model feature is extremely high. It consists of many feature subsets formed by different approaches. Rich model made a break through by detecting steganography with high accuracy. Due to its high dimensionality, Kodovský and Fridrich [7] put forward the ensemble classifier for steganalysis by Rich model feature. Such ensemble classifier trains several Fish Linear Discriminate (FLD) classifiers as base classifiers. And each classifier only use a part of features randomly selected from the whole Rich model feature set. The final result is an ensemble result from base classifiers by voting. To the best of our knowledge, so far using the ensemble classifier and rich model feature is the most effective steganalysis method, especially in detecting high secure adaptive steganography.

The motivation of our work is to enhance the accuracy of multi-class steganalysis by modified ensemble classifier with different base classifier and different ensemble strategies. Considering the extraordinary ability of rich model which is able to sensitively capture the disturbances of different steganographic embedding, we develop our multi-class steganalysis method based on it for its potential to serve multi-class steganalysis. The key problem of using rich model for multi-class steganalysis is to design a proper multi-class classifier. Inspired by the success of ensemble FLD classifier mentioned above, we propose two schemes of multi-class ensemble classifier based on Linear SVM [10]. Since multi-class steganalysis is more difficult than detecting the presence of stego images, we choose linear SVM as base classifier for its robustness and accuracy. And more importantly, it can be trained by primal method efficiently. We will discuss it in detail in Sect. 3.1. Besides new base classifier, our schemes apply different ensemble strategies. Scheme 1 simply aggregates results from multiple multi-class linear SVM classifiers, and fuses them to the final result by voting. In Scheme 2, the conventional multi-class classifier is updated by replacing its binary classifiers with ensemble binary Linear SVM classifiers.

In this paper we choose to verify our multi-class steganalytic schemes for JPEG images. Therefor the rich model feature for JPEG image, named Cartesian Calibration JPEG Rich Model (CC-JRM), is used. Without loss of generality, our method also can be applied to multi-class steganalysis on spatial steganography. One can easily modify it just by replacing CC-JRM with spatial rich model feature or PSRM feature [11, 12]. We compare our method with a state-of-art method which adopts the Cross-Domain Feature (CDF) [13] and Kernel SVM (KSVM). Experimental results show that our method performs better than CDF with KSVM method.

The remaining of this paper is organized as follow: In Sect. 2, we review CC-JRM feature for JPEG steganalysis. And our method is presented in Sect. 3. Section 4 is experimental results and analysis. Finally, we discussed this method and draw a conclusion in Sect. 5. To prevent confusion over these two similar terminologies in this paper, we define them in detail here. Multi-class ensemble classifier is the general term of ensemble classifier for multi-class steganalysis. Ensemble multi-class classifier is a new terminology, which is similar to conventional ensemble classifier except selecting multi-class classifier as base learner. Ensemble multi-class classifier is proposed in Scheme 1.

2 Review of CC-JRM Feature

Feature provides basic information for steganalysis. Cartesian Calibration JPEG Rich Model (CC-JRM) feature is extracted from JPEG coefficients. It conforms to the philosophy of Rich model feature. As Fridrich et al. point out, enlarging the "diversity" is important for the steganalysis feature [6]. Thus CC-JRM is composed of several different feature sets which characterize different statistical properties of JPEG coefficient. CC-JRM feature was successfully applied to detecting JPEG stego images. Because of the diversity of CC-JRM feature, it not only captures the disturbance introduced by steganographic embedding, but also reflects the difference of them. This is desirable for multi-class steganalysis.

CC-JRM feature respectively extract the feature on image and its calibrated image with the same procedure. "Cartesian Calibration" stands for combining them by concatenating. Calibration image is obtained by a special operation on candidate image. It first decompress the candidate image to the spatial domain, and then crop pixels of 4 columns on left and 4 rows on top, finally it compress cropped image to JPEG with the quantitation matrix of candidate image. Although it is hard to explicitly explain the mechanism of calibration, so many works on JPEG steganalysis confirmed the effectiveness of calibration. In [14], Kodovský et al. discussed several possible functions of calibration.

The sub-models of CC-JRM can be divided into two parts: DCT-mode specific components and Integral components. The former regards 64 DCT coefficients as parallel channels to capture inter and intra block dependencies on different directions. The latter is a powerful supplement to submodels extracted from the single channels, because they take all DCT modes into account and also form co-occurrence matrices on five directions from an integral perspective. Therefore, these components can detect statistical dependencies which may be omitted by DCT-mode specific components.

The feature of CC_JRM includes: (1) the co-occurrence matrices is based on the absolute value, intra-block differences, and inter-block differences of DCT coefficients; (2) the submodels are compact and robust due to removing redundant elements and further fusion between those matrices which have similar statistics dependencies; (3) the feature extracted from one natural image which is mirrored about the main diagonal is completely the same as that from the original image; (4) some submodels are based on a small portion of DCT coefficients in the blocks, while others cover all DCT modes in order to increase the diversity of the model; (5) like many advanced feature space, Cartesian calibration [14] is applied to improve the performance.

The total dimensionality is 22510. More details of CC-JRM feature can be found in [6].

3 Proposed Method

In this section we describe our method. CC-JRM is a powerful feature set in steganalysis for JPEG images due to its diversity. It is consist of many kinds of submodels extracted from partial and integral DCT coefficients and can capture different types of dependencies which may be disturbed by embedding artifact. Therefore we select CC-JRM as our model for identifying different steganographic schemes. However, high dimensionality may bring new problem named Curse of Dimensionality [7]. In order to utilize rich model for multi-class steganalysis, we adopt ensemble machine learning approach. To the best of our knowledge, ensemble classifier is a suitable and successful choice for handling high model dimensionality and large training sets flexibly. It has been proved that ensemble classifier can significantly improve the performance of steganalyzers across various embedding algorithms and payload in the case of binary classification [8]. The contribution of our work is modifying binary ensemble classifier for multi-class detector. As explained in Sect. 1, we choose Linear SVM as the base classifier in our ensemble classifier. The key problem is how to design multi-class ensemble classifier based on Linear SVM. For this purpose, we propose two schemes constructed by different multi-class ensemble strategies respectively. Before we present them in Sect. 3.2, we first introduce linear SVM classifier trained by primal method, which underlies our proposed schemes.

3.1 Linear SVM Trained by Primal Method

SVM classifier is well known for its accuracy and robustness. The decision rule of Linear SVM is in form of linear function which require less computational and storage cost in applications. For these reasons, we select linear SVM as base classifier in our schemes. The training of SVM is to solve following "max margin" model:

$$\min_{\omega,b,\xi_j} \omega^T \omega + C \sum_{j=1}^{l} \xi_j$$
$$\text{s.t} \quad y_i(\omega^T x_i + b) \geq 1 - \xi_j$$
$$\xi_j \geq 0 \, j = 1,2\ldots,l$$

Where ω and b are parameter of classifier $\omega^T x + b$. $y_i \in \{-1,1\}$ and x_i are label and feature of the ith training sample, respectively. C is the parameter in training, and it trade off the "prediction error" on training samples and the "generalize ability" of classifier.

Typically, the training of linear SVM is converted to a dual problem and solved, which is utilized by popular SVM toolbox LibSVM [15]. However, there is a more adequate method for training linear SVM, which is called primal method. Primal method solves SVM training by trust region Newton method. Compared to dual methods, primal method can train linear SVM with larger number of training samples in much less time. LibLinear is a popular open source library for large-scale linear classification [16]. LibLinear toolbox implements linear SVM by dual method (default) and as well primal method. Thanks to it, for our multiclass ensemble classifier we are enabled to train dozens of linear SVM classifiers by primal method.

Linear SVM can be used as binary classifier and multi-class classifier, which is denoted as BLSVM and MLSVM for clear illustration, correspondingly.

3.2 Ensemble Schemes for Multi-class Steganalysis

Firstly, let's discuss internal workings of general multi-class classifier here. For N-classes multi-class steganalysis, let $C = \{c_1, c_2, \ldots, c_N\}$ denotes labels of N classes of steganographic methods. Generally, multi-class classifiers perform multi-class classification by dividing it into several binary classifications. There are 3 approaches for this task. Respectively they are "one-against-one", "one-against-all" and "directed acyclic graph". "one-against-one" and "directed acyclic graph" only need to load training data of two classes in training each binary classifier, thus require less memory and are more suitable for practical use. A comparison among these three approaches can be found in literature [17]. In this paper, we involves "one-against-one" in Scheme 2 because it is convenient and effective. "one-against-one" trains binary classifiers for each pair of different classes in $\mathbf{C}$, which means a multi-class classifier comprised $\binom{N}{2} = N(N-1)/2$ binary classifiers. In multi-class classification step, a sample is input into these classifiers and thus receive $N(N-1)/2$ classification results $R_:, i = 1, 2\ldots,$ $N(N-1)/2$. For each class c_i, correspondingly there are $n-1$ binary classifiers that output decision results between c_i and other $n-1$ classes $\{c_1, \ldots, c_{i-1}, c_{i+1}, \ldots, c_N\}$. After $N(N-1)/2$ binary results are obtained, the final result of multi-class classification is determined by the class with the largest number of related classification results against other $n-1$ classes, which is known as "Max Wins".

Next, we proposed two schemes to assemble linear SVM for multi-class steganalysis. They are elaborated as follows:

Scheme 1: Scheme 1 can be viewed as the multi-class extension of conventional ensemble binary classifier proposed by Kodovský et al. [8]. Formally, ensemble classifier for multi-class steganalysis contains L base multi-class classifiers $f_i, i = 1, 2, \ldots, L$, which are trained on different feature subsets $d_i, i = 1, 2 \ldots L$. Each subset d_i includes indexes of features randomly selected from CC-JRM feature set, and dimensionality of selected feature sets is denoted as d. Finally we simply assemble the multi-class classification results from L classifiers by voting strategy. Figure 1 shows the detailed structure of ensemble multi-class classifier.

In Scheme 1, we simply use MLSVM as the base multi-class classifier $f_i, i \in \{1, 2, \ldots, L\}$. Each base MLSVM simply accepts N classes of training images in the training phase and generates a Linear SVM model. We do not care about its detailed implementation.

For a candidate JPEG image to be tested, firstly its CC-JRM feature x is extracted. Let $x(d_i)$ denotes the feature component selected by d_i in x, and classifiers $f_i, i = 1, 2, \ldots, L$, individually predict the multi-class classification results on $x(d_i), i = 1, 2, \ldots, L$. That is to say, consequently ith classifier MLSVM produces its prediction value $f_i(x(d_i))$ in the testing phase. Note that $f_i(x(d_i)) \in \mathbf{C}$. Following formula describes the ensemble rule by voting:

$$result = \arg \max_{c \in C} \sum_{i=1}^{L} \delta(f_i(x(d_i)) = c)$$

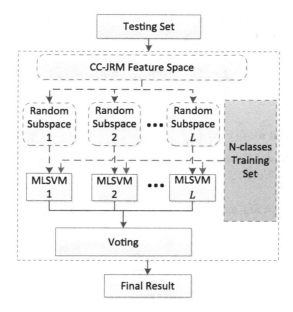

Fig. 1. The structure of Scheme 1: ensemble multi-class classifier.

where $\delta(\cdot)$ is defined as: $\delta(k) = \begin{cases} 1 & \textit{if k is true} \\ 0 & \textit{else} \end{cases}$.

Formula above shows that the final result is the class with the most prediction support from MLSVM $f_i, i = 1, 2 \ldots L$.

Scheme 2: Multi-class classifier of Scheme 2 derives from the classifier proposed by Kodovský et al. [2]. It follows the principle of "one vs. one" strategy. $\frac{N(N-1)}{2}$ binary classifiers are trained for N classes. Each binary classifier is BLSVM. That means a set of BLSVM cooperate to implement multi-class classification according to "one-against-one" algorithm. For each pair of different classes $\{c_m, c_n\} \subseteq \mathbf{C}, m, n \in \{1, \ldots, N\}$, there is a corresponding binary classifier that maps feature of image x to prediction result between c_m and c_n:

$$h_{c_m, c_n} : x \rightarrow \{c_m, c_n\}$$

However, rather than using single classifier, each binary classifier in scheme 2 is formed by L binary classifiers $h_{c_m, c_n, i}, i = 1, 2, \ldots, L$. Accordingly, each $h_{c_m, c_n, i}$ also employs feature subset $x(d_i)$ randomly selected from CC-JRM feature x to predict the decision result. It can be written as:

$$h_{c_m, c_n, i} : x(d_i) \rightarrow \{c_m, c_n\}$$

Where d_i is the subset that includes feature indices randomly selected for classifier $h_{c_m, c_n, i}$.

After all the decision results $h_{c_m,c_n,i}(x(d_i)), i = 1, 2, \ldots, L$, have been output, h_{c_m,c_n} assemble them by voting:

$$h_{c_m,c_n}(x) = \begin{cases} c_m, & \text{if } \sum_{i=i}^{L} \delta(h_{c_m,c_n,i}(x(d_i)) = c_m) > L/2 \\ c_n, & else \end{cases}$$

where $\delta(\cdot)$ is defined as: $\delta(k) = \begin{cases} 1 & \text{if } k \text{ is true} \\ 0 & else \end{cases}$.

The final result of multi-class classification in Scheme 2 is calculated by the same procedure as "Max Wins":

$$result = \arg \max_{c \in C} \sum_{m=1}^{N-1} \sum_{n=m+1}^{N} \delta(h_{c_m,c_n}(x) = c),$$

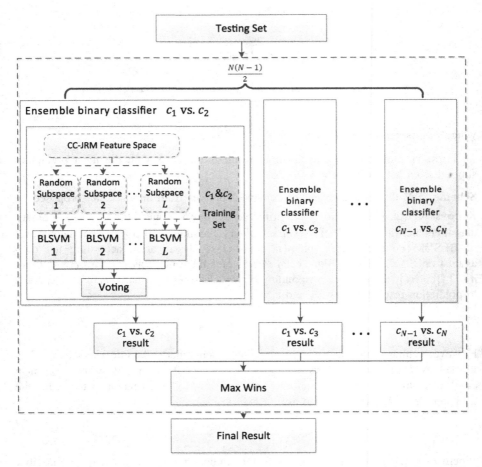

Fig. 2. The structure of Scheme 2: multi-class classifier by one vs. one approach based on ensemble binary classifier

where $\delta(\cdot)$ is defined as above. The structure of Scheme 2 is showed in Fig. 2.

Ensemble schemes only use part of high dimension feature in training of each classifiers, so it can avoid "over learning" problem and relieve the training burden for high dimension feature and large scale data. Similar to ensemble FLD classifier proposed by Kodovský et al. [7], both schemes of our multiclass ensemble classifier need to set two parameters: number of base classifiers L and dimension of randomly selected feature subset d. We search the optimized parameter L and d by trials of repeatedly tuning and training, and the stop criterion is the same of training ensemble FLD classifier.

On another hand, classifiers can be simultaneously trained on parallel or distribution computer systems with multiple cores, which make it possible to deal with large scale dataset of more steganographic schemes for multi-class steganalysis.

4 Experiments on Multi-class Steganalysis

4.1 Experimental Setup

We evaluate proposed method on standard image dataset. The experiments are carried out on BOSS V1.01 image dataset. BOSS V1.01 includes 10000 images photographed by cameras of 6 types. They are resized to 512×512 resolution and converted to gray images. BOSS V1.01 is the latest version of BOSS image dataset. So far it is the most standard database for steganalysis research.

Four Modern JPEG steganographic methods are included in our experiment. They are nsF5 [18], Model Based(MB1) [19], MME3 [20], Uniward [21]. Along with cover images, there are 5 classes in our multi-class steganalysis experiment. Although we know other JPEG steganographic methods, however, our experiment is designed to verify the effectiveness of our multi-class steganalysis method. Thus we select these 4 steganographic methods as benchmark in our experiment because they are the most secure and undetectable among proposed JPEG steganographic methods so far. We also explain why we select MB1 but not its updated version MB2 [22]. Although MB2 revised some problems of MB1, such revision incurs additional weakness so that MB2 is less secure than MB1 in CC-JRM feature based steganalysis [23].

Cover images are original images in BOSS V1.01 dataset. Stego images are generated by embedding cover images by these four steganographic methods. We test 0.1 bpnc and 0.2 bpnc embedding payload. The terminology bpnc is "bit per non-zero AC coefficient". Higher payload means larger divergence on feature among different steganographic methods. Both these two settings of payload are relatively small for multiclass steganalysis. For stego images of each class and cover images, 50 % of them were randomly selected as the training samples and the rest the testing samples. Totally there are $5 \times 5000 = 25000$ images playing as training sample and other 25000 images as testing samples. The implementation of Linear SVM we select is the LibLinear toolbox (version 1.94) [16]. It includes a family of linear SVM classifiers for large-scale linear classification and regression. The software package is downloaded from http://www. csie.ntu.edu.tw/~cjlin/liblinear/. After one-dimensional grid search for best parameters, we fix the dimensionality of feature subset at $d = 1500$ and the number of base classifiers at $L = 60$.

We compare our methods with the method using CDF feature and KSVM classifier. CDF is proposed by Kodovský et al. and combines 686-D SPAM feature and 548-D Cartesian calibration PEV feature. SPAM feature is extracted from the spatial domain [24] and Cartesian calibration PEV feature the JPEG coefficients [4]. The 686-dimensional SPAM is one of the most sensitive features in spatial domain steganalysis. Many previous JPEG multi-class steganalysis methods rely on the PEV-274 feature for its superior performance, and Cartesian calibration PEV feature is revised version of PEV-274 feature which leads to further improvement. It has been proved that cross-domain feature outperform the single domain feature by [6] and [13]. Thus, ascribe to more feature sets from two domains, 1234-dimensional CDF feature performs better. CDF feature is usually analyzed by KSVM. KSVM employs kernel function to map original feature to kernel feature space which is more discriminative. KSVM is proper for multi-class steganalysis by a single classifier on low dimensional feature. We use prediction accuracy as benchmark measure.

We also compare the Scheme 2 with FLD-based multi-class ensemble classifier. We implement the latter in the framework of Scheme 2. As we mentioned, the ensemble binary classifier in the framework of Scheme 2 is a set of BLSVMs. However, As its name implies, FLD-based multi-class ensemble classifier uses a set of FLD to construct ensemble binary classifier of the framework. This is the only difference between them. Since FLD had outstanding performance in binary steganalysis, through comparison of classification accuracy, the role of LSVM in Scheme 2 and the prospect of LSVM in multi-class ensemble classifier will be concluded.

Experiments are implemented on 64bit Matlab and Windows 7. 64bit system is necessary, because training classifiers consumes a large amount of memory,[1] and only 64bit system is affordable.

4.2 Experimental Results

Experimental results are described by confusion matrices. Confusion matrix contains classification accuracy of each class in multi-class steganalysis. In our experiment, there are 5 classes: cover, nsF5, MB1, MME3, Uniward. Thus the size of confusion matrix is 5×5. The element of the ith column and the jth row in confusion matrix indicates the proportion of the jth class samples that has been classified as the ith class. That is to say, the diagonal elements indicate the portion of samples in classes that has been correctly classified.

Tables 1 and 2 include comparison among experimental results of CDF + KSVM, FLD-based multi-class ensemble classifier and our methods method on 0.1 bpnc and 0.2 bpnc embedding payload. We can see that for overall results of 5 classes both our schemes are better than CDF + KSVM method. The Scheme 2 consistently achieves the best performance. And in the framework of Scheme 2, LSVM performs as well as FLD. The classification accuracies of both are very close except the nsF5 class on 0.1bpnc, where LSVM performs better than FLD by 5.77 %. It means that in the

---

[1] In our experiments, training 5-classes classifiers consumes about 10G memory.

Table 1. Confusion matrices of four methods on 0.1 bpnc payload

CDF+KSVM					
	Cover	nsF5	MME3	MB1	Uniward
Cover	**39.50**%	23.32%	1.43%	2.10%	33.65%
nsF5	15.18%	**63.38**%	1.80%	3.65%	16.00%
MME3	0.95%	1.38%	**94.85**%	2.45%	0.38%
MB1	1.83%	2.45%	2.30%	**92.35**%	1.08%
Uniward	38.35%	23.88%	1.40%	2.08%	**34.30**%

Proposed Scheme 1					
	Cover	nsF5	MME3	MB1	Uniward
Cover	**36.15**%	19.93%	1.95%	3.83%	38.15%
nsF5	4.83%	**76.65**%	2.33%	2.23%	13.98%
MME3	0.07%	0.10%	**99.40**%	0.30%	0.13%
MB1	0.07%	0.07%	0.47%	**99.30**%	0.07%
Uniward	35.00%	20.98%	1.93%	3.75%	**38.35**%

Proposed Scheme 2					
	Cover	nsF5	MME3	MB1	Uniward
Cover	**45.85**%	22.95%	0.03%	0.28%	30.90%
nsF5	8.00%	**84.65**%	0.07%	0.17%	7.10%
MME3	0.03%	0.17%	**99.55**%	0.17%	0.07%
MB1	0.17%	0.10%	0.07%	**99.58**%	0.07%
Uniward	41.85%	23.80%	0.03%	0.28%	**34.05**%

FLD-based multi-class ensemble classifier					
	Cover	nsF5	MME3	MB1	Uniward
Cover	**48.05**%	17.43%	0.00%	0.07%	34.45%
nsF5	11.13%	**78.88**%	0.00%	0.13%	9.88%
MME3	0.03%	0.05%	**99.72**%	0.15%	0.05%
MB1	0.07%	0.05%	0.07%	**99.67**%	0.13%
Uniward	43.58%	18.60%	0.00%	0.10%	**37.73**%

Table 2. Confusion matrices of four methods on 0.2 bpnc payload

CDF+KSVM					
	Cover	nsF5	MME3	MB1	Uniward
Cover	**50.30**%	7.10%	0.13%	0.35%	42.13%
nsF5	5.10%	**88.03**%	0.25%	0.80%	5.83%
MME3	0.45%	0.40%	**98.70**%	0.42%	0.03%
MB1	0.72%	1.00%	0.25%	**97.95**%	0.07%
Uniward	45.65%	8.30%	0.13%	0.35%	**45.58**%

Proposed Scheme 1					
	Cover	nsF5	MME3	MB1	Uniward
Cover	**54.83**%	12.15%	0.35%	3.38%	29.30%
nsF5	1.25%	**97.65**%	0.07%	0.33%	0.70%
MME3	0.05%	0.00%	**99.95**%	0.00%	0.00%
MB1	0.03%	0.03%	0.00%	**99.95**%	0.00%
Uniward	42.17%	14.88%	0.25%	3.58%	**39.13**%

Proposed Scheme 2					
	Cover	nsF5	MME3	MB1	Uniward
Cover	**55.33**%	2.48%	0.00%	0.03%	42.17%
nsF5	1.05%	**97.38**%	0.00%	0.03%	1.55%
MME3	0.00%	0.00%	**100.00**%	0.00%	0.00%
MB1	0.00%	0.00%	0.00%	**100.00**%	0.00%
Uniward	42.00%	3.17%	0.00%	0.03%	**54.80**%

FLD-based multi-class ensemble classifier					
	Cover	nsF5	MME3	MB1	Uniward
Cover	**54.27**%	2.63%	0.00%	0.00%	43.10%
nsF5	1.63%	**96.13**%	0.00%	0.00%	2.25%
MME3	0.00%	0.00%	**100.00**%	0.00%	0.00%
MB1	0.00%	0.00%	0.00%	**100.00**%	0.00%
Uniward	41.05%	3.63%	0.00%	0.00%	**55.33**%

framework of multi-class ensemble classifier which utilizes "one vs. one" strategy, LSVM is more stable. We can conclude that LSVM is a promising machine learning tool in steganalysis. We noticed that Uniward is the most difficult to be correctly classified. CC-JRM is not sensitive enough to Uniward. We carefully checked the binary detection by ensemble classifier described in [8] which distinguishes Uniward images from cover images, and that supports our claim. This result is coincident with the security character of Uniward [21, 25].

We can draw some conclusion about the ensemble classifier and linear SVM. We test the effect of the number of base classifiers on final accuracy. The result is showed in Fig. 3. The predicting accuracy converges fast and keeps steady close to the highest accuracy even though the number of the base classifiers increases. It shows that the number of base classifiers cannot be too large which means more training time or too small which cannot gives satisfied result. On the other hand, linear SVM is suitably used in multi-class ensemble classifiers for it consumes less time and gives better accuracy. Multi-class steganalysis usually has to deal with more training samples than binary steganalysis due to more classes, and ensemble classifier need to train dozens of base classifiers, leading to more training time, e.g., in our experiment of Scheme 1, each multi-class classifier has $5000 \times 5 = 25000$ samples in training phase. Since linear SVM is designed for large data, it can handle the training process well with acceptable time spent. Our experiments show KSVM + CDF takes the most time, Scheme 1 less, and Scheme 2 least. We also discover that there exists an interesting phenomenon about linear SVM. For each base classifier in ensemble classifier,

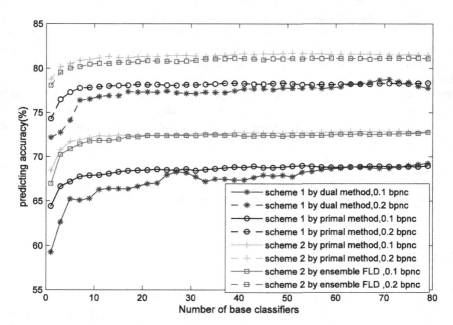

Fig. 3. Effect of the number of base classifiers L on the final predicting accuracy of ensemble classifier in different schemes

Linear SVM trained by primal method has superior prediction accuracy, about 5 % higher contrasted with that by dual method, which again explain why we use primal method. However, along with the increase of the number of the base classifiers L, the final accuracy of ensemble classifier trained by dual method is close to even exceeds the accuracy of that trained by primal method.

The experimental results also reveal some interesting properties of four methods. In Table 1 we can see that Scheme 1 is the best one for Uniward with 0.1 bpnc, however Scheme 2 is better for Uniward with 0.2 bpnc. Besides, in experiment of 0.1 bpnc payload, Scheme 2 is take advantages over CDF + KSVM for 4 classes, but not better for Uniward. Suppose Uniward manipulate modifications JPEG coefficients according to the loss function computed from spatial domain, and SPAM feature in CDF also extracted from spatial domain, perhaps feature from spatial domain is helpful for Uniward with small payload in multi-class steganalysis.

5 Conclusion

Multi-class steganalysis is an important part for steganalysis system in real applications. In this paper we proposed two schemes for multi-class steganalysis. They are based on ensemble classifier, linear SVM and CC-JRM feature. The experimental results demonstrate that a proper ensemble scheme and rich model feature can formulate a multi-class steganalyzer to enhance accuracy of multi-class steganalysis. We introduce primal trained linear SVM to ensemble classifier and designed two ensemble schemes for multiclass steganalysis. Experimental results also prove that Scheme 2 is better scheme for multi-class steganalysis. This is the main contribution of this paper.

Our work shows a prospect of multi-class steganalysis by rich model feature and ensemble classifier. The future works about this topic will focus on 3 aspects. First, it is possible to investigate more ensemble strategies for ensemble classifier. Second, a heuristic feature selection for multi-class steganalysis is beneficial, because it can remove some redundant or ineffective component in feature set, especially for high dimensional feature such as rich model feature. Finally, we need to find a feasible approach to incorporate the multi-class steganalysis with targeted steganalysis. These are still open problems and worth further studying.

Acknowledgements. This work was supported by the NSFC under 61170281, 61303259 and 61303254, the Strategic Priority Research Program of CAS under XDA06030600, and the Project of IIE, CAS, under Y4Z0031102 and Y3Z0071502.

References

1. Pevný, T., Fridrich, J.: Multiclass detector of current steganographic methods for JPEG format. IEEE Trans. Inf. Forensics Secur. **3**(4), 635–650 (2008)
2. Pevný, T., Fridrich, J.: Towards multi-class blind steganalyzer for JPEG images. In: Barni, M., Cox, I., Kalker, T., Kim, H.-J. (eds.) IWDW 2005. LNCS, vol. 3710, pp. 39–53. Springer, Heidelberg (2005)

3. Dong, J., Wang, W., Tan, T.: Multi-class blind steganalysis based on image run-length analysis. In: Ho, A.T.S., Shi, Y.Q., Kim, H.J., Barni, M. (eds.) IWDW 2009. LNCS, vol. 5703, pp. 199–210. Springer, Heidelberg (2009)
4. Pevný, T., Fridrich, J.: Merging Markov and DCT features for multi-class JPEG steganalysis. In: Electronic Imaging 2007. International Society for Optics and Photonics (2007)
5. Lubenko, I., Ker, A.D.: Steganalysis using logistic regression. In: IS&T/SPIE Electronic Imaging. International Society for Optics and Photonics (2011)
6. Kodovský, J., Fridrich, J.: Steganalysis of JPEG images using rich models. In: IS&T/SPIE Electronic Imaging. International Society for Optics and Photonics (2012)
7. Kodovský, J., Fridrich, J.: Steganalysis in high dimensions: fusing classifiers built on random subspaces. In: Proceedings of the SPIE, Media Watermarking, Security, and Forensics III, vol. 7880, p. 78800L, 10 February 2011
8. Kodovský, J., Fridrich, J., Holub, V.: Ensemble classifiers for steganalysis of digital media. IEEE Trans. Inf. Forensics Secur. **7**(2), 432–444 (2012)
9. Fridrich, J., Kodovský, J.: Rich models for steganalysis of digital images. IEEE Trans. Inf. Forensics Secur. **7**(3), 868–882 (2012)
10. Fan, R.E., Chang, K.W., Hsieh, C.J., Wang, X.R., Lin, C.J.: LIBLINEAR: a library for large linear classification. J. Mach. Learn. Res. **9**, 1871–1874 (2008)
11. Holub, V., Fridrich, J., Denemark, T.: Random projections of residuals as an alternative to co-occurrences in steganalysis. In: Proceedings of the SPIE, Media Watermarking, Security, and Forensics 2013, vol. 8665, p. 86650L, 22 March 2013
12. Holub, V., Fridrich, J.: Random projections of residuals for digital image steganalysis. IEEE Trans. Inf. Forensics Secur. **8**(12), 1996–2006 (2013)
13. Kodovský, J., Pevný, T., Fridrich, J.: Modern steganalysis can detect YASS. In: Proceedings of the SPIE, Media Forensics and Security II, vol. 7541, p. 754102, 27 January 2010
14. Kodovský, J., Fridrich, J.: Calibration revisited. In: Dittmann, J., Craver, S., Fridrich, J. (eds.) Proceedings of the 11th ACM Multimedia & Security Workshop, Princeton, NJ, pp. 63–74, 7–8 September 2009
15. LIBSVM – A Library for Support Vector Machines. http://www.csie.ntu.edu.tw/~cjlin/libsvm/
16. LIBLINEAR – A Library for Large Linear Classification. http://www.csie.ntu.edu.tw/~cjlin/liblinear/
17. Hsu, C.W., Lin, C.J.: A comparison of methods for multiclass support vector machines. IEEE Trans. Neural Netw. **13**(2), 415–425 (2002)
18. Fridrich, J., Pevný, T., Kodovský, J.: Statistically undetectable JPEG steganography: dead ends challenges, and opportunities. In: Proceedings of the 9th Workshop on Multimedia & Security, pp. 3–14. ACM (2007)
19. Sallee, P.: Model-based steganography. In: Kalker, T., Cox, I., Ro, Y.M. (eds.) IWDW 2003. LNCS, vol. 2939, pp. 154–167. Springer, Heidelberg (2004)
20. Kim, Y.H., Duric, Z., Richards, D.: Modified matrix encoding technique for minimal distortion steganography. In: Camenisch, J.L., Collberg, C.S., Johnson, N.F., Sallee, P.(eds.) IH 2006. LNCS, vol. 4437, pp. 314–327. Springer, Heidelberg (2007)
21. Holub, V., Fridrich, J.: Digital image steganography using universal distortion. In: Proceedings of the First ACM Workshop on Information Hiding and Multimedia Security (IH&MMSec 2013), pp. 59–68. ACM, New York (2013)
22. Sallee, P.: Model-based methods for steganography and steganalysis. Int. J. Image Graph. **5**(01), 167–189 (2005)

23. Ullerich, C., Westfeld, A.: Weaknesses of MB2. In: Shi, Y.Q., Kim, H.-J., Katzenbeisser, S. (eds.) IWDW 2007. LNCS, vol. 5041, pp. 127–142. Springer, Heidelberg (2008)
24. Pevný, T., Bas, P., Fridrich, J.: Steganalysis by subtractive pixel adjacency matrix. IEEE Trans. Inf. Forensics Secur. **5**(2), 215–224 (2010)
25. Denemark, T., Fridrich, J., Holub, V.: Further study on the security of SUNIWARD. In: Proceedings of the SPIE, Electronic Imaging, Media Watermarking, Security, and Forensics, vol. 9028, pp. 2–6 (2014)

Enhanced Matching Method for Copy-Move Forgery Detection by Means of Zernike Moments

Osamah M. Al-Qershi and Bee Ee Khoo[✉]

Engineering Campus,
Universiti Sains Malaysia, Nibong Tebal, Penang, Malaysia
beekhoo@usm.my

Abstract. Copy-move is one of the most popular and efficient operations to create image forgery. Many passive detection techniques have been proposed to detect such a forgery in digital images. The performance of the detection algorithms depends mainly on the features used for matching image blocks or keypoints and the matching method as well. Among the existing detection algorithms, those which employ Zernike moments as features provide remarkable detection accuracy. The robustness of Zernike moments comes from the fact that they are invariant to rotation and scaling. However, Zernike moments-based algorithms can be improved further by adopting more efficient matching methods. In this paper, we propose a new matching method in order to enhance the detection accuracy. Compared to the lexicographical sorting-based matching method, the proposed method improved the detection accuracy by 40 %.

1 Introduction

The advances in hardware and software made manipulating digital images at the fingertips of a wide range of regular computer users. Sophisticated and low-cost editing tools are widely used to create misleading images with no obvious trace. However, the reliability of images is essential in many applications such as journalism, criminal investigation, and surveillance systems [1]. A famous example of exploiting image forgery is the case of the Korean scientist; Dr. Hwang Woo-Suk [2]. In 2004, he published ground-breaking results in stem cell research in the journal Science based on faked images. Hwang was charged with embezzlement and bioethics law violations after it emerged much of his stem cell research had been faked. After this scandal, other journals realized the importance of investigating images in submitted papers. The editors of the Journal of Cell Biology have been testing images since 2002 and they estimate that 25 % of accepted manuscripts have images that are modified beyond their standards, while one percent contains fraudulent images [3]. Besides this clear example, faked images may be used as evidence in the court and may mislead the justices.

The different types of digital image manipulation operations can be classified into three main categories, based on the method used in creating forged images. The categories are Copy-move forgery, Image splicing, and Image retouching. Among the three categories, Copy-move is one of the most popular method

© Springer International Publishing Switzerland 2015
Y.-Q. Shi et al. (Eds.): IWDW 2014, LNCS 9023, pp. 485–497, 2015.
DOI: 10.1007/978-3-319-19321-2_37

for manipulating the semantics image [4]. It is achieved by simply copying a region of an image and pasting it into the same image with the intent to hide undesired objects or to replicate objects. In copy-move forgery, the tampered region still shares most of its inherent characteristics such as color palette or pattern noise with the rest of the image. Besides, a structural analysis of image regions might reveal high similarities between the duplicated regions. Thus, it is not easy to detect the forgery parts, especially when some processing, such as scaling or rotating, is used before pasting the copied region. Moreover, some post-processing operations, such as adding noise or blur, may be used to remove any detectable traces of the copy-move like sharp edges which makes detection even harder [5].

A simple method of finding duplicated regions is based on using exclusive search to find match image regions. It is obvious that the drawback of such a method is its computational complexity and inefficiency. To overcome this challenge, several approaches have been proposed, and the first attempt in detecting copy-move forgery was described in [6]. They suggested looking for matches among DCT coefficients of image blocks. To reduce the cost of computation and complexity of comparisons, DCT coefficients are sorted lexicographically. After the sorting, the adjacent identical pairs of blocks are considered as potentially tampered regions. To refine the selection results, a histogram that counts the number of matching blocks separated by the same distance is calculated. Finally, a predefined threshold is used to select regions that have the high number of pairs located at the same distance, and the corresponding regions are marked as tampered. Higher number of pairs located at the same distance indicates a high probability that those blocks belong to copy-moved regions.

Despite the wide range of algorithms proposed for copy-move forgery detection, most of the algorithms adhere to a common pipeline [7]. First, the image is optionally pre-processed (downscaling and/or conversion to greyscale). It is then subdivided into overlapping blocks of pixels. On each of these blocks, a feature vector is extracted. Highly similar feature vectors are matched as pairs. Known methods for matching are lexicographic ordering on the feature vectors and nearest neighbor determination in a Kd-tree. The similarity of two features can be determined by different similarity criteria, e.g. Euclidean distance. In the verification step, outliers are removed and holes are filled which may be achieved using a basic filtering such as morphological operations. The overall performance of copy-move detection methods depends mainly on two stages of that pipeline; the type of the features that are extracted from image blocks and the matching method [8].

The extracted features play a crucial role because the robustness of the detection algorithm comes from the characteristics of those features. For example, rotation invariant features make the detection algorithm able to detect duplicated regions, even if the copied region underwent some rotation operation before pasting it and vice versa. Based on that, researchers have used a wide range of features to enhance the accuracy of detection. The list of the features that have been used includes Discrete Cosine Transform (DCT) coefficients [9–11], Log-polar transform [12,13], Texture and intensity [14–16], Zernike moments [17,18], Singular Value Decomposition (SVD) [19,20].

On the other hand, an efficient matching method is necessary to find similar image blocks with high True Positive Ratio (TPR) and low False Positive Ratio (FPR), which leads to high detection accuracy. Most of the existing techniques employ lexicographic sorting along with Euclidian distance as a matching method [6,10,15,17]. This method is popular due to its simplicity and efficiency. However, it can be improved even further to achieve higher detection accuracy. In this paper, we propose a new matching technique that exploits lexicographic sorting, while Zernike moments is used as features. An overview of Zernike moments is presented in Sect. 2. Section 3 presents a copy-move detection algorithm based on Zernike moments and a straightforward lexicographic sorting. The proposed algorithm is presented in Sect. 4. The Experimental results are presented in Sect. 5, while Sect. 6 concludes the paper.

2   Zernike Moments

Moments and invariant functions of moments have been extensively used for invariant feature extraction in a wide range of pattern recognition, digital watermark applications and etc. [21,22]. Of the various types of moments defined in the literature, Zernike moments have been proved to be superior to the others in terms of their insensitivity to image noise, information content, and ability to provide faithful image representation [22,23]. The Zernike moments of order n with repetition m for a continuous image function $f(x,y)$ that vanishes outside the unit circle are:

$$A_{nm} = \frac{n+1}{\pi} \iint_{x^2+y^2 1} f(x,y)V_{nm}^*(\rho,\theta)dxdy \tag{1}$$

where n is a nonnegative integer and m is an integer such that $n - |m|$ is nonnegative and even. The complex-valued $V_{nm}(x,y)$ functions are defined by:

$$V_{nm}(x,y) = V_{nm}(\rho,\theta) = R_{nm}(\rho)exp(jm\theta) \tag{2}$$

where ρ and θ represent polar coordinates over the unit disk and R_{nm} are polynomials of ρ (Zernike polynomials) given by:

$$R_{nm}(\rho) = \sum_{s=0}^{(n-|m|)/2} \frac{(-1)^s[(n-s)!]\rho^{n-2s}}{s!(\frac{n+|m|}{2}-s)!(\frac{n-|m|}{2}-s)!} \tag{3}$$

For a digital image, the integrals are replaced by summations. To compute the Zernike moments of a given block, the center of the block is taken as the origin and pixel coordinates are mapped to the range of the unit circle. Those pixels falling outside the unit circle are not used in the computation [17].

3   Copy-Move Forgery Detection Using Zernike Moments

In order to detect copy-move forgery, it is remembered that the detection algorithm should be insensitive to additive noise or blurring since a forger might slightly manipulate the tampered region to conceal clues of forgery. In this perspective, Zernike moments have been adopted due to their desirable properties such as rotation invariance, robustness to noise, and multi-level representation [23,24]. A copy-move detection algorithm with a straightforward lexicographical sorting-based matching method can be found in [17]. We added a verification stage to enhance the accuracy of their algorithm, and the final algorithm can be described as follows:

A. Pre-processing: The image is downscaled, to reduce the processing time, and then converted into a grayscale image.

B. Block Tiling: Then the grayscale image of size $m \times n$ is divided into $k \times k$ overlapping blocks, with a step of one pixel in each direction.

C. Feature Extraction: The Zernike moments A_{ij} of degree $(n = 5)$ are calculated from each block and vectorized. The entire number of moments in the vector is 12 according to the following equation:

$$N_{moments} = \sum_{i=0}^{n} \left(\left\lfloor \frac{i}{2} \right\rfloor + 1 \right) \tag{4}$$

The total number of calculated moments is 12 moments. Then, a set $\mathbf{Z}$ of vectorized magnitude values of the moments A_{ij} is formed:

$$\mathbf{Z} = \begin{bmatrix} |A_{00}| \\ \cdots \\ |A_{(m-k)(n-k)}| \end{bmatrix} \tag{5}$$

D. Matching Features: The set $\mathbf{Z}$ is then lexicographically sorted since each element of $\mathbf{Z}$ is a vector. The sorted set is denoted as $\hat{\mathbf{Z}}$. Then each vector in $\hat{\mathbf{Z}}$ is paired with the next r vectors, the Euclidean distance between the vectors in each pair is calculated as D_E. If the distance is smaller than the pre-defined threshold D_1, the corresponding blocks are considered as a pair of candidates for the forgery. Due to the fact that the overlapped blocks might have relatively similar Zernike moments, the actual distance between the candidate blocks is calculated as D_A. If it is greater than a pre-defined threshold D_2, the corresponding blocks are considered as copy-move blocks.

E. Verification: To refine the selection results, a histogram that counts the number of matching blocks separated by the same distance is calculated. To do so, the shift vector s between the two matching blocks is calculated as:

$$S(s_1, s_2) = (x_1 - x_2, y_1 - y_2) \tag{6}$$

where (x_1, y_1) and (x_2, y_2) are the positions of two matching blocks. For each matching pair of blocks, the shift vector counter C is incremented by one:

$$C(s_1, s_2) = C(s_1, s_2) + 1 \qquad (7)$$

At the end of the matching process, the counter C indicates the frequencies with which different shift vectors occur. Finally, a threshold D_3 is used to group shift vectors corresponding to regions that are located within the same distance if:

$$s_1, s_2 < D_3 \qquad (8)$$

This step minimizes the number of the shift vectors, and the blocks corresponding to the shift vector with the highest frequency are marked as tampered.

4   The Proposed Matching Method

Due to the way of calculating Zernike moments, their magnitude values may have a very wide range as we can see from Table 1. Besides, the first moment always has a very large magnitude compared to the other monuments. As a result of this, it is not necessary that similar blocks are always adjacent to each other after lexicographical sorting. It means that matching a vector with the next r vectors may not be enough to find similar vectors, and this may reduce the TPR. To overcome this issue, all vectors should be considered in the matching process. Such an extensive matching process will increase the computational complexity dramatically. Moreover, when the Euclidean distance is used for matching blocks, the magnitude of the first moment, $A_{0,0}$, has the highest contribution because of its higher value compared to the others. Two different blocks may be considered as similar blocks just because their first moments are close, and thus may increase the FPR. To overcome the first issue, we adopted a grouping method introduced in [16]. Instead of matching all blocks with each other, the blocks are first divided evenly into G groups. Then G buckets are created so that the i bucket contains the blocks from group i, group $i - 1$, group $i + 1$. Each block will be placed into 3 buckets except the blocks in the first and last groups which are placed in only two buckets as shown in the example in Fig. 1. The blocks are matched with those blocks within the same bucket. In [16], the authors used pixel values of blocks as features, and a statistical hypothesis to match blocks. The statistical-based matching showed a very good performance as the copy-moved blocks did not undergo any affine transformation. When the copied region is rotated or resized, the similar blocks cannot be detected. So, we opted not to use statistical-based matching to overcome the issue of Euclidean distance based matching. We used relative error for matching blocks within each bucket. The matching stage can be described in the following steps:

Table 1. Example of the first 12 Zernike moments for an image block

$A_{0,0}$	$A_{1,1}$	$A_{1,-1}$	$A_{2,0}$	$A_{2,-2}$	$A_{2,2}$	$A_{3,-1}$	$A_{3,1}$	$A_{3,-3}$	$A_{3,3}$	$A_{4,0}$	$A_{4,2}$
10093.63	470.15	881.96	884.02	196.46	302.15	1895.84	682.32	941.27	371.59	56.16	714.38

1. The feature vectors set $\mathbf{Z}$ is sorted lexicographically and then divided into G groups. After that, G buckets are created as described earlier.
2. Within each bucket $\mathbf{B}_i$, vectors are paired, and the actual distance between paired blocks is calculated as D_A. A new set of paired vectors is created as:

$$\mathbf{P}_i = \{(\mathbf{B}_{i_j}, \mathbf{B}_{i_k})\}, j \neq k \quad \forall i = 1 \ldots G \tag{9}$$

$$\text{If } D_A(\mathbf{B}_{i_j}, \mathbf{B}_{i_k}) > D_2 \tag{10}$$

3. Within each set $\mathbf{P}_i$, the relative error is calculated between vectors of each pair as the ratio of the absolute error and the minimum value of the two components:

$$\left| \frac{\mathbf{P}_{i_j} - \mathbf{P}_{i_k}}{min(\mathbf{P}_{i_j}, \mathbf{P}_{i_k})} \right| < D_1, j \neq k \; \forall i = 1 \ldots G \tag{11}$$

If all the relative errors are below threshold D_1, the two corresponding blocks are considered as candidate forgeries. Otherwise, the pair of vectors is omitted from $\mathbf{P}_i$.

After that, all pairs in all $\mathbf{P}$ sets are scanned to calculate shift vector s between each matched blocks as described in the previous section.

5   Experimental Results and Discussion

5.1   Image Dataset Preparation

We started preparing the dataset with 20 BMP authentic images from a personal collection. The images selected carefully such as they have relatively similar regions to make copy-move detection quite challenging which simulate real situations. The authentic images are shown in Fig. 2.

The size of the images is 400×300 pixels, and the size of the copied region is 80×80, which is about 5 % of the image size. The copied regions are pasted in different locations for each image in order to provide kind of spatial synchronization and homogeneity between the copied region and its neighbors. Copy-move forgery with various combinations of manipulations such as scaling, rotation, JPEG compression, Additive White Gaussian Noise AWGN, blurring was performed. The final dataset has 900 images. Table 2 shows the settings used to generate those images.

The level of blur in the Table 2 is equal to the radius of the disk-shape filter used to generate the blur. The level of Gaussian noise in the table is used to calculate the variance of the Gaussian Noise according to the following equation $v = 25 \times 10^{l-5}$, where v is the variance and l is the value in the table. For Multiple operations images, only one level of blur and noise was used because higher levels affect the overall quality of the images dramatically.

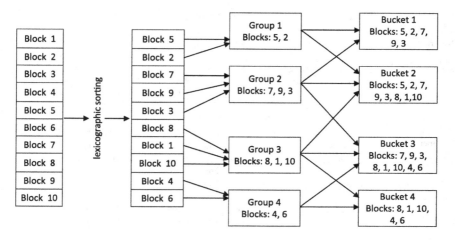

Fig. 1. An example of placing block into buckets

5.2 Metrics

Detecting copy-move forgery in images can be considered as a classification problem, where image blocks, the dataset, are classified into copy-move blocks and non-copy-move blocks. Generally, the size of copy-move region is quite small compared to the size of the image. This makes the image an unbalanced dataset because the number of copy-move blocks is way smaller than the number of non-copy-move blocks. Measuring the detection accuracy as the total number of predictions that were correct may not be an adequate performance measure when the dataset is imbalanced [25].

To detect copy-move forgery, we need appropriate metrics to measure the accuracy of the detection method. In this paper, we adopted Precision (P), Recall (R), and F1-measure which are often-used measures in the field of information retrieval [17,26]. The Precision is a measure for the probability that a detected region is correct, while the Recall is the ratio of True Positive components to elements inherently ranked as the positive class. They can be calculated as follows:

$$P = \frac{True\ positive}{True\ positive + False\ positive} \tag{12}$$

$$P = \frac{True\ positive}{True\ positive + False\ negtive} \tag{13}$$

Due to the trade-off between Precision and Recall, the accuracy of detection is measured using $F_{1-measure}$, which is the harmonic-mean of Precision P and Recall R:

$$F_{1-measure} = \frac{2PR}{P + R} \tag{14}$$

Table 2. The settings used for preparing the dataset

No processing		Levels							
		-	-	-	-	-	-	-	-
Single operation	Scaling (percentage)	80 %	90 %	110 %	120 %	-	-	-	-
	Rotating (angle)	15°	45°	90°	135°	-	-	-	-
	Blur (radius)	2	3	4	5	-	-	-	-
	Gaussian noise (variance)	0	1	2	3	-	-	-	-
	JPG compression (quality)	100 %	90 %	80 %	70 %	-	-	-	-
Multiple operations	Scaling	90 %	90 %	110 %	110 %	90 %	90 %	110 %	110 %
	Rotating	15°	45°	15°	45°	15°	45°	15°	45°
	JPG comp.	100 %	100 %	100 %	100 %	70 %	70 %	70 %	70 %
	Scaling	90 %	90 %	110 %	110 %	90 %	90 %	110 %	110 %
	Rotating	15°	45°	15°	45°	15°	45°	15°	45°
	Blur	2	2	2	2	2	2	2	2
	JPG comp.	100 %	100 %	100 %	100 %	70 %	70 %	70 %	70 %
	Scaling	90 %	90 %	110 %	110 %	90 %	90 %	110 %	110 %
	Rotating	15°	45°	15°	45°	15°	45°	15°	45°
	Noise	0	0	0	0	0	0	0	0
	JPG comp.	100 %	100 %	100 %	100 %	70 %	70 %	70 %	70 %

5.3   Experimental Setup

Several experiments have been carried out in order to setup the initial values and the thresholds required for the straightforward lexicographical sorting-based method and the proposed method. The initial values the thresholds are in Table 3.

5.4   The Results

As stated earlier, the dataset which we prepared includes different images with various operations are applied on the copied region to create the copy-move forgery. When no operation is involved in creating forgery, the straightforward lexicographical sorting-based method has an average accuracy of $F_1 = 71.51\,\%$, while the proposed method has an accuracy of $F_1 = 70.42\,\%$. A comparison between the accuracy of the two methods is illustrated in Tables 4, 5, 6, and 7.

5.5   Discussion

In this paper, we aimed to propose an enhanced matching method to overcome the disadvantages of straightforward lexicographical sorting-based method. When no operation is involved in creating copy-move, the proposed algorithm illustrates a slightly lower accuracy. Also, there is not much difference between the two methods when blur, noise, or JPG compression is applied as shown in Table 4. However, when scaling or rotation is applied, the proposed method has a higher accuracy especially with rotation.

Table 5 shows clearly the advantage of the proposed method in terms of higher accuracy (24.26 %–51.08 %) compared to (8.11 %–34.81 %). The same thing can

Fig. 2. The authentic used for preparing the dataset

Table 3. Parameters and thresholds used for evaluation

	Straightforward lexicographical sorting-based method	The proposed method
k	16	16
$N_{moments}$	12	12
D_1	50	0.25
D_2	32	32
D_3	2	20
r	7	-
G	-	256

Table 4. A comparison between the two methods when single operation is applied

Operations	Levels	Straightforward lexicographical sorting-based method			The proposed method		
		Recall (R)	Precision (P)	F_1	Recall (R)	Precision (P)	F_1
Scaling	80%	25.25	20.06	17.96	23.46	23.99	18.19
	90%	49.72	45.54	43.10	64.17	53.79	55.72
	110%	56.87	65.42	56.97	73.35	55.311	61.09
	120%	38.51	48.73	38.98	57.34	82.28	53.44
Rotating	15°	39.31	48.18	39.92	73.64	56.67	61.80
	45°	14.26	14.76	11.34	49.88	50.06	46.31
	90°	16.08	13.35	12.11	52.50	51.90	48.96
	135°	13.97	14.58	11.81	51.24	50.85	47.15
Blur	2	89.78	70.47	76.79	92.23	62.04	71.32
	3	83.88	70.12	74.23	94.24	63.13	72.65
	4	82.94	62.55	69.23	94.16	60.66	70.81
	5	87.27	62.61	70.76	94.89	59.50	70.11
Gaussian noise	0	85.87	67.95	79.71	93.57	62.83	72.04
	1	82.20	66.60	66.74	89.50	63.85	70.70
	2	54.17	50.98	53.68	50.25	42.04	42.22
	3	7.92	12.40	8.82	1.05	1.85	1.11
JPG compression	100%	85.43	65.75	72.20	89.80	62.04	71.30
	90%	85.79	72.08	76.38	93.30	62.18	71.49
	80%	82.93	65.32	70.56	93.83	63.08	72.13
	70%	77.38	63.70	67.48	91.77	61.57	70.81

Table 5. A comparison between the two methods when multiple operations are applied (Scaling + Rotating + JPG compression)

Operations		Levels							
	Scaling	90%	90%	110%	110%	90%	90%	110%	110%
	Rotating	15°	45°	15°	45°	15°	45°	15°	45°
	JPG comp.	100%	100%	100%	100%	70%	70%	70%	70%
Straightforward lexicographical sorting-based method	Recall (R)	24.59	12.66	27.64	13.20	34.10	14.02	32.20	11.17
	Precision (P)	19.20	9.19	40.08	18.21	30.88	10.29	48.81	10.27
	F_1	17.99	8.11	28.66	12.64	28.48	10.08	34.81	9.69
The proposed method	Recall (R)	57.30	27.26	58.06	41.44	60.94	27.80	55.93	41.17
	Precision (P)	49.18	31.05	50.76	45.28	50.73	30.47	49.31	45.81
	F_1	48.73	24.26	52.48	39.99	51.39	25.08	51.08	39.70

Table 6. A comparison between the two methods when multiple operations are applied (Scaling + Rotating + Blur + JPG compression)

Operations		Levels							
	Scaling	90 %	90 %	110 %	110 %	90 %	90 %	110 %	110 %
	Rotating	15°	45°	15°	45°	15°	45°	15°	45°
	Blur	2	2	2	2	2	2	2	2
	JPG comp.	100 %	100 %	100 %	100 %	70 %	70 %	70 %	70 %
Straightforward lexicographical sorting-based method	Recall (R)	33.66	17.83	36.12	17.38	29.07	15.63	37.23	15.43
	Precision (P)	31.90	10.66	41.82	17.89	26.56	9.90	42.14	12.21
	F_1	27.59	12.12	35.23	14.01	23.18	9.76	34.34	12.56
The proposed method	Recall (R)	57.25	28.95	66.80	34.94	63.10	28.53	63.84	41.52
	Precision (P)	52.25	27.76	54.92	40.08	44.44	29.95	48.52	44.21
	F_1	52.13	25.70	57.83	34.56	47.84	25.52	52.93	40.36

Table 7. A comparison between the two methods when multiple operations are applied (Scaling + Rotating + Noise + JPG compression)

Operations		Levels							
	Scaling	90 %	90 %	110 %	110 %	90 %	90 %	110 %	110 %
	Rotating	15°	45°	15°	45°	15°	45°	15°	45°
	Noise	0	0	0	0	0	0	0	0
	JPG comp.	100 %	100 %	100 %	100 %	70 %	70 %	70 %	70 %
Straightforward lexicographical sorting-based method	Recall (R)	29.54	15.06	34.04	15.48	27.61	14.94	33.92	14.34
	Precision (P)	28.86	7.95	41.12	10.21	29.79	9.33	39.30	11.35
	F_1	23.91	9.17	34.26	11.45	23.52	8.82	32.57	10.68
The proposed method	Recall (R)	61.53	18.21	57.90	32.12	54.06	30.47	60.11	33.74
	Precision (P)	47.65	23.63	52.31	33.67	50.17	30.90	49.51	43.78
	F_1	48.26	16.31	52.69	30.02	49.28	27.01	52.46	33.59

be seen from Tables 6 and 7 as the proposed method demonstrates higher accuracy. It is obvious that the proposed method enhanced the robustness of detection against rotation and scaling. Whenever, scaling and/or rotation are applied, the proposed method shows better accuracy. This can be considered as an important contribution because copy-move forgery is often created with rotation and/or scaling in real life situations.

The proposed method achieved an overall accuracy of 48.93 % compared to 34.88 % for the straightforward lexicographical sorting-based method. These values seem to be very low compared to what it can be found in the literature. The reason behind those low values is the relatively similar regions which originally exist in the images before creating the copy-move forgery. In addition, multiple operations with high levels make the detection accuracy even lower. The enhanced accuracy of the proposed method is due to the high number of the comparisons within each bucket. When a computer with an Intel i7 processor is used to run a MATLAB code to simulate the two methods, the average processing time is $440\,s/image$ and $26\,s/image$ for the proposed method and the original method respectively. It is obvious that the proposed method is slower than the straightforward lexicographical sorting-based method. Nevertheless, the proposed method enhanced the detection accuracy by 40 %.

6   Conclusion

Exploiting straightforward lexicographical sorting-based matching method in copy-move forgery detection is very popular due its simplicity and efficiency. However, this matching method has disadvantages that may increase the FPR and decrease the TPR so that high detection accuracy cannot be achieved. In this paper, we proposed an enhanced matching method that can be used to detect copy-move forgery based on Zernike-moments. By dividing the blocks into buckets and adopting relative error instead of Euclidean distance, the proposed method enhanced the detection accuracy significantly. The accuracy is enhanced because of the robustness of the proposed method against rotating and scaling.

Acknowledgment. The authors would like to acknowledge the financial assistance provided by Universiti Sains Malaysia via TPLN USM. They would also like to thank S.J. Ryu et al. [17] for sharing their code.

References

1. Mahdian, B., Saic, S.: A bibliography on blind methods for identifying image forgery. Signal Process.: Image Commun. **25**, 389–399 (2010)
2. Normile, D.: Hwang convicted but dodges jail; stem cell research has moved on. Science **326**, 650–651 (2009)
3. Wade, N.: It May Look Authentic. Here's How to Tell It Isn't. New York Times, New York (2006)
4. Redi, J.A., Taktak, W., Dugelay, J.L.: Digital image forensics: a booklet for beginners. Multimedia Tools Appl. **51**(1), 133–162 (2011)
5. Liu, G., Wang, J., Lian, S., Wang, Z.: A passive image authentication scheme for detecting region-duplication forgery with rotation. J. Netw. Comput. Appl. **34**, 1557–1565 (2010)
6. Fridrich, J., Soukal, D., Lukáš, J.: Detection of copy-move forgery in digital images. In: Proceedings of Digital Forensic Research Workshop (2003)
7. Christlein, V., Riess, C., Angelopoulou, E.: On rotation invariance in copy-move forgery detection. In: IEEE International Workshop on Information Forensics and Security, WIFS (2010)
8. Al-Qershi, O.M., Khoo, B.E.: Passive detection of copy-move forgery in digital images: state-of-the-art. Forensic sci. Int. **231**, 95–284 (2013)
9. Zhao, J., Guo, J.: Passive forensics for copy-move image forgery using a method based on DCT and SVD. Forensic Sci. Int. **233**, 158–166 (2013)
10. Gupta, A., Saxena, N., Vasistha, S.K.: Detecting copy move forgery using DCT. Int. J. Sci. Res. Publ. **3**, 3–6 (2013)
11. Wandji, N.D., Xingming, S., Kue, M.F.: Detection of copy-move forgery in digital images based on DCT. Int. J. Comput. Sci. Issues **10**, 1–8 (2013)

12. Wu, Q., Wang, S., Zhang, X.: Log-polar based scheme for revealing duplicated regions in digital images. IEEE Signal Process. Lett. **18**, 559–562 (2011)
13. Wu, Q., Wang, S., Zhang, X.: Detection of image region-duplication with rotation and scaling tolerance. In: Pan, J.-S., Chen, S.-M., Nguyen, N.T. (eds.) ICCCI 2010, Part I. LNCS (LNAI), vol. 6421, pp. 100–108. Springer, Heidelberg (2010)
14. Langille, A., Minglun, G.: An efficient match-based duplication detection algorithm. In: The 3rd Canadian Conference on Computer and Robot Vision, 2006, p. 64 (2006)
15. Ardizzone, E., Bruno, A., Mazzola, G.: Copy-move forgery detection via texture description. In: Proceedings of the 2010 ACM Workshop on Multimedia in Forensics, Security and Intelligence, MiFor, 2010, pp. 59–64. ACM Multimedia (2010)
16. Lynch, G., Shih, F.Y., Liao, H.Y.M.: An efficient expanding block algorithm for image copy-move forgery detection. Inf. Sci. **239**, 253–265 (2013)
17. Ryu, S.-J., Lee, M.-J., Lee, H.-K.: Detection of copy-rotate-move forgery using Zernike moments. In: Böhme, R., Fong, P.W.L., Safavi-Naini, R. (eds.) IH 2010. LNCS, vol. 6387, pp. 51–65. Springer, Heidelberg (2010)
18. Yang, J., Ran, P., Xiao, D., Tan, J.: Digital image forgery forensics by using undecimated dyadic wavelet transform and Zernike moments. J. Comput. Inf. Syst. **9**, 6399–6408 (2013)
19. Ting, Z., Rang-Ding, W.: Copy-move forgery detection based on SVD in digital image. In: Proceedings of the 2009 2nd International Congress on Image and Signal Processing, CISP 2009 (2009)
20. Li, G., Wu, Q., Tu, D., Sun, S.: A sorted neighborhood approach for detecting duplicated regions in image forgeries based on DWT and SVD. In: Proceedings of 2007 IEEE International Conference on Multimedia and Expo, pp.1750–1753 (2007)
21. Hu, M.K.: Visual pattern recognition by moment invariants. IRE Trans. Inf. Theory **8**, 179–187 (1962)
22. Kim, H.S., Lee, H.K.: Invariant image watermark using Zernike moments. IEEE Trans. Circuit Syst. Video Technol. **13**(8), 766–775 (2003)
23. Teh, C.H., Chin, R.T.: On image analysis by the methods of moments. IEEE Trans. Pattern Anal. Mach. Intell. **10**(4), 496–513 (1988)
24. Ryu, S.J., Kirchner, M., Lee, M.J., Lee, H.K.: Rotation invariant localization of duplicated image regions based on Zernike moments. IEEE Trans. Inf. Forensics Secur. **8**, 1355–1370 (2013)
25. Chawla, N.: In: Maimon, O., Rokach, L. (eds.) Data Mining and Knowledge Discovery Handbook SE - 40. Springer, Heidelberg (2005)
26. Manning, C.D., Raghavan, P., Schutze, H.: Introduction to Information Retrieval. Cambridge University Press, Cambridge (2009)

An Iterative Management Model of Exploring Windows Date-Time Stamps in Cloud Storage Forensics

Da-Yu Kao[✉] and Ying-Hsuan Chiu

Department of Information Management, Central Police University,
Taoyuan 333, Taiwan
camel@mail.cpu.edu.tw

Abstract. The law enforcement community has faced difficulties on how best to tackle the complex and dynamic developments on the internet, cloud services, or communications technology. This creates difficulties in the consistency of handling a digital crime scene. Offenders could use cloud storage service as a media to save others' data through the internet. This study explores the challenges of digital investigation on Windows file system, and proposes an iterative management model to explore date-time stamps in the file metadata of Windows system. We further observe the file metadata and compare their differences in the date-time stamp issues. The analysis techniques of this study may help establish event timeline, and clarify the offender's actions to the file. It will be useful in investigations and mitigate the impact of time bias across multiple systems.

Keywords: Date-time stamp · Cloud storage forensics · File metadata · Action research · Dropbox service

1 Introduction

Computer has progressed by leaps and bounds; it has become an indispensable tool in our lives. But offenders can steal the data from our storage devices and share some confidential information with others in a cloud network. Those who making decisions about the conduct of a digital investigation must often make judgments about the focus and scope of an investigation, and take into account available intelligence and investigative resources [1]. If computers are not handled properly, digital evidence may be altered or destroyed. It will make it difficult to make strong assertions about the evidence they contain [3]. A file system in turn is organized logically into files and folders. Actual magnetic data are translated into sectors, which are grouped into clusters in a file system. A common problem in forensic examination tools is incomplete or incorrect interpretation of file metadata. This study discusses related problems, and issues to corresponding countermeasures. Most forensic examiners only see a representation of that data, but it sometimes may encounter issues on operation error or information loss [4].

The related works on cloud storage forensics and Windows file system are discussed in Sect. 2. Section 3 describes the key experiment components in a cloud storage device and its experiment design on date-time stamp. An iterative management

© Springer International Publishing Switzerland 2015
Y.-Q. Shi et al. (Eds.): IWDW 2014, LNCS 9023, pp. 498–512, 2015.
DOI: 10.1007/978-3-319-19321-2_38

model of exploring windows date-time stamps is presented to solve building event timeline problems in Sect. 4. The finding on date-time stamp is proposed in Sect. 5. The conclusion is drawn in Sect. 6.

2 Reviews

2.1 Cloud Storage Forensics

On June 2014, the National Institute of Standards and Technology (NIST) had issued a draft report which was prepared by cloud and digital forensic experts from industry, government and academia [10]. Some challenges are illustrated to forensics investigators who uncover, gather, examine and interpret digital evidence to help solve crimes in a primary category below [13].

- Role management: Data owners, identity management, users, and access control.
- Incident first responders: Trustworthiness of cloud providers, response time, and reconstruction.
- Training: Forensic investigators, cloud providers, qualification, and certification.
- Legal: Jurisdictions, laws, service level agreements, contracts, subpoenas, international cooperation, privacy, and ethics.
- Data collection: Data integrity, data recovery, data location, and imaging.
- Standards: Standard operating procedures, interoperability, testing, and validation.
- Architecture: Diversity, complexity, provenance, multi-tenancy, and data segregation.
- Anti-forensics: Obfuscation, data hiding, and malware.
- Analysis: Correlation, reconstruction, time synchronization, logs, metadata, and timelines.

Actions taken by users on a computer may leave traces that help investigators figure out what occurs on the system. Adequate training will enable cybercrime related person to handle digital devices that contain potential digital evidence. This study focuses on the analysis challenge issues, and explores the date-time stamps that are relevant to the investigation with important characteristics.

2.2 Windows File System

Computer file systems provide good performance for user's usage patterns, which often vary over time. To help understand offenders' digital action patterns, we decided to measure a wide range of file systems in a number of different processes in Windows 7. Since the relative performance of personal action is different from each other, we collect traces from experimental data and focus on date-time stamp behavior. Digital information placed in a storage area is one large body of data. By separating the data into individual pieces in order, the information is easily separated and identified in a file. The structure and logic rules used to manage the groups of information and their names are called a file system. There are many different kinds of file systems. Each one has different structure and logic. A file system is used to control how data is stored and retrieved. Windows makes use of the following file systems [2]: FAT (File Allocation Table), NTFS (New Technology File System), exFAT (Extended File Allocation Table), and ReFS (Resilient File System). Some patent-protected file systems have been designed to be used for specific applications. For example, hackers will create their own to hide their 'secret' data.

Windows File System Algorithm. People use computer system every day, but we rarely recognize the attributes of an electronic file. There are a few ways to view and change file metadata. Investigators seek to preserve and maintain file metadata in its initial request. Two of them are via the file or folder properties from Windows Explorer or using the forensic tool of Guidance Encase. This study tries to use different method to explore about the attributes of file metadata, and to better understand how the file system works in a Windows environment [9]. The file metadata has lots of associated information that includes additional file/directory data about the file itself or its contents. It only exists in the following two states [5]: Set or Cleared (similar to On or Off). The file metadata is used by the operating system or software applications to define file system behavior and to meet their file system algorithm. After users take lots of operations, it become more essential to know what kinds of date-time stamp are touched, accessed, modified, changed, or saved. The more date-time stamps are collected, the more evidences are proved. That would be of great help in establishing an event timeline.

Windows File System Metadata. A file system is a collection of file metadata and file attributes. Various file systems differ in the maintenance of file metadata, which includes file attributes such as file permissions, file creation date, or other information. File metadata is updated whenever a file is created, accessed, modified, obtained, deleted or dropped. When the file is created or written, additional file system blocks are requested. Each extent request updates the file metadata [11]. Characterizing file system behavior is difficult in obtaining data to analyze. For example, last write time is the time of last data modification. Dynamic traces of continuous access patterns yield more detailed information about file system usage [2, 8].

3   Our Experiment in a Cloud Storage Device

Computer investigators are better served by simpler methodologies that guide them in the right direction, while allowing them to maintain the flexibility to handle diverse situations [3]. In the following experiment, the operational processes are undertaken by the offender, and the investigator has no idea about his complete process. This kind of experiment would like to simulate the practical investigation process in which an investigator has to explore their findings and prepare some questions for the offender.

3.1   Key Experimental Components

This growing interest and need of experiment in a cloud network has sparked heated debates about terminology and many other fundamental aspects of cloud storage forensics field [3, 7]. The primary aim of this experiment is to help the examiners tackle the challenging process of seeking scientific truth through objective and thorough analysis of cloud storage service. The flowing definitions are implemented in this experiment.

Synchronous or Asynchronous Date-time Stamp. Date-time stamps are very important when transactions are done in a cybercrime investigation. Sometimes, the date-time stamp of file metadata does not match with the actual time. The synchronization of date-time stamp from a single standard time source is critical for investigators.

Sequential or Decompressing Processing

(1) *Sequential Processing.* To implement sequential processing, operations are processed by asynchronous adapters during each occurrence of a batch job. We can control the sequence, and run a single task each time. The order of the experimental files are sequentially processed applies only during a single occurrence of a batch job.
(2) *Decompressing Processing.* To improve the performance of file processing, we can carry out of more tasks by decompressing the test file.

Browser Interface and Synchronization Folder. Dropbox service provides file-backup services, and grants online access to our files when we are away from our desktop. We can directly upload/download our files to the site from the two methods below.

(1) *Cloud Browser Interface.* After we log in to the Dropbox account, a pop-over box will appear with options to select the files we want to upload or download.
(2) *Cloud Synchronization Folder.* If we use the Dropbox desktop application, we can drag or copy files to our "My Dropbox" folder. That will allow us to sync that folder with Dropbox.

3.2 Experiment Design on Date-Time Stamp

Experiment Environment. In order to minimize the complexity of trace collection, this study uses oCam software to record the snapshots, and concentrates on static data, which is collected by examining the date-time stamp of file system metadata. We create some test files and observe their different attributes on date-time stamp issues. The experiment design on date-time stamp is divided into two parts: client side and server side. The client side is further composed of client preparation, client compression and client access. The cloud side focuses on the cloud sharing status on upload/download process. In this experiment design, we prepare the following environment:

(1) *Hardware Tool*
  - ASUSTeK Computer Inc.

(2) *Software Tool*
- OS: Windows 7 Home Premium Version Service Pack1
- File system: exFAT.
- Office: Microsoft Office 2010
- Forensic Tool: Guidance Encase v7
- Capture Tool: The oCam. v2.1 software is a program for taking screenshots or recording the desktop screen.

(3) *Cloud Service: Saas*
- Cloud storage service: Dropbox 2.6.31

Action research is an interactive inquiry process which is initiated to understand underlying causes, to improve a reflective process of progressive issue, or to solve an immediate problem [6]. This action research involves actively participating in a change situation with the aim of improving their practices and knowledge of the environments.

Experiment Process. In client compression (client side), we compress the test file into RAR file, decompress the test file, and observe the difference of date-time stamp. In cloud sharing (cloud side), we upload the test file to the cloud, download it from the cloud, and observe the difference of date-time stamp. In client access (client side), we observe the difference of date-time stamp from the process below.

(1) *Access, open, and close the test file.*
(2) *Modify, save, and close it.*
(3) *Copy and paste it.*

Experiment Operation. It is a time consuming job and sometimes almost impossible to fully capture or preserve file metadata at the point of collection without any errors or mistakes [7]. The observation of date-time stamp is operated by the following operations to produce guidelines for best practice:

(1) *Viewing the Date-time Stamp from Windows Explorer.* Right-clicking and selecting properties on any file or folder in Windows Explorer will bring up the properties window, which shows the attributes of file metadata.
(2) *Viewing the Date-time Stamp from Guidance Encase.* The file metadata associated with digital files may be preserved, maintained and produced in the process of legal investigation.

4   An Iterative Management Model of Exploring Windows Date-Time Stamps

This section can be undertaken from two four-step spiral processes in iterative management model and exploring date-time stamp. This iterative management model, which is depicted as a cyclical process of change, can be initiated to solve a reflective process of progressive problem, to help a team improve its work practices, and to improve the immediate issues [6]. We also hope this model assist law enforcement in identifying cyber criminals and clarifying the offender's actions to the file.

4.1   Four Stages of Iterative Management Model

Table 1 and Fig. 1 summarizes our stages, phases and processes involved in planned change of our experiment through the inheritable attribute observation of file metadata. The four stages of iterative management model are reconstructed for the following processes [6]: Plan, Action, Observation and Reflection. Those processes are also shaped like the PDCA (Plan–Do–Check–Act) management model.

(1) **Plan Stage.** Included in this stage is the iterative activity which is carried out jointly by the offender and the investigator. The cycle begins with the 'plan' stage initiated by the intent of exploring date-time stamp. The principal elements of this stage include data gathering, preliminary preparation, and joint action planning. This is the input stage, in which we believe file time issues are important in an investigation. It may need further examination to clarify their created, updated or unchanged status.

(2) **Action Stage.** The second stage of management model is to do something. This stage includes actions relating to operational processes (perhaps in the form of role analysis) and to executing behavioral changes by users.

(3) **Observation Stage.** Following the experimental sessions, these stages are carried out as part of the observation stage. Feedback at observation stage would have the effect of altering previous planning to bring the learning activities of this experiment into better alignment with change objectives on date-time stamp issues.

(4) **Reflection Stage.** The fourth stage of management model is the output or results stage. This stage includes actual changes from corrective action steps. Data are gathered from the above stages so that follow-up phases can be determined and necessary adjustments in experimental activities can be made.

4.2   Four Phases on Exploring Date-Time Stamp

Many places can show the date-time stamp. It is important to have a methodical approach to analyze the digital data when computers and networks are involved. In order to clarify the offender's action and mitigate the impact of time bias across multiple systems, the exploring metadata of date-time stamp plays a crucial role. In Table 1, this study explores the experiment form the following phases [12, 13]: Observe Date-time Stamp, Analyze Inheritable Attribute, Compare Date-time Stamp, and Conclude Inheritable Attribute.

(1) **Observe Date-time Stamp Phase.** In Table 2a, a sequential processing on a test source file is undertaken (see #A). Through the browser interface of cloud services, we find that date-time stamps have inheritable attributes. A plan of adding the compression/decompression processing is formed and we observe its changes in date-time stamps.

(2) **Analyze Inheritable Attribute Phase.** In Table 2b, a decompressing processing on a test source file is undertaken (see #B). Through the synchronization folder of cloud services, we find that different operations have different influences on the inheritable attribute of date-time stamps. Another plan of using browser interface

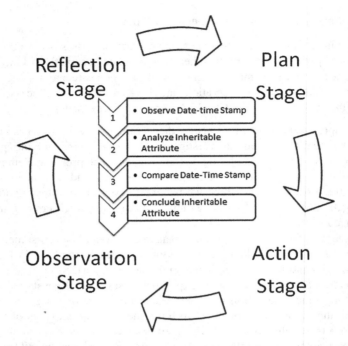

Fig. 1. Two four-step spiral processes in action research

Table 1. Inheritable attribute observation of date-time stamp

Stage / Phase	Plan Stage — Plan the Experiment	Action Stage — File Processing	Action Stage — Cloud Operation	Observation Stage — Check the Findings	Reflection Stage — Act for the Follow-up Plan
1	Observe Date-time Stamp	Sequential Processing	Browser Interface	Date-time stamps have inheritable attributes.	Plan: Add the compression/decompression to observe changes in date-time stamps.
2	Analyze Inheritable Attribute	Decompressing Processing	Synchronization Folder	Different operation has different influence on the inheritable attribute of date-time stamps.	Plan: Use browser interface is formulated to check the difference between two cloud operations.
3	Compare Date-time Stamp	Decompressing Processing	Browser Interface	There is no different influence between two cloud operations.	Plan: Explore time deviation between local client and cloud server.
4	Conclude Inheritable Attribute	Sequential Processing	Synchronization Folder	The time deviation between server and client is about 2 seconds.	Findings: 1. A second or two with network timing issues is acceptable. 2. M-time is influenced by the upload/download operation.

Table 2a. Observe date-time stamp phase by browser interface

	1. Client Preparation	1.1 Prepare an environment: hardware, software, Saas 1.2 Prepare a test file: Create a test file and observe date-time stamp. (# A1)		
Client Side	2. Client Compression	2.1 Compression (# A2) 2.1.1 Compress the test file into RAR file. 2.1.2 Observe the difference of date-time stamp.	2.2 Decompression (#A3) 2.2.1 Decompress the test file. 2.2.2 Observe the difference of date-time stamp.	
	3. Client Access	3.1 Access (# A4) 3.1.1 Access, open, and close the test file. 3.1.2 Observe the difference of date-time stamp.	3.2 Modification (# A5) 3.2.1 Modify, save, and close it. 3.2.2 Observe the difference of date-time stamp.	3.3 Movement (# A6) 3.3.1 move it to another disk. 3.3.2 Observe the difference of date-time stamp.
Cloud Side	4. Cloud Sharing	4.1 Upload Cloud (# A7) 4.1.1 Share test file to cloud(by using the web interface). 4.1.2 Observe the difference of date-time stamp.	4.3 Download Cloud (# A8) 4.3.1 Download it from the cloud(by using the web interface). 4.3.2 Observe the difference of date-time stamp.	

Table 2b. Analyze inheritable attribute phase by synchronization folder

	1. Client Preparation	1.1 Prepare an environment: hardware, software, Saas 1.2 Prepare a test file: Create a test file and observe date-time stamp (# B1)		
Client Side	2. Client Compression	2.1 Compression (# B2) 2.1.1 Compress the test file into RAR file. 2.1.2 Observe the difference of date-time stamp.	2.2 Decompression (# B3) 2.2.1 Decompress the test file. 2.2.2 Observe the difference of date-time stamp.	
	3. Client Access	3.1 Access (# B4) 3.1.1 Decompress the test file. 3.1.2 Access, open, and close the test file. 3.1.3 Observe the difference of date-time stamp.	3.2 Modification (# B5) 3.2.1 Decompress the test file. 3.2.2 Modify, save, and close it. 3.2.3 Observe the difference of date-time stamp.	3.3 Movement (# B6) 3.3.1 Decompress the test file. 3.3.2 Move it to another disk. 3.3.3 Observe the difference of date-time stamp.
Cloud Side	4. Cloud Sharing	4.1 Upload Cloud (# B7) 4.1.1 Decompress the test file. 4.1.2 Share test file to cloud(by copying the test file to synchronous folder). 4.1.3 Observe the difference of date-time stamp.	4.3 Download Cloud (# B8) 4.3.1 Download the test file from the cloud(by copying the test file from synchronous folder). 4.3.3 Observe the difference of date-time stamp.	

Table 2c. Compare date-time stamp phase by browser interface

Client Side	**1. Client Preparation**	1.1 Prepare an environment: hardware, software, Saas 1.2 Prepare a test file: Create a test file and observe date-time stamp (# C1)		
	2. Client Compression	2.1 Compression (# C2) 2.1.1 Compress the test file into RAR file. 2.1.2 Observe the difference of date-time stamp.	2.2 Decompression (#C3) 2.2.1 Decompress the test file. 2.2.2 Observe the difference of date-time stamp.	
	3. Client Access	3.1 Access (# C4) 3.1.1 Decompress the test file. 3.1.2 Access, open, and close the test file. 3.1.3 Observe the difference of date-time stamp.	3.2 Modification (# C5) 3.2.1 Decompress the test file. 3.2.2 Modify, save, and close it. 3.2.3 Observe the difference of date-time stamp.	3.3 Movement (# C6) 3.3.1 Decompress the test file. 3.3.2 Move it to another disk. 3.3.3 Observe the difference of date-time stamp.
Cloud Side	**4. Cloud Sharing**	4.1 Upload Cloud (# C7) 4.1.1 Decompress the test file. 4.1.2 Share test file to cloud (by using the web interface). 4.1.3 Observe the difference of date-time stamp.	4.3 Download Cloud (# C8) 4.3.1 Download the test file from the cloud (by using the web interface). 4.3.3 Observe the difference of date-time stamp.	

Table 2d. Conclude inheritable attribute phase by synchronization folder

Client Side	**1. Client Preparation**	1.1 Prepare an environment: hardware, software, Saas 1.2 Change local time by minus 40 minutes 1.3 Prepare a test file: Create a test file and observe date-time stamp. (# D1)		
	2. Client Compression	2.1 Compression (# D2) 2.1.1 Compress the test file into RAR file. 2.1.2 Observe the difference of date-time stamp.	2.2 Decompression (#D3) 2.2.1 Decompress the test file. 2.2.2 Observe the difference of date-time stamp.	
	3. Client Access	3.1 Access (# D4) 3.1.1 Access, open, and close the test file. 3.1.2 Observe the difference of date-time stamp.	3.2 Modification (# D5) 3.2.1 Modify, save, and close it. 3.2.2 Observe the difference of date-time stamp.	3.3 Movement (# D6) 3.3.1 move it to another disk. 3.3.2 Observe the difference of date-time stamp.
Cloud Side	**4. Cloud Sharing**	4.1 Upload Cloud (# D7) 4.1.1 Share test file to cloud (by copying the test file to synchronous folder). 4.1.2 Observe the difference of date-time stamp.	4.3 Download Cloud (# D8) 4.3.1 Download it from the cloud (by copying the test file from synchronous folder). 4.3.2 Observe the difference of date-time stamp.	

is formulated to check the difference between two cloud operations (browser interface and synchronization folder). After comparing their differences in the date-time stamp issues, investigators can figure out actions taken by the offenders and have a better idea on what has happened on the past.

(3) **Compare Date-time Stamp Phase.** In Table 2c, a decompressing processing on a test source file is undertaken (see #C). Through the browser interface of cloud services, we find that there is no different influence between two cloud operations. Another plan of exploring time deviation between local client and cloud server is formulated to check the time from the cloud server. Note that any errors in the setting of the local computer clock would be evident in any operation which is processed on the computer. If the computer clock were several minutes slow, it would place an incorrect date-time stamp in file metadata. This can cause great confusion when trying to reconstruct events, as it can give the wrong impression or accuse on the file content. Moreover, it is important to pay attention to the actual date and time, any inconsistency between the current time and the computer time, the time zone of the file source, and the time stamps on different digital objects. File differences will often exist between apparently similar date-time stamps. It may be slightly different on data content, or process procedure.

(4) **Conclude Inheritable Attribute Phase.** In Table 2d, a sequential processing on a test source file is undertaken (see #D). Looking at the whole file metadata will show correct date-time stamps from any possible upload, download, or modification procedure while it was being processed. Therefore, we do an experiment to verify the updated time from the cloud server. Through the synchronization folder of cloud services, we find the following [12, 13]:

- Time Delay: The time deviation between server and client is about 2 s. A second or two with network timing issues is acceptable.
- Influenced Time: Modification time (M-time) is influenced by the upload/ download operation. Additional examination is required to determine the precise relationship between date-time stamp and its operation.
- Access the Original: Some investigators have directly operated the original evidence file. Digital evidence contamination also puts the forensic analyst into great troubles. It is also necessary to clarify what kind of data is modified and what we can explore from the obtained file.
- Explore the Fact: Office documents contain some details that can be useful for possible evaluation of their past process such as directory locations, creator, and date-time stamps. Further examination of network activities is necessary to explore and find the fact.

5 Findings on Date-Time Stamp

The data will be changed on the time when the computer is on. Operating systems and other programs may automatically alter, add and delete the contents of electronic storage. The date-time stamps of file metadata may differ from different circumstances [12]. It is of great help for investigators to infer the associated actions when the file metadata is changed. Exploring the content of date-time stamp can be complex. The simplest way is to create, modify, or copy a list of files.

5.1 Notice Date-Time Stamp Types

Digital forensic examiners use date-time stamps both to timeline activity as well as locate other potentially suspicious files. The results of these examinations are often used in court. The different OS or file system has different date-time stamp. Some file systems may implement only a subset of these date-time stamps. A single file can have multiple analyzed tools or methods and the same file can be processed by different programs for different needs. However, the output format of date-time stamp may differ from various software (such as Encase for Entry Modified Time; Windows Explorer for Text-establishment Date-time and Last write Date-time). Date-time stamps are queried and set via the information class 'FileBasicInformation' or 'FileRenameInformation' [8, 9]. Windows has some types of date-time stamps as follows:

(1) **Internal Metadata: General Date-time Stamp for the File Itself.** The Internal Metadata of date-time stamp can be found in the general information ('一般') of Windows Explorer Program (see Fig. 2a). These date-time stamps are created by the file themselves, but they often have different names in different operation System (e.g., Window, Unix/Linux, or Macintosh) [8].
   - Creation Date-time Stamp (C-time or '建立時間'): C-time is set to the current time when the file was created during data processing.
   - Last Access Date-time Stamp (A-time or '存取時間'): A-time is set to the current time when the file is created. When the file is last accessed, A-time is updated.
   - Modification/Change Date-time Stamp (M-time or '修改時間'): M-time is set to the current time when the file is created. When the file's metadata or contents were last modified or changed, M-time is updated.

(2) **External Metadata: Detailed Date-time Stamp for Application Program or File System.** The external metadata of date-time stamp can be found in the detailed information ('詳細資料') of Windows Explorer Program (see Fig. 2b). These date-time stamps are created by application program or file system [9].
   - Text-establishment Date-time (T-time or '已建立的本文'): T-time is set to the current time when the file is created. Sometimes, it would be different from C-time if there is editing time.
   - Last Write Date-time Stamp (L-time or '上次儲存日期'): L-time is set to the current time when the file is created. When the files contents were last modified, L-time is updated.
   - Entry Modified Date-time Stamp (E-time): E-time is the time at which the 'TunnelCacheEntry' system call created. The function will automatically purge this entry from the tunnel cache once the entry is 15 s old.
   - File Acquired Date-time Stamp (F-time): F-time is the time at which the Guidance Encase acquires the file. Sometime, it would appear empty value (see Fig. 3).

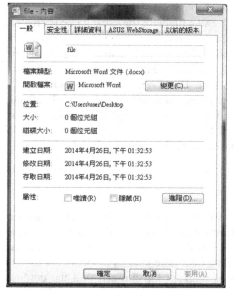

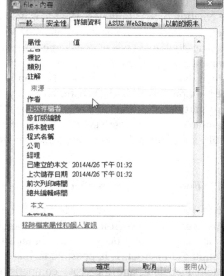

2a. General Date-time Stamp for the File Itself

2b. Detailed Date-time Stamp for Application Program or File System

Fig. 2. Observe date-time stamp through windows explorer

Fig. 3. Observe Date-time stamp through guidance EnCase

5.2   Observe the Date-Time Stamps

Most operating systems keep track of the C-time, M-time, and A-time of files and their folders. These date-time stamps can be very useful in determining what occurred on a computer. Windows Explorer or other third party's software would rely on the Windows API (Application Interface) function calls to translate the binary time values into human readable format. Figure 2 shows the effect of date-time stamp against an entire volume viewed through Windows Explorer. There is still additional T-time and L-time). This vulnerability has the greatest impact on 3rd party forensics software that relies on the Windows API to translate the binary time stamps. Figure 3 shows the effect of date-time stamp on a single file viewed through Guidance EnCase. By default, the creation time is tunneled. If a file is deleted, and a file with the same name is created later, we find that some metadata attributes are inheritable in our experiment. If a forensic tool displays at the same format all the time, it is almost impossible to guarantee what investigators acquire is always correct. In Fig. 3, there is no T-time or L-time, but it appears Entry-modification Date-time. However, when the Windows API does not properly translate them, it displays no information instead. It adversely affects third-party applications that rely upon the Windows API to perform the translation. For example, the date-time stamps of E-time and F-time are missing (see Fig. 3). As a result, some forensic tools have different time formats from the original OS.

5.3   Find the Time Conflict

When investigators prosecute a crime, it is usually desirable to know the time and sequence of events. Sometimes the general information and detail data of date-time stamp in file content does not match, and it means that some operation was processed through the internet. It is possible to manipulate date-time stamps associated with file system metadata, and the cross comparison of relevant log file can find the conflict part. Fortunately, in addition to storing, retrieving, manipulating, and transmitting data, computers keep copious account of time.

5.4   Correct the System Clock

Difficult situations arise where a computer or network was involved in a crime. Without additional verification, an investigator cannot ascertain whether this event occurred on certain time. The correcting date-time stamp issues are discussed below [3, 5].

(1) **Incorrect Setting Issue.** The system clock on a computer or a server can be incorrect, and the date-time stamps in auditing logs can be interpreted incorrectly. Without additional information, a digital investigator cannot ascertain the actual time of the event. It is necessary to estimate uncertainty in a heuristic manner.

(2) **Time Zone Issue.** The date-time stamp in auditing records or metadata files could be configured with a time zone in either Universal Standard Time (UTC) or local time. One digital forensic examiner may not initially realize that the date-time stamps in a file are in UTC rather than local time. The potential errors can be addressed by documenting the system clock time and by examining the time zone configuration. That may lead to a wrong suspect. Therefore, digital forensic analysts should care about the differences in time zones and daylight savings, and consider the possibility that date-time stamps may have been altered or are inaccurate.

(3) **Daylight Saving Time Issue.** Daylight saving time is the practice of advancing clocks during summer months so that people get up earlier in the morning and experience more daylight in the evening. Origination uncertainty can be further compared by cross-drive analysis, related computer or auditing logs.

(4) **Check Date-time Synchronization.** Data retrieved or recovered from a computer can indicate that something was happened at a specific time. When a suspect claimed that he/she was not using the internet at the time of a crime, investigators should explore digital evidence which is relevant to the investigation, and should understand his/her computers' role in the crime [3]. When investigators deal with digital evidence, it is necessary to compare its date-time stamp with a reliable time source for time synchronization.

5.5   Build Event Timelines

The date-time stamp on digital file is embedded on a file metadata. Sometimes some software or operations will not update the date-time stamp when they processed digitally. Some operations just re-digitize that stamp in a standard form. However, each OS has different file system, and each file system also has different file metadata on date-time stamp. This situation often confuses lots of investigators. If a case hinges upon a single form or source of digital evidence such as date-time stamps on computer files, then the case is unacceptably weak [3]. Without additional clues, it could be reasonably argued that someone else did it at the time. Timeliness of evidence seizure may be critical. It is also crucial to understand their differences on the date-time issues. The above experiment was taken without the help of any digital forensics tools. That makes it easier to explore the changing status of date-time stamp issues. The event timeline is often associated with a particular crime or incident and provides some possible answers for the where, when, or sometimes how. All individuals' activities are likely fused from a variety of related sources such as client records, or server logs. All service providers almost keep some records about their customers. This information from ISPs (Internet Service providers) or telephone companies can reveal the location and time of an individual's activities. The changing history of date-time stamp can be observed by building event timelines. The effort of generating timeline representation is necessary to give juries, judges and other decision makers a better chance of understanding important details.

6   Conclusion

Even though cloud computing changes the form of digital data and provides great help to our lives, the potential crisis cannot be overlooked. This study has considered the date-time stamp of file system and cloud computing storage service on digital forensics investigations. The experiment and findings of date-time stamp evaluation have given us the impression that without a careful consideration of comparison and correction these date-time stamps might prove to be less fruitful. It also proposes a practical method to explore the metadata of file system, and mitigate the impact of time bias across multiple drives or locations. Based on our results, we believe the iterative management model of exploring Windows date-time stamps can assist law enforcement in identifying cyber criminals and also help examiners establish event timeline, and clarify the offender's actions to the file. It will be useful in investigations and mitigate the impact of time bias across multiple systems. Findings from this research will be of importance to forensic practitioners, as well as in criminal investigations and civil litigation matters.

Acknowledgements. This research was partially supported by the Ministry of Science and Technology of the Republic of China under the Grants MOST 103-2221-E-015-003-.

References

1. ACPO (Association of Chief Police Officers), ACPO Good Practice Guide for Digital Evidence (2012). http://www.digital-detective.net/digital-forensics-documents/ACPO_Good_Practice_Guide_for_Digital_Evidence_v5.pdf
2. Arpaci-Dusseau, R.H., Arpaci-Dusseau, A.C.: Operating Systems: Three Easy Pieces. Arpaci-Dusseau Books Inc, Madison (2014)
3. Casey, E.: Digital Evidence and Computer Crime Forensic Science Computers, and the Internet, 3rd edn. Elsevier Inc, London (2011)
4. Casey, E.: Handbook of Digital Forensics and Investigation. Elsevier, New York (2010)
5. Conrad, C.: 2BrightSparks.: Understanding File Attributes (2014). http://www.2brightsparks.com/resources/articles/understanding-file-attributes.html
6. Denscombe, M.: Good Research Guide for Small-Scale Social Research Projects, 4th edn. Open University Press, Berkshire (2010)
7. Federici, C.: Cloud data imager: a unified answer to remote acquisition of cloud storage areas. Digit. Invest. **11**(1), 30–42 (2014). Elsevier Ltd., New York
8. Microsoft Corporation, File System Algorithms (2014). http://msdn.microsoft.com/en-us/library/ff469524.aspx
9. Microsoft Corporation, File System Behavior in the Microsoft Windows Environment (2014). http://download.microsoft.com
10. NIST Cloud Computing Forensic Science Working Group, NIST Cloud Computing Forensic Science Challenges (Draft NISTIR 8006) (2014). http://csrc.nist.gov/publications/drafts/nistir-8006/draft_nistir_8006.pdf
11. SAS Institute Inc., A Survey of Shared File Systems- Determining the Best Choice for your Distributed Applications (2013)
12. Thorpe, S.; Ray, I., Grandison, T., Barbir, A.: Cloud log forensics metadata analysis, In: IEEE 36th Annual on Computer Software and Applications Conference Workshops (COMPSACW), pp. 194−199, Izmir, Turkey (2012)
13. Zawoad, S. Hasan, R.: Cloud Forensics: A Meta-Study of Challenges, Approaches, and Open Problems, University of Alabama at Birmingham (2013)

Tag Detection for Preventing Unauthorized Face Image Processing

Alberto Escalada Jimenez[1]([✉]), Adrian Dabrowski[2], Noburu Sonehara[3],
Juan M. Montero Martinez[1], and Isao Echizen[3]

[1] E.T.S. Ing. Telecomunicacin, Universidad Politcnica de Madrid, Madrid, Spain
alberto.escalada.jimenez@alumnos.upm.es
[2] SBA Research, University of Technology, Vienna, Austria
adrian.dabrowski@tuwien.ac.at
[3] National Institue of Informatics, Tokyo, Japan
iechizen@nii.ac.jp

Abstract. A new technology is being proposed as a solution to the problem of unintentional facial detection and recognition in pictures in which the individuals appearing want to express their privacy preferences, through the use of different tags. The existing methods for face de-identification were mostly ad hoc solutions that only provided an absolute binary solution in a privacy context such as pixelation, or a bar mask. As the number and users of social networks are increasing, our preferences regarding our privacy may become more complex, leaving these absolute binary solutions as something obsolete. The proposed technology overcomes this problem by embedding information in a tag which will be placed close to the face without being disruptive. Through a decoding method the tag will provide the preferences that will be applied to the images in further stages.

Keywords: Privacy · Face detection · Tag detection · Unauthorized face processing

1 Introduction

Face detection and face recognition technologies have been highly developed during the last decades [1,2] and they have achieved a high efficiency being capable of detecting faces at long distances or in low visibility conditions. As a representative fact, facial recognition systems are aimed to be installed in surveillance of public places, and access and border control at airports [3] while it is already a fact that for instance it is estimated that there are over 10,000 webcams focused on public spaces around the United States. This last fact was aggravated with the terrorist attacks of September 11, 2001, which immediately focused attention on the field of biometrics [4]. This development has been made only in favor of the technology and not taking into account its social implications, which means that the individuals whom their faces have being detected have not intervened in the process. This scenario has made that the individuals being recorded or

© Springer International Publishing Switzerland 2015
Y.-Q. Shi et al. (Eds.): IWDW 2014, LNCS 9023, pp. 513–524, 2015.
DOI: 10.1007/978-3-319-19321-2_39

photographed have a few means to express their privacy preferences or their posture about being subjected to these new technologies. Lately, due to the improvement of portable devices with built-in cameras and the popularization of Social Networks in which photos are daily posted, like the case of Facebook, in which daily are uploaded 350 million photos on average [5], the widespread of a photography has a bigger impact than some years ago, and the access to these information is easier, and more out of the users control than what is generally conceived [6]. If we take a closer look at what some Social Networks use about face detection or recognition software, we find that Facebook, in which everyday people add more than 100 million tags to photos, offers a tag suggestion feature in which they use a face recognition software [7]. The facial recognition software uses an algorithm to calculate a unique number called template, based on some facial features appearing in the already tagged photos and profile pictures [8]. In this situation, a person who desires to block their faces in order to not being subject of a face recognition software has no means unless he is the one who has uploaded the picture.

In this paper we present a technology which allows the individuals that are being subject to a face processing method to express their privacy preferences through a visual code in which the information is embedded. In further steps, this flag-based system which is being worn by the individuals who want to protect their privacy under certain situations, is detected with a code detection algorithm, and thus the information contained can be extracted and applied to the image. These privacy preferences are set according to a policy framework presented by Adrian Dabrowski called Picture Privacy Policy Framework (P3F) which consists in a central database of privacy policies using a flag-based system [9]. In its work, the author developed a policy framework providing a solution to the problem of unauthorized face image processing. It covered all the aspects regarding how the desired system should work since the moment the policy was obtained from a code that the individuals would wear. That is the main difference with the work presented in this paper, which presents the a new novel technology that will be capable of encoding the privacy preferences of the user, and will therefore make this system feasible. An example of use of the P3F policy framework can be seen in Fig. 1.

2   Previous Methods

In this section we will try to have a look at the two different approaches of methods that have been used for de-identification purposes: first the methods protecting privacy right before pictures are taken as a way of showing their attitude and preferences regarding their privacy in pictures, and then the methods that have been used for protecting the privacy of the individuals once a video or a photograph have been taken. We will also consider the commonly used and available visual encoding schemes and will explain in what they consist at the end of this section.

As time passes, Social Networking Services (SNS) develop faster coming up with new ideas for sharing our lives and being connected to each other. That is

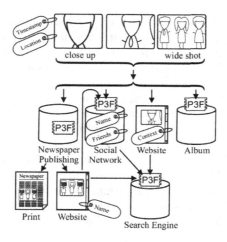

Fig. 1. Example where P3F sists in the distribution path [9].

the main reason why the preferences about our privacy become more and more complex and we need a new method as the one presented here to enable the individuals to express their preferences in different contexts and situations.

There are already some methods to protect the privacy and express the privacy preferences before the photos are taken. The most famous ones are called face mummification, but they are not successful because they are too radical and intrusive. The solutions for providing privacy once the pictures have being taken are called ad hoc and consist in making the face unrecognizable so the people appearing in a picture can maintain their anonymity. Some examples of ad hoc solution are blurring, pixilation, other distortion filters, or a more recent one called k-Same algorithm [10].

When we check the methods that already exist, we see that they consist in absolute binary solutions, in which the person decides, in a notably difficult way if it is possible (we always do not know where we have been photographed or recorded), whether they want their face in a picture or not, and this mechanism in today's more complex context as the SNS grow it is likely not to fulfill the users requirements and expectations. That is the reason why our solution outstands, it is an easy way to express more difficult decisions about privacy in an easy, non-time consuming, and less obtrusive way. As an example of the increasing complexity and the convenience of the hereby proposed technology, we can decide that we do not want to show our face to anyone with the same technology as if we were saying that we do not want to be recognized by any algorithm, but we still allow showing our face in certain SNS.

Some of the related work regarding already existing technology used for encoding information in a visual way are:

1. *1D Barcodes:* Linear bar codes are an obvious choice since it is a widespread technology and they are computationally easy to detect using frequency analysis. Nevertheless, the fact that they are a black and white technology might interfere with our face or eye detection algorithms. Since they are composed of several bars with different widths, their feasibility is relatively low when the distance to the code increases.
2. *2D Barcodes:* This is a more feasible scheme, since some of them can be customized almost from scratch (e.g. Microsoft Tag [11]). Most of them require an easily spottable wynchronization marker or a quite zone around them, and they are recognizable pattern which question the discretion required for such a technology, and thus questioning the validity of this method.
3. *Watermarking Techniques:* Watermarking and stenography are often used in the context of digital rights management. These technologies are mainly used in digital surfaces and means, and therefore are difficult to implement in any physical device.
4. *Augmented Reality Markers:* This technology is similar to the 2D Barcodes, and furthermore it is highly resistant to distortion and enable calculation of the relative distance and angle of the barcode surface to the camera. On the other hand, they lack of the discretion, and probably, the unobtrusiveness requirements, since it is used and optimized for real-time applications.

There is a slight difference between the two kind of methods presented in first place which are technologies that have the purpose of protecting the privacy of individuals once their faces have been detected, and the methods presented later for embedding information in a visual platform, which are closely related to the technology presented in this paper.

3   Requirements of the Technology

Right before finding the perfect solution, we have to come up with a group of requirements that the desired technology has to fulfill. These requirements fall within 2 different categories, which will set a framework that may be used in future steps to compare different potential technologies as possible implementations for our system.

3.1   Technical Requirements

1. *Data Payload:* The code has to be able to embed a certain amount of information (6 bits if we are going to use the P3F scheme) which will express in a visual way the privacy preferences chosen by each individual appearing in an image. If the policies that are desired to be expressed increase, then the data payload has to increase as well.
2. *Redundancy:* This feature is desirable in our code since the more redundant the information in the code is, the higher the chances of successfully detecting and decoding will be under worse conditions.

3. *Noise Robustness:* The technology has to be resistant to the noise that can appear in a picture due to environmental causes such as smoke, or due to the camera device, especially in low-light and low-contrast situations.
4. *Filter Resistant:* A lot of SNS offer a wide variety of popular filters that can be applied easily. For instance, Instagram (which offers the direct option of posting the image also in Facebook) offers 19 different filters which modify different aspects of the image appearance by adding a border or frame, making color space transformations to increase contrast, or make color cast [12].
5. *Blurriness:* The technology has to be immune to blurriness that can be added manually (again a popular feature offered by today's SNS), or because of external causes.
6. *Illumination:* Some pictures are taken in a low illumination environment such as night scenes and thus, the code is not exposed in the picture in desirable lighting conditions.
7. *Distance:* The code has to be detectable from long distances. This requirement comes from the big development that all face detection methods have been subject of. Now we have really accurate face detection methods and therefore, the code has to be also detectable and decodable for a successful technology.
8. *Compression Stability:* Digital photography is subject to several compression algorithms which commonly destroy details in pictures. The most common compression method for photographs on the Internet is JPEG.
9. *Cropping Invariance:* Some user editing tools available in any smartphone device as well as some popular SNS offer the option of cropping pictures so it can fill a desired size or they just show a certain part of the picture. Therefore, our code has to be decodable even if it has suffered some cropping or some cut in it.
10. *Physical Support:* We need a place where we can put our code without being too annoying for the user. For a first approach in this technology, a frame of the user's glasses would be an ideal solution.
11. *Non Blind Decoding:* This requirement is desirable instead of a blind decoding because although the latter is more flexible, the former is easier to implement for a new research topic as it is the one presented in this article. The technology has to be identifiable with a database which contains all the possible options in which the code can take form (can be presented as).

All these requirements are only applicable if the face detection algorighm succeeds. That means that if for any reason the picture has not the appropriate characteristics so the faces are detected, our code does not have to be visible or fulfill the requirements either.

3.2 Aesthetic Requirements

1. *Unobtrusiveness:* When a subject decides to use the P3F technology, it has to be as simple as possible and does not require too much effort without causing any disturbance for the user.

2. *Location:* The location of the code has to be as close as possible to the face, since placing the code somewhere else would be useless when a picture just shows the face. We have also agreed that the code has to be placed always in the same location (that will be a requirement for the user), because that way the algorithm will be much more efficient and lighter.
3. *Discretion:* The technology has to be as discreet as possible since otherwise it will not be used. This might seem as a minor requirement, but it is not. For the feasibility of this technology, the tags have to cause the smallest discomfort to the user as possible, and also for other people's eyes.

In the proposed requirements we can see that there could be some requirements that seems opposite, for instance for fulfilling the distance requirement we could think of making a bigger code which would be seen from longer distances, but that would make the Discretion requirement to fail, since a big object close to the face seems to compromise the feasibility and success of such a technology. Therefore we cannot meet all of them although they are all desirable, and some of them will have more priority or importance than others.

4 Proposed Tag

For the tag that we are going to use to express our policy, we are going to use a novel way to put information through a visual way, and that is by using different sets of colors which will be scanned at the same time that a facial detection or recognition software takes place.

4.1 Color Space

The selected color space for the colors that will be used in the tag is the RGB color model, an additive color model in which red, green, and blue light are added in order to reproduce a certain color. There are many different ways of defining the different RGB colors through numeric representations, and we will use the digital 8-bit per channel representation, in which a RGB color is defined by three 8-bit numbers each of them corresponding to the red, green, and blue lights.

   According to the P3F framework, we would need to embed 6 bits in our tag to fulfill the requirements. That is 64 different possibilities. We decide to use only 5 different colors of the RGB color space in order to use the strongest options maintaining a wide margin of distance in between the chosen colors in the RGB color space. These colors and their 8-bit representations are: Red (255,0,0), Green (0,255,0), Blue (0,0,255), White (255,255,255), and Black (0,0,0). This way we are ensuring a robustness in our code through the use of five different and strong colors.

4.2   Tag Design

In order to embed 6-bit of data, which was the data payload needed to implement the P3F policy, using the five colors we already named we find a simple problem of combinations. With a 6-bit word, we can obtain 64 different words, and using 5 colors we need to know how many use in a combination of them to obtain a number equal or greater of possible combinations.

We have decided, for simplicity and creating a stronger code, that the order of the colors appearing in the tag will not be taken into account, and the information will only come from the colors appearing and not the place they occupy. Therefore, we come up with a simple problem of combinations in which we have to figure out how many colors to use from the set of 5 colors from the RGB color space so we can obtain a number equal or greater than 64 combinations. The equation used for combinations is (1) where r stands for the unknown number of colors that need to be used, and n is the set of 5 different colors selected. The result, is the number of possible combinations when r objects have been selected from a set of n objects.

Thus we obtain that placing 4 colors in a tag, we could obtain a number of 70 different combinations in which the order is not taken into account.

$$_nC_r = (\frac{n!}{r!(n-1)!}) \tag{1}$$

We can see a first approach to this technology in the tag sketched in Fig. 2.

Fig. 2. Proposed tag which will be composed of a white background and four different circles in which will be placed the different RGB colors.

4.3   Tag Size and Other Features

In this section some of the physical features of the tag will be explained, as well as the criteria that is going to be used to base our decisions.

The size of the tag will be, in the beginning, such that all the aesthetic requirements are fulfilled, which means that it will have a width and length that will not be too intrusive in someone's face, but at the same time they will be big enough to be seen and processed correctly by the algorithm explained in this paper. We have already make a test plan, which includes testing how accurate is the processing of the tag according to its size and the size of the circles which appear in it (both sizes are closely linked). Therefore, we will be able to extract an ideal size which will be transported to reality and thus, will optimize the results of this novel technology.

As it has already said, the colors used in this TAG belong to the RGB color space, and they are quite simple and robust since they are, or composed by, the extreme colors of the named space. This scenario makes the generation of the tags that will be worn extremely cheap and easy, since everyone with access to a computer can create a tag with the desired colors and with an optimal size which will be provided in the near future.

5   The Detection Algorithm

Once the technology has been implemented and the codes have been created, we will implement an algorithm which will be capable of detecting, locating, and analyzing the codes that appear in a picture. This algorithm is composed of two different parts that will lead to a lighter and more efficient search of the different codes shown in the picture. The phases and the explanation of the algorithm are given below, and an outlook of the whole algorithm can be seen in Fig. 3.

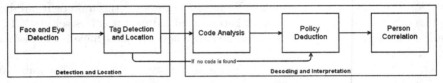

Fig. 3. Different stages of the detection and interpretation algorithm.

Furthermore, the algorithm proposal we are presenting here is composed of one more stage which does not depend on us. It is a watermarking phase which would be executed by the publishing entities, since they are responsible too of using the proposed algorithm for detecting and decoding the tags.

5.1   Detection and Location

In this project, for the computer image processing which will be hold during the whole development of the technology, it was decided to use an open source computer vision software such as OpenCV. This powerful tool will help us to analyze the different images subject of our research being capable of detecting and decoding the tags in which the information will be contained. We can differentiate two main stages in which this phase is divided.

The first step is to use a face detection algorithm in the image we are going to analyze, which will be critical to reduce the heaviness of the whole process. Since the location of the code in the facial area (in a fixed place, as it was previously said) is an important requirement, we will first locate the faces appearing in a picture and this way we will reduce the area in which we will look for the code making the algorithm faster, lighter, more accurate, and more efficient. For this task, we have opted for the most commonly used method for face detection, which is the one reported by Viola and Jones in 2004 [13]. This method achieves highly accurate rates and high-speed detection since it is based on a multi-scale detection algorithm that uses cascade composition of the Haar-like features, image integration, and a cascade architecture with strong classifiers. By using a face detection method that uses Haar Cascades in OpenCV, we can obtain results similar as the shown in the second picture in Fig. 4. Thus, being easier to reduce the area of searching to a smaller and lighter location close to one of the eyes of each face detected. If the image that is being analyzed does not meet some size requirements, the algorithm will resize it since we have proved that the eye detection stage has better results when the images are not so small.

As a result from the face and eye detection algorithm we obtain a matrix containing rectangles in which the faces are framed. The next step is the detection and location of the code. This step will be easy using the software already named. We first will use some geometrical approximations to reduce the area in which we are going to look for the code. Since the eyes and the face have been identified and placed, some parameters arise from that calculation, like the radius of the eyes, or face. Using those parameters, we create a rectangular space within the picture limits in which we frame both eyes, and we add a dynamic margin which will ensure that also the code is included in that rectangle. We use the radius of the face to create the margin, so if the face is bigger than expected, the margin will be bigger as well granting that the colors of the code will remain in the limits of the rectangle which will be subject of study. After that, a simple shape detection algorithm is enough for finding a rectangular shape. If this algorithm does not succeed, then we will just submit the whole rectangle to the proper color filtering process.

5.2   Decoding and Interpretation

Once the code has been placed within the limits of the image, the picture will be subject to some color filters that will determine which colors are appearing in our tag. If the tag has been detected in the shape detection part, then it will be easier that the colors are detected with a lower mistakes.

For detecting the different colors that appear in the tag, we will use again the OpenCV software that has been previously mentioned. Since the tag has a white background, we will just look for the other four RGB colors and unless four colors are detected in the tag, the white color will be supposed and there will be as many circles as the difference between the total number of circles, four, and the detected colored circles.

For detecting which circles are colored we will use a tool for detecting the existing colors between a certain range in the RGB color space, and since we have selected four different colors with wide margin we will use the mean of those two extreme values to set the range limits. For instance, a colour will be considered black always that its three RGB components are greater than 128 in the 8-bit representation, that would be (128,128,128).

Once this step is complete the results will be compared with a data base in which all the policies are saved. We are using a non-blind decoding so all the possible codes have to be placed in the algorithm to finally obtain the information which is embedded in the tag.

5.3   Watermarking

With this schema we are trusting the publishing entities as the ones responsible of using this detecting and decoding technology in order to preserve the privacy of people. We can introduce a further step which will ensure that the privacy preferences information is maintained even out of the publishing entity space.

If we add a secure and invisible watermarking step to our schema, the privacy preferences now will be embedded in the picture and not just in the privacy code anymore. Therefore if any third party uses the picture and modifies it in such a way that the tag is not visible, or the code cannot be decoded properly, there will be still a secure way of knowing and proving what the individuals appearing in the picture opted for their privacy. This is step has to be provided by the publishing entity, in which we completely trust.

6   Evaluation

In this section we will present some of the results obtained in our attempt of using the already explained algorithm, and see how the results have been so far. In the following figures we will explain what are steps followed in the evaluation of a certain picture.

First we place a tag in a photo where a recognizable face appears. If we apply the face detection and eye detection methods, we obtain an image like the original one but with the eyes and the face framed in a circle, a consequence that they have been detected. Once we have that, we can extract a smaller area as it is shown in the third picture in which we will look for our tag. All these three pictures can be seen in Fig. 4.

 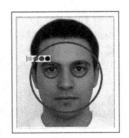 

Fig. 4. The first picture shows the original photo with the policy tag. The second picture shows the photo after the eyes and face detection. And the third picture shows the tag area which will be scanned for extract information.

In the following images in Fig. 5, we can see the result of a number of transformations that the image suffer in order to determine the number of existing circles in the tag, and its colors.

Fig. 5. In the image on the left we can see the contour of three out of the four circles. On the right we can see a method that detects green pixels.

Because we are adding the tag manually, and there is not time to analyze the picture under different and worse conditions, it is very likely that the accuracy will close to 100.

After the paper is submitted, the research about this topic will continue and will have as an objective the quantification of its features. This means that the algorithm will be tested with different tag sizes, applying different filters to the pictures, changing the margins of colors, seeing how does all this work in a group picture, etc. And the results will quantify the quality of this proposed new technology.

7   Future Work

While the research was conducted, the potential of this technology was seen, but was not fully developed because of the time limitations. Because of this reason, we are proposing some guidelines that the research topic could follow in order to obtain a more successful technology.

A big future improvement that would improve the results of security preserved, and the immunity obtained in a picture would be to convert the whole system into a sensor-trusted one. That would mean that the decoding and application of each policy would be made right at the same time as the face detection takes place in any camera.

Another further step that could be taken in this research would be the implementation of the watermarking or steganography function that would provide, as it has already been explained, a more secure technology. That would be implemented also as a instant feature in the desired sensor-trusted improved technology.

Finally, a big improvement could be done for the success of this technology having to do with the appearance of the device that has to be worn. It seems that the discretion of this technology is a major concern for people, therefore, a new way of applying the already existing technology could be possible. For instance by placing different color spots within the limits of the frame of the eyeglasses, or using removable stickers that perfectly match the size of the frame. The only requirement here would be again the one asking for a detectable place.

8   Conclusion

The technology we have presented facilitates and allows the individuals appearing in any picture to express their preferences regarding privacy preferences within a framework already created.

The technique presented here makes the transmission of information through a novel way using colors located in a tag that will be worn in the proximity of the face. This technology enables a new way of expressing new and more complex preferences regarding the privacy of people appearing in pictures than existing previous methods.

A fast evaluation shows that the technology is feasible and that a possible quantification of its most important parameters would be ideal to improve it. Therefore, that is the direction the research will follow.

Acknowledgments. This work was performed under the National Institute of Informatics international internship program.

References

1. Yang, M.-H., Kriegman, D., Ahuja, N.: Detecting faces in images: A survey. IEEE Trans. Pattern Anal. Mach. Intell. **24**(1), 34–58 (2002)
2. Zhang, C., Zhang, Z.: A survey of recent advances in face detection, Technical report, Microsoft Research (2010)
3. Sadeghi, A.-R., Schneider, T., Wehrenberg, I.: Efficient privacy-preserving face recognition. In: Lee, D., Hong, S. (eds.) ICISC 2009. LNCS, vol. 5984, pp. 229–244. Springer, Heidelberg (2010)
4. Bowyer, K.W.: Face recognition technology: security versus privacy. IEEE Technol. Soc. Mag. **23**(1), 9–19 (2004)
5. A focus on efficiency, internet.org, Techical report (2013)
6. Besmer, A., Lipford, H.R.: Moving beyond untagging: photo privacy in a tagged world. In: Proceedings of the SIGCHI Conference on Human Factors in Computing Systems. ACM, pp. 1563–1572 (2010)
7. Making photo tagging easier, June 2011. https://www.facebook.com/notes/facebook/making-photo-tagging-easier/467145887130
8. How does facebook suggest tags?, May 2014. https://www.facebook.com/help/122175507864081
9. Dabrowski, A., Weippl, E., Echizen, I.: Framework based on privacy policy hiding for preventing unauthorized face image processing. In: 2013 IEEE International Conference on Systems, Man, and Cybernetics (SMC), pp. 455–461, October 2013
10. Gross, R., Airoldi, E.M., Malin, B., Sweeney, L.: Integrating utility into face de-identification. In: Danezis, G., Martin, D. (eds.) PET 2005. LNCS, vol. 3856, pp. 227–242. Springer, Heidelberg (2006)
11. M. Corporation. Microsoft tag - implementation guide (2011). http://tag.microsoft.com/resources/implementation-guide.aspx
12. How does instagram develop their filters?, May 2012. http://www.quora.com/Instagram/How-does-Instagram-develop-their-filters
13. Viola, P., Jones, M.J.: Robust real-time face detection. Int. J. Comput. Vis. **57**(2), 137–154 (2004)

Detecting Fake-Quality WAV Audio
Based on Phase Differences

Jinglei Zhou, Rangding Wang$^{(\boxtimes)}$, Chao Jin, and Diqun Yan

College of Information Science and Engineering,
Ningbo University, Ningbo 315211, China
wangrangding@nbu.edu.cn

Abstract. With the continual growth of the requirements of digital audios, some people have been selling the fake-quality audio which was transcoded from the audio with worse quality and lower price for profits. For protecting the legitimate rights of consumers to some extent, a method for telling whether the WAV audio has been compressed with the audio encoders (MP3, AAC or OGG) is presented by using the statistical features of phase difference in this paper. The experimental results show that the proposed method can effectively detect whether the given WAV audio is original or not, and furthermore, it can identify the type of the codec. The overall hit rate can reach over 97 %.

Keywords: WAV · Fake-quality detection · Encoder type · Phase differences

1 Introduction

With the development of multimedia information technology, people can easily obtain the audio, video and various kinds of multimedia which bring a lot of convenience to our life. On the other hand, unscrupulous people seek illegitimate benefits in the field of multimedia trade, such as counterfeiting, piracy and transcoding. This paper focuses on the transcoding of consumer digital audios. It is cheap for someone to buy a compressed and lossy audio, such as an MP3 [1], AAC [2] and OGG [3] file. For obtaining the unlawful profits, the criminals sell the audio with a higher price by either decoding the compressed audios to the raw format audio – WAV file (fake-quality audio of lossless format), or further recoding them to the same format as the compressed audio with higher bitrate (fake-quality audio of lossy format).

Up to now, some schemes have been proposed for detecting the fake-quality audio of lossy format. Yang et al. [4] utilized the numbers of small-value MDCT coefficients as features to discriminate fake-quality MP3 from normal MP3. Liu and Qiao et al. [5, 6] present an effective algorithm to detect double MP3 compression for both up-transcoding and down-transcoding based on the statistical features of MDCT coefficients. Yu et al. [7] took the Huffman table index as the classification features for detecting the fake-quality MP3 audio successfully. Bianchi et al. [8] proposed a single measure to decide if an MP3 file is single compressed or double compressed based on the statistical properties of quantized MDCT coefficients. And the method can also detect the bit-rate of the first compression. However, there are few work concentrate on the detection of fake-quality audio of lossless format. Luo et al. [9] proposed a method

Y.-Q. Shi et al. (Eds.): IWDW 2014, LNCS 9023, pp. 525–534, 2015.
DOI: 10.1007/978-3-319-19321-2_40

for detecting whether the WAV files has been previously compressed or not, and further to estimate the compression type (MP3 or WMA). Similarly, the features of this approach were also constructed according to the MDCT coefficients which were acquired during the compression process.

In this paper, the phase spectrums of the original WAV and its processed versions encoded and decoded by MP3, AAC and OGG encoders were analyzed, and furthermore the mean and variance of the phase differences which were calculated based on the given WAV and the corresponding version were compared. Then the variance which performs better than the mean on classification was chosen as the feature for our detection approach. Finally, libSVM [10] was applied as the classifier. Experimental results show that our method is able to identify the WAV is original or decoded from the compressed audio file by the three popular encoders, namely Lame 3.99.5 [11] (MP3), FAAC 1.28 [12] (AAC) and Oggenc2.87 [13] (OGG).

The rest of the paper is organized as follows. Section 2 mainly analyses the phase spectrum, and describes the extraction process of the features. Section 3 shows the experimental setup, and then the experimental results will be given. And the summary will be shown in the last section.

2   The Proposed Method

A certain amount of audio distortion will be produced during the audio compression process. The distortion can be clearly detected by the phase spectrum of the audio, although cannot be perceived by human's ears. In this section, the impact of audio phase generated in the compression process has been brief analyzed, and then the extraction process of the features has been described.

2.1   Phase Spectrum Analysis

The lossy compression codecs (including MP3, AAC and OGG) utilize the characteristic which human ear is not sensitive to high frequency sound signal, transforming the time domain signal into frequency domain signal and removing the redundancy. Different encoders have some similar parts, such as the modified discrete cosine transform (MDCT), psychoacoustics model, as well as quantification and frame data stream formation, though they are not following the same standard. The psychoacoustics mode and quantification are result in the difference of phase spectrum in audio signal.

In order to facilitate the description, the different WAV audio versions proposed in this paper were defined as the abbreviations given in Table 1. W represents the original uncompressed WAV audio, M, A, and O depict the WAV audios which were encoded and decoded by MP3, AAC, and OGG compressions, respectively. MM, AM, OM were defined as the WAV audios which were encoded and decoded by MP3, AAC and OGG at the first compression and processed by MP3 at the second compression. Whereas the other two similar definitions (MA, AA, OA, and MO, AO, OO) share the same rule of MM, AM and OM. In order to figure out the alteration of the phase

Table 1. The abbreviations of the WAV audios with different versions.

W1	W2		
	The encoder used for compression		
	MP3	AAC	OGG
The original WAV(W)	M	A	O
The MP3 decompressed WAV	MM	MA	MO
The AAC decompressed WAV	AM	AA	AO
The OGG decompressed WAV	OM	OA	OO

spectrum caused by compression, a randomly-selected WAV audio of our audio dataset was considered as the W for generating the corresponding M, A, O, MM, AA and OO which were all compressed at the bit-rate of 128 kbps; and the phase spectrums of the WAVs were plot and shown in Figs. 1, 2 and 3. Figure 1 shows the phase spectrum of one frame which belongs to W. Figure 2 shows the phase spectrums of the corresponding frame of M, A and O, and Fig. 3 illustrates the counterparts of MM, AA and OO. It is observed from the comparison of Figs. 1, 2(a) and 3(a) that the phase spectrum changes a lot after the first compression while alters little after the second compression with the same encoder. The similar changes of phase spectrums for the other two encoders (AAC and OGG) are shown in Figs. 2(b), (c) and 3(b), (c).

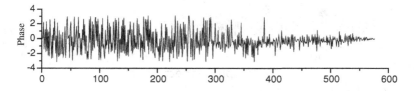

Fig. 1. The phase spectrum of the frame randomly selected from W.

From the observation of the above figures, the phase differences between the given WAV audio (W, M, A and O) and their processed versions which were encoded and decoded by the three encoders, can be taken for constructing the effective features. Then the two widely-used statistics, namely the mean and variance of the phase differences were calculated according to Fig. 4, wherein the W1 is the given WAV and the W2 is the processed version. Each WAV was divided into overlapping frames and every frame was multiplied a hamming window. The FFT algorithm was used to get the phase spectrum of each frame. The phase spectrum of the *ith* frame in W1 and W2 were defined as $\varphi_{W1}(i)$ and $\varphi_{W2}(i)$ respectively. The phase differences denoted by $\varphi_d(i)$ were obtained by subtracting the phase spectrums $\varphi_{W1}(i)$ from $\varphi_{W2}(i)$. Finally, the mean and variance of the phase differences calculated according to Eqs. (1) and (2).

$$\text{MEAN} = \frac{1}{N}\sum_{i=1}^{N} \{E[\varphi_d(i)]\}, \, i = 1, 2, \ldots, N \tag{1}$$

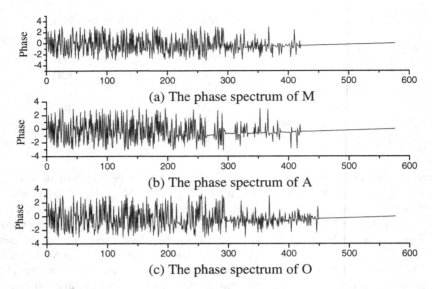

Fig. 2. The phase spectrums of the corresponding frame of M, A and O.

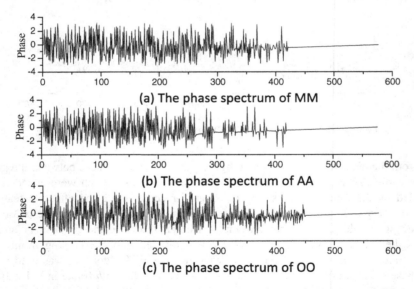

Fig. 3. The phase spectrums of the corresponding frame of MM, AA and OO.

$$\text{VAR} = \frac{1}{N}\sum_{i=1}^{N}\{D[\varphi_d(i)]\},\ i = 1, 2, \ldots, N \tag{2}$$

where N is the number of frames, $E(\cdot)$ and $D(\cdot)$ are the functions for calculating the mean and variance.

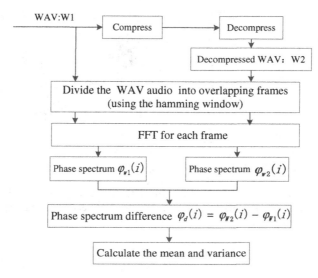

Fig. 4. The process of feature extraction.

Figure 5 (a) and (b) respectively show the mean (M1) and variance (V1) of the phase differences between the given WAVs (W, A, M and O) and the processed versions (M, MM, AM and OM) compressed and decompressed by MP3 encoder. Figures 6 and 7 illustrate the counterparts of which the processed versions were encoded and decoded by AAC encoder and OGG encoder respectively. It is observed from Figs. 5, 6 and 7 that compared to the mean values, the variance values of the phase differences of W, M, A and O separate each other more distinctly. So the variances would be more effective for classification and the simulation results shown in the following part have testified our inference.

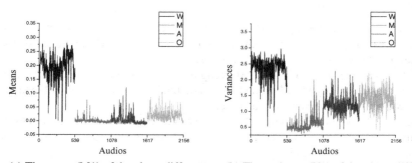

(a) The mean (M1) of the phase difference   (b) The variance (V1) of the phase difference

Fig. 5. The mean and variance of the phase difference calculated based on the W, M, A, O (128 kbps) and their corresponding WAVs processed by MP3 encoder (192 kbps).

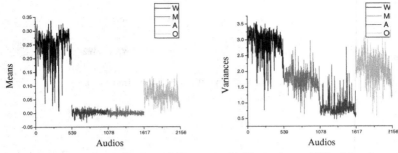

(a) The mean (M2) of the phase difference   (b) The variance (V2) of the phase difference

Fig. 6. The mean and variance of the phase difference calculated based on the W, M, A, O (128 kbps) and their corresponding WAVs processed by AAC encoder (152 kbps).

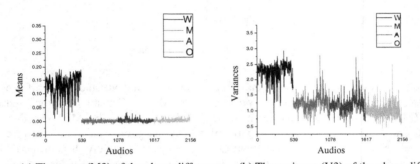

(a) The mean (M3) of the phase difference   (b) The variance (V3) of the phase difference

Fig. 7. The mean and variance of the phase difference calculated based on the W, M, A, O (128 kbps) and their corresponding WAVs processed by OGG encoder (192 kps).

2.2   The Detection Method

Based on the analysis in Sect. 2.1, V1, V2 and V3 have been designed as the classification features for the detection method and the entire procedure of the detection method can be illustrated by the following steps:

Step 1: The questionable WAV audio is compressed and decompressed by MP3 at 192 kbps, AAC at 152 kbps, and OGG at 192 kbps, respectively, and then the three processed versions are acquired.

Step 2: Calculate the three variances (V1, V2 and V3) of phase difference values of the questionable WAV and the processed versions generated in Step 1 according to the Eq. (2).

Step 3: Take the feature set constructed in Step 2 as the input of libSVM classifier and sort it into the version (W, M, A and O) which it belong to according to the model trained by a big amount of W, M, A and O samples. Consequently, the classification result would be output and the detection is finished.

3 Experiments and Results

3.1 Experimental Setup

To support our results and to reduce the risk of tautological finding, a basic audio dataset which consists of 839 mono WAV audios was constructed for evaluating the performance of our algorithm. Each audio has duration of 10 s and a sample rate of 44.1 kHz. The whole dataset contains several musical genres of classical, pop, folk, rock, hip-hop and so on. Herein 539 WAV audios were randomly selected for training the classification model and the remaining for testing. Besides, 539 WAV audios for training were compressed by MP3, AAC and OGG at 128 kbps respectively, and then decompressed to obtain 539 MP3 audios (M), 539 AAC audios (A), 539 OGG audios (O). To acquire the processed versions (MM, AM, OM, MA, AA, OA, MO, AO and OO), M, A and O were processed by MP3 at 192 kbps, AAC at 152 kbps, and OGG at 192 kbps respectively. Please note that the actual bit-rate of the OGG audio floats around the set bit-rate during the process of OGG encoding and the highest bit-rate of AAC audio is 152 kbps.

The training and testing procedure was shown in Fig. 8. In order to grantee the testing results comprehensive and convincing, the 300 testing WAV audios were respectively processed at five bit-rates (64, 96, 128, 160 and 192 kbps) to obtain M, A and O, and then doubly processed versions were obtained according to the previously processed audios (MM, AM, OM, MA, AA, OA, MO, AO and OO). The entire experiment process was repeated 10 times for every condition of the 5 bit-rates (64, 96, 128, 160 and 192 kbps), and the averaged detection accuracy were given in the next section.

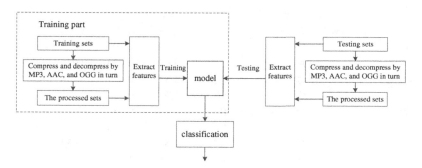

Fig. 8. The training and testing process.

In the experiment, the libSVM classifier has been used for constructing the classification model which would be utilized for predicting which category the testing sample belongs to. The kernel function of *svmtrain*($\cdot$) was set as the RBF function, that is *svmtrain*($\ldots,' -t2'$), and other parameters were set as the defaults.

3.2 Experimental Results

In this experiment, we aim to determine whether a given WAV file has been compressed and decompressed by MP3, AAC or OGG encoder previously. Table 2 shows the overall hit rates at the compressed bit-rates of 64, 96, 128, 160 and 192 kbps. It is observed that the proposed features can achieve good performance for all five bit rates.

Table 2. The overall hit rates at different bit-rates(%).

Bit-rate	64 kbps	96 kbps	128 kbps	160 kbps	192 kbps
Accuracy	95.25	97.42	97.67	98.17	97.67

Table 3 shows the multi-classification results for the testing sets at the compressed bit-rates of 64, 96, 128, 160, and 192 kbps. Taking the condition of 64 kbps as an example, the first row in Table 3 shows that 96.33 % of the original WAV audios were classified as original WAV audios, and 1.00 %, 0.67 % and 2.00 % of the original WAV audios were detected as M, A and O, respectively. The table shows that the detection accuracy of M can reach 100 %, and the achieved minimum detection accuracy of W is still reach 93 %. It indicates that the proposed method can effectively detect whether the WAV was original or decompressed from the MP3, AAC or OGG encoders.

Table 3. Confusion matixes of the detection accuracy under the 5 conditions of 64, 96, 128, 160, and 192 kbps (%).

Compression conditions		Accuracy (%)			
		Predict version			
Bit-rates	True version	W	M	A	O
64 kbps	W	96.33	1.00	0.67	2.00
	M	0	95.00	5.00	0
	A	0	0.67	98.33	0.67
	O	2.33	2.33	0	91.33
96 kbps	W	96.33	1.00	0.67	2
	M	0	99.67	0.33	0
	A	0	0	98.33	1.67
	O	2.33	1.67	0.67	95.33
128 kbps	W	95.33	2.33	1.67	0.67
	M	0	100	0	0
	A	0	0.33	99.67	0
	O	1.00	2.00	1.33	95.67
160 kbps	W	95.00	3.67	0.67	0.67
	M	0	100	0	0
	A	–	–	–	–
	O	1.00	0.67	0.33	98.00
192 kbps	W	93.00	5.67	0.33	1.00
	M	0	100	0	0
	A	–	–	–	–
	O	0.33	1.33	0.33	98.00

Table 4 shows the detection accuracy for W and A, M, O at the random bit-rate. For each original uncompressed WAV audio in this experiment, the M, A, and O were obtained at a random bit-rate respectively. As shown in Table 4, it is observed that the detection accuracies are still satisfactory for distinguishing the four types of audio. And the average detection accuracy obtained from the experiment as high as 97.58 %.

Table 4. Confusion matixes of the detection accuracy for W and A, M, O at the random bit-rate (%).

True version	Predict version			
	W	M	A	O
W	96.33	1.00	0.67	2.00
M	0	99.67	0.33	0
A	0	0.33	99.67	0
O	0.33	1.33	0.67	94.67

4 Conclusions

In this paper, by analyzing the statistical properties of the phase difference of the WAV audio decompressed by different encoders, a novel algorithm was proposed for identifying the original WAV audio from the WAV audio which has been processed by MP3, AAC or OGG compressions. However, our method also has some limitations; for example, it can only detect the three most widely-used encoders. And further research for detecting other encoders is needed in our future work. In addition, this method is unable to figure out which bit-rate has been used for encoding and what is the compression history of the questionable WAV audio. The above limitations will also on our research schedule.

Acknowledgements. This work was supported by the National Natural Science Foundation of China (Grant No. 61170137, 61300055, 61301247), Zhejiang Natural Science Foundation (Grant No. LY13F020013), Ningbo Natural Science Foundation (Grant No. 2013A610057, 2013A610059), Ningbo University Fund (Grant No. XKXL1313, XKXL1310) and K.C. Wong Magna Fund in Ningbo University.

References

1. Information technology - coding of moving pictures and associated audio for digital storage media up to about 1.5 mbit/s – part 3: audio. ISO/IEC International Standard IS 11172-3 (1993)
2. Information technology - generic coding of moving pictures and associated audio information - part 7: advanced audio coding. ISO/IEC International Standard IS 13818-7 (1997)
3. Xiph.org: OGG. http://xiph.org/ogg/

4. Yang, R., Shi, Y.Q., Huang, J.W.: Defeating fake-quality MP3. In: Proceedings of the 11th ACM Workshop on Multimedia and Security, pp. 117–124 (2009)
5. Liu, Q.Z., Sung, A.H., Qiao, M.Y.: Detection of double MP3 compression. Cogn. Comput. **2**(4), 291–296 (2010)
6. Qiao, M.Y., Sung, A.H., Liu, Q.Z.: Revealing real quality of double compressed MP3 audio. In: Proceedings of the International Conference on Multimedia, pp. 1011–1014 (2010)
7. Yu, X.M., Wang, R.D., Yan, D.Q., Ma, P.F.: Detecting fake-quality MP3 based on Huffman table index. J. Softw. **9**(4), 907–912 (2014)
8. Bianchi, T., De Rosa, A., Fontani, M., et al.: Detection and classification of double compressed MP3 audio tracks. In: Proceedings of the first ACM Workshop on Information Hiding and Multimedia Security, pp. 159–164 (2013)
9. Luo, D., Luo, W., Yang, R., et al.: Compression history identification for digital audio signal. In: IEEE International Conference on Acoustics, Speech and Signal Processing (ICASSP), pp. 1733–1736 (2012)
10. Chang, C.C., Lin, C.J.: LIBSVM: a library for support vector machines. ACM Trans. Intell. Syst. Technol. (TIST) **2**(3), 27 (2011)
11. Lame MP3 Encoder. http://lame.sf.net
12. FAAC-1.28. http://www.linuxfromscratch.org/blfs/view/svn/multimedia/faac.html
13. Rare Wares. http://www.rarewares.org/ogg-oggenc.php

Non-integer Expansion Embedding
for Prediction-Based Reversible Watermarking

Shangyi Liu and Shijun Xiang$^{(\boxtimes)}$

School of Information Science and Technology, Jinan University, Guangzhou, China
xiangshijun@gmail.com

Abstract. This paper proposes a new reversible data hiding algorithm in encrypted image by referring to MSBs (Most Significant Bits) of image blocks. While inserting one bit in a block, MSBs' value of a block is computed for deciding the number of LSBs (Least Significant Bits) to be flipped. In such a way, image block's smoothness characteristics can be exploited for improving data recovery rate for the same embedding distortion by comparing with the two existing state of the art works. Experiment results have proven the validity of the proposed method.

Keywords: Encrypted image · Reversible data hiding · Most Significant Bits · Block classification

1 Introduction

Reversible data hiding is a technique which embeds additional data in covers and the original covers can be completely recovered after the extraction of the embedded data. It is often used for covert communication, integrity certification of multimedia works, etc. At present, researchers have proposed many reversible data hiding algorithms [1–6]. In [1–3], authors used difference expansion, lossless compression and histogram shifting to achieve the goal of reversible data hiding respectively. Improvement for the classical reversible data hiding performance was made in [4–6].

As we know, encryption is another technique, which transforms multimedia plaintext into incomprehensible ciphertext for safe communication. To further strengthen the security, encryption and reversible data hiding are often combined in some scenarios [7–9]. Traditionally, this procedure is accomplished by encrypting the carriers which contains additional data. However, in some application, this traditional fashion is unapplicable. For example, in medical system, it is obligatory to encrypt the original medical images firstly for protecting the patients' privacy. Then, the personal information of patients, such as names and id numbers are embedded for identification. Moreover, medical images usually require very high fidelity, that is to say, they don't allow any distortion. Therefore, it is very important to perform reversible data hiding in the encrypted multimedia carriers. Actually, such algorithms have been proposed in [10,11]. The sketch of scheme proposed in [10] or [11] is given in Fig. 1. In [10], the

© Springer International Publishing Switzerland 2015
Y.-Q. Shi et al. (Eds.): IWDW 2014, LNCS 9023, pp. 535–543, 2015.
DOI: 10.1007/978-3-319-19321-2_41

3 least significant bits (LSBs) of encrypted image are flipped for data embedding and the correlation of natural image is used for extraction at the decoder. However, [10] doesn't exploit the edge pixels of image blocks in the fluctuation function when extracting, which increases the error rate of data restoration. In order o avoid this defect, a new fluctuation function which contains all the pixels of image blocks is defined in data extraction phase of [11]. Moreover, a side-match scheme is adopted. Experimental results revealed that the work [11] offers better performance than [10].

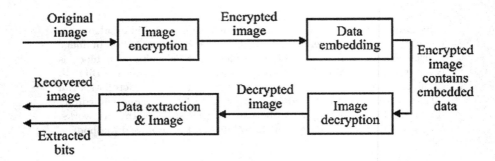

Fig. 1. The sketch of scheme proposed in [10] or [11].

The two excellent algorithms [10,11] share a common weakness, that is in all the blocks 3 LSBs of each pixel will be flipped for data embedding. Such a way may result in higher embedding distortion or larger data extraction error rate. In fact, according to the experimental results of [10] and [11], we find out that the extracted-bit errors are mainly occurred in texture areas due to the weak spatial correlation among pixels. In these regions, more number of flipped-bits are needed to obtain better effect. For an image, there are always some smooth areas with strong spatial correlation, where the embedded data and the blocks can be restored correctly even the number of flipped-bits is less than 3. Considering that MSBs of a block can better represent the block's smoothness characteristics, in this paper we propose a new reversible data hiding algorithm by computing the value of MSBs of a block as a reference to decide the number of flipped-LSBs for data embedding. Experimental results have shown that data recovery rate can be improved for the same embedding distortion by comparing with the algorithms [10,11].

In the next section, the proposed block classification is described. This is followed by a description of test results against other two methods. Finally, we draw the conclusions.

2   Proposed Scheme

The sketch of the proposed scheme is similar to that in Fig. 1, including image encryption, data embedding, image decryption, data-extraction/image-recovery phases. In our scheme, the image encryption and image decryption operations are the same as that of [10] and [11]. The difference is that the MSBs' value of an image block is adopted in data embedding and data-extraction/image-recovery stages to judge the number of to-be flipped LSBs. The process on how to classify blocks in the proposed scheme is described as follows.

2.1 Block Classification

In a natural image, different blocks may have different smoothness character-istics. In the literature, there are many methods on how to compute a block's smoothness. But these methods are not fit to the proposed data hiding scheme because the LSBs of the pixels will be flipped in the embedding. Consider that MSBs of a pixel are not changed in the embedding, in this paper we compute the MSBs' value of a block to classify all the blocks into three categories for flipping different number of LSBs for different category. Our motivation is that to some extent, the block smoothness of original image can be reflected by that of IM's.

For the images of 256 ($256 = 2^8$) gray scales, if the number of the flipped LSBs reaches to 4, the 4 MSBs of the pixels in a block are keep unaltered though the 4 LSBs have been changed after decrypting. At the encoder, we firstly construct an image named IM by utilizing the 4 MSBs of original image. This process is done by setting 0 to the 4 LSBs. Then, we segment IM into a number of non-overlapping blocks sized by $S \times S$ as described in the embedding phase of [10,11]. The number of the blocks (denoted by R) is computed as:

$$R = \frac{N}{S \times S},\tag{1}$$

where N denotes the amount of pixels of an image. Here, we adopt the fluctu-ation function in [11] to compute the smoothness of each block of IM. A large smoothness value indicates the weak correlation of the pixels in the block and vice verse. Actually, for a natural image, if the correlation between the adjacent pixels is high, the smoothness values constructed by the different block's MSBs should be very close or even the same. Contrarily, if greatly poor, their MSBs' values would be very different.

The smooth values of all the blocks are computed at first, then we sort them in ascending order to construct a matrix F. Divide the matrix into three areas (texture area, midst area and smooth area, as shown in Fig. 2) by referring to two thresholds T_1 and T_2:

$$T_1 = F(x)\tag{2}$$

and

$$T_2 = F(R - y)\tag{3}$$

where x and y denote the number of the blocks in the smooth area and texture area, respectively.

Denote the kth block smoothness value (computed by the fluctuation function of [11]) in IM be f_k. To sort all the smoothness values f_k. If f_k is less than T_1, the block I_k is a smooth area. Identically, if f_k is larger than T_2, we name I_k as a texture block. When f_k is between T_1 and T_2, we call I_k as midst area. Figure 2 shows the basic idea of block classification clearly.

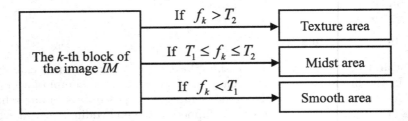

Fig. 2. The sketch of block classification.

2.2   Data Embedding Using Block Classification

At the sender, let the encrypted image be IE and we segment it using the same way as that of [10] and [11]. The k-th block of IE denoted by IE_k. In former works, the authors flip 3 LSBs for all the blocks of IE for embedding additional data, which results in high embedding distortion or large extracted-bit error rate. For better performance, we will flip 4 encrypted LSBs of half pixels in IE_k if I_k is a texture area and 3 if I_k is a midst area and 2 if I_k is a smooth area. Here, I_k denotes the kth block of the image IM. As mentioned before, f_k is the smooth value of I_k. If $f_k > T_2$, indicates I_k is a texture area and IE_k will be flipped 4 LSBs; If $T_1 \leq f_k \leq T_2$, indicates I_k is a midst area and IE_k will be flipped 3 LSBs; If $f_k < T_1$, indicates I_k is a smoothness area and IE_k will be flipped 2 LSBs. After that, the embedded fashion is done as that of [10] and [11]. Figure 3 shows the embedded procedures of the proposed method and the former works.

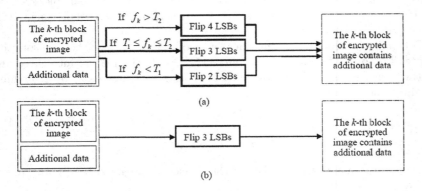

Fig. 3. The embedding sketch. (a) The proposed. (b) The former works.

Fig. 4. Eight example images. (a) Lena. (b) Baboon. (c) Sailboat. (d) Splash. (e) House. (f) Darkhair. (g) Cameraman. (h) Pirate.

In 8-bit image, 2 LSBs denote 4 gray scales and 4 LSBs denote 16 gray scales. In this work, the relation of x and y is

$$y = x/4. \tag{4}$$

That is to say, the number of the blocks in the smooth area is 4 times of that in the texture area. This is beneficial to comparing with the former two works [10,11] for the same PSNR value.

In addition, x and y vary with the block size S. The smaller S is, the fewer available pixels can be used by the fluctuation function, and that would result in bigger randomness at extraction or restoration phases. For ensuring the correctness rate of extracted-bit, the proportion of the blocks flipped 2 LSBs should be lower. However, when S is larger, the correctness rate will not decrease even the proportion of the blocks flipped 2 LSBs are higher since the fluctuation function has a nice robustness when the available pixels included in a block are plenty.

When the block size $S = 8$, extensive testing shows that a satisfactory performance can be got with $x = \lfloor \frac{R}{16} \rfloor$ and $y = \lfloor \frac{R}{64} \rfloor - 1$. When S increases to S_k, x and y change to x_k and y_k correspondingly. The relation of x and S can be defined as

$$x_k = \frac{S_k}{S_0} \cdot x_0 \tag{5}$$

Then, according to (4), the relation of y and S can be:

$$y_k = \frac{x_k}{4} = \frac{S_k}{4S_0} \cdot x_0 = \frac{S_k}{S_0} \cdot y_0 \tag{6}$$

We can see from (5) and (6) that when the block size is fixed, we can find out the corresponding x and y values for a satisfactory performance.

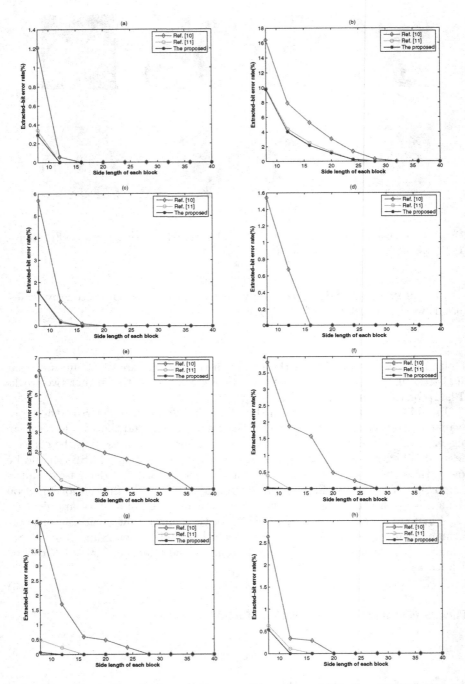

Fig. 5. The error rate comparison. (a) Lena. (b) Baboon. (c) Sailboat. (d) Splash. (e) House. (f) Darkhair. (g) Cameraman. (h) Pirate.

2.3   Data-Extraction/Image-Recovery Using Block Classification

At the receiver, we firstly decrypted the received image according to the encryption key. Because of the maximal number of the flipped LSBs is 4, the 4 MSBs will be not changed after decrypting when an image represented by 8 bits. Let the decrypted image be ID. For the blind extraction, we use the 4 MSBs of ID to reconstruct the image IM and then segment it in the same way used in the encoder. By computing the smoothness values, we can get f_k. According to the magnitude of f_k, we can know the number of flipped-bits in the k-th block. If $f_k > T_2$, indicating the k-th block should have been flipped 4 LSBs; If $T_1 \le f_k \le T_2$, indicating the k-th block should have been flipped 3 LSBs; If $f_k < T_1$, indicating the k-th block should have been flipped 2 LSBs. The rest extraction procedure is the same as that of [11]. As a result, the data can be extracted and the original can be restored.

3   Experimental Results and Analysis

In experiment, we used several standard grayscale images of size 512×512 as the test images. To compare with the former methods, we show the test results of all methods using the same four classic pictures (Lena, Baboon, Sailboat, Splash). Meanwhile, to prove the superiority of the proposed algorithm, we use another four images (House, Darkhair, Cameraman, Pirate) for performance comparison. The eight images, which are shown in Fig. 4, could be obtained from USC-SIPI [12] and ImageProcessingPlace [13] database.

Figure 5 plots the block size S versus the extraction error rate of [10,11] and the proposed method. It shows that the proposed method offers lower error rates than that of [11], not to mention that of [10]. For instance, for the Lena image at block size 8×8, the error rate of [11] is 0.34 %, but the error rate of the proposed method is 0.29 %, which offers a 1.17 times lower error rate than that of [11]. For the Sailboat image, when block size is 12×12, the error rate of the proposed method is 1.35 times lower than that of [11]. For the Splash image, the error rates of the proposed method are always 0, which are the same as that of [11]. For the Darkhair and Cameraman images at block size 8×8, the improvements of the proposed method are the most significant. We can see the error rates of [11] are respectively 0.39 % and 0.49 %, but the error rates of the proposed method are separately only 0.024 % and 0.073 %, which decreases the error rate by 93.85 % and 85.1 % compared with that of [11].

Figure 6 shows the PSNR comparison with the image *Lena*. According to [10], we know that the PSNR values of the three methods should be about 37.9 dB no matter what the value of S is. From Fig. 6, we find the PSNR value of the proposed method is always fluctuating around 37.9 dB. For other images, the results are similar.

Overall, we can see that the proposed method can provide better performance by using MSBs of a block a reference for block classification. Basic reason is that the proposed scheme has less distortion for the smooth area and higher data recovery rate for the texture area.

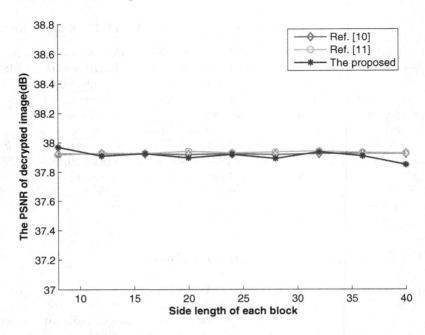

Fig. 6. The PSNR comparison with the image *Lena*.

4   Conclusions

This paper proposes a reversible data hiding for encrypted image using block classification. Noticing the MSBs of decrypted image are always not changed in [10] and [11], in this paper we compute the MSBs' value of each block, which is used as reference for embedding and blind extraction. The experimental results have proven that the performance of the proposed method is better than that of the existing two state art of works [10,11].

In our future research, to test more images with different block sizes for further optimization of the parameters used in this paper is a consideration.

Acknowledgements. This work was supported by NSFC (No. 61272414).

References

1. Tian, J.: Reversible data embedding using a difference expansion. IEEE Trans. Circuits Syst. Video Technol. **13**(8), 890–896 (2003)
2. Celik, M.U., Sharma, G., Tekalp, A.M., Saber, E.: Lossless generalized-LSB data embedding. IEEE Trans. Image Process. **14**(2), 253–266 (2005)
3. Ni, Z., Shi, Y.Q., Ansari, N., Su, W.: Reversible data hidding. IEEE Trans. Circuits Syst. Video Technol. **16**(8), 354–362 (2006)

4. Luo, L., Chen, Z., Chen, M., Zeng, X., Xiong, Z.: Reversible image watermarking using interpolation technique. IEEE Trans. Inf. Forensics Secur. **5**(1), 187–193 (2010)
5. Hong, W., Chen, T.-S., Chang, Y.-P., Shiu, C.-W.: A high capacity reversible data hiding scheme using orthogonal projection and prediction error modification. Signal Process. **90**, 2911–2922 (2010)
6. Chang, C.-C., Lin, C.-C., Chen, Y.-H.: Reversible data-embedding scheme using differences between original and predicted pixel values. IET Inf. Secur. **2**(2), 35–46 (2008)
7. Kundur, D., Karthik, K.: Video fingerprinting and encryption principles for digital rights management. Proc. IEEE **92**, 918–932 (2004)
8. Lian, S., Liu, Z., Ren, Z., Wang, H.: Commutative encryption and watermarking in video compression. IEEE Trans. Circuits Syst. Video Technol. **17**(6), 774–778 (2007)
9. Cancellaro, M., Battisti, F., Carli, M., Boato, G., Natale, B., Neri, A.: A commutative digital image watermarking and encryption method in the tree structured haar transform domain. Signal Process. Image Commun. **26**(1), 1–12 (2011)
10. Zhang, X.: Reversible data hiding in encrypted image. IEEE Signal Process. Lett. **18**(4), 255–258 (2011)
11. Hong, W., Chen, T.-S., Wu, H.-Y.: An improved reversible data hiding in encrypted images using side match. IEEE Signal Process. Lett. **19**(4), 199–202 (2012)
12. Image database. http://sipi.usc.edu/database/
13. Image database. http://www.imageprocessingplace.com/root_files_V3/image_databases.htm

Definition of Private Information for Image Sharing in Social Networking Services

Erwan Chaussy[1]([✉]), Shimon Machida[2], Noboru Sonehara[2,3],
and Isao Echizen[2,3]

[1] Polytech Paris-Sud at University of Paris-Sud, Orsay, France
erwan.chaussy@u-psud.fr
[2] The Graduate University for Advanced Studies, Hayama, Japan
shmachid@gmail.com
[3] National Institute of Informatics, Tokyo, Japan
{sonehara,iechizen}@nii.ac.jp

Abstract. With the increasing use of online image sharing and social networks, such as Facebook or Instagram, people share more and more personal information and privacy issues can arise. Such issues are already occurring and people are becoming aware of it. Helping them managing their privacy and improving privacy awareness has become essential. Recent studies have gathered testimonies of regrets and users' concerns or created access control systems that help the users to manage their privacy. However, there is no guidelines to define privacy-sensitive information contained in images. In this work, we propose a classification table of private information for images in Social Networking Services as such guidelines in order to improve privacy awareness and prevent future privacy invasion. We then verify it by submitting the table to the users and asking them to rank information according to privacy level. Results reveal that people agree to it and feel the need of such classification table. Finally propose a method that uses these guidelines in order to create settings for access control.

Keywords: Privacy invasion · Photo sharing · Social Networking Services

1 Introduction

Social Networking Services (SNS), such as Facebook and Twitter, are widely used in 2014, with over 1,100 million and 255 million monthly active users on the sites respectively [1,2]. Users share a lot of information via texts or images. For example, Facebook has over 219 billion images uploaded [1]. New services appear and make image sharing even easier, such as Instagram that has 200 million monthly active users and an average of 60 million photos shared every day [3]. As using SNS has become common, privacy invasion issues have appeared. For example, a holiday picture taken few years before and posted on an SNS led a teacher to lose her job in 2011 [4]. A more recent example proved that an image

© Springer International Publishing Switzerland 2015
Y.-Q. Shi et al. (Eds.): IWDW 2014, LNCS 9023, pp. 544–556, 2015.
DOI: 10.1007/978-3-319-19321-2_42

shared with friends can spread easily on the Internet and lead to problems [5]. These examples of SNS users losing their jobs indicate that privacy awareness is important.

According to research by Ahern et al. [6], users share images online following specific privacy patterns. This proves that users are concerned when posting on SNS. But users often inadvertently leak their own private information only to realize and regret it later [7]. It is important to realize that these kinds of posts can stay online for a long time so users need to be careful. SNS provide access control mechanisms to make posts readable for certain audiences, e.g. "Everyone" or "Friends", in order to prevent privacy-related problems. Strater et al. [8] have shown that users apply these mechanisms but it is often an "One time event" or an "All or nothing strategy", i.e. users do not update their settings when the SNS evolve, which can create problems later. One strategy used to prevent issues is self-censorship [9]. Users restrain themselves from sharing for various reasons, e.g. identity management and avoidance of discussion or offend. They have difficulties targeting the right audience in SNS, making it easier not to post. In order to satisfy the users' need for privacy, information analysis is needed to help them manage access control rules.

To prevent privacy invasion due to images, we need guidelines to classify information which they contain. Using previous surveys [6,7,10], we define a privacy invasion classification table for image sharing in SNS. To prove that this classification is needed and correct, we asked users what they think about it by ranking the different pieces of information contained in the table. This gave us the opportunity to refine the table according to the users concerns. We also asked some feedback and testimonies to have a better insight of what is privacy according to the users. Finally we propose a method for setting access control using the classification table of privacy invasion for images in SNS.

The remaining of this paper is organized as follow. First, we introduce related work in Sect. 2. Then we present the privacy invasion table in Sect. 3. Section 4 reports the results of the user study. We propose in Sect. 5 a method to set access control that uses the privacy invasion table. Finally, Sect. 6 concludes the paper and outlines future work.

2   Related Work

Users are privacy-aware when they share images online [6,10]. The content is important when posting, for example pictures of persons or locations tend to be more private on Flickr [6]. Henne et al. [10] revealed that users are concerned about online images of themselves they did not post. It emphasizes the idea that the content is important and location or identification of individuals are a problem when strangers can access the image. SNS users have regrets when posting [7] and these posts give insight about what should be kept private.

These research shows what users consider as privacy-sensitive information and systems to manage their privacy exist. On Facebook, to help users deal with images of themselves shared by others, Besmer et al. [11] proposed a way to restrict access to tagged images. The problem is that the image is already online and it only restricts the access. On Flickr, a system using user-defined tags makes access control easier for the user [12]. The user needs to define rules for every friends he/she has, which becomes burdensome when the number of friends is high, e.g. 130 friends on average on Facebook [1]. The Adaptive Privacy Policy Prediction system [13] was developed to help users to set up access control according to previous settings. After a learning phase, the system adapts the settings to the content, making it easier to share to the right audience. For the content analysis of images, the system classifies it using only 5 general classes where a more fine grained classification is needed. Furthermore, it only adapts to what the user has decided and does not make him/her more privacy-aware. Last but not least, PicAlert! [14] is better for privacy-awareness. It gives a privacy score to the image submitted, making people aware of what they are sharing. The system used crowd sourcing as a learning phase, which reflects what users think is private or not. But here is the problem, it only considers the users' point of view and does not bring new thought to the users. Finally, a privacy invasion table already exist [15], but it only focuses on texts. The content of the image is also important when one try to infer privacy settings [13], therefore a fine grained classification of privacy-sensitive information for images is required.

3   Definition of the Privacy Invasion Table

3.1   Construction of the Table

The classification used in this work is similar to the one used by Machida et al. [15]. It is composed of 2 axes, with the information that should be kept private in 3 main categories along the vertical axis and the degree of importance of the information along the horizontal axis. We restricted the categories on the vertical axis to the ones that emerge as the most likely in SNS. These categories are described later. The disclosure level along the horizontal axis represents the importance of information that should be kept private, as mentioned before. This was chosen considering the interaction in SNS where the purpose is to share information with an audience. Therefore, we want to restrict the people that can see the information to the intended ones. We thus define a privacy invasion classification table for images according to the information that should be kept private and its importance.

3.2   Disclosure Range Expressing the Level of Importance

We first describe the horizontal axis which is the disclosure range of posts given the importance of the content included in it. One uses SNS to share information with an audience. When posting privacy-sensitive information, unintended users may see it. Thus, the idea is to restrict the disclosure of the content to prevent the leak of private information using access control mechanisms. Gala et al. [17] have researched about ego network in online social networks and the classification of friends to create access control within SNS. An ego network is a network centered on a specific user in social network analysis. For instance, the friends list on Facebook can be seen as an ego network centered on the user himself. They have applied Dunbar's circle [16] to online ego network, and used the frequency of contact to determine the strength and weakness of ties with friends within the SNS network. In addition, they have shown that their classification in four circles derived from tie strengths and weaknesses is similar to the real-world classification. Dunbar's circles represent the social capacities of individual according to cognitive sciences. The maximum number of people someone can maintain stable relationship with is on average 150 people. This means that users with more than 150 friends on Facebook have very weak ties in their ego network, which increases the risk of privacy leaks. We define disclosure levels based on the frequency of contact within SNS as access control in accordance with the degree of importance of information that should be kept private. The disclosure levels for ego network in online social networks are shown in Table 1.

The recipients of Disclosure Level 1, which is the strictest level, are "family" and "close friends", where close friends are between 1 and 5 persons that the user communicate with at least once a week. Recipients of Disclosure Level 2 are people with whom the user communicates at least once a month, which is between 6 and 15. Disclosure Level 3 refers to "more than acquaintances but less than friends" that are people who the user communicate with at least once every 6 months. This number of people is between 16 and 50. Then the Disclosure Level 4 is for "acquaintances". This is used for content that does not contain private information. It includes between 51 and 150 people but it is not used in our classification table. Finally, Disclosure Level 5 includes all other people that the user do not necessarily communicates with or has not heard of for years. Note that disclosure levels include intended recipient from the previous levels. The classification always uses the strictest disclosure level for every piece of information.

Table 1. Disclosure levels in SNS ego network within an online social network

Disclosure level	Intended recipients	Number of persons	Frequency of contact
1	Family and close friends	1 to 5	At least once a week
2	Friends	6 to 15	At least once a month
3	More than acquaintances but less than friends	16 to 50	At least once every six months
4	Acquaintances	51 to 150	At least once a year
5	Other people	151 or more	Less than once a year

3.3   Detail of the Information that Should Be Kept Private

When considering the information that should be kept private, we review events where SNS users expressed regrets after posting on social networking sites. Wang et al. [7] exposed that users tend to inadvertently leak their own private information when posting in a "hot" state of emotion or under the influence of alcohol and regret it later. From previous research [6, 7, 10], we extract the contents of posts that users are concerns about and group them as in Table 2.

The location is important because it allows someone to track the individual's whereabouts. An example of issue arising from that is burglary [18]. Considering the different behavior a user can have reflects the identity management concern that arise when using SNS [11, 19]. The criminal actions are also related to this topic aside from the legal issue. We added the sensitive photography category to capture images that are not always considered in studies but that can be exposed. As mentioned earlier, images online stay for a really long time and users' sharing preferences evolve [20]. Thus, it is important to make users aware of that. Identification of individuals appears in the classification because of the over exposure to face detection systems. This technology is already used in some SNS, like on Facebook, and security agencies want to use it too [21]. Being aware of potential misuse of one's face is essential.

3.4   Privacy Invasion Classification Table

The two axis have been presented and we now can combine the informations to create the privacy invasion classification table. Table 3 combine what we have presented just above to create the guidelines to prevent privacy issues when sharing images online.

Table 2. Groups of information to be ranked

Main group of information	Detail of information contained in the group
Information relating to social activities	Regular activity or destination
	Photographs that indicate an individual's travel location
	Aberrant behavior
	Day-to-day behavior
	Criminal action (severe)
	Criminal action (light to moderate)
Information relating to identification of individuals	Photographs that can identify the user
	Photographs that can identify relatives
	Photographs that can identify friends
	Sensitive photographs (Highly exposed body)

Table 3. Privacy invasion table for images in SNS according to information that should be kept private

Classification according to the information that should be kept private	Access control according to the degree of importance of information	Disclosure level 1 — Family and close friends (1-5 persons), communication at least once a week	Disclosure level 2 — Friends (6-15 persons), communication at least once a month	Disclosure level 3 — More than aquaintances but less than friends (16-50 persons), communication at least once every 6 months
Information relating to social activities	Location			Photographs that indicate an individual's location
	Behavior	Aberrant behavior		Day-to-day behavior
	Criminal and unlawful action	Criminal action (severe)	Criminal action (light-to-moderate)	
Information relating to identification of persons	Identification of individual		Photographs that can identify the user	
	Identification of social circles	Photographs that can identify relatives		Photographs that can identify friends
Sensitive photographs	Sensitive photographs	Nude, lustful or highly exposed body photographs		

4   Verification of the Privacy Invasion Table

In order to verify our privacy invasion classification table for images we conducted an online survey to have the users' point of view on the information presented in the table. We also used this survey to ask for testimonies about privacy invasion experience, and comments on the classification table to have a better insight of what users think about privacy. This section presents the procedure used for the survey and the results.

4.1   Study Method

We created the survey using SurveyMonkey[1] and posted it on Facebook. Using an SNS as a recruiting system will select participants that know about these systems.

Procedure. The survey consists on 2 ranking questions and 2 comment questions. We divided the categories of privacy-sensitive information in 2 main groups, one containing information relating to the user's activities and one about identification of individuals. Participants were asked to rank pieces of information from the most private to the least one. Two distinct items could not have the same rank. Groups of information are visible in Table 2. Example of images were provided, along with explanation of some categories. We then asked participants to remember an event where they felt their privacy invaded and describe it. The second comment was about what participants thought about the privacy table itself.

Participants. As explained earlier, we published the survey on Facebook. 20 participants answered. The demographics information are as follow:

- Gender
  - 13 Males (65.0 %)
  - 7 Females (35.0 %)
- Age group
  - 16 between 20 and 29
  - 3 between 30 and 39
  - 1 between 40 and 49
- Frequency of use of SNS
  - 19 use SNS Everyday
  - 1 use SNS At least once a week
- Purpose of use of SNS
  - 90.0 % for communication with friends
  - 40.0 % for communication with family
  - 35.0 % for communication with people (not necessarily friends)
  - 30.0 % for other purposes

The participants being mostly in a young age group, the results might not reflect properly older SNS users. We might have introduced bias by having participant to whom English is not their mother tongue. We provided as much information and example to make the classification more explicit and ranking item needs visual content more than explanation.

4.2   Result

We used the data collected from the ranking method to convert ranks into scale values [22]. This allowed us to order the pieces of information according to users. We then applied an one tail t-test between following ranks to know if they

---

[1] http://www.surveymonkey.com.

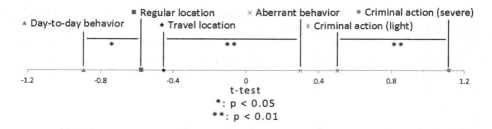

Fig. 1. Ordering of scale values for information relating to social activities

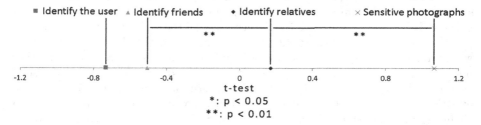

Fig. 2. Ordering of scale values for information relating to identification of persons

are significantly different. This confirms or not separation between pieces of information in distinct disclosure level. Figures 1 and 2 sum up the results. Every pieces of information are placed on a scale according to their mean rank, the least important information being on the left of the scale and the most important one on the right. The differences between the groups revealed by the t-test are illustrated.

With these results we updated the privacy invasion table by moving pieces of information between disclosure levels, which led to Table 3 presented earlier. The ranks of information about location are not significantly different, $t(38) = 0.57$, $p < 0.05$, we therefore decided to merge them together. We first separated these pieces of information to reflect the users' concerns found by Ahern et al. [6] but this difference did not appear in our work. We kept photographs that can identify the user and friends separated from photographs that can identify relatives to reflect the difference between theses pieces of information, $t(38) = 4.28$, $p < 0.01$. Identification of relatives remained in disclosure level 1 because it seems more logical to share information about them only with one's family, despite the significant difference between sensitive photographs and identification of relatives, $t(38) = 6.94$, $p < 0.01$. The other results confirmed the placement of the pieces of information in the appropriate disclosure level.

When calculating the Cohen's d effect size [23] for every t-test, we were able to calculate the minimal sample size needed for each of them. We found that the distinction between 2 pieces of information can either need a small sample size or a big one. For example, the minimal sample size to compare criminal actions is 11 ($d = 1.14$). On the contrary, in order to differentiate individual's travel location from regular destination a minimum sample size of 367 ($d = 0.19$) is needed. Overall, the number of participants being rather small is not a problem since the main pieces of information were separated with an effect size greater than 1. The other pieces of information were manipulated by merging them together which make the comparison disappear and avoid the problem of a huge minimal sample size.

Testimonies and Comments. 16 Participants answered the open questions. This number being small, no relevant conclusion can be extracted but it reflects a few tendencies. First, comments about the privacy invasion classification table showed that users want these kinds of guidelines to help them manage their privacy. We can then conclude that access control tools and research to improve privacy are needed. The most interesting comment about the table was a user wondering how to manage the shift of a friend from one disclosure level to another one. This echoes with information aging on SNS and the need to control disclosure of old posts more easily [20]. Then, testimonies about privacy invasion experiences confirmed that users are concerned when people share pictures of them, as previous research has shown [11]. SNS users want better control on image of oneself shared by someone else.

5   Proposed Method for Setting Access Control

5.1   Access Control Available on SNS

As of June 2014, Facebook provides "Public" (i.e., "Everyone"), "Friends", "Only Me", "Specific group created on the SNS side", "User-customizable group" and "Custom" (i.e., restriction to specific friends or list) as access control mechanism. On Twitter or Instagram, accounts can be public or private, forcing acceptance by the users for people requesting access to their posts. Strater et al. [8] underlined that users tend to set access control mechanism once and do not change the settings later. Therefore, even if they restrict posts to "Friends", it still includes weak ties as there is different social circles merged together [24]. On Facebook, it is possible to define access control for each post but this become burdensome and targeting the right audience is harder than not posting [9]. We then propose a system that evaluates the content of a post according to the privacy invasion classification table described in Sect. 3 and notifies the user of potential leaks of privacy-sensitive information and recommends a privacy policy.

5.2   Previously Proposed Systems

Squicciarini et al. [13] proposed a method to predict and provide access control settings for a new post according to the content of the post and previous settings the user has chosen. However, the presented privacy policy is based on groups provided by the SNS which includes weak-tie friends. Another system, closer to what we propose, as been presented by Machida et al. [15]. It evaluates the content posted according to privacy guidelines they created and proposes access control policy to the user who can review it before posting. Unfortunately, the system only analyzes texts and as mentioned previously, the content of the image is also important.

5.3 System Presentation

The system we propose is utilized before posting content on an SNS. It determines if private information is contained in an image and if so, it proposes a disclosure policy to the user according to frequency of contact and the importance of the information that should be kept private. The user can modify this policy to include or exclude intended recipients for this specific content before posting to the SNS. This revision will be considered for further access control suggestions. It allows SNS users to share more easily by helping them managing their access control, avoiding unintended users to see privacy-sensitive information.

Analysis of the Method. Figure 3 present the process flow of our method. It is composed of 3 main processes which are private information detection, access control derivation and policy notification. We describe these processes below.

Step 1: Detection of private information disclosure.
> The system analyses the submitted content in order to detect privacy-sensitive information. It applies the classification of the privacy invasion table described in Sect. 3, but the policy analysis follows different steps. It first tries to detect faces in the photo. Then it uses more advance image analysis to infer its content, such as behavior or sensitive photographs, to classify it more accurately. If private information is detected, the system proposes a disclosure level in accordance to the privacy invasion table.

Step 2: Derivation of access control.
> The system calculates the distances by frequency of contact with friends in the online ego network centered on the user. It then decides on the intended recipients for the post according to the disclosure level decided on Step 1. During this step, the system considers revision of information from previous posts and includes or excludes recipients. This is done to considerate strong friendship ties but low frequency of contact between the 2 users.

Step 3: Policy notification.
> The system notifies the user of potential leak of privacy-sensitive information and presents the suggested access control policy. The SNS user can decide to post or not, and if the user decides to do so, the privacy policy can be adjusted. Revisions are stored in access control suggestions for future posts.

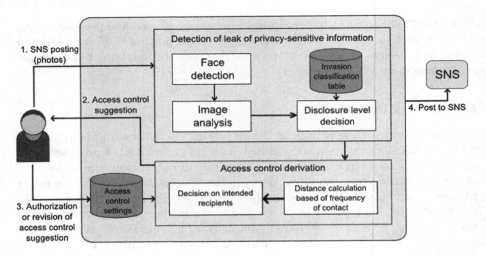

Fig. 3. Process flow of the system

5.4 Limitations

Image analysis while powerful cannot be used completely automatically. For example, face detection is used in many systems and is easy to implement, but it can detect people in the background. Suggesting to blur faces selected by the user is an option that can be provided in a final system. Interpretation of the semantic of the image, such as criminal action or aberrant behavior, is complicated and a work in progress. This means that for an effective implementation of the system, crowd sourcing might be needed while machine learning is not effective enough. The human interpretation is better than the computer's one but not all images can be reviewed by a human given the quantity of shared images. Detecting certain information can help narrow the amount of images to be reviewed. In other words, the actual technical abilities limit the effectiveness of such system but the guidelines are still relevant and can be used in the future. The solution is to combine image analysis with text analysis as Machida et al. [15] did.

6 Conclusion and Future Work

In this work, we defined guidelines to classify private information contained in images. By gathering users' concerns, we provide a new way to look at privacy issues in SNS. We verified that this classification reflects users' concern of privacy and updated our work according to their answers. Results showed that SNS users feel the need of such guidelines and agree to what we introduced. Finally, we proposed a method for setting access control by detecting leak of private information in images using the classification table for privacy invasion. In future work, we plan to implement the access control system introduced by the proposed method and present it to users. In this way, we can gather statistical results and proof of effectiveness of our method. This will also allow us to compare different methods such as watermark based access control to improve privacy protection for users. We will be able to improve the classification table and add new categories to help users to manage their privacy online.

References

1. Facebook Inside. http://www.insidefacebook.com/2014/01/16/infographic-10-years-of-facebook/
2. Twitter Statistics. https://about.twitter.com/company
3. Instagram. http://instagram.com/press/
4. Teacher sacked for posting picture of herself holding glass of wine and mug of beer on Facebook (2011). http://www.dailymail.co.uk/news/article-1354515/Teacher-sacked-posting-picture-holding-glass-wine-mug-beer-Facebook.html
5. KFC Mashed Potatoes Photo: Woman Fired for Sharing Image of Licking Food (2013). http://www.huffingtonpost.com/2013/02/20/kfc-mashed-potatoes-photo-licking_n_2726022.html
6. Ahern, S., Eckles, D., Good, N., King, S., Naaman, M., Nair, R.: Over-exposed? privacy patterns and considerations in online and mobile photo sharing. In: Proceedings of the SIGCHI Conference on Human Factors in Computing Systems, CHI 2007, pp. 357–366 (2007)
7. Wang, Y., Norcie, G., Komanduri, S., Acquisti, A., Leon, P., Cranor, L.F.: "I regretted the minute I pressed share": a qualitative study of regrets on facebook. In: Proceedings of the 7th Symposium on Usable Privacy and Security, SOUPS 2011, article n° 10 (2011)
8. Strater, K., Lipford, H.R.: Strategies and struggles with privacy in an oline social networking community. In: Proceedings of the 22nd British HCI Group Annual Conference on People and Computers: Culture, Creativity, Interaction, BCS-HCI 2008, vol. 1, pp. 111–119 (2008)
9. Sleeper, M., Balebako, R., Das, S.: The post that wasnt: exploring self-censorship on facebook. In: Proceedings of the 2013 Conference on Computer Supported Cooperative Work, CSCW 2013, pp. 793–802 (2013)
10. Henne, B., Smith, M.: Awareness about photos on the web and how privacy-privacy-tradeoffs could help. In: Adams, A.A., Brenner, M., Smith, M. (eds.) FC 2013. LNCS, vol. 7862, pp. 131–148. Springer, Heidelberg (2013)
11. Besmer, A., Lipford, H.R.: Moving beyond untagging: photo privacy in a tagged world. In: Proceedings of the SIGCHI Conference on Human Factors in Computing Systems, CHI 2010, pp. 1563–157 (2010)
12. Klemperer, P.F., Liang, Y., Mazurek, M.L., Sleeper, M., Ur, B., Bauer, L., Cranos, L.F., Gupta, N., Reiter, M.: Tag, you can see it! using tags for access control in photo sharing. In: Proceedings of the SIGCHI Conference on Human Factors in Computing Systems, CHI 2012, pp. 377–386 (2012)
13. Squicciarini, A., Sundareswaran, S., Lin, D.: A3P: adaptative policy prediction for shared images over popular content sharing sites. In: Proceedings of the 22nd ACM Conference on Hypertext and Hypermedia, HT 2011, pp. 261–270 (2011)
14. Zerr, S., Siersdorfer, S., Hare, J.: PicAlert!: a system for privacy-aware image classification and retrieval. In: Proceedings of the 21st ACM International Conference of Information and Knowledge Management, CIKM 2012, pp. 2710–2712 (2012)

15. Machida, S., Shimada, S., Echizen, I.: Settings of access control by detecting privacy leaks in SNS. In: International Conference of Signal-Image Technologies and Internet-Based Systems (SITIS), pp. 660–666. IEEE Press (2013)

16. Dunbar, R.I.M.: The social brain hypothesis. Evol. Anthropol. **6**(5), 178–190 (1998). Wiley-Liss, Inc

17. Gala, M., Arnaboldi, V., Passarella, A., Conti, M.: Ego-net digger: a new way to study ego networks in online social networks. In: Proceedings of the First ACM International Workshop on Hot Topics on Interdisciplinary Social Networks Research, HotSocial 2012, pp. 9–16 (2012)

18. Twitter user says vacation tweets led to burglary (2009). http://www.cnet.com/news/twitter-user-says-vacation-tweets-led-to-burglary

19. DiMicco, J.M., Millen, D.R.: Identity management: multiple presentations of self in facebook. In: Proceedings of the International ACM Conference on Supporting Group Work, GROUP 2007, pp. 383–386 (2007)

20. Ayalon, O., Toch, E.: Retrospective privacy: managing longitudinal privacy in online social networks. In: Proceedings of the Ninth Symposium on Usable Privacy and Security, SOUPS 2013, article n° 4 (2013)

21. Interpol wants facial recognition database to catch suspects (2008). http://www.theguardian.com/world/2008/oct/20/interpol-facial-recognition

22. Smith, S.M., Albaum, G.S.: Fundamentals of Marketing Research, Chap. 10. SAGE Publications Inc., Thousand Oaks (2005)

23. Thalheimer, W., Cook, S.: How to calculate effectsizes from published research articles: A simplified methodology (2002). http://work-learning.com/effect_sizes.htm. Accessed on 26 June 2014

24. Stutzman, F., Kramer-Duffield, J.: Friends only: examining a privacy-enhancing behavior in facebook. In: Proceedings of the SIGCHI Conference on Human Factors in Computing Systems, CHI 2010, pp. 1553–1562 (2010)

Steganography and Steganalysis

Variable Multi-dimensional Co-occurrence for Steganalysis

Licong Chen$^{(\boxtimes)}$, Yun-Qing Shi, and Patchara Sutthiwan

New Jersey Institute of Technology, Newark, NJ 07102, USA
{lcchen,shi,ps249}@njit.edu

Abstract. In this paper, a novel multidimensional co-occurrence histogram scheme has been presented, in which the numbers of quantization levels for the elements in the co-occurrence are variable according to the distance among the elements, referred to as the co-occurrence with variable number of quantization levels, abbreviated as the VNQL co-occurrence or variable co-occurrence. Specifically, the longer the distance the smaller the number of quantization levels used. The dimensionality of the variable co-occurrence is therefore flexible and much smaller than that used in the traditional multidimensional co-occurrence of the same orders. Furthermore, the symmetry existed in the multidimensional co-occurrence is skillfully utilized in the proposed variable co-occurrence. Consequently, the feature dimensionality has been lowered dramatically. Thus, the fourth order variable co-occurrence applied to the residuals used in the spatial rich model results in $1,704$ features, which work with a G-SVM classifier, can achieve an average detection rate similar to that of achieved by the TOP10 (dimension approximately 3,300) in the spatial rich model with a G-SVM classifier against the HUGO at 0.4 bpp on the same setup. The time consumed by the proposed $1,704$ features is much shorter that used by the latter. Furthermore, the performance achieved by the proposed $1,704$ together with a G-SVM classifier is on par with that achieved by the TOP39 with $12,753$ features and an ensemble classifier on the same setup against two steganographic schemes, the HUGO and the edge adaptive. With another proposed set of $1,977$ features, generated from the residuals used in the spatial rich model and from a few newly formulated residuals, and the G-SVM classifier, the performance achieved is better than that achieved by using the TOP39 feature-set with ensemble classifier on the same setup against the HUGO.

Keywords: Co-occurrence · High order co-occurrence · Variable co-occurrence · Steganalysis · Steganography

1 Introduction

Steganography and steganalysis are a pair of modern technologies that have been moving ahead swiftly in the last decade. The conflicting between these two sides is a driving force for the rapid development. That is, each side learns from its

© Springer International Publishing Switzerland 2015
Y.-Q. Shi et al. (Eds.): IWDW 2014, LNCS 9023, pp. 559–573, 2015.
DOI: 10.1007/978-3-319-19321-2_43

counterpart. As expected, there is no end in the competition between steganography and steganalysis just like mouse versus cat. In [1] the SPAM feature was proposed to defeat the LSB (Least Significant Bit) matching steganography. A modern adaptive steganographic scheme, named HUGO (Highly Undetectable steGO algorithm) [2], has been developed so as to fail the SPAM by using the content adaptive technology and advanced coding of Syndrome - Trellis Codes [3] on its data embedding. Hence the security of the HUGO has been significantly improvement. In the BOSS (Break Our Steganogaphic System) competition [4], two stegnalystic methods [5,6] have been reported to break HUGO, which achieved the detection rates of 76.8 % and 80.3 % on the BOSSRank [4] with 1000 images. In [6], working on the image-set of BOSSBase ver. 0.92, a complicated steganlytic model called HOMELS (Higher-Order Local Model Estimators of Steganographic changes) was proposed, which achieved an average detection rate at 83.90 % against HUGO with $T = 90$ at 0.4 bpp (bit per pixel). The ensemble classifier has been first introduced and utilized in steganalysis to handle feature dimensionality as high as $33,963$. In [7], another novel scheme inspired by the textual classification, an active research area having five decades history, was proposed and has achieved an average detection rate of 83.92 % against HUGO at 0.4 bpp, which is similar to what reported in [6] on the same experimental setup. Specifically, the LBP (local binary pattern), instead of the high order co-occurrence used in [6], was introduced in steganalysis for first time. Afterward, Fridrich and Kodovský proposed the spatial rich model (SRM) in [8], which moves the steganalysis by a big step. i.e., the detection rate has been lifted to 86.45 % against HUGO with $T = 255$ by using $12,753$ features. Here, note that HUGO with its embedding parameter $T = 255$ is a slightly more secure than $T = 90$. In [8], the fourth order co-occurrence has been utilized on five groups of different and carefully selected residuals as classification feature, and the symmetry existing in these kinds of co-occurrence are used to deduce the feature dimensionality. In [9], the mapping co-occurrence together with a procedure like Huffman coding instead of the traditional high-order co-occurrence. From seven groups of residuals which extended from those used in [8], a total number of $15,840$ features have been extracted. The average detection rate is 87.17 %, which is higher than that reported in [8] on the same setup against HUGO at 0.4 bpp. In [10], a simplified mapping function is used to replace the procedure like Huffman coding, the number of residuals is deduced so as to only $6,000$ features. It achieved the similar detection rate as compared to [9].

Take a look at the SRM, one can find that there are $1,344$ zero-valued features among the proposed $12,753$ features of the SRMQ1 (or the TOP39). Noted that these features are always zero-valued no matter from what specific image in the dataset the features are extracted. Obviously, these zeroed features are redundant and should be removed. This verified that the traditional fourth order co-occurrence exists redundant bins among the features. The PSRM is current state-of-the-art steganalysis scheme. An obvious issue with it is a very large amount of computation for convolution is needed. Consequently its execution is time consuming. For instance, it takes about 396 s in extracting the proposed

$12,870$ features on a single image of size 512×512, while the time consumed in extracting the $12,753$ SRMQ1 or TOP39 features on the otherwise same running environment is only 1.5 s. As mentioned in [11], a new algorithm on calculating the PSRM features will be presented, which is based the GPU (Graphic Process Unit). Hence in this paper, we cannot provide the experimental comparison to the PSRM because of its unbearable time consuming in feature extraction.

In recent years, it seems to be a trend that the modern steganalysis schemes are always working on a large number of features in order to achieve a good performance. All of them are using the ensemble classifier which is based on a simple classifier, i.e., Fisher Linear Discriminants (FLD).

In this paper, the new concept of variable co-occurrence, i.e., the number of quantization levels for each element in the high order co-occurrence array is variable instead of fixed is utilized. Furthermore, the symmetry existed in the high-order co-occurrence array which has been used in [8] is skillfully utilized for the variable co-occurrence. Consequently, the feature dimensionality has been dramatically reduced. Specifically, the feature dimension of each $SPAM$ sub-model is only 43, and the feature number of each $MINMAX$ sub-model is 36. Noted that the $SPAM$ and $MINMAX$ are two kinds of sub-models introduced in [8] and their dimensionalities have been lower to 169 and 325, respectively. Obviously, the dimensionality of 43 and 36 verses that of 169 and 325 indicates a large reduction in feature dimensionality. Based on the same residuals used in [8], the feature-set resulted in the proposed scheme has only $1,704$ features. As a result, the G-SVM classifier can be utilized, to achieve a similar, or even slightly better performance than that achieved by using the TOP39 with ensemble classifier on the same setups. Furthermore, another case is presented in this paper, that is, we add an additional group of residuals into the residuals used in [8], hence resulting in a set of $1,977$ features. Note that with such a feature-set, the average classification rate achieved is better than that achieved by using the TOP10[1] with a G-SVM classifier against the HUGO with embedding parameter $T = 255$.

The rest sections are organized as follows. In Sect. 2 the high-order co-occurrence for steganalysis is described. The high-order co-occurrence with variable numbers of quantization levels, i.e., the VNQL co-occurrence, is presented in Sect. 3. The VNQL co-occurrence feature-sets consisting of the 475,$1,704$ and $1,977$ features, extracted from the same set of residuals used in [8] together with some proposed additional residuals have been present in Sect. 4. Experimental works are reported in Sect. 5. Finally, the discussion and conclusion are made in Sect. 6.

2   High-Order Co-occurrence for Steganalysis

The co-occurrence matrix was proposed as textural features for image classification for the first time [12]. In [6,8], the second to sixth order co-occurrences

---

[1] TOP10 is assembled with the best 10 sub-models by using the strategy ITERATIVE-BEST-q in [8], and its dimension is approximately $3,300$.

were used in the steganalysis. The vector quantization for the high order co-occurrence used in steganalysis has shown that this scheme could not improve the capacity of the steganalysis, which was reported in [13]. Since the proposed variable co-occurrence is derived for the case where the high order co-occurrence is used, we describe the conception of variable co-occurrence according to the description of the high order co-occurrence in [14]. The kth order co-occurrence has been mathematically defined in [14], which is shown below.

2.1   Definition of kth Order Co-occurrence

Denote an $M \times N$ image by $I = I(x, y)$, $x = 0, \ldots, M - 1$, $y = 0, \ldots, N - 1$. The kth order co-occurrence, indexed by gray levels of k pixels, is computed by first taking a displacement vector associated k elements, i.e., $\Delta_1 = (\Delta_{1,x}, \Delta_{1,y}), \ldots, \Delta_k = (\Delta_{k,x}, \Delta_{k,y})$, then collecting all k-tuples of pixels with these mutual displacements from the image and forming

$$C_{\Delta_1, \ldots, \Delta_k}(g_1, \ldots, g_k) = \#\{(x, y)| \tag{1}$$
$$I(x + \Delta_{1,x}, y + \Delta_{1,y}) = g_1, \ldots, I(x + \Delta_{k,x}, y + \Delta_{k,y}) = g_k\}$$

where $\#$ denotes cardinality of a set, $g_1, \ldots, g_k$ are discrete gray levels. Here, $\Delta_{i,x}$ and $\Delta_{i,y}$, $i = 1, \ldots, k$ stand for the offset of X and Y axes of the image, respectively. In general, the $C_{\Delta_1, \ldots, \Delta_k}(g_1, \ldots, g_k)$ has G^k elements, where G is the total number of different gray levels [14]. Note that this definition of the high order co-occurrence is only a simple version, it can be easily extended to color image and any 2-dimensional array.

2.2   High-Order Co-occurrence Used in Steganalysis

In [8], a novel spatial rich model has been presented, which utilizes eight directions of first order and third order difference arrays, four directions of second order arrays, four EDGE masks and SQUARE mask of 3×3 and 5×5 on an image to generate a large number of residual images. All of residual images have been quantized, rounded and truncated to five levels: $-2, -1, 0, 1, 2$. The fourth order co-occurrence has been extracted from the residual images to form the feature-set. Noted that two kinds of the fourth order co-occurrence are used. One is along the horizontal direction with the displacement vector, i.e., $\Delta_{1h} = (0, 0)$, $\Delta_{2h} = (1, 0)$, $\Delta_{3h} = (2, 0)$, $\Delta_{4h} = (3, 0)$, the other along the vertical direction, with the displacement vector, i.e., $\Delta_{1v} = (0, 0)$, $\Delta_{2v} = (0, 1)$, $\Delta_{3v} = (0, 2)$, $\Delta_{4v} = (0, 3)$.

Residual Images. It is well known that steganography would change in some way the distribution of spatial neighboring pixel values. The features used for steganalysis are often extracted from the so-called residual images generated by applying high-pass filtering to the target images. The generation of residual images is shown in Formula (2).

$$R = Trunc_T(round(\frac{filter(X, h)}{q})) \tag{2}$$

where h is a high-pass filter, $filter(X, h)$ means image X is filtered by the filter h; followed by quantization with step q; and then rounded to integers; finally truncated with a threshold T. Here, the filter can be linear or non-linear. The purpose of working on residual image for steganalysis is to remove the image content and boost stego information for steganalysis. The filtered image is often referred to as residual image. The quantization is used to reduce the dynamic range of the residual image, thus reducing the feature dimensionality. In [8], T is set to 2. The quantization step has been set as $q = 1c$, $q = 1.5c$ and $q = 2c$, where c is the value of the center pixel of the filter h.

Feature-Set Generated in Spatial Rich Models. Here, we briefly describe all of five categories of residual images used in [8], which are also used in this work for the performance comparison. They are denoted by R_{1st}, R_{2nd}, R_{3rd}, $R_{3\times3}$ and $R_{5\times5}$, respectively. The R_{1st} and R_{3rd} residual images are generated by applying Formula (2).with eight directions of the first order and third order difference arrays as filters. The R_{2nd} residual images are created by Formula (2) with four directions of the second order difference arrays as filter. The $R_{3\times3}$ and $R_{5\times5}$ are generated by Formula (2) by using 3×3 and 5×5 masks that includes one SQUARE mask and the corresponding four EDGE masks, respectively. The 3×3 and 5×5 SQUARE masks are shown in Fig. 1, respectively. The EDGE mask is similar to the SQUARE mask, but a part of elements has been set to zero. For the detail, readers are referred to Sect. II-B of [8]. Noted that in this paper, we don't merger two $SPAM$ features into one sub-model. that is why we have 45 sub-models in the proposed scheme, but the SRM includes 39 sub-models in [8].

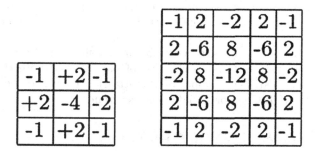

Fig. 1. 3×3 and 5×5 SQUARE mask

Based on the R_{1st} and R_{3rd} residual images, the following 12 kinds of feature subsets can be generated. They are $SPAM14h$, $SPAM14v$, $MM22h$, $MM22v$, $MM24$, $MM34$, $MM34h$, $MM34v$, $MM41$, $MM48h$, $MM48v$ and $MM54$. Based on the R_{2nd} residual images, the following seven kinds of feature subsets can be generated. They are $SPAM12h$, $SPAM12v$, $MM21$, $MM32$, $MM24h$, $MM24v$ and $MM41$. Based on the $R_{3\times3}$ and $R_{5\times5}$ residual images, another group of seven feature subsets can be extracted, It contains $SPAM11$, $SPAM14h$, $SPAM14v$, $MM24$, $MM22h$, $MM22v$ and $MM41$.

In [8], the whole feature-set can be classified into two different types, i.e., *type SPAM* feature subset that are similar to the SPAM feature vector in [1] and *type MM* feature subset. There are 45 feature subsets in total that included 12 *type SPAM* feature subsets and 33 *type MM* feature subsets. According to the symmetry of the high order co-occurrence used, the dimensionality of a single *type SPAM* feature-set has been lowered from 625 to 169 dimensions, and each pair of minimum and maximum feature subsets, generated by the pair of corresponding minimum and maximum residual images, have been reduced from 2×625 to 325, so the dimensionalities of *type SPAM* and *type MM* are of 169 and 325, respectively. As there are three quantization steps, i.e., $q = 1c$, $q = 1.5c$, $q = 2c$ for each residual image [8], except that the first order residual images that have only two versions, i.e., $q = 1c$, $q = 2c$. So there are three versions for each single feature except that the first order features have only two versions of features. So the dimensionality of the whole feature-set reaches $34,671$. The TOP39 feature-set, which use one kind quantization step among the steps of $q = 1c, 1.5c, 2c$ for every sub-model, has $12,753$ features.

3   High Order VNQL Co-occurrence

It is well known that the closer the distance between two elements (in our case, pixels of residual images), the higher the correlation between the two elements. Hence, it makes sense for us to give the different numbers of quantization levels to the elements whose co-occurrence is under consideration according to the distance between the elements. When the distance between elements under consideration becomes large we use a smaller number of quantization level. Vice versa, if two elements are close to each other, we use a larger number of quantization levels.

This new concept of co-occurrence with variable number of quantization levels is described in this section. In the rest of paper, we denote this new type of co-occurrence as Variable Number of Quantization Levels co-occurrence, and abbreviated as VNQL-Cooc or variable co-occurrence.

3.1   Representation of VNQL Co-occurrence

Here we describe a scheme to represent the VNQL-Cooc, which will be utilized late in this paper. The displacement vector of the VNQL-Cooc is defined as $(\Delta_{1,x}, \Delta_{1,y}), \ldots, (\Delta_{k,x}, \Delta_{k,y})$. L is a set of values that $I(x, y)$ can assume. For each coordinate (x, y) of an image (or a residual) $I = I(x, y)$, the corresponding k elements are represented as $I_{(x+\Delta_{1,x}, y+\Delta_{1,y})}, \ldots, I_{(x+\Delta_{k,x}, y+\Delta_{k,y})}$. We can construct k mapping functions f_i $(i = 1, \ldots, k)$ as shown in Formula (3).

$$f_i(I(x + \Delta_{i,x}, y + \Delta_{i,y})) = d_i, d_i \in 0, \ldots, M_i - 1 \tag{3}$$

where $i = 1, \ldots, k$, and $M_1, \ldots, M_k$ are positive integer numbers. Formula (3) has shown that the element $I(x + \Delta_{i,x}, y + \Delta_{i,y})$, $i = 1, \ldots, k$ can be mapped from L to $\{0, \ldots, M_i - 1\}$, where $i = 1, \ldots, k$. The functions $\{f_i\}$, $i = 1, \ldots, k$ can be defined according to the actual needs in different scenarios. A simple scheme to construct these k mapping functions is described in the next section.

Note that d_i $(i = 1, \ldots, k)$ is a number like 0 to 9 for the decimal number. These k numbers can form a special k-digit number, denotes as $(d_k d_{k-1} \ldots d_1)$, just like three digits 3, 6 and 0 can form a decimal number 360. As d_i is an integer from 0 to M_i, $i = 1, \ldots, k$, generally, $M_i \neq M_j$, when $i \neq j$. The number represented by $(d_k d_{k-1} \ldots d_1)$ has different weights in the k-digit positions. This special number can be converted to a decimal number according to Lemma 1.

Lemma 1. A k-digit number $(d_k d_{k-1} \ldots d_1)$, where d_i is an integer number from 0 to $M_i - 1$ and M_i is a positive integer, can be converted to a decimal number, d, by using the Formula (4), and the decimal number d ranges from 0 to $M - 1$ with $M = M_1 \times M_2 \ldots \times M_k$.

$$(d_k d_{k-1} \ldots d_1) = d_1 + M_1 \times d_2 + \ldots + M_1 \times M_2 \times \ldots \times M_{k-1} \times d_k \quad (4)$$

For $(d_k d_{k-1} \ldots d_1)$, the weight of d_1 is 1, the weight of d_2 is $M_1, \ldots$, the weight of d_k is $M_1 \times M_2 \times \ldots \times M_{k-1}$. So the k-digit special number can be calculated according to Formula (4).

In this way, there is a number $(d_k d_{k-1} \ldots d_1)$ formed by the above defined way for each coordinate (x, y) of the image $I(x, y)$. So we could denote the k-digit special number as $d(x, y)$ for the coordinate (x, y). Of course, all of these $d(x, y)$ formed a matrix $D = d(x, y)$. In fact, we can consider the process as a function F, this function F maps a target image to a matrix, It can be mathematically denoted as $F(I) = D$.

We calculate the histogram of D as the VNQL co-occurrence. Note that the range of $d(x, y)$ of D is from 0 to $M - 1$, here $M = M_1 \times M_2 \times \ldots \times M_k$. In this sense the VNQL co-occurrence becomes a one-dimensionality vector. Obviously, the dimensionality of the kth order VNQL co-occurrence is M. We denoted the kth order VNQL co-occurrence as VNQL-Cooc$_{(M_1, \ldots, M_k)}$.

3.2   Mapping Function Used in VNQL-Cooc

As discussed in Sect. 3.1, for the kth order VNQL co-occurrence, the k mapping functions should be defined first. In [8], all of residual images have been quantized to five levels from -2 to 2 with step 1. In this paper, we have adopted the fourth order VNQL co-occurrence. So we also have $k = 4$, and the four mapping functions f_1, f_2, f_3 and f_4 have been defined as follows.

1. f_1 and f_2: five levels $-2, -1, 0, 1, 2$ are mapped to $0, 1, 2, 3, 4$, respectively.
2. f_3: $\{-2, 2\}$, -1, 0, 1 are mapped to $0, 1, 2, 3$, respectively.
3. f_4: $\{-2, -1\}$, 0, $\{1, 2\}$ are mapped to $0, 1, 2$, respectively.

where $\{-2,2\}$ means the levels -2 and 2 are merged as one, the $\{-2,-1\}$ and $\{1,2\}$ have the same meaning. As mentioned in Sect. 3.1, we denote the above defined VNQL co-occurrence as VNQL-Cooc$_{(5,5,4,3)}$. Obviously, the dimensionality of the VNQL-Cooc$_{(5,5,4,3)}$ is 300. If we replace the above-mentioned f_4 with the f_{4a}, which maps $\{-2,-1\}$, $\{0,1,2\}$ to 0, 1, respectively, then we have the following four mapping functions $\{f_1, f_2, f_3, f_{4a}\}$, we can then have another VNQL co-occurrence, i.e., VNQL-Cooc$_{(5,5,4,2)}$, its dimensionality reduces to 200.

In this paper, we extracted the VNQL-Cooc$_{(5,5,4,3)}$ from the *type SPAM* residual images, and extracted the VNQL-Cooc$_{(5,5,4,2)}$ from the *type MM* residual images (minimal and maximal residual images). That is, we use the different mapping functions in the VNQL co-occurrence for the different kinds of residual images. Our aim is to reduce the dimensionality of the entire VNQL co-occurrence feature-set as many as possible while keeping the high performance.

To further reduce the dimensionality of the VNQL-Cooc feature-set, we replace the above mapping function f_4 with f_{4b}. The mapping function f_{4b} maps $\{-2,-1,0,1,2\}$ to 0. In the case of mapping functions $\{f_1, f_3, f_3, f_{4a}\}$ and $\{f_1, f_3, f_3, f_{4b}\}$, we can achieve VNQL-Cooc$_{(5,4,4,2)}$ and VNQL-Cooc$_{(5,4,4,1)}$, respectively.

4   VNQL-Cooc for Steganalysis

As said in the previous sections, we work on the same set of residual images that have been developed and utilized by Fridrich et al. in [8] in order to have a fair performance comparison so as to demonstrate the advantage possessed by the proposed scheme. We mainly replace the conventional high-order co-occurrence with the VNQL co-occurrence in this work. Now we describe the setting of VNQL co-occurrence used for the steganalysis.

4.1   Feature-Set Generation

In [8], the whole feature-set with 34,671 features are generated from residual images with all of three different kinds of quantization steps, and the TOP39 feature-set with 12,753 features are extracted from residual images with only one kind of quantization step. In this article, to reduce feature dimensionality, we only use R_{1st} residual images with quantization step $q = 1c$, $c = 1$, and R_{2nd}, R_{3rd}, $R_{3\times3}$ and $R_{5\times5}$ with quantization step $q = 2c$, where the meaning of c has been mentioned in Sect. 2.2. These five categories of residual images, used in [8], have been introduced in Sect. 2.2. We apply the proposed VNQL co-occurrence on these residual images to generate the new feature-set, here we denote the new feature-set as VNQL-Cooc$_{45subset}$, the subscript '45*subset*' indicates the 45 feature subsets described in Sect. 2.2.

To further enhance the performance of VNQL co-occurrence, we add one kind of residual images, denoted as $R_{7\times7}$ that includes both the SQUARE and EDGE residual images. The $R_{7\times7}$ is generated similar to the $R_{3\times3}$ and $R_{5\times5}$ except the size is 7×7. The 7×7 filter used shown in Fig. 2. Analogously, based on the residual images $R_{7\times7}$, we can extract the following seven kinds of feature subsets, i.e., $SPAM11$, $SPAM14h$, $SPAM14v$, $MM24$, $MM22h$, $MM22v$, $MM41$. Here, we denoted the extended feature-set as VNQL-Cooc$_{52subset}$ that includes VNQL-Cooc$_{45subset}$ and the additional seven feature subsets. The performance of adding these additional residual images to that used in [8] is also presented below in this paper.

-1	4	-7	8	-7	4	-1
4	-16	28	-32	28	-16	4
-7	28	-49	56	-49	28	-7
8	-32	56	-64	56	-32	8
-7	28	-49	56	-49	28	-7
4	-16	28	-32	28	-16	4
-1	4	-7	8	-7	4	-1

Fig. 2. The SQUARE mask of 7×7

4.2   Symmetry Used in VNQL-Cooc

As mentioned above, the residual images that were used in [8] are used in this work; these residual images are calculated by the uniform quantization as well. The co-occurrence generated from these residual images have the symmetry which have been used in [8]. The symmetry also can be used for the proposed variable co-occurrence. The detail is described below.

The fourth order co-occurrence can be represented by using our variable co-occurrence, denoted as VNQL-Cooc$_{(5,5,5,5)}$. It includes 625 bins whose indexes are calculated from the $d = (d_4d_3d_2d_1)$ that has been describe in Sect. 2.2, where d_i $(i = 1, \ldots, 4)$ is an integer number ranging from 0 to 4. According to the symmetry of $type\ SPAM$ co-occurrence, for every bin whose index represented is $d = (d_4d_3d_2d_1)$, together with the other three bins whose indexes represented by $\{(4 - d_4, 4 - d_3, 4 - d_2, 4 - d_1), (d_1d_2d_3d_4), (4 - d_1, 4 - d_2, 4 - d_3, 4 - d_4)\}$ can be added into one. So we can have 169 bins from the 625 bins according to this rules. According to the symmetry of $type\ MM$ co-occurrence, for every bin whose index is represented as $d = (d_4d_3d_2d_1)$, together with another bin whose index is $\{(4 - d_4, 4 - d_3, 4 - d_2, 4 - d_1)\}$ can be added into one, so the number of bins has been lower to 325. In this process, we can have the corresponding table consisting of 169 rows. The 169-row table that indicates which bins have been merged in each row for the $type\ SPAM$ VNQL-Cooc$_{(5,5,5,5)}$. Analogously, we can get the 325-row table that indicats which bins have been merged in each row for the $type\ MM$ VNQL-Cooc$_{(5,5,5,5)}$.

According to the variable co-occurrence, we can construct a table of 300 rows and a table of 200 rows which record, respectively, how the VNQL-Cooc$_{(5,5,4,3)}$ and VNQL-Cooc$_{(5,5,4,2)}$ can be generated from the bins of VNQL-Cooc$_{(5,5,5,5)}$, i.e., the conventional co-occurrence. For the time being we first consider the case of VNQL-Cooc$_{(5,5,4,3)}$ generated from $type\ SPAM$ residual images. A table is used to record what elements of VNQL-$\text{Cooc}_{(5,5,5,5)}$ have been merged to generate an elements of the VNQL-$\text{Cooc}_{(5,5,4,3)}$. We also know which elements of VNQL-$\text{Cooc}_{(5,5,5,5)}$ will be able to merge to generate the 169 elements utilizing the symmetry, which has been reported in [8]. Hence, we can map each of all the elements of VNQL-$\text{Cooc}_{(5,5,4,3)}$ to 169 elements accordingly. Since our method works on VNQL-$\text{Cooc}_{(5,5,4,3)}$ instead VNQL-$\text{Cooc}_{(5,5,5,5)}$, the 169 elements can be further reduced to 43 elements. Now we see that the same method can be similarly applied to the VNQL-$\text{Cooc}_{(5,5,4,2)}$ used for *type MM* residual images, the number of bins for *type MM* feature subset is only 36.

After applying the symmetry property existed in the variable co-occurrence, the dimensionality of VNQL-$\text{Cooc}_{(5,5,4,3)}$ used for *type SPAM* and VNQL-$\text{Cooc}_{(5,5,4,2)}$ used for *type MM* have been reduced drastically. As the VNQL-$\text{Cooc}_{45subset}$ includes 12 *type SPAM* feature subsets and 33 *type MM* feature subsets, so the dimensionality of VNQL-$\text{Cooc}_{45subset}$ is $1,704$ since $12 \times 43 + 33 \times 36 = 1,704$, denoted as VNQL-$\text{Cooc}_{1704}$. Analogously, because the VNQL-$\text{Cooc}_{52subset}$ has 15 *type SPAM* feature subsets and 37 *type MM* feature subsets, the dimensionality of the VNQL-$\text{Cooc}_{52subset}$ is 1977 as $15 \times 43 + 37 \times 36 = 1,977$, and this $1,977$ dimensional feature-set has been denoted as VNQL-Cooc_{1977}.

To further reduce the dimensionality of the feature-set, the VNQL-$\text{Cooc}_{(5,4,4,2)}$ and VNQL-$\text{Cooc}_{(5,4,4,1)}$ described in Sect. 3.2 can be applied for the *type SPAM* and *type MM* residual images, respectively. According to the above-mentioned strategy, the dimensionality of each *type SPAM* feature subset is 7, and each of *type MM* feature subset has 10 bins. Consequently, the VNQL-$\text{Cooc}_{52subset}$ has 475 bins as $15 \times 7 + 37 \times 10 = 475$ in this case, we denote this 475 dimensional feature-set as VNQL-Cooc_{475}. To evaluate performance of the proposed VNQL co-occurrence, we have constructed three different dimensional feature-sets, i.e., VNQL-Cooc_{475}, VNQL-Cooc_{1704} and VNQL-Cooc_{1977}. The performance of these three feature-sets has been reported in Sect. 5.

5   Experimentation

To evaluate the performance of the proposed VNQL co-occurrence, we have conducted experiments to break two steganographic algorithms with a few different embedding rates. The first one is typical high adaptive steganography, i.e., HUGO [2], the other updated and better steganographic methods, WOW, UNIWARD and S-UNIWARD have not been involving in this paper. In fact, this also have an comparable on the proposed schemes with the SRM. Noted that the HUGO with embedding parameters, that is $\delta = 1$, $\gamma = 1$, and $T = 255$, this setting is the same as used in [8]. Another steganography, Edge-Adaptive (EA) algorithm [15], which embeds the secret message into the sharp edge regions adaptively according to a threshold determined by the size of secret message and the gradients of the image content edge. Both the HUGO and EA algorithms embed data into those locations of images that are hard to be modeled. The four different embedding rates, i.e., 0.1, 0.2, 0.3 and 0.4 bpp, have been applied to the HUGO and EA algorithms in our experiments.

For the objective performance comparison, we work on the BOSSBase ver. 0.92 [4] that consists of 9,074 cover images. These images have been taken with seven digital cameras in the RAW format, converted to grayscale, and then cropped to 512 × 512. We randomly split the 8094 images for training and the rest 1000 images for testing. We evaluate the performance using the detection error and MAD (median absolute deviation) on the testing set which is used in [8].

$$P_E = \frac{1}{2}(P_{FA} + P_{MD}) \tag{5}$$

where P_{FA} and P_{MD} are the probabilities of false alarm and missed detection.

The G-SVM (Gaussian support vector machine) classifier instead of the ensemble classifier are used to evaluate the proposed feature-sets, i.e., VNQL-Cooc$_{475}$, VNQL-Cooc$_{1704}$ and VNQL-Cooc$_{1977}$. In applying the G-SVM, a five-fold cross-validation search for the optimal hyper-parameters, i.e., the cost parameter C and the kernel with γ, has been carried out on the grids G_C and G_γ, with $G_C = \{2^\alpha\}$, $\alpha = \{9, 11, 13, 15\}$, $G_\gamma = \{2^\beta\}$, $\beta = \{-8, -9, -10\}$. The publicly available package of LIBSVM [16] has been used in the experiments.

Table 1. The median detection errors of VNQL-Cooc$_{475}$, VNQL-Cooc$_{1704}$ and VNQL-Cooc$_{1977}$ are calculated from ten splits of Bossbase ver. 0.92, 8074 images for training and the rest 1000 images for testing on the HUGO algorithm with $T = 255$ at four different embedding rates.

HUGO	VNQL − Cooc$_{475}$		VNQL-Cooc$_{1704}$		VNQL-Cooc$_{1977}$		TOP39 in [8]	
Dim	475		1,704		1,977		12,753	
Classifier	G-SVM		G-SVM		G-SVM		Ensemble	
Payload	PE	MAD	PE	MAD	PE	MAD	PE	MAD
0.1	0.3848	0.0055	0.3703	0.0056	**0.3613**	0.0041	0.3640	0.0023
0.2	0.2895	0.0050	0.2695	0.0039	**0.2603**	0.0069	0.2658	0.0053
0.3	0.2018	0.0059	**0.1865**	0.0043	**0.1795**	0.0042	0.1915	0.0033
0.4	0.1423	0.0064	**0.1305**	0.0063	**0.1283**	0.0050	0.1355	0.0035

The experimental results on HUGO algorithm have been shown in Table 1 and Fig. 3, and the results on EA algorithm have been shown in Table 2 and Fig. 4, respectively.

From Tables 1 and 2, it is clear that HUGO is by far more secure than EA algorithm at the same embedded rate, For instance, the median detection error on HUGO algorithm at 0.4 bpp achieved by VNQL-Cooc$_{1977}$ is 12.83 % while the median detection error on EA algorithm at 0.4 bpp is 6.63 % for the VNQL-Cooc$_{1977}$. In addition, the performance of VNQL-Cooc$_{1977}$ is better than that of TOP39 while its feature dimensionality is only 15.5 % of that of TOP39. In the case of Table 1 and Fig. 3, the median detection error achieved by VNQL-Cooc$_{1977}$ on HUGO at 0.4 bpp is about 0.72 % lower as compared with TOP39

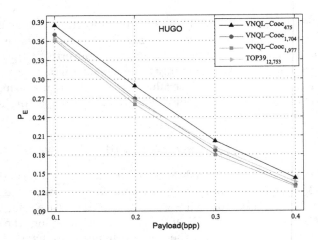

Fig. 3. The comparison of the median detection error on the HUGO over the BOSSBase ver. 0.92 for ten splits, 8074 pairs of images for training and the rest 1000 pairs of images for testing

Table 2. The median detection errors of VNQL-Cooc$_{475}$, VNQL-Cooc$_{1704}$ and VNQL-Cooc$_{1977}$ are calculated from ten splits of Bossbase ver. 0.92, 8074 images for training and the rest 1000 images for testing on the edge-adaptive algorithm at four different embedding rates.

EA algorithm	VNQL-Cooc$_{475}$		VNQL-Cooc$_{1704}$		VNQL-Cooc$_{1977}$		TOP39 in [8]	
Dim	475		1, 704		1, 977		12, 753	
Classifier	G-SVM		G-SVM		G-SVM		Ensemble	
Payload	PE	MAD	PE	MAD	PE	MAD	PE	MAD
0.1	0.2650	0.0065	0.2400	0.0045	0.2353	0.0062	**0.2335**	0.0067
0.2	0.1675	0.0046	0.1460	0.0026	**0.1443**	0.0050	0.1445	0.0037
0.3	0.1130	0.0040	0.1000	0.0037	0.1005	0.0057	**0.0958**	0.0038
0.4	0.0740	0.0030	**0.0663**	0.0051	**0.0663**	0.0045	0.0695	0.0020

in [8]. In other embedding rates such as 0.1, 0.2 and 0.4 bpp, the detection rate of VNQL-Cooc$_{1977}$ on HUGO is slightly better than TOP39. Even the performance of VNQL-Cooc$_{1704}$ on HUGO at 0.4 and 0.3 bpp is better than that of TOP39, but it is slightly worse than TOP39 at 0.1 and 0.2 bpp. On all of the four embedding rates, the VNQL-Cooc$_{1977}$ is better than VNQL-Cooc$_{1704}$. This indicates that the additional seven feature subsets on $R_{7 \times 7}$ residual images are helpful to decrease the detection error in breaking HUGO. In the case of VNQL-Cooc$_{475}$, the median detection error on HUGO at 0.4, 0.3, 0.2 and 0.1 bpp increased 0.68 %, 1.03 %, 2.37 % and 2.08 %, respectively comparing with TOP39, but the dimensionality of VNQL-Cooc$_{475}$ is far smaller than that of TOP39, that is, 475 vs 12, 753. By the way, the detection rate of VNQL-Cooc$_{475}$

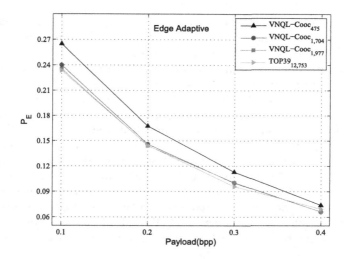

Fig. 4. The comparison of the median detection error on the Edge-Adaptive over the BOSSBase ver. 0.92 for ten splits, 8074 pairs of images for training and the rest 1000 pairs of images for testing

on HUGO with $T = 255$ at 0.4 bpp has reached 85.77 % (e.g., the detection error is 14.23 %), compare with TOP10 feature-set (about 3286 features) in [8], the detection rate of TOP10 is lower than 85 % from Fig. 6 in [8].

In the case of the EA algorithm, the results have been shown in Table 2 and Fig. 4. The detection rates of VNQL-Cooc$_{1704}$ and VNQL-Cooc$_{1977}$ are slightly better than TOP39 at 0.4 bpp, The performance of VNQL-Cooc$_{1977}$ is similar with TOP39 at 0.2 bpp, but when the embedding rate at 0.1 and 0.3, the performance of TOP39 is slightly better than that of VNQL-Cooc$_{1704}$ and VNQL-Cooc$_{1977}$. From Table 2, the performance of VNQL-Cooc$_{1977}$ is slightly improved as comparing with VNQL-Cooc$_{1704}$ at 0.1 and 0.2 bpp while keeping the similar performance at 0.3 and 0.4 bpp. In the case of VNQL-Cooc$_{475}$, the detection error on EA algorithm at 0.4 bpp is slight increased 0.45 % comparing with TOP39, but the detection errors of VNQL-Cooc$_{475}$ on EA algorithm at 0.2, 0.3 and 0.4 bpp are increased from 1.72 % to 3.15 % comparing with TOP39, while the dimensionality of these two feature-sets are 475 vs 12, 753.

6   Discussion and Conclusion

In this paper, A new concept of variable number of quantization levels in multi-dimensional co-occurrence, abbreviated as VNQL co-occurrence or variable co-occurrence has been presented. With one-dimensional histogram representation, the proposed framework, i.e., VNQL co-occurrence histogram, has been applied to steganalysis. The symmetry existing in the high-order co-occurrence has been used to largely reduce the feature dimensionality. These two measures have drastically reduced the feature dimensionality used by the proposed variable co-occurrence. For example, the scheme VNQL-Cooc_{1977} has used only $1,977$ features, which is less than one sixth of $12,753$ features used in the TOP39 feature-set [8] while the detection accuracy rates achieved by $1,977$ features with a G-SVM classifier have been improved by 0.27% to 1.2% for the following four different embedding rates: 0.1, 0.2, 0.3 and 0.4 bpp, on the HUGO with embedding parameter $T = 255$. The proposed VNQL co-occurrence achieves the similar detection rates on the edge adaptive steganograpic algorithm as achieved the TOP39 as reported in [8]. The proposed three feature-sets, i.e., VNQL-Cooc_{475}, VNQL-Cooc_{1704}, and VNQL-Cooc_{1977} can afford to work with the efficient G-SVM classifier instead of the ensemble classifier that has been broadly used in steganalysis recently. In order to show the performance of VNQL co-occurrence compared with that achieved by the high-order co-occurrence in steganalysis, we work on almost the same residuals used in the spatial rich models, and the same test image-set BOSSBase ver. 0.92 [4], and all of the average results are calculated from the ten splits with the same evaluation indicator.

References

1. Pevny, T., Bas, P., Fridrich, J.: Steganalysis by subtractive pixel adjacency matrix. IEEE Trans. Inf. Forensics Secur. 5(2), 215–224 (2010)
2. Pevný, T., Filler, T., Bas, P.: Using high-dimensional image models to perform highly undetectable steganography. In: Böhme, R., Fong, P., Safavi-Naini, R. (eds.) IH 2010. LNCS, vol. 6387, pp. 161–177. Springer, Heidelberg (2010)
3. Filler, T., Judas, J., Fridrich, J.: Minimizing additive distortion in steganography using syndrome-trellis codes. IEEE Trans. Inf. Forensics Secur. 6(3), 920–935 (2011)
4. Bas, P., Filler, T., Pevný, T.: Break our steganographic system: the ins and outs of organizing BOSS. In: Filler, T., Pevný, T., Craver, S., Ker, A. (eds.) IH 2011. LNCS, vol. 6958, pp. 59–70. Springer, Heidelberg (2011). http://dx.doi.org/10.1007/978-3-642-24178-9_5
5. Gul, G., Kurugollu, F.: A new methodology in steganalysis: breaking highly undetectable steganograpy (HUGO). In: Filler, T., Pevný, T., Craver, S., Ker, A. (eds.) IH 2011. LNCS, vol. 6958, pp. 71–84. Springer, Heidelberg (2011). http://dx.doi.org/10.1007/978-3-642-24178-9_6
6. Fridrich, J., Kodovský, J., Holub, V., Goljan, M.: Steganalysis of content-adaptive steganography in spatial domain. In: Filler, T., Pevný, T., Craver, S., Ker, A. (eds.) IH 2011. LNCS, vol. 6958, pp. 102–117. Springer, Heidelberg (2011)
7. Shi, Y.Q., Sutthiwan, P., Chen, L.: Textural features for steganalysis. In: Kirchner, M., Ghosal, D. (eds.) IH 2012. LNCS, vol. 7692, pp. 63–77. Springer, Heidelberg (2013). http://dx.doi.org/10.1007/978-3-642-36373-3_5
8. Fridrich, J., Kodovsky, J.: Rich models for steganalysis of digital images. IEEE Trans. Inf. Forensics Secur. 7(3), 868–882 (2012)
9. Chen, L., Shi, Y.Q., Sutthiwan, P., Niu, X.: A novel mapping scheme for steganalysis. In: Shi, Y.Q., Kim, H.-G. (eds.) IWDW 2012. LNCS, vol. 7809, pp. 19–33. Springer, Heidelberg (2013)
10. Chen, L., Shi, Y.Q., Sutthiwan, P., Niu, X.: Non-uniform quantization in breaking HUGO. In: Shi, Y.Q., Kim, H.-J., Pérez-González, F. (eds.) IWDW 2013. LNCS, vol. 8389, pp. 48–62. Springer, Heidelberg (2014)

11. Holub, V., Fridrich, J.: Random projections of residuals for digital image steganaly-
    sis. IEEE Trans. Inf. Forensics Secur. **8**(12), 1996–2006 (2013)
12. Haralick, R.M., Shanmugam, K., Dinstein, I.: Textural features for image classifi-
    cation. IEEE Trans. Syst. Man Cybern. **SMC–3**, 610–621 (1973)
13. Pevný, T.: Co-occurrence steganalysis in high dimensions. In: IS&T/SPIE Elec-
    tronic Imaging. International Society for Optics and Photonics, pp. 83 030B–83
    030B (2012)
14. Oja, E., Valkealahti, K.: Compressing higher-order co-occurrences for texture
    analysis using the self-organizing map. In: Proceedings of IEEE International Con-
    ference on Neural Networks, vol. 2, pp. 1160–1164 (1995)
15. Luo, W., Huang, F., Huang, J.: Edge adaptive image steganography based on lsb
    matching revisited. IEEE Trans. Inf. Forensics Secur. **5**(2), 201–214 (2010)
16. Chang, C.-C., Lin, C.-J.: LIBSVM: a library for support vector machines. ACM
    Trans. Intell. Syst. Technol. **2**(3), 27:1–27:27 (2011)

Steganography Based on High-Dimensional Reference Table

Bingwen Feng[1], Wei Lu[1], Lu Dai[1], and Wei Sun[2]([✉])

[1] School of Information Science and Technology, Sun Yat-sen University,
Guangzhou 510006, China
bingwfeng@gmail.com, {luwei3,dailu}@mail.sysu.edu.cn
[2] School of Software, Sun Yat-sen University, Guangzhou 510006, China
sunwei@mail.sysu.edu.cn

Abstract. In this paper, a high dimensional reference table-based embedding is proposed for steganography. It employs an N-length cover vector to embed $B(K, N)$-ary notational digits, which causes a Euclidean distance-based distortion no more than K. By choosing the appropriate values of K and N, a embedding strategy suitable for arbitrary relative capacity can be achieved. Further, we introduce the One-by-One Search Algorithm (OOSA) to optimize the mapping function, which maps the elements in the codeword set to those in the neighborhood set. Due to the high dimensional embedding, the proposed scheme provides a higher embedding efficiency or relative capacity compared with other similar approaches. Experiments on both grayscale images and H.264 video show the effectiveness of the proposed scheme.

Keywords: Steganography · Data hiding · High dimensional reference table · Embedding efficiency · Relative capacity

1 Introduction

Steganography aims to conceal secret information into a digital cover so that no one, apart from the sender and receiver, can detect the existence of the secret. Undetectability and embedding capacity are two major considerations when designing a steganographic method. In this paper, the relative capacity α, change rate ρ, and embedding efficiency ϵ [1] are utilized to measure the performances of different steganographic schemes. Supposing n bits are embedded into N pixels with average K embedding change (in the term of, for example, Hamming distance), α, ρ, and ϵ can be calculated by

$$\alpha = n/N \tag{1}$$

$$\rho = K/N \tag{2}$$

$$\epsilon = \alpha/\rho = n/K \tag{3}$$

High embedding efficiency indicates less distortion caused by unit message embedding, while high relative capacity indicates that more information can

© Springer International Publishing Switzerland 2015
Y.-Q. Shi et al. (Eds.): IWDW 2014, LNCS 9023, pp. 574–587, 2015.
DOI: 10.1007/978-3-319-19321-2_44

be concealed in each cover vector. In essence, a steganographic method should maximize either embedding capacity or relative capacity.

Least Significant Bit (LSB) replacement is usually suggested for its high embedding capacity and low computational complexity. However, LSB replacement introduces asymmetry noise, which leads to the consequence of easy detection [2,3]. Therefore, LSB match revisited (LSBMR) [4] was presented for decreasing the modification rate of LSB replacement, while maintaining the same payload. The relative capacity and embedding efficiency of LSBMR are 1 and 2.67, respectively. The Exploiting Modification Direction (EMD) scheme [5] further improves the embedding efficiency of LSBMR. By embedding one $(2N+1)$-ary digit into an N-length pixel vector by at most 1 pixel adding or subtracting 1, EMD can reach arbitrarily high embedding efficiency. However, its relative capacity is very low. For example, using cover vectors of length 4 can obtain an embedding efficiency as $\epsilon = 3.17$ but a low relative capacity as $\alpha = 0.8$.

In contrast, the diamond encoding (DE) [6] tries to increase the relative capacity as much as possible. In DE, the gray-scale change amount of each pixel pair is no more than K, so the relative capacity is $\alpha = log_2(2K^2 + 2K + 1)/2$, and the embedding efficiency is $\epsilon = log_2(2K^2 + 2K + 1)/K$. Since Euclidean distance-based distortion measurement is usually employed in practice, Hong and Chen [7] proposed an Adaptive Pixel Pair Matching (APPM) scheme by minimizing the embedding distortion in the term of MSE. For instance, when the relative capacity is 2.322, the embedding efficiency of DE in the term of Manhattan distance is 2.073, while that of APPM is 1.935. However, when measured with MSE, the embedding efficiencies of DE and APPM are 1.116 and 1.161, respectively, showing that the former is smaller than the latter. Reported results have supported the advantage of using Euclidean distance-based measurement. As a result, we also employ it to measure the embedding change K in this paper.

These schemes, usually referred as the reference table-based embedding [7], employ a pixel vector to embed message digits. There are other similar approaches [8–10] as well. However, these schemes could not outperform EMD, DE, or APPM since the optimum embedding efficiency is not achieved. Simulation indicates that relative capacity increases with increasing the vector length while embedding efficiency increases with increasing the maximum distortion. Therefore, a better scheme could be achieved by increasing both the maximum distortion and the vector length.

We know that matrix embedding such as the Hamming codes [1] and BCH codes [11] can also employ cover vectors of changeable length to embed message bits. In [12], Munuera presented a unified construction of matrix embedding from Error Correcting Codes (ECC). However, the perfect codes, or covering codes, are too few [13] to satisfy the requirement of adjustable relative capacity. On the other hand, the insufficient utilization of syndromes in practical ECCs that are not perfect limits its embedding efficiency.

When the embedding distortion on each pixel equally affects the image, a fewer change of cover images will be more statistically undetectable. However, this assumption is failure in practice. For example, the dependency among neighboring pixels dramatically affects the detectability of the local distortion [14,15].

Many schemes that consider image contents were also suggested [16–19]. Nevertheless, for schemes with the same embedding mechanism (e.g., a wet paper channel [20]), a fewer embedding distortion will be more secure. Furthermore, it is sometimes difficult to assess the content-based distortion in some cover types, such as the video components [21], the 3D mesh [22], and special sensor signal [23]. As a result we are herein devoted to developing a good steganographic code without considering the image content, and applying it to different cover types.

In this paper, a steganography that uses K-distance N-dimensional reference table is proposed. The maximum distortion K and the pixel vector length N are used to provide the tradeoff between relative capacity and embedding efficiency. Given K and N, an optimization algorithm, namely One-by-One Search Algorithm (OOSA), is proposed to search the parameter vector that nearly maximizes the codeword set. Experimental results are demonstrated, illustrating the superiority of the proposed method.

2   Generalized Reference Table

Reference table-based steganographic technique embeds message digits into pixel vectors [24]. For imperceptibility, some constraints are imposed on the embedding distortion. For example, EMD [5] only allows each pixel group changing one gray-scale at most. DE [6] is designed to limit the total distortion on each group no more than K gray-scales. All these reference table-based schemes schemes try to find a mapping function to assign B-ary notational digits to elements in the defined neighborhood set. Consequently, an appropriate neighborhood, which directly impacts the size of codeword set and the maximum embedding distortion, should be determined firstly.

2.1   Generalized Neighborhood Set

The shape and size of a neighborhood set are fixed when constraints are given. In EMD, the shape of its neighborhood is a hypercube, whose dimensionality is the length of the pixel vector. The distance between the center and each vertex is 1, and the volume of the hypercube, i.e., the cardinality of the neighborhood set, is $2N + 1$. In DE, the shape of the neighborhood is a square, whose vertices are all on the axes and of distance K to the center, and the cardinality of the neighborhood set is the area of the square, which is $2K^2 + 2K + 1$.

We now consider an N-dimensional neighborhood with Euclidean distance no more than K, which we denote as $\Phi_{K,N}$. The shape of this neighborhood is an N-dimensional hypersphere with radius K. The volume can be calculated by adding up all the volumes of its $N - 1$ dimensional projections. A recursive definition of the cardinality of $\Phi_{K,N}$ is

$$B(K,N) = |\Phi_{K,N}| = 2\sum_{i=1}^{\lfloor K \rfloor} |\Phi_{\sqrt{K^2-i^2},N-1}| + |\Phi_{K,N-1}| \qquad (4)$$

where $|\cdot|$ denotes the cardinality of the set. $|\Phi_{0,N}| = |\Phi_{0,1}|$ and $|\Phi_{K,1}| = 2\lfloor K \rfloor + 1$.

Let $\Psi_{K,N}$ denote the codeword set, i.e., $\Psi_{K,N}(\mathbf{p}) \triangleq \{y : y = \mathrm{f}(\mathbf{p}'; \mathbf{a}), \mathbf{p}' \in \Phi_{K,N}(\mathbf{p})\}$. Then, the maximum number of codewords is no more than the number of elements in the neighborhood set. Each codeword is assigned with a digit, which means that we can embed at most one $B(K, N)$-ary digit in a pixel vector. Such a steganographic method is named as the K-distance N-dimensional reference table-based embedding (denoted by (K, N)-scheme). In essence, the Euclidean distortion in this method is no more than K and the dimensionality of pixel vector is N. Note that, when $K = 1$, the (K, N)-scheme reduces to EMD.

2.2   Optimization of the Mapping Function

Given a defined neighborhood, a bijective function should be determined so that each $B(K, N)$-ary digit can be mapped to an unique element in the neighborhood, i.e., a mapping function satisfying $|\Psi_{K,N}| = |\Phi_{K,N}|$. However, When $K \geq 2$ and $N \geq 3$, there seldom exists a polynomial solution. Therefore, to maximize $|\Psi_{K,N}|$, a mapping function, whose parameters are the solution of the following optimization problem

$$\arg\max_{\mathbf{a}} |\Psi_{K,N}|, \tag{5}$$

should be given.

Herein, a simple linear function is considered, which is defined as

$$\mathrm{f}(\mathbf{p}; \mathbf{a}) = \mathbf{a}^T \mathbf{p} \bmod B(K, N) \tag{6}$$

$$= a_1 p_1 + a_2 p_2 + \cdots a_N p_N \bmod B(K, N) \tag{7}$$

Thus, Eq. (5) can be refined as

$$\arg\max_{\mathbf{a}} |\{y : y = \mathbf{a}^T \mathbf{p} \bmod B(K, N), \ \mathbf{p} \in \Phi_{K,N}\}| \tag{8}$$

$$\text{s.t.} \quad a_1 = 1,$$

$$1 < a_2 < a_3 < \cdots < a_N < \lfloor \frac{B(K, N)}{2} \rfloor.$$

where the constraint follows the properties of modular arithmetic.

However, the feasible solution space for Eq. (8) is large. The computational complexity of exhaustive search is $\mathcal{O}(\lfloor \frac{B(K,N)}{2} \rfloor^{N-1})$. Experimentally we observe that, if the global maximum point is achieved when one axis is assigned with a certain value, then nearly all the local maximum points can be reached by fixing this axis on this value and changing other axes. Inspired by this, the One-by-One Search Algorithm (OOSA) is introduced to solve Eq. (8), as described as follows. When the being-optimized axis n, the initialized parameter vector $\mathbf{a}$, the cardinality of the neighborhood set $B(K, N)$ and the cardinality of the temporarily optimized codeword set $|\Psi_{K,N}|^{\mathrm{opt}}$ are given, the Search on One Dimension (SOD) function, denoted by $\mathrm{SOD}(n, \mathbf{a}, B(K, N), |\Psi_{K,N}|^{\mathrm{opt}})$, fixes all but the n-th axis and sequentially searches the only left axis to find the local maximum value and its corresponding feasible solution, as described in Algorithm 1.

Algorithm 1. Search on One Dimension (SOD)
___

Require: $n, \mathbf{a}, B(K, N), |\Psi_{K,N}|^{\mathrm{opt}}$.
 1: initialize the temporary value list, $\mathbf{b} \leftarrow \mathbf{0}$.
 2: $\mathbf{a}^{\mathrm{opt}} \leftarrow \mathbf{a}$.
 3: **for** $i = 1$ to $\lfloor B(K, N)/2 \rfloor$ **do**
 4:     $a_n \leftarrow i$.
 5:     assign b_i, $b_i \leftarrow |\Psi_{K,N}(\mathbf{0})|$.
 6:     **if** $|\Psi_{K,N}|^{\mathrm{opt}} < b_i$ **then**
 7:         $|\Psi_{K,N}|^{\mathrm{opt}} \leftarrow b_i$.
 8:         $a_n^{\mathrm{opt}} \leftarrow a_n$.
 9:     **end if**
10: **end for**
11: **return** $\mathbf{b}, \mathbf{a}^{\mathrm{opt}}, |\Psi_{K,N}|^{\mathrm{opt}}$.

Then the search of the best feasible solution is performed by successively calculating the best value on each axis via converging its temporary best index set. Given the maximum distance K and the vector length N, the initiation is set as $\mathbf{a} = \mathbf{1}$, and the proposed One-by-One Search Algorithm (OOSA) is outlined in Algorithm 2.

Algorithm 2. One-by-One Search Algorithm (OOSA)
___

 1: $\mathbf{a} \leftarrow \mathbf{1}, |\Psi_{K,N}|^{\mathrm{opt}} \leftarrow 0$.
 2: $B(K, N) \leftarrow |\Phi_{K,N}|$.
 3: **for** $n = 2$ to $N - 1$ **do**
 4:     $a_{n-1} \leftarrow a_{n-1}^{\mathrm{opt}}$.
 5:     $(\mathbf{b}, \mathbf{a}^{\mathrm{opt}}, |\Psi_{K,N}|^{\mathrm{opt}}) \leftarrow \mathrm{SOD}(n, \mathbf{a}, B(K, N), |\Psi_{K,N}|^{\mathrm{opt}})$.
 6:     set the best index set, $\Omega \leftarrow \{i | b_i = |\Psi_{K,N}|^{\mathrm{opt}}\}$.
 7:     **repeat**
 8:         $a_{n+1} \leftarrow a_{n+1} + \Delta$.
 9:         $(\mathbf{b}, \mathbf{a}^{\mathrm{opt}}, |\Psi_{K,N}|^{\mathrm{opt}}) \leftarrow \mathrm{SOD}(n, \mathbf{a}, B(K, N), |\Psi_{K,N}|^{\mathrm{opt}})$
10:         remove $\{i | b_i < |\Psi_{K,N}|^{\mathrm{opt}}\}$ from set Ω.
11:         **if** $\Omega = \emptyset$ **then**
12:             $\Omega \leftarrow \{a_n^{\mathrm{opt}}\}$.
13:         **end if**
14:     **until** $|\Omega| = 1$
15:     $a_n^{\mathrm{opt}} \leftarrow i$ where $\{i\} = \Omega$
16: **end for**
17: $a_{N-1} \leftarrow a_{N-1}^{\mathrm{opt}}$.
18: $(\mathbf{b}, \mathbf{a}^{\mathrm{opt}}, |\Psi_{K,N}|^{\mathrm{opt}}) \leftarrow \mathrm{SOD}(N, \mathbf{a}, B(K, N), |\Psi_{K,N}|^{\mathrm{opt}})$.
19: **return** $\mathbf{a}^{\mathrm{opt}}, |\Psi_{K,N}|^{\mathrm{opt}}$.

The space complexity of OOSA is $\mathcal{O}(B(K, N) + 4N)$. Considering the mapping function $f(\cdot; \cdot)$ as a computational unit, the time complexity is $\mathcal{O}(c\lfloor \frac{B(K,N)}{2} \rfloor (N - 1) \cdot \lfloor \frac{B(K,N)}{2} \rfloor)$, where $c\lfloor \frac{B(K,N)}{2} \rfloor$ is determined by the the step size Δ in Step 8 of Algorithm 2. Δ can be adaptively set to increase the convergence speed. In implementation, $\Delta = \lceil |\Omega|/100 \rceil$ is employed, achieving an average c smaller than 0.01.

Although the global optimum solution is not usually obtained by OOSA, the yielded best feasible solution is closed to the global optimum one. We compare our algorithm with the exhaustive search, which gives the global optimum solution. The comparison result reported in Fig. 1 indicates that the proposed algorithm is closed to the upper bound and comparable with the exhaustive search. Some parameters obtained by OOSA and their corresponding cardinalities of neighborhood sets and codeword sets are given in Table 1.

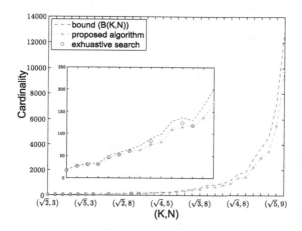

Fig. 1. The cardinalities of codeword sets using different algorithms. The first 15 points are amplified in the subpicture. Notice that for many situations the exhaustive search is beyond the computational power, so only a few points can be found.

Table 1. List of $|\Phi_{K,N}|$, $|\Psi_{K,N}|$ and corresponding parameters obtained by OOSA

(K, N)	$|\Phi|$	$|\Psi|$	$\mathbf{a}$	(K, N)	$|\Phi|$	$|\Psi|$	$\mathbf{a}$
$(\sqrt{2}, 3)$	19	17	$[1, 2, 6]$	$(1, 2)$	5	5	$[1, 2]$
$(\sqrt{3}, 3)$	27	27	$[1, 3, 9]$	$(1, 4)$	9	9	$[1, 2, 3, 4]$
$(\sqrt{4}, 3)$	33	29	$[1, 3, 13]$	$(1, 5)$	11	11	$[1, 2, 3, 4, 5]$
$(\sqrt{2}, 4)$	33	31	$[1, 3, 10, 15]$	$(1, 7)$	15	15	$[1, 2, 3, 4, 5, 6, 7]$

As mentioned previously, when $K = 1$, the (K, N)-scheme reduces to EMD. In Table 1, it can be noted that the parameters obtained by using the proposed algorithm are identical with those by using EMD.

Figure 2 illustrates the assignment of digits in $\Phi_{\sqrt{4}, 3}(\mathbf{0})$, which are represented by all its projections in the $p_1 p_2$ plane. It should be noted that $5_{(33)}$, $8_{(33)}$, $25_{(33)}$

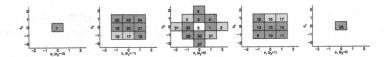

Fig. 2. Assignment of 33-ary digit in $\Phi_{\sqrt{4},3}(\mathbf{0})$, which is represented as each projection in the $p_1 p_2$ plane. The repeat digits are colored yellow. Note that this assignment is obtained by the proposed algorithm and is not the best solution, in which there are only two repeat digits.

and $28_{(33)}$ are absent in $\Phi_{\sqrt{4},3}(\mathbf{0})$. This is because the mapping function is no longer bijective, some digits have not been assigned to any entry. When the to-be-embedded digit is one of these absent codewords, a readjustment of current pixel group will be in need.

2.3   Embedding and Extraction Functions

We can employ the mapping function to reveal embedded message digits. The received stego pixel group is used as input to calculate the value of the mapping function, which gives the concealed message digit.

In the case of embedding, the entry of the message digit in the neighborhood set corresponding to the cover vector is required. The neighborhood set at the origin, i.e., $\Phi_{K,N}(\mathbf{0})$, can be generated in advance. It is then considered as the reference table and used in each vector embedding. For a coming cover vector, the original value of the mapping function (denoted as y) is calculated first. Assuming the embedded digit is m, the modulus distance between y and m is obtained as $d = y - m \bmod B(K,N)$ and found in the reference table. Then the adjustment index (denoted as $\mathbf{q}$) corresponding to this distance value is subtracted from the cover vector, which gives the stego vector $\mathbf{p}'$. The message digit m can be extracted correctly as $f(\mathbf{p}';\mathbf{a}) = f(\mathbf{p} - \mathbf{q};\mathbf{a}) = f(\mathbf{p};\mathbf{a}) - f(\mathbf{q};\mathbf{a}) \bmod B(K,N) = y - d \bmod B(K,N) = m$.

However, as shown in Fig. 2, some $B(K,N)$-ary digits are absent in the codeword set. If such a digit need to be embedded, the cover vector must be readjusted to a new vector $\mathbf{p}'$, so that in the new vector's neighborhood set, the obtained modulus distance can be found. Based on this, the embedding procedure that embeds one $B(K,N)$-ary message digit m into a cover vector $\mathbf{p}$ can be performed as:

1. Calculate the value of the mapping function $y = f(\mathbf{p})$ and the corresponded modulus distance $d = y - m \bmod B(K,N)$;
2. If d can be found in the reference table $\Psi_{K,N}(\mathbf{0})$ and its adjustment index is $\mathbf{q}$, compute the stego pixel vector as

$$\mathbf{p}' = \mathbf{p} - \mathbf{q}$$

and goto Step 4;

3. Otherwise, exhaustively search $d_1, d_2 \in \Psi_{K,N}(\mathbf{0})$ which satisfies $d_1 + d_2 \bmod B(K, N) = d$. Compute the stego pixel vector as

$$\mathbf{p}' = \mathbf{p} - \mathbf{q}_1 - \mathbf{q}_2$$

where $\mathbf{q}_1$ and $\mathbf{q}_2$ are the corresponded adjustment indices of d_1 and d_2, respectively;

4. Output $\mathbf{p}'$.

We can confirm the correctness of the obtained stego vector by

$$\begin{aligned}
f(\mathbf{p} - \mathbf{q}_1 - \mathbf{q}_2; \mathbf{a}) &= f(\mathbf{p}; \mathbf{a}) - f(\mathbf{q}_1; \mathbf{a}) - f(\mathbf{q}_2; \mathbf{a}) \bmod B(K, N) \\
&= y - d_1 - d_2 \bmod B(K, N) \\
&= y - d \bmod B(K, N) = m
\end{aligned}$$

Note that $d_1 + d_2 \leq 2K$. Therefore, the distortion distance caused any embedding will be no more than $2K$. Furthermore, the cardinality of the absent set is very small, as shown in Fig. 1, hence major fraction of message digits can be embedded with a distortion no more than K. We can also employ some search strategy to further decrease the distortion when finding d_1 and d_2.

3   Experimental Results and Analysis

3.1   Performance and Analysis

The relative capacity α, change rate ρ and embedding efficiency ϵ described in [1] are utilized to measure the performances of different steganographic methods. Both α and ϵ are expected to be large. Let $\Psi_{K,N}^c$ denote the absent codeword set, i.e., $\Psi_{K,N}^c = \{y : y \notin \Psi_{K,N}\}$. Since $\frac{|\Psi_{K,N}^c|}{|\Phi_{K,N}|}$ fraction of pixel vectors are changed in range $[K, 2K]$ in our scheme, the average embedding change K can be calculated as

$$K = \frac{|\Psi_{K,N}| + 2|\Psi_{K,N}^c|}{(|\Phi_{K,N}|)^2} \sum_{\mathbf{p} \in \Phi_{K,N}(\mathbf{0})} \|\mathbf{p}\|^2 \tag{9}$$

where $\|\mathbf{p}\|$ denotes the Euclidean norm of $\mathbf{p}$.

The curves of relative capacity α and embedding efficiency ϵ w.r.t. the proposed scheme are given in Fig. 3(a) and (b), respectively. It can be found that α increases when K increases or N decreases, while ϵ increases when N increases or K decreases. Further, EMD reaches the best ϵ given N, and $\pm k$ LSB reaches the largest α given K. But our scheme gives tradeoffs between them.

For an appropriate tradeoff between α and ϵ, we maximize the latter when the former is given. Figure 4(a) gives the ratio of relative capacity to embedding efficiency, which also gives the ratios with DE [6] and APPM [7]. For a fair comparison, K and N of each scheme are selected no larger than $\sqrt{5}$ and 10, respectively. As shown in Fig. 4(a), EMD is the best solution for the lowest

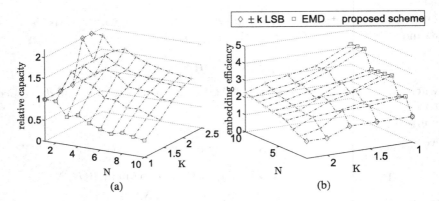

Fig. 3. Relative capacity (a) and embedding efficiency (b) curves of the proposed scheme. Note that EMD and $\pm k$ LSB schemes are special versions of the proposed scheme.

capacity. However, our scheme offers the best solution for most capacity values. For example, the $(\sqrt{3}, 10)$-scheme performs best given $\alpha = 1.0$, and the $(\sqrt{3}, 4)$-scheme performs best given $\alpha = 2.0$. Due to the parameter constraints, APPM(C_{16}) outperforms the others when $\alpha = 2.0$. However, better performance can be achieved in our method when larger K and N are allowed.

Some schemes based on matrix embedding are also employed for comparisons. Codes from Hamming, Golay and BCH families are adopted to construct matrix embedding by the method suggested in [12]. Figure 4(b) gives the comparison of ratios of relative capacity to embedding efficiency. As shown in Fig. 4(b),

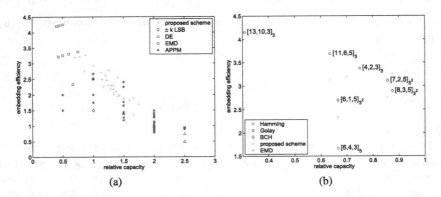

Fig. 4. The ratios of relative capacity to embedding efficiency. In (a) we compare our scheme with $\pm k$ LSB, EMD, DE and APPM. The K and N for all the schemes are constrained to no larger than $\sqrt{5}$ and 10, respectively. In (b) we compare our scheme with well known matrix embedding. The matrix embedding is labeled with its corresponded ECC. The $[n, k, d]_{q^m}$ code means a linear code of length n and dimension k over $\mathbb{F}_{q^m}$, whose minimum distance is d.

± 1 Hamming codes are equivalent to EMD, and our scheme outperforms other matrix embedding except the ± 1 Golay code. This is because the global optimum solutions are not usually achieved by the proposed optimization algorithm, hence the perfect $(\sqrt{2}, 11)$-scheme equivalent to Golay code is not achieved.

3.2   Application in Grayscale Image

The proposed high-dimensional reference table-based embedding can maximum the embedding efficiency when given the relative capacity. A straightforward application of this property is the grayscaly image steganography, where each N pixels are employed as a cover vector to embed one B-ary notational message digit. In this section, we compare this grayscaly image steganographic scheme with DE, EMD, and APPM. 10000 images from the BOSSBase1.01 database [25] are selected as the cover images. Pseudorandom binary sequences of certain length are used as secret messages to guarantee relative capacities equal to 1 and 1.5. Table 2 shows the average results in the term of PSNR under different relative capacities, which also gives the employed parameters.

The maximum relative capacity of EMD is 1, so it cannot be compared with when the relative capacity is larger than 1. Similarly, we cannot compare with DE when the relative capacity is smaller than 1.5. Given the capacity, our method minimizes the Euclidean based distortion, which yields better image qualities w.r.t. Euclidean based measurements (e.g., MSE, PSNR) than the others. Moreover, Our scheme can choose more suitable parameters for specified message length to reduce the redundant codewords, and thus further decreases the embedding distortion. These are summarized in Table 2. Further, Table 2 also coincides with the analysis in Sect. 3.1.

Table 2. PSNR comparison of different schemes with different relative capacities

α (bpp)	proposed scheme (parameters)	EMD [5] (parameters)	DE [6] (parameters)	APPM [7] (parameters)
1.0	**53.0589** $(K = \sqrt{3}, N = 10)$	52.1011 $(N = 2)$	—	52.3760 $(C_4 = 2)$
1.5	**50.1690** $(K = \sqrt{3}, N = 4)$	—	47.7876 $(K = 2)$	50.1509 $(C_8 = 3)$
1.5259	**49.0064** $(K = 2, N = 3)$	—	46.0944 $(K = 3)$	47.9927 $(C_{16} = 6)$

Furthermore, more appropriate parameters for an arbitrary relative capacity are available. For example, a 100 000 bits message needs to be embedded, reaching a relative capacity $\alpha = 1.5259$. In this case the best choice of APPM is C_{16}, which will waste 31.1 % payload. However, the best strategy of the proposed scheme is $(2, 3)$ and only 9.2 % payload is wasted. Comparison results are also given in Table 2.

We further compare the securities of these schemes. The Subtractive Pixel Adjacency Matrix (SPAM) features [14] combined with soft-margin SVM are employed to attack different schemes on the BOSSBase1.01 database. For a fair comparison, the embedding positions are randomly chosen to guarantee that all the schemes are with the same payload. The decision error probability P_E defined in [14] is employed here.

Comparison results with payloads of 0.1 and 0.25 are given in Table 3. It demonstrates that our $(\sqrt{3}, 10)$-scheme outperforms the others. Furthermore, we can observe that a heavier embedding distortion usually indicates that the corresponded stego image will be detected more easily. It is because that, when embedding distortion on each pixel equally influences the image, a fewer change of cover image will be more statistically undetectable [12].

Table 3. Security comparison on BOSSBase1.01 [25] using SPAM features [14]

	bpp= 0.1		bpp= 0.25	
	Average PSNR	P_E	Average PSNR	P_E
Proposed scheme $(\sqrt{3}, 10)$	**63.0341**	**0.1701**	**59.0552**	**0.0963**
EMD [5] $(N = 2)$	62.0821	0.1480	58.1028	0.0796
APPM [7] (C_4)	62.3704	0.1405	58.3976	0.0710
Proposed scheme $(\sqrt{3}, 4)$	61.8930	0.1277	57.9141	0.0700
DE [6] $(K = 2)$	59.5245	0.0712	55.5392	0.0404
APPM [7] (C_8)	61.8794	0.1256	57.8995	0.0690

3.3 Application in H.264 Video

When embedding efficiency do not affect the performance of data hiding seriously, we can employ the proposed scheme to maximum the relative capacity. As an example, an information hiding scheme is proposed for H.264 in this section by applying the high-dimensional reference table-based embedding to the motion estimation (ME). When encoding a sub-block in a P frame, the best motion vector (MV) is first searched in the location of integer-pixel, then the sub-pixel around the best integer pixel position, and finally the quarter-pixel around the sub-pixel position [26]. The search graph of ME based on quarter-pixel is demonstrated in Fig. 5(b). In [27], these quarter-pixel positions were divided into two groups, and the search point is modulated to embed one message bit. Herein, we employ the $(\sqrt{3}, 4)$-scheme. The entry, $\mathbf{p}'$, corresponding to the embedding message digit is first searched in $\Phi_{\sqrt{3},4}(\mathbf{0})$. Then each element in $\mathbf{p}'$, which is denoted as p', is successively embedded into MVs by applying the similar method in [27]. Experimentally we find that the probabilities of $p' = 1$, $p' = -1$, and $p' = 0$ are approximaly equal to 0.2, 0.2, and 0.6, respectively, thus the mapping rule between the search points and p' is defined as

$$\begin{cases} \{1, 3, 0, 6, 8\} & \text{if } p' = 0 \\ \{2, 7\} & \text{if } p' = -1 \\ \{4, 5\} & \text{if } p' = 1 \end{cases} \tag{10}$$

We compare the proposed scheme with the original version in [27]. The first 100 frames of three video sequences, that is, Carphone, Foreman, and Salesman, of resolution QCIF (176 × 144) are used in the test. They are encoded in the fashion of "IPPP" style to comply with the baseline profile. Further, quantization parameters (QPs) are set with {23, 28, 36, 40} successively. Figure 5(b) illustrates the coding efficiency losses incurred by different schemes. It can be seen that hiding data does not affect the bit-rate or quality of video in either scheme. However, the proposed scheme can embed more message bits due to its high relative capacity. The payloads of different schemes with different QPs are listed in Table 4.

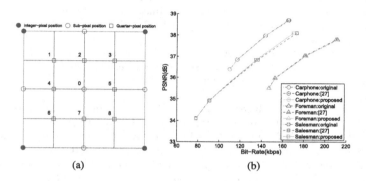

(a)   (b)

Fig. 5. (a) The search graph of quarter-pixel ME. (b) The rate-distortion curves before and after embedding message bits by using different schemes.

Table 4. Payload comparison of different schemes with different quantization parameters

	QP = 23		QP = 28		QP = 36		QP = 40	
	Proposed	[27]	Proposed	[27]	Proposed	[27]	Proposed	[27]
Carphone	20844	14875	19206	13250	14880	10131	13116	8848
Foreman	30180	20900	26100	18260	20560	14573	17960	12500
Salesman	8736	8024	8874	7619	8016	5848	7182	5220

4   Conclusion

In this paper, a generalized K-distance N-dimensional reference table-based embedding is proposed. The adaptive choice of K and N allows to construct a better steganographic scheme given arbitrary relative capacity. Furthermore, due to the introduction of high dimensional embedding and optimization algorithm, the proposed scheme offers nearly optimum embedding efficiency, which improves the quality of the stego. In the experiments, we apply the proposed scheme in both grayscale images and H.264 video. In the case of images, the proposed scheme is more secure against steganalysis since less modification is taken compared with other schemes. We can further construct a content-adaptive scheme by combining the proposed scheme with the edge region [17]. In the case of H.264, the proposed scheme provides a higher capacity compared with the original scheme. Applying the proposed high-dimensional reference table-based embedding to more cover types is our future work.

References

1. Westfeld, A.: F5-A steganographic algorithm. In: Moskowitz, I.S. (ed.) IH 2001. LNCS, vol. 2137, pp. 289–302. Springer, Heidelberg (2001)
2. Johnson, N.F., Jajodia, S.: Steganalysis of images created using current steganography software. In: Aucsmith, D. (ed.) IH 1998. LNCS, vol. 1525, p. 273. Springer, Heidelberg (1998)
3. Westfeld, A., Pfitzmann, A.: Attacks on steganographic systems. In: Pfitzmann, A. (ed.) IH 1999. LNCS, vol. 1768. Springer, Heidelberg (2000)
4. Mielikainen, J.: LSB matching revisited. IEEE Signal Process. Lett. **13**, 285–287 (2006)
5. Zhang, X., Wang, S.: Efficient steganographic embedding by exploiting modification direction. IEEE Commun. Lett. **10**(11), 781–783 (2006)
6. Chao, R.M., Wu, H.C., Lee, C.C., Chu, Y.P.: A novel image data hiding scheme with diamond encoding. EURASIP J. Inf. Secur. **2009**, 1–9 (2009)
7. Hong, W., Chen, T.S.: A novel data embedding method using adaptive pixel pair matching. IEEE Trans. Inf. Forensics Secur. **7**(1), 176–184 (2012)
8. Yang, C.H.: Inverted pattern approach to improve image quality of information hiding by LSB substitution. Pattern Recogn. **41**(8), 2674–2683 (2008)
9. Hong, W.: Adaptive image data hiding in edges using patched reference table and pair-wise embedding technique. Inf. Sci. **221**, 473–489 (2013)
10. Wang, J., Sun, Y., Xu, H., Chen, K., Kim, H.J., Joo, S.H.: An improved section-wise exploiting modification direction method. Signal Process. **90**(11), 2954–2964 (2010)
11. Schönfeld, D., Winkler, A.: Embedding with syndrome coding based on BCH codes. In: Proceedings of the 8th Workshop on Multimedia and Security, pp. 214–223. ACM (2006)
12. Munuera, C.: 3. In: Algebraic Geometry Modelling in Information Theory. Coding Theory and Cryptology, vol. 8, p. 83. World Scientific Publishing Co., Pte. Ltd., February 2013
13. Bierbrauer, J., Fridrich, J.: Constructing good covering codes for applications in steganography. In: Shi, Y.Q. (ed.) Transactions on Data Hiding and Multimedia Security III. LNCS, vol. 4920, pp. 1–22. Springer, Heidelberg (2008)
14. Pevný, T., Bas, P., Fridrich, J.: Steganalysis by subtractive pixel adjacency matrix. IEEE Trans. Inf. Forensics Secur. **5**(2), 215–224 (2010)
15. Fridrich, J.J., Kodovský, J.: Rich models for steganalysis of digital images. IEEE Trans. Inf. Forensics Secur. **7**(3), 868–882 (2012)
16. Pevný, T., Filler, T., Bas, P.: Using high-dimensional image models to perform highly undetectable steganography. In: Böhme, R., Fong, P.W.L., Safavi-Naini, R. (eds.) IH 2010. LNCS, vol. 6387, pp. 161–177. Springer, Heidelberg (2010)
17. Luo, W., Huang, F., Huang, J.: Edge adaptive image steganography based on LSB matching revisited. IEEE Trans. Inf. Forensics Secur. **5**(2), 201–214 (2010)

18. Holub, V., Fridrich, J.: Designing steganographic distortion using directional filters. In: IEEE International Workshop on Information Forensics and Security (WIFS), 2012, pp. 234–239. IEEE (2012)
19. Holub, V., Fridrich, J.: Digital image steganography using universal distortion. In: Proceedings of the first ACM Workshop on Information Hiding and Multimedia Security, pp. 59–68. ACM (2013)
20. Fridrich, J., Goljan, M., Lisoněk, P., Soukal, D.: Writing on wet paper. In: Delp, E.J., Wong, P.W., (eds.) Proceedings of SPIE on Security, Steganography, and Watermarking of Multimedia Contents. vol. 5681, pp. 328–340. SPIE, San Jose, September 2005
21. Tew, Y., Wong, K.: An overview of information hiding in H.264/AVC compressed video. IEEE Trans. Circuits Syst. Video Technol. 24(2), 305–319 (2014)
22. Vasic, B., Vasic, B.: Simplification resilient LDPC-coded sparse-QIM watermarking for 3D-meshes. IEEE Trans. Multimedia 15(7), 1532–1542 (2013)
23. Ibaida, A., Khalil, I.: Wavelet based ECG steganography for protecting patient confidential information in point-of-care systems. IEEE Trans. Biomed. Eng. 60(12), 3322–3330 (2013)
24. Anderson, R.J., Petitcolas, F.A.: On the limits of steganography. IEEE J. Sel. Areas Commun. 16(4), 474–481 (1998)
25. Bas, P., Filler, T., Pevný, T.: "Break Our Steganographic System": The ins and outs of organizing BOSS. In: Filler, T., Pevný, T., Craver, S., Ker, A. (eds.) IH 2011. LNCS, vol. 6958, pp. 59–70. Springer, Heidelberg (2011)
26. Recommendation, I.T.U.T. H 264: Advanced video coding for generic audiovisual services. ITU-T Rec. H 264, pp. 14496–14510 (2003)
27. Zhu, H., Wang, R., Xu, D.: Information hiding algorithm for H.264 based on the motion estimation of quarter-pixel. In: 2nd International Conference on Future Computer and Communication (ICFCC), 2010. vol.1, pp. 423–427. IEEE (2010)

Steganography Based on Grayscale Images Using (5, 3) Hamming Code

Cheonshik Kim[1]([✉]) and Ching-Nung Yang[2]

[1] Department of Digital Media Engineering, Anyang University,
Anyang-si, Gyeonggi-do, Korea
mipsan@paran.com
[2] Department of Computer Science and Information Engineering, National Dong
Hwa University, Hualien, Taiwan, ROC
cnyang@mail.ndhu.edu.tw

Abstract. Steganography is a technique to hide secret data in cover images securely. This technique is used for secret communication. However, steganography is not as strong as watermark against various attacks. "Hamming+1" scheme is a well known scheme in the steganography. In this paper, we propose new data hiding scheme that showed better performance compared to "Hamming+1". The proposed scheme conceals 3 bits per 5 pixels of an image. The experimental result showed that the proposed scheme achieves an 0.599 bpp embedding payload and a higher visual quality of stego images compared to the previous schemes.

Keywords: Steganography · Data hiding · LSB · Hamming code

1 Introduction

Nowadays, due to the advancement of the computer and network technology, people can easily send or receive secret information in various forms to or from almost any places through the Internet. However, important secret messages mayleak out while they are being transmitted or exchanged over public communication channel (i.e., e-mail, ftp, web browser) [1,2]. Therefore, achie nving safe secret communication is an important field of research. Recently, many people have started using cryptography and steganography [1–7] to protect their precious data from the attackers. Steganographic technologies are a very important part of future Internet security and privacy on open systems, such as the Internet. The steganography is the least secure means by which to communicate secretly because the sender and receiver can rely only on the presumption that no other parties are aware of the secret message. Using Steganography, information can be hidden in carriers, such as images.

Steganography can be classified into two domains, the spatial [1,2] and frequency [1,2]. In the spatial domain, the secret message is inserted directly into the pixels. In the frequency domain, the common method of data hiding are discrete cosine transform (DCT)-based method, discrete wavelet transform (DWT)-based

© Springer International Publishing Switzerland 2015
Y.-Q. Shi et al. (Eds.): IWDW 2014, LNCS 9023, pp. 588–598, 2015.
DOI: 10.1007/978-3-319-19321-2_45

method, or other methods based on similar mechanisms. The most common methods are histogram-based and least-significant bit (LSB) techniques in the spatial domain. The embedding by flipping LSB of pixels is relatively easy to detect even at very low embedding rates. Essentially, senders and receivers agree on a steganographic system and a shared secret key that determines how a message is encoded in the cover medium. Steganographic schemes have a vulnerable point from steganalysis attacks; thus, many researchers proposed various schemes.

Chang et al. [4] proposed (7, 4) Hamming code for data hiding, which improves on the "Hamming+1" scheme. *Westfeld's* F5 [5] is the first implementation of matrix encoding. OutGuess [5]was the first attempt to explicitly match the DCT histogram. Crandall [9] showed that linear codes could markedly improve the embedding efficiency. *Rongyue et al.* [14] proposed an efficient BCH coding for steganography, which embeds the secret information inside a block of cover data. The CPT scheme [15] showed the embedding efficiency by hiding messages based on the weighted value of a block. *Zhang et al.* [6] proposed the ternary Hamming codes using the concept of efficiency by exploiting the modification direction (EMD) [13,16,17]. The performance of "+/- steganography" was introduced by the [8]. Mielikainen [8] presented a method based on a pair of two consecutive secret bits [11].

In this paper, we proposed (5, 3) hamming code scheme, which can be used to embed 3 bits per 5 pixel blocks in an image. Our proposed scheme is very efficient and steganographic, so it can be used in many various application fields. The rest of this paper is organized as follows. In Sect. 2, we review related pre-vious research schemes. In Sect. 3, we introduce our proposed scheme for grayscale images. In Sect. 4, we explain the experimental results. Section 5 presents our conclusions.

2   Related Works

2.1   Error Correction Code

Many secret data are sent through noisy channel, and it is common for an occasional bit to flip. The channel is "noisy" in the sense that what is received is not always the same as what was sent. Thus if binary data is being transmitted over the channel, when a 0 is sent, it is hopefully received as a 0 but sometimes will be received as a 1 (or as unrecognizable). Noise in deep space communications can be caused, for example, by thermal disturbance. If no modification is made to the message and it is transmitted directly over the channel, any noise would distort the message so that it is not recoverable. The basic idea is to add some redundancy to the message in hopes that the received message is the original message that was sent. The redundancy is added by the encoder and the redundancy message is called a codeword c.

2.2   Hamming Code

Linear codes with length n and dimension k will be described as $[n, k]$ codes. Hamming codes are linear codes and are described as a $[n, k]$ q-ary Hamming code, where q is the size of the base field, F_q. A generator matrix G for an $[n, k]$ linear code c (over any field F_q) is a k-by-n matrix for which the row space is the given code. In other words, $c = \{xG|x\}$. Matrix encoding conceals messages with the parity check matrix of a linear codes. If H is the checker matrix for c, H is an $(n-k)k$ matrix, the rows of which are orthogonal to c and $\{x|Hx^T = 0\} = c$. This matrix contains a canonical generator matrix G and a parity-check matrix H. For (7,4) code, the matrices are as follows [10].

$$G = \begin{bmatrix} 1 & 0 & 0 & 0 \\ 0 & 1 & 0 & 0 \\ 0 & 0 & 1 & 0 \\ 0 & 0 & 0 & 1 \\ 0 & 1 & 1 & 1 \\ 1 & 0 & 1 & 1 \\ 1 & 1 & 0 & 1 \end{bmatrix} \tag{1}$$

$$H = \begin{bmatrix} 0 & 1 & 1 & 1 & 1 & 0 & 0 \\ 1 & 0 & 1 & 1 & 0 & 1 & 0 \\ 1 & 1 & 0 & 1 & 0 & 1 & 1 \end{bmatrix} \tag{2}$$

The 4-bit information word is the first bit-wise multiplied (logically anded) by each column in the generator matrix G. Each bit in each of the column products is then added, modulo-2, to create a parity bit for each product. An example of a 4-bit infoword $p = [1010]$ and its generated codeword is $c = [0011010]$.

$$c = Gp^T \tag{3}$$

In Eq. (3), c is the codeword, which includes redundancy for error checker.

$$s = Hc^T \tag{4}$$

In Eq. (4), the vector Hc^T is called the syndrome (or error syndrome) of the vector c. If the syndrome is zero, then c is a codeword; otherwise, the syndrome represents one of the integers $1, 2, \cdots, 7$ in binary. This tells us which of the seven bits of c to switch to recover a valid Hamming codeword from c.

[**Example 1**] For information sequence $q = [0110]$, we get the following transmitted codeword of length 7. Now all we have to do is multiply the information vector q with matrix G to get a codeword c.

[**Example 2**] We assume that the codeword c is $[1101001]$. It is easy to calculate the syndrome using Eq. (4) with the parity check matrix H and the codeword $= ([000])^T$. If the syndrome is zero, then c is a valid code; otherwise, c is a wrong code so we need to switch to recover a valid Hamming codeword from c. In this example, s is zero, so there is no need to flip any bit.

3 Our Proposed Scheme

3.1 (5, 3) Hamming Code

Every codeword in a Hamming code [5,3] has a distance of minimum 3 to another codeword, making it possible to correct 1 corrupt bit in each codeword. Let us assume that the sender is transmitting data r to the receiver. The r consists of codeword c and error bit e, as shown in Eq. (5).

$$r = c + e \tag{5}$$

For example, if the codeword is $r = [1\ 0\ 0\ 0\ 0]$, the matrix in Eq. (6) (error detection matrix) and Eq. (7) can be used to identify an error in it. In this case, the first bit is the error. If the error is removed, it becomes $r = c$. That is, Eq. (6) is a matrix that is used to identify errors in [5,3] Hamming code.

$$H = \begin{bmatrix} 1 & 0 & 1 & 0 & 0 \\ 0 & 1 & 0 & 1 & 0 \\ 1 & 1 & 0 & 0 & 1 \end{bmatrix} \tag{6}$$

Equation (7) is used to verify syndrome.

$$s(r) = rH^T = (c+e)H^T = eH^T \tag{7}$$

In Eq. (7), rH^T is called syndrome and relies on error vector.

Table 1. Represents a relationship between r and the syndrome table

Order	Error vector	Syndrome
0	[0 0 0 0 0]	[0 0 0]
1	[0 0 0 0 1]	[0 0 1]
2	[0 0 0 1 0]	[0 1 0]
3	[0 0 1 0 0]	[1 0 0]
4	[0 1 0 0 0]	[0 1 1]
5	[1 0 0 0 0]	[1 0 1]
6	[1 1 0 0 0]	[1 1 0]
7	[0 1 1 0 0]	[1 1 1]

$s(r)$ means a syndrome of r. Therefore, the error correction algorithm is as follows.

- The syndrome is computed by Eq. (7) with the codeword of receiver.
- The errors $s(r)$ are searched in Table 1.
- Flipping error position in codeword r.

Suppose that a codeword c is sent and the received vector is $r = c + e$ (addition modulo 2). The first decoding step is to compute the syndrome $s = rH^T = (c + e)H^T = eH^T$. The error position i is the column i of H that is equal to the (transpose of) the syndrome s^T.

Algorithm 1. Hamming Code Decoding

Step 1: For the received codeword r, compute the syndrome $s = rH^T$.
Step 2: If $s = 0$, then the decoded codeword is $r = c$.
Step 3: If $s \neq 0$, then let i denote the column of H, which is equal to s^T.
Step 4: There is an error in position i of r. The decoded codeword is $r = c + e_i$, where e_i is a vector with all zeros, except for a 1 in the ith position.

This decoding procedure fails if more than one error occurs.

3.2   Encoding Procedure

Our scheme is described below in terms of the embedding procedure for hiding secret data in a grayscale image. A cover image is divided into non-overlapping 5-pixel blocks. We present step-by-step description of the embedding procedure:

Input. Cover image I size $H \times W$, a binary secret message δ of maximum length $H \times W - 1$, and the parity check matrix H, cnt$= \lfloor (H \times W)/5 \rfloor$.
Output. Stego image I' size $H \times W$.

Step 1: Divide cover image I into 1×5 blocks, let $r_i = (b(x_1), \cdots, b(x_n))$, where $b(.)$ denotes LSB of a pixel. Further, c denotes codeword and a set of LSB.
Step 2: Read partitioned pixels and secret messages into array variable x and δ, respectively.
Step 3: Calculate the syndrome s by applying Eq. (7) to the parity check matrix H and c, i.e., $s = rH^T$. Compute $s = s \oplus \delta_j^k$, where $\oplus$ is XOR operation and $j = 1 \cdots n, j = j + k$. The pos is the position for error correction.
Step 4: Find the syndrome corresponding to *pos* in Table 1. Then, find the row of *pos* in Table 1 and flip the value in that position in the corresponding error vector in r. That is, $0 \leftarrow 1$ or $1 \rightarrow 0$.
Step 5: cnt $=$ cnt $- 1$; If *cnt* is not 0, go to Step 2.
Step 6: Return the completed stego image.

3.3   Decoding Procedure

Our scheme is described below in terms of the extracting procedure of secret message bits from the stego image. A stego image is divided into non-overlapping 5-pixel blocks. We present step-by-step description of the extracting procedure:

Input. Stego image I' sized $H \times W$ and parity-check matrix H, cnt $= \lfloor (H \times W)/5 \rfloor$.

Output. A secret message δ.

Step 1: Divide cover image I into 1×5 blocks, let $r_i = (b(x_1), \cdots, b(x_n))$, where $b(.)$ denote LSB of a pixel. Let c denote codeword and a set of LSB.

Step 2: Read partitioned pixels and secret messages into array variable x and δ, respectively.

Step 3: Calculate the syndrome s by applying Eq. (7) to the parity check matrix H and c, i.e., $s = rH^T$. The calculation result is the hidden message bit, and its value is assigned to δ in the following way.
$$\delta_i = \delta_i + rH^T$$

Step 4: $cnt = cnt - 1$; If cnt is not 0, return to Step 2.

Step 5: Return when operation is complete.

[Example 3] We assume that the codeword is $r = [11001]$ and secret code is $\delta = [101]$. Apply the Eq. (7) to the codeword and secret code, $pos = exor(rH^T, \delta)$. In this case, $pos = 2$. Find the syndrome pos in Table 1 and search the error vector in the corre-sponding row of pos. Since pos is 2, the position of '1' in the corresponding error vec-tor is fourth from the left. Therefore, flip the $4th$ value in r to complete the encoding procedure. That is, $r = [11011]$. From the receiver, it is easy to find the concealed secret bits by simply solving Eq. (7) for r.

4   Experimental Results

We proposed a (5,3) Hamming scheme for data hiding. To prove our proposed scheme is correct, we performed an experiment to verify that it ensures the restoration of the hidden image. In addition, the quality of stego image is very important for resisting detection from attackers. Therefore, our method is feasible for making good quality stego images from the original grayscale image. To carry out our experiment, 512512 grayscale images were used as cover images. Figure 1 shows cover images [12] for experiment to verify our proposed scheme. The two most important elements in the experiment are quality of stego images (resolution, PSNR) and the embedding rate of the data stored in the stego image. Such evaluation criteria are commonly used to evaluate the performance of data embedding. In this paper, PSNR (Peak Signal to Noise Ratio) [13] was used to prove such evaluation more objectively.

$$PSNR = 10log_{10} = \left(\frac{I_{max}^2}{MSE}\right), \tag{8}$$

That is, in Eq. (8), the Eq. (9) was applied to the value of the difference between the original image I and stego image I'.

$$MSE = \frac{1}{MN} \sum_{i=1}^{M} \sum_{j=1}^{N} \left(|I_{i,j} - I'_{i,j}|\right)^2, \tag{9}$$

Here, M is the width of the image and N is the height. High PSNR means the stego image is similar to the original image and low PSNR means no resemblance

(a) Baboon   (b) Barbara   (c) Boat

(d) Goldhill   (e) Jet(F16)   (f) Lena

(g) Pepper   (h) Tiffany   (i) Zelda

Fig. 1. The original images used in the experiment

between the original and stego images. In general, PSNR over $30\,dB$, indicates that it is not easy to detect stego images visually. In order to measure the capacity of data hiding in stego images, *bpp* (bits-per-pixel) means embedding payload. Embedding rate is calculated using the Eq. (10).

$$p = \frac{||S||}{M \times N}(bpp), \tag{10}$$

In Eq. (10), p denotes *bpp*, which is an embedding payload. Our experiment compares the number of secret bits that can be carried by a cover pixel. $|d|$ is the number of bits of a secret message d.

Table 2. Comparison between the performance of "Hamming+1" scheme and the proposed scheme

Method / Images	Hamming + 1		Our proposed scheme	
	PSNR	p	PSNR	p
Baboon	53.71	0.499	54.61	0.599
Barbara	48.6	0.499	54.63	0.599
Boats	49.37	0.499	54.62	0.599
Goldhill	53.73	0.499	54.6	0.599
Jet (F16)	51.61	0.499	54.62	0.599
Lena	52.43	0.499	54.62	0.599
Pepper	47.26	0.499	54.63	0.599
Tiffany	47.46	0.499	54.64	0.599
Zelda	54.04	0.499	54.6	0.599
Average	50.91	0.499	54.6	0.599

Figure 2 shows the stego images from the results of the experiments and their respective PSNR. Table 2 shows the comparison between the performance of "Hamming+1" scheme and the scheme proposed in this paper. "Hamming+1" scheme has the average data embedding rate of 0.499 and the average PSNR for the cover image of 50.91 dB. However, the scheme proposed in this paper showed better performance in the experiment, as the data embedding rate was 0.599 and the average PSNR was 54.62 dB. This proves that our proposed scheme is better compared to "Hamming+1".

Table 3. Connection between change density and embedding rate

k	n	Change density	Embedding rate	Embedding efficiency
1	1	50.00 %	100.00 %	2
2	3	25.00 %	66.67 %	2.67
3	**5**	**16.67 %**	**60.00 %**	**3.60**
3	7	12.50 %	42.86 %	3.40
4	15	06.25 %	26.67 %	4.27
5	31	03.13 %	16.13 %	5.16
6	63	01.56 %	9.52 %	6.10
7	127	00.78 %	5.51 %	7.06

The embedding efficiency of the $(1, n, k)$ code is always larger than k. Table 3 shows that the rate decreases with increasing efficiency [5]. Hence, we can achieve high efficiency with very short messages. Our proposed (5, 3) code scheme show higher embedding rate and efficiency compared to (7, 3) hamming code.

(a) Baboon : 54.61 (dB)   (b) Barbara : 54.61 (dB)   (c) Boat : 54.62 (dB)

(d) Goldhill : 54.60 (dB)   (e) Jet(F16) : 54.62 (dB)   (f) Lena : 54.62 (dB)

(g) Pepper : 54.63 (dB)   (h) Tiffany : 54.64 (dB)   (i) Zelda : 54.60 (dB)

Fig. 2. The original images used in the experiment

Figure 3 shows the result from the steganalysis [18] with a database of 200 grayscale images. The circle is the original grayscale image, and crosses are stego images. The crosses are located around the circles, so it is impossible to detect our proposed method from this steganalysis tool. Therefore, our method is very strong related security.

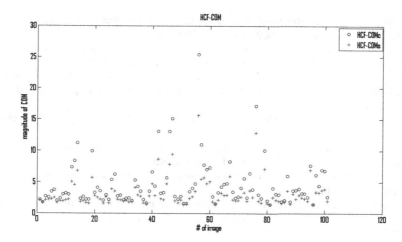

Fig. 3. Cover image (circles) and Stego image (crosses) after embedding for 200 images

5 Conclusions

Matrix Coding and "Hamming+1" are steganographic data hiding schemes. Therefore, these schemes are very good safety channel in many dangerous communication environment. Our scheme is motivated from the matrix coding method. This paper described the use of steganography and its functions. The paper also introduced researches related to this topic and provided explanations for error correction code and Hamming codes. Finally, we proposed a steganographic data-hiding scheme. We proved that our proposed scheme performs better (embedding rate and image quality) compared to "Hamming+1" scheme.

Acknowledgement. This research was supported by the Basic Science Research Program Through the National Research Foundation of Korea (NRF) by the Ministry of Education, Science and Technology (20120192).

References

1. Bender, W., Gruhl, D., Mormoto, N., Lu, A.: Techniques for data hiding. IBM Syst. J. **35**, 313–336 (1996)
2. Provos, N., Honeyman, P.: Hide and seek: an introduction to steganography. IEEE Secur. Priv. **1**(3), 32–44 (2003)
3. Zhang, W., Wang, S., Zhang, X.: Improve embedding efficiency of covering codes for applications in steganography. IEEE Commun. Lett. **11**(8), 680–682 (2007)
4. Chang, C.-C., Kieu, T.D., Chou, Y.-C.: A high payload steganographic scheme based on (7, 4) Hamming code for digital images. In: International Symposium on Electronic Commerce and Security, Guangzhou, China, pp. 16–21 (2002)

5. Westfeld, A.: F5: A steganographic algorithm. In: Moskowitz, I.S. (ed.) IH 2001. LNCS, vol. 2137, pp. 289–302. Springer, Heidelberg (2001)
6. Zhang, X., Wang, S.: Efficient steganographic embedding by exploiting modification direction. IEEE Commun. Lett. **10**(11), 781–783 (2006)
7. Chang, C.C., Chen, T.S., Chung, L.Z.: A steganographic method based upon JPEG and quantization table modification. Inf. Sci.-Informatics Comput. Sci. **141**(1–2), 123–138 (2002)
8. Mielikainen, J.: LSB matching revisited. IEEE Signal Process. Lett. **13**(5), 285–287 (2006)
9. Crandall, R.: Some notes on steganography. Steganography Mailing List (1998). http://os.inf.tu-dresden.de/westfeld/crandall.pdf
10. Hamming, R.W.: Error detecting and error correcting codes. Bell Syst. Tech. J. **29**(2), 147–160 (1950)
11. Chan, C.S., Chang, C.Y.: Hiding secret in parity check bits by applying XOR Function. In: 2010 9th IEEE International Conference on Cognitive Informatics (ICCI), pp. 835–839 (2010)
12. University of Southern California. The USC-SIPI Image Database. http://sipi.usc.edu/database/. Accessed 1 March 2011
13. Kim, C.: Data hiding by an improved exploiting modification direction. Multimedia Tools Appl. **69**(3), 569–584 (2014)
14. Zhang, R., Sachnev, V., Botnan, M.B., Kim, H.J., Heo, J.: An efficient embedder for BCH coding for steganography. IEEE Trans. Inf. Theory **58**, 7272–7279 (2012)
15. Huy, P.T., Kim, C.: Binary image data hiding using matrix encoding technique in sensors. Int. J. Distrib. Sens. Netw. **2013**, 1–7 (2013). Article ID. 340963
16. Kim, H.J., Kim, C., Choi, Y., Wang, S., Zhang, X.: Improved modification direction methods. Comput. Math. Appl. **60**(2), 319–325 (2010)
17. Kim, C., Shin, D., Shin, D., Zhang, X.: Improved steganographic embedding exploiting modification direction in multimedia communications. In: Park, J.J., Lopez, J., Yeo, S.-S., Shon, T., Taniar, D. (eds.) STA 2011. CCIS, vol. 186, pp. 130–138. Springer, Heidelberg (2011)
18. Goljan, M., Soukal, D.: Higher-order statistical steganalysis of palette images. In: Proceedings of the SPIE, Electronic Imaging, Security, Steganography, Watermarking of Multimedia Contents V, Santa Clara, California, pp. 178–190 (2003)

Steganographic Greedy Algorithms for Data Hiding Based on Differences Under SMVQ

Wei-Jen Wang[1], Cheng-Ta Huang[2],
Shiau-Rung Tsuei[3], and Shiuh-Jeng WANG[3(✉)]

[1] Department of Computer Science and Information Engineering,
National Central University, Taoyuan 320, Taiwan
[2] Graduate Institute of Biomedical Engineering,
National Taiwan University of Science and Technology, Taipei 106, Taiwan
[3] Department of Information Management,
Central Police University, Taoyuan 333, Taiwan
sjwang@mail.cpu.edu.tw

Abstract. In this study, we present the idea of using secret bits to repair SMVQ-compressed images. The idea can be viewed as the optimization problem of Using Secret Bits for Image-block Repairing based on Differences under SMVQ (USBIRDS). We propose a novel algorithm named Greedy-USBIRDS to find a near optimal solution for the USBIRDS problem. The experimental results show that, the proposed method provides excellent stego-image quality and large embedding capacity, in particular for complex cover images. While compared with Chen and Lin's steganographic method, which is the known best method based on VQ/SMVQ, the proposed method achieves about 53 % more dB of PSNR of the stego-image quality and about 4.2 % more bits of the embedding capacity on average.

Keywords: Information hiding · Steganography · Side-match vector quantization (SMVQ)

1 Introduction

The Internet has become a common media for people to share and to distribute information. However, the Internet is also known for its publicity and openness nature, which may expose security weakness, such as eavesdropping, fabrication, and plagiarism. Steganography is one possible way to alleviate the security threats from the Internet. Unlike cryptography that encrypts the secret data into meaningless cipher texts, steganography conceals the secret data into cover media to avoid detection, such that no one suspects the existence of the embedded secret data. Thus, a steganographic method, or a data-hiding method, can enhance data protection in many Internet applications, such as steganographic communication, copyright protection, and tampering detection [1–3].

In the area of digital data hiding, many techniques have been proposed for various purposes. The techniques for image data hiding [4–19] can be assorted to three kinds of technique domains - the spatial domain [4–9], the frequency domain [10–14], and the

© Springer International Publishing Switzerland 2015
Y.-Q. Shi et al. (Eds.): IWDW 2014, LNCS 9023, pp. 599–612, 2015.
DOI: 10.1007/978-3-319-19321-2_46

compression domain [15–19]. All of the methods produce either raw images or compressed images as their outputs.

A method of the spatial technique domain usually embeds secret data in each pixel; it may utilize the relationship among pixels to encode the secret data along with each pixel. Generally, a data-hiding method of this technique domain produces stego-images with excellent visual quality and large embedding capacity. The major weakness of the domain is that it may not pass statistical steganalysis [20]. The most representative methods in the domain are the least-significant-bit (LSB) embedding method [4–6], the pixel-value-differencing (PVD) embedding method [7, 8] and the histogram embedding method [9].

A data-hiding method of the frequency technique domain uses a frequency-oriented mechanism, such as the discrete cosine transformation (DCT) method [10–12] and the discrete wavelet transformation (DWT) method [13, 14], to transform the cover image into coefficients in the frequency domain. Then the secret data are embedded in the coefficients and produce a stego-image. A method in this domain usually produces stego-images with high visual quality and limited embedding capacity. Those methods are usually employed by watermarking applications [12, 13] due to their robustness against image distortion attacks.

A method of the compression (block-substitution) domain transforms a master copy of the cover image into small substitutes, and then applies various techniques to encode the secret data and the small substitutes into a stego-image. Since the compression is lossy, the compressed image has smaller size and lower signal-to-noise ratio. Vector quantitation (VQ) is one of the typical compression methods that are used for image data hiding. Some VQ-based methods encode the cover images along with the secret data and produce compressed VQ images [16, 17], while some may produce stego-images in other formats, such as raw images [19]. The VQ partitions an image into small image blocks, typically blocks of 4×4 pixels, and then uses a given codebook to map each image block to an index value, which points to a codeword in the codebook, such that the codeword can best represent the image block. Side-match vector quantitation (SMVQ) is another lossy compression method that is popular in the compression technique domain. It follows the concept of VQ encoding, and uses state codebooks, which are calculated based on the edge pixels of the neighboring blocks, to compress an image to a smaller data representation. Compared with the methods of the other two technique domains, the methods of the compression technique domain provide more confidential communication since they can pass many existing detection approaches of statistical steganalysis. Most of them [21] have relatively low stego-image quality and relatively small embedding capacity for secret data because the stego-images are compressed. However, this kind of method can achieve large embedding capacity for secret data if the stego-image is not compressed [19].

This study focuses on the issue of steganographic communication employing VQ-based encoding schemes. There are two major challenges in this area. The first challenge is to improve the embedding capacity for secret data, and the second challenge is to improve the visual quality for the stego-images. The latter is a harder problem since prior VQ-based steganographic methods cannot provide better visual quality than the VQ-based encoding. We propose a new VQ-based steganographic method that can be classified into the compression technique domain. The proposed method provides larger embedding capacity for the secret data and significantly better visual quality for the stego-images while compared with the best of the known methods in this technique domain, the Chen-Lin method [19]. Therefore, the proposed method is as secure as the other methods in the compression technique domain, and has large capacity for secret data and high visual quality for stego-images.

The rest of the paper is organized as follows. Section 2 introduces the background of this study. Section 3 describes how the proposed method encodes and decodes the cover image along with the secret data. Section 4 provides the experimental results and comparisons on other similar studies. Section 5 draws the conclusions.

2 Related Work

This section introduces the state of the art of the VQ-based methods that produce raw images as the output stego-images.

2.1 State-of-the-Art

The VQ-based image steganography is defined to hide secret data into a cover image using VQ-based compression techniques. The VQ-based steganographic methods can be classified into three groups according to their outputs: VQ-based codes as outputs [22, 23], VQ-based codes with control messages as outputs [24, 25], and raw images as outputs [18, 19]. Wang et al. has presented a more complete study in [21] for the first two groups. The first group, VQ-based codes as outputs, is constrained by the VQ encoding scheme since the output stego-images are VQ-based images. As a result, the average visual quality of stego-images in this group is about 28 dB to 30 dB in PSNR, which is very close to but smaller than the visual quality of typical VQ-based images. The second group, using VQ-based codes with control messages as outputs, provides VQ-reversibility, which means the ability to recover the input VQ-compressed image (the cover image) along with the secret data from the output compressed codestream. The third group, raw images as outputs, uses the VQ-based encoding schemes as the intermediate tool to hide secret data. This sub-section focuses on the related work in the third group. There are two representative steganographic methods. One is the method proposed by Chang et al. in 2006 [18] and the other is the method proposed by Chen and Lin in 2010 [19].

Chen and Lin [19] proposed two similar steganographic methods based on SMVQ. Their methods embed multiple secret bits per pixel while Chang et al.'s method embeds a secret bit per image block. Therefore, they are able to embed much more secret data than Chang et al.'s method. Figure 1 shows the concept of Chen and Lin's methods. To encode a block R, the methods retrieve the closest codeword X to R and the closest codeword Y to X from the state codebook. The half of the distance between X and Y is the distance radius of X, namely t. Any codeword within the distance radius of X is mapped to X, which represents the same result of using the SMVQ to map block R into X. Chen and Lin pointed out that, for a 4×4 block, the constraint to embed v bits per pixel is:

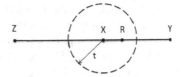

Fig. 1. The concept of Chen and Lin's method, where X is the closest codeword in the state codebook to the encoding block R, Y is the closest codeword in the state codebook to X, Z is any other codeword in the state codebook, and t is the radius of X that every block within the range is mapped to X by the SMVQ.

$$16 \times (2^v - 1)^2 \leq t^2 \tag{3}$$

Chen and Lin's first steganographic method is derived from Eq. 3. That is, each pixel in the block can embed v secret bits, such that the block can still map to X. To retrieve the secret data from a stego-image block, the method constructs a state codebook for the block in the first step, calculates the distance radius t in the second step, and retrieves the r least significant bits from the block as the secret bits.

The first steganographic method proposed by Chen and Lin is shown below:

The first steganographic method proposed by Chen and Lin is shown below:

Input: Cover image G, Codebook C, Secret data S
Output: Stego-image Z
Step 1: Divide the image G into non-overlapping blocks of 4×4 pixels.
Step 2: For each block R, do Steps 3 to 6.
Step 3: If R is on the first row/ column, do VQ encoding. If not, go to Step 4.
Step 4: Do SMVQ encoding to establish a state codebook.
Step 5: Find the closest codeword X to R and the closest codeword Y to X in the state codebook. Set $v = \lfloor \log_2 (\lVert X - Y \rVert / 2) \rfloor$ bits to be the largest embedding capacity for each pixel of R.
Step 6: Retrieve v bits of secret data, namely I, and then replace the least significant v bits of a pixel in X by the secret bits I. The block is saved in Z. Go back to Step 2 until all blocks are processed.
Step 7: Output Stego-image Z.

In order to increase the embedding capacity, Chen and Lin proposed the second method, which embeds $v + 1$ secret bits, instead of v secret bits, into the first w pixels of a block R. The w is the maximum number of the first pixels in a block R to hide $v + 1$ secret bits, such that the closest codeword of block R is always codeword X. The key concept of the second method is to use the residual vector space to embed more secret bits.

3   The Proposed Scheme

This section introduces the proposed steganographic method, which tries to provide better visual quality for the stego-images than prior similar work and to maintain large embedding capacity for secret data. We will explain the concept of the proposed steganographic method, the major techniques used in the proposed method, and the details of the embedding and the extracting algorithms.

3.1   Concept of the Proposed Method

The proposed method uses two major techniques based on SMVQ: the image repairing technique using secret bits, and the codeword reversibility checking technique. While encoding an image block, the image repairing technique uses various bits of secret data and converts them into integers. Then, each converted value is added to or subtracted from a pixel of the SMVQ codeword that represents the image block, such that the new codeword becomes more similar to the cover image block. The codeword reversibility checking technique verifies whether the secret bits can be embedded. The embedding procedure embeds nothing in an image block if the reversibility checking fails. Here we employ a greedy strategy (described in Subsect. 3.4) to calculate a good embedding solution.

To embed secret data into a cover image, the proposed method partitions the image into non-overlapping blocks of 4×4 pixels, and transforms each of the blocks into an index value of the SMVQ. Then, the proposed method retrieves several secret bits for each pixel and converts them into an integer with a prefixing "1." It embeds the integer by using addition or subtraction on the corresponding pixel of the SMVQ codeword, such that the new pixel becomes closer to the corresponding pixel of the original cover image. To achieve reversibility of the SMVQ codeword, the proposed method checks if the step of embedding secret bits into a pixel of a block causes the block to map to a different codeword. If the answer is yes, the pixel is not embeddable and should be bypassed.

3.2   Image Repairing Using Secret Bits

The SMVQ encoding phase of the proposed method generates a compressed image as the output. The compressed image is then recovered to a transformed raw image, which is used for data embedding. Before any secret data is embedded in the transformed raw image, its visual quality is ranging from 25 dB to 31 dB of PSNR in most cases. The image repairing technique described in this sub-section can improve the visual quality of the stego-images by about 10 more dB of PSNR.

To embed the secret data into the transformed raw image, the proposed method uses the secret data to adjust each pixel of the transformed raw image block, such that the stego-image block becomes more similar to the cover image block than the transformed raw image block. There are two major challenges to overcome. First, the adjustment must be reversible. That is, there exists a deterministic method that can retrieve those secret data back from the stego-image. Second, the secret data are given and cannot be modified, and thus the effect of the adjustment is constrained by the input secret data.

The key technique to maintain reversibility of the embedded secret data in the proposed method is to make each stego-image block reversible to the corresponding transformed raw image block. To be more specifically, when we use the SMVQ to compress the stego-image and then to transform the result to a raw image, the raw image must be the same as what we obtained in the encoding phase.

To embed secret bits into a pixel, the proposed method uses addition and subtraction operations. The proposed method calculates the absolute difference value of each stego-image block and its corresponding SMVQ codeword to extract secret bits. The step of secret-data-embedding needs to convert the secret bits into integers for the addition/subtraction operations. The problem is that many combinations of secret bits can map to the same integer based on direct type conversion. For example, "1," "01," and "001" all map to integer 1. To avoid the ambiguity, we employ the following mapping rules for encoding and decoding:

- The secret-bits-string S is null if and only if the integer value to be embedded is 0 or 1.
- The secret-bits-string is S of length $k = LEN(S)$ if and only if the integer value to be embedded is equal to the integer value of S, denoted as $INT(S)$, plus 2^k.

The mapping function $H(S)$, which encodes a secret-bit-string S into an integer, can be defined as follows:

$$H(S) = \begin{cases} 0 \, or \, 1 & ...if \, LEN(S) = 0 \\ INT(S) + 2^{LEN(S)} & ...if \, LEN(S) > 0 \end{cases} \tag{4}$$

The inverse mapping function of H converts an integer into a secret-bit-string. Let $STR(I,k)$ be the function that converts a positive binary integer I into a string of length k, where the string consists of '0' and '1'. If the length of the converted string is smaller than k, the STR function puts enough '0' in front of the converted string, such that the new length becomes k. The inverse mapping function is defined as follows:

$$\bar{H}(I) = \begin{cases} EMPTY \, STRING \, \varepsilon & ...if \, I \leq 1 \\ STR(I - 2^{\lfloor \log_2 I \rfloor}, \lfloor \log_2 I \rfloor) & ...if \, I > 1 \end{cases} \tag{5}$$

Given a secret string S, a codeword pixel W_i for embedding, and the original pixel O_i, it is possible to produce several stego-image pixel Z_i by using addition or subtraction. The proposed algorithm for pixel embedding chooses the one that has the shortest distance to O_i. Extraction of secret-bit-string is done by computing the inverse function of H, given the parameter of the absolute difference value of Z_i and W_i. The two functions, PE that stands for Pixel Embedding and SE that stands for Secret Extracting, are shown below:

Function PE

Input: Original pixel O_i, Codeword pixel W_i, Secret string S
Output: Stego-image pixel Z_i
1. if $LEN(S) = 0$
2. Compute three candidates of $Z_i = \{W_i+1, W_i-1, W_i\}$
3. Pick the candidate Z_i' that is in the range of 0~255 and minimizes $|O_i - Z_i'|$
   4. $Z_i = Z_i$'
   5. **else**
   6. Compute two candidates of $Z_i = \{W_i+H(S), W_i-H(S)\}$
7. Pick the candidate Z_i' that is in the range of 0~255 and minimizes $|O_i - Z_i'|$
8. $Z_i = Z_i$'
9. **return** Z_i

Function SE

Input: Stego-image pixel Z_i, Codeword pixel W_i,
Output: Secret string S
1. $S = \overline{H}(|Z_i - W_i|)$
2. **return** S

The major problem in the proposed image repairing technique is to pick a right secret-bits-string from the secret data to fix each pixel, such that the image quality is optimized. Our strategy is to pick the secret-bit-string that can minimize the difference between the stego-image pixel and the codeword pixel (the transformed raw image pixel). However, the step of visual quality optimization may violate codeword reversibility. That is, a stego-image block can be mapped to a wrong codeword if we do not check whether an embedding operation on a pixel leads to a wrong state. We will describe our solution in in following sub-section.

3.3 Block-Level Embedding and Reversibility Checking

One way to check whether an embedding operation preserves reversibility is to remap a stego-image block to a SMVQ codeword. If the remapped SMVQ codeword remains identical to the original image block, then we can conclude that the embedding operation is reversible between the stego-image block and the corresponding cover image block. Following this idea, we can identify the problem of Using Secret Bits for Image-block Repairing based on Differences under SMVQ (USBIRDS) as follows:

Problem Definition: Given a secret-bit-string S and an image block O that maps to a codeword W under a state codebook SC of 2^k codewords, the USBIRDS problem is to pick and to partition the first m secret bits of S into sixteen sub-strings, of which the maximal length are seven (restricted by the Eq. 4), denoted as $SS = <SS_1, SS_2, ..., SS_{16}>$, and to produce the stego-image block $Z = < PE(O_1,W_1,SS_1), PE(O_2,W_2,SS_2), ..., PE(O_{16},W_{16},SS_{16}) >$, such that $\|Z-O\|^2$ is minimized and Z maps to W under SC.

The optimal solution for the USBIRDS problem can be obtained by enumerating all the combinatorial cases of the lengths of the sixteen sub-strings. Since the length of a sub-string ranges from 0 to 7, the total cases to verify is 8^{16}. Since the naïve approach to find the optimal solution is impractical, we choose to find a good solution instead of the optimal solution. Our strategy for the USBIRDS problem is to repair each pixel of a cover-image block one by one. Since the goal is to minimize the squared difference between the original image block and the stego-image block, we can retrieve a secret-bit-string to repair each stego-image pixel Z_i, such that is minimized, subject to that the stego-image block Z still maps to the same codeword under a given SMVQ state codebook.

Let the original cover image block be $O = <O_1, O_2, ..., O_{16}>$, and the stego-image block be $Z = <Z_1, Z_2, ..., Z_{16}>$ that is initially equal to SMVQ codeword $W = <W_1, W_2, ..., W_{16}>$. Let the cost function, named $Cost$, denotes the squared distance between O and Z, represented as $\|O - Z\|^2$, subject to that Z still maps to W under SMVQ state codebook SC. We can employ a greedy strategy, given four parameters O, W, S, and SC, to find a feasible solution by minimizing function $Cost$ as follows:

Algorithm Greedy-USBIRDS

Input: Secret-bits-string S of length n, Image block O of 16 pixels, and Codeword W of 16 bytes, State codebook SC

Output: Stego-image block Z, and Array of sixteen secret-bits-strings SS

1. $length = 0$
2. $Z = W$
3. $Cost = \sum_{k=1}^{16} (O_k - Z_k)^2$
4. **for** $i = 1 \sim n$
5. $SS_i = \varepsilon$
6.   **for** $j = 1 \sim 7$
7. $Ztemp = PE(O_i, W_i, substring(S, length +1, length + j))$
8. $Costtemp = \sum_{k=1}^{16} (O_k - Z_k)^2 - (O_i - Z_i)^2 + (O_i - Z_{temp})^2$
9.   **if** $Ztemp$ maps to W under the state codebook SC **and** $Costtemp \leq Cost$
10. $Cost = Costtemp$
11. $Z_i = Ztemp$
12. $SS_i = substring(S, length +1, length + j)$
13.   **else**
14. $length = length + j - 1$
15.   **break**
16. **return** Z and SS

Lines $1 \sim 3$ of Algorithm Greedy-USBIRDS initializes the worst acceptable solution for the USBIRDS problem, which embeds nothing into the cover image block,. Variable $length$ denotes the number of secret bits to be embedded by the current solution. Line 5 initializes the sub-string to be embedded into the i_{th} pixel of the cover image. Lines $6 \sim 15$ iteratively test the longest length that the i_{th} pixel of the cover image can be embedded, such that $\|Z-O\|^2$ is minimized. Note that in Line 7, we use the condition, $Costtemp \leq Cost$, instead of the condition, $Costtemp < Cost$. This is because we want to embed one more bit into the cover-image block for the same $\|Z-O\|^2$.

3.4 Embedding and Extracting

The pseudo code for Algorithm Embedding is listed below:

Algorithm Embedding

Input: Cover image O, State codebook size 2^k, Codebook C, and secret bit stream S

Output: Stego-image O'
1. SMVQ image G = SMVQ_Encoding(O, 2^k, C)
2. G' = the recovered raw image of G
3. Partition O', O, and G' into images of 4×4 blocks
4. **for each** block $O'_{i,j}$ in O'
5.   **if** $O'_{i,j}$ is in the first column or in the first row
6. $O'_{i,j} = O_{i,j}$
7.   **else**
8.   Retrieve 16×7 = 112 secret bits from S, where 16 is the size of a codeword in bytes and 7 is the maximum number of bits that can be embedded in a pixel
9.   Let the 112 secret bits be S_p
10.   Get the state codebook SC of $G_{i,j}$
11.   Retrieve the codeword W from SC that best represents $O_{i,j}$
10.   Call Greedy-USBIRDS(S_p, $O_{i,j}$, W, SC) to get the stego-image block Z and the sixteen secret-bits-strings SS
12. $O'_{i,j} = Z$
13.   Remove SS from S
14. **return** O'

In Algorithm Embedding, lines 1 ~ 2 calculate the SMVQ-compressed image from the cover image. Line 5 checks whether the block to be embedded is in the first column or the first row. If the answer is yes, we should directly use the content of the corresponding cover-image block as the output stego-image block, which is described in Line 6. We do not embed anything into these blocks because we should follow the principle of SMVQ encoding to achieve SMVQ reversibility. Lines 8 ~ 13 call Algorithm Greedy-USBIRDS to embed secret bits into a cover-image block, and obtain the corresponding stego-image block and the sixteen secret-bit-strings from Algorithm Greedy-USBIRDS. Note that Algorithm Greedy-USBIRDS uses Function PE to embed secret bits in a cover-image pixel, and Function PE uses Eq. 4 to encode a piece of secret bits into a reversible integer. In Line 8, we retrieve 112 secret bits because the maximum secret bits a cover-image block of sixteen pixels can be embedded is 112 bits. The situation occurs when each pixel embeds seven bits, which is the maximum number of bits Eq. 4 can embed. Note that the 112 secret bits may not be totally embedded into a cover-image block. The residue secret bits are embedded into the next cover-image blocks.

The extracting algorithm is relatively simple since it only uses Function SE (in subsection 3.3) to decode the embedded secret bits. The key idea to retrieve secret data correctly is that both Algorithm Embedding and Algorithm Extracting generate the same SMVQ-compressed image. That is, both the cover image and the stego-image map to the same SMVQ-compressed image. This invariant is ensured by Algorithm Greedy-USBIRDS while producing each stego-image block. The pseudo code of Algorithm Extracting is listed below:

Algorithm Extracting

Input: Stego-image O', State codebook size 2^k, Codebook C
Output: Secret bits S
1. S = EMPTY
2. SMVQ image G = SMVQ_Encoding(O', 2^k, C)
3. G' = the recovered raw image of G
4. Partition O', and G' into images of 4×4 blocks
5. **for each** block $O'_{i,j}$ in O'
6.   **if** $O'_{i,j}$ is in the first column or in the first row
7.   **continue**
8.   **for each** pixel z in $O'_{i,j}$
9.   Find the corresponding pixel w in $G'_{i,j}$
10. sb = call Function SE(z, w)
11. $S = sb \parallel S$
12. **return** S

4 Experimental Results

We have conducted some experiments to evaluate the performance of the proposed method. The results are used to compare the proposed method with Chen and Lin's method. Both the proposed method and Chen and Lin's method are implemented in C ++ programming language, and we used six 512 × 512 gray-level cover images, including three smooth images, "Lena," "Boat," "F16," and three complex images, "Baboon," "Barbara," and "Bridge. We used two VQ codebooks in the experiments, one has 256 codewords and the other has 512 codewords. The codebooks are generated by the LBG algorithm [26].

Table 1 shows the image quality (PSNRs) of the VQ-compressed images and the SMVQ-compressed images, which are generated based on the six testing cover images. In the experiment, we used two VQ codebooks of 256 codewords and 512 codewords, and five different sizes of state codebooks for SMVQ: 8, 16, 64, and 128 entries. From the SMVQ-compressed images, we found the larger the state codebook, the better the image quality. We can also found that, the effect of increasing the size of the VQ codebook is not significant on PSNR improvement rate.

Tables 2 and 3 shows the image quality (in PSNR) and the embedding capacity (in bits) of the stego-images that are produced by the proposed method, given two VQ codebooks of 256 codewords and 512 codewords. The results show that, given the same testing cover images, the image quality of all the stego-images are significantly better than the image quality of the corresponding VQ-compressed images and the corresponding SMVQ-compressed images. We have observed two features of the proposed method from Tables 2 and 3. First, the complex cover images, such as Baboon, Barbara, and Bridge, provide larger embedding capacity than the smooth

Table 1. The PSNR of the VQ-compressed images and the SMVQ-compressed images on different state codebooks, given different codebooks of 256 codewords and 512 codewords for SMVQ encoding.

Image	VQ size		State Codebook size							
			8		16		64		128	
	256	512	256	512	256	512	256	512	256	512
Lena	31.18	32.07	24.07	23.55	26.37	25.74	29.84	29.58	30.80	31.12
Boat	29.25	30.02	23.99	23.25	25.71	25.05	28.20	27.89	28.94	29.05
F16	30.61	31.58	24.43	23.74	26.45	25.58	29.44	29.29	30.26	30.59
Baboon	23.91	24.21	21.14	20.77	21.88	21.52	23.21	22.89	23.72	23.60
Barbara	25.81	26.42	21.25	20.89	22.76	22.35	24.74	24.46	25.53	25.44
Bridge	24.34	24.79	21.17	20.74	22.42	21.93	23.89	23.75	24.23	24.37

cover images do. Second, the complex stego-images still maintain good image quality, which is about 3 dB less than the image quality of the smooth stego-images. The two features are the evidences for that, the proposed method can use secret data to repair the cover images effectively. On the other side, the smooth cover images, such as Lena, Boat, and F16, have less room to be repaired because their SMVQ-compressed images have relatively good image quality (3 ~ 10 more dB) than the complex SMVQ-compressed images. As a result, the smooth cover images provide less embedding capacity and better image quality than the complex cover images do. All the results in Tables 2 and 3 indicate that, the proposed method optimizes the image quality as well as the embedding capacity of the stego-images. The results also indicate that, the proposed method does not sacrifice the image quality in return of embedding capacity.

Table 2. The image quality in PSNR and the embedding capacity (EC) in bits of the stego-images, using different state codebooks and the codebook of 256 codewords.

Image	Codebook size 256									
	8		16		32		64		128	
	PSNR	EC	PSNR	EC	PSNR	EC	PSNR	EC	PSNR	EC
Lena	37.43	336,652	39.23	278,077	40.54	246,585	41.40	229,615	41.95	221,306
Boat	37.41	357,818	38.75	317,331	39.84	291,186	40.46	275,438	40.95	266,770
F16	37.77	289,856	39.29	248,466	40.45	221,837	41.28	205,893	41.74	197,820
Baboon	34.94	634,210	35.59	592,840	36.25	561,146	36.75	538,069	37.27	521,737
Barbara	34.94	542,972	36.31	484,944	37.29	448,510	37.60	424,645	38.60	409,006
Bridge	34.87	649,933	36.05	597,630	36.78	562,587	37.32	540,730	37.60	529,353

We have implemented Chen and Lin's method [19] and used the six testing cover images as the input to evaluate its performance. To compare the proposed method and Chen and Lin's method, we put the measured performance numbers of Chen and Lin's method and the proposed method in Table 4, given the codebook of 512 codewords and the state codebook size of 16 entries. The results show that, the image quality of the stego-images produced by Chen and Lin's method is almost identical to the image quality of the SMVQ-compressed images. The stego-images produced by our method achieve 54 % better image quality on average than the stego-images produced by Chen and Lin's method. In addition, the proposed method provides 4 % larger embedding capacity on average than Chen and Lin's method.

Table 3. The image quality in PSNR and the embedding capacity (EC) in bits of the stego-images, using different state codebooks and the codebook of 512 codewords.

Image	Codebook size 512									
	8		16		64		128		256	
	PSNR	EC	PSNR	EC	PSNR	EC	PSNR	EC	PSNR	EC
Lena	36.87	339,033	38.68	272,799	41.35	214,260	42.15	201,031	42.51	194,884
Boat	36.73	365,403	38.18	318,438	40.29	261,791	41.09	247,141	41.54	239,249
F16	37.21	295,086	38.68	248,041	41.34	193,335	30.59	180,242	42.50	173,700
Baboon	34.63	645,814	35.22	599,943	36.47	535,441	37.10	512,438	37.53	498,377
Barbara	34.57	561,142	35.92	491,477	37.74	417,127	38.55	393,759	39.23	380,358
Bridge	34.49	667,267	35.58	609,000	37.19	533,110	37.68	512,755	37.97	502,237

Table 4. A comparison on the proposed method and Chen and Lin's method.

Image	Codebook 512 State Codebook 16				
	SMVQ	Chen and Lin		Proposed method	
	PSNR	PSNR	EC	PSNR	EC
Lena	25.74	26.51	355,952	38.68	272,799
Boat	25.05	25.79	375,021	38.18	318,438
F16	25.58	26.39	296,154	38.68	248,041
Baboon	21.52	22.16	456,286	35.22	599,943
Barbara	22.35	22.51	439,678	35.92	491,477
Bridge	21.93	22.23	514,967	35.58	609,000
Average	23.70	24.27	406,343	37.04	423,283

Now let us interpret the performance numbers of Table 4 from two different perspectives using the smooth images and the complex images. We found that, the proposed method provides smaller embedding capacity than Chen and Lin's method. This is because the proposed method does not sacrifice image quality in return of embedding capacity. As a result, the proposed method achieves 38 dB in PSNR for the smooth cover images, and 3 less dB in PSNR for the complex images. When we compare both methods on the performance numbers of the complex images, we found that, the proposed method is significantly better than Chen and Lin's method in terms of embedding capacity and image quality. The reason why the proposed method is better resides in how SMVQ encodes an image. Since a complex image usually contains very different neighboring pixels in each image block, the SMVQ-compressed image is hard to represent it well. Therefore, the difference between a pixel in the complex cover image and the corresponding pixel in the SMVQ-compressed image could become very random. Since Chen and Lin's method embeds a fixed number of secret bits in each pixel of an SMVQ-compressed image block, it thus cannot repair the large difference very well. In fact, Chen and Lin's method can enlarge a very small difference between a pixel of the cover image and the corresponding pixel of the SMVQ-compressed image. This is because their method always embeds a fixed number of secret bits in an image block and enlarges the difference. On the contrary, the proposed method can adapt to different sizes of differences, resulting in significantly better image quality and better embedding capacity on average.

5 Conclusions

In this paper, we have presented a steganographic method based on SMVQ. The proposed method uses secret bits to repair an SMVQ-compressed image and produces a stego-image accordingly. In other words, it turns secret data embedding into image repairing. This concept enables an algorithm to pursue the goals of optimizing image quality and embedding capacity at the same time. The problem we aimed to tackle is defined as the problem of Using Secret Bits for Image-block Repairing based on Differences under SMVQ, or the USBIRDS problem for abbreviation. We developed an algorithm, the Greedy-USBIRDS algorithm, to repair each SMVQ-compressed image block efficiently. We employed the codeword reversibility checking technique in the Greedy-USBIRDS algorithm to ensure that the embedded secret bits can be recovered from each stego-image block correctly. We have conducted several experiments using six cover images, consisting of three complex images and three smooth images, to evaluate the performance of the proposed method. The experimental results showed that the proposed method outperforms Chen and Lin's method, the existing best SMVQ-based steganographic method that provides large embedding capacity and good image quality, even though the proposed Greedy-USBIRDS algorithm sacrifices one bit of embedding capacity to transform secret bits into integers. When compared with Chen and Lin's method, the proposed method achieves about 53 % more dB of PSNR of the stego-image quality and about 4.2 % more bits of the embedding capacity on average. In addition, the proposed method performs significantly better in complex cover images based on the experimental results.

Acknowledgements. This research was partially supported by the National Science Council of the Republic of China under the Grants NSC 99-2218-E-008-012, NSC 98-2221-E-015-001-MY3, NSC 99-2918-I-015-001, NSC 102-2221-E-015 -001, MOST 103-2221-E-015 -002, and the Software Research Center, National Central University.

References

1. Chen, W.M., Lai, C.J., Wang, H.C., Chao, H.C., Lo, C.H.: H.26 video watermarking with secret image sharing. IET Image Process. **5**, 349–354 (2011)
2. Phan, R.C.W.: Tampering with a watermarking-based image authentication scheme. Pattern Recognit. **41**, 3493–3496 (2008)
3. Run, R.S., Horng, S.J., Lai, J.L., Kao, T.W., Chen, R.J.: An improved SVD-based watermarking technique for copyright protection. Expert Syst. Appl. **39**, 673–689 (2012)
4. Xu, H., Wang, J., Kim, H.J.: Near-optimal solution to pair-wise LSB matching via an immune programming strategy. Inf. Sci. **180**, 1201–1217 (2010)
5. Zhang, T., Li, W., Zhang, Y., Zheng, E., Ping, X.: Steganalysis of LSB matching based on statistical modeling of pixel difference distributions. Inf. Sci. **180**, 4685–4694 (2010)
6. Lou, D.C., Hu, C.H.: LSB steganographic method based on reversible histogram transformation function for resisting statistical steganalysis. Inf. Sci. **188**, 346–358 (2012)
7. Peng, F., Li, X., Yang, B.: Adaptive reversible data hiding scheme based on integer transform. Signal Process. **92**, 54–62 (2012)

8. Yang, C.H., Weng, C.Y., Wang, S.J., Sun, H.M.: Varied PVD + LSB evading detection programs to spatial domain in data embedding systems. J. Syst. Softw. **83**, 1635–1643 (2010)

9. Lin, C.C., Tai, W.L., Chang, C.C.: Multilevel reversible data hiding based on histogram modification of difference images. Pattern Recognit. **41**, 3582–3591 (2008)

10. Chang, C.C., Lin, C.C., Tseng, C.S., Tai, W.L.: Reversible hiding in DCT-based compressed images. Inf. Sci. **177**, 2768–2786 (2007)

11. Noda, H., Niimi, M., Kawaguchi, E.: High-performance JPEG steganography using quantization index modulation in DCT domain. Pattern Recognit. Lett. **27**, 455–461 (2006)

12. Phadikar, A., Maity, S.P., Verma, B.: Region based QIM digital watermarking scheme for image database in DCT domain. Comput. Electr. Eng. **37**, 339–355 (2011)

13. Keyvanpour, M.R., Merrikh-Bayat, F.: Robust dynamic block-based image watermarking in DWT domain. Procedia Comput. Sci. **3**, 238–242 (2011)

14. Chan, Y.K., Chen, W.T., Yu, S.S., Ho, Y.A., Tsai, C.S., Chu, Y.P.: A HDWT-based reversible data hiding method. J. Syst. Softw. **82**, 411–421 (2009)

15. Lu, Z.M., Wang, J.X., Liu, B.B.: An improved lossless data hiding scheme based on image VQ-index residual value coding. J. Syst. Softw. **82**, 1016–1024 (2009)

16. Tsai, Y.S., Tsai, P.: Adaptive data hiding for vector quantization images based on overlapping codeword clustering. Inf. Sci. **181**, 3188–3198 (2011)

17. Yang, C.H., Wang, W.J., Huang, C.T., Wang, S.J.: Reversible steganography based on side match and hit pattern for VQ-compressed images. Inf. Sci. **181**, 2218–2230 (2011)

18. Chang, C.C., Tai, W.L., Lin, C.C.: A reversible data hiding scheme based on side match vector quantization. IEEE Trans. Circuits Syst. Video Technol. **16**, 1301–1308 (2006)

19. Chen, L.S., Lin, J.C.: Steganography scheme based on side match vector quantization. Opt. Eng. **49**, 0370081–0370087 (2010)

20. Guillermito: Steganography: a few tools to discover hidden data (2004). http://guillermito2.net/stegano/tools/index.html

21. Wang, W.J., Huang, C.T., Wang, S.J.: VQ applications in steganographic data hiding upon multimedia images. IEEE Syst. J. **5**, 528–537 (2011)

22. Tsai, P.: Histogram-based reversible data hiding for vector quantisation-compressed images. IET Image Process. **3**, 100–114 (2009)

23. Chang, C.C., Lin, C.Y.: Reversible steganography for VQ-compressed images using side matching and relocation. IEEE Trans. Inf. Forensics Secur. **1**, 493–501 (2006)

24. Wang, J.X., Lu, Z.M.: A path optional lossless data hiding scheme based on VQ joint neighboring coding. Inf. Sci. **179**, 3332–3348 (2009)

25. Yang, C.H., Lin, Y.C.: Fractal curves to improve the reversible data embedding for VQ-indexes based on locally adaptive coding. J. Vis. Commun. Image Represent. **21**, 334–342 (2010)

26. Linde, Y., Buzo, A., Gray, R.: An algorithm for vector quantizer design. IEEE Trans. Commun. **28**, 84–95 (1980)

Evaluation of a Zero-Watermarking-Type Steganography

Hirokazu Ishizuka[1]([⊠]), Isao Echizen[2], Keiichi Iwamura[3], and Koichi Sakurai[1]

[1] Faculty of Information Science and Electrical Engineering,
Kyushu University, 744 Motooka, Nishiku, Fukuokashi, Fukuoka, Japan
hirokazu.ishizuka@inf.kyushu-u.ac.jp, sakurai@csce.kyushu-u.ac.jp
http://itslab.inf.kyushu-u.ac.jp/en/members.html
[2] Digital Content and Media Sciences Research Division,
National Institute of Informatics, 2-1-2 Hitotsubashi, Chiyodaku, Tokyo, Japan
iechizen@nii.ac.jp
[3] Faculty of Engineering Division I, Department of Electrical Engineering,
Tokyo University of Science, 6-3-1, Niijuku, Katsushikaku, Tokyo, Japan
iwamura@ee.kagu.tus.ac.jp

Abstract. We evaluated the resistance of image compression for the zero-watermarking-type steganography which proposed by us in 2005. As a result, even if we compressed to 1/100 of an original image, it still can extract its watermark information with an accuracy of 99 % or more. We also proposed a new type of sparse filtering for low-frequency spatial extraction, and confirmed its performance by computational experiments. Finally, we mentioned a study on the relevance of the proposed filter and biological visual systems.

Keywords: Steganography · Watermarking · Similar image search · Probabilistic frequency transform · Secret sharing

1 Introduction

Digital watermarking technology is used to prevent piracy of video and audio data content such as movies and music. Since digital watermarking embeds watermark information into the luminance, color, spectrum, etc. of the host data, degradation of the host data quality is inevitable [1–5,7,11].

We have developed a method that does not degrade host data quality. Secret information is extracted from the host data using simple arithmetic operations and a separate file. This method can be applied in various areas including steganography, content protection, probabilistic secret sharing, and similar image search. Although it can be considered a kind of zero-watermarking [6,8,9], we will show some differing points in this paper. In addition, we evaluate the resistance of image compression, we got a result that even if we compressed to 1/100 of an original image, it still can extract its watermark information with an accuracy over 99 %.

© Springer International Publishing Switzerland 2015
Y.-Q. Shi et al. (Eds.): IWDW 2014, LNCS 9023, pp. 613–624, 2015.
DOI: 10.1007/978-3-319-19321-2_47

2   Overview

A novel by Ango Sakaguchi published in 1948 contained the inspiration for our method. The novel's title is "Angou," which in Japanese, means cipher. In this novel, secret information was extracted from a set of digits written on a piece of paper and in a corresponding book (Fig. 1). That is, according to the set of digits, words are extracted from page numbers, line numbers, and character numbers in the book. Similarly, our method uses a file describing the coordinates of points in the host data to extract secret information from the host data [10] (Fig. 2). We describe the algorithm used in the next section. We also discuss why zero-watermarking and our method are necessary for copyright protection.

Generally, the host data is more important than the secrecy data in watermarking. On the other hand, the secrecy data is more important than the host data in steganography. However, as for the world of digital media, they are almost similar technology. With a conventional watermark embedding method, which depends on the content of the host data, there is a trade-off between host data quality and watermarking robustness. Moreover, a counterfeit watermark embedding attack cannot be defended against with only a watermark embedding method. In contrast, our method and zero-watermarking dare to create a watermark on the conspicuous but robust part of the image. The part is that we could not embed large amount of watermark conventionally. This means that we release digital watermarking from the shackles of the human visual characteristics.

3   Algorithms

Our proposed steganography method comprises two algorithms. The first one is for detecting the low-frequency spaces. This algorithm can be roughly substituted for a discrete Fourier transform including fast Fourier transformation (FFT) and conventional convolution. It substantially reduces the amount of calculation in comparison with conventional methods for the low-frequency calculation. After the low-frequency space is detected, we will bind the watermark (steganography) data to the low-frequency space. This is an essential point of our method and is described below.

3.1   Low Frequency Space Detection Algorithm

In general, the low-frequency components of an image are no less important than the high-frequency ones and are also noticeable. This property can be applied to digital watermarking. Although, a lot of information can be embedded in the high-frequency components, which do not easily stand out, by rewriting the information, they can be easily eliminated. Conversely, the low-frequency components tend to stand out and cannot be used to embed much information, but they cannot be easily removed. This is a law of the human visual system.

With digital watermarking, watermarks that are not easily erased are used to embed secret information in the low-frequency spaces, resulting in image degradation [12, 13]. In contrast, our method does not change any image data, so

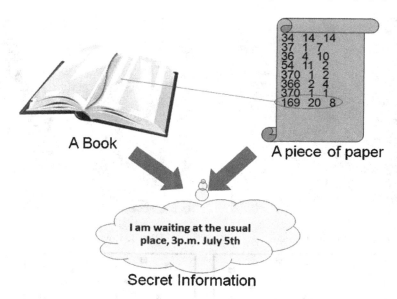

Fig. 1. Method introduced in the novel

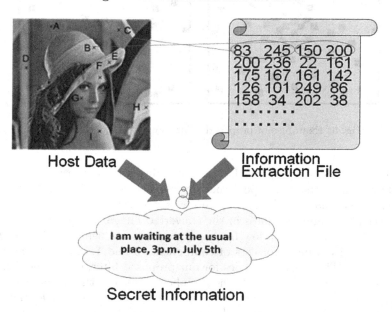

Fig. 2. Proposed method

there is no degradation. However, our method needs to detect the low-frequency spaces. For comparison, we first describe the detection of low-frequency spaces using Fourier transformation. Fourier transformation converts an original image

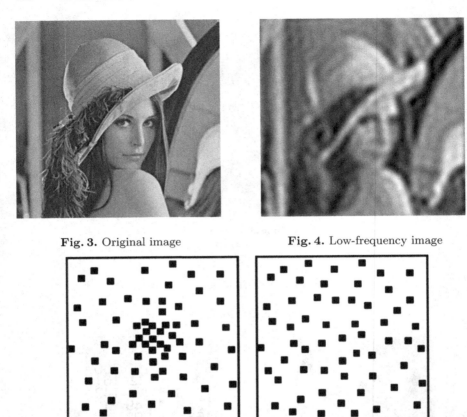

Fig. 3. Original image   **Fig. 4.** Low-frequency image

Fig. 5. Examples of proposed filter (Type I (Left), II (Right))

(Fig. 3) to an frequency space. It then cuts the domain containing the high-frequency components, and performs inverse Fourier transformation (Fig. 4). Looking at the image in the figure, we see that discontinuity of the cut-off frequency results in unnaturalness in the converted image.

Our method detects the low-frequency components using the following procedure. Basically a filter consists of components 0 and 1, and only the part of 1 is processed. There are two types for our proposed filter, one is the density of sampling points decreases toward the periphery, and the other is having the constant sampling density. Representing 1 as a small black square hole, those filter images are shown in Fig. 5. In addition, we should decide following thresholds (t_1, t_2) in advance. The low-frequency space extracting algorithm is as follows:

1. Overlap the filter as shown in Fig. 5 to the host image and read the pixel intensity $I(p_0)$ corresponding to the center of the filter.
2. Read another pixel intensity ($I(p_i)$) in the image through the filter's hole in order.

3. If $|I(p_i) - I(p_0)| \leq t_1$ then increment a counter($c(p_0, p_i)$), otherwise do nothing.
4. Continue until all holes have been processed.
5. If the counter c exceeds the threshold (t_2), let the corresponding point to the filter center be a low-frequency space ($O(p_0) = 255$). This means if almost all pixel intensities are same to the center pixel intensity, then the center may be a center of the low-frequency space.
6. Shift the filter on a constant value and perform steps 1–5 for the whole image.

The low frequency space (LFS) is expressed by the formula shown below. Where F is a partial set of the host image corresponding to our proposed sparse filter. Numbers 0 and 255 are the case of gray-scale image.

$$O(p_0) = \begin{cases} 0 & if \ \sum_{p_i \in F} c(p_0, p_i) \leq t_2 \\ 255 & if \ \sum_{p_i \in F} c(p_0, p_i) > t_2 \end{cases} \tag{1}$$

where

$$c(p_0, p_i) = \begin{cases} 1 & if \ |I(p_0) - I(p_i)| \leq t_1 \\ 0 & if \ |I(p_0) - I(p_i)| > t_1 \end{cases} \tag{2}$$

Next, we discuss computational complexity. The number of arithmetic operations for N samples is estimated as follows:

– Ordinary two-dimensional discrete Fourier transformation

$$DFT(N) \propto O(N^4) \tag{3}$$

– Fast Fourier transformation (however, the input must be powers of 2)

$$FFT(N) \propto O((N \log N)^2)) = O(2N^2 \log N) \tag{4}$$

– Convolution (neglecting sampling theorem), where F is the filter size

$$CONV(N, F) \propto O(N^2 * F^2) \tag{5}$$

– Proposed method where F is the filter size and S is the degree of filter sparseness.

$$OurMethod(N, F, S) \propto O(N^2 * F^2 / S) \tag{6}$$

Although FFT is fast, the low-frequency space provided by FFT may not necessarily be the best choice in watermarking (It depends on the size of the frequency area to be cut, i.e. frequency dependence). Figure 6 contains a little high-frequency region which is the result of the band-pass filter according to the Fourier transform, and Fig. 7 shows the binary image obtained by the left side filter in Fig. 5. Depending on the filter size, our method detects not only the low-frequency spaces but also the high-frequency ones. Figures 8 and 9 show the result of applying the type-II filter (the right side of Fig. 5). These converted images are very well matched to the result of FFT. We confirmed that both our filters mainly extract the low-frequency space and slightly contains the high-frequency space.

Fig. 6. Binarization after band-pass FFT

Fig. 7. Filtered image (Applied type I filter)

3.2 Proposed Algorithm

Our proposed steganography algorithm works as follows. We assumed that the low-frequency spaces have already been extracted by the above-mentioned algorithm.

1. Take one concealment bit from the secret information.
2. Chose two points, A and B, from the low-frequency space by random numbers.
3. If the absolute difference between the brightness of the two points is smaller than the threshold t_2, go to 2. Otherwise go to 4.
4. If the concealment bit is "1" and the value of the brightness (A - B) is positive, set the order of the two points as A, B in the information extraction file. If (A - B) is negative, set the order as B, A. If the concealment bit is "0", reverse the order in each case.
5. Continue until all the information has been concealed.

The arithmetic operation $(A - B)$ can switch to a more complex one with a slight modification of the algorithm.

When both information extraction file and the host image file is not aligned, our method can not extract the secret information. This is a precondition of our method when we use it as steganography or digital watermarking. However, if we encrypt the information to be concealed using a certain cryptography, such as the one-time pad cipher, we can further enhance the safety.

4   Evaluation

We evaluated the resistance of the JPEG image compression for our method. The result is summarized in Tables 1 and 2. The left most column is the image ID. Some of the compressed images are displayed in Figs. 10 and 11. The second

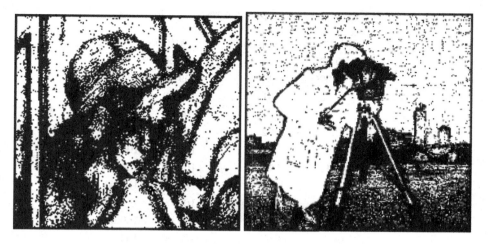

Fig. 8. Applied type II filter to Lena

Fig. 9. Applied type II filter to Camera-man

Fig. 10. Compressed images for Lena (L1,L3,L7 from left)

column from the left shows the file size of the compressed images where the original image size is 66 KB. The third column is the percentage ratio of the compressed size (second column) to the original size. The fourth and fifth column are the bit accuracy ratio for extracting the watermark. The difference is only a bit reading scheme. The fourth column is the bit accuracy ratio when it is read by an intensity average of $9=(3 \times 3)$ vicinity of the target bit, and the fifth column is that is $25=(5 \times 5)$ neighbors. The size of the neighborhood for reading depends on the type of image. Two kinds of images show that the larger average is not necessarily good.

Decoding process of our method, we don't need any preprocessing (see Fig. 15). We only read the pixel whose coordinate is written in the information extraction file and we also read its neighborhood pixels (3×3 pixels or 5×5 pixels or more) in order to increase degradation resistance. We evaluate the probability of correct bit extraction against the compression quantity.

Table 1. Image compression resistance for Lena

Image ID	Size(KB)	Comp. ratio(%)	BAR(*1)	BAR(*2)
L1	0.830	1.26	99.50	99.53
L2	0.966	1.46	99.78	99.44
L3	1.72	2.61	99.69	100.00
L4	2.40	3.64	100.00	100.00
L5	3.91	5.92	99.86	99.87
L6	4.92	7.45	100.00	100.00
L7	5.11	7.74	100.00	100.00
L8	6.95	10.53	99.86	100.00
L9	9.88	14.97	100.00	100.00
L10	11.6	17.58	100.00	100.00
L11	14.3	21.67	100.00	100.00
L12	27.6	41.82	100.00	100.00
L13	40.1	60.76	100.00	100.00
L14	42.8	64.85	100.00	100.00

The vertical axis of those graphs in Figs. 12 and 13 represents the bit accuracy ratio (BAR:=[#correct_bits/#all_bits] × 100) at which we were able to extract concealed bits definitely at a percentage, and the horizontal axis represents the image compression ratio. These graphs show that you can still extract the watermark information in over 99 % accuracy, even if the original image was compressed to 1/100. Furthermore, application of an error correction code to the secret data may improve the correct bit ratio.

5   Application to Secret Sharing

One potential application of our method is to secret sharing. Suppose the host data was temporarily divided into four pieces (Fig. 14), and a different carrier carries each piece. However, the information extraction file is based on the assumption of no division. The information to be carried by each messenger is about $1/4^2 = 1/16$=(the probability that any two points belong to the same 1/4 pieces). If the information extraction file is created by duplicating the secret information, the amount of information is $2/4^2 = 1/8$. This redundancy of the secret information and the image size splitting enables the use of an arbitrary probabilistic secret sharing scheme. Conversely, if the image is left as it is and the information extraction file is divided into four pieces, the amount of information that can be extracted is one-fourth per division. Furthermore, if the image and information extraction file are divided in other suitable ways, various probabilistic secret sharing systems can be realized.

Table 2. Image compression resistance for Cameraman

Image ID	Size(KB)	Comp. ratio(%)	BAR(*1)	BAR(*2)
C1	0.899	1.36	98.96	99.44
C2	1.005	1.52	99.40	99.05
C3	1.35	2.05	99.88	99.72
C4	2.23	3.38	100.00	100.00
C5	3.67	5.56	99.87	100.00
C6	4.84	7.33	99.87	100.00
C7	4.92	7.45	99.54	100.00
C8	6.75	10.23	99.87	100.00
C9	9.84	14.91	99.88	99.87
C10	11.7	17.73	100.00	100.00
C11	14.6	22.12	100.00	100.00
C12	28.4	43.03	99.60	100.00
C13	41.5	62.88	99.77	100.00
C14	44.5	67.42	99.71	100.00

Fig. 11. Compressed images for Cameraman (C1,C3,C7 from left)

6 Application to Similar Image Search

If a similar image, i.e., one with the same background and the same composition as the original, is used, the secret information could be extracted against an intention for watermarking. We postulated that if a sufficient number of water-marked bits were taken from the information extraction file, our system could distinguish the difference. We tested this by using two images of the same person taken with the same camera at almost the same time. The difference in PSNR between the two images was 15.9 dB. The images were almost the same image, dare to say the facial expressions were slightly different. We applied our algorithm to the almost same image and we get the probability of the correct extraction of hiding bit was about 97 %, which is close to the visual impression.

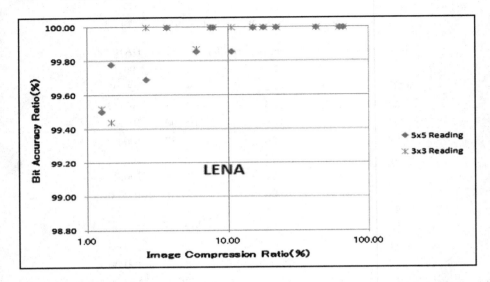

Fig. 12. Relationship of extracting bit accuracy ratio with image compression ratio for Lena

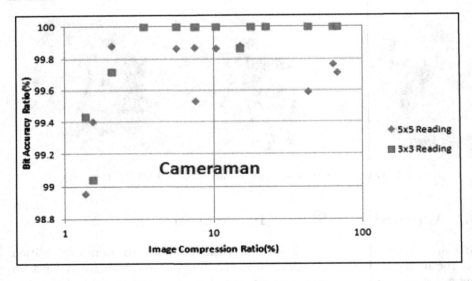

Fig. 13. Relationship of extracting bit accuracy ratio with image compression ratio for Cameraman

Application of this characteristic in the opposite manner would enable a similar image search. As evidenced by its use on Google, similar image search has become an important application in the handling of big data. Decoding of our method simply compares the luminance difference between two points (Fig. 15), it is faster than conventional image search methods. Since the application of

Fig. 14. Four separated images

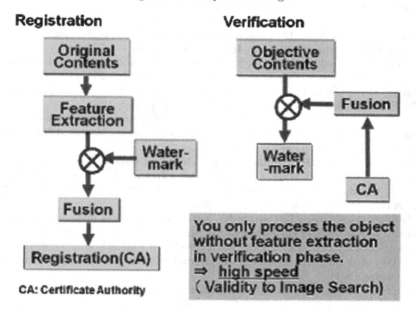

Fig. 15. Encoding and decoding

similar image search does not need secrecy, we can use additional information such as signed difference of intensity to the information extraction file.

7 Conclusion and Prospects

Our proposed digital steganography method does not degrade host data quality. Secret information is extracted from the host data and the separate file using simple arithmetic operations. The evaluation by simulation showed compression

624   H. Ishizuka et al.

immunity of our method. This method has following features. They are a simple and fast frequency analysis, rapid decoding, and a wide range of potential applications.

By the way, the creatures such as humans have low-frequency spatial extraction in their visual system is known. The frequency analysis at near the retina can be explained with the Gabor filter is also known. However, the frequency analysis at advanced stages of integration is not known very well. We are currently investigating whether the frequency characteristics at advanced stages can be explained in the filter structure proposed by us. Since the neural circuit consists of simple elements called sum-of-products operation and threshold value comparison like our filter operation, we expect that there is a similar structure of our filter somewhere in the two paths through the area V2 from V1 field toward the parietal or temporal lobe.

References

1. Liu, R., Tan, T.: An SVD-based watermarking scheme for protecting rightful ownership. IEEE Trans. Multimedia 4(1), 121–128 (2002)
2. Lancini, R., Mapelli, F., Tubaro, S.: A robust video watermarking technique in the spatial domain. In: VIPromCom-2002, 4th EURASIP, pp. 251–256 (2002)
3. Suhail, M.A., Obaidat, M.S.: Digital watermarking-based DCT and JPEG model. IEEE Trans. Instrum. Measur. 52(5), 1640–1647 (2003)
4. Nikolaidis, A., Pitas, I.: Asymptotically optimal detection for additive watermarking in the DCT and DWT domains. IEEE Trans. Image Process. 12(5), 563–571 (2003)
5. Bao, P., Ma, X.: Image adaptive watermarking using wavelet domain singular value decomposition. IEEE Trans. Circ. Syst. Video Technol. 15(1), 96–102 (2005)
6. Chen, N., Zhu, J.: A robust zero-watermarking algorithm for audio. EURASIP J. on Adv. Sig. Procession 2008, 1–7 (2008)
7. Cheddad, A., Condell, J., Curran, K., Kevitt, P.M.: Digital image steganography: survey and analysis of current methods. Signal Process. 1, 727–752 (2010)
8. Zhang, L., Cai, P., Tian, X., Xia, S.: A novel zero-watermarking algorithm based on DWT and Edge detection. In: 4th International Congress on Image and Signal Processing (2011)
9. Han, S.C., Zhang, Z.N.: A novel zero-watermark algorithm based on LU decomposition in NSST domain. In: ICSP 2012, pp.1592–1596 (2012)
10. Ishizuka, H., Nishioka, T., Hasegawa, T., Tsurumaru, T.: An Evaluation of a Digital Steganographic Method(ANGO). In: SCIS 2005 (2005) (in Japanese)
11. Chanu, Y.J., Singh, K.M., Tuithung, T.: Image steganography and steganalysis: a survey. Int. J. Comput. Appl. 52(2), 1–11 (2012)
12. Raja, K.B., Sindhu, S., Mahalakshmi, T.D., Akshatha, S., Nithin, B.K., Sarvajith, M., Venugopal, K.R., Patnaik, L.M.: Robust image adaptive steganography using integer wavelets. In: Communication System Software and Middleware and Workshops (COMSWARE), pp. 614–621 (2008)
13. Hashad, A.I., Madani, A.S., Wahdan, A.E.M.A.: A robust steganography techniquie using discrete cosine transform insertion. In: Proceedings of IEEE/ITI, pp. 255–264 (2005)

Author Index